# PUBLIC ADMINISTRATION IN THE NEW MILLENNIUM

## Challenges and Prospects

# PUBLIC ADMINISTRATION IN THE NEW MILLENNIUM
## Challenges and Prospects

*Editors*

Shiv Raj Singh
P.P.S. Gill
Sewa Singh Chauhan
Sanjeev K. Mahajan

ANAMIKA PUBLISHERS & DISTRIBUTORS (P) LTD.
4697/3, 21A, Ansari Road, Daryaganj
New Delhi 110 002
Phones: 3201531, 3281655

*First Published 2003*



ISBN 81-7975-021-3

PRINTED IN INDIA

Published by Anamika Publishers & Distributors (P) Ltd., 4697/3, 21A, Ansari Road, Daryaganj, New Delhi 110 002. Typeset by VGA, MU-61D, Vishakha Enclave, Pitampura, Delhi 110 088 and Printed at Nagri Printers, Delhi.

# Preface

The present book is the outcome of a National Seminar organized by the Department of Public Administration, Himachal Pradesh University on the Theme "The Public Administration in New Millennium: Challenges and Prospects" on April 19-20, 2001. The Seminar was inaugurated by His Excellency Dr. Suraj Bhan, Governor of Himachal Pradesh and Chancellor of H.P. University. About 60 Academicians practising civil servants, Army Officer, participated in the seminar. In his inaugural address His Excellency emphasized that administration should not only be responsible but also responsive. There has to be a proper accountability at all levels and persons doing good work must be rewarded and given due recognition in their service career. Transparency can help to solve many maladies with which the administration of today is afflicted. Narrating his long experience in administration and politics, he emphasized that administration needs to be oriented to subserve the interest of weaker sections of society. Attitudinal changes are required in dealing with the issues and problems of common masses, only then we can move in an era of new public management. For achieving this a well structured and well formulated training system at different levels has to be developed.

In the wake of new forces unleashed by liberalization, globalization, knowledge, economy, social economy and political development in this age of information technology, there is need to reorient the vast expanding apparatus of public administration. Public administration must perform active role in the changing scenario to bring desirable change in the socio-economic life of the masses and it must be ensured that the people are benefited by the new technology. Great changes can take place in a 21st century if necessary restructuring and reforms are undertaken in the educational sector. The Nobel Prize Winning research of Amartya Sen has shown that India cannot develop without providing for primary health care and elementary education to all. The theory of administration is common to both public administration and business management. We often take recourse to western theories even for getting a better understanding of our administration or management which catered to find solutions for the problems encountered by their own society. Western theories arose in their own specific environment. So India should evolve a theory which fits into its socio-economic setting. It is because of this reason that we have selected this theme i.e. Public Administration in the New Millennium: Challenges and Prospects which includes more vital areas than law and order.

The editors owe great debt to late Professor S.K. Gupta former Vice-Chancellor, H.P. University, Shimla who was a source of inspiration and strength for organizing the Seminar. We are grateful to him for delivering the Presidential address. We take this opportunity to thank Professor N.K. Sharda, Hon'ble Pro-Vice Chancellor, H.P. University, Shimla for delivering the valedictory address to the seminarians. We are also thankful to Shri Dhruv Vashist the Registrar of the University and Dr. Sudesh Kumar Garg, Dean College Development Council for their cooperation and administrative support to the organizers. Special thanks to distinguished participants who contributed articles in the seminar. We are also thankful to Shri Gian Chand and Shri Ami Chand for providing ministerial assistance and the Research scholars as well as the students of the Department of Public Administration who contributed a lot in the completion of this work.

Last but not least we are thankful to our Publisher Anamika Publishers and Distributors (P) Ltd., New Delhi for brining out this volume in a record time.

Editors

# Contents

# Contributors


1. **Professor R.K. Sapru**, Department of Public Administration, Panjab University Chandigarh.
2. **S.K. Baldi**, IAS, Managing Director, H.P.M.C.
3. **Manoj Dixit**, Senior Lecturer, Department of Public Administration, University of Lucknow.
4. **Jaya Chaturvedi**, Research Scholar, Deptt. of Public Administration, University of Lucknow.
5. **D.S. Kheora**, Asstt. Professor, Economic Administration, H.P. Institute of Public Administration, Shimla.
6. **Dr. Mohinder Singh**, Reader, Deptt. of Public Administration, Kurukshetra University, Kurukshetra.
7. **Brij Pal**, Research Scholar, Deptt. of Public Administration, Kurukshetra University, Kurukshetra.
8. **Professor M.A. Hussain**, Deptt. of Pol. Science & Public Administration, Sri Venkateswara University, Tirupati (A.P.).
9. **Dr. R.K. Prabhakar**, Reader, Deptt. of Public Administration, M.D. University, Rohtak.
10. **Dr. Sansar Singh Janjua**, Reader, Deptt. of Pol. Science, Panjabi University, Patiala.
11. **Dr. Sanjeev K. Mahajan**, Reader, Deptt. of Public Administration, H.P. University, Shimla.
12. **Anupma Mahajan**, Research Scholar, Deptt. of Public Administration, H.P. University, Shimla.
13. **Professor Shiv Raj Singh**, Chairman, Deptt. of Public Administration, H.P. University, Shimla.

14. **Dr. Pawan Kumar Banta**, Research Scholar, Deptt. of Public Administration, H.P. University, Shimla.
15. **L.N. Sharma**, Lecturer, Political Science, G.C. Sarkaghat, Mandi (H.P).
16. **Dr. Charanjeev Singh**, Lecturer, Deptt. of Public Administration, Panjab University, Chandigarh.
17. **Vandana Disodia**, Research Scholar, Deptt. of Public Administration, Panjab University, Chandigarh.
18. **Dr. Manjusha Sharma**, Lecturer Public Administration, Kurukshetra University, Kurukshetra.
19. **S.N. Joshi** (I.A.S.) Retd., Bharari, Shimla.
20. **Dr. S.C. Arora**, Reader & Chariman, Deptt. of Public Administration, M.D. University, Rohtak.
21. **Subhash C. Sharma**, Deputy Director (Law), H.P. Institute of Public Administration, Shimla.
22. **Dr. S.S. Dhaliwal**, Technical Director, State Urban Development Authority Panjab, Chandigarh.
23. **Dr. S.S. Chauhan**, Reader, Deptt. of Public Administration, H.P. University, Shimla.
24. **Dr. Mamta Mokta**, Lecturer, Public Administration, R.K.M.V., Shimla.
25. **Professor S.L. Kaushik**, Chairman, Deptt. of Public Administration, Panjab University, Chandigarh.
26. **Dr. Kiran Bala**, Lecturer, Public Administration, D.A.V. College, Chandigarh.
27. **Dr. Mohan Jharta**, Reader, Deptt. of Sociology, H.P. University, Shimla.
28. **Brig. V.S. Tonk**, Station Commander Kasauli, Solan.
29. **Rakesh Kanwar**, Joint Director, H.P. Institute of Public Administration, Shimla.
30. **Suman Gupta**, Research Scholar, Deptt. of Public Administration, Kurukshetra University, Kurukshetra.
31. **Dr. Sudesh Negi**, Director, Centre for Adult, Continuing Education and Extension, H.P. University, Shimla.

32. **Rajinder Singh Chauhan**, Asstt. Director, Physical Education & Youth Programme, H.P. University, Shimla.
33. **Dr. Pradeep Vaid**, Sr. Lecturer, Public Administration, ICDEOL, H.P. University, Shimla.
34. **Himani Vaid**, Research Scholar, Deptt. of Public Administration, H.P. University, Shimla.
35. **Professor S.L. Goel**, Professor, Emeritus, Panjab University, Chandigarh.
36. **Professor Aruna Goel**, Deptt. of Correspondence Studies, Panjab University, Chandigarh.
37. **Professor Arvind Sharma**, Vice-Chancellor, Mizoram University, Aizol.
38. **Professor Bal Ram Dogra**, Director, Institute of Management Studies, H.P. University, Shimla.
39. **Professor R.B. Jain** (Retd.), Deptt. of Pol. Science, University of Delhi, Delhi.
40. **Professor S.S. Tiwana**, Deptt. of Public Administration, Punjabi University, Patiala.
41. **Dr. Pradeep Saxena**, Asstt. Professor Public Administration, University of Rajasthan Jaipur.
42. **Devinderjit Kaur**, Research Scholar, Deptt. of Public Administration, Panjab University, Chandigarh.
43. **Dr. Ravinder Sharma**, Associate Professor, University of Rajasthan, Jaipur.
44. **Rajbans Gill**, Lecturer, Deptt. of Public Administration, Punjabi University, Patiala.
45. **Professor Satya Deva** (Retd.), Deptt. of Public Administration, Panjab University, Chandigarh.
46. **Professor Harbans Pathak**, Chairman, Deptt. of Public Administration, Punjabi University, Patiala.
47. **Parul Pathak**, Lecturer, Pol. Science, Govt. Mohindra College, Patiala.
48. **Professor C.S. Panwar**, Head, Deptt. of Political Science, Vikram University, Ujjain (M.P.).

49. **Dr. P.P.S. Gill**, Reader, Deptt. of Public Administration, H.P. University, Shimla.
50. **Dr. Rajesh Kumar**, Lecturer, Public Administration, Shimla.
51. **Dr. Simmi Agnihotri**, Lecturer, Centre for Evening Studies, H.P. University, Shimla.
52. **Dr. Saroj Malik**, Reader, Deptt. of Political Science, Kurukshetra University, Kurukshetra.
53. **Dr. Hiteshwar Thakur**, Research Scholar, Deptt. of Public Administration, H.P. University, Shimla.
54. **Dr. Om Pal**, Range Officer, Deptt. of Forest, H.P. Government.

# Part 1

# New Public Management

# 1

# New Public Management: A Negation to Bureaucratic Approach

*R.K. Sapru*

## Introduction

New Public Management (NPM), Managerialism, Market-based Public Administration, or Reinventing Government are a few incarnations of a new model of public sector management which emerged in the beginning of the 1990s in response to the challenges of globalisation, international competitiveness and technological change. It is argued that it represents a paradigm shift from a traditional model of public administration,[1] dominant for most of the twentieth century to managerialism or what is popularly known as "New Public Management". This new approach manifests a change in the role of government and bureaucracy in society and the relationship between government and citizenry.

### Problems with Traditional Bureaucratic Model

The Traditional Model of Public Administration (TPA) theorised and contributed largely by writers like Woodrow Wilson. (The Study of Administration written in 1887 in the United States), the Northcote-Trevelan Report (published in 1854 in the United Kingdom) and Max Weber (German Sociologist who developed bureaucratic model) remained in operation in most Western countries until the third quarter of the twentieth century. This model can be characterised as: an administration under the formal control of the political leadership, based on a strictly hierarchical model of bureaucracy, staffed by permanent, neutral and anonymous officials, motivated only by the public interest, serving any governing party equally, and not contributing to policy but merely administering those policies taken by the politicians.

Developing countries emerged from dependence to independence with government becoming by far the most important societal actor, controlling the details of the economy in addition to its normal functions. The World Bank[2] argued:

> "The new interventionist credo had its counterpart in the development strategy of the day, adopted by many developing countries at independence, which emphasised the prevalence of market failures and accorded the state a central role in correcting them. Centralised planning, corrective interventions in resource allocation, and a heavy state hand in infant-industry development were part and parcel of this strategy. Economic nationalism was added to the mix, to be promoted through state enterprise and encouragement of the indigenous private sector. By the 1960s, states had become involved in virtually every aspect of the economy, administering prices and increasingly regulating labour foreign exchange, and financial markets."

In developing countries the administration was true bureaucracy, meaning government by officials. In this context Smith observed:

> "The bureaucracy controls and manages the means of production through the state. It provides the necessary organisation. It proliferates opportunities for bureaucratic careers by the creation of public bodies needing public managers—marketing boards, development corporations and other parastatal organisations and their subsidiaries. It articulates an ideology of state ownership and planning. It organises the

> means of its own reproduction bypassing on to the offspring of bureaucrats disproportionately advantageous opportunities to obtain the qualifications needed for entry into bureaucratic occupations and therefore the new class."[3]

As Dunleavy observed:

> "During the 1970s, conventional public administration approaches began to look tired and undynamic. By contrast, political economy offered a logical/deductive model of how government agencies behave, with clear directions for policy analysis and simple normative recommendations for reform. Public choice accounts became widely accepted because they fitted closely with everyday or common-sense views of bureaucracy. Officials and civil servants are basically portrayed as wanting to maximise their budgets, within external political constraints. Many people experience bureaucracies as expansionist organisations, constantly seeking to increase their size, staffs, financing and scope of operations."[4]

This administrative rigidly bureaucratic model is now being denounced and replaced by new managerial approach (NPM). Several rationales for the replacement include: the realisation that public service functions are managerial in nature, responses to the attacks on the scale and size of government, changes occurring in a range of different countries in the world. Recent changes in the public sector have led to fundamental questioning of its role and place in the economy. Here this may be called the public choice critique. A 1991 OECD report argues that an administrative system is economically sub-optimal:

> "It is argued that traditional administrative organisation is now reaching fundamental limits: the political/administrative system is not an efficient allocator of resources to meet demand: administration is not an efficient producer; untested and uneconomic burdens are being placed on business and individuals; the size and complexity of tasks overwhelm the capacities of traditional administration. Economic theory, and the evidence of performance measured in economic terms, suggest that there are inherent costs of public

sector provision which may only be justified in rigorously defined circumstances. Within the constitutional framework, political authorities have the responsibility to decide the balance of economic efficiency and other values; but the extent of the associated economic losses will depend on the cost-effectiveness of the public sector. However, the information available may be inadequate for such decisions to be made without risk."[5]

The period since the mid-1980s has seen the criticism and attack on the size and capability of the public sector. Government, particularly its bureaucracy has always been a source of some tension in the public as more services were demanded of it. There are mainly three reasons to this attack on the public sector and its administration.

First, the scale of the public sector was criticised with arguments advanced that governments were simply too big, consuming scarce resources. Second, there is the criticism about the scope of government. It was argued that government involved itself in too many services and that these could be returned to the private sector. Third, there was a scathing attack on the methods of government, with bureaucracy, especially becoming a highly unpopular form of social organisation. It is argued that bureaucracy greatly restricts the freedom of individual and is inefficient compared with the market. Formal bureaucracy may have its advantage but it is also argued that it encourage administrators to be risk-averse rather than risk-taking and to waste scarce resources instead of using them efficiently. Weber saw bureaucracy as the "ideal type" (rather than advocating it) but it is also attacked producing inertia, red tape, mediocrity and inefficiency. There seems to be two main problems with the theory of bureaucracy: one, its problematic relationship with democracy; and second, it is inefficient.

1. With its characteristics of rationality, hierarchy, rigidity and secrecy, bureaucracy inevitably comes into conflict with democracy. Weber noted: "every bureaucracy seeks to increase the superiority of the professionally informed by keeping their knowledge and intentions secret", adding that "the concept of the official secret is the specific invention of bureaucracy."[6]

Bureaucracy is seen by some as abrogating the power of the citizen or the politician with its political accountability problematic. To some in society this poses a problem as politicians see bureaucrats having wide powers over their lives. It did not make sense for a democracy to have a distinct elite acting secretively.

Theoretically the bureaucracy is accountable to the minister. But it seems that the accountability is not clarified and explicit, it is entirely to the minister to interpret the accountability in a manner that is most convenient to him. Similarly there is missing accountability of the bureaucrat to the citizens who get the services from the bureaucrats. Whenever bureaucratic control becomes all-encompassing it also creates an obsession with power. Detailed bureaucratic control over individuals and markets led to the fall of communist regimes in the former Eastern Block in the early 1990s.

2. The second problem of bureaucracy is that it is no longer regarded as a particularly efficient form of organisation. The technical superiority of bureaucracy was no longer accepted for two reasons.
   (i) First, there was some divergence in practice from Weberian principles, particularly in the personnel system, which was created more rigid, more formal and less elitist than Weber described.

   The principle of career service came to mean it was practically impossible to dismiss an employee in spite of the incumbent's incompetence. The principle of seniority came to be understood that promotions were ensured purely by length of service. Without considering the justification for the creation of posts in terms of workload at higher levels or the justification for initial recruitment, posts are often created and upgraded in the sheer fulfilment of the career prospects of the bureaucracy. Thus in some states, the State Civil Service officers rise automatically up to the level of Additional Secretary to the Government of India. This leads to an increase in the levels of government hierarchies so that in place of one Under Secretary, say, there would be an Under Secretary, a Deputy Secretary, a Joint Secretary, an Additional Secretary and a Special Secretary in addition to the Secretary. A major consequence of such promotions on service length would be an increase in the number of levels through which a proposal passes leading to delays and confusion, a missing principle of selection based on performance, the splitting of functional charges into additional posts with a reduced span of responsibility, giving rise to disgusted unemployment and the problem of administering each other.

Another glaring defect in the bureaucracy is its ever-growing size. This is in sharp contrast to functions it performs in comparison to the private sector employment. Statistical figures show that the share of government employment in the organised sector in India has increased from 58.3 per cent in 1961 to an estimate 72 per cent in 1999 which is one of the highest in the world. The number of posts in the Central Government increased from 17.37 lakh in 1957 to 39.50 lakh in 1999. Further figures show that the average wage of a bureaucrat in India is 7 times that of per capita GDP in any case, much higher than in other countries of Asia. All this has led to the financially burdensome as the wage bill puts a heavy squeeze on the funds available for development. In Punjab and Haryana more than 65 per cent of the funds in the budget are eaten up by the salaries, not to say anything of other perquisites and expenses. In other words agents of socio-economic progress and nation-building have become its principal, if not sole beneficiaries.

The unionisation of the bureaucracy, especially the lower bureaucracy, has destroyed not only the work culture and discipline but also demoralised the supervisory levels into withdrawal and the line of least resistance. The higher and the middle levels of bureaucracy are too powerless and marginalised to give any relief to citizens in cases of corruption and unresponsiveness by lower level staff at the cutting edge of the administration. Further endemic political interference by the political executive has compounded the marginalisation of the higher buraucracy, thereby undermining its capacity to deliver goods and services to the citizens.

Further the principle of political neutrality is being interpreted as the idea of "service to the nation", beyond that of rendering advice and carrying out the policy decisions of the political executive. This created problems of accountability in that bureaucrats did what they wanted, instead of what the elected politicians wanted them to do. Now there is a symbiosis between the politicians and the bureaucrats in that both share a power in pursuit of their self-interested ends. Some evidence in support of this is provided by an Indian bureaucrat who observed: "The bureaucracy is the instrument by which the politicans in power tend to extract rent from the clients of the bureaucracy. The bureaucrats, in turn, have happily extracted rent, kept a part of it for themselves, and passed on the remainder to their official and political superiors."[7]

(ii) Second, behavioural theories of organisations argue that formal bureaucratic models are no longer particularly efficient in comparison to more flexible forms of management. The bureaucratic organisation follows certain operating procedures but, consequently, the attainment of results may become less important than maintaining the processes and rules. Robert Merton argued: "Adherence to rules, originally conceived as a means, becomes transformed into an end-in-itself, there occurs the familiar process of displacement of goals whereby an instrumental value becomes a terminal value".[8] In other words, rigid adherence to rules leads to reduction in efficiency. Michel Crozier also argued that bureaucratic organisations were axiomatically inefficient, even that "a bureaucratic organisation is an organisation that cannot correct its behaviour by learning from its errors".[9]

Instead of bureaucracy becoming efficient as Weber argued, it is proving to be inefficient. S.K. Das noted:

"The bureaucracy in India is too big, costs too much and what is worse, does not have the capacity for delivering services. It is over-extended. Bureaucrats have appropriated a wide array of functions and the unhappy result for the user public is mounting non-performance.

Under-priced and overstaffed public utilities have performed poorly".[10]

Thus the Indian bureaucracy in its present-day functioning exhibits all the characteristics of a badly managed bureaucratic organisation. The bureaucracy in India is now under severe attack because of its vices of corruption, inefficiency, politicisation and criminalisation. Fixed procedures and orderly working patterns do not work well in the changed circumstances. Contemporary writers on New Public Management, Public Choice Theory, New Managerialism argue that bureaucracy is not appropriate for non-routine activities that involve creativity and innovation. With globalisation, privatisation waves, the private sector is moving away from formal bureaucratic structures toward greater flexibility in structure and staffing and to an increased emphasis on performance and speedy response. The focus of subsequent reforms in the public service has been to move away from the idea of a rigid and bureaucratic career service towards a more flexible structure which is capable of achieving results.

Despite the fact that the bureaucratic model, as outlined by Weber, has attracted many criticisms, "his model", according to Blau and Meyer, "has not been abandoned".[11] They draw three conclusions: first, that bureaucratic principles do achieve coordination and control in administration. Second, conclusion is that "bureaucratic principles may achieve efficiency in administration, but even when they do not, alternative forms of administration may prove even less desirable". Their third conclusion is that "bureaucratic organising principles can effectively serve many purposes, which may be in opposition to one another".[12] Bozeman and Straussman argue that organisation theorists are constantly "grappling with alternatives to the hierarchical image of bureaucracy, but the Weberian closed bureaucracy has staying power."[13]

With the introduction of liberalised policies, a change in public sector organisations has been to introduce business like flexibility and accountability in order to achieve desired results. While a new model is not fully in place, apparently there is now a greater focus on results than process, on accountability than its evasion and on management than administration.

## Focus in New Public Management

As noted earlier, the various names for new public management reflect differing views what is occurring, but they do have some points in common as:

- (i) First, the NPM represents a major shift from traditional public administration with much more attention paid to the achievement of results and the personal responsibilities of managers.
- (ii) Second, there is an intention to move away from classic bureaucracy to make organisations, personnel and employment terms and conditions more flexible.
- (iii) Third, the organisational and personnel objectives are to be set clearly in order to measure their achievement through performance indicators.
- (iv) Fourth, higher civil servants are more likely to be politically committed to the government of the day rather than being neutral.
- (v) Fifth, government functions are more likely to face market tests, such as contracting out in what Osborne and Gaebler call separation of "steering from rowing".[14]
- (vi) Sixth, there is also a trend towards reducing government functions through privatisation and other forms of contracting.

New public management looks at results first, with no preconceived idea as to how these should occur.

R.A.W. Rhodes[15] saw managerialism in Britain (the first country which initiated the privatisation of public enterprises) as a "determined effort to implement the '3Es' of economy, efficiency and effectiveness at all levels of British government" and argued: "The 'new public management' has the following central doctrines: a focus on management, not policy, and on performance appraisal and efficiency; the disaggregation of public bureaucracies into agencies which deal with each other on a user-pay basis; the use of quasi-markets and contracting out to foster competition; cost-cutting, and a style of management which emphasises, amongst other things, output targets, limited-term contracts, monetary incentives and freedom to manage".

Osborne and Gaebler in the United States are of the view that government needs to be "reinvented". Osborne and Gaebler's volume *Reinventing Government* is a book that has guided a great deal of recent thinking about management in the public sector including Clinton's *National Performance Review* in the United States. They propose to reorganise government by creating entrepreneurial incentives for the purpose of giving priority to the consumer, reducing bureaucracy, and empowering employees. By doing this the writers expect to create a "governmental market" that will:

1. save the government money and significantly decrease wasteful spending or bad investment choices.
2. increase the efficiency of governmental employees and the entire system of government, and
3. reduce the amount of 'red tape' within the systems.

In theory these proposed changes will result in a consumer-empowered, competitive, and market-oriented government that will reduce regulations, create revenue through fees and charges, and concentrate on the decentralisation of authority, the privatisation of management, and quality improvement in public services. Osborne and Gaebler set out a ten-point programme for what they term entrepreneurial governments:

> Most entrepreneurial governments promote *competition* between service providers. They *empower* citizens by pushing control out of the bureaucracy into the community. They measure the performance of their agencies, focusing not on inputs but on *outcomes*. They are driven by their goals—their *missions*—not by their rules and regulations. They redefine their clients as customers and offer them choices... They *prevent* problems before they emerge, rather than simply offering services afterward. They put their energies into *earning* money, not simply spending it. They *decentralize* authority, embracing participatory management. They prefer *market* mechanisms to bureaucratic mechanism. And they focus

not simply on providing public services, but on *catalyzing* all sectors—public, private and voluntary—into action to solve their community's problems.[16]

## Managerial Programme (Elements to NPM)

The emergence of a new managerial approach in the public sector marks a shift from earlier reforms. Instead of being reforms to the public sector, NPM represents a transformation of the public sector and its relationship with government, bureaucracy and society. Governments found that traditional model of administration did not work any more. They began to hire people trained in management in place of generalist officials, borrowed management technology and techniques from the private sector, erased the line of demarcation between public and private sector activity with the objective of reducing costs, and set out to change working environment which was not conducive. Faced with declining real revenue and political demands to maintain services, governments adopted new managerialism approach.

As to what is involved in managerialism or NPM, the OECD[17] argues that many of its members "are trying to make their public sectors more managerial" with a common feature being the introduction of "a more contractual, participative, discretionary style of relationship: between levels of hierarchy; between control agencies and operating units; and between producing units, be they public or private". The main elements in the OECD view could be briefed as: (i) improving human resources, including performance pay; (ii) staff involvement in decision-making, (iii) relaxing controls, but imposing performance targets; (iv) using information technology; (v) service to clients; (vi) user charges; (vii) contracting out; and (viii) deregulation of monopolies.

For Massey,[18] elemental threads intrinsic to goals of reforms have been:

(i) to reduce the role and extent of the 'state' in order to enhance that of the private sector.
(ii) to facilitate the acquisition of entrepreneurial skills and activities within society generally;
(iii) to prevent future expansion of the public sector, often

through the creation of a powerful coalition of interests to counter the perceived welfare-demanding coalitions which have linked their interests to those of the bureaucrats;

(iv) to de-politicise many (mainly economic) policy decision and their being entrusted to professional experts, rather than the whim of politicians and bureaucrats perceived to be in the thrall of self-serving interest groups;

(v) to inculcate public sector organisations with the best techniques of private sector practice in order to bring the discipline and inherent efficiencies of the marketplace to the activities of the state;

(vi) to entrench the divisions between the private and public in such a way that individual civil liberties are protected by inalienable property rights, which act as a flexible bulwark against the power of the state and the temptations of state employees and elected politicians to behave in an arbitrary and capricious manner, abusing their power, power loaned to them in trust by the citizenry.

Hood[19] considers the managerial programme or what he calls "new public management" as comprising seven main points.

1. ***Hands-on professional management in the public sector:*** This means letting the managers manage, or as Hood puts it "active, visible, discretionary control of organisational from named persons at the top". The typical justification for this is that "accountability requires clear assignment of responsibility for action".
2. ***Explicit standards and measures of performance:*** This acquires goals to be defined and performance targets to be set, and is justified by proponents as accountability requires (a) clear statement of goals; efficiency requires a "hard look" at objectives.
3. ***Greater emphasis on output controls:*** Resources are directed to areas according to measured performance, because of the "need to stress results rather than procedures".
4. ***A shift to disaggregation of units in the public sector:*** This involves the breaking up of large entities into "corporatised units around products", funded separately and "dealing with one another on an "arm's-length" basis. This is justified by

the need to create manageable units and to gain the efficiency advantages of franchise arrangements inside as well as outside the public sector."

5. ***A shift to greater competition in (the) public sector:*** This involves, "the move to term contracts and public tendering procedures" and is justified as using "rivalry as the key to lower costs and better standards".
6. ***A stress on private sector style of management practice:*** This involves a "move away from military-style 'public service ethic' and flexibility in hiring and rewards", and is justified by "need to use 'proven' private sector management tools in the public sector".
7. ***A stress on greater discipline and parsimony in resource use:*** Hood sees this as "cutting direct costs, raising labour discipline, resisting union demands, limiting 'compliance costs' to business" and is typically justified by the "need" to check resource demands of public sector and "do more with less".

## Ideological and Theoretical Bases for New Managerialism

### *Ideological basis*

It is generally argued that the new managerialism is an ideological movement. Pollitt argues that

> "managerialism is the 'acceptable face' of new-right thinking concerning the state. It is an ingredient in the *pot pouri* which can attract support beyond the new right itself. For that wider constituency 'better management' sounds sober, neutral, as unopposable as virtue itself. Given the recent history of public service expansion the productivity logic has a power of its own which stands independently of the political programme of the new right. Yet simultaneously for new right believers, better management provides a label under which private sector disciplines can be introduced to the public services, political control can be strengthened, budgets trimmed, professional autonomy reduced, public service unions weakened and a quasi-competitive framework erected to flush out the 'natural' inefficiencies of bureaucracy".[20]

The focus of managerialism is on improving performance and reducing government and involvement as far as possible. Managerialism was adopted by both the Thatcher and Reagan governments because these had a profound distaste for the public service. Public choice can be another basis of managerialism.

***Theoretical basis***

Unlike traditional public administration founded on (i) the theory of bureaucracy, and (ii) the theory of separation between politics and administration. New Public Management (NPM) is theoretically based on economics and private management. Pollitt,[21] for example, argues that management is "clearly an activity which is intimately concerned with directing flows of resources so as to achieve defined objectives "and these objectives" are defined predominantly in the language of economics". At another point he claims the driving force behind management change was a "a generic model of management" and the particular species of genericism tended to be "of a neo-Taylorian character".

It is argued that the economic basis to managerialism allows it to draw on 'public choice theory' (1980s). The key assumption of public choice is the view of individual rationality. According to Stigler: "A rational man must be guided by the incentive system within which he operates.... The carrot and the stick guide scientists and politicians as well as donkeys".[22]

The "public choice theory" gave theoretical backing to the attack on bureaucracy, politicians (motivated by selfish interest instead of public interest) reducing government in general and gave a methodology for designing market-oriented public policies. Economic thinking dominated the government and public administration in both theory and practice. The focus on managerial models on results, productivity and measurement could be said to derive from economics and private management.

It may be emphasised that public management has largely been influenced by the theories and techniques of private management. Much more attention now paid to the strategic planning and management in the public sector is attributed to the private sector. What is more now observed is the adoption of private sector personnel practices including the greater use of rewards throughout the organisation, such as paying more for good performance, or less for poor performance, or terminating staff relatively easily (the voluntary retirement schemes have been offered to the staff working in the public sector banks and many public enterprises in India recently). The traditional model of public administration was criticised for its focus on structure and process rather than results. New public management like the private management looks at results first, with no preconceived notion as to how these occur.

Thus economics and private management do largely contribute to the formation of theoretical bases of new public management. Two issues which have direct relevance to the NPM practice are: (i) Relationships with politicians, and (ii) New contractualism.

(i) *Relationships with Politicians*

In the traditional model of public administration, the relationship between the political leadership and the bureaucracy was one of the master and servant, of one giving the order and one carrying it out. The main characteristic of the NPM approach is that responsibility is taken by managers for the achievement of results. Public managers are now involved in matters of policy, they are equally involved in matters of strict politics, they are more often personally accountable if something goes wrong. An effective manager is one who is good political player. The traditional model attempted to de-politicise what is essentially political. New public management, on the other hand, does recognise the essential political character of government managers and the public servants are supposed to work with politicians in an interactive process. Further there is the recognition of the need for direct responsibility between public managers and the public.

(ii) *New Contractualism*

Any government service can be provided by contract either externally through private providers or internally with other parts of government. "Contracting can replace traditional bureaucractic hierarchy and command with networks of providers loosely clustered around government funding agencies, delivering services once the exclusive domain of the State".[23] The resort to contracts is to reduce the scope of the public sector. Davis adds that a contract state might turn being akin to the traditional model of public administration, containing a small elite of core officials.

## Criticism of New Managerial Approach

New public management, managerialism or market-based administration which has been followed by most developing countries since 1990s is fraught with serious criticisms. "Managerialism" is seen as a derogatory term in some quarters particularly in India. There are several aspects of new public management which have attracted criticism.

1. ***Revival of Taylorism:*** Pollitt, a staunch critic, sees managerialism representing a revival of Frederick Taylor's scientific management ideas which, according to him, are contrary to the development of the organisational behaviour (human relations approach). Pollitt argues that the managerial reform programme in the 1970s and 1980s "was dominated by the values of efficiency and economy, with effectiveness a poor third", while "other values—for example, fairness, justice, representation, or participation—were either off the agenda or were treated as constraints on the drive for higher productivity.[24]
2. ***Basis in Public Choice Theory:*** The basis in public choice theory forms one of the criticisms of managerialist thinking. Public choice advocates the maximisation of choice by individuals, a maximum role for market forces and a minimal role for government. The key assumption of public choice is a view of rationality. However, in the real world all individuals do not behave rationally and all bureaucrats do not maximise their own utility (that is increasing their own power, prestige and security). It could be said that the assumption of individual rationality is too sweeping and ignores any selfless or public-spirit behaviour by public officials. The question about bureaucrats maximising budgets to achieve their personal ends suffers from a marked lack of empirical test.[25]
3. ***Ethical and Accountability Problems:*** It is argued that politicisation of the public service leads to erosion of ethical stand-

ards. Stillman argues that the emphasis on "an enlarged, politically partisan cadre of loyalists to carry out the work of public administration can and does lead to wholesale corruption and ethical misconduct in office, not to mention poor and inefficient performance as well". It can open up the government to shady practices, but "limited state literature remains largely silent on these vital accountability issues".[26] A few ethical problems may arise in contractual matters. Corruption may be resulting from such as secret commissions to individual public officials giving contracts, political interference in the selection of contractors, collusion among tenderers and acceptance of tenders for prices above the cost of public provision. It is largely felt that there are greater opportunities for the dishonest with the adoption of new managerialism. In addition there are difficulties in ascertaining accountability.

4. ***Problem of Politicisation:*** Under the new managerial approach political leaders are now more likely to select their departmental head, and require some sympathy with their political goals. On the contrary it is argued that politicisation of the public service could lead to the emergence of spoils system. If public managers are to be made accountable for their own results, and the system becomes more political and personal, the same kinds of problems could happen. In such a changed situation when public servants became politically committed, there might be demands to emphasise the notion of civil service neutrality.
5. ***Other Problems of the Managerialism:*** First, new public management is associated with reducing government and developing markets instead. However, it is one thing to apply market principles and adopt managerial approach, yet another to have markets work. Developing countries do not have much experience in the operation of markets. Markets require rule of law to ensure compliance with contracts. Where goals are vague and not clearly specified, or where corruption is endemic, using contracts is not likely to be successful.

In developing countries where capital markets are underdeveloped, there is likely to be greater domination by foreign or multinational corporations. In addition, changing from bureaucracy to markets might lead to corrupt practices, although the World Bank in its report in 1997 argues: "Reforming the civil service, restraining political patronage, and improving civil service pay have also been shown to reduce corruption by giving public officials more incentive to play by the rules." The reality is, however, that the bureaucracy remains more important than in Western countries and that in order for the market-oriented changes to work, a powerful institution will have to give up a substantial amount of its power and, in the absence of other power centres in the polity or the markets will have to do so voluntarily.

Frederickson (1992) states that the major problem areas of *Reinventing Government* (by Osborne and Gaebler) are the idea that the government is a "market" and the citizens are the "customers" that downsizing will decrease the size and cost of government without diminishing its effective level of functioning, and the assumption that the employees of government are the primary problem. These criticisms suggest that government could possibly become more complicated, less effective and authoritative, and ultimately weaker and unsuccessful in serving its citizens.

## Conclusion

New public management, it is argued by (World Bank and most developed countries, including United States, United Kingdom and France) does offer much to developing countries, at least by comparison to the traditional model of public administration which did not work. However, by itself it is unlikely to produce good results in developing countries. Developing countries are faced with problems of poverty, institutions, the rule of law, inadequate capital and retail markets, lack of educated and trained staff and so on. Moreover, developing countries have different cultures, histories and are not homogeneous. New public management accompanied by the use of welfare-oriented private sector may help the transient of developing economies into developed ones.

## REFERENCES

1. The traditional model of Public Administration tended to be rigid and bureaucratic, was based on process instead of outcomes, and

on setting procedures to follow instead of focusing on results.
2. World Bank, *World Development Report, 1997*, Washington: World Bank, 1997, p. 23.
3. B.C. Smith, *Understanding Third World Politics: Theories of Political Change and Development*, Bloomington: Indiana University Press, 1996, pp. 235-36.
4. Patrick Dunleavy, *Democracy, Bureaucracy and Public Choice: Economic Explanations in Political Science*, London: Harvester, Wheatsheaf, 1991, p. 147.
5. OECD, *Serving the Economy Better, Occasional Papers on Public Management*, Paris: OECD, 1991, p. 13.
6. H.H. Gerth and C. Wright Mills (eds.), *From Max Weber: Essays in Sociology*, London: Routledge and Kegan Paul, 1970, p. 233.
7. S.K. Das, "Managing the Bureaucracy", in S.L. Rao, *Managing the Indian State*, New Delhi: All Indian Management Association, 1999, p. 64.
8. Robert Merton, *Social Theory and Social Structure*, 3rd edn., New York: Free Press, 1968, p. 260.
9. Michel Crozier, *The Bureaucratic Phenomenon*, Chicago: University of Chicago, 1964, p. 187.
10. Das, *op. cit.*, p. 60.
11. Peter M. Blau and Marshall W. Meyer, Bureaucracy in Modern Society, 3rd edn., New York: Random House, 1987, p. 162.
12. *Ibid.*, pp. 186-87.
13. Barry Bozeman and Jeffrey D. Straussman, *Public Management Strategies*, San Francisco: Jossey-Bass, 1990, p. 142.
14. David Osborne and Ted Gaebler, *Reinventing Government: How the Entrepreneurial Spirit is Transforming the Public Sector*, Reading, M.A.: Addison-Wesley, 1992.
15. R.A.W. Rhodes, "Introduction", *Public Administration*, vol. 69, No. 1, 1991, pp. 1-2.
16. Osborne and Gaebler, *op. cit.*, p. 20.
17. OECD, *Public Management Developments: 1991*, Paris: OECD, 1991, p. 11.
18. Andrew Massey, *Managing the Public Sector*, Aldershot: Edward Elgar, 1993, pp. 7-8.
19. Christopher Hood, "A Public Management for all Seasons", *Public Administration*, vol. 69, no. 1, 1991, pp. 4-5.
20. Christopher Pollitt, *Managerialism and the Public Services: The Anglo-American Experience*, Oxford: Basic Blackwell, 1990, p. 49.
21. Pollitt, *op. cit*, p. 5.
22. George Stigler, *The Citizen and the State*, Chicago: University of Chicago Press, 1975, p. 171.

23. Glyn Davis, "Implications, Consequences and Futures", in Davis and others (eds.), *The New Contractualism*, Melbourne: Macmillan, 1997, p. 236.
24. Pollitt, *op. cit.*, p. 138.
25. Jan-Erik Lane (ed.),*The Public Sector: Concepts, Models and Approaches*, 2nd edn., London: Sage, 1995, pp. 64-65.
26. Richard J. Stillman, *Preface to Public Administration: A Search for Themes and Direction*, New York: St. Martin's Press, 1991, p. 183.

# 2

# New Public Management

*Shrikant Baldi*

## Introduction

The new public management (NPM) represents the thrust of managerial reforms in the public sector of developed market economies over the past two decades notably in the U.K., New Zealand and Australia. Since 1990 some of the developing countries have also adopted variants of NPM.

NPM has become a collective term and a shorthand name for a bundle of particular management approaches and techniques, which dominated the government sector reforms in most of the O.E.C.D. countries from the late 1970s. Many of these techniques were borrowed from private sector and applied to public sector. The term NPM thus captures most of the structural, organisational and management changes in the government services, which seek to shift the emphasis from traditional public administration to market-based public administration.

## Factors Driving NPM

The fiscal and economic crisis leading to shrinking budget compelled most of the developed countries to refocus on the government services. The rapid expansion of information technology made the various traditional activities in the government sector redundant. The good governance debate, which emphasised on better public service delivery, required a re-look on government services. With advent of WTO most of the countries were to become internationally competitive. It was also felt that government had over-extended and unaffordable and citizens were largely dissatisfied. Moreover the new technologies like IT, etc., opened up new methods of service delivery. All these factors were catalyst in bringing new approach in the public administration.

## NPM Goals

The main goals of NPM are

1. Improving economy, efficiency and effectiveness of public service delivery.
2. Improving the quality of public services.
3. Making the government sector customer-oriented.
4. Bringing the much desired performance orientation in the government sector.

## Key Components of NPM

### 1. *Decentralisation, Disaggregation and Downsizing in Public Services*

(a) ***New structures:*** The emphasis was given on breaking up of huge bureaucracies by separating the strategic policy and operational arm of government like in UK executive agencies have been formed which are separate and independent from the Ministries. The formation of executive agencies reform took place in UK on the basis of IBBS Report and which is continuing now as next step programme. The main change in the separation is that the relationship between the Ministries and executive agencies is now not have the traditional hierarchy but based on contractual agreement. The stress is on corporatisation and managerialism. These agencies are given full autonomy in financial, personnel and in professional management. In UK the executive agencies are formed when prior option of abolition, privation and contracting out has been considered and not found feasible.

(b) ***Flatter hierarchies:*** The stress is given on replacing traditional tall hierarchies with flatter, flexible and more responsive structures formed and reformed around specific processes, e.g., issuing licenses, paying benefits rather than traditional functions like finance and personnel.

(c) ***Separation between the role of funder, purchaser and provider of services:*** Making a clearer separation (organisational and financial) between defining the need for and paying for public services on one hand and the actually providing these services.

(d) ***Decentralised management authority:*** Giving top management freedom to manage with clear responsibility and reducing the management goal like in case of grant-maintained schools in UK.

(e) ***Devolving budget and financial control:*** Delegation of financial responsibility gives manager some leeway to consider alternative methods of ensuring the provision of required services.

### 2. *Market and Quasi-Market*

Introducing market and quasi-market type mechanism to stimulate competition between service providing agencies, in the belief that this will promote cost savings and responsiveness (OECD, 1993). Fostering competition between service providers is key to increasing efficiency and effectiveness. The common instrument used for market type mechanism include:

(a) ***Contracting out (out-sourcing):*** The main objective of public services should be steering and not rowing. If the teachers and taught becomes the same, then the quality of public services would deteriorate like if the municipal administration itself take up the cleaning services or if transport department directly provide the bus services. To ensure that the contracting out is successful, it is necessary that service requirement are ascertained, there is a transparent bidding system and there is a regular monitoring of performance, based on output and outcome.

(b) ***User charges:*** The user charges should be based on actual cost of service so the benefit of the service is properly evaluated by the users and secondly the charges are paid by the beneficiary and not by someone else through taxes like if Municipal Committee is required to charge full cost of water supply then the consumers will evaluate whether it is providing proper water supply as per the cost or not. They will also consider whether it is better to take water supply from Municipal Committee or through some other source like tube-wells. While levying user charges consultation with users integrating equity considerations and efficient collection system are *sine qua non*.

(c) ***Internal pricing:*** There should be market testing of in-house operation like photostat section, building department and the budget for these purposes is provided to the user departments.

(d) ***Internal market:*** Budget is required to be provided to the user department to get a better service like for construction of a school building budget is provided to Education Departement than to PWD. Similarly a particular school is provided budget on the number of students admitted in that school and a particular PHC is provided budget on the number of indoor and outdoor patients treated by it.

### 3. *Customer Orientation*

The delivery of public services should meet the need of the citizens not the convenience of the service provider like the timings of public library should not be based on the convenience of the library employees (10 to 5) but on the convenience of the public who may like to use it in the evening and on Sundays. To ensure customer orientation, most of the developed countries have published citizen charters, which focus on end-result and service standards. It is also to be ensured that public should be involved in decision-making about how services should be provided. The delivery should be targeted like subsidised seeds and food should be given to the poor and needy in place of giving to everyone and diluting its effect. It is also important that government should be open and transparent and there should be freedom of information. Moreover, government should be joined up and budget of various departments doing the similar activities should be pooled. By these measures public services are made more responsive to the wishes of the users. In UK customer views and demands are increasingly being used for shaping service provisions by formulating citizen charters and NHS patient charters.

4. ***Changing Employment Relations***

In most of the developed countries limited term contract is being given to senior staff in place of traditional career tenure. In place of fixed salary, performance related pay based on performance appraisal is increasingly being adopted. All the recruitment and promotions are strictly based on merit and not on the basis of length of service. There is an emphasis on mobility within and between public and private sectors.

5. ***Performance Orientation***

Most of the public services are evaluated on the basis of performance indicators based on output and outcome in place of traditional process and input accountability. In UK, Audit Commission publishes performance review of all the government departments. Moreover, all the executive agencies have to publish their performance for the consumption of the general public. The emphasis in public services is on result-based accountability and most of the departments are moving from accountability for inputs (obeying the rules on spending and staffing) to accountability for outputs (performance).

6. ***Others***

In addition to the above-mentioned principles and practices, there is emphasis on regulatory reforms in economic, social and administrative sectors. There is emphasis on re-thinking role of the government.

## Applicability of NPM in India

1. ***Decentralisation, Disaggregation and Downsizing the Public Services***

The new public management emphasises on corporatisation by

separating the policy-making and execution role of the government. The corporatisation is not a new thing for Indian public services and many public sector units are already working under the government of India and State Governments based on the principal of separation of operational work and autonomy. However, this has not resulted into any efficieny in delivery of public services, as there is a complete lack of performance orientation. There are excessive controls from the government and legislature, the staff works as government employees and are amenable to political interference. The audit of these undertakings is based on inputs and not on performance. Moreover, the discretion in working leads to arbitrariness and corruption. The government also faces the problem of monitoring these undertakings effectively.

The reforms of flatter organisations is not possible as retrenchment in the public services is not possible due to complex socio-political conditions. Regarding the reform of decentralised management, most of the autonomous bodies like universities, etc., have not shown any perceptible improvement in the performance. In fact, in the Indian condition it appears that central control and procedures are the only safeguard against discretion leading to corruption and nepotism.

**2. *Market and Quasi-Market***

(a) ***Contracting out:*** The system of contracting out is already in vogue in many departments like PWD and IPH. But contracting out in place of improving performance and bringing economy has been the den of corruption, patronage and discretion. This is basically because of lack of transparent rules and tendering system. Moreover there is lack of accountability due to undesired secrecy in all the procedures for purchases (this has also been revealed by Tehlaka exposure). In many departments contracting out becomes dfficult because of institutional weakness and transaction cost. Our legal system also tends to procrastinate such matters.

(b) ***User charges:*** In India levying of user charges is beset with many problems. Due to populist political system it is not possible to levy user charges in most of the cases. Even if it is levied, it is levied only partially. Moreover if full cost is levied then it will put the poor people in difficult position because of lack of safety nets. In addition of this, government sector is by and large inefficient, hence the cost of service delivery is very heavy which cannot be transferred to the users. In most of the cases, the collection cost of user charges is very heavy and there is a problem of evasion.

(c) ***Internal market:*** There is a problem of proper accounting and also of the transaction cost in creating internal market.

Hence subjecting the State to more competition in India is beset with the problem of rule-based compliance, weak capacity and non-transparency.

### 3. *Customer Orientation*

In India most of the government departments lack the customer orientation because of feudal mindset. Most of the government officials are treated as higher/above than the public to whom they are supposed to serve. In such a mindset it is very difficult to expect a customer orientation in the government departments. Moreover, there is a lack of transparency and inadequate grievance redressal mechanism in most of the government departments. Most of the government departments do not publish the service standards and they are not accountable to the public.

### 7. *Changing Employment Relations*

Most of the reforms proposed by new public management are not feasible in India as strong trade unions do not allow any change in employment relations. The labour laws in India are very stringent and over-protective for labourers. Moreover, there is a lack of safety valves and employment opportunities if employees are given only the short-term employment. This system is also susceptible to misuse because of patronage system based on region, religion and caste. The performance related pay could easily be abused by senior officers to build personal empire.

### 8. *Performance Orientation*

Performance-based accountability does not work in India because of existence of separate formal and informal rules based on political, regional and caste connections. It is also difficult to hold anyone responsible for performance, as there is hardly any control on staff and funds and over control by the government. The information collection system is unreliable which hampers performance-monitoring system. In general obedience and loyalty is considered more important than the actual performance. In addition to this, there is hardly any incentive to perform better in the government. I am reminded of one quote that who is a good government officer? A good government officer is who is "*baat main chust, file per drust* and *kaam main sust*".

### 9. *Others*

In addition to the above points, in India large number of people are illiterate, the law enforcing institutions are weak, there is no freedom of information and most of the decisions are on extraneous considerations than on merit because of complex socio-political situation. This leaves very little room to apply the techniques of new public management in Indian public sector.

## What Needs to be Done

### 1. *Matching the role of the state to its capability*

In general the State should do what it is capable of. But reducing or diluting the State role cannot be the end of the reform story. For human welfare to be advanced the State's capability—defined as the ability to undertake and promote collective actions efficiently, must be increased. The capability of State could be raised by reinvigorating public institutions.

### 2. *Steps needed to reinvigorate public institutions*

(a) ***Establishing a foundation of law:*** The first and foremost requirement in India is rule-based compliance. All the law and rules should be enforced without any distinction of rich or powerful or VIPs. This requires that the rules should be clear and transparent and they should be enforced impartially, effectively and quickly through efficient judicial system. Writing laws are the easy part, enforcing them in fairness is difficult.

(b) ***Maintaining non-distortionery policy environment:*** For government's credibility the predictability of rules and policies and the consistency with which they are applied, are very important factors in attracting private investment. Weak and arbitrary state institutions often compound the problem with unpredictable and inconsistent behaviour.

(c) ***Giving people a voice:*** Greater information and transparency are vital for informed public debate for increasing popular trust and confidence in the State. Users need to be involved in planning and supervision. There are clear evidences that government programmes work better when they seek the participation of potential user.

(d) ***Subjecting the State to more competition:*** Government can improve their capability and effectiveness by introducing much greater competition in variety of areas in hiring and promotion, in policy-making and the way services are to be delivered.

(e) ***Boosting competition within the civil service:*** The recruitment in civil service should be based on merit not favouritism and there should be a merit-based promotion system.

(f) ***Strengthening watchdog institutions:*** For government reforms to succeed, it is necessary that watchdog institutions like Judiciary, Press, Comptroller and Auditor General, Institutions of Lokpal and Lokayukt are properly strengthened so that they could ensure proper vigil on the government service delivery.

(g) ***Bringing accountability through transparency:*** Most of the government departments lack accountability due to non-transparent way of working. It is very necessary that Right to Information Act be passed by the Parliament so that citizens have right to access information in all the public offices.

(h) ***Effective regulations:*** Well-designed regulatory system can help societies influence market outcome for public ends.

Regulation can protect consumers, workers and the environment. It can foster competition and innovation while constraining the abuse of monopoly power. Due to regulatory reforms initiated in 1980s Chile's telecommunication industry has enjoyed sustained private investment increasing service quality and reducing prices.

(i) ***Sequencing reforms:*** All the reforms should not be taken at one go. In place of this we should proceed with caution. Giving public managers more flexibility may increase arbitrariness and corruption with no commensurate improvement in performance. Hence step-by-step reforms should be undertaken.

(j) ***Strengthening database:*** For performance monitoring and evaluation correct data and management information system is essential.

(k) ***Combating entrenched corruption:*** A major thrust should be to reduce the opportunity for corruption by cutting back on discretionary authority. Policies that lower controls on trade, remove entry barriers for private industry, privatise state firms in a way that ensure competition—all of these will fight corruption. The renowned expert Klitgart has rightly said that *corruption is equal to monopoly plus discretion minus accountability and transparency*. Hence we need to cut monopoly and discretion and increase accountability and transparency.

(l) ***Strengthening democratic decentralisation:*** We have to strengthen the Panchayats in true spirit of 73rd Constitutional amendment to work as institution of self-government.

(m) ***Others:*** There is a need to develop performance indicators based on output and outcome for all public services. Accountability should be built in the system for bureaucracy as well as for politicians by ensuring transparency in all public dealings. There is a need to promote literacy and awareness. The use of IT in all walks of public life should be encouraged to cut down delays and red-tapism. There is a need to bring attitudinal change in bureaucracy, which make them customer oriented. All the laws and rules should be reviewed to measure their customer orientation and simplicity of enforcement. Last but not the least, is the effective political commitment for reforms, which was shown by Margaret Thatcher as Prime Minister of Britain.

At the end I would like to say that market and governments are complementary. The State is essential for putting in place the appropriate institutional foundation for markets. An effective State is not a luxury but it is vital for provision of goods and services, rules and institutions that allow market to flourish. Hence by having effective State we can ensure that the public services are geared effectively for the users and general public.

# 3

# Redefining Public Administration

*Manoj Dixit & Jaya Chaturvedi*

Ideas have to be in keeping with the times to escape the charge of redundancy. If the aforesaid be not the case, things appear out of context and are unsuited to tackling the problems at hand. If such be the case, ideas need to be redefined or reassessed as the need be. Public administration likewise needs to be redefined in the changed context. The chief contextual factors can be identified as Globalisation, knowledge era, liberalisation and political pluralism. Administration needs to be considerably *resilient* to face up to the multifarous challenges.

Theoretically public administration has been understood as follows.

- Getting things done
- Co-operative rational action
- Consciously co-ordinated activity of two or more persons
- Determined action taken in pursuit of a conscious purpose
- Concerned with the "what" and "how"of government.

According to Merson, "The administrator gets things done and just as the science of politics is an enquiry into the best means whereby the will of the people may be organised for the formulation of the policies, so the science of administration is an enquiry as to how policies may best be carried into operation".

Such an understanding suggests a routine administration and not one that is proactive or one that can make things happen instead of passively getting things done. Administration has to plan as well as administer. There is the question then of division of labour between political and administrative institutions. One of the persistent problems of administrative science has been to work out an acceptable separation of jurisdictions between the two. If public administration really is concerned with the what and how of government, a strict policy administration dichotomy may not be feasible in practice. Pfiffner's understanding of public administration as "organisation and direction of human and natural resources to achieve desired ends" echoes at this point and seems most pertinent, especially when one is tempted to discount policy/administration dichotomy in the interest of a new and revolutionary public administration. One talks of both institutional and attitudinal transformation in order to bring about real development administration. Development policies for instance have relied/concentrated on engineering change. Engineering of change involves social craft in that attitudes, beliefs and culture change along with occupation and outlook towards life. Engineering of change will depend on how change is understood. If change is taken to mean a drastic reordering of affairs, it will entail reformatory/transformatory alteration of existing affairs, which may or may not lead to desirable change in the long run. For instance, opening of public schools imparting liberal education with regular higher secondary curricula in a backward area inhabited mostly by tribals can at best be described as an unthinking strategy, totally devoid of rationality. The other approach is to have administration aiding and abetting and thereby expediting/facilitating the natural course of evolution that any community of people undergo. To make matters clearer, development administration is about attempts at discovering the real needs of a specific group of people, and making provisions for their fulfilment so their natural evolution is not obstructed. Tribals, instead of History and Geography may be in need of technical know-how and finances to revive or preserve traditional handicraft or some such occupation which makes them subsist and possibly thrive as a community.

Likewise, different regional/linguistic/ethnic groups of people may have specific interests to be answered and attended to. Education packages in the above cases should include vocational assistance in the identified area so people are technically equipped besides being aware of their rights and privileges. Similarly, and for instance, there is need for incorporating agriculture science in school curriculum in predominantly rural areas. The medium of instruction should preferable be the regional language so people establish a sense of identity with what is imparted to them by way of education. Certain innovative strategies may also need to be adopted as far as primary education is concerned. It may unquestionably be a good idea to teach what people wish to learn. Education has to evoke interest, especially, adult education. It may be a good idea to include traditional Indian scriptural knowledge, which is both interesting and knowledgeable in literary campaigns in traditional regional pockets. One is referring to *Amar Chitra Kathas* and the like to boost cultural values and possibly moral calibre in subjects. It may be apt to remark here that *New public administration* has to aim at sustainable development, i.e., development that is in consonance with and not antithetical to Indian cultural values. Here it should be remembered that culture implies a set of ideas and not a set of redundant or conservative practices. There is no suggestion of obscurantism or even a reactionary or revivalist prescription. Sustainable development has to be understood in the wider cultural context and not simply ecological, as it is generally understood/appreciated. The difference thus in engineering change and aiding and abetting change that is naturally ordered/directed, is that the former aims at changing the existing state of affairs for a completely new one while the latter seeks to understand the exigencies/requirements of a situation and answers them so that the natural process of change sees the light sooner and in a surer fashion than is ordained. In the same vein, obstruction of any sort is ruled out. This will mean a catalytic administration and not one, which claims omniscience and insists on dictation.

Again, public administration has to be far-sighted. It has to be aware of all possible consequences running even into the distant future if it has to be development orientated in the real sense. One has to move from short run to long-term objectives.

Administration today is more reactive than proactive in nature. It reacts to emergent situations rather than anticipate pre-empt them or apply far-sight and modify them in the desired fashion. The other alternative may be to introduce policy packages designed to bring about far-reaching economic, socio-cultural changes. Simon's mean end chain must be remembered at this point. Every end is a means to a further end. The ultimate end has to be kept in view and achievement of every intermediate end assessed continually in the light of the final value aimed at. To serve an example, the government recently gave ownership rights to slum dwellers (refugees) to lands they had inhabited for a long time. The immediate unrest was laid to rest. Values sacrificed were not if at all taken into account. Values referred to could range from those involving town planning issues, hygiene/sanitation with possible consequences for health care administration, demographic/cultural consequences, crime situation, etc. Obviously, any long-term strategy for municipal administration was non-existent or ruefully sacrificed if at all in existence. Needless to point out, specialist institutions like town planning agencies obviously had nothing to do with that particular decision. As has been pointed out earlier, the nature of relationship between politics and administration has been difficult to define. If politics makes unruly inroads into administration, the impact on administration is bound to be unsavoury. While policy and administration are integrally connected/related, the same can/cannot be said about politics and administration. While the two are integrally related, the onus for maintaining the integrity, efficiency, morale as also neutrality of administration falls on the political institutions. Crippling directives like the one listed above do not help the cause at all. Besides, politically motivated decisions like the aforesaid negate the understanding of administration as a co-operative and rational exercise. In the above case it comes across as very much an arbitrary exercise as also an irrational one.

Another facet that has to be considered in the context of redefining public administration is the relationship between administration and democracy. Democracy is the most acceptable form of government. Democracy however is at best an occasional occurrence in that it is in evidence once every five years when the country goes to polls. For the interregnum when the elected party is functional as the government, democracy is all but elusive; more so in case of absolute majority for the party in power. Another way to put is that the most disquieting thing about democracy is that it is an intermittent phenomenon. It has been the contention of leading political theorists, that democracy is visible/evident only during the time of elections when people exercise their franchise and chose their representatives. It is held hostage for the intervening period between two elections. Democracy on a sustained basis is the desired virtue/ state of affairs. In the absence of right to information as a recognised fundamental right, what transpires in the corridors of power is very much a secret. Democracy in practice is more a mirage that shows up every now and then and helplessly fades away.

Policy is the chief instrument by which administration functions. Democracy can be secured by invoking the device of public interest via public policy. Public interest then has to be articulated on a sustained basis. Advocacy of public interest as an instrument of democracy is based on a positive assumption of its veracity as a rational guide of public policy. There can be two broad assumptions as far as public interest is concerned. First, that people are rational and people know what is best/ desirable. Second, that governance is esoteric business, which should be left to a chosen view; "rabble does not reason". The latter view does not hold ground any more. Each man is as much a master of destiny as any other. Democracy is constitutional rule.

Aristotle discusses the cardinal principles of constitutional rule. It is:

- Rule in the public or general interest as distinguished from a factional or tyrannous rule in the interest of a single class or individual.
- Government is carried on by general regulations and not by arbitrary decrees and also in the vaguer sense that the government does not flout standing customs and conventions of the constitution.
- Constitutional government means the government of willing subjects as distinguished from a despotism that is supported merely by force.

Political and administrative institutions partake equally in governance. Needless to assert then, administration has to be as value-based as politics itself. The fact-value dichotomy thus could be said to be predicated on the politics-administration dichotomy. If both are taken to be equal partners in governance, the distinction is rendered fallacious. The conceptual separation of fact and value and political and administrative activities is more a matter of degree than kind. Thus, administration is primarily concerned with facts and politics with values.

It is also held by political theorists that public opinion must be admitted to be not only an unavoidable force but also, up to a point, a justifiable standard in politics.

Direct democracy seems to be the only sure way of practising/ensuring real democracy. It is however not practicable except in cases of gram sabhas or city states. While the former exist in present times, the latter are not found any more. Direct democracy however can be made to function in a different way; via policy formation. Direct democracy is about legislation based on public opinion, preferably, General Will (Rousseau). Government functions by way of policies. The process of policy formation has to have democracy built into it. This is the only way to ensure publicness of public administration. The idea of publicness of public administration often dissolves in the maze of uncertainty/indeterminancy. Public is an unwieldy unit and hence, public opinion too abstract and indeterminate a concept. There will be in every case however, an effective public, i.e., that section of population which happens to be directly concerned with the policy under review/determination. Efforts would need to be made to identify the effective public in every case and articulate its opinion. That will make the process of policy formation democratic. To serve an example, the NDA government recently outlined the new education policy that incorporated propositions like the introduction of Sanskrit as in primary and secondary education programmes on a mandatory basis. While the importance and utility of Sanskrit especially in the context of computer application cannot be denied, it has to be accepted that the proposition had more to do with the revivalist/reactionary philosophy/programme of the party in power that any scientific/literary progress. There could be arguments put, both for and against the proposition but they would be put by people who matter or who have a say, i.e., members of political parties, academicians, prominent social servants, etc. The process is all but democratic. While it is only likely that the party in power will push its agenda, party ideology should not be allowed to obfuscate public opinion. It is erroneously concluded by some political scientists and also forwarded as major ideological endorsement of the ways of the political parties by political parties themselves that since the electoral battle is won on the basis of the party manifesto, party agenda can be taken to be an expression of public opinion. This is an a *priori* conclusion, more a rhetoric, as the electoral process is not wholly a rational exercise. In case of developing countries, politics is hardly an informed or a rational/educative exercise. Party manifestos can hardly be taken to reflect public opinion. The *effective public* in the above case is the student community, which is treated at best, as *passive public,* i.e., without a say in the determination of its own destiny. Instead of making an arbitrary policy incident on a passive public, it is advisable to seek/ascertain the opinion of the effective public prior to the determination of a policy statement by means of intelligent research design. Good sampling effort and a questionnaire incorporating quetions like should Sanskrit be a compulsory part of secondary education would do the trick. This might sound like a referendum. One might question its applicability as sampling that is acceptable and representative may be a problem. One might also be tempted to think that it is probably too bulky and copious an exercise to undertake every time and in respect of every policy. It should be asserted as a counter argument that the potentiality will be realised if academics gets its due as an institution. Research institutions across the length and breadth of the country would be expected to stay in a state of readiness preferably in synergy with universities. One can visualise a state of readiness where all conceivable samples are kept prepared in *tandem* with the political parties, especially the one in power, to be applied as and when they are required to be, so meaning and substance is imparted to governance. It is thus an application of two prime political devices, viz., Direct Democracy and referendum via the administrative system.

Another aspect of the administrative system that has to be

looked at is the co-ordination between departmental agencies engaged in work that is of a related/integrated nature. No department can hope to function in isolation and still deliver the goods. To serve an example, maintenance of hygiene and sanitation in public places will be the responsibility of the local municipal council or corporation as the case may be. Checking epidemics or achieving reductions in death rate would be the responsibility of the department of health. One cannot see the latter performing its task well if the former stays oblivious of its duties. This is the general scenario as far as Indian administration is concerned. One has to visualise a situation where the latter is in a position to legally enforce the former to perform its duty. Legal intervention as things stands presently, is only invited in case of public interest litigations field against errant executive agencies, or *suo motu* action by the Supreme Court which is obviously construed as judicial activism. Actually it should be one executive agency making the other with a direct and significant bearing on its own work that should ensure (legally if need be) that the other does its job. Necessary steps should be taken to ensure an integrated administration as envisaged.

Applying the systems paradigm, administration has to relate to the market in a new and a big way. Wealth has to be created/generated employing innovative strategies. This is the age of the market and public administration needs to be redefined in the context of the new liberalised dispensation. The market one feels can offer solutions that have defied political and administrative institutions. Public administration has to work more in consonance with the market than political institutions. Government departments, which have for long relied almost wholly on government grant have to start thinking in terms of raising their own resources. The modalities will of course, have to be worked out. One need mention that municipal bonds were successfully used in America to help local Governments raise resources independently. In the age of the market, the potentiality thrown open by the market will have to be exploited with innovative strategies such as government departments initiating entrepreneurial activity on their own. One can talk in terms of financial advisors for co-operatives, police, *et al.* that channelise employee savings and surplus funds in profitable enterprise.

Certain innovative strategies such as the one listed above would need to be employed if wealth has to be created.

Administration one feels has to be far-sighted and result-oriented than being simply concerned with getting things done or organising co-operative action in pursuit of determined purposes. One feels purposes determined for public administrative systems are intermediate and myopic in nature. There has to be perspective planning involved even in setting targets for administration to achieve.

It is pertinent to discuss Simon's views on the end-mean chain and the efficiency criterion in the above stated context. Discussing the technique of budget making adopted by modern Governments, Simon has a few suggestions to offer. According to him, budget should not be a singular document composed for the ensuing year. It should in fact comprise of two separate documents-annual, which is how modern day budgets are framed, and a long-term document which spells out the government programme for development for the next twenty years or so. Besides, long-term planning should be detailed enough to spell out government programmes and projects in sufficient enough detail to let the administration and citizens know exactly what is to be expected when, and not simply, broad forecasts, which is the practice today.

With such an approach administration would acquire the much needed end orientation which is one of the hallmarks of development administration. Presently, the pursuit of intermediate goals as even goal displacement in administrative functioning mar attempts at efficient/effective service delivery. This is one aspect of public administration that needs to be looked at with a reversionary temper. To that end, public administration needs to be redefined.

The other thing derived out of the above recount of academic opinions is that collective and planned functioning is at the heart of administrative activity. The emphasis has varied from one on procedure (getting things done) to one on content itself which includes the domain of policy-making. Academic opinion about the nature and scope of public administration has veered around the discipline's relationship with political science/politics, both academically and in practical terms. This, the authors feel has restricted the area that can be possibly explored as far as the extent/reach of the discipline is concerned.

Another point that needs to be raised is that public administration hitherto has been conceived in terms of the civil service or the government bureaucracy. Its practical domain needs to be enlarged to include other institutions like the NGOs or even the university which have a significant contribution to make to the cause of development. To this extent, public administration needs to be redefined.

Redefinition of public administration has to be sought also in terms of accountability and ethics.

## Ethics in Administration

It is difficult to define ethics as it is difficult to define morality.

In the words of Paul Appleby, "Morality begins in arrangements between human beings, ordering relationships to mutual advantage but with mutual discipline."

A few cardinal virtues held as desirable as far as the issue of impregnating administration with ethics is concerned can be recounted as follows:

- Publicness
- Representation
- Efficiency
- Effectiveness
- Responsibility
- Responsiveness
- Accountability
- Public interest
- Citizen obligation and
- Citizen participation in governance.

It is in order to discuss each one with a view to suggesting ways of their incorporation in administrative behaviour. Publicness of public administration has especially been stressed upon in academic literature. It is both a present and a desirable virtue as far as the nature of public administration is concerned. What is public? That which is governed or subject to governance by the government is public. Public thus, refers to the clientele and publicness, the orientation of service towards the clientele so identified. The difficulty however is with *identifying the clientele* that is "public" in nature as opposed to that which is "private". The distinction however a subtle one. Public is the passive, politically inert segment of society whose needs and interests remain largely inarticulate. It is for this public that administration functions or ought to function with professed socialistic/welfare objective. Organised interest on the other hand that determines policy content by active lobbying for vested interests is understood as private interest. Both however are part of the governed and difficult to distinguish in practice. Besides, a constituent element once part of a private interest could be part of the passive public at some other particular time at the instance of some other policy and so on. It is up to the sagacious judgement of the individual administrator to identify public interest and safeguard it against private interest aggression. This is precisely where, questions of value impinge upon administrative acts and so they should. Public interest has to be defined in the same context. As publics are diffused and the contours of identifiable public change every time so public interest has to be determined on a case by case basis. The individual judgement morality, sagacity and responsibility of the individual administrator come into play every time something *indeterminate/inchoate* has to be *determined/made cogent*. The idea of discovering the effective public was underlined earlier. This will have to be attempted successfully to impart real publicness to public administration.

### *Responsibility and Responsiveness*

Responsibility and responsiveness are the two guiding principles/maxims of governance or administrative behaviour. It is ascribed equally to the political and administrative systems. Democratic governance is more in the nature of a potentiality that gets realised in practice by the level of sensitivity displayed by its instrumentality in dealing with the clientele. It purports to exist for them. The *instrumentality* referred to above, is administration, by means of which goals of government are operationalised and met. *Sensitivity* is understood as composed of three specific virtues, viz., responsibility, responsiveness and accountability. The nature of the exercise of the three, or the way in which they get manifest however, differs in case of the political and administrative systems.

Paul Appleby attempts to enumerate the components of responsibility and responsiveness as they apply to the political system. In his words,

> "Democratic Government must be both responsive and responsible. The first need of operating democracy is to achieve response to a public sense of some particular disorder. The second need is to fix and identify officials whom the public may hold accountable for the response as it has been governmentally formulated. The third is the need to differentiate within the ordered unity brought about in response to a particular need, deferring to the pluralistic character of democratic unity. The first is the enduring problem of *e pluribus unnun*. The third is the problem of *ad plura unnum*. These two are together the problem of *responsiveness*. The second is the peculiar problem of *responsibility*."

Prof. S.R. Tiwari, brings out the implications of the virtues outlined for administrative behaviour. According to him, "a civil servant should be responsible to the political master and responsive to the people in a democracy. Responsiveness is a subjective virtue to be ingrained in the mind of a public employee. Bureaucracy in a democracy should respond to, reflect and give expression to, the will of the people, ... when we idealise the 'responsive role' of the administrator, it requires him to be articulate even with regard to the inchoate demands and representations of the people". An administrator has to play the vanguard role in that he has to assume responsibility to go by more than what his role stipulates in letter and be a friend philosopher and guide to the inarticulate masses. Responsiveness however, as all higher virtues, is contingent on innate morality that gets manifest as responsibility. In the words of Chester Barnard, "responsibility is the property of an individual by which whatever morality exists in him becomes effective in conduct". Accountability is more a legal concept in that the subordinate has to account for his actions to the superior. In the process there is the requirement of his being responsible without reservations for the authority reposed in him by virtue of the position vested by the organisational scheme of things. The function of responsibility again is crucial to the exercise/enforcement of accountability. Responsibility thus is the *common denominator* as far as the exercise of responsiveness or accountability is concerned. The exercise of responsibility poses moral dilemmas. Often deference has to be made in favour of official organisational morality as distinguished from personal morality. The two may be the same on occasions. On a few others, the difference may need to be understood/worked out.

Appleby identifies leadership with a representative character with responsibility. "Pluralism is both the presupposition and precipitate of democracy". The practical implication of the above statement is that values abound, and have to be brought into some sort of a reconciliation/adjustment so action may be taken pursuant to any of them. It should be remembered that there are opportunity costs involved in selecting values to the deferment of a few others. Values selected/sacrified count in ethical terms. The function is ascribed to leadership in that the leader is trusted with the task of assigning differential values to interests pressing for identification and grant a few recognition to the exclusion of a few others. The task is often a contentious one in that processes of politics and power struggle are often intertwined with those of interest articulation. There are however, limits to the exercise of leadership. There are limits beyond which influences and persuasions do not work. The effective public is a wide public, and assent assumes a content of higher as well as broader willingness. The dictum applies as well to administration as it does to politics. Administration often has to contend with interest or pressure groups that impute a certain representative character to the bureaucracy. "A truly representative bureaucracy is in its several parts variously representatives of special interests and functions and highly representative altogether of the public at large." Pressure groups functioning from outside create pressure groups even inside the bureaucracy. A section of academic opinion contends that the sociological make up of administration has an important bearing on the allocation/selection of values. The viewpoint underscores the sociological perspective to understanding administration. If an administrator is a social arbiter, he has to be an unbiased champion of public good which he is called upon to determine subjectively. Hence the need for a representative bureaucracy that is representative of a cross-section of needs and interests. For actuating the above possibility, recruitment has to be broad based and special interests kept sight of. There could be a scenario crystallising, of consolidated interests developing into monopoly pressure groups; in the form of minority power blocs, championing a few dominant values and submerging other less potent ones. It is the imperative need of articulating these special interests and weaving them in the fabric of public interest along with the inevitably forceful ones, that administrators and politicians encounter their worst moral predicaments. It is here that the personal predilection and sense of empathy of the individual administrator assumes importance/comes into play. Consumer interest provides the instance of one such interest. It often gets lost amidst producer and business and political cliques' interests. The question often is how much how far and in what way to insist upon these public interests. Hierarchy serves as a tool for exercise of responsibility in that it furnishes occasions in increasing order of occurrence for the sieving and sifting of interests. The task invariably involves moral questions more than it does technical because subjective value judgements impinge upon the design activity preceding choice. Often a decision has to be taken about what is public as opposed to what is parochial or private. In such an environment, consideration has to be tempered with propriety". This search points to developing techniques and to imaginative interpretations of responsibility which mitigate but do not nullify the intent of public policy. As one moves up the hierarchy the substantive content of work augments as opposed to procedural or technical. Value judgements to the extent of arbitrating between or reconciling interests to arrive at an integral public interest are involved increasingly/progressively as one climbs up the hierarchy. Occasions for the exercise of responsibility arise at each stage.

An Administrator is most inconveniently placed in between majority and minority assent. There is an obligation attendant/placed upon him to seek consensus especially in case of redistributive policies. Where a policy is specially designed to benefit a minority populace, the exercise of responsibility inheres in seeking majority assent to it. Conversely, when a policy concedes to majority opinion, it is an obligation placed upon a bureaucrat to seek/secure minority agreement". In this pursuit, there must be care not to confuse one's professional viewpoint, functional preoccupation, or personal prejudices with public interest. Concern for public interest has to be exercised in the face of attendant influences identified, as the pull of organised vested interest.

This is almost a super human conception of an administrator/human being which is, one dare say/admit, difficult to realise in practice. It is important to involve an impartial institution such as the academia in neutral assessment/monitoring of policies even while they are in progress. One is talking of policy analysis which is all but absent in India. Not only will it ensure responsiveness on the part of administration, but also equitable treatment of the populace in procurement of distributive benefits. The technical aspects of policy implementation would also be looked into.

Responsibility inheres in taking on tasks beyond those expressly stipulated. It comes forth in the exercise of delegated functions and initiative in the matter of taking on more than is organisationally stipulated and being self-motivated. A responsible person will show flexible/adaptive tendencies, exhibit qualities like loyalty, synergy, deference and be readily socialised in the environment of the organisation; regard its objectives as his own and establish a sense of identity with its larger purposes. Instances for responsible behaviour are thus infinite/multifarious.

### Value and Fact in Administration

Value is the intangible and fact the tangible aspect of administrative phenomenon. Values are roughly identified, as *ought* statements having *ideological/emotional* content that aim at producing a desired state of affairs. They are also held to be unrealistic and utopian. Values to be realised are not uniform, desired values in turn are matters of opinion and differ with time, place, culture and circumstance. They cannot therefore be put to a scientific analysis and prescribed as principles to be followed by administrative systems around the globe. Facts on the other hand, are matter-of-fact statements that *are there to see*. They can be succinctly put and are amenable to logical analysis and interpretation. They even show certain amount of uniformity in the matter of occurrence *sans* culture, time and place. Fact is what imparts scientism to administrative theory. What then should administration be concerned with? Fact? Value? or both?

It may be pertinent to look at two broad orientations that inform public administration theory as far as the questions of fact and value are considered.

### *Logical Positivism*

Herbert Simon is among a few chief proponents of this school. Logical positivism was a part of the behavioural school where it was maintained that administration could be set up as a science if indeterminate variables could be ejected out of its concern. Indeterminate variables are the normative criteria that govern administrative behaviour and effectively thwart attempts to set administration up as a science. Values are generally understood as statements of preferences, i.e., a preferred state of affairs; more in the realm of imagination. They have been held to be abstract and speculative phenomenon, more the irrational and emotional elements of human behaviour and hence far removed from reality. Fact belongs to the tangible world, the world of observable phenomenon and states *what is* without any qualifications attached to what is, i.e., there are no *should* and *ought* judgements involved in a statement of fact. It just has to be taken at *face value*. It is the *intrinsic* worth however, of a value statement, i.e., what it can potentially lead to that has to be appreciated. It is the difficulty involved in such an attempt that deters academic quest in the field of possible value-analysis.

The converse view seeks to establish inseparability of facts and values and is more in accord with real life situation. Values and facts are inextricably intermixed, i.e., occasions for decision making present issues involving both objective and subjective factors. Facts are indispensable and values unavoidable as the concern/subject-matter of governance is human being.

In the words of Marshall Dimock, "POSDCoRB is important only in so far as they are related to the larger problems of culture, economics and human relations". The viewpoint saw its logical culmination in the New Public Administration Movement, which advocated emphatically the value-based character of public administration and called for refurbished efforts to make public administration dominated by ethical notions. Dimock called for an "Instrumentalist emphasis in that ethics and action have to be combined, which together cause growth and vitality and prevent erosion and decay.... Value orientation makes ends and means consistent with each other. Every decision needs to be built on the bedrock of philosophy. If not, it'll be built on something else. The alternative is too often, rules and procedure which when not understood in their ultimate significance result in behaviour by rote. According to Arnold Toynbee the combination of challenge and response is the key to both survival and growth. The greatest source of true efficiency is derived from internal challenge and response which is primarily individual rather than from external sources which are primarily group.

Instead of assuming that the administrator ought to conform to what the institution demands it is more accurate to say that the institution is more in the process of adjusting to what the leadership wants. An organisation is forever subject to change; it is the executive that is in the process of engineering most of this change. If employees are given a free environment, we would get a much more fundamental type of institutional loyalty as an unsolicited by product. The modern trend in administration is to administer by objectives not orders.... Individuals are bound together by ideas and not coercive authority and this atmosphere is the one that seems to produce efficiency in the long run.

The veracity or otherwise of the above stated claim may be tested by exploring the relativity involved in emotion and reason. There is perhaps no pure emotion or reason. There could be reason inherent in emotion. Cognisance needs to be taken of the fact that modern psychology has been talking of an emotional quotient or E.Q., apart from the I.Q. or the intelligence quotient. You can think with the heart. The Heart's wisdom is held to be different from mind's. The stricture however is that emotional value procured/imparted by a specific administrative act cannot be empirically ascertained or validated. Simon, the high priest of efficiency however stressed upon the need to look at the intangibles (values procured) in the context of decision-making. According to Simon, decisions entail both factual and ethical elements and make preferences as among strategies to be adopted towards goal fulfilment. Since decisions involve valuations of this kind, says Simon, they cannot be objectively described as correct or incorrect. For instance, Just what is a good decision? That which maximises liberty? Or that which sublimates the idea of equality? Welfare, to give another instance has never been precisely defined. It again, could imply any of the two aforesaid propositions. Simon says it is easy to arrive at an efficiency standard for commercial organisations that are guided solely by the profit motive. The criterion of efficiency simply involves a cost/benefit equation in case of a private agency. In case of a public agency however it will imply an exercise at oversimplification as the overall impact of the policy has to be assessed, especially with a view to ascertaining its distributive impact, externalities/indirect outcomes ensuing thereby; in other words the overall effectiveness. According to Simon, a "mechanistic, profit directed, stop watch theory of administration should not be stressed upon. Any attempt to establish an input-output ratio to judge efficiency does not work as efficiently in case of social sciences as it does in case of physical sciences. Simon refers to two dominant views with regard to efficiency; efficiency in the sense of a ratio between input and output, efforts and results, expenditure and income, cost and the resulting pleasure and efficiency in the sense of a relation between what is accomplished and what might be accomplished. There is no "perfect efficiency" in administration as can be in natural sciences where output equals input and output never exceeds input. Simon offers the analogy of 'the law of conservation of energy' whereby output of energy cannot exceed the energy input. Such rules/stipulations do not/cannot apply to administration. Simon says efficiency is always relative and never absolute. Greater or lesser efficiencies between available alternatives have to be looked at" under these circumstances, the definitions of efficiency as ratio of output to input and as a ratio of the actual to the maximum possible amount to the same thing. Resources are scarce and have to be addressed to multifarious problems. "The criterion of efficiency dictates that choice of alternatives which produces the largest result for the given application of resources … even though all decisions be made in terms of alternative applications of the same resources, the problem still remains of comparing the values which are attained by the different courses of action. The efficiency criterion neither solves nor avoids this problem of comparability". Simon feels the solution lies in statement of objectives of the activity, and by the construction of indices that measure the degree of attainment of these objectives. The objectives should be set in terms of relatively final ends/values targeted by organisational activity. The problem however is that that broad aims or values cannot be stated specifically and objectives are stated in terms of more quantifiable intermediate goals or means. Further difficulty is posed by lack of a common denominator of value. One activity may lead to two or more values and there could be the issue of effecting a choice between the two. Simon gives the example of Health department having to choose between investing in decreasing infant mortality or increasingly the facilities of the venereal disease clinic". The two values can be compared amongst themselves only when they are directed towards a common, broader value. Rationality then would lie in assigning weights to conflicting values as they function (are likely to) in pursuance of the said value. The responsibility does not end here, it extends thereafter to considering even the indirect results of a decision. Policy analysis is again being hinted at. It is a highly specialist task which demands exclusive and informed attention from academic circles. Final values have to be established and sought by persistent effort. The process of establishing final value it should be asserted, has to be both rational and democratic. Irrational rhetoric might spell danger.

Consideration of public opinion like public interest involves value judgements, which a conscientious public administrator will take into account. As has been pointed out earlier, it is held that elections are expressions of public opinion and it is legitimate therefore on the part of representatives so chosen to harbour a general will sort of a notion to understanding/enforcing public opinion. There is almost an assumption of the idea of general will inhering in peoples' mandate. General will is a collection/desideratum of individual wills in a way that it forms a whole that is greater than the sum of its parts and once in existence, holds coercive power to enforce what is the good of the people even contrary to people's wishes. *Party agenda is not general will.*

Public interest is any policy or act that strengthens individuals by making them grow in self-reliance and in balanced effectiveness which in turn enables institutions to do a better job of their appointed tasks and makes the country as a whole more able to survive and prosper in the long run. Research effort to *ascertain final values* in every case is the panacea.

The understanding of ethics has to be enriched by providing the Indian perspective to it. Western psychologist have regarded/understood human nature in very simple and average terms/sense. There is, for instance, no if any research into the higher mind. Freud talked of the lower mind laying bear all mischief and insinuation it was capable of. While there is no denying the fact that man basically is actuated by self-interest often regardless of others' interest, and moved to work by material fear/favour, it is wrong to assume there are no higher impulses at all. Self-motivation is one that has to be looked. Extension motivation is another. Indian psychologists must take up the subject so recruitment policies and training programmes are better designed. Character of people also differs with time and place. Indian character exhibits a few traits that are distinctive to it. This particular fact about people' lives should also be taken into account while hypothesising on human behaviour at work.

Clue should be taken from the *Gita* which talks about doctrines like *nishkama karma* or action not actuated by desire for benefit and *dharma* of a Kshatriya.

*Nishkama karma* is extolled as a virtue over and above all others which leads the practitioner to salvation and also perfection in this life. It is explained as a sort of self-motivation that makes the subject oblivious of the consequence of action. It is action for the sake of perfection and excellence at work. The sense of satisfaction derived from work is a more credible source of satisfaction and happiness than material benefit hoped to be procured from action. Original academic effort on the part of Indian Scholars in the direction of reinventing and to that end, redefining public administration need to be invited. Instead of "getting things done", it is probably, *aiding things get done.*

# Part 2

# Good Governance

# 4

# Decentralised Planning

*D.S. Kheora*

Modern age is the age of planning and development. The planning has become a popular slogan, a catchy phrase and a common craze with Government as well as the people of UDE (under-developed countries). It became popular in under-developed countries because of its unique achievements in the field of economic development in Russia and other socialist and East-European countries. After Second World War due to the end of colonial era and rapid expansion of scientific and technical knowledge, the under-developed and newly emerged countries began a struggle to meet the challenges of development. They adopted the system of economic planning for achieving economic development and social justice. As of today one quarter of global population lives in absolute poverty and 90 per cent have no control over their lives despite grass-root activities (U.N. Reports). The world's poorest 20 per cent find that the top 20 per cent enjoy 150 times their earning level with the rural masses in developing nations getting less than half of the income opportunities. On an average two-thirds may only receive less than a quarter of education, health, water, sanitation, housing services. The UNDP report on *Human Development Index* says the disabled and the poor do not participate in societies. Women and disabled often have no power to change their lives and this dis-empowerment can extend to entire nations.

## Decentralised Planning

The concept of decentralised planning is not new to India. It started with the Government of India's resolution of December 14, 1870 and finally culminated in the passing of India Act, 1931. However decentralisation in planning had not been accorded the role and importance which it actually deserved in the initial phases of planning. It has been passed largely at the national and state level areas. It has not been operationalised due to variety of constraints, like inadequacy of planning machinery, lack of uniform enthusiasm on the part of states.

India has been familiar with the concept of social and economic planning for a long time. As early as 1876 Dada Bhai Nauroji wrote a paper on poverty in India asserting that poverty under the Raj was increasing and demanding organised remedial action. In 1931 M. Visewarya, the well-known engineer and statesman, prepared a blue print on a comprehensive economic plan for India. The public opinion in the country was thus getting created in favour of economic planning. In 1938 the Congress set up the National Planning Committee under the Chairmanship of Jawaharlal Nehru which published 16 final and 16 interim reports, one of them being on National Planning, Principles and Administration itself. It is important to note all these were unofficial exercises in planning. Mention must be made of the 3 famous plans made public during the Second World War—the Bombay Plan, the Gandhian Plan and the M.N. Roy's People's Plan. In addition to this government of India under the British regime appointed the Department of Development and Planning under the Chairmanship of Sir A. Dalal. On 15th August 1947 India got Independence with Partition of the country. The overall condition of the economy was shattered economy with agrarian base and the complete absence of basic and key industries. How to start with was the biggest question and on 6th April, 1948 the first policy of Industrial Development was announced with the mixed economy as the nature and structure of Indian Economy. Pt. Nehru was the brain behind the economic development of India and his vision of development is still in operation, though more than three decades of his death had been over.

One of the earliest action of independent India's Government was to set up the Planning Commission with the commencement of Constitution of India and Planning Commission as part of the Constitution. On 26th January, 1950 the Constitution was implemented and its various wings along with Planning Commission also came into being. It is the entire responsibility of the Planning Commission to prepare, implement, analyse and go into the failures of plans and its objectives. The Planning Commission itself could not undertake the challenging task of plan formulation single handedly because the country being federal and plural in character India's commitment to planning made it necessary to set up a number of associated policies making programming and evaluation agencies at the centre and later on in states and district level also. So that the complex problem which planning in a country of India's size and diversity and necessary involves are addressed to.

The three principal components of parameter within which planning in India is undertaken are as follows:

1. India is a democracy of the parliamentary type in which the executive is accountable to the parliament.
2. The country is federal in character in which the programmatic responsibilities vest with the states, the later being the theatre of action and execution.
3. India's economic development is based on mixed economy with a large private sector. Since the nineties the country is committed to the economic policies of liberalisation and free market.

## Decentralised Planning in Present Set-up

Centralised planning refers to the entire plan prepared, implemented and monitored from a central planning office for the country as a whole. On the other hand decentralised planning stands for planning at different levels, formulated, implemented and evaluated at each level. Decentalised planning is based on micro level or local planning. Decentalised planning is based on concept of sub-national economic regeneration. It is process of economic development by which lower level government and other popular institutions mobilise resources, formulate the plan for a defined reason and implement it. These planning are better geared to the specific needs of the area and its growth potential. It is based on the success of local area development which gives further encouragement for the implementation of other objectives. It thus marks among others, a rejection of the 'Tickle Down' theory of economic development.

Multilevel planning is based on local level initiative and leadership. It marks a search for an alternative to the presently operative centralised planning. It gives a new direction and meaning to the transfer of knowledge. It is a new strategy of creative innovation. The case for decentralised planning is mainly based on four objectives:

1. To cover effectively the resources of local significance.
2. Bring the peripheral groups of poor and underprevileged within mainstream.
3. Make stable and dependable arrangements for provisions of relief and supply of minimum needs to the poor.
4. Have participatory mechanism in the planning in the resources and needs with a view to promoting among people motivation habits of self-help, local level leadership and active role in strategic and planning decisions.

Thus the importance of decentalised planning at present stage of development in our country is obvious. It will enable a better preception of local needs, provide the rationale for taking planning to the grass-root levels. It will ensure effective participation of the people, make better inform, decisions-making possible, will leave to better exploitation of local resources and potentials. The centralised theme of decentralised planning is "Spatially Based" or "Developmental Locale" organisation of administrative system. According to P.R. Dubashi, decentralisation is however not a mere matter of weighing costs and benefits, it is also a question of community attitude and cultural pattern. With the implementation of 73rd Constitutional Amendment, the utility of decentralised planning has further increased as a development of local area have been given special attention.

The essence of decentralised planning lies in the listing of people's participation in the planning process. The local people must effectively participate in planning, decision-making, target fixing and implementation. On such mobilisation hinges the success of planning, which in turn demands a certain level of education in the society. Such plannings must be flexible and broadly framed to make it understandable to a common man. Decentralised planning must equally promote another attribute local resource mobilisation is at the core of decentralised planning. The local community must generate at least a respectable part of local resources.

One of the part of decentralised planning is district level planning. In India planning begins as a centralised macro effort as the country was inspired by the Soviet model of planning. District level planning is a macro exercise, requiring thereby an entirely new approach. It is decentalised in its approach and methodology and thus constitute so to say a reversal of the centralised planning approach. Moreover, district planning has to be multi-level, its realism depending on its capabilities to monitor and to assimilate development impulses at various territorial levels.

The socio-economic planning began in India in 1950 and the attention was concentrated on the national and state plans. Though the need for decentalised planning began to be indicated in the Second Five Year Plan onwards, planning activity remained centered around the centre and state. It was later realised that the distributive fruits of development and social justice can only be imparted with the decentralisation. In the mean time various developments in the process of the economic path of India like green revolution and distributive justice through social justice were set as the goals of planning. The occurrence of green revolution was the biggest event and country began to realise the need of the decentralised planning. Moreover in order to give the big push to Indian Economy the removal of regional disparities was one of the principle underlying decentralisation. The district level planning assumes that planning has to incorporate the felt needs of the local people and region covered. These needs differ from region to region. One of the agency of district planning is the existence in each district of the District Rural Development Authority (DRDA). DRDA is the agency entrusted with the responsibility of area planning to ensure that the local needs and resources are taken into consideration while formulating the plan for the said regions.

At present the District Level Planning needs improvement in its working. There must be a single body functioning as a District Planning Board at the district level with the seniormost ministers from the district as the chairman. Elected representatives and district officers should be associated with the same. The district collectors role should be defined and must be involved in the District Level Planning, implementation and monitoring of each schemes. The nature of the present set of planning and the development activities of district planning boards are being substituted by the micro planning.

### Decentralised Planning in Five Year Plans

The planning has recognised the problems of inter-regional and inter-state imbalances. Consequently, a great deal of efforts were made in the 1950s and 1960s. It was in the First Five Year Plan document that "no plan can have any chance of success unless millions of small farmers accept the objectives, share in its making and regards it as their own". It was in 1967 the ARC stressed the need for greater decentralisation of planning and recommended the setting up of State Planning Board. During the Fourth Five Year Plan State Planning Boards were set up and in 1969 the Planning Commission issued a set of guidelines for the formulation of district plans. The Fifth Plan document recommended a "National Programme of Minimum Needs" to take care of phenomenal deficiency in social consumption in backward areas by offering the facilities of elementary education, rural health and water supply, nutrition, rural roads and rural electrification. 1977 was the year of new Janata Party regime at the centre and it saw the introduction of Block Level Planning in the country. 1980 was the return of Congress regime at the centre and Mrs. Indira Gandhi was more concerned about the involvement of village level functionaries in the development work. Planning Commission set up a working group in September, 1982 on the District Planning, wherein the group recommended participatory approach right from pre-planning. In the Sixth Plan, planning at the local level had an important role to play in investment decisions in agriculture, minor irrigation, animal husbandry, fisheries, etc.

The Seventh Plan listed decentralisation of planning as its first important features and strived to achieve the decentralisation on the lines recommended as model by working group on district planning. In 1985 at the close of Seventh Plan Mr. G.K.V. Rao Committee was established to review the administrative arrangements for rural development and poverty alleviation. Again 1986 when Singhvi Committee on re-vitalisation on Panchayati Raj Institutions was constituted, it also emphasised the concept of district planning. Rajiv Gandhi, the then Prime Minister, in 3-day's workshop of District Magistrates at Combaitore said that district planning has to be married to Panchayati Raj to make both of them effective instrument of democracy and development. It was in the Chief Secretaries conferences held in July, 1988 that a consensus was reached and called for creating planning board as adjunct of Zila Parishad. Eighth Five Year Plan really recognised the utility of decentralised planning. The then Prime Minister Mr. P.V. Narasimha Rao had expressed a pious hope while writing a foreward to Eighth Five Year Plan document that implementation strategy for this plan relies on building and strengthening people's institutions and making people active participants.

The biggest contribution for decentralisation emerged from the drastic changes made through 73rd Constitutional Amendment passed in December, 1992. Credit goes to Narasimha Rao government for bringing such a far-reaching changes in the Constitution. With these amendments the Panchayats have been empowered with such power and authority as may be necessary to enable them to function as Institutions of self-government.

After the subsequent attempts in the form of CAARD, Singhvi Committee, Thungun Committee, Sarkaria Commission, Congress Committee on Policy and Programme, etc., express the realisation of the mood of revival of these institutions. It was followed by the constitutional 64th Amendment Bill (1989) and 74th Amendment Bill (1990) and finally the 73rd Constitutional Amendment Act, 1992. But even after giving constitutional status to the Panchayati Raj Institutions (PRIs) one is sceptical about revival all the more because there is sharp polarisation of opinion about its functioning. The following few points in regard of revival of PRIs and more of people's participation will clearly throw light on the future of these institutions in the country:

(i) With activitisation of Panchayati Raj at the grass-root level a system of Rural Local Government Democracy in India would come in the picture. With its implementation, there is revival of both Urban and Rural Local Self Government institutions.
(ii) For the development of the country people's participation in the process of development is essential. Development in India has suffered because it has failed to mobilise people's participation to the required extent.
(iii) The Revival of Panchayats relates to planning from below or decentralised planning on which Dantawala Report laid particular emphasis.
(iv) These amendments has removed the gulf between the people and administration. Bureaucracy cannot continue to look upon the people with contempt as illiterate and ill-fed masses who cannot be left alone to look after themselves, they have to promote their own welfare with their own help.
(v) For the smooth functioning of the democracy again the leadership from bottom upwards, leading the emergence of linkage politics and linkage administration in the country is also to be met by democratic decentralised institutions.
(vi) The state rural communication is really poor in the country and the revival of PRIs would provide proper auspicious for rural communications.

All the above-mentioned points clearly shows that the dreams of Mahatma Gandhi where he visualised a complete republic for India in Indian villages, the amendments are a way to realise his dreams.

### Problems of Decentralised Planning

The various approaches and intensive efforts made by our planners to defuse the administrative powers towards the fields to formulate, execute and implement are praiseworthy. Yet the sincerity and political will are lacking on the part of politicians and administrators. Most of the Panchayati Raj Institutions do not receive directions and encouragement from the government to fruitfully participate in the process of development. Some of the practical problems which are commonly faced by these institutions are as below:

1. Lack of political will to handover administrative authority to lower functionaries;
2. Lack of public participation due to their neglect in the past more than four decades.
3. Lack of financial resources at lower level to make decentralised planning operational;
4. Absence of self-reliance of local authorities in financial matters;
5. Lack of co-ordination between different departments of government;
6. Large number of agencies and programmes of ad hoc nature in rural areas which are caught and trapped in bureaucratic jungle and local elite.

The problems in a country with vast rural base of the population require mass popular education and training programme both for the staff, rural institutions and the people to generate interest and participation for any development programme.

In Himachal Pradesh, advent of decentralisation can be seen with setting up of Panchayat Election Commission and Panchayati Raj Finance Commission. It ensures the participation of people at the grass-root level. This three-tier system of Gram Panchayat, Block Panchayat Smiti and Zila Parishad has a special role in the process of rural upliftment and development.

Today we are in twenty-first century which is expected to change the lives of rural poor. It is very sad that there was time when India used to contribute more than 20 per cent of world GDP and at present it is less then 3 per cent of GDP. Moreover, by going through the index for the last 30 years the percentage of middle-class has increased in very slow progression and it is 18 per cent today. Had India adopted the policies of libralisation, privatisation and globalisation in 1970s there would have been a great impact on our economy. Though 1990s can be regarded as the golden age in the Indian economy yet the fruit of economic planning, sometime bears long gestation period. With the introduction of new concepts like micro planning for Indian villagers and their participation at the grass-root level, we hope the fruit will reach the common masses who deserve them the most.

# 5

# Democratic Decentralisation in India After 73rd Amendment: Some Issues and Challenges

*Mohinder Singh*

"Local institutions constitute a strength of nations. A nation may establish a system of free government but without local institutions, it cannot have the spirit of liberty". (De-tocqueville). It is a fact that a system of democratic form of government for its success requires local self-governing institutions. Lord Bryce had rightly said, "the best school of democracy and the best guarantee for its success is the practice of local self-government". A close examination of the history of the local government in India shows that the Resolution of Lord Ripon in 1882 had merely paid lip service to the decentralisation of powers. After Independence, the Constitution through Article 40 provides that the State shall take steps to organise village Panchayats and endow them with such powers and authority as may be necessary to enable them to function as units of self-government. But the Panchayati Raj Institutions (PRIs) could not develop into units of self-government as these were visualised as instruments of community participation in developmental programmes at the grass-roots level rather than becoming real units of self-government. The Balwantray Mehta

Committee (1957) concluded that development cannot progress without responsibility and power and the community development can be real when the community understands its problems, realises its responsibilities and maintains a constant and intelligent vigilance on local administration. The committee *inter alia* recommended a three-tier system of rural local government namely village Panchayat at the village level; the Panchayat Samiti at the block level; the Zila Parishad at the district level so as to evoke local interest. On the recommendation of Committee, Panchayati Raj was first inaugurated on 2nd October 1959 by Pt. Jawaharlal Nehru at Nagaur in Rajasthan and the other States to follow the suit were Andhra Pradesh, Punjab and Uttar Pradesh. Gradually other States introduced it. But these institutions remained failure in acquiring status and dignity of viable units of local self-government. "This sorry State of affairs was due to absence of regular elections prolonged super-sessions, variation in structure, powers and functions from State to State, insufficient representation to weaker sections, inadequate devolution of powers, lack of financial powers and political will".[1] Asoka Mehta Working Group on District Planning, G.V.K. Rao and a number of other committees appointed to revitalise the PRIs identified shortcomings in their functioning. To overcome the bottlenecks in the functioning of the PRIs, the institutions were constitutionalised as the third stratum of government through 73rd constitutional Amendment.

In the present paper an attempt has been made to discuss in brief the main features of the 73rd Amendment, some issues and challenges before the PRIs; and suggest suitable measures to tackle them.

## Features

Here some of the main features of the 73rd Constitution Amendment are presented to have an overview of them.

### Gram Sabha

Gram Sabha is a body consisting of all registered voters in the area of the Panchayat. According to Article 243A, "A Gram

Sabha may exercise such powers and perform such functions at the village level as the Legislature of a State may by law provide".

**Panchayats**

A three-tier system has been provided thereby bringing some amount of uniformity in the Panchayati Raj structure throughout the country. Accordingly, PRIs are to be established at the village, intermediate and district levels. Such States as have a population not exceeding 20 lakh have been given the option of not having the middle tier.

**Election**

The Amendment provides that the elections of all membes of Panchayats at the village, intermediate and district levels will be direct. As regards the election for the Chairpersons at the intermediate and district levels, it has been provided that they will be elected indirectly by and from amongst the elected members. But it has been left to the State Legislature to decide about making the Chairpersons of the Gram Panchayats as ex-officio members of the intermediate level and the Chairpersons of the intermediate level as ex-officio members of the Panchayat at the district level. The mode of election of Chairpersons of the Gram Panchayats has also been left to the State Legislature. The State Legislature may also by law, provide for the representation to the MPs and MLAs at intermediate and district levels. The Chairperson and all the members whether chosen by direct election or ex-officio shall have the right to vote in the meetings of the Panchayats.

**Reservation of Seats**

There is a provision of reservation of seats for the persons belonging to the Scheduled Caste and Scheduled Tribe at all the three levels in proportion to their population and in proportion of the area. One-third of the total number of seats reserved for SCs and STs shall be reserved for women belonging to the SCs or as the case may be, the STs.

One-third of the total number of seats in a Panchayat has been reserved for women (including the number of seats reserved for women belonging to the SCs and STs). The seats reserved for women may be allotted by rotation to different constituencies in a Panchayat.

Not less than one-third of the total number of offices of Chairpersons in Panchayats at each level has been reserved for women by rotation at each. Similarly, reservation for SCs and STs has also been provided in case of office of Chairperson at each level.

### Tenure of Panchayats

Article 243E provides for a term of five years for every Panchayat unless it is dissolved earlier on specific ground. If some Panchayat is dissolved, election to constitute the Panchayat has to be completed before the expiration of a period of six months from the date of its dissolution.

### Financial Resources of Panchayats

Article 243H empowers the Legislature of a State to:

"(a) authorise a Panchayat to levy, collect and appropriate such taxes, duties, tolls and fees in accordance with such procedure and subject to such limits;
(b) assign to a Panchayat such taxes, duties, tolls, and fees levied and collected by the State Government for such purposes and subject to such conditions and limits;
(c) provide for making such grants-in-aid to the Panchayats from the Consolidated Fund of the State; and
(d) provide for costitution of such funds for crediting all moneys received, respectively, by or on behalf of the Panchayats and also for the withdrawl of such moneys, therefrom as may be specified in a law".

### State Finance Commission

According to Article 243-1, the Governor of a State shall at the expiration of every fifth year, constitute a Finance Commission to review the financial position of the Panchayats and recommend the pattern of distribution of funds between the State and Panchayats.

## State Election Commission

There is a provision of a separate State Election Commission to be appointed by the Governor for the superintendence, direction and control of the preparation of electoral rolls for, and the conduct of, all elections to the Panchayats.

## Functions of the PRIs

The Panchayati Raj Institutions are responsible for the preparation of plans for economic development and social justice and the implementation of such schemes for economic development and social justice as may be entrusted to them including those in relation to the 29 items listed in the Eleventh Schedule (see Appendix 1).

## District Planning Committee

The 74th Constitution Amendment Act provides for constitution of District Planning Committee having representation of both the elected representatives of rural and urban areas in proportion to their population to prepare a plan for the entire district. Although this provision has been made in the 74th Amendment Act yet the States have agreed to extend the provision in the 73rd Amendment Act.

As regards application of this Amendment Act, it shall not apply to the States of Nagaland, Meghalaya, Mizoram, the hill areas of Manipur for which District Councils exist and the District of Darjeeling in the State of West Bengal.

## Issues and Challenges

It is hoped that the Constitutional status accorded to PRIs will definitely check the State to tamper with the life of these institutions. This will also enable them to function as instruments of vibrant and viable rural local self-government and acquire the capacity to learn, to respond to change and to mobilise better people participation in managing the local affairs. Under the process of political and administrative decentralisation, the PRIs have to be instruments of decision-making having autonomy and administrative capabilities, ability for proper planning and sufficient resources for effective implementation. But if we look at the real scenario, we find a lot of gap between theory and practice. It has been observed that mere holding elections of Panchayats and Municipalities does not mean decentralisation. They require sufficient powers and resources.[2]

### Half-Hearted Devolution of Powers and Functions

A close examination of the tasks assigned to the PRIs clearly shows that there is a lack of delineation of functions between the three tiers of the PRIs. No doubt, 29 items have been included in the Eleventh Schedule of the Constitution but it is not clear as to what functions are to be performed by each tier. Thus, absence of clear functional jurisdiction for PRIs is serious flaw in the Amendment Act. There is also a wide variation in functions assigned to the PRIs by the States. Regarding specifying the powers of the PRIs, the Chief Minister of M.P. had rightly opined that "... the key problem is that unless the Constitution is amended again to clearly specify the powers of the Gram Panchayats, Block Panchayats and Zila Parishads, the ultimate power would remain with the person sitting in the Chief Minister's chair—how much he wants to give and how much he wants to keep with himself. This is how I see the Panchayati Raj as it stands today". A study of 19 States conducted by the National Institute of Rural Development (NIRD) while focusing on growth, structure, election, status, devolution of powers and functions, etc. The study has *inter alia* found that "States such as Karnataka, Gujarat, Maharashtra and West Bengal where some of the departments had already been brought under the administrative control of the Panchayat Raj earlier continue to function as before. Some other States, namely, Madhya Pradesh, Kerala and Himachal Pradesh have issued orders to transfer some of the departments to PRIs. Even in these States the process of transfer has yet to be completed in real sense. In some other States such as U.P., the orders to transfer some 24 departments have been issued but these do not vest then PRIs with powers to exercise full control over the staff, budget and schemes. The budgets of departments which have been transferred has also not been placed at the disposal of the PRIs in majority of the States".[3] Thus, sincere and objective devolution of powers and functions are required for the success of the PRIs.

## Absence of Autonomy

It is hoped that the PRIs will become solid and strong autonomous in institutions for good governance at all levels. But the question arises as to how these institutions will enjoy full measure of self-governance in the absence of local autonomy. In this context, it is pointed out that "at the district, there is little autonomy for planning as national and State plans have to be accommodated many of these schemes are centrally funded—and the norms and targets are more or less defined. There is no room at best for slight adjustments. As such, for district plan to be meaningful there has to be a district list. If there is such a list, planning pertaining to these items at the district level can become functional. Otherwise, in the midst of the present system of Central and State lists, the district will be more or less has a post office function.... The efforts at decentralisation for rural areas seem to be cosmetic than functional. In Maharashtra, Minister of State Government holds charge of a district. The measures for financial decentralisation introduced in Karnataka, were soon withdrawn, which is retrograde step. MPs and MLAs are members of the Zila Parishads and Panchayats Samiti. In some States, the chairman of the DPC to be a Cabinet Minister. More than 95 per cent of PRI budget is committed—as it pertains to various schemes and programmes. There is neither functional nor financial autonomy...."[4]

## Dominance of Bureaucracy

The State Acts have retained the upper hand of bureaucracy in managing the rural local affairs. The Chief Executive Officers of the Zila Parishads enjoy enormous powers. They will not implement any resolution that in their opinion is inconsistent with the respective Acts. Actually they enjoy veto power. The

CEOs have been given sweeping powers for suspension of Zila Parishad resolutions by the State Government. Section 47(1) of the Haryana Panchayati Raj Act 1994, says, "the District Development and Panchayat Officer or Divisional Officer (Civil), as the case may be, can with their order, suspend the execution of any resolution or order of the Gram Panchayat, prohibit the doing of any act which is about to be done or is being done under the provision of this Act". Moreover, in the State of Haryana, the heads of Zila Parishads are ordinary members of the DPCs whereas, the Divisional Commissioner has been made the Chairman. The Kerala Panchayat Amendment Bill, 1994 provides that the government shall appoint an officer not below the rank of a secretary to government as Commissioner, who will be assisted by the Deputy Commissioner, who besides superintending the operations of the Panchayats in his jurisdiction shall exercise such powers and perform such duties as are vested in him by or under this Act and the Rules made thereunder. The government may appoint as many officers as it deems necessary for superintending the Panchayats. In this way the village, block and the districts would be brought under the complete control of the State level bureaucracy. Thus, it would pave the way for bureaucratic centralisation rather than democratic decentralisation.[5]

## Lack of Sufficient Resources

The Panchayati Raj Institutions do not have sufficient resources for providing better services to the rural masses. No doubt, the Constitutional Amendment has made specific provisions regarding financial matters relating to the PRIs but the question is whether or not States are willing to share their financial resources with these institutions. The issue of finance involves practical problems for the PRIs. "If the size of funds is minimal in comparison to local requirements, it results in a shortage of funds for a large number of activities.... Normally, PRIs have low level of external funding as compared to their local requirements. They are mostly dependent on outside funds which, in the form of grants and aids, are distributed over a large number of PRIs and are quite insufficient to cater to the monumental task of strengthing local development base".[6]

The recent past experience shows that the States constituted their Finance Commissions but most of them have not implemented the recommendations made by them. These Commissions could not become instrumental in bringing about a substantial transfer of funds from State governments to the PRIs.

## Little Impact of Reservations

There is a provision of reservations for women and the weaker sections in the PRIs. But these reservations in general and especially in case of women have not fully helped them to participate more actively in the Panchayats at lower level due to lack of sufficient time, increased workload, illiteracy, cultural inhibitions, male resistance, poverty, caste factor, etc. Regarding participation of SCs/STs, it has been observed that in some cases, those belonging to upper castes intentionally ignore the elected representatives of Panchayats belonging to this category. A study conducted in Karnataka by James Manor and Richard Crook for the Overseas Development Administration pointed out that despite reservation of seats for SCs and women, in practice, males from the upper castes dominated discussions and decision-making. Sometimes agenda are not brought to their notices. Some of them lack confidence. As most of them are new and going to shoulder greater responsibilities, therefore, there is a need to organise regular training for the elected members of the PRIs. They will have exposure to the art of governance.

## Over Dominance of Legislators

The provision of voting right to MPs and MLAs in the capacity of ex-officio members is also questioned on the ground that it would lead to over domination of Panchayats by them. Thus, it is contrary to the spirit of decentralisation. Funds under the Local Area Development Scheme and at the disposal of MLAs also lead towards centralisation of powers. Most of the works being completed are the same as contained in the lists of the XIth and XIIth Schedules of the 73rd and 74th Amendment Acts.

## Inactive Gram Sabha

According to Article 243(A), "A Gram Sabha may exercise such powers and perform such functions at the village level as the Legislature of a State may by law provide". This clearly shows that the Act does not specify functions to be performed by the Gram Sabha. So this basic institution at the grass-root level has been paid up service. Mostly the States have established the Gram Sabhas but their powers have been restricted and the procedures for the exercise of the powers have not been clearly spelt out. "In most laws the decisions of the Gram Sabhas are not mandatory on the Gram Panchayats. Although Gram Sabhas are expected to carry out important functions like mobilising voluntary labour and contributions in kind and cash for the community welfare programmes, consideration of the accounts of Gram Panchayats, report of administration, audit reports, implementation of development programmes, they have hardly carried out these functions".[7] However, to some extent, the Gram Sabhas are involved in process of making selection of beneficiaries of anti-poverty programmes. The State of Kerala and M.P. have attempted to strengthen the Gram Sabhas, the other States should learn from the experience thereof.

## Lack of Transparency

It has been observed that the development funds placed at the disposal of the PRIs are often misutilised and people complain about the poor quality of services and goods delivered to them. If they seek some clarification and information about the manipulations in the works completed, they are generally ignored. Only openness and transparency can insure the quality services and fair deal. Openness and transparency are the most potent weapons against corruption and ensure a responsive administration through which the true will and aspirations of the people are reflected. Their significance cannot be ignored, therefore, efforts should be made to observe and follow them.

The study conducted by the Institute of Social Sciences on Panchayats Acts of 11 States has concluded that the constitutional mandate of making Panchayats institutions of self-government has not been fulfilled and the overall scenario of

Panchayati Raj in the country is dismal. Although there are certain weaknesses, yet a new era has begun in which desired results would be obtained supported by strong political will. Following suggestions may prove useful in the establishment of democratic decentralisation on sound footing.

**Suggestions**

- As the PRIs are vibrant institutions of local self-government, therefore necessary powers and functions should be clearly defined for each tier. It would be better to incorporate them in the Constitution itself instead of placing them at the disposal of the State legislatures. It is also in the interest of decentralised good governance.
- To improve the financial position of the PRIs, at least 50 per cent of total allocations in the respective State budget should be earmarked for the PRIs to perform the functions assigned more effectively. Not only this, the institutions should also not hesitate in mobilising resources in their respective areas. In this context the Local Finance Enquiry Committee had rightly pointed out: "Local bodies which do not utilise their powers of taxation can have no claim on the financial resources of the State". The recommendations of the State Commissions should be considered without any delay and must be given practical shape.
- Appropriate measures should be adopted to make the bureaucracy subordinate to the elected bodies. Unwarranted powers of bureaucracy should be curtailed by incorporating requisite changes in the PR Acts. The District Rural Development Agencies in all the States should be placed under control of the Zila Parishads. The Chairman of Zila Parishads should be made the Chairpersons of the DRDAs. The overriding powers, leading towards centralisation should be withdrawn.
- As the PRIs are in a great need of training, therefore, regular training through well-established institutions should be arranged for all the elected representatives of the PRIs. For capacity building, the training modules should include all the relevant provisions of the State Act, development programmes, planning, budgeting, project formulation, imple-

mentation, monitoring and evaluation.

- To ensure openness and transparency, it is suggested that each tier should let all to be completed and future courses of action effective people participation should be there and no document relating to the ongoing and completed works should be kept confidential. Work should be completed through committees, bulk purchase should be through the committees. People concerned should be well informed and their doubts should be cleared.
- The time has come when the Gram Sabha has to be activated. Powers and functions should be specified and it should be ensured that each Gram Sabha meets twice a year. The Gram Panchayats be made accountable to the Gram Sabha. The services of the NGOs, the NSS, the woman cells and the Mahila Mandals should be used to generate awareness among the voters about the role and relevance of the Gram Sabhas.
- It is found that in some of the States, the District Planning Committee is placed under the administrative control of some higher authority. It undermines the elected representations of the Zila Parishad; therefore, the DPC should be placed under the Chairmanship of the concerned Zila Parishad.
- In order to provide real benefits of reservation to the weaker sections and women, special campaign should be launched to bring them in the main stream of decentralised government by creating awareness, motivation and updating knowledge and skills. Efforts should be made through street plays, "Nukur Nataks", etc., to instill confidence and boost their morale.
- The success of the PRIs also depends on the attitude of MPs, MLAs, officials and those in power. All of them should join hands to extend the wholehearted support so that various political, social, economic and cultural hurdles in the smooth functioning of the PRIs could be removed. Thus, the ultimate success is in the hands of people itself.

## REFERENCES

1. Singh, Mohinder, "Capacity Building in Panchayati Raj Institutions

with special reference to Gram Panchayats", paper presented in NIRD Foundation Day Seminar on Emerging Institutions for Decentralised Rural Development, January 7-8, 2001 organised by NIRD Hyderabad.

2. Singh, Raj, "Problems and Prospects of New Panchayati Raj Institution", *Kurukshetra*, vol. 47, no. 2, November 1998, pp. 5-6.
3. Choudhury, R.C. and Jain, S.P. (eds.), "Pattern of Decentralised Governance in Rural India", vol. 1, *NIRD*, Hyderabad, pp. 9-10.
4. Barnabas, A.P., "Good Governance at Local Level", *IIPA*, vol. XLIV, no. 3, July-September 1998, pp. 450-51.
5. Namboodiripad, E.M.S., "Kerala Panchayat Bill: An Exercise in Bureaucratic Centralisation", *People's Democracy*, April 24, 1994.
6. Mukherjee, Neela, "Resource Sustainability: Developmental Goals and Panchayati Raj Institutions", *Kurukshetra*, vol. XLIV, no. 7 April 1996, p. 25.
7. See, *Panchayati Raj in India-Status Report 1999*, Rajiv Gandhi Foundation, New Delhi, March 2000, pp. 10-11.

# 6

# Constitution's 73rd Amendment Act and Gram Sabha: Problems and Prospects

*Mohinder Singh & Brij Pal*

The success of democracy depends on the effective involvement of grass-root institutions. Mahatma Gandhi said, "The democracy could not be worked by some men sitting at the top. It has to be worked from below by the people of every village". To ensure the participation of the people, there is a provision of local self-governments both in urban and rural areas. A three-tier system of Panchayati Raj has been in operation to bring about an element of transparency between the people and the government system. Apart from three-tier, there is another institution known as Gram Sabha—a general body of all the voters in the jurisdiction of a Gram Panchayat. Virtually, it is the "house of the villagers". It is hoped that all the activities carried out by the Gram Panchayat would be approved by the Gram Sabha. This provision is meant for developing a system of internal checks and balances on the working of the officials of different departments at the village level. In other words, it is the ultimate repository of power over development decision-making, over the local bureaucracy, over the management of natural resources, etc.

If we look into the history of the local self-government, it was Lord Ripon's famous Resolution of 1882 in which he had recommended: "the smallest administrative unit, the sub-division or taluka or tehsil, small ordinarily be placed under a local board, which would further be controlled by the district boards". According to Resolution, the Governor-General-in-Council did not believe that the introduction of local self-government would, by itself, immediately bring about an improvement in administration, as a matter of fact that there may initially, be some deterioration. He also felt that "it is not bad policy but sheer waste of power, to fail to utilize".

Indian National Congress in its 24th Session at Lahore, urged the government to take early steps to make all local bodies from village Panchayats upwards elective and to provide them the requisite financial powers.

Both the Royal Commission and the Congress in its Allahabad session had recommended the constitution of village panchayats and endow them with real powers so as to enable them efficiently manage the local affairs.

The Lord Ripon's scheme of local self-government could not take much progress due to a number of reasons. Similarly, the other efforts made by the commissions, committees and the Acts also could not make a dent in promoting real decentralisation.

Gandhiji also laid emphasis on decentralisation of powers at the village level and wanted that every village should become a republic having full powers. On 25 January 1948, he noted that, "the charter of India's independence as conceived by the congress was based on village autonomy". In fact, he was the pleader of decentralisation. He had clear idea of the Gram Sabha even before the framing of Indian Constitution.

The local self-government ministers' conference held at Shimla in 1954 mooted the concept of Gram Sabha as more than as electorate. It was suggested that the entire village should meet at least twice a year.

On the recommendations of the Balwant Ray Mehta Committee (1957), a three-tier system of Panchayati Raj was first inaugurated by the then Prime Minister Pt. Jawaharlal Nehru on 2 October, 1959 at Nagour in Rajasthan, the other states also followed the suit.

## 73rd Amendment and Gram Sabha

Constitution 73rd Amendment Act, 1992 provides constitutional status to Gram Sabha. But as regards its powers and functions, it has been left to the state legislature. Thus, this institution performs such functions and exercises such powers as are entrusted to it by the state legislature.

Regarding the body of Gram Sabha, Article 243(B) says, "Gram Sabha means a body consisting of persons registered in the electoral roles relating to a village comprised within the area of panchayat at the village level". Article 243(g) of the Act defines a village as one specified by the Governor by public notification to be a village for the purpose of the Act and may include a group of villages so specified. To fulfil the constitutional obligation, all the state governments have made provision for the institutions of Gram Sabhas in their respective Panchayati Raj Acts. The Gram Sabha being a statutory body is an integral part of the Panchayati Raj system. It facilitates direct participation of the people in local activities. The membership of the Gram Sabha is confined only to the registered residents.

Gram Sabha should meet frequently for the effective functioning. For this purpose, every Gram Sabha should meet at least twice a year. It has been observed that in a number of states, the meeting has been called mostly on the direction of the Zila Parishad or the Panchayat Samiti concerned at a very short notice. Such meeting will be presided over by the Sarpanch. The Secretary of the Gram Panchayat will act as Secretary of the Gram Sabha. A prescribed number of members will form the quorum. It is the duty of the Sarpanch to ensure the quorum. In some states, the Sarpanch is empowered to call a special meeting of the Gram Sabha. The special meeting will be called on the written demand not less than one-fifth members of the Gram Sabha. The period within which such a meeting is to be called is generally of 21 days. The quorum in U.P. and Punjab is one-fifth of the total members. Whereas, in M.P. and West Bengal is one-tenth. In Maharashtra and Gujarat the meeting can be presided by the third person elected by the Gram Sabha in the absence of Sarpanch and co-sarpanch.

The paper is devoted to discuss in brief the historical perspective, provisions in the 73rd Amendment about Gram Sabha and its problems. On the basis of discussion, some measures have been suggested for strengthening of the institution of Gram Sabha.

## Functions and Responsibilities

Some of the common functions and responsibilities of the Gram Sabha relating to village development are:

(a) to examine the annual statement of accounts and the audit report of the Gram Panchayat for the preceding financial year;
(b) to discuss the annual report of the administration of the Gram Panchayat for the preceding financial year;
(c) to discuss the programmes proposed to be undertaken next year;
(d) to discuss the budget of the Gram Panchayat for the next financial year;
(e) to discuss the report of the development programmes implemented by the Gram Panchayat in the preceding year;
(f) to scrutinise the ongoing and completed schemes and works of the Gram Panchayat;
(g) to identify the beneficiaries of various rural development programmes to be implemented in the village;
(h) to undertake programmes of adult education and family welfare in the village;
(i) to maintain records of all development works undertaken by Gram Panchayat and by other governmental and non-governmental agencies;
(j) to render assistance in the implementation of village development schemes;
(k) to mobilise voluntary labour and contributions in kind or cash or both, for community welfare programmes;
(l) to seek clarifications from the Sarpanch and members of the Gram Panchayat about any particular activity, scheme, income and expenditure;
(m) to examine and act upon the reports of the vigilance committee; and
(n) to promote unity and harmony among all sections of society in the village.[1]

## Problems

There is no doubt in it that a number of functions and

responsibilities have been given to the Gram Sabha by some of the States. But in practice, there are several problems due to which this institution could not prove its utility. Some of them are being discussed in the following paragraphs:

### *Inadequacy of powers*

No institution can become effective in the absence of adequate powers. So far as the powers of the Gram Sabha are concerned, these are not reported adequate. For example, if the meetings of the Gram Sabha are convened, it is with the Gram Panchayat as to whether it convenes the same or not. Generally, it has been observed that most of the Gram Panchayats do not take keen interest in convening the meetings of the Gram Sabhas. If some meeting is convened that too lacks sincerity. Sometimes bogus signatures are obtained just to fulfil the requirements of quorum. As this institution does not enjoy sufficient powers, therefore, villagers also do not take keen interest in attending the meetings of the Gram Sabha. In some of the states, the Gram Sabha has been empowered for social audit. This has also been laid down in the "Provisions of the Panchayats (Extension to the Scheduled Areas) Act, 1996". According to the Act, the completion certificate for all village development works can only be accorded by the Gram Sabha. This power needs to be made mandatory because the power of the Gram Sabha for such audit is necessary corollary of and arguably even more important than the power of development planning and implementation. Another reason for the necessity of social audit power is that the untrammelled power of the development bureaucracy and even elected representatives to implement and monitor these programmes have led typically to huge leakages and malfeasance, and official channels of control and redress have mostly proved ineffective. This provision would potentially enable a despairing and victimised public to rein in corruption.[2]

### *Problems regarding meetings, agenda, time, venue and quorum*

The meetings of Gram Sabha as provided in the Constitution

73rd Amendment Act to be held at least once in a period of 6 months. On the basis of the working of the Gram Sabhas, it has been found that the meetings of the Gram Sabhas are more often convened by the Sarpanches, under pressures from the Zila Parishad or the Panchayat Samiti.

"Meetings called are mostly without or adequate notice. Despite special efforts, very few Panchayats convened the minimum prescribed number of meetings. In most places, only a formality was observed; proxy meetings at times were convened and proceedings were written even without the knowledge of those who attended".[3]

Meetings are also not convened timely with adequate notices. Agenda of the meeting is also not made available. As regards quorum, the presence of a minimum number of persons is insisted upon and there is no uniformity in the provisions of the state Acts. Thus, the quorum does not determine the maximum number of individuals. Only those having vested interests attend the meetings.

### *Lack of keen interest*

It has been observed that those living below the poverty line do not take interest in the meetings of Gram Sabha as they fear that attending the meeting will render them jobless for the day. On the other hand, those belonging to the middle class think that it is mainly for the persons living below the poverty line. In this way, people do not take keen interest in the meetings of the Gram Sabhas as they are not going to get any benefit.

### *Lack of awareness*

If the people concerned are well informed and fully aware, they may take active part in the activities of some institution. In the case of Gram Sabha, the general masses do not have sufficient knowledge and information about the importance of the Gram Sabha. What to talk about this institution even the members of the Panchayat are not fully aware of their powers, functions and responsibilities. Had the rural people in general been made fully aware of the role of relevance of Gram Sabha, the scenario would have been different one.

***Problem of bigger size and scattered area***

There is problem of bigger size of Panchayat and scattered area, sometimes spread over distance of 5 km. The membership of Gram Sabha varies from state to state ranging from 250 to 5,000. The size of a panchayat in a state like Kerala is reported to be in the range from 10,000 to 75,000 persons. It becomes difficult rather impossible for a Gram Sabha to meet at one place. However, the Kerala Panchayati Raj Act, 1994, provides for the constitution of Gram Sabha separately for each ward. In a number of cases, more than one village have been grouped together to form a Gram Sabha. But it is argued that in the case of a multi-village Gram Sabha, it becomes difficult for the members from the villages, other than the one where the meeting is held, to attend due to long distance to be covered. The problem is more serious in case of tribal areas or the hilly areas as the members do not attend the meetings of Gram Sabha on the pretext that they will have to cover longer distance causing wastage of time.

***Lack of recognition***

Most of the States have not recognised the contribution of the Gram Sabha that is why they have not shown commitment in giving appropriate and required powers. As a result of it, this institution has remained mere consultative/advisory body. It has been pointed out by those scholars who have conducted their studies on the Gram Sabhas that usually no care is taken about the recommendations of Gram Sabhas by the Gram Panchayats. If we want to imbibe real democratic values, the state governments should not allow bypassing the Gram Sabhas by the Gram Panchayats. Specific provision should be made through the legislation.

***Problem of relationship***

As the Gram Panchayat is the executive body of the Gram Sabha, therefore, it has to be made more powerful to control the Gram Panchayat. But there is a problem in determining the role of both the institutions. If the Gram Panchayat is made a part of Gram Sabha, it is doubted that day-to-day working of the Panchayat will be effected. However, greater harmony and better relationship between both the institutions can be achieved by making the Gram Panchayat a part of the Gram Sabha.

***Rare participation of women***

The Gram Sabha is considered to act as a larger forum for the participation of all sections of the rural community. But it is a matter of greater concern that women rarely participate in the Gram Sabhas due to hesitation, traditional ideology and idealisation of self-effacement. The Gram Sabhas cannot be considered more effective in the absence of active participation of women.

***Indifferent attitude of the sarpanches***

Most of the Sarpanches of the Gram Panchayats generally avoid to meet the people in Gram Sabha meetings because they do not want to share informations and seek active participation of the villagers in the related discussion and in the decision-making. They fear that their manipulations and other corrupt practices may be exposed by the members of the Gram Sabha while seeking the related clarifications. Thus, they try to avoid the electorate.

***Problems of accountability***

There is no substitute of making Panchayats accountable to the Gram Sabha. Our past experience shows that accountability has not been ensured as "Gram Sabhas have turned into discussion forums and at many places these discussions are hijacked by the rural elite. In some other cases, holding of a Gram Sabha meeting has become more ritualistic, where locally powerful people come to give sermons. There is no fixed agenda for the meetings. A number of studies conducted have shown that there is a gradual decrease in people's participation in the Gram Sabha meetings. These studies have attributed ineffective functioning of Gram Sabha due to lack of awareness among rural people about the functioning of Gram Sabha; dominance of Sarpanches; absence of people understanding between the members of village panchayat and Gram Sabha; and interference by the politicians.[4]

On the basis of various facets of the Gram Sabha discussed, we can infer that the institution of the Gram Sabha is not playing an effective role in expediting the process of democratic decentralisation due to the problems and weaknesses such as inadequacy of powers, bigger size and scattered area, lack of keen interest and awareness, problems of relationship, lack of recognition, poor participation, procedural drawbacks, and lack of accountability which require immediate attention of the state governments. The following suggestions may go a long way in the establishment and effective working of the Gram Sabha.

### Suggestions

To strengthen the Gram Sabhas and provide them with necessary powers, the message of the President of India which was given wide publicity on 4 July, 1999 requires special attention. In his words,
"Concerted efforts are necessary, therefore, to equip the Gram Sabha and other Panchayati Raj Institutions, through effective dvolution of powers, finance and responsibilities along with necessary training and capacity building."

- It is suggested that appropriate provisions in the Acts of the states relating to the PRIs should be made so as to make the Gram Panchayat an executive body of the Gram Sabha. All aspects of village governance falling within the jurisdiction of the Gram Panchayat should be approved by the concerned Gram Sabha.
- The Gram Panchayat should not be given the power to overrule the decisions taken by the Gram Sabha.
- There is a need to establish linkages of Gram Sabha with the Gram Panchayat, Panchayat Samiti and Zila Parishad. Clear-cut relationship should be provided in the Act itself.
- As the Gram Sabhas are generally ineffective, therefore, they are in the need of supportive and facilitative attitude of the lower level of functionaries including the teacher, panchayat

secretary, health workers, etc. These officials should act as guides, friends and philosophers. There has to be better rapport of lower level officials with the village electorate.

- Efforts should be made to develop general consensus among the villagers with regard to the constitution of Committees of the Gram Sabha and at the time of deciding about the planned development of the village.
- As there is a lack of general awareness about the Gram Sabha's role and relevance, therefore, a special campaign should be launched by involving the NGOs, Youth Clubs, NSS volunteers, officials, retired personnels and elder leaders to make the common masses fully aware. As regards women's participation which is almost negligible, a special channel for women should be started.
- In such cases where the size of Gram Panchayat is bigger and the population scattered, Sub-Gram Sabhas/Ward Sabhas should be created and as suggested by the Satya Brata Sen Committee, the Gram Sabha should meet as frequently as possible, at any rate not less than once in three months; there should be written invitations to every household to ensure 10 per cent quorum; and every member should be given a copy of the government order detailing the rights and responsibilities of Gram Sabhas with a covering letter by the Gram Panchayat President.[5]
- If openness and transparency are ensured and people have clear vision about the activities of the Gram Sabha, it can make them more vigilant and confident. Their active participation may keep working of the Gram Panchayat on right track.
- To facilitate villagers' participation in the process of governance, need-based committees of the Gram Sabha should be constituted and they will be responsible for their activities. Moreover, it must be ensured that the weaker sections of society including women, SCs/STs are not ignored at all rather their adequate representation should be mandatory.
- For the success of democratic decentralisation committed leadership is required not only at the lower but also at the block, district, state and national level. The Gram Sabhas should be kept aloof from political interference. Special awards should be introduced for those Gram Sabhas which

really play an effective role in the establishment of good governance at the grassroot level.

## REFERENCES

1. Jain, S.P., "The Gram Sabha: Gateway to Grassroots Democracy", *Journal of Rural Development*, vol. 16(4), 1997, pp. 566-67.
2. Mander, Harsh, "Towards Direct Democracy: The Legal Empowerment of Gram Sabha", *Kurukshetra,* vol. 48, no. 1, Oct. 1999, p. 12.
3. Jain, S.P., "Working of Gram Sabhas: Some Issues", Background paper, National Conference on Gram Sabha (28-29 July, 1999), NIRD, Hyderabad.
4. Aslam, M., "Towards Empowering Gram Sabha", *Kurukshetra, ibid.*, p. 32.
5. "Committee on Decentralisation, Second Interim Report", Government of Kerala, Thiruvananthapuram, 1997, p. 17.

# 7

# Good Governance and Public Management with Special Reference to the Andhra Pradesh Experience

*M.A. Hussain*

The term "Governance" is derived from Greek word "Kybernan" and "Kybernates". It means to steer and to pilot or be at the helm of things. While the term "Government" indicates a political unit for the function of policy-making as distinguished from the administration of policies, the word "Governance" denotes an overall responsibility for both the political and administrative functions. It also implies ensuring moral behaviour and ethical conduct in the task of governing, i.e., the continuous ethical exercise of authority on both the political and administrative units of Government.[1]

There are three main regimes involved in good Governance. They are the (1) State, (2) the Civil Society, and (3) the Private Sector. The state maintains the rule of law, regulate socio-economic standards, develops social and physical infra-structure and ensuring social safety nets and civic protection. The state provides the foundation of equity, justice and peace, creating a conducive political and legal environment for development. Civil society provides the foundation of liberty, equality, responsibility and self-expression through organising the communities;

educating the communities, mobilising groups to participate in the economic and social life of society; facilitating political and social interaction, supporting solidarity actions and watch-dog functions and fostering culture. The Private Corporate Sector provides the foundation of economic growth and development, service delivery, setting and consultancy, upgrading, corporate standards.

From the Prime Minister down to the Andhra Pradesh Chief Minister Sri N. Chandrababu Naidu these days talk about SMART government. SMART being the acronym for simple, moral, accountable, responsive and transparent elements that captures the essence of good government.[2] The recent initiatives of the Central Vigilence Commissioner to combat corruption by adopting transparent procedures addresses themselves only to the government departments and agencies. The Infotech initiative in Andhra Pradesh to put the government on the Website is largely a one track approach that placing the government and its agencies on a pedestal and displaying information they condescend to share with the public. Though the intention is laudable, it is doubtful whether this will lead to open governance in the absence of any radical change. E-Government however, confuses the goal with the methods to reach it. The goal should be good government rather than E-government and information technology should only be a means and not an end in achieving this goal. It is for this reason that the Government of Andhra Pradesh considers its objective to be not E-Government but SMART Government. Under the leadership of Sri Chandrababu Naidu, Andhra Pradesh Government has given top priority to establish SMART Government. Andhra Pradesh is the first state in the country which came out with the Vision 2020 Document. The Vision-2020 spells out the aims and objectives of development in the first two decades of the next millennium. So far it has been a professional job completed by hiring an Australian firm and providing it all the inputs from the government through more than a dozen task forces, the basic assumptions and data must now be in place. What is needed is political consensus among the major parties to ensure that this vision gets implemented without any major slippage. Even during his first visit abroad in 1997 to Singapore and Malaysia, Sri Naidu crystallised his vision for

Andhra Pradesh. Sri Naidu deeply inspired by the Malaysian Vision 2020 implemented then with great zeal by the Premier Dr. Mahathir Mohamad.[3] Andhra Pradesh emerges as the first state to draw up a plan for two decades. But this is no more than a comprehensive long-term growth strategy for economic growth. It focuses on 19 primary growth sectors, 6 in agriculture, 6 in industry and 7 in services to achieve in 9 to 10 per cent rate of growth annually for the next 20 years. It may be possible but it is also quiet a challenge to sustain that level of growth. Sri Naidu sought the expertise of the economist, Dr. C. Rangarajan to serve as Governor of Andhra Pradesh, to help transform the state into a leader and pioneer in the country. Sri Naidu has attempted to depoliticise the exercise. If he succeeds in the task and wins political support for a broad policy framework of development, Andhra Pradesh despite its present financial crunch will have the potential to emerge as a frontline state in industrial and economic growth even in the medium term. Sri Chandrababu Naidu's mantra nowadays is good governance. It is indeed heartening to see a political establishment talk this language and even have a concrete agenda for achievement. Let us take a closer look at the broader issues governing the concept of good governance.

As things stand today, the electronic concept of transparent governance may remain just that and the people at large will continue to suffer the arbitrariness and inefficiencies of a closed and secretive administrative system. This will be so unless they seek to understand what governance is and what the imperatives and features of open and good governance are. As a first step it should be understood that governance extends beyond governments and includes all institutions and organisations that serve the citizens, whether in a public, private, co-operative voluntary capacity. The strengthening of these institutions and organisations for collective decision-making and the resolution of conflicts is an essential function of governance. This in a sense, implies building up of new alliances and partnerships in which the government may play an enabling role. It should further be recognised that the government is only one of the components of governance, though the most prominent one. In a democracy that India is, governance is of the people and the government is only a part of it. For open and good governance a public-private-popular partnership approach is far more appropriate and relevant than the over-blown government machinery running solo and making a mess of people's lives.

As the ultimate goal of governance in the Indian context is the economic upliftment and the well-being of the masses. The imperatives of such governance would be: (1) an enabling framework giving the government a central role in setting the agenda for overall development. (2) A participative process of building and developing the state and the social economy. (3) Creation of capacity and capability to absorb and manage rapid changes taking place in the technology and management systems. (4) Encouraging initiative, innovation and creative thinking at all levels. (5) An interactive citizen's information system, opening up the entire decision-making process to full public view. (6) Replacing the colonial revenue-oriented administrative machinery with a democratic, development-oriented proactive management system.

These imperatives call for adoption of the concept which envisages distinct roles for the different players in this process:

(a) Government departments, organisations and agencies act as policy-makers, facilitators and regulators.
(b) Private ventures and entrepreneurs as innovators and partners.
(c) Individuals and citizen groups as originators of ideas and think-tank.
(d) Community-based and non-government organisations as enablers mediators and advisors.[4]

For more than half century now the country and its people have put up with a closed system of government and the phenomenon of inefficiency and corruption. Individual initiative and private enterprise have been blocked. A mindset has been created as if the government exists only to provide support to its employees and not to look after public interest or welfare. Nearly 75 per cent of the taxpayers money being spent on the pay and perks of the government employees. It is difficult to understand how a stagnant and inefficient administrative system, allergic to openness and transparency will ever be able to give good governance to a country like India with so much of diversity and complexity with the one billion Indians who constitute one-sixth of the human race, enter this millennium and mendicant quality and stagnant economy which are the drawbacks of closed governance? Or will expeditious measures be taken to usher in an era of open, transparent and participative governance? The answer lies with the people because in a democracy it is their right to decide how they are to be governed.

## Governance in Andhra Pradesh

Sri Chandrababu Naidu has demonstrated for greater political courage and reformist outlook on account of fiscal compulsions. He has reduced unsustainable food subsidies and abandoned prohibition. He has initiated radical reforms of the power sector and gone in for a tough four billion dollars loan from the World Bank that enforces financial discipline on the state and demands a major reorientation of public expenditures and privatisation. All this is done in Andhra Pradesh though it is one of the six most educationally backward states in India. Andhra Pradesh's agriculture is prosperous. Sri Naidu is working in an environment which is conducive as a technocratic moderniser. He is in a long distinguished line of development-oriented, investor friendly Chief Ministers. The record of successive Andhra Pradesh governments in fastering entrepreneurs who have made a name for themselves is outstanding. It was late N.T. Rama Rao who carried out India's first privatisation by selling Allwyn's commercial vehicles to Mahindras way back in 1987. The Andhra Pradesh has excellent infrastructure. And in a remarkable testimony to what has been happening in Andhra at the grass-root level the state now stands poised to reach the replacement level of fertility in 2001, the third state to do so.[5]

## E-Governance in Andhra Pradesh

Sri Chandrababu Naidu realises the importance of information technology in governance. He wanted to build super class infrastructure in the state. He wants fast results in IT revolution in

A.P. IT does not require huge investments, yet it is skill-based and employment-generating. Moreover it is the industry of the twenty-first century. But what is there in Andhra Pradesh and Hyderabad that will attract IT companies to set up IT parks. According to Randeep Sudan, special secretary to Chief Minister who is known to be the IT brain behind Sri Naidu, "IT professionals require a good quality of life and IT company's require good infrastructure. That is why we are trying to revamp Hyderabad and beautifying the city. 32 flyovers are being built". A hitec city in Hyderabad is being built near the state capital in the Madapur area over 160 acres providing office space and township. Already the first phase of the city was commissioned and the hitec city has an international gateway and earth station putting the world within the easy reach. 23 per cent of the NRIs in software are from Andhra Pradesh. The Microsoft, IBM and Oracle invested their capital in IT at Hyderabad. Hyderabad will become number one centre in IT. Bangalore is lagging behind Hyderabad in this regard. A massive infrastructure development programme is also underway. 12 ports are to be developed on the state's long coast line and for many of them bids have been received from foreign companies. Six toll ways, totalling over 1,500 km, have been thrown open for privatisation and 3 small airports and 2 international airports are being planned.[6]

The present advancement in computers and communications have become timely boons for us. The infrastructure facility provided by the government attracted the attention of various foreign visitors including Mr. Bill Clinton, the former President of the U.S. It is time for the scientists, administrators, and the business people to use the information technology for efficient management. The recent national level budget gave a boost to use information technology very effectively. As the prices of computers decreased day by day they are now within the reach of the number of organisations and common people. The benefit of such advancements and price reductions should reflect in serving the poor and needy in our country. Availability of right information at right time should get extended to the benefit of the common man. Information is power if it reaches the right person in right time. Individualised information dissemination is now possible even to the common man. A large number of internet cafes made even the illiterates to make use of the internet. We have well trained manpower which is the base for effective e-governance. Computer education in A.P. has already attracted students at various levels. The school children are the real force making their elders computer literates. The mental block of the officials to change over to computerisation is the cause for delays in computerisation in the government or in public sector undertakings. Even today there is a need for computer awareness amongst the senior officials and administrators.[7]

Andhra Pradesh has taken the lead in introducing electronic governance and has achieved considerable progress in this field. Several projects have been launched for better service delivery to the citizens.

## Twin Cities Network and Services

Through a pilot project 19 citizens' services have been provided across one counter. For providing this front-end service to citizens, computerisation and updating of data in the line departments and utility services is essential. Replication of similar services through more such centres throughout the twin cities will be taken up very soon and based on this experience, it will be the endeavour of the government to extend similar facilities to other parts of the state.

## Computer Aided Administration of Registration Department

Through this project, important activities like registration of documents, issuance of encumbrance certificates, valuation certificates, etc., have been computerised and service in these areas are being provided speedily and efficiently at 214 Sub-Registrar offices throughout the State.

## Fully Automated Services of Transport Department (FAST)

Transport is another department which has a major interface with citizens. Therefore, important activities like registration of vehicles and issue of driving licenses are fully automated to ensure efficient service to citizens.

### Multi-Purpose Household Survey (MPPHS)

Through a massive house to house survey, a database of all citizens of the State has been created. This data will not only help the Revenue Department in the effective maintenance of revenue records and issuance of certificates but also help others in socio-economic planning and the monitoring of social sector programmes.

### Andhra Pradesh Statewide Area Network (APSWAN)

Through this scheme a dedicated communication network has been set up from the State Headquarters to the districts and all other important centres. This has vastly improved administration, co-ordination and response time at all levels.

### Secretariat Knowledge and Information Management Systems

The A.P. State Campus Area Network has already been operationalised. Through the SKIMS project, all Acts, Rules, Regulations, government orders and all other relevant information will be digitised and made accessible, leading to transparency and accountability through sharing of knowledge.[8]

People come into contact with the government when they need birth, death or registration certificates, when they have to pay taxes, obtain land records, register deeds or apply for passport or when they have to apply for permits and licenses. More often than not, they dread the contact. In Andhra Pradesh the government had decided that the citizen should be made the focus of information technology applications in the government. IT can provide what good governance needs; speed, efficiency, transparency, consistency and reliability. It can smoothen the interface citizens and business have with the government by making the latter more responsive. With information technology it becomes possible to improve internal efficiencies, integrate services and to introduce new services. Some applications have already gone onstream in the state.

One of the first citizen-oriented applications was the computerisation of Registration of Stamps Department. People come here to get their immovable properties valued to register sale deeds and then pay the stamp duty on sales. They come to register property transactions and obtain non-encumbrance certificates. They also come to register societies, firms, chit funds and non-trading companies. Statewide this department services some 50 lakh citizens a year and earns substantial revenue for the state through stamp duty sales. In 1998-99 gross revenue from it was Rs.650 crore. It employs 4,000 people in 387 subdistricts across the state.[9]

Sri Chandrababu Naidu highlighted the transformation of Hyderabad into Cyberabad with the establishment of knowledge-based industries and a number of centres for higher education and research. He already provided world class infrastructure required for developing it as a coveted technology hub. The state already had 22 thousand km of optic fibre lines set up by the department of telecommunications while high speed digital backbone was being set up by reliance company to provide for data speed in the terabit range. The government of Andhra Pradesh had taken the lead in providing one stop services to its citizens through a portal which was being established with private sector partnership. By end 2001 the Government of A.P. hoped to provide 25 per cent of government services online. In the power sector already the government has taken a number of reforms including privatisation of distribution and in the next two years plan to add an additional 3000 MW of electricity.[10]

Chief Minister N. Chandrababu Naidu is increasingly chanting the mantra of outsourcing of services in government and is pushing for privatisation wherever possible. He said that pruning the government and outsourcing of services is essential. He said government would have to be trimmed and surplus employees redeployed or surrendered to a "Surplus Manpower Cell" to be created in the Finance Department. The surrendered employees would continue to draw their salaries from their parent departments till their redeployment. This will come into force in 160 government departments from 2002-03 financial year.[11] Further, the Chief Minister Naidu said that the government was depending on private sector participation for resource mobilisation and felt that a suitable regulatory mechanism should be developed. Further A.P. government policy was to make government smaller. "You should increase outsourcing of services instead of recruiting people". Naidu said citing the example of the Municipal Corporation of Hyderabad, which is spending just 23 per cent of its revenues on establishment costs and utilising 77 per cent revenues on creating capital assets.

## Strategy for Good Governance

We will have to do some heart searching as to whether we have been able to develop the right concepts of good governance to suit the Indian context. We were deeply disturbed to learn of a UNDP report, which rated India as one of the least well governed countries. In the estimate of World Bank we are also highly corrupt. We should search our conscience and in the light of our own culture of moral strength create governance best suited to the country. Unless we improve the government and corporate image in the minds of our people we may not improve governance very much and may even retrograde.

Good governance is the art of public leadership. There are three distinct dimensions of governance: (1) the form of political regime; the process by which authority is exercised in the management of country's states economic and social resources and the capacity of governments to design, formulate, and implement policies and discharge functions. The criteria that constitute good governance have been drawn from (a) legitimacy of government, (b) accountability of political and official elements of government (media of freedom, transparency of decision-making, accountability mechanisms) and (c) competence of governments to formulate policies and deliver services, the respect for human rights and rule of law. Good governance puts people into the centre of development.

Andhra Pradesh should be the fastest growing state in the country and should surpass the growth rates of many of the fastest growing countries in the world. The growth engines identified include pharmaceuticals, mining, labour intensive, export intensive units, contract farming, agro-based industry, tourism and of course information technology. Sri Naidu knows that a critical factor determining his success is support from the people. The Chief Minister also embarks off and on what is called the Janma Bhoomi programme. Along with officials Sri Naidu travels from district to district exhorting the people to take up activities like road building on a voluntary basis. In the field of social engineering in Andhra Pradesh Sri Naidu had set up watershed committees, Vana Samrakshaka Samitis, Youth groups, DWCRA groups and Water-users Associations. These organisations are voluntary units manned by the people. However, they will get funds directly from the Government of Andhra Pradesh for undertaking developmental works.

The Government of Andhra Pradesh recently have evolved a detailed strategy for good governance. A strategy paper approved by the Council of Ministers on 1 January 2001 concentrated on the following reforms:

1. Decentralisation
2. Accountability
3. Convergence at Gram Panchayat level
4. Strengthening of planning at district level
5. Development of backward areas
6. Capacity Building at community level
7. Consolidation of schemes already initiated and future initiatives planned

We urgently need to look for innovative options in governance. How can we redesign our democracy so that costs of entry into politics are lowered for the gifted the decent and concerned? How can we bring greater stability to governments so that the costs of insecurity of tenure are reduced, and yet at the same time accountability of the government to citizens is increased? How can we improve the quality of governmental decision-making? How do we strengthen local self-government and how do we deligate more powers to the states but also ensure that resources are not misused. A number of innovative possibilities exist. No alternative is perfect, of course, but if you look around both within India and outside India many interesting ideas are available that can contribute to better governance. The presidential form of government, proportional representation two-third vote of no confidence rather than a simple majority vote to bring down government have been practised in various parts of the world.

## REFERENCES


1. *The Hindu*, Madras, dated 9-1-2001.
2. Sudan, Randeep, "Towards SMART Government: The Andhra Pradesh Experience", *The Indian Journal of Public Administration*, vol. XLVI, no. 3, July-September, 2000, p. 401.
3. *The Hindu*, Madras, dated 4-2-1999.
4. M.G. Devasahayam, "The Approach to Good Governance", *The Hindu*, Madras.
5. Jayaram Ramesh, "Tale of Two CMs", *India Today*, 20 Sept. 1999.
6. *The Sunday Times of India*, Bangalore, August 9, 1998.
7. Smt. Uma Madhava Reddy, Minister, Govt. of Andhra Pradesh, Inaugural address delivered at Southern Regional Seminar on E-governance organised by Regional Branch of Indian Institute of Public Administration, A.P. Regional Branch, Hyderabad, held on 10 March, 2001.
8. Strategy paper on Governance and Public Management, Govt. of Andhra Pradesh, Hyderabad, 2001, pp. 4-5.
9. N. Chandrababu Naidu with Sevanti Ninan, *Plain Speaking*, Viking Publications, New Delhi, 2000, p. 86.
10. Asia Society Technology Conference held on 12-3-2001 at Bangalore.
11. *Times of India*, Bangalore dated 20-3-2001.

# 8

# Holding Local Body Elections—An Inside Story

*R.K. Prabhakar*

Periodic elections are indispensable for the success of indirect democracy as they provide legitimacy to the governing body. Further, they offer an opportunity to the people at large to participate in the political process. They assume all the more importance in the case of local self-governing institutions because of their close proximity to the people. These, in fact, serve the training ground for the people to elect their representatives at the state and national levels. Keeping this in view there had always been a provision for regular elections of local bodies in the Acts passed by the state governments from time to time primarily on the initiative of the Central Government. However, holding of regular elections at specified intervals both for rural and urban local bodies have been made a constitutional obligation for the first time under the 73rd and 74th Amendment Acts. Article 243E of the Constitution provides that:

Every panchayat, unless sooner dissolved under any law for the time being in force, shall continue for five years from the date appointed for its first meeting and no longer.

Further, Article 243E and 243U mandate that elections to panchayats, panchayat samities and zila parishads apart from municipal committees "shall be held before the expiry of tenure of existing bodies".

The state governments were required to incorporate these provisions in their respective panchayat and municipal acts in the spirit of the Constitutional Amendments. Consequently, now onwards it has become a constitutional obligation on the part of the state governments to hold elections well within time frame.

Despite this, the Haryana government has not reconciled to the very spirit enshrined in these Amendments as it had made every possible attempt and ultimately succeeded in postponing the elections. The objective of the paper is to analyse the motive behind this move and the ways and means adopted to achieve to end.

In Haryana, elections to the local self-governing institutions under the amended Acts were held for the first time in December, 1994. Five year tenure of these bodies expired on January 15, 2000 and the next elections became due. But the ruling alliance of INLD-BJP in the State was interested in holding Assembly elections prior to that of local bodies. The logic behind this was that if the elections to local bodies are held before the Assembly elections and the ruling alliance performs less spectacularly than in the Lok Sabha Elections, held recently in which it won all the ten seats, the present buoyant mood will dissipate. Contrary to this, if the main opposition party the Congress does creditably in these panchayat elections, it will regain its lost vigour and put up a tough fight in the Assembly elections.

This logic led the officialdom to support a private petition for seeking to quash a government notification for timely polls to the local bodies. The petition was filed in the Punjab and Haryana High Court on 7 September 1999 by Mr. Bhag Singh, counsel for Mr. Surjit Singh, a resident of Naharishi village in Ambala district's Naggal constituency praying that Ambala district elections should be postponed and electoral rolls be revised because voters lists were not consistent with the Assembly list. The petition was admitted by the Bench which had issued notice of motion for 30 September, 1999. When the petition came up for hearing, the then Advocate-General of Haryana made a statement before the Bench saying that the electoral rolls of all panchayats and municipal committees in the State would be revised by June, 2000. The Bench disposed off this petition with the direction that all electoral rolls should be completed by June, 2000. By Virtue of this, the panchayat and municipal elections scheduled for 1999 stood postponed.[1] In this way the ruling alliance succeeded in its endeavours.

When the Haryana Congress Legislative Party—the main opposition—came to know of this decision of the Court, Mr. Surjewala, Mrs. Kartar Devi, the leader of the HCCP and certain other persons filed a joint review petition praying the Court *inter alia* to permit them to be impleaded as parties. It also urged the Court to recall its orders of 30 September, 1999 permitting the State Government to defer panchayat, municipal committees and zila parishad elections till June, 2000 and diect the State Election Commission (SEC) to conduct the elections before the expiry of tenures of existing bodies. It was alleged in the review petition that the earlier original petition dated 7 September was filed on the behest of the ruling alliance. It further charged that the State Election Commission in collusion with the State Government played a fraud on the Court by withholding the Constitutional provision contained in Articles 243E ande 243U.

Allowing the application of Mr. Surjewala, the Court impleaded applicants as respondents in the writ petition and recalled its order of 30 September 1999 admitting that the same had been passed in ignorance of the Constitutional provisions given in part IX and part IX-A and in the Haryana Panchayati Raj Act, 1994, and the Haryana Municipal Act, 1973. While dismissing the writ petition of 7 September, 1999 the Bench issued show-cause notice to State Election Commission and Chief Secretary, Haryana as to why contempt proceedings should not be initiated against them for deliberately misleading the Court. However, the then newly appointed Advocate General stated that the Government was unaware of the statement made by his predecessor which the Court found difficult to accept.[2]

As a result of Court's recalling its decision, it now became a constitutional obligation on the part of the State Government and the State Election Commission to conduct local bodies' elections before January 15 when the term of existing bodies expires. With this the game-plan of the ruling alliance for holding Assembly elections prior to that of local bodies got jeopardised.

The Hon'ble Court further directed the State Government and the SEC to file affidavits spelling out the schedule for holding panchayat elections failing which the Bench itself would issue an interim order specifying the schedule for holding the elections. It further made it clear in no uncertain terms that the "state government has to adhere to the schedule".[3]

After failing initially in its game-plan, the State Government thought of another strategy to postpone the local bodies' elections. This strategy came in the form of a plea from the Secretary, Development and Panchayat Department before the Bench suggesting that the Government should be allowed to hold panchayat and other local bodies' elections between 25 March and 10 April, 2000 to get away with an anomalous situation. This anomalous situation as explained by the Secretary was that the State Poll Panel was getting the voter's lists of 92 gram panchayats prepared with 1 January, 2000 as the qualifying date while earlier the State Poll Panel had got the remaining voter's list of panchayati raj institutions with 1 January, 1999 as the qualifying date.

It would not be out of place to mention that the SEC had stated in its affidavit that it was willing to conduct poll to the panchayati raj institutions within 40 days. However, Advocate General of Haryana pleading in line with the Secretary stated that the State Government could get the elections conducted only between March 25 and April 10 but gave different arguments. He pointed out that the difficulty in holding the local bodies' elections as per Court orders was that the Vidhan Sabha (Legislative Assembly) had already been dissolved and the Election Commission of India was likely to announce the election schedule for the Assembly poll itself. It would not be possible for the Election Commission and Government of Haryana to hold both elections simultaneously for want of sufficient equipment in terms of ballot boxes and security forces.

However, the Court rejected the plea put forward by Secretary and the State Advocate General as it felt that it had already been cheated by the former AG in withholding the constitutional provisions about the holding of panchayat elections. While doing so the Court observed:

> "It is the conceded position that the State Assembly has been dissolved some 17 months before its normal tenure by the voluntary act of the present Government.... It is, therefore, not open to State Government to say that "there could be administrative problems as a unilateral and deliberative action taken by the State Government cannot nullify a constitutional and statutory duty".

The Court further observed:

> "We are not concerned with the Vidhan Sabha elections. These can be held after 17 months. Moreover, if the Election Commission can hold parliamentary elections all over the country, why cannot it hold panchayat and Assembly election in Haryana. We shall not permit the Government to dilly-dally in discharging its statutory obligations."[4]

In the light of the above observations the Court directed the State Government and its Election Commission on 27 December, 1999 to hold elections to panchayats, panchayat samities, zila parishads and municipalities by the end of February, 2000 positively except in the case of 92 gram panchayats and 20 municipal committees in which the voters' list has not been prepared.[5]

This verdict of the Hon'ble Court has thwarted the attempt of the Haryana State Government to skipover the law by postponing the election to a date more suitable to the ruling party and its prospective allay—the BJP. But the subsequent efforts by the Government show that it was not ready to give way so easily. It filed a petition in the Punjab and Haryana High Court on 10 January, 2000 praying to the Court for reviewing its order of 27 December directing it to hold elections to panchayati raj institutions in the State by 28 February, positively. A week later, i.e., on 17 January the Haryana State Election Commission also filed a petition in the same Court seeking direction to the State Government to issue the necessary notification for holding elections to panchayati raj institutions and providing it election material.

The Election Commission stated in its petition that it wrote to the Chief Secretary on 27 December for issuing the necessary notification for holding these elections as was required under section 211(i) and 161 of the Haryana Panchayati Raj Act. It added that it also requested the Financial Commissioner and Secretary, Printing and Stationery Department, to complete the printing of forms and other election material immediately. It also claimed that a series of reminders were sent to the Government in this regard on January 7, 9 and 13. However, the Government did not accept its request. The concern of the State Election Commission thus exhibits its objectivity in this regard.

The Court while considering both the petitions simultaneously, dismissed the review petition preferred by the Haryana Government and reiterated its earlier orders that elections to panchayati raj institutions must be held by the end of February under any circumstances. Finding no justification, it even declined to allow the State Government to appeal to the Apex Court as envisaged under Article 134A of the Constitution.[6]

Thus as per the decision of the High Court it became mandatory for the State Government to hold elections to local bodies by the end of February, 2000. The Government found itself in a fix as the time left was too short. So it preferred to file an S.L.P.[7] In the Supreme Court seeking some more time as it would serve its very motive for holding these elections after the Assembly elections scheduled to be held on 22 February, 2000.

The State Advocate General apprised the Bench of the Supreme Court about the difficulties to be faced by the Haryana Government in holding these elections as directed by the High Court. The Bench considering the difficulties, granted more time for holding local body election in the State and directed it to complete the panchayat and municipal body elections by 31 March and 7 April, 2000 respectively.

From the preceding discussion, it becomes quite clear that the holding of elections to local bodies was beret with political considerations. The ruling Alliance was interested to hold these elections after the Assembly elections which was dissolved about 17 months before the completion of its term. As per its calculations, this move would have paid it sufficient political dividend. As against this, the opposition wanted to take political mileage by getting these elections held as per the schedule, i.e., before assembly elections. This led to the legal wranglings and in the ultimate analysis the ruling alliance succeeded in its game-plan. The net result of this whole episode has been that the sacrosanct constitutional provisions contained in Articles 243E and 243U became the casuality having serious repercussions about self-governing status of local bodies. The phenomenon requires a countrywide examination to see whether this is an isolated case or its type of there is a general tendency of such nature and if the findings go with the later, some corrective measures must be taken immediately.

## REFERENCES

1. *The Tribune*, Chandigarh, 11 December, 1999.
2. *Ibid.*
3. *Ibid.*, 22 December, 1999.
4. *Ibid.*, 27 December, 1999.
5. *Ibid.*
6. *Ibid.*, 22 January, 2000.
7. SLP (C) Nos 1598-99 of 2000.

# 9

# Good Governance

*Sansar Singh Janjua*

India has chosen for itself a republican, democratic, and secular form of governance. These values and goals are enshrined in our Constitution. Yet religious discords, communal conflicts and ethnic strifes can be seen everywhere due to the lack of political will of good governance. Good governance as a concept has suddenly entered the vocabulary of administration since the 1990s.

The term "Governance" which means a political unit for the functioning of policy-making for both the political and administrative units of Government.[1] Good governance is based on the conviction that man has the moral and intellectual capacity, as well as the inalienable right, to govern himself with reason and justice.[2] This acceptable form of governance is the most distinguished thing that has happened in this century, says Nobel Laureate Amartya Sen.[3]

The concept of good governance is associated with efficient and effective administration in democratic set-up. In practical terms, there are three particular aspects of good governance. First, the empowerment and capacity of government to formulate and implement policies and discharge functions. Second, the form of political will and third, the process by which authority is exercised in the management of country's economic and social resources for development. Therefore, the test of good governance for any government lies in its goals and objectives, in its policies and the manner these are executed in order to achieve the desired results. Further, it also reflects the attitudes of the people towards the functioning of the so many agencies of the government.[4]

The conference of Chief Secretaries held on November 20, 1996, all of a sudden woke up to the realisation that there was a crisis in Indian Administration.[5] The reality is that our administrative system where the politico-bureaucratic order which rules most thrives on status-quaism of the negative type. The old order of 53 years has challenges ahead in the new millennium for a modern outlook. The crisis in administration calls for a redefining of the role of the government and its functions and also its real focus to serve the public effectively as much as to ensure efficiency and cost effective administration. Accountability, transparency and cleansing public services are all inter-connected issues, for ensuring a clean and responsive[6] administration.

The system of government and the structure of institutions in India are a legacy of British rule and were built around the requirements of general administration such as revenue collection, the maintenance of law and order and the upkeep of minimum infrastructure and facilities for trading.[7] There have been different patterns of governance at different times. At one time absolute monarchy was considered the best way to govern and to redress the grievances of the governed. But as the burden of governing increased, the ruler came to depend on his close friends and relations. They in turn assumed not only significant roles in governances but, were also given vested interests.[8]

Good governance comes only from good laws. Basically, it emanates from wise interpretations, effective and fair implementation of those laws. It also originates from honest intentions and their implementation, devoid of politicisation of every issue. Fixity of tenure or irremovability are important components of good governance. Normally, when a crisis occurs, governments tend to find scapegoats to compensate for its own failure in dealing with any situation. It is true that it may not be humanly possible for the minister concerned to monitor the working of all aspects of his department. But there is nothing to prevent him from devising a mechanism or having people in his team who would deliver results. It has been noticed that a set of people, irrespective of the party in power, manage to surround the political masters.[9]

The critical role of the state in the delivery of public goods and services can be realised only through an efficient, effective and responsive administration delivering quality public service. Measures for administrative reforms have, therefore, acquired an urgency as the framework for an effective administration, capable of quality service needs to be sensitively achieved. High quality and effective public services are a vital part of a modern welfare state as people are entitled to expect that services which are often central to their lives, should be responsive, sensitive to their needs, easy to use, flexible and efficient. Unfortunately, too many public services are still unnecessarily complex and many are uncoordinated in their parameters. Thus, we in government now, intend to focus on quality in government joining hands with the private sector.[10]

Although the government ensures that all public services should set out clear standards of services, against which the quality of service delivery can be measured, and provide effective remedies when things go wrong. Yet, the service has to be responsive and accessible with equality and fairness of treatment. It should be open and provide full information while using resources effectively to provide best value to users. It should also be sensitive to innovations for improvement through its dynamic interaction with users.[11] In the present scenario, a simple achievement may, considering the level and quality of our existing services, these standards may appear to be difficult to achieve in a short time span. But, we do want public services that respond to the needs and wishes of people who use them and people are entitled to expect that services, which are often central to their lives, should be responsive to their needs, easy to use and efficient.[12] In fact, considerable improvements are necessary to achieve this. This therefore, is a key theme for which significant issues arise, such as:

(a) exchange of information between organisations.
(b) geering measurement of performance to provide incentives for joint working.

(c) and, maintaining clear accountability for delivering value for money, need to be carefully addressed.

Although government is very sensitive to this expectation of the people and sincere efforts in this direction have already been initiated. Good governance, is an overreaching component of the agenda of our government which has taken measures to make administration accountable, responsive and transparent through and through by adopting such measures as,

(a) Need to ensure that standards focus on quality of output and not simply on process.
(b) Review of administrative laws and regulations for quality of output.
(c) Formulation of a freedom of information bill.
(d) Need to ensure, quality in government but "What is quality[13] in Government"?

In fact, the concept of quality in government is about responsiveness to people's needs and expectations. It is about accountability, transparency, efficiency and effectiveness of a corruption free administration. These major issues have been engaging the attention of the government for a long time. Although, the agenda for reform initiatives in government was set up by the Chief Ministers'[14] conference held in May, 1997 which emphasised the need for making administration accountable and citizen-friendly, strengthening of grievance redressal mechanism, review[15] of administrative laws, etc.

The present government's commitment to administrative reforms is highlighted in the Election Manifesto of the National Democratic Alliance which commits it to provide a stable, honest, transparent and efficient government. It also emphasises the need to introduce time bound programmes of administrative reforms. Our worthy Prime Minister, in his address to the nation, spoke of the need for an administrative system which is responsive, transparent, efficient and caring. He also wanted it to respond to citizen's concerns and complaints with efficiency and dedication. He also pleaded for an administrative system that has a heart that feels for the poor and a mind that cares for their needs. The fact, that in spite of the rich administrative resource, the reality is that we have not succeeded in creating a system that meets people's[16] expectations.

Quality in government has a very strong link with elimination of corruption. In fact, India has been rated as one of the most corrupt countries by the transparency internationally. Probity in public as well as private sector is of the essence for good governance. The central government from time to time has taken various initiatives to integrate and strengthen the vigilance machinery. The Central Vigilance Commissioner is being given a statutory status. A Lok Pal Bill to deal with corruption in high places has been drafted. Moreover, the use of Information Technology tools would also facilitate increasing the transparency and accountability in the government sector. There is, therefore, considerable emphasis on promoting E-governance.[17] The term E-governance is new and essentially implies upgradation of the efficiency and effectiveness of the administrative machinery through the combination of information technology and sophisticated multimedia to deliver better, cost-affective and speedy services to the citizens. Although, E-governance gives the extraordinary pace of changes in the IT industry but, government functions as a servo-mechanism, joining the polity and economy to achieve public objectives. In government the transition to electronic delivery of services will not only involve changes to the system, procedures and processes of the relevant services but will also effect the way in which the public and the business community deals with the government. These new trends will influence the nature of government, administration and management, thereby reinventing the government to make its experience seemless to the citizens.

We are now on the threshold of the twenty-first century. In the new millennium, the government would need to become more citizen-friendly. Greater delegation and decentralisation of authority and responsibilities would need to be introduced at all levels. Besides this, ethical standards would also need to be adopted by the civil servants as well as politicians. The change in the attitude of the bureaucracy however, cannot be brought about by merely amending conduct of rules or issuing of circulars. The need for it has to be realised by each and everyone of us and the urge for change has to come from within. M.V. Kamath thinks that switching to the presidential form of government will solve our problems of good governance. Failures of governance have generated continuing debate and criticism. One view, often expressed, is that the existing failures in the functioning of executive can be set right if the country shifts from the cabinet system to a presidential system. Whatever be the merits of such argumentation, it must be remembered that almost maximum population still lives in the villages. Thus, whatever may be done to make the functioning of the centre more effective, but we have to remain more careful about the quality in administration at the ground level, from which our problems originate and some of which, due to sustained mismanagement, develop into national issues. The government and Parliament understand the needs to enforce wide-ranging reforms in the continuing system of elections. After the study of N.N. Vohra criminal/nexus report, it requires to at least keep persons with known criminal backgrounds out of the state legislatures and Parliament. The basic objective has still to see fruition, to say nothing of the other important reforms, as required in the electoral process. Some people even suggest that only educated Indians should be allowed to vote. These people have never paid attention to the constituents of our political parties the building blocks of our political system. Once you are the boss in a political party you are there for life. What kind of democracy is this? New blood just does not get in. And the best agency to do this is the Election Commission. It should not recognise parties which do not have democratic set-up. Party tickets should be decided by the people and not by the party bosses.

The USA system is successful because people choose the candidates. This way anyone can enter the election fray. Once the President retires, he is never heard of. So let us take a long and hard look at our parties and throw out the crooks. We should never lose sight of the fact that we are the third most corrupt nation[18] and also the poorest. It is time we started looking at ourselves more critically.

In a globalised world there is no place for the kind of politics that our present-day leaders practise. It is not easy to educate the public at large, and government does not have much time to convince ordinary Indians who is not a victim of its own inaction. It is suffering from a Parliament that has run amok, but that should not paralyse the executive authority. The political commentators have not done much to confront the nation with the problems arising from a political system run on black money. They wrote their articles, made there remarks, however, dissipated a golden opportunity to encourage new thinking on political funding. Vajpayee was voted to power as being the able leader who could lead the country towards a corruption-free nation. Will the Prime Minister and his party rise to the moment and meet the challenges? It is the credibility of the governemnt that is at stake. The present government should strive to come out of the mess that the various agencies have created and prove its worthiness and stand the test of the times.

The present times have become turbulent and frightening. At this hour the country needs statesmanship in politics, promptness, fairness and responsiveness in administration and sagacity in the people. The need for remoralisation of politics and the reconstruction of administrative integrity is both vital and urgent. Attention needs to be paid to the management of values and culture in the country and this should be the pre-eminent task of our leadership. We need "politics" and government of "meaning".[19] We need a new ethos of sharing and caring of tolerance and accommodations, of unity and co-operation. We need statesmanship from our leaders. We need tolerance from our peoples. We need inspiring acts from our intellectuals, scientists, professionals and those who maintains the integrity of management in administration.

## REFERENCES

1. *The Hindu,* Madras, 9 January, 2001, p. 4.
2. M.G. Devasahayam, "Growth Institutions Need for a Focused Role", *The Tribune,* 23 April, 1997, p. 8.
3. Mohit Bhattacharya, "Conceptualising Good Governance", *Indian Journal of Public Administration,* vol. XLIV, no. 3, July-September, 1998, p. 289.
4. World Bank (1994) Governance: *The World Bank's Experience* World Bank, Washington, p. 407.
5. The Conferences of Chief Secretaries, Nov. 20, 1996 in New Delhi, See fn. 3.
6. The Conference of Chief Ministers (24 May, 1997) *Action Plan for Affective and Responsive Government,* Deptt. of Administration

Reforms and Public Grievances, New Delhi, p. 7.

7. Joginder Singh, "Governance Without Gimmicks, Performance as the Criterion", *The Tribune,* 9 July, 1998, p. 8.
8. *Ibid.*
9. Prabhat Kumar, "A Responsive and Effective Government in Management in Government", *A Journal of Administrative Reforms,* vol. XXXI, no. 4, January-March, 2000, New Delhi, p. 1.
10. *Ibid.*
11. *Ibid.*
12. B.B. Tandon, "Quality in Government", *Management in Government,* January-March, 2000, New Delhi, p. 5.
13. B.B. Tandon, "Management in Government", January-March, 2000, New Delhi, p. 5.
14. The Conference of Chief Minister's, 24 May, 1997, See fn. 6.
15. *Ibid.*
16. O.P. Sharma, "Looking Inwards", *The Tribune,* 18 April, 2001, p. 10.
17. *Ibid.*
18. B.B. Tandon, "Quality in Government", See fn. 12.
19. T.N. Dhar, in Government Administration, *Police and Civil Order in Current Trends in Indian Politics,* Edited by N.S. Gehlot, Deep & Deep Publications, 1998, New Delhi, p. 305.

# 10

# Good Governance at Panchayati Raj Institutions

*Sanjeev K. Mahajan & Anupama Mahajan*

Indian federal Constitution provides major guidelines and sets the determining parameters. Local self-government is the direct responsibility of the sub-national government.[1] Under the Indian Constitution, it is obligatory of the State Governments to establish Panchayati Raj Institutions (PRIs) at the village, intermediate and the district levels. Further, it has been clearly mentioned in the Constitution with regard to their composition, term and reservation of seats for the scheduled castes and scheduled tribes and also for women at the various levels. 73rd Amendment also provided for new provisions like establishment of independent state institutions, viz., Electoral Commission (to conduct and supervise elections) and a Finance Commission (to review the existing financial positions of PRIs and suggest ways and means to improve the financial positions of these institutions to the Governor of the State).

73rd Amendment of the Constitution followed by a national policy resolution was thought to provide the much needed impetus for resuscitation of PRIs and the extent to which it will promote sustained development and democracy. Still, PRIs have fallen short of criteria which have been discussed in later part of the article.

## Concept of Good Governance

The concept of good governance is associated with efficient and effective administration in a democratic framework. The World Bank has identified three distinct aspects of governance: (i) the form of political regime; (ii) the process by which authority is exercised in the management of country's economic and social resources for development; and (iii) the capacity of government to design, formulate and implement policies and discharge functions.[2] Therefore, the test of good governance for any government lies in its goals and objectives, in its policies and the manner these are executed in order to achieve the desired results. Further, it also reflects the attitudes of the people towards the functioning of the various agencies of the government.

## Origin of Panchayati Raj Institutions

Panchayati Raj represents grass-root democracy. The success of the democratic process depends largely on the active involvement and participation of the people at the village level. Majority of the population which resides at the village level is socially and economically backward in comparison with the urban population. Ignorance, poverty and helpless resignation to a hostile environment have retarded rural progress. After Independence, the development of rural community became the principal concern of our national government.[3]

The development of Panchayati Raj can be said to be the logical outcome of the Community Development Programmes. But the programmes failed to achieve their objectives of development goals. Balwant Rai Mehta Committee, realising the popular participation, recommended the creation of institutions which were to be statutory elective, comprehensive in duties and functions, equipped with necessary executive machinery with adequate resources and with enough autonomy and freedom. The creation of PRIs with the object of entrusting the authority and responsibility for rural development to the rural people was considered not only an innovation, but also a resolution.

The Committee felt that the main thrust would be reawakening of public keenness for community development through the institution of PRIs. As the Committee felt that development cannot progress without responsibility and power. Community development can be reality only when the community understands its problems, realises its responsibilities, exercises the necessary power through its chosen representatives and maintains a constant and intelligent vigilence on local administration. Hence, the significance of PRIs must be seen to build up a system of democratic structure of administration by establishing statutory elective local bodies.

The high expectations with regard to PRIs have not resulted in fulfilling the desired hopes. The Government of India acknowledged the shortcoming of the PRIs. Hence, various committees were established to rejuvenate or to suggest measures to strengthen the PRIs (Ashok Mehta Working Group on District Planning, G.V.K. Rao Committee to review the existing administrative arrangements for rural development, committee headed by Dr. L.M. Singhvi prepared a Concept Paper on the revitalisation of PRIs, etc.), Narasimha Rao's Government enacted the Constitution (73rd) Amendment Act, 1992 passed in April 1993, aimed at providing de facto powers to PRIs and to ensure genuine decentralisation right up to the level of village panchayats. The Act envisages States to establish three-tier system of strong, intermediate and district levels. States are expected to devolve adequate powers, responsibilities and funds upon these bodies so as to enable them to prepare plans and implement schemes for economic development and social justice.[4]

Prior to this Act, the rural development was the responsibility of government administrators. After the enactment of Act, the task of rural development lies with the democratically elected members at the various levels in the district. As the time progressed, there are many constraints which have led to disillusionment with regard to PRIs.

## Arena of Constraints

The thrust of the Act was to increase the effectiveness of the democratic system by filling up the organisational gaps between the masses and the governing elite. But the experience of the working of PRIs has reflected that the major constraints are related to the implementation of plans and schemes falling under its jurisdiction.

### Ambiguous Functions

There is no specific mention in the Constitutional (73rd) Amendment about the functions to be performed by different institutions at different levels of the Panchayati Raj system. However, a Schedule entitled "Eleventh Schedule" has been appended as per Article 243G, wherein 29 functions have been brought under the Panchayati Raj system.[5] But which tasks are to performed at each tier has not been classified. The amended Act does recognise Gram Sabha as body consisting of persons registered as voters within area of panchayat at village level but this does not specify the powers and functions to be performed by Gram Sabha. It is mentioned in the Act that the Gram Sabha shall perform such functions which may be assigned to it by the respective State through State Legislation. This gives the state a upper hand in assigning functions. Under these circumstances formulation of objectives, identification of priorities, formulation of plans and programmes, etc., depends upon the moral responsibility and political obligation of the respective State Government in the devolution of powers and functions to the PRIs.

### Incompatible Administration Procedures

The performance of PRIs, over the years have suffered from the uncertainties and rigidities in the procedures for provision of financial assistance which make it difficult for the PRIs to draw up plan of action in advance. The lack of resources at all the levels have discouraged the PRIs from undertaking special programmes for their area. Most of them have been made available out of the community development budget or the developmental allocations from time to time. These resources are again at the disposal of District Rural Development Agency. This leads to the conflict between the District Rural Development Agency and the PRIs. This results in confusion at the local level as responsibilities are not clearly defined. There are numerous agencies involved in carrying out the developmental programmes and also the political factors play a prominent role in the implementation of the plan schemes under PRIs. In the present scenario, the political rivalries between the various political parties and local groups have over shadowed the functioning of the PRIs.

## PRIs Controlled by Rural Elites

The 73rd Amendment provides for the much higher levels of people's participation. In the present scenario most of the PRIs are controlled by rural elites. The major reason for their dominance was their position in the village, though members belonging to weaker sections and backward classes are also given representation in PRIs. Further, the Act also provide that not less than one-third (including the number of seats reserved for women belonging to scheduled castes and scheduled tribes) of the total number of seats to be filled up by direct election in every panchayat shall be reserved for women. But in practice, it has oftenly seen that most of these women member exist on paper. And in real terms, their work is being looked after by their counterpart. Unless the empowerment of women is there in real terms, it will not be possible to remove their inequality, invisibility and powerlessness.

## Lack of Autonomy

Although PRIs has control of certain development funds but it is not a full-fledged planning or budgeting body. At the PRIs level, there is little autonomy for preparing planning. As many national or State plans have to be accommodated from time to time. Further, there are certain schemes which are either fully or partially sponsored by the agencies working directly under the control of Central or State Governments. Though the plan is prepared by the district planning unit but ultimate say lies with State Planning Board.

The administrative system is also hierarchical which leaves a little scope for the culture of decentralisation. In order to develop the rural India, it is necessary to understand that unless the greater responsibilities and powers are transferred to the PRIs, it will not be possible to function independently as far away as possible from the Central and State Governments.

### Lack of Technical Assistance

The execution of developmental plans and works is also handicapped by the lack of effective technical assistance from the concerned departments. Most of the governmental departments concerned with the co-ordination of developmental activities with PRIs do not show the interest in implementing these programmes within the framework of time. This also results in delay in the completion of the developmental works. Further, employees working at the different district levels are overburdened and have to handle large area and paper work which leaves little time to spare at the unit level.

### Good Governance at the Grassroot Level

The crisis in administration calls for a redefining of the role of the government and its functions and also its real focus to serve the public effectively as much as to ensure efficiency and cost-effective administration. Accountability, transparency and cleansing public services are all interconnected issues, for ensuring a clean and responsive administration.[6]

### Improving Service Ethics

Public functionaries generally consider themselves as the masters in their respective jurisdiction rather than as public servants. In India, the bureaucracy lacks in desire to serve the people of the country. In order to enforce a work culture and ethnical value system in the governmental organisations, it is must that the people ought be aware to exercise their powers and rights in the right direction. So that the people are encouraged to give their feedback and proper follow up action is taken on where good performers are suitably rewarded and action is taken against the guilty officials. This will help in improving good governance as good governance should help in building delivery system of services. Therefore, responsive administration requires that service delivery and administration of support schemes are decentralised through the PRIs. This will help in making meaningful democracy as envisaged in the 73rd Constitutional Amendment.

## Recognising the Role of Non-Governmental Organisations

In the present context, it has been seen that non-governmental organisation cannot be side tracked in tackling the problem of rural poverty. Mostly non-governmental organisations operate at the grass-root level. Such organisations do render valuable supplemental services to government efforts by extending them to the people. As these organisations help in building public opinion, in fighting corruption and injustice done to the weaker sections of the society by exposing misdeed of the governmental agencies. The major role played by these organisations is to empower the people so that "people first" become the guiding principle of the governmental agencies. That is only possible when non-governmental organisations and governmental agencies join hands in the upliftment of rural masses. What is required under such circumstances is the complete transparency and accountability both in non-governmental organisations and PRIs.This will also give impetus to the people's effective participation towards good governance at the local level. It will also ensure that the delivery system operates efficiently as all the schemes could be reoriented and integrated under the PRIs with the help of non-governmental organisations.

## Summing Up

The Act ensures full freedom to plan according to the local needs but this not merely require delegation of power and resources but also peolple's participation. This also lays the foundation of giving power to the people which is one of the basic fundamental to strengthen the Indian democracy. Further, PRIs have to responsive towards their needs. This can only be possible, when the administration has to responsive and good governance has to accessible. Finally, citizens first has to be guiding motto for every responsive government.

## REFERENCES

1. Reeta Chowdhari Tremblay and Prema Kunitakar, "Governance and Representation: A Study of Women and Local Self government" *The Indian Journal of Public Administration,* July-September, 1998, IIPA, New Delhi, p. 460.
2. World Bank, *Governance: The World Bank's Experience,* World Bank, Washington, 1994, p. 407.
3. Government of India, *Gram Sevika,* Ministry of Community Development and Cooperation, New Delhi, July, 1960, p. 1.
4. A. Vijay Kumar, "Management of Panchayati Raj Institutions: A New Thrust Needed" in Ratna Ghosh and Alok Kumar Pramanik (eds.), *Panchayat System in India,* Kanishka Publishers, New Delhi, 1999, pp. 225-226.
5. V. Venkatakrishnan and B.S. Bhargava, "Tardy Progress of Panchayati Raj Movement in Tamil Nadu" in Ratna Ghosh and Alok Kumar Pramanik (eds.), *Panchayat System in India,* Kanishka Publishers, New Delhi, 1999, p. 125.
6. The Conference of Chief Ministers, *Action Plan for Effective and Responsive Government,* Department of Administration Reforms and Public Grievances, New Delhi, 24 May, 1997, p. 7.

# 11

# Good Governance at Grassroot Level: Challenges and Prospects

*Shiv Raj Singh*

Any government is to rule effectively and in a citizen-friendly manner, has to ensure good governance. In this context, one could say that state craft is an instrument which enables government to preserve their authority, pursue their goals and provide security to their citizens. The prime duty of the state is to protect its citizens and promote growth, sustain development and social justice. It is required to defend its citizens from enemies within and enemies without. Both protection and equity driven development are essential and, in order to achieve the goals of welfare, peace and order have to be ensured. Otherwise development cannot take place.[1]

In terms of the broad values which are historically rooted in our cultural, social and spiritual systems and traditions, the good of one and all in the community has been, in the past, and are still, the prime goals of the society. In other words, the main thrusts of governance in India has been on the widest possible social good which is well expressed by the metaphor, *bahujan hitaye, bahujan sukhaya*. Laws, regulations, codes and behavioural guidelines were laid down in different *Smritis* and *Nitis* said to have been authored by Manu, Narada, Shukra, Yajnavalkya, Kautilya and others.[2]

## Concept of Good Governance

Traditionally, governance refers to forms of political system and the manner in which power is exercised in utilising country's economic and social resources for development.[3] It also deals with the capacity of government to design, formulate and implement policies and, in general, to discharge government functions. In brief governance means the act and manner of managing public affairs. Good governance is associated with efficient and effective administration in a democratic framework.[4] It is equivalent of purposive and development-oriented administration which is committed to improvement in quality of life of the people. It implies high level of organisational effectiveness. Good governance is thus, a function of installation positive virtues of administration and elimination of vices of dysfunctionalities. In short, it must have the attributes of an effective, credible and legitimate administrative system citizen-friendly value-carrying and people-sharing.[5] Kautilya in his treatise *Arthasastra* propounded the traits of good governance by the ruling king as follows:

> In the happiness of his subjects lies his happiness, in their welfare his welfare, whatever pleases himself he shall not consider as good, but whatever pleases his subjects, he shall consider as good.[6]

The concept of good governance has been receiving considerable attention in recent years. However like decentralisation and democratisation it does not enjoy uniformity of meaning. For instance, international organisations like the world bank, associate good governance primarily with capacity building and the exercise of political power needed for efficient and effective management of concrete national programmes, whether the political system is democratic or not.[7] Similarly for authors like Dunn, good governance implies a high level of organisational effectiveness without any choice as to its ideological premise.[8] For Jefferies, good governance is equivalent to purposive and development-oriented administration which is committed to improvement of quality of life of the mass of the people, without necessarily being democratic in style. For another group of writers good governance implies presence of Rule of law, safeguarding basic human rights, presence of honest and efficient government, accountability, transparency, predictability, and openness.

Through the process of governance the essentual link is established between the civil society and the state, giving a shape to the way decisions are made for serving public interest. Constitution and laws provide the legal framework of governance. The institutions, embodying the governing process, include the executive, legislature, judiciary, army, bureaucracy, political parties and interest groups. Public administration is an aid to the process of governance, which needs the help of ethics for achieving stability and excellence.[10]

## Challenges

The basic purpose of public administration in a democracy is, in broad sense to bring in a just order to serve the interests of the people. It would be closer to truth to say that justice can be effectively administered in everyday life by the representatives of the people at the grassroot and the administrators appointed primarily to realise the goal of good governance. Building vibrant local government in order to strengthen the process of democratic governance is an off-repeated promise made by political leadership. It all began with the Balwantrai Mehta Study Team (1957), recommending democratic decentralisation or Panchayati Raj for the purpose of enlisting people's participation in rural development.[11] After some ups and downs with the experiment of Panchayati Raj, the faith in democratic decentralisation was reiterated by the Ashoka Mehta Committee (1978).[12] Prime Minister Rajiv Gandhi wanted to proceed further in this direction and porposed Constitutional Amendment for strengthening local government, both in the rural and urban areas. Stiff opposition to his proposals came from the state governments, who feared loss of their powers and influence if the proposed amendments were enacted. The measure could not be carried through. In 1992 the Rao government has been successful in pushing through the 73rd and 74th amendments to the Constitution with the declared purpose of enabling Panchayats and municipal bodies to function as institution of self-government". But the Panchayati Raj administration is not informed by this noble ideal and the most successful system in West Bengal is found to be suffering from a pervasive "JRY fixation" since the Panchayats at all the three-tiers of district, block and village are overly engrossed in routine work of implementing schemes assigned to them from above under Jawahar Rojgar Yojana.[13] The 73rd Constitutional Amendment envisages devolution of powers and responsibilities upon Panchayat with respect to "(a) the preparation of plans for economic development and social justice; (b) the implementation of schemes for economic development and social justice as may be entrusted to them including, those in relation to the matters listed in the Eleventh Schedule". This schedule containing 29 items, most of them related to local rural development, does not create any exclusive jurisdiction of Panchayats, nor does it preserve any tax or source of finance for exclusive exploitation by Panchayats. What the constitutional Amendment has achieved is merely to ensure the continued survival of Panchayats against supersession and dissolution. It has not ensured adequate financial support for them, nor has it sought to realise the goal of "Self-government" for Panchayats laid down in Article 40 of the Constitution. The history of modern local government in India extends to more than a century, yet its progress has been slow, halting and till today somewhat uncertain. The high hopes with regard to the Panchayati Raj Institution have not been fulfilled. There is recognition in the government of the shortcomings of the Panchayati Raj Institutions. This is born out by findings of a number of committees appointed to revitalise the Panchayati Raj Institutions (Ashoka Mehta Working Group on Distt. Planning, G.V.K. Rao, L.M. Singhvi, P.K. Thungan, etc.). The aim of 73rd Constitutional Amendment is to overcome some of the bottlenecks in the functioning of the Panchayati Raj Institutions. The rationale for the constitution amendment is that though the Panchayati Raj Institutions have been in existence for a long time, they have not been able to acquire the status and dignity of viable and responsive people's bodies. Obstacles, such as irregular elections, prolonged suppression, inadequate representation of weaker sections, insufficient devolution of powers, absence of administrative and financial autonomy, coupled with lack of resources inhibited the growth of these institutions. While there was positive response for the amendment, initially, but the enthusiasm has warned substantially now. In fact, some are now suggesting to introduce amendments to the provisions made in the 73rd Amendment itself.

As mentioned earlier the role envisaged originally for local government was an educative one. Other dimensions have been added subsequently and the concept has become quite enlarged. Jawaharlal Nehru was in favour of giving lot of importance to the Panchayats. However, at the same time, he was keen that these institutions should not be officialised. The official element should act primarily as advisors and allow these bodies to function smoothly without much interference.[14] He was all in favour of panchayat members making mistakes and learning from it, rather than consistently being supervised by the officials. From this point of view, he was keen that there is need to study the administrative problems between the officials and the non-officials". The mistakes of the Panchayats will not endanger the security of the country we can survive it. But they will not suffer for it, they will learn from it, and the public learn from it too. He was convinced that with the coming of the Panchayati Raj, "the basis of our politics is going to be powerfully affected. He was convinced that highest importance should be given to the administrative problems of panchayats. He pointed out further that: we must make Panchayats the sheet-anchor of our administration.[15] The local man knows the local conditions, the local people, the local needs and he generally also knows who is the deserving person in the locality. If he is not invested with authority and the authority is vested in the higher level, to that extent that man in the rural areas suffers. Even if there is some mistake made by the Panchayat, it is likely to be corrected by the people becuase in the Panchayat system, the man has to go and stand for elections next time and if he has been errant he is not likely to be returned.

Local self-government now refers to where people of a locality, possess certain responsibility and direction in the administration of local public affairs and in raising required finances to meet the expenses related thereto. The state with multitudinous activities, which affect all aspects of life, tends to become monolithic and apersonal. The local government, therefore, can provide a human tough in the performance of their assigned duties.

An investigation into the legislations on Panchayati Raj in various states, clearly reveals that the original proposal of decentralisation has neither been honestly tries nor achieved. In spite of all the cry for local autonomy and "Gram Swaraj during the Freedom Movement and even after the attainment of freedom almost all the statutes pertaining to the Panchayati Raj system in different states seem, uniformally to have continued British legacy of relying more upon regulatory rather than autonomous aspects of local government.

Seventy-third Amendment to the Constitution of India is a historical step to liberate the people from the clutches of the big government and the total state system. However, there are some operational maladies which can be outlived as under.

A major flaw of the new Act is that it has adopted a uniform three-tier structure without consideration to requirements and socio-historical conditions of the states. Again the Bill had defined the Panchayats as an institution of self-government but narrowed down the functions to development only as per Article 243G(a) and (b). Without policing (law and order) as a function at each level no institution of self-government is worth the name.[16]

There is no delineation of functions between the three-tiers. The Eleventh Schedule in the Constitution lists the functions that can be performed by the Panchayati Raj Institutions. But what tasks are to be performed at each level is not clear. There is wide variation in the assignment of functions in different states. At times there is reference to the role of the Gram Sabha and Village Panchayats in planning but this is more a rhetoric than reality.[17]

Good governance means empowering people to manage their affair. Panchayati Raj is an institution through which people can be empowered. The concept of political and economic decentralisation in the Indian context, has always been associated with the Gandhian philosophy of non-violent social order consisting of self-sufficient village republics. "Centralization as a system" according to Mahatma Gandhi is in consistant with non-violent structure of society (*Harijan* 18-1941) because "Centralization cannot be sustained and defended without adequate force". He therefore, suggested that if India is to evolve along non-violent lines it will have to decentalise many thing".[18] (*Harijan* 30.12.1939).

In view of Gandhi, political decentralisation means distribution of power among people. "The centre of power," he said, "now is in Delhi, or in Calcutta and Bombay, in the big cities. I would have it distributed among the seven hundred thousands villages of India". So far as economic decentralisation is concerned. Gandhi opposed both industrialisation and urbanisation.[19] Panchayati Raj Institutions have undergone vicissitudes since their launching in 1952. Increasing bureaucratisation of development programmes minimised their importance.

Everybody thinks that after the enacting the 73rd Amendment to the Constitution by India and the provincial acts of Panchayat Raj, the system would work effectively with full vibrancy. In reality it cannot be so. To make this institution a new system of governance, all the old acts relating to the subjects indicated in the 11th Schedule have to be modified or new Acts have to be passed.

Yet another aspect is that mere passing of legislations cannot alter the existing scenario. What is seen today in the Indian society is total apathy and non-understanding of the issues and mass inaction. Most of the Acts are not in operation as the mass never created an opportunity to invoke them. For any act for its success people co-operation, initiative and understanding is imperative. It is also true that all along for the four decades the people had been oriented towards receiving benefits from the government officials without taking any responsibility and it is difficult to make them to take up the responsibility. People's alienation from the grassroot policy for several years created a gap between the people and the government and the government has been playing hide and seek with the people. As a result the officials have become corrupt and a corrupt system has been established legitimately with the approval of politicians.

Gandhi visualised a democratic government in evolutionary form gradually instead of imposing a best system unknown to the people and known to the intellectuals is not suitable to the people. It was clearly indicated by Gandhi's himself when he was asked by the press reporters at the time of framing of the Constitution in the Constituent Assembly. He unequivocally said that the representatives of the millions of people who live in five lakh villages can alone frame a Constitution suitable to the people. The intellectuals who have assembled in the Constituent Assembly had no connection with the rural people and the members were intellectuals but they had no inclination to know the feelings, desires and needs of the people. Our intellectuals and political pundits have enacted a constitution which is against the wishes of the father of the nation and now we are facing the crisis due to what we have done at the dawn of independence. Concentration of power at the centre has completely made the people slaves and the government so powerful.[20]

Everybody is talking about decentralisation of power. It does not mean political power alone, without economic power, there is no meaning of political power. Resource mobilisation and management is the vital part in Panchayati Raj System.

Once villages have got rich resources potentials but they were all destroyed by the politicians with the help of officials. Nowadays as such there is no resource base for effective administration of Panchayats the villagers should have right over land, water, forest and other resources. Village Panchayats can function effectively only with land reforms and without which attempts would yields only negative results. At present village atmosphere is polluted because of the waste water of the industries in the towns. What right do the villages have in the present Act to protect the villages from environmental degradation? Village Panchayats should have rights to decide whether the industries (major) could be started in the villages or not. In the present Act there is no mention about it.[21]

One thing is clear from the attitude of the political parties towards the new Act that all political parties are not interested in sharing power with grassroot institutions. They feel that their importance will be lost. The nation is in a critical decade. As we have invited companies from foreign countries our economic sovereignty is at stake.[22] On the one hand, we are talking about political power decentralisation, on the other, our government is determined to usher in more globalisation and liberalisation.

Democracy, parliament, legislature, judiciary and bureaucracy, etc., are only for the privileged class not for the poor. Until the poor get minimum needs there is no meaning for all those concepts. The political executive the instrumentalists of public administration and the police are, in a manner of speaking at crossroads. People have begun to lose faith in governments and institutions. The question often asked as "whose reality counts". An intensifying polarisation has developed in the society between "privilage and deprivation, between security and vulnerability and between power and impotence". There is so much talk about democracy, decentralisation, empowerment, accountability and the securing of people's rights and freedoms. Yet the common citizens often finds himself trapped between the dual vice of state power on the one hand, and the market forces (often translated as anarchic licence to do what you wish) on the other. The present times have assumed many characteristics of intolerance, confrontary ethos, fear and distrust.

The Indian governance scenario during the last 50 years is a rather gloomy one, uninspiring, and dismal. In the first one or two decades after independence kindled some hope, it was extinguished thereafter. The system had failed on several fronts, the major ones being: vision and mission, corruption, population, education, character, values integrity, nationalist spirit, factorisations of political parties, social and institutional reforms and leadership vacuum.[23]

## Prospects

In all the provisions of the 73rd Amendment, the provision relating to Gram Sabha is the landmark in the Act. It is in the history of Constitution of India, first of its kind in giving power to the people to participate in decision-making process. Through Gram Sabha the whole democracy can be perfected. Gram Sabha is a place where people are to be socialised. It is more or less a mini parliament. By conducting the Gram Sabha in such a fashion, almost all the eligible voters can oriented in a representative form of government.

First step should be taken to instill in the minds of the people that the responsibility should be taken by people not given by the officials. Indeed time has come to people-ise government and power. Unless people can share real power in the government not in the mechanical sense of sending unknown, unwanted and useless representatives once in five years during the election time the government tends to treat people as avoidable distraction or as bothersome clients, not as citizen (the source of power) to be served. Democracy needs citizens and not clients. Real democracy means real empowerment, government is not business, it is service, born in sympathy and empathy.[24]

The lower level of administration also needs effective decentralisation through the three-tier, popularly elected Panchayati Raj Institutions (PRIs) at the district, block and village levels. These institutions for proper discharge of their functions need to be made financially viable. Being close to the people they ought to be legally empowered to enforce many laws through their own agencies. Panchayat level Lok Adalats could also deal with minor civil and criminal disputes to relieve the higher judicial courts of their mounting case work. There should, of course, be proper supervision and guidance at the initial stages to these PRIs to ensure impartiality and fairness in their functioning. Retired judicial officials could also be made honorary advisers to Panchayat Adalats. In fact, a beginning has already been made in many states to hand over all developmental activities to the PRIs. What could be additionally given to them is legal dispute settlement duties. They could also be empowered to give various kinds of legal certificate, i.e., birth, death, marriage, caste, character, etc. The Panchayats should be entrusted with maintenance of peace and security in their respective areas. Administration in many respects should be self-managed and closer to the people.[25]

Initially, there may be understandable reluctance in expanding the roles of the Panchayats. There is, however need to use democratic institutions in the service of the people and reduce the role of bureaucracy. These bodies could be less formal and more accommodating in taking care of the many day-to-day problems of the people.[26]

Cutting short needless discussion on details, it may be added that 73rd Amendment Act has the potential of establishing at least the procedure part of good governance. The decentralised system of elected governance has certain inherent advantages. For example, it will bring efficiency as decision-makers, who live locally are likely to know about local conditions and would be in a position to match resources and needs more precisely. Second, it will also bring accountability in the sense that the decision-makers live and work in close contact with the users and as such are exposed to more effective scrutiny and greater pressure to deliver the goods.[27]

Apart from these advantages there are also more opportunities for rural people to participate in planning services and to pay for them in the form of local taxes. It is an established world-view that local governments tend to give high priority than central government to human development. The most striking point in regard to 73rd and 74th Amendments is one-third reservation of elected offices for women and for SCs and STs in proportion to their population. Adequate representation of women and dalits will certainly bring qualitative change in the functioning of Panchayats. In initial stages some cases of functioning by proxy may be reported. But once women taste, power they would assert their independence as is evident in case of West Bengal, Kerala, Karnataka, Madhya Pradesh and to certain extent Himachal Pradesh. Added to this is the fact that with regular elections and performance audit by the electorate, the existing power elite would lose power gradually and thus transfer of power to the weaker sections will be a smooth fair.[28]

While not boasting the people's participation through Panchayats will prove is to be a panacea for all the evils of misgovernance, yet we would like to assert, that they have the potential for good governance at the grassroot level provided they are institutionally, financially and legally supported by the existing power structure.[29] Similarly only insertion of Eleventh Schedule in the body of the Constitution specifying 29 subjects to be performed by Panchayat is not enough. What is required is that there should be a drastic reduction and restructuring of central and state governments apparatus, especially in respect of items included in this Schedule. Another important thing which is left out in the 73rd Amendment the old concept of Naya Panchayat which must be introduced without further delay.

A determined popular movement is necessary for empowerment of Panchayats, because the intrenched interests would not like to part with their existing power. In this connection a lead has to be taken by enlighted citizens, social activists and NGOs. But to play an effective role in good governance, the NGOs themselves need adequate training and capacity building.[30] It is better to follow the model of West Bengal for realistic implementation of Panchayati Raj, however, we are imperfect. In West Bengal 50 per cent of the sales tax is being earmarked for Panchayati Raj bodies.

## Conclusion

To make it more vibrant, accountable and sensitive, people are to be oriented in the new system. Cleaning village polity will help cleansing national polity, creating healthy democratic practice in the village bodies will help the national bodies to create healthy practice. By doing all activities in the villages in a systematic way through a new value system nation's political scenario can be transformed. Panchayati Raj Act is only an opener and it is not all in all. To make the Panchayati system to work effectively the present Acts relating to agriculture, forestry, industry, education, co-operation and few others have to be reenacted in consonance with the provision of the 73rd Constitutional Amendment Act and state Acts.

Governance, as an issue has undoubtedly emerged as one of the critical importance in the country. We can plan, mobilise, investments, train manpower, raise financial resources, induct the most modern technologies and set for ourselves the goals of economic development, equity, social justice and better quality of life for all. We can time and again, reaffirm our resolve to wash off the lost tear drop from the eye of the weakest and the humblest. We can evolve policies and programmes key to the goals of the state. But it must be remembered that, the good governance is the indespensable, enabling condition for converting fine intentions into concrete actions.

There is need to set out house in order. There is need to mount as much pressure as possible through collective action, debate, dialogue, media, articulation and by all other legitimate means for speedy political, administrative, judicial reforms to ensure good governance. At this hour what is require is statesmanship in politics, firmness, discipline, transparency, accountability and responsibility in administration.

## REFERENCES


1. T.N. Dhar, "Governance, Policing and Human Rights", *The Indian Journal of Public Administration,* vol. XLVI, no. 2, 2000, p. 199.
2. *Ibid.*, pp. 199-200.
3. O.P. Minocha, "Good Governance: New Public Management and Perspective", *The Indian Journal of Public Administration,* vol. XLIV, no. 3, 1998, p. 271.
4. *Idem.*
5. Bata K. Dey, "Defining Good Governance", *The Indian Journal of Public Administration,* vol. XLIV no. 3, p. 414.
6. *Idem.*
7. H.K. Asmerom (et al.), "Good Governance, Decentralisation and Democraticisation", *The Indian Journal of Public Administration,* vol. XLI no. 4, 1995, p. 736.
8. *Idem.*
9. *Idem.*
10. Ashok Mukhopadhyay, "Ethics in Governance, The Indian Perspective", *The Indian Journal of Public Administration,* vol. XLI, no. 3, 1995, p. 395.
11. India Report of Team for the Study of Community Projects and Extension Service, Committee on Plan Projects, New Delhi, Govt. of India, 1957.
12. India Report of Panchayati Raj Institutions, New Delhi, Department of Rural Development, Government of India, 1978.
13. Nirmal Mukherji and D. Bandhyopadhyay, *New Horizons for West Bengal's Panchayats,* Calcutta, Government of West Bengal, 1993, p. 4.
14. Presidential address in Fifth Annual General Body Meeting of Indian Institute of Public Administration, New Delhi, April 25, 1959.
15. Presidential address in Thirty Second Annual General Body Meeting of Indian Institute of Public Administration, New Delhi, October 19, 1986.
16. Biju M.R., *Dynamics of New Panchayati Raj System, Reflections and Retrospection,* Kanishka Publishers, Distributors, New Delhi, 1999, p. 290.
17. A.P. Barnabas, "Good Governance at Local Level" *The Indian Journal of Public Administration* Special Number on Towards Good Governance, vol. XLIV, no.3, 1998, p. 450.
18. P.N. Bora, "Panchayati Raj: Experiment of Decentralisation" in *The Bi-Annual Journal of Public Administration,* Department of Public Administration, Lucknow University, vol. 1, no. 1, 1996, p. 55.

19. *Idem.*
20. G. Palanithurai, "View from Grassroots" in his (ed.) book, *New Panchayati Raj System: Status and Prospectus,* Kanishka Publishers, New Delhi, 1996, p. 17.
21. *Ibid.*, p. 116.
22. *Ibid.*, p. 119.
23. Bata K. Dey, "Defining Good Governance", *The Indian Journal of Public Administration,* vol. XLIV no. 3, p. 419.
24. *Ibid.*, p. 423.
25. U.C. Aggarwal, "Good Governance, Cutting edge of Administration" *The Indian Journal of Public Administration,* vol. LIV no. 3, 1998, p. 436.
26. *Ibid.*, p. 437.
27. S.N. Mishra and Sweta Mishra, "Good Governance, People's Participation and NGOs". *The Indian Journal of Public Administration,* vol. XLIV, no. 3, 1998, p. 443.
28. *Ibid.*, p. 444.
29. *Idem.*
30. *Idem.*

# 12

# Panchayati Raj and Rural Development in India

*Pawan Kumar Banta*

When Panchayati Raj was started in India the basic idea was that at the local level there should be certain amount of democracy which would give to people a sense of involvement, otherwise what was happening that there was democracy at the state level, and democracy at the national level, i.e., election to the state legislative assemblies, election to the Parliament, but at the local level there was no democracy, it was ruled by administrators. That's what was felt. If the people are to be involved they have to be given some sort of involvement in the functioning of the institutions or development programmes. This is the only way to take democracy to the masses. In fact, in a real democracy, people have an opportunity to get involved in development programmes. So the idea at that time was that decision-making level should be closer the people.

The Panchayati Raj aims at establishing democracy at grass-root level and giving a sense of involvement to the people at the village level. As Mahatma Gandhi said: "In a democracy, decentralisation of political and economic power is essential, because a few centres of power cannot realise or fulfil the needs of vast multitudes of people. If India is to develop the power and responsibilities must be shared by all." The failure of our poverty alleviation and rural development programmes to achieve their avowed goals fully highlights this fact. These programmes were designed by few people at the top and have been implemented without the involvement of people at grassroot level. They do not reflect the needs and aspirations of people and thus fail to satisfy them.

## Historical Background of Democratic Decentralisation

When Mahatma Gandhi discovered that there was no mention of Panchayati Raj (PR) in the earlier draft of the Constitution, he insisted on its inclusion in the revised draft, because PR was an important component of his vision of future India in which economic and political power was decentralised and each village was self-reliant economically. He felt that people's voice should be reflected in our independence through panchayats, and therefore, "the greater is the power of panchayats, the better is for the people". Article 40 of the Constitution of India which was included in the chapter on Directive Principles of State Policy, said that "the state shall take steps to organize village panchayats and endow them with such powers and authority as may be necessary to enable them to function as units of self-government".

In the post-Independence era, the introduction of the Community Development Programme (CDP) in 1952, with people's participation as its central concern, was perceived as a project which would transform the socio-economic life of the village community. But, the entire programme suffered due to the lack of involvement to the beneficiaries and their representatives in the planning and execution of development schemes meant for them. It was realised that CDP would be meaningless unless it becomes a people's programme with officials guiding them and supplying them with technical knowledge.

Towards the closing years of the decade of fifties the Balwant Rai Mehta Study Team (Committee) was appointed in January 1957 to study and report on the Community Development Projects and National Extension Service. The Study Team offered two broad directional thrusts: (i) there should be administrative decentralisation for effective implementation of development programmes, and (ii) the decentralised administrative system should be under the control of elected bodies.

The Committee further realised that development cannot progress without responsibility and power, community development can be real only when the community understands its problems, realised its responsibilities and exercises the necessary powers through its chosen representatives. With this objective the Committee recommended an early establishment of statutory elective local bodies and devolution to them necessary resources, powers and authority. The Committee, therefore thought PR system as a means of involving people and their representatives in development programmes of the government. While explaining its philosophy, the Committee remarked the PR system establishes a linkage between local leadership enjoying confidence of local people and the government.

The three-tier PR system is recommended by the Mehta Team was first launched in Rajasthan and Andhra Pradesh in 1959. Almost all the states were quick to introduce the PR as per the Directive Principles of the Constitution. PRIs in different states and UTs have been set up under different legislations.

The basic theory behind the PR is to ensure people's participation in development programmes. Initially, it was intended that they will unleash the arrested process of change and growth, but after sometime it was observed by several state level committees as well as by various studies that PR system was suffering from a number of weaknesses, and the other. Ashok Mehta Committee was set up in 1978 to look into its working in various states and to make recommendations for strengthening it.

The Ashok Mehta Committee viewed that PR system was not only meant for decentralisation of power and people's participation, but also for supporting rural development and strengthening the planning process at the micro level. The Committee, therefore, wanted PRIs to participate in development activities in the areas of agriculture, forestry, cottage industries, welfare activities, etc.

With the launching of anti-poverty programmes and setting up of district rural development agencies (DRDAs) and other related organisations at lower levels, the need for integration of PR system with development programmes and administration was felt. C.H. Hanumanth Rao's Working Group on istrict Planning (1983) and G.V.K. Rao Committee (1985), set up to review the existing administrative arrangements for rural development and poverty alleviation programmes, have given recommendations for this purpose. The G.V.K. Rao Committee, for example, has recommended strengthening of Zilla Parishads and district level planning as well as integration of block and lower level planning with lower level PRIs. In 1986-87 the Singhvi Committee prepared the concept paper on Panchayati Raj. It to be closely involved in planning implementation of rural development programmes at lower levels. The Singhvi Committee has recommended that village Panchayats of groups of small villages if necessary should be made viable. It has also supported the recommendations of the G.V.K. Rao Committee for integrating administrative structures with Panchayati Raj Institutions. The Singhvi Committee as well as Ashok Mehta Committee suggested suitable constitutional amendments for the purpose.

## Limitations of PRIs

Indeed, the concept of Panchayati Raj has undergone some changes over the years. Though it began as a narrow concept, it has expanded to cover the areas of rural development and economic planning to a reasonable extent. However, there are certain limitations that have been broadly identified as follows: (i) the concept is still very narrow as it does not view PR institutions that can play an important role in the overall development of rural areas or in other words, the present concept does not see a PRI as a planning as well as implementation agency of various rural development programmes, and as an agency that can take care of routine administration, infrastructure and socio-economic welfare of rural population; (ii) there is no clarity about how to involve the weaker sections in the functioning of PRIs; (iii) there is, therefore, considerable confusion about the role of PRIs in rural development programmes, specially anti-poverty programmes; and (iv) there is no clear trend emerging in the context of decentralisation of power to district and lower level bodies, on the other hand central schemes are increasing both in number and size.

## Past Experience

The past experience of PRIs had been a state of neglect and impoverishment. Even after being in existence for about four decades PRIs could not acquire the status and dignity of a viable unit of self-government and responsive people's body. Several factors are responsible for the slow growth of PRIs; e.g., absence of regular and periodic elections within a stipulated period, prolonged supersession, variation in structure, powers and functions from state to state, insufficient representation of weaker sections including SCs, STs, OBCs and women, inadequate devolution of powers, lack of financial resources and above all lack of political will. PRIs being the potential centres of people's power, aroused apprehensions in the minds of bureaucracy and elected representatives at the national and state level bodies so they were not quite willing to share power.

## Rural Development Programmes: Historical Perspective

In free India, the Community Development Programme (CDP) was started in October 1952. This humble beginning had very ambitious objectives. The CDP was launched with the goal of transforming the outlook of the people, inculcating the spirit of self-reliance and generating the habit of co-operation through public bodies. The National Extension Service (NSS) scheme was introduced in October 1953, throughout India for assisting the process of development planning. These programmes ensured people's participation by organising non-statutory committees at the village and block levels. Notwithstanding the many criticisms of CDP, it has made a positive contribution, howsoever small it may be, to the economic and social development of rural India.

### *Broad spectrum of activities*

There are three stages of rural development. The first stage of rural development includes co-operative village management, rural extension programmes, community development, abolition of intermediaries, land reforms, democratic decentralisation, additional investment in agriculture, irrigation, industry and so on. These development activities were expected to change the rural scenario divert rural people from agriculture to other occupations and reduce the pressure of population on agriculture. But there was no spectacular change in the rural economy even though the economy as whole made some progress.

In the second stage, new technology in agriculture was introduced. Production increased but did not improve the economic condition of rural people. From the starting of the Fourth Plan (1969-74) an attempt was made to attack poverty by poverty eradication programmes like Small Farmers Development Agency (SFDA), Marginal Farmers and Agricultural Labourers Agency (MFAL) and Drought Prone Area Programme (DPAP). In the Fifth Plan (1974-79), the Minimum Needs Programme was introduced to improve the quality of life of the poor.

Since all this did not bring about substantial improvement in rural area, a number of radical poverty eradication programmes were introduced in the Sixth Plan 1980-85 which continued during the plan 1985-90. These programmes included:

1. Employment planning at block level through National Employment Programme (NREP) and Rural Landless Employment Guarantee Programme (RLEGP).
2. Integrated Rural Development Programme (IRDP) which extended the scope and content of SFDA, MFALA, etc., and which aimed at the real integration of various programmes.
3. Revised minimum needs programmes.
4. Special area programmes for hilly and forest areas and for other backward areas.
5. Emphasised distributive justice through land reforms, extended public distribution system for mass consumption goods, etc.

Another item of rural development which elicited wide public attention is the Jawahar Rozgar Yojana (JRY), a programme for providing additional gainfully employment for the unemployed and underemployed persons in rural areas. Representing a merger of NREP and RLEGP, the scheme atempts to provide fuller employment opportunities to at least one member of each family below the poverty line who seeks unskilled employment.

An Employment Assurance Scheme (EAS) for providing assured employment to as many as 2,470 rural poor blocks of 261 districts was started in October 1993. The objective of the scheme was to provide about 100 days of assured casual manual labour employment during the lean agricultural season at the statutory minimum wages. Under EAS more than 4.30 million person have been registered and more than 4.81 crore mandays have been generated.

As to self-employment for educated youth, both in urban and rural areas, the Prime Minister's Rozgar Yojana (PMRY) has been launched. It is meant for setting up micro-enterprises by educated unemployment youth. The earlier scheme for Self-Employment of Educated Unemployed Youth (SEEUY) has been amalgamated with PMRY.

But unfortunately, the rural development programmes failed to involve people in the planning and implementation of programmes. It was noticed that CDP as well as other rural development programmes, instead of being people's programmes with government's assistance, were becoming more and more government's programmes with varying degree of people's participation. PRIs were also found weak and ineffective to mobilise the masses in support of the programmes.

Experience of various rural development programmes reveals that mere project approach or a sectoral approach is not adequate to lead to an overall development of the area and distribution of benefits to local population, particularly the weaker sections of the society. The distribution of unemployment and poverty and the potential for development of agriculture and related activities vary widely from region to region and also within region. Different areas in the country are at different levels of development and have varying degrees of potential, depending on local endowments. The efforts will now be to make the programme area-specific and utilise the local endowments for growth, social justice and full employment. It will, therefore, be necessary to plan for integration of various programmes and establish appropriate linkages for optimal utilisation of local endowments in consistent with the plan objectives, local needs and environmental balance.

Though development has taken place, but its gains have not yet reached every family in the rural India. There still remains a vast majority of the rural poor and the landless labourers for whom greater efforts need to be made in terms of creating employment opportunities and providing assistance in income generating with a view to enabling them to cross the poverty line. Though the government has in the past, tried to solve this gigantic problem with the help of available resources through various rural development programmes, but still the poverty of the rural areas calls for more effective and efficient rural services.

Besides, as the experience indicates though despite initiatives by the government to help rural poor have reduced the incidence poverty, many of the programmes could not yield desired results, mainly due to lack of people's participation and well-organised institutional support, particularly at the grassroot level. Therefore, a number of measures were taken to ensure that the benefits of these special schemes reach the real poor. For instance people belonging to weaker sections were given priority in the development efforts so that the benefits of planned investment can go to the relatively backward sections of the community.

## Panchayati Raj and Rural Development

PRIs have been assigned the most important task of rural development. They inevitably occupy the most prominent place in our democracy. The new PR system has two main objectives: the first is to strengthen the democratic set-up at the lowest level and the second is the socio-economic upliftment of the rural masses. The main motive is to bring about socio-economic development of villagers and to raise their standard of living by their active participation. As we have seen in the past, the overall picture of the working of the PRIs has not been very impressive and satisfactory.

The 73rd Constitutional Amendment Act, 1992 has broken a distinctly new ground. The PRIs deserve to succeed as the principal vehicles for rural development. The economic development through various programmes that are to be taken up during the Eighth Plan, which has a massive provision for rural development, has to be channellised by provision of adequate funds and powers to the PRIs with the active involvement of the grassroot organisations in both planning and implementation. The quality of implementation will also improve as the PRIs are ideally suited to effective implementation of the programmes entrusted to them.

Involvement of people at the grassroot level been considered as the most effective means through which economic development can meet aspirations of the people and to ensure that the benefits really percolate down to the lowest strata of the society.

The Eleventh Schedule of the Constitution of India lists twenty-nine subjects which ought to provide an effective role to the PRIs in planning and implementation of works of local significance ranging from drinking water, agriculture, land and water conservation to communications, poverty alleviation programmes, family welfare, education libraries and cultural activities, maintenance of community assets, etc.

The 73rd Constitutional Amendment Act has introduced a new PR system throughout the country. The primary goal has been to proceed with decentralisation, dispersal and redistribution of power. It seeks to give responsibilities to the three-tier PRIs to make them the true decision-making centres with local power.

It is notable that the PRIs are the primary institutions of democracy where people from village, block and district could participate. Devolution of power has to start here and this is also where people at local levels get into the mainstream of development as well as public affairs. The PRIs, especially the "Gram Sabha", make the concept of "direct democracy". The Gram Sabha has been designed to be the place where development issues should be discussed, development programmes initiated and beneficiaries of development schemes selected. It may be added that the prospects of the PRIs would be on the increase keeping in mind the pace of economic liberalisation in India. In fact, they would become watch-dog bodies to ensure proper implementation of the employment generation programmes. In fact, the PRIs would play an important role in accelerating socio-economic development in the rural areas.

It is hoped that administration of rural development and welfare schemes would be greatly facilitated through democratic decentralisation and the three-tier structure of self-government envisaged in the 73rd Constitutional Amendment Act the question of devolving adequate powers on PRIs is being vigorously pursued by the centre with the states. Together with this, the rural development programmes have received added impetus in the wake of substantial set-up in central allocation, which have gone up to Rs.30,000 crore in the Eighth Plan from Rs.11,000 crore in the Seventh Plan.

In the Ninth Plan (1997-2002), the PRIs in rural areas will be directly involved in the development process. People's involvement through their elected representatives will be realised through genuine democratic decentralisation.

## REFERENCES

Desai, Vasant, *Panchayati Raj*, Himalaya Publishing House, New Delhi, 1990.

Gandhi, Mahatma, "India independence must begin at the bottom", *Kurukshetra*, February 1989.

Government of India, *Constitution of India,* New Delhi.

Government of India, *First to Eighth Five Year Plans,* Planning Commission, New Delhi.

*Gramin Vikas Newsletter,* Ministry of Rural Development, New Delhi, May 1993 and April 1994.

Hirway, Indira, "Panchayati Raj at Grassroots", *Economic and Political Weekly*, vol, XXV. no. 29, July 1989.

Mehta, B.R., *Committee Report on Plan Projects,* vol. I, Planning Commission, New Delhi, 1959.

Mishra, B.N., "Rural Development", *Kurukshetra*, March 1991.

Mishra, S.N., *New Horizons in Rural Development*, Mittal Publications, New Delhi.

Prasad, Mahesh, "Planned Development to End Inequality", *Yojana*, January 1996.

Ramanujam, K.N., "The Philosophy of Rural Development", *Kurukshetra*, January 1995.

Rao, P.V. Narasimha, "Education expansion will help strengthen Panchayati Raj", *Yojana*, vol. 33, nos. 1 & 2, January 1989.

Report of the Committee on Panchayati Raj Institutions, Government of India, New Delhi, 1978 (Chairman: Ashok Mehta).

Report of the Working Group on District Planning, vols. 1 & 2.

Planning Commission, New Delhi, 1983 (Chairman: C.H. Hanumantha Rao).

73rd Constitution Amendment Act, Government of India, New Delhi.
Singh, S.K., *Towards Effective Rural Self-Government.*
Trivedi, Bhupat J., "What it holds for rural development", *Kurukshetra*, January 1992.
Vasant, V. Sathe, "Panchayati Raj: Its Validity", *Yojana*, vol. 33, nos. 1 and 2, January 1989.

# 13

# Democratic Decentralisation in Relation to 73rd and 74th Amendments

*L.N. Sharma*

Democracy, to be real and vibrant must originate at the local level, which is termed as grassroots democracy. It, thus, envisages a political structure which ensure the participation of the people at the local level in a widest possible manner.

The question may be asked: In what does the essence of grassroots democracy consist? Grassroots democracy stands for a political structure in which democracy is not merely confined to the national and regional levels but is also extended to local levels in a real and large measure. It is thus a medium of people's participation, which is not remote and intermittent, and is not limited to electing representatives for a rather distant government—say, national or regional once in two, three or five years, but is based on their participation in the day-to-day conduct of their own local area, village or town, as the case may be. Grassroots democracy is thus essentially decentralised democracy in which the management of public affairs does not begin and end at the top but operates through a wide network of people's participating units in the local area which form more or less a miniature government in themselves and are thus real centres of power and, therefore, of democratic thought and action.[1]

As such the creation of centres of power at the local level inherit the idea of democratic decentralisation.

## Democratic Decentralisation: The Real Issues

The idea of decentralisation is in a way inherent in the democratic ideal in its application to political organisation. Democracy as a form of political organisation is an attempt at right ordering of people's partnership not merely in the sovereign power of the state but also in the day-to-day conduct of government. Though democracy as a form of political organisation has been differently described by political thinkers, yet the idea of maximum participation by the people is the common factor in their analysis. Thus according to Mill, "the only government which can fully satisfy all the exigencies of the social state is one in which the whole people participate".[2] People's participation forms the heart of democracy. The larger and more continuous and the more active, constructive and closer (qualitatively speaking) is the people's participation in the operation of their own government in a country, the nearer is it to democracy as a political ideal. Democratic decentralisation is one of the media of people's participation. It aims at associating people with the work of government to the maximum possible extent and in a living manner.[3]

It might be asked: when the idea of decentralisation inherent in the democratic principle, why should the adjective "democratic" be prefixed to it? The prefix is not superfluous. It emphasises the purpose of decentralisation which is to provide a larger, greater and closer association of the people with the work of their own government. The adjective "democratic" also distinguishes democratic decentralisation from administrative decentralisation. Administrative decentralization originates in a quest for efficiency in terms of initiative, performance and speed of administrative personnel, particularly at the lower operative levels, while democratic decentralisation has its roots in the desire to associate more and more people with the work of government at all levels, national, regional and more particularly, local. Democratic decentralisation implies people's right to initiate their own projects for local well-being and the power to execute and operate them in an autonomous manner.[4]

The words, "democratic" and "decentralisation" form the key to the understanding of the synthetic compound expression democratic decentralisation. The word "democratic" explains at once the nature and purpose of the concept as also its basic postulates in its institutional aspect. The word "decentralisation" is essentially indicative of the method to realise the end as contained in the word "democratic". By itself, thus the word decentralisation hardly has a democratic content and as Montague Harris has pointed out, "decentralisation also means what deconcentration signifies, in spite of the fact that according to French usage, the former stands for local self-government and the latter for local state governments".[5] It is thus only the prefix democratic that enriches the content of decentralisation. The latter when read with the former stands for transfer of authority and grant of autonomy from top levels to the people at the lower levels in a three-dimensional manner:[6]

(i) taking of decision about the programme and policy in a wide and duly specified area of activity—a function which is essentially political;
(ii) controlling and managing of material resources needed to cope with the responsibilities thus devolved—a function essentially financial; and
(iii) supervising, guiding, and conducting the actual operation, a function essentially administrative—all these without undue interference from the top levels.

So it can be concluded that the democratic decentralisation is a political concept, which aims at devolution of powers and authority to the people at the lowest level in matters of political decision-making, financial management and administrative management without any interference from top levels. Democratic decentralisation, as such, is closer participation of the people at the local level with their own government, directly or through their representatives, in political decision-making, financial control and administration without interference from the above.

## Democratic Decentralisation: Operational Dimension

After having analysed the reality of democratic decentralisation the next important issue is the operation of the concept. As clarified the democratic decentralisation is dispersion or devolution of powers to the people to manage their political, financial and administrative affairs at the local level. This management requires certain organisational arrangement and the system of local self-government is the natural corollary to democratic decentralisation. Democratic decentralisation is a political concept whereas the local self-government is an institutional arrangement to put the idea into operation. However both the terms are neither identical nor vitally different.

Both aim at greater participation by the people and more autonomy to them in the management of their affairs. Both of them incidentally limit the control from the above. What are the points of difference? It can be said that democratic decentralisation is a political idea and local self-government is its institutional form. There is also a difference of emphasis between the two, the former laying greater stress than the latter in positive terms, on more or less complete autonomy at the bottom and, in negative terms on no or limited exercise of control from above. On the other hand, democratic decentralisation is in fact a plea to further democratise local self-government to enable it to enjoy more authority, shoulder greater responsibility, take more initiative and experience greater autonomy in the management of the affairs of the local area than what the local self-government institutions have been doing so far.[7]

## Democratic Decentralisation: The Indian Panorama

The concept of democratic decentralisation is not new to the Indian soil and the institutions of local self-government used to exist in India since Vedic times.

Both during the ancient and medieval period Indian villages were administered by their own people. But formally the villages as the local self-governing units were accepted by the British government which had a two-fold purpose—(i) to inculcate the responsiveness among the Indian masses and (ii) to redress their legitimate grievances. Liberal local self-government institutions were introduced by the British rulers in India as a response to the gorwing nationalistic upsurge and rising discontent within the country. But, true to the psychology of the Dominion-masters, these measures, too, were devised as an advantageous bargain wherein local representative elements were introduced without, in any way relenting the hold of dominant bureaucratic control of the foreign masters. The centres of political powers were kept intact at every level be it central, provincial or district. Thus, emerging as a component of a clearly-designed scheme, giving the appearance of democratic framework, yet-retaining the overall predominance of the bureaucracy—the local government institutions in India grew with an in-built tradition of strong bureaucratic controls.[8]

After achieving independence, with India's tryst with destiny, it was only legitimate to hope that the spirit of freedom and self-rule would percolate down to the very grassroot of the Indian polity. Indian National Congress's strong commitment to the principles of decentralisation and the vociferous and repeated statements of the Father of the Nation (Mahatma Gandhi) and the first Prime Minister Pandit Jawaharlal Nehru made before independence and afterwards warranted this conclusion and hope on the part of the people. This hope was further strengthened when the Constituent Assembly took up the task of Constitution-making and speaker after speaker rose to champion the cause of the "Panchayati Raj" as a necessary prerequisite of rural uplift and development, resulting in making numerous provisions in the Constitution particularly in the Directive Principles of the State Policy.[9]

The Constitution of India provides in Article 40 that, "The state shall take steps to organise village panchayats and to endow them with such powers and authority as may be necessary to enable them to function as units of self-government".[10] Also Article 246 empowers the State Legislature to legislate with respect to any subject relating to self-government. These provisions in the Constitution indicates a clear-cut policy directive with regard to the manner how local government was to be developed. As a result, it became obligatory on the part of the state governments to ensure the proper functioning of the local bodies.[11]

Soon, Indian leaders took vigorous steps to fulfil the aims of the Constitution through planning and community development. The Community Development Programme (CDP) was started on 2 October, 1952 with 55 Community Development Projects under the Indo-US Operational Agreement. On the suggestion of the Grow More Food Enquiry Committee, the Government of India introduced another programme, called the National Extension Service (NES) on 2 October, 1953.[12] The programme had an encouraging start. There was enthusiasm among the people and development officials. But in three to four years, it lost its initial momentum and the participation and involvement of the people showed a considerable decline.[13] Therefore, the Planning Commission urged the National Development Council to have the whole issue investigated. The National Development Council constituted a committee on Plan Projects which, in turn, appointed a study term for community. Projects and National Extension Service in 1957, headed by Balvantrai G. Mehta, as its Chairman. The Study Team submitted its report in late 1957. The Committee observed that the CDP and NES Programmes had failed to evoke popular initiative, that local bodies at the higher level than the panchayat had evinced but little enthusiasm in the CDP and even the panchayats had not come into the field of community development in any significant way.[14]

The Balvantrai Mehta Team offered two broad directional thrusts; first it argued that there should be administrative decentralisation for the effective implementation of the development programme and that the decentralised administrative system should be under the control of elected bodies.[15] The committee recommended that the old district boards be replaced by a three-tier system of rural self-government with each tier linked by indirect election and genuine transfer of power and responsibility of planning and development. The three tiers suggested were: Gram Panchayat at the village level, Panchayat Samiti at block level, and Zila Praishad at the district level.[16] The Team further pointed out: if this experiment of democratic decentralisation was to yield maximum results, it was necessary that all the three tiers of the scheme, viz., village panchayat, panchayat samiti and zila-parishad should be started at the same time and operated simultaneously in the whole district.[17]

The recommendation about the establishment of three-tier system was discussed in the Parliament as accepted by the

National Development Council in January 1958. For evoking popular appeal among the masses the name of democratic decentralisation was changed to Panchayati Raj. The states were given option to adopt it with such modification as suited their special conditions.[18]

In 1957, Madras started a pilot block of democratic decentralisation on an experimental basis in its own way. Then Andhra Pradesh introduced it in twenty selected blocks, one in each district, but Rajasthan was the first to give the practical shape to this scheme throughout the state. Pandit Jawaharlal Nehru inaugurated it in Rajasthan on Mahatma Gandhi's birthday on 2 October, 1959. Then followed Andhra Pradesh with full scale implementation of the new scheme on 1 November, 1959. Madras followed it on 2 October, 1961.[19] As on 31 March, 1984, there were 2,17,319 Gram Panchayats covering 5,61,135 villages and about 95 per cent of the rural population, 4526 Panchayat Samitis and 297 Zila Parishads.[20]

Since the implementation of panchati raj in India in terms of the recommendations of the Balvantrai Mehta Study Team several state level committees and regional studies observed that the system was suffering from number of weaknesses and the successive governments have shown very little regard for these institutions of local self-government.

Therefore, with a change of government at the centre in 1977, there was a revival of interest in panchayt raj. The central government appointed a High Level Committee on Panchayati Raj Institutions in 1977 under the Chairmanship of Ashok Mehta. This committee submitted its report in August 1978 and made 132 recommendations.[21] However the report of the Ashok Mehta Committee could not be implemented because of the change of ruling party at the centre in 1980. A potentially viable and useful structure of panchayati raj existed in form but its effectiveness had been limited in practice.[22] Similar was the position with the urban institutions of local self-government.

With the change of government in 1980, the Draft Sixth Plan (1978-83) was replaced by the Sixth Plan (1980-85). During the Sixth Five Year Plan, it was proposed to strengthen the process of Democratic Decentralisation. The question of the involvement of panchayati raj institutions became an important issue of debate since the beginning of 1980s when the question of district planning modalities became important aspect of the decentralisation process.[23] Thereafter numerous committees such as Hanumantha Rao Committee (1983), GVK Rao Committee (1985), Singhvi Committee (1986-87), Sarkaria Commission on Centre-State Relations (1988), Thungon Committee (1988), made several recommendations to strengthen the process of democratic decentralisation in India.

As a result of recommendations of various committees, the Government of India felt the need to amend the Constitution because it was felt that the state governments are not very enthusiastic about implementing panchayati raj in their respective states. They are also not prepared to share power with lower level bodies. In fact, it was argued that some state governments had grabbed the power back from panchayati raj bodies gradually. Second, local self-government and panchayati raj bodies are in the state list in the present Constitution, with the result that central government cannot pass any legislation in these areas unless the Constitution is amended for the purpose. Therefore, there was a need to amend the Constitution to ensure power to the panchayati raj bodies.[24]

The Government of India found the solution in the form of the constitutional 64th Amendment Bill to all the weaknesses of panchayati raj. It was argued that this Bill sought to enshrine democracy at grassroots, as it intended to give power to people.[25] Rajiv Gandhi introduced the 64th Constitutional Amendment Bill (1989) in the Lok Sabha on the last day of the extended budget session. The Bills got through in the Lok Sabha but the government suffered a major setback when the Constitutional Amendment Bill on the Panchayati Raj fell through in the Rajya Sabha. It was through the two Constitutional Amendment Bills, 64th and 65th, defeated in Rajya Sabha, the government wanted to take democracy to the rural masses and toiling people in the urban areas.[26]

Soon the Congress found itself out of power. But the successor of Rajiv Gandhi, Mr V.P. Singh introduced the Seventy-Fourth Amendment Bill in September, 1990. But it could not be passed due to collapse of the V.P. Singh government. The new Congress government headed by P.V. Narasimha Rao picked up the thread initiated by Rajiv Gandhi. But one noticeable feature was that unlike Rajiv Gandhi, Rao had consulted all major political parties in the drafting of the bills. This is known as the Seventy-Third Amendment Bill which became operative in May 1993 on its ratification by 50 per cent of the states.[27] Similarly another Constitution Amendment Bill relating to urban local self-government bodies was also approved and implemented as the Seventy-fourth Constitution Amendment Bill.

## 73rd and 74th Constitution Amendments and the Democratic Decentralisation

Democratic decentralisation as a political concept aims at widening the area of people's participation, authority and autonomy through dispersion or devolution of powers to people's representative organisation from the tope levels to the lowest levels in all the triple dimensions of "political decision-making, financial control and administrative management" with least interference and control from higher levels.[28]

In terms of the above objectives, the process of democratic decentralisation in India was the logical outcome of the Community Development Programme. Panchayati raj as described by Harrison as the most important potential invention of Independent India, is a complex system of rural local self-government. With the rise of panchayati raj, a new phase of local government was ushered in by democratic decentralisation to make the lower units of administration more popularly elected, more socially broad-based and more engaged in the wider range of activities than hitherto.[29]

Since then, the process has passed through four distinct phases within its short span. In the first phase of ascendancy (1958-64) the basic pillar of panchayati raj were erected following the recommendations of Balvantrai Mehta Committee. The second phase (1964-69) marked the stagnation in which no serious attempts or efforts were made either to revamp or to revitalise panchayati raj structure. The third phase (1969-83) which is termed as the period of decline marked the neglect of Panchayat Raj Institutions (PRIs) as no serious attempts were made to revamp them in early seventies during the Congress rule at the centre. The appointment of Ashok Mehta Committee in 1977 was the only major step taken in this direction. Panchayati raj in India entered the last and the latest phase of revival after 1983 when the central government headed by Mr. Rajiv Gandhi made certain serious attempts to involve local self-government institutions in the mainstream of Indian politics. The process initiated by Rajiv Gandhi was brought to the logical conclusion by Narasimha Rao when the 73rd and 74th Constitutional Amendments relating to local self-government in India were introduced and approved by the Parliament and implemented in May 1993 after necessary ratification by 50 per cent of the States.[30]

## Characteristics of the New System

The system of rural and urban local self-government constitutionalised by virtue of 73rd and 74th Constitutional Amendments to strengthen the process of democratic decentralisation is based on the following characteristics:[31]

(i) The new system has been given a constitutional status, by which it has got permanence in the Indian Political System as a third government.

(ii) It has a three-tier structural arrangement namely, district panchayat; middle level panchayat and gram panchayat for the rural area and municipal panchayat, municipal council and municipal corporation for the urban area.

(iii) One-third of the total seats in all the local bodies at all levels including the offices of the chairpersons have been reserved for the women and likewise seats and offices of the chairpersons have also been reserved for the scheduled castes and scheduled tribes in proportion to their respective population.

(iv) The institutions of local self-government are to be assigned the powers, authority and responsibilities with respect to the preparation of plans for economic development and social justice and the implementation of schemes for economic development and social justice including the power of taking decision on 29 subjects mentioned in the 11th Schedule.

(v) To alter the planning process in the country, a statutory planning body—District Planning Committee has to be created at the district level.

(vi) To maintain periodicity in conducting elections to the local bodies, State Election Commission has to be created by which it is declared that elections will be conducted to local bodies regularly in every five years and even if the local bodies are dissolved or dismissed, elections would be conducted within six months.

(vii) Local body institutions are not merely to carry out schemes evolved by central and state governments with the resources allocated by the federal and state governments. They have more responsibilities than the assigned and they have to chalk out various programmes based on the local needs peculiar to the local areas with the resources available locally.

(viii) To make the local body institutions sound in financial resources to meet the requirements, a State Finance Commission has to be constituted to make recommendations. The inherent weakness in the previous system with regard to finance has been eliminated by this provision.

(ix) People's participation is *sine qua non* for democratic decentralisation and development and it has been realised through the creation of a body at grassroot level called "gram sabha". All eligible registered voters are members of gram sabha. The gram sabha has to be assigned many functions.

## Operationalisation of the Amendments

The models of democratic decentralisation have been outlined in the 73rd and 74th Constitutional Amendments as a framework, however, the operationalisation of new system depends upon the Act to be enacted by the State Government. State Governments were given the time frame of one year after May 1993 and almost all the state governments where these amendments were to be made applicable, have enacted new legislations to give operational dimension to the key characteristics of 73rd and 74th Constitutional Amendments. Though all the states have developed the structure of the local bodies in conformity with the provisions of the amendments yet the functions vary from state to state. The following two case studies support this contention.

### *Himachal Pradesh*

To strengthen the democracy at grassroot level and to make Panchayati Raj Institutions viable the State Government devolved powers, functions and responsibilities relating to 15 departments on 31.7.96 and the chairpersons of zila parishads have also been notified as the chairpersons of the governing body of the respective District Rural Development Agency.[32]

### *Madhya Pradesh*

Although the functions related to 23 departments have been transferred to the three-tier panchayati raj system in the State, a clear picture has not yet emerged at the grassroot level as gram panchayats are not fully aware of the powers and functions which they have to perform.[33]

Attempts are ongoing to earmark from the subjects given in the 11th Schedule. However, the institution of gram sabha is the most vital arrangement of democratic decentralisation in the new system. It can bring peace, harmony, development and nurture democracy at the grassroot level. So far, people have not been involved in the decision-making, financial management and local administration at the grassroot level and they were kept aloof in the development process from planning to implementation of schemes and programmes. It has created a gap between the government and the people and as a result there was no transparency in the transactions of the government. All these weaknesses will be avoided by involving the people in the development process through gram sabha. Gram sabha will enable the people to share their knowledge with others. It provides opportunity to the people to express their grievances and demands. It creates avenues to reduce the social tension and the gram sabha develops a new democratic culture through its meetings where everybody gets a chance to speak and listen to others.[34] As such the gram sabha is the mini Parliament in the new arrangement and the most vital institution of decentralised democracy. All other rural as well as urban institutions created in terms with the key provisions of the 73rd and 74th Constitutional Amendments do provide ample scope and opportunities to take decisions and implement them as per local requirements and conditions. Hence, the 73rd and 74th Amendments are historical steps in democratic decentralisation.

## Operational Problems

From the legal point of view the process of democratic decentralisation is complete and real as the 73rd and 74th Amendments have been carried out through the state legislations. All the rural as well urban institutions have been created and they are enjoying the constitutional status and wide powers. However, the following operational problems questions the efficacy of the new arrangement:

The new institutional arrangement in terms of 73rd and 74th Constitutional Amendments providing uniform structure throughout the country is a historical step yet it is not the product of popular demand but the arrangement thrust upon the people. Hence, it will take sometime to secure the acceptance for the new system.

The seats and offices have been reserved for the women and the scheduled castes and scheduled tribes population in all the institutions of local self-government at all the levels. However, some critics point out that the provision of reservation for women will be only "*naam ke waste*" (for the sake of name) and the women will be panchayats as proxies to their male counterparts.[35] As a result of reservation, a large number of women belonging to SCs and STs have got an opportunity to participate in the decision-making process. The irony is that majority of them are housewives without having any interest in politics and public life being unlettered. Most of women have no clear idea of their role as a member (functionary) of panchayat. For women panches and sarpanches, belonging to SC and ST, the leadership role is rather a curse and much worse than their upper caste counterparts for the apparent reason that the former is subjected to ostracism on caste grounds.[36]

The Constitutional Amendments provide for altering the planning process in the country and it is to be initiated from the grassroot level institutions and co-ordinated at the district level by the statutory District Planning Committee. Yet the new process of planning is yet to take root and above all the people as well as representatives at the grassroot level are not trained and aware about the planning process.

Dispersion and devolution of powers from the top levels to the lower levels along with autonomy are the vital ingredients of democratic decentralisation. But the amendments have assigned this role and responsibility to the Legislature of the State and used the word "may" to devolve powers and authority, with the result that all and effective powers are not being given to the local level institutions. State governments are reluctant to share the powers and authority. Above all number of restrictions have been imposed on these institutions, such as provision of dissolution of these institutions by the state governments or removal of chairpersons or members of these institutions on the ground of abuse and misuse of power. These provisions are permanent threat to the autonomy of local self-government institutions hence serious bottlenecks in effective democratic decentralisation.

Financial viability, control and management of the local self-government institutions is the most important dimension of the democratic decentralisation. The amendments provide not only for giving effective powers of taxation to these institutions but also the constitution of State Finance Commission to make necessary recommendations for the allocation of resources to these institutions. However, the devolution of financial powers so far by the state government has not been very effective. State governments and their officials enjoy more powers on the local finance than these institutions. State governments decides the budgets of the local self-government institutions and the latter cannot levy even the local taxes as the range of taxation is decided by the state government. District and block level panchayats have either no or very little financial powers. Only Gram Panchayats can levy some local taxes and collect certain fees with the approval of the state government. State Finance

Commission has also not been able to provide financial stability to local self-government institutions as the state governments themselves are facing financial crunch. Hence the financial viability of these institutions is still in doubt.[37]

## Conclusion and Suggestions

In spite of some weaknesses of the new system there is no need to be unduly pessimistic. The democratic process is a steadying process which has its own corrective mechanism. The problems appearing at the initial stages of the new system are bound to disappear once the system acquires the acceptability of the masses.

It is true that all along for the fifty years the people had been oriented towards receiving benefits from the government officials without taking any responsibility. But the Amendments have exchanged the roles and now the government has assumed the role of facilitator in place of provider. Now the people themselves have to take initiative and own responsibilities leaving aside the dependency syndrome.[38]

The need of the hour is people's awareness towards the changes that are brought in the local bodies. They should understand the new opportunities for them. For the effective functioning of the new system people are to be oriented and leaders are to be trained in the new direction.[39]

The 73rd and 74th Constitutional Amendment are landmark Acts for the democratic decentralisation. However, some bottlenecks appearing at the initial stage can be overcome by suitable legislative and administrative measures. The following suggestions can be considered in this regard:

(i) People should be made aware of the implications of the new system created through 73rd and 74th Amendments. The task is difficult yet the joint efforts of the government, voluntary organisations, academic activists and service-minded people can conscientise the masses.

(ii) Elected leaders of local self-government institutions should be trained about their role and responsibilities. Women, scheduled caste and scheduled tribe leaders should be imparted special training so that they acquire necessary knowledge, understanding, skills and confidence for decision-making, implementation and evaluation.

(iii) Elected leaders should be trained in the art of micro level planning so that they can initiate the planning process from below.

(iv) All the institutions of local self-government should be equipped with the adequate financial resources and they should also have the power and authority to generate local resources.

(v) People as well as elected leaders should have adequate information on the subjects earmarked for local body institutions.

These steps can help to attain the objectives of democratic decentralisation and above all proper co-operation and co-ordination among the masses and functionaries, officials as well as non-officials can further the cause of democratic decentralisation.

## REFERENCES

1. Iqbal Narain, "Democratic Decentralisation: The Idea, The Image and the Reality", in T.N. Chaturvedi (ed.), *Panchayati Raj*, Indian Institute of Public Administration, New Delhi, 1981, pp. 10-11.
2. Quoted in *Masters of Political Thought*, edited by Lane W. Lanester, vol. III, George H. Harrap & Co. Ltd., London, 1959, p. 141.
3. Iqbal Narain, *loc. cit.*
4. *Ibid.*, pp. 11-12.
5. G. Montague Harris, *Comparative Local Government*, Hutchison University Library, London, 1948, p. 9.
6. Iqbal Narain, *op. cit.*, p. 15.
7. Iqbal Naraian, *op. cit.*, p. 17.
8. Shariful Hasan, "Panchayati Raj—Constants of Democratic Decentralisation", in R.S. Rajput and D.R. Megha (eds.), *Panchayati Raj in India*, Deep & Deep Publications, New Delhi, 1984, p. 102.
9. *Ibid.*, p. 103.
10. The Constitution of India, Article 40.
11. Sahib Singh and Swinder Singh, *Local Government in India*, New Academic Publishing Co., Jalandhar, 1986, pp. 88-89.
12. S. Bhatnagar, *Rural Local Government in India*, Life and Light Publishers, New Delhi, 1978, p. 17.

13. Srivastava, "Structure and Pattern of Panchayati Raj", *The Indian Journal of Public Administration*, vol. VIII, no. 4, Oct-Dec., 1962, p. 460.
14. Report of the Team for the study of Community Projects and National Extension Service, vol. I, Committee on Plan Project, (known as Balvantray Mehta Study Team), New Delhi, 1957, p. 5.
15. Balvantray Mehta Study Team Report, *op. cit.*, p. 6.
16. *Ibid.*, pp. 7-8.
17. *Ibid.*, pp. 127-28.
18. Sita Ram Singh, "Revitalisation of Panchayats", *Kurukshetra*, vol. XXXIV, no. 6, 1986, p. 5.
19. B. Maheshwari, *Studies in Panchayati Raj*, Metropolitan, Delhi, 1963, p. 11.
20. Annual Report 1984-85, Department of Rural Development, Quoted in Sita Ram Singh, *op. cit.*, p. 5.
21. Reports of Committee on Panchayati Raj Institutions, Ministry of Agriculture and Irrigation, Department of Rural Development, Govt. of India, New Delhi, 1978. (Hereinafter known as Ashok Mehta Committee Report.)
22. Vijay Ranjan Dutta, "Dynamics of Panchayati Raj", *Kurukshetra*, vol. XXXII, no. 7, April 1984, pp. 17-18.
23. Indira Hiraway, "Panchayati Raj at Crossroads", *Economic and Political Weekly*, vol. XXIV, no. 29, 22 July, 1989, p. 1663.
24. D.D. Guru, "New Economic Policy Initiative: Panchayat Raj Amendment", *Employment News Weekly*, vol. XIV, no. 18, Saturday, 29 July, 1989, p. 2.
25. Indira Hiraway, *loc. cit.*
26. Mario D. Zamora, *The Panchayat Tradition: A North Indian Village Council In Transition, 1947-1962*, Reliance Publishing House, New Delhi, 1970, p. 33.
27. M.R. Biju, *Dynamics of New Panchayati Raj System, Reflections and Retrospections*, Kanishka Publishers, Distributors, New Delhi, 1999, p. 46.
28. Iqbal Narian, *op. cit.*, pp. 15-16.
29. M.R. Biju, *op. cit.*, pp. 23-24.
30. *Ibid.*, pp. 1-3.
31. *Ibid.*, pp. 15-16.
32. R. Gangadhar Reddi, "Himachal Pradesh" in Patterns of Decentralised Governance in Rural India, R.C. Choudhary and S.P. Jain (eds) *NIRD*, Hyderabad, pp. 283-85.
33. C.P. Vithal, "Madhya Pradesh", *op. cit.*, p. 396.
34. M.R. Biju, *op. cit.*, p. 16.

35. *Ibid.*, p. 291.
36. C.P. Vithal, *op. cit.*, pp. 397-98.
37. Palanithurai, *New Panchayati Raj System at Work: An Evaluation*, Concept Publishing Co., New Delhi, 1999, pp. 19-20.
38. G. Palanithurai, *New Panchayati Raj System, Status and Prospectus*, Kanishka Publishers, Distributors, New Delhi, 1996, pp. 17-18.
39. G. Palanithurai, "Panchayati Raj for Prosperity", *ibid.*, p. 23.

# 14

# Rural Democratic Decentralisation in Himachal Pradesh: Rhetorics and Reality

*S.K. Baldi*

## Introduction

The State of Himachal Pradesh came into existence on 15th April, 1948 with the merger of 30 princely States of Shimla and other Himalayan regions. In Himachal Pradesh Gram Panchayats were constituted first time on statutory basis vide HP Panchayati Raj Act, 1952. In November 1966 hilly areas of the State of Punjab were merged in this State. In the merged area a three-tier Panchayati Raj system was working whereas in old area only two levels, i.e., Gram Panchayats and Panchayat Samitis were established. With a view to bring uniformity in all the areas Himachal Pradesh Panchayati Raj Act, 1968 was enacted. The State of Himachal became full-fledged State on 25th January, 1971 but the Panchayats continued to be governed by the Act of 1968. In 1994 Himachal Pradesh Legislature enacted H.P. Panchayati Raj Act, 1994 by repealing the old Act of 1968 in view of the historic 73rd Constitution Amendment. The new Act made the changes in conformity with the Constitutional Amendment like establishement of three-tier Panchayati Raj, reservation of seats for scheduled castes and scheduled tribes, reservation of 1/3rd seats for women, constitution of State Finance Commission and State Election Commission.

In addition to these provisions, the article 243(g) of the Constitution provided that the Legislature of a State may be law endow the Panchayat with such powers and authority as may be necessary to enable them to function as institutions of self-government. In this paper I would like to consider whether the legislature of Himachal Pradesh has given sufficient powers and authority to the Panchayats or not to function them as institutions of self-government. The Panchayats could function as institution of self-government only if they have sufficient power, authority and resources in their assigned responsibilities and have real autonomy in their functional domain.

## The Present Level of Devolution to Panchayati Raj in H.P.

### *Functions*

As per section 11 of HP Panchayati Raj Act 1994, Gram Panchayats have been assigned 29 functions. However, Gram Panchayats in practice, are doing very few functions. The HP State Finance Commission in its report dated November, 1996 observed "The Commission understood that these functions were not being performed by the Gram Panchayats on account of lack of resources on one hand and also due to the fact that many of the functions are getting performed through the decentralised planning scheme of the State Plan." Similarly Panchayat Samitis have been assigned many functions in section 81 of the HP Panchayati Raj Act but due to lack of resources, they are not performing most of the functions. It is paradoxical that most of the functions assigned to Panchayat Samitis are being performed by the extension officers of various Departments posted in the development blocks but the elected members of the Panchayat Samitis have no control over the working of these extension officers. As far as Zila Parishad is concerned, the Act has envisaged it as a Advisory Body devoid of any large service delivery responsibility. The H.P. Government vide its notification dated 31st July, 1996 further devolved powers, functions and responsibilities relating to various programmes of 15 departments. Though the notification of the State Government runs into 26 pages but it lists actually more responsibilities than assigning any real power or authority in PRIs.

***Panchayats and Civil Servants***

In HP on every two Panchayats one Gram Panchayat Avam Vikas Adhikari (Panchayat Secretary) is posted. All the records and proceedings of the Panchayats are maintained by him. His transfer and posting is vested with Director, Panchayati Raj. Thus, Gram Panchayat virtually has no control over the lone employee they are dependent upon. In case of Panchayat Samiti, BDO is the ex-officio Secretary of the Panchayat Samiti. BDO and all staff functioning at block level are posted and transferred by State Government. As far as Zila Parishads are concerned, they were established in Himachal Pradesh only since 1996. Each Zila Parishad has been provided with one stenographer, one clerk, one driver and one peon. This bare minimum staff is also controlled by the State Government.

***Finances***

In Himachal Pradesh Panchayat Samitis and Zila Parishads have no power to impose any tax. In case of gram panchayat it could impose house tax and property tax up to a limited extent. Thus Panchayati Raj institutions in Himachal Pradesh are dependent on grants receoved from the State Government. The grants to PRIs are dependent on the recommendations given by the State Finance Commission which has been constituted in Himachal Pradesh in conformity with the provisions of the 73rd Constitutional Amendment.

From the aforesaid discussions it is clear that PRIs in Himachal Pradesh are heavily dependent on State Government for finances as well as for staff to discharge their obligatory functions. They hardly have any autonomy in any sphere to function as institutions of self-government.

## Steps Needed to Make them Institution of Self-Government

The functioning of PRIs as institution of self-government is very important as it is well known that Panchayats are best placed to know the exact nature of the needs of the local people and how they could be met in cost-effective way. Panchayats as a representative body is presumed to be closure to the aspiration of the public and hence are more responsive to the needs of the local people. Panchayats are more open and transparent in their working compared officials of the State Government. Further Panchayat representatives are much more accessible to general public compared to State Government officials who are considered socially remote. The decision-making at Panchayat level is quicker and easier. Moreover, Panchayats are accountable to the general public to whom they are to serve. Due to these features the strengthening and devolution of powers is very vital. To make Panchayats functions as institutions of self-government, following measures are suggested:

***Functions to be Assigned to Panchayats***

The strengthening of the Panchayats is to be matched with the service delivery responsibility assigned to these institutions (Bahl Linn, 1992). Hence it is necessary to have clear-cut devision of functional responsibility between State Government and Panchayats.

As per Article 243(g) of the Constitution of India "State Legislature may endow Panchayats with such powers and authority as may be necessary to enable them to function as institution of self-government and for that purpose they may be entrusted with implementation of schemes in relation to matters listed in the 11th Schedule." The 11th Schedule list out 29 matters which could be entrusted to Panchayats. At the same time State Government is empowered to perform all these functions under the power vested to it in the State List prescribed in the 7th Schedule of the Constitution. Moreover, provisions of the article 243(g) of the Constitution, as per the article itself are subject to other provisions of the constitution. "Due to these weaknesses of the constitutional provisions, the State Governments have so far ignored the 11th Schedule for functional devolution to the panchayats under their confirmity legislation after enforcement of the 73rd Constitution Amendment Act". (Datta, A.,1995)

Thus there is an overlapping of functions between State Government and PRIs.

> "For decentralisation to work, assignment of service delivery responsibility amongst the level of government should be as clear and simple as possible. Vagueness in the division of responsibility can undermine local accountability like in Brazil all levels of government could open hospital, which leads to duplicity and confusion." (WDR, 1988)

Thus in place of having joint responsibility for providing the same service, the State Government and PRIs should have a clear division of functions like is the case in Britain. The exclusive functional domain to Panchayats could be either ensured by inserting a local list in the 7th Schedule of the Constitution or clear-cut State Government commitment to exclusively devolve functional responsibility to PRIs on the same anology as is the case between Union Government *vis-a-vis* State Government in India.

Now the second issue is which function should be exclusively devolved to PRIs. For division of functions the first criterion is the economy efficiency (Davey, K., 1989). By this test the services which benefit exclusively the local people should be provided by Panchayats if they benefit most of the people living in their local area and by the State Government if they benefit the entire State. The second criterion is, the nature of task. If standardised, uniform provisions and procedures are important then it should be administered by the State Govt. If adoption to local circumstances and preferences is important, it should be the Panchayat's responsibility (Davey, K.,1989). The third criterion that entrustment of function should be based on technical competency and professional skill available at a particular level. According to Mahipal (1998) the cardinal principle of devolution is what can be done at a particular level, should be devolved to that level and not at a higher level. Following this in Karnataka the Act, itself has spelled out the powers and functions to take decentralisation forward on the basis of the cardinal principal that what is appropriate at given level of three tier system should be done at that level and not unnecessary at a higher level.

***Devolution of Functions and Responsibilities to PRIs in H.P.***

Given the above framework I would like to proceed to discuss the devolution of power and responsibilities to the Panchayats with respect to first of the twin task mentioned in Article 243(g), i.e., preparation of plans for economic development and social justice.

In H.P. before the enactment of Panchayati Raj Act 1994, Zila Parishads were not in existence. Hence district level plans were never prepared by a democratically elected body. With the 73rd Constitution Amendment there is a new dimension to district planning namely the mandatory provision of "District Planning Committee" which will consolidate the plans prepared by Panchayats and Municipalities in the district. The Chairman of the DPC is to be chosen in such a manner as may be prescribed by the State Government. Accordingly section 185 of H.P. Panchayati Raj Act, 1994 prescribes the constitution of DPC. H.P. Government has further notified the Rules for constitution of this committee but even after lapse of six years these Committees have not been constituted. Thus, even the mandatory provisions of the Constitution have not been implemented in this regard. For PRIs to work as institution of self-government first and foremost requirement is that whatever functions are to be implemented by them, they should be actively associated in their planning. If PRIs are involved only in implementation of various schemes by placing funds at their disposal, then they would be merely doing the agency work of the State Government in place of articulating the local needs. Thus, the State Government should immediately constitute District Planning Committees. The scope of DPC should be based on the cardinal principle of planning that whatsoever is responsible for implementation of a particular function or activity, should also be assigned the task of its planning under the overall budgetary ceiling. After preparation of District Plan, the same should be sent to State Planning Department who should convene a meeting of DPC functionaries to finalise the plan for the District. The Head of Department at the State level should be actively associated in scrutinising these plans. If State Government or HOD feels that there is a need to amend the District Plan, then these amendments should be referred to DPC for reconsideration. After reconsideration DPC should send its final recommendations to State Government which should be accepted by the Government in toto. If the State Planning Department feels that certain areas of public importance have been left uncovered in the District Plan then the same should be covered by them by making suitable provision in the State portion of State Plan.

The second of the twin task is stated in Article 243(g)(b) of the Constitution which says that the legislature of a State may devolve powers and responsibilities to Panchayats for the implementation of schemes for economic development and social justice as may be entrusted to them including those in relation to the matter listed in the 11th Schedule.

The 11th Schedule does not specifically provide for the total range of govermental functions at the Panchayat level like law and order and other regular responsibilities. At present this appears to be reasonable as Panchayats as institution of local government are yet to take firm roots. Presently, it is important that they win the acceptability and confidence of the people through efficient implementation of development programmes.

What constitutes an optimum package of powers and functions for local government in a State would depend on its unique historical background for evolution of its present administrative and institutional pattern. However, the functions assigned should not be illusory or mere agency functions. The package of power and functions should be such which put the Panchayats on the path of evolution as effective unit of local self-government.

In HP Panchayats have statutory duties prescribed in the Act and they have also been delegated some functions under the state government notification dated 31-7-1996. Though the list of functions under the Act is quite impressive but, they are more like a list of subjects, without clarifying which functions or projects are to be performed at which level of PRIs. Moreover, at present many functions assigned to PRIs are routinely being performed by the departments of state government, leading to lack of functional responsibility for both levels of government. As Slater (1994) emphasised in case of Sri Lanka that a clear demarcation of responsibilities with associated spending authority is essential for strengthening decentralisation, therefore I propose that the following functions should be exclusively done by Panchayats by amending the HP Panchayati Raj Act, 1994. The allocation of functions is being proposed keeping in view the principle of economic efficiency, nature of task and technical competency available at three levels.

*Gram Panchayats*

(i) Sanitation, conservancy and drainage in panchayat area.
(ii) Supply of drinking water and cleansing and disinfecting the source of supply and storage of water.
(iii) The construction and maintenance of public streets, community buildings and culverts.
(iv) Construction of primary school buildings and assisting ZP in management of primary education.
(v) Agriculture extension
  (a) To conduct demonstration on improved technology and training of farmers through extension staff of agriculture department.
  (b) Implementation of bio-gas programme.
  (c) To organise crop protection and pest management programmes and to release subsidy on pesticide.
(vi) Lighting of village street and other public places.
(vii) Plantation and preservation of panchayat forest.
(viii) Running of Anganwari centre of Integrated Child Development Services (ICDS).
(ix) Organising horticulture input distribution with the help of extension staff.
(x) Identification and selection of beneficiaries of various developmental schemes of government.
(xi) Running and maintenance of minor irrigation scheme and kulhs.
(xii) Preparation of development plan for GP.
(xiii) Poverty alleviation programmes.

*Panchayat Samiti*

(i) Running and maintenance of large water supply schemes.
(ii) Construction and maintenance of village link roads.

(iii) Assisting ZP in establishment and running of primary schools.
(iv) Undertaking scheme or financial assistance through GP for the development of agriculture, livestock, cottage industries, co-operatives, horticulture and fisheries.
(v) Arrangement of supply of agriculture and horticulture inputs.
(vi) Release of funds under various development schemes to GP and monitoring thereof.
(vii) Organisation of health and family welfare camps and promotion of awareness of national health programmes.
(viii) Running of ICDS programme.
(ix) Formulation of development plans of PS, consolidating plans all the GPs.
(x) Minor irrigation.

*Zila Parishad*

(i) Establishment and running of primary and middle schools in the district.
(ii) Agriculture/horticulture and animal husbandry activities benefiting the whole district.
(iii) Schemes relating to soil conservation.
(iv) Minor irrigation schemes.
(v) Social forestry and management of waste-land in the district.
(vi) Feed and fodder development schemes of the veterinary department.
(vii) Rural housing.
(viii) Construction of village link roads in the district.
(ix) Community development programmes of fisheries, welfare and health departments.
(x) Economic planning for the rural area of the whole district.
(xi) Poverty alleviation programmes.
(xii) Welfare of SC/ST.
(xiii) Public distribution.
(xiv) Co-operation.

From the above it is clear that in place of present limited

advisory role, Zila Parishads should have larger role in planning, co-ordinating and implementing various developmental functions as District is the most suitable unit for systematic planning and implementation below the State level. District has sufficient administrative and technical resources for functional efficiency. The intermediate level Panchayat (Panchayat Samiti) and Gram Panchayats would be implementing agencies in consonance with administrative and technical competency available at their level.

## Measures Needed to Make PRIs as Institution of Self-Government

Now, after assignment of exclusive service delivery responsibility to PRIs we need to match it with appropriate administrative and financial authority. In my opinion following measures are required to make PRIs the real institutions of self-government.

### *Commitment of State Level Political Leadership*

The first and foremost requirement is that Chief Minister and Ministers should be fully committed to the cause of democratic decentralisation. At present the general feeling amongst the State level politicians is that if anything beyond the agency function is entrusted to PRIs, the State Government will become powerless. But this fear is unfounded as State Government would continue to have larger role and the PRIs, in fact, would help in improving the State Government image by better delivery of various services assigned to them.

### *Organic Link between the Three-Tiers of Panchayats*

As per the constitutional provision all the three tiers of Panchayats in a District are directly elected. Due to directly elected independent members they could have the feeling that they are independent of other levels of PRIs and may start working for cross-purpose. In my view this would not be healthy situation as we cannot have three institutions of self-government at district level. I propose that there should be only two levels of elected representatives, one at Zila Parishad level (District level) and second at Gram Panchayat level. The intermediate level should consist of elected representatives of Zila Parishads as well as Gram Panchayats. This would ensure proper co-ordination amongst the three tiers and a feeling that they are part of a whole. Till that is done all the Pradhans of Gram Panchayats should be made member of Panchayat Samitis and Members of Zila Parishad should be made members of Gram Panchayat falling in their area. Similarly Members of Zila Parishad should also become Member of Panchayat Samiti of their area and President of Panchayat Samitis should be member of Zila Parishads. This would lead to an organic link amongst the three levels of Panchayats in a District and all the three levels would work in tandem.

***Integrated Administration and Institutional Changes***

(a) *Changes at Zila Parishad and District Administration Level*

In HP the district is the basic unit of administration. State government therefore, has posted district level officers in all the districts with sufficient administrative and financial delegations, to run its affairs. Deputy Commissioner is the head of district administration who co-ordinates the activities of all the departments.

Zila Parishad and other tiers of Panchayati Raj are required to implement the developmental schemes of various development departments, but at present, ZP has no control over the functioning of district level officers of various departments (like agriculture, horticulture, education and rural development department, etc.), whose schemes they are responsible to implement. This diarchy, at district level is the crux of the problem of poor service delivery and weak position of PRIs in HP. The Ashok Mehta Committee (1978) recommended for strong executive Zila Parishad. Similarly, GVK Rao Committee (1985) recommended that district should be the basic unit for policy planning and programme implementation. According to Kamal Siddiqqi (1992), the Zila Parishad should become the principal body for the management of all development programmes, which can be handled at that level. Thus there is a need of forging and integrating district development administration under the supervision of Zila Parishad. To translate this into reality, following suggestions are made—

(i) *Merger of DRDA in ZP*: Government of India vide its letter dated 6-11-95 (Mahipal, 1998), asked the state governments to restructure the DRDA's by making ZP chairman to be ex-officio chairman of the governing body of DRDA. Accordingly in HP, the chairman of Zila Parishads have been made chairman of governing body of DRDA, relieving Deputy Commissioner of this charge. But this is only a partial integration as DRDA still remains an independent body and DC continues to exercise all the executive and financial powers in it. Secondly, members of ZP except chairman are not associated with the working of DRDA. As DRDA is the most important body of rural development at district level therefore, its complete merger with ZP should be done.

(ii) An I.A.S. officer equivalent to the Deputy Commissioner in seniority and status should be posted as the Chief Executive Officer (CEO) of the Zila Parishad as is the practice in the state of Karnataka, Maharashtra and Gujarat. Moreover, the office of ZP should be suitably strengthened by posting sufficient staff.

(iii) The district level officers of department of Agriculture, Horticulture, Animal Husbandry, Rural Development and Education who deals primarily with the functions to be performed by the Zila Parishad at district level should be brought into the fold of Zila Parishad and should be accountable to them. The CEO should be the head of the multi-disciplinary team of officers. He should be responsible for horizontal co-ordination amongst the head of various functional departments. As far as technical inputs are concerned the line hierarchy should not be broken and technical guidance to the extent necessary from higher level should be available to the line hierarchy (Mahipal, 1998).

(iv) At Zila Parishad level the system of committees needs to be strengthened, so that specialised subjects could be discussed in depth and experts from outside could be also co-opted to the committees. Moreover, the committee system ensures fuller participation of elected members in the decision-making. The various committees should have important role of preparing budget proposal in their respective spheres and should decide about various programmes as is the case in UK local government.

(b) *Changes at Panchayat Samiti Level*

Panchayat Samiti is required to execute programmes of various development departments. The BDO is the ex-officio executive officer of the Panchayat Samiti. State government has also posted extension officers of various departments in the Development Block. Though, the office of Panchayat Samiti and Development Block is in the same building, yet these extension officers are neither under the control of PS nor under the control of BDO, and they report to their respective district heads. This ambiguity and dyarchy needs to be removed by placing all the extension officers, directly under the control of PS. It is also suggested that, all the BDOs should be from Himachal Administrative Service. Moreover, at present BDO is to play dual role. One as a BDO in which he reports to DC, and another as executive officer of Panchayat Samiti in which he reports to PS. Now this dual role should end, and he should solely be under the control of PS. Moreover, like CEO of ZP he should be captain of all the extension officers posted in the Block, to provide technical and administrative support to PS. "This will end the rock departmentalism, with the establishment of a structured relationship between locally elected politician and departmental officers" (Webster, 1990).

(c) *Change at Gram Sabha and Gram Panchayat Level*

(i) In the union budget for 1999-2000, the year 1999-2000 has been designated as the year of the Gram Sabha. The purpose is to enhance resources transfer and participation of local bodies in the implementation of developmental schemes. "Gandhiji also envisaged a primary role for village republic in the attainment of economic self-sufficiency" (Multalib, M., 1982, p. 94). It is therefore, recommended that Gram Sabha would be vested with the power of selection and approving the names of eligible persons for all the developmental schemes run by state government. It should function like "communes in Switzerland which decide all the important matters at local level" (Allen, Hubert, 1998).

(ii) In Himachal Pradesh GP Pradhans (chairman) are directly elected. This leaves a gap between him and other elected members of GP as he is not accountable to them. The accountability to electorates comes only after five years in election, which is not sufficient to stop him becoming authoritarian. It has been observed by me that many Pradhans start taking decisions without consulting other members of GP therefore, to ensure day-to-day accountability to members of GP, it is proposed that GP Pradhan should be indirectly elected from amongst the elected members of GP as is the case in West Bengal and Karnataka. Day and Klein cited in Crook and Manor (1998) has aptly remarked "it is day-to-day accountability, in which the ruler explain and justify their action to the ruled, which distinguishes a democratic society from an elected tyranny".

(iii) In HP, at present two panchayats shares one Panchayat secretary, who is the lone official to maintain office record and accounts. Considering the increase in the workload each Panchayat should have an independent Panchayat secretary, who should be under the control of GP.

***Personnel System***

Mahwood as cited in (Allen, H. 1998) suggests that, there are three principal systems governing the management of appointed local government personnel:

(i) *Separate*: in which local authority acts as a complete autonomous employer.

(ii) *Integrated*: in which each local authority administration is composed of state government officials who could be moved freely between state government and local authorities.

(iii) *Unified*: in which local authorities staff is employed on a collective basis by all local governments.

Davey, K. (1989) explains that there are four main problems surrounding the staffing of local government, i.e.,

1. Merit
2. Mobility
3. Loyalty
4. Discipline and control.

In case of a separate system loyalty and discipline is ensured, but merit and mobility is compromised. Moreover, in a separate system chances of promotion of staff are less. In case of integrated and unified system merit and mobility is there but loyalty and discipline are divided. Thus there is no perfect personnel system and a trade off is required to be made. In HP at present integrated system is prevalent, under which all the staff in PRIs is posted by state government, which creates the problem of loyalty and discipline. As Slater and Watson (1989) puts it "ultimate control over departmental staff tends to be exercised by state ministers who determine transfer, promotions and leave entitlements". To rectify the problem following suggestions are made:

- All the class III and class IV employees of PRIs should be appointed and controlled by respective panchayat (i.e., ZP/PS/GP). For that purpose there should be a separate "Panchayat Service" as is the case in state of Gujarat.
- There should be a district cadre of panchayat secretaries and ZP should control their transfer and postings.
- Class I and II officers should remain integrated with the state government services. However, chairman of Zila Parishad and PS, respectively should be given powers like writing of ACR (Annual Confidential Report) and sanctioning of leave, to have control over them.
- To ensure merit in recruitment, the recruitment of class III and IV employees of "Panchayat Services" should vest in State Public Service Commission.
- The complete control of officials under the PRIs could affect the impartial working of the officers and officials working in these institutions. Therefore, accountability of bureaucrats should be to both elected representatives and to legal-administrative mechanism as suggested by Crook and Manor. The

state government and director of concerned department should provide sufficient protection to ensure balance in both the things. For that purpose the ACR written by elected representative at district level should be subject to review by the director of concerned department.

### *Finances*

(i) *Background*

The financial position of PRIs has been weak since the very beginning. They always depend on grant received from the state government, which is given to them on ad-hoc basis. "The decentralised governance system to operate effectively, should have financial autonomy" (Aziz, 1996). To improve the financial position of PRIs, the 73rd Constitutional Amendment provided for constituting State Finance Commission in every state "to review the financial position of PRIs and to make recommendation to the governor for transferring resources from state to panchayats". Accordingly State Finance Commission has been constituted in HP and it has submitted its report in November 1996. From the perusal of the report of State Finance Commission it is evident that it recommended for transfer of 10.06 crore rupees to PRIs to fulfil the expenditure requirement of delegated functions only. No additional funds were recommended for obligatory functions as these were being done by other agency/department of state government from other funds.

For financial autonomy, PRIs should have sufficient resources, so they are in a position to meet their financial responsibility in executing various functions.

(ii) *The resources* for PRI could be generated from the following sources:

(a) User charges
(b) Taxation
(c) Grants from state and central government.

As per efficiency criteria for raising local revenue (World Developemnt Report 1988):

(i) The cost of providing local services should be recovered to the extent possible from charges on beneficiaries (those who benefit).
(ii) Services whose cost cannot be recovered from charges should be financed from general taxes.
(iii) If the benefit of local service produces statewide benefits, it should be financed from grants.

**(a)** ***User Charges:*** In Himachal Pradesh the present level of user charges by PRIs is very low. The State Finance Commission in its report observed, "the issue of user charges for various services has been evaded for long, but it will increasingly become imminent that such charges will need to be levied. Resources which can legitimately be raised will required to be raised and no alibis will help sustaining the current scenario for long". Thus now user charges on utilities like water supply, irrigation, etc., should be based on the criterion of cost recovery.

**(b)** ***Taxes:*** The income from taxes of PRIs in HP is only 2 per cent of its total resources. Generation of such a low tax revenue shows that, the cost of servicing rural area is being met by other tax-payers. To improve the tax collection following action should be taken:

(i) At present only GP has the power to raise resources through taxation. Now the taxing power should be given to all the three tiers. "The taxing power should be on natural local fiscal domain, i.e., levies on the use of common resources in the form of forest and quarriable material and minor minerals; levies on privately owned property and on production originating from their respective jurisdiction" (Indira Rajaraman, 1999).
(ii) There should be some penalty for non-collection of taxes. Like State Finance Commission in its report recommended that, "in case some local bodies do not collect the statutory levies, the resources transfer recommended through this report of Commission should not be released. Compliance to collect taxes at the local level should only qualify these bodies for availing the resource transfer from the consolidated fund of the state".

(iii) There should be obligatory minimum tax rate to ensure tax efforts and to reduce scope of subversion (Indira Rajaraman, 1999).
(iv) There is need to strengthen local "technical capacity" to collect taxes, like technical competence to properly evaluate the properties for property taxation.

**(c) *Inter-Governmental Transfers:*** Considering the rural base of PRIs, whatever funds arc raised by them through user charges and taxation, would always be short of their requirement. This gap needs to be filled by the state government on the recommendation of State Finance Commission. The transfer should be based upon the fair assessment of gap between tax potential in the jurisdiction of PRIs and expenditure responsibility with them. The transfer should be based upon a formula to ensure stability and predictability of grant. This would help PRIs to plan their spendings (WDR, 1997). As per Bird and Rodriguez (1999), decentralised poverty reduction strategy requires "equalisation grant" in sense of larger transfer to poorer regions and it should be supported with specific grant, targeted to poor people. Indira Rajaraman (1999) has favoured taxwise sharing between state government and PRIs. In 1999-2000 HP state budget, the state government has announced complete transfer of land revenue to panchayats, which is a welcome step.

**(d) *Explicit Incentives for Raising Local Revenues*** To improve revenue generation by PRIs incentives should be offered by state government. Like in state of Rajasthan, cash award for development work are given linked with revenue generation by PRIs. In Tamil Nadu, 15 per cent of the transfer from general state revenues are set aside for incentives like matching grants for rural local bodies.

(iv) For integrated functioning it is recommended that budget, non-plan and plan of the departments (for the functions transferred to PRIs) should become part of Zila Parishad budget. The state budget should be split into two, providing separate budget for PRIs as is the case in state of Karnataka (Raghavalulu, 1991).
(v) Accounting wing in PRIs should be strengthened to ensure

proper maintenance of accounts.

(vi) Last but not the least, as the *State Finance Commission* has a very crucial role to play in improving the financial position of PRIs, therefore it is recommended that chairman and members of the Commission should be eminent persons, who are well versed about the working of PRIs. Second on the receipt of the report of the Commission, state government should by and large accept the recommendation, as is the practice in union government *vis-a-vis* Union Finance Commission.

### *Training of Elected Members*

For smooth functioning of PRIs, the training of elected representatives is must. In HP, with the conduct of three-tier PRIs elections in December 1995, the number of elected representatives have considerably increased. Moreover, due to the reservation of seats, most of them are first timers. Proper training to them is must for smooth functioning of these institutions. To fulfil this work, the PRI training institute situated at Mashobra and at Baijnath needs to be vitalised.

### *Accountability*

Accountability of elected members to citizens needs to be ensured for effective service delivery. Accountability through "auditability" after the event is over is not very useful, but accountability through "transparency" of operation at the time, the resources are used is crucial (Allen, Hubert, 1998). Thus the working of these institutions should be transparent. General public should have the right to observe the proceedings of the meeting, as is the practice in UK. Similarly, they should have the right to obtain a copy of any record kept by these institutions.

### *Performance Indicators and Performance Targets*

For effective service delivery from PRIs, designing of performance indicators is essential. The indicators should be designed to focus attention on what services have delivered (outcomes), rather than what resources have been devoted to them (inputs). The indicators will help PRIs to know where they stand, on the range of services which they provide and where they want to get to (Modern Local Government: UK, 1998).

Moreover, there should be a "Performance Competition" amongst various PRIs. Good ZP/PS should be rewarded with substantial prize money and trophies to motivate them. "In local government in Sri Lanka, such schemes had an influence on performance improvement across a range of functions". (Slater, 1994)

### *Preparation of Guidelines and Manuals*

In view of the fact that Article 243(g) of the Constitution has clearly assigned the preparation of plan for economic development and also its implementation to the Panchayats, suitable guidelines and manuals need to be prepared by State Government for the use of elected representatives and officials associated with Panchayats.

### *There should be Balance between the Power Shared by the MLA's and the Members of PRIs*

For proper working of democracy, there should be a balance between the power exercised by the state level and local level politicians. If a majority of the MLAs are dissatisfied in this respect. It leaves scope of a determined backlash from above resulting in myriad pressure on the state administration to hamper the functioning of these institutions. Moreover, as local government is a creature of state legislature, the MLAs would never support, more decentralisation if they find, in the process, that they would loose power. Therefore, in my view as MLAs and MPs are members of ZP and PS, their views should be given due weightage by other members of these bodies. Moreover, the chairperson of District Planning Committee should be a minister of the state government. This would balance the power between both the level, as being chairperson of DPC a minister would be able to have his say, similarly ZP members would also continue to have their voice as "4/5 member of DPC would be from ZP" (section 185 of HP PR Act, 1994).

### *Need of Attitudinal Change in the Bureaucracy*

The sub-state level administrative space has long been the exclusive domain of bureaucracy, as such accountability to democratic representative at local level is still an anathema to a bureaucrat (Budhadeb Ghosh). Bureaucracy at district and state level exercises substantial power under the state level politician, because their number is much smaller than the PRIs representatives. Thus bureaucracy has vested interest in making the local government ineffective. However, they should realise that like MLA's, members of PRIs are also people's representatives and they have to accept working under them. This requires a cultural change, which could be initiated by giving regular training to employees. Moreover, bureaucracy could be made to change if there is political will at state level to do so. "Examples such as Korea's Saemaul Undong and Sri Lanka's million house programmes demonstrate that if there is a real political commitment at the highest level then the most conservative bureaucracy will come into line and desist from obstruction" (Allen, H. 1990, p. 112).

## To Sum Up

The road of making Panchayats as institution of self-government in hilly State of Himachal Pradesh is tortuous and bumpy. At present the State Government was virtually failed to endow sufficient powers to PRIs in the true spirit of democratic decentralisation. While the Constitutional sanctions binds the State Government to establish the three-tier system of Panchayati Raj, operationalisation of the spirit of the amendment is at present fully dependent on the degree of commitment at the level of State political leadership and bureaucracy. This needs an attitudinal change in the bureaucracy coupled with strong political will in the State level political leadership towards making the decentralisation work. In the present context adding a local list/district list in the 7th Schedule of the Constitution which assigns exclusive functional domain to Panchayats independent of State Government, appears to be only viable solution to ensure that Panchayats become real institutions of self-government as envisaged in article 243 of the Constitution of India.

## REFERENCES

Agarwal, Govind (1996), *Decentralization for Rural Development in Nepal,* Tribhuvan University, Kathmandu.

Allen, Hubert (1990), *Cultivating the Grass Roots, why Local Government Matters,* International Union of Local Authorities, Hague.

Allen, Hubert (1998), "Crystal Clear? Accountability and Transparency in the Public Sector" *Course HandBook, The State and Civil Society,* School of Public Policy, University of Birmingham.

Allen, Hubert (1998), Lecture Notes, Local Government DAG 12, School of Public Policy, University of Birmingham.

Aziz, A., Arnold and David (1996), *Decentralised Governance in Asian Countries,* Sage Publication India Ltd, New Delhi.

Awotukum, A.M. (1995), *New Trends in Nigerian Local Government,* Ile-life.

Babu, Devendra (1996), "Karnataka Mandal Panchayats Finances: Imbalances in needs and Resources", *The Indian Journal of Public Administration* 1996, pp. 53-65.

Bahl, Roy and Linn, J (1992), *Urban Public Finances in Developing Countries,* Oxford, UP 992.

Barnabas, AP (1998): "Good Governance at Local Level", *The Indian Journal of Public Administration,* July-September 1998.

Bird, R and ER Rodriguez (1999), "Decentralisation and Poverty Alleviation. International Experience and the case of Phillippines," *Public Administration and Development,* vol. 19, issue no 3, p. 299-319.

Byrne, T (1992), *Local Government in Britain,* Penguin Books.

CIRDAP (Centre for Integrated Rural Development for Asia and the pacific), 1992, *Impact of Decentralisation on Rural Poverty an Asian Perspective,* Dhaka.

Crook, Richard and Aif Mortem Jerve (1991), *Government and Participation: Institutional Development, Decentralisation and Democracy in the Third World,* CHR Michelsen Institute, Norway.

Crook, Richard and Manor, James (1998), *Democracy and Decentralisation in South Asia and West Africa, Participation, Accountability and Performance,* Cambridge University Press.

Constitution of India: http:/www.nic.in/constitution.

Datta, A. (1995), Constitutional Strengthening of Local Government in a Third World Federation, Seminar on Municipal Administration, Centre for Economic Studies (Calcutta University) at Calcutta June 10-11, 1995.

Davey, Kenneth (1989), Strengthening Municipal Government, the World Bank Policy, Planning and Research Staff, Discussion Paper, 1989.

Department of Environment, Transport and Region, Britain (1998): Local Government in Touch with People CM 4014.

Devas, N (1998-99), Lecture Notes, Regional/Local Government Finance DAG43H, University of Birmingham.

Dillinger, W (1994), Decentralisation and Its Implementation for Urban Service Delivery, Urban Management Programme, Discussion Paper 16, Washington DC: World Bank.

Dutta, Vijay, R (1991), "New Experiment of Panchayti Raj in Karnataka: Towards Grassroots Democracy and Swaraj", *Gandhian Perspectives* vol. IV, no. 2, 1991 pp-43-73.

*Economic Survey* (1998-99), Government of India, Chapter 10.

Echeverri-Gent, J.G. (1992), "Public Participation and Poverty Alleviation. The Experience of Reform Communist in India's West Bengal", *World Development,* vol. 20, pp-1401-22.

Foreign and Commonwealth Office London, *Local Government in Britain,* 1998.

Flynn, N. (1997), *Public Sector Management,* chapter 10 (managing performance).

Government of Himachal Pradesh (1997), Department of Panchayati Raj, *Annual Administrative Report, 1997,* Shimla.

Government of Himachal Pradesh (1994), Rural Development and Panchayati Raj Department, *The Himachal Pradesh Panchayati Raj Act, 1994,* Shimla.

Government of Himachal Pradesh (1996), *Panchayati Raj Department, Notification*, Dated Shimla-2, the 31st July 1996.

Government of Himachal Pradesh (1997), *Department of Panchayati Raj Rules, 1997,* Shimla.

Government of Himachal Pradesh (1997), Department of Rural Development, *Annual Administrative Report 1997,* Shimla.

Hirway, Indira (1989), "Panchayati Raj at Cross Roads", *Economic and Politically Weekly,* July 22, 1989.

Hooja, Meenakshi and Hooja Rakesh (1998), "Panchayati Raj in Rajasthan—Policy Issues and Concern", *The Indian Journal of Public Administration,* July-Sept. 1998.

Joshi, BM (1996), "State Finance Commission in India: Organisation and Emerging Issues", *Indian Journal of Public Administration,* 1996, pp. 179-84.

Khan I.H. (1969), *Government in Rural India,* Aligarh Muslim University, Aligarh.

Kuldeep Singh (1988), *Performance of Block Development Administration with reference to Jubbal-Kothkhai Block,* Department of Public Administration, HP University, Shimla.

Kurian, N.J. (1981), "Anti Poverty Programme: A Reappraisal", *Economic and Political Weekly*, vol. XXIV, no. 2, March 1981.

Maheswari, Shriram (1987), *Local Government in India*, (4th edn), Educational Publisher, Agra.

Mathur Kuldeep (1996) (eds), *Development Policy and Administration—Reading in Indian Government and Polities*, Sage Publication, Delhi.

Mahwood, P. (1993), *Local Government in the Third World—The Experience of Decentralization in Tropical Africa*, second edition.

Mehta, A.K. *Poverty Trends and Incidence in India*, Indian Institute of Public Administration.

Mishra, S.N. and Sweta Mishra (1998), "Good Governance, Peoples Participation and NGO", *Indian Journal of Public Administration*, July-Sept 1998.

Multalib, M. and Khan, M. (1982), *Theory of Local Government*, Sterling Publishers, New Delhi.

Mahipal (1998), *Panchayati Raj, Five Year of Experience*, Society for Participatory Research in Asia, New Delhi.

National Productivity Council (1984), *Report on Concurrent Evaluation of IRDP in Kangra District*, Shimla 1984.

Nickson, Andrew (1995), *Local Government in Latin America*, Lynne Rienner Publisher, London.

Panth, A and Bohra O.P. (1995), "Finances of Panchayati Raj Institutions", *Indian Journal of Public Administration, 1995*, pp. 69-77.

Raghavulu and Narayana, E.A. (1991), "Reforms in Panchayati Raj: A Comparative Analysis of Andhra Pradesh, Karnataka and West Bengal", *Indian Journal of Public Administration*.

Rajaraman, Indira (1999), Fiscal Features of Rural Local Government in India, Paper Presented at Conference on Governance and Development, University of Bonn, May 1999.

Rondinelli, D. et al. (1984), *Decentralisation in Developing Countries, A Recent Review of Experience*, World Bank Staff Working Paper, number 581.

Roy, W. Bahl and Linn (1992), *Urban Public Finances in Developing Countries*, NY, Oxford UP.

Shankar, Kirpa (1994), "Jawahar Rojgar Yojna: An Assessment in UP", *Economic and Political Weekly*, July 16, 1994.

Singh, S., et al. (1997), *Legislative Status of Panchayati Raj in India*, IIPA; New United Process, New Delhi.

Siddiqui, Kamal (1992), *Local Government in South Asia*, The University Press Limited, Dhaka.

Shiviah, M. and Srivastava (1990), *Factors Affecting Development of the Panchayati Raj System*, National Institute of Rural Development.

Slater Richard and Watson, John (1989), "Democratic Decentralisation or Political Consolidation: The case of Local Government reform in Karnataka", *Public Administration and Development*, vol. 9, pp. 147-57.

Slater, Richard (1994), *Strengthening Decentralisation and Local government in Sri Lanka*, Paper Presented at the International Conference on Democratic Decentalisation in Africa and Asia, Institute of Common Wealth Studies, London, 21-23 September, 1994.

Smith, B.C. (1985), *Decentralisation: The Territorial Dimension of the State.*

State Finance Commission, *Himachal Pradesh: Report of the State Finance Commission*, November 1996, Shimla.

Swaminathan, M. (1990), "Village Level Implementation of IRDP", *Economic and Political Weekly*, Nov. 1990.

Ter-Minassian, T, "Decentralising Government", *Finance and Development*, September 1997.

Turner, Mark and Hulme, David (1997), *Governance, Administration and Development, Making the State Work*, Mackmillan Press Ltd.

UNCHS (1996), *An Urbanizing World, Global Report on Human Settlements*, 1996, Chapter-5.

Webster, Neil (1990), *Panchayati Raj and Decentralisation of Development Planning in West Bengal*, Centre for Development Research, Denmark.

Webster, Neil (1994), *Panchayati Raj and Democratic Decentralisation in West Bengal, India*, Centre for Development Research, Copenhagen.

World Bank (1988), *World Development Report, 1988*, chapter 7.

World Bank (1997), *World Development Report 1997*, chapter 7.

# 15

# Good Governance: Empowerment of Women in Urban Areas

## A Case Study of Haryana

*Charanjeev Singh & Vandana Disodia*

### Introduction

The traditional view of governance implies the political system and the manner in which power is exercised in utilising country's economic and social resources for development. It also includes in its ambit the capacity of the government to formulate and execute policies. It, in a sense, implies sustainable development, catering to the needs of the people at present keeping in view the future requirements. Rather, in more concrete terms, it implies an administration having the qualities of organisational effectiveness, efficiency, legitimacy, credibility and responsiveness.[1]

The World Bank has identified three distinct aspects of governance:[2]

(a) Form of political regime,
(b) Process by which authority is exercised for managing a country's economic and social resources for development;
(c) Capacity of the government to design, formulate and implement policies and discharge functions.

This definition of governance has given a concrete shape through accountability for transparency in administration, and above all welfare services on the part of the government for the masses as a whole.

## Good Governance Defined

Good governance consists of five fundamental factors:

> First, it requires accountability of government officials (both political leaders and career civil servants) in, for example, their disposition of public funds, providing for the safety and security of citizens, and in the equitable pursuit of economic well-being for society.
>
> Second, good governance implies that there be transparency in government procedures, processes, investment decisions, contracts and appointments.
>
> Third, predictability in government behaviour is particularly crucial to the carrying out of economic transactions between individuals and in investment decisions.
>
> A fourth aspect of good governance is openness in government transactions, and reliable flow of the information necessary for economic activity and development to take place; the media for example, should have full access to social and economic information germane to the well-being of society.
>
> Fifth, government and its citizens must adhere to observance of the rule of law: that is, governments and institutions should be subject to rules and regulations, which are understood by everyone in society.[3]

Good governance, therefore, implies:

(i) Fiscal hygiene, and sound management of national resources.

(ii) Building the capacity for the analysis and formulation of sound economic policies, and then utilising it.

(iii) A respect for economic agents—management and labour included. The government should foster their activities and abilities, rather than dampen them.

(iv) Providing an enabling environment for private-sector activities through the effective and efficient provision of vital government services.

(v) A withdrawal of the State from economic activities better handled by the private sector.

(vi) Equity and social justice in the allocation of national resources.

(vii) An end to corruption, nepotism and political manipulation of public institutions.

In 1989, the concept of "governance" was for the first time highlighted in a World Bank document on Sub-Saharan Africa.[4] Good Governance at that time came to signify sound development management. In this context four key areas were highlighted:

(a) Public sector management
(b) Accountability
(c) Legal framework for development
(d) Information and transparency

But, during the past 53 years of Independence, this concept of governance has received a setback in India. The system has failed on certain fronts like corruption, population, education, character, values and integrity, fracturisation of political parties, social and institutional reforms, etc. The government became paradoxically prisoner of its magnificent obsession and lost initiative, drive and direction. To overcome these lacunae, there is inherent need of certain administrative reforms catering to the needs of the people as a whole in the light of the changing circumstances. The government has to play the role of "a facilitator" so as to have a people-oriented government. In order to have a real democratic set-up, empowerment of the masses as a whole is required. For this, people should be made conscious of their heritage through social, institutional and human reforms.[5]

**Decentralisation and Governance**

Good governance is increasingly cited as a key component in any successful strategy to reduce poverty. Decentralisation of authority and responsibility is a key factor in good governance. Good governance is concerned with institutionalising democracy in such a way that the structure produces the expected functions.[6] A recent study has argued that the persistence of poverty in most countries has its origins in problems of governance rather than in an inadequacy of resources. The basic argument about the role of governance in development holds that weak governance is the result of failure of the state to do the following:

(a) Project a developmental vision;
(b) Demonstrate a commitment to realise the vision, through putting in place policies and programmes, as well as calibrating priorities to realise the vision; and
(c) Develop the administrative, technical and political capacity to mobilize the necessary support within the civil society to translate the vision into reality.

The lack of a pure vision having it's roots within the country and projected through its political leadership results in the loss of ownership over the country's developmental agenda, usually to aid donors. A more serious hazard is that special interest groups pursuing sectional concerns at the expense of a set of national goals appropriate different areas of policy-making.

Decentralisation policy is generally considered constructive for efficiency, equity and participation. So far as efficiency is concerned, decentralisation contributes to identifying local priorities, potentialities and resources for the formulation, implementation and sustainable management of projects. With regard to equity, local government often co-ordinates services in a better way having re-distributive implications, for instance primary health care, education, child care, housing and public transportation, etc. As regards participation, the identification and mobilisation of all available resources and their deployment in accordance with common requirements accentuates direct participation. Local self-government can surely contribute to the health of a nation's democracy by providing opportunities for greater participation in the business of governance and by creating a democratic climate of opinion. Through a local electoral process, the political parties aggregate the demands of the dispersed population, represent political interests, ensure electoral competition and form governments, thereby facilitating the participation of people in governance.

The role of local bodies in the development effort has been gradually increasing over the years, irrespective of the stage of economic growth in the country. In Nepal, the introduction of the Local Self Governance Act, 1999 was a right step in this direction so far as decentralisation and participatory development is concerned. In Thailand, the new constitution of 1997 envisioned a more decentralised and participatory structure in which government institutions at all levels would operate in a more transparent, accountable and responsive fashion. At the local level, a holistic development concept is being conceptualised with the increasing realisation that an urban development paradigm guided by the notion of economic growth alone fails to enable urban communities to achieve self-reliant and sustainable development. In Indonesia, new laws enacted in May 1999 provided administrative decentralisation consistent with the devolution of responsibilities.

The experience of several countries of the Asian and Pacific region, however, show that decentralisation policies, though enacted in several forms, suffer from the following drawbacks:

(a) There is a possibility of power vacuum at the Centre after devolving power to the lower levels. The Centre is therefore reluctant to have full-scale decentralisation, eventually creating confusion in the regulatory and promotion functions of the local bodies. For instance, in Thailand, there is complex and multi-level administrative structure comprised of local, regional and central levels. The regional and central structures play a major role in the management of natural resources, while local administration is less involved in planning. The authority to monitor and enforce compliance with environmental regulations is scattered among several agencies, each operating under the mandate of a different set of laws and regulations. This situation has often resulted in open competition and disagreement among the various resource agencies, like fisheries, forestry, lands and irrigation. This policy requires rejuvenation so that roles and responsibilities are assigned to different tiers of governance in accordance with their comparative advantages. There has to be proper standardisation of work at different levels. For example, the lower level should be more involved with implementation aspects, while the higher levels could be involved in policy formulation, monitoring, setting standards and research. This can improve the efficiency of governance at all levels.

(b) There is overlapping of the functions of local and central authorities. The decentralisation policy can hardly function at the local level without corresponding reforms at the central level. In order to make policy functional, several supporting institutions should be strengthened and activated to train local functionaries in their duties. A proper, continuous, comprehensive, monitoring and evaluating process is the need of the hour.

(c) Planning and plan implementation at the macro- and micro-levels in a decentralised system are still the cause of confusion in many countries. For example, at the central level, there is a system of obtaining prior approval for the sectoral policies, programmes and budget. Likewise, each ministry is answerable to the Comptroller and Auditor General and to the Parliament for its finances and expenditure. A question still lingers as to how to make the local self-governments, which are autonomous and responsive to local needs and aspirations, answerable to the Parliament.

(d) Active participation of people through NGOs or the co-operatives proves to be more effective at the local level because a link between the project officials and the public is directly maintained. This enhances greater transparency in the implementation of projects and programmes and greater accountability among public officials in charge of implementation, thereby enhancing the sense of ownership among project beneficiaries for project sustenance. Still, the task of the empowerment and social mobilisation of the poor remains unfulfilled. For this, the concerned institutions and political capacity will have to be furnished 'if empowerment is to become a political reality. There has to be plurality of initiatives along with the broad framework of the decentralised planned development process.

**Peoples Participation in Urban Areas**

Urbanisation is an essential component of development, a necessary transformation which society will and must go through if it is to move from one stage of development to another. However, the transition from rural to urban, often painful, can take many paths with profound effects for the future well-being of society. Crucial choices must be made which require a sound knowledge base. The manner in which society copes with urbanisation the governance of its cities will in no small part determine the nature of its social and economic development.

The participation of the urban poor is both encouraged and supported in all the developing nations. Liberalisation and privatisation has resulted in changes in local governance through decentralisation in many developing Asian countries. The Human Development Report, 1999 shows that the benefits of competitive markets can be preserved and can meet the needs of human development only with strong governance, local, national, regional and global, having a clear decentralised framework of established practices, thus, setting standards and giving incentives to individuals, organisations and firms.

The experience of the participation of the urban poor in governance has been mixed. In recent years, with more countries installing an open and democratic system of governance, political participation through elections has expanded at both national and local levels. Still, the majority of the people have not been active partners in governance, rendering the systems of governance less responsive and relevant to the needs and concerns of the masses.

In India, for example, in recent years legal and financial provisions have been decentralised substantially. But institutional capabilities and human resources have not been enhanced commensurate with the decentralised responsibilities. Consequently, certain local bodies remain incapable of discharging the functions that have been devolved to them. Furthermore, the majority of urbanities lacks little or no training and is unable to have access to the available opportunities and resources. This in a way arises due to complicated rules and regulations. The NGOs, no doubt, work in the areas of social mobilisation, awareness-raising, environmental protection and income generation but the absence of proper mechanisms for co-ordination with different tiers of government structure is a hindrance. So, the NGOs and representatives of civil society should complement each other and avoid overlaps, so that the outcomes of the macro-level policy liberalisation reach the household levels in a much better way.

People's participation and empowerment is, thus, a pre-requisite for a system, which is responsive and sustainable. In the light of good governance, empowerment of women in urban areas in today's scenario occupies a deep thought. The local government in India by way of its 74th Constitutional Amendment Act, has boosted the status of women by providing them reservation in Municipal Committees/Councils. Now, women have been empowered to have their say in local administration in urban areas. This enables them to get elected to the urban local councils as chairman/members and contribute by way of active participation.[7]

## Empowerment and Governance

The key ingredients for empowerment are summed up below:

(a) ***Motivation:*** Poor households should be encouraged and motivated to form groups for organising and pursuing community development activities. This would enable them to develop routine interaction and the power to assert themselves as citizens and members of the society. The groups should be encouraged to engage in income-generating activities using their own resources and capabilities.

(b) ***Awareness and training:*** Raising awareness in several areas, such as immunisation, sanitation and primary education should be pursued. Similarly, vocational skills should be imparted through participatory methods, where local knowledge, mainly based on experience, can be clubbed with outside knowledge. Such training can assist the poor to set-up their own self-employment activities or go outside for seasonal employment.

(c) ***Resource mobilisation:*** The mobilisation of resources is a method of pooling individual resources through regular savings and voluntary contributions to create social capital.

This generalisation could improve their individual situation substantially. Careful consideration should be given to developing a proper system of resource generation, allocation and utilisation, so that all members have equal opportunities. This would ensure ownership and sustainability.

(d) ***Self-management:*** People should be capable of electing their own leaders and managing their own activities, such as the conduct of meetings, record-keeping, savings and credit operations, conflict resolution and community property management. In the initial stages, an outside agent can assist them in developing a system. Later the groups can be given full autonomy over the system.

(e) ***Building linkages:*** Organising self-help groups at the grassroots is a method of activating the "demand side" of decentralised policies by enhancing the capability of the poor to access the resources, opportunities and organisations of the state that work for their development. As such, it is crucial for the poor to have linkages with decentralised institutions in order to gain access to opportunities and resources.

## The Indian Experience

In India, in urban areas, poverty alleviation programmes like Swarna Jayanti Shahari Rozgar Yojna (SJSRY) has provided empowerment to women by setting up community-based structure like Neighbourhood Groups (NHGs), Neighbourhood Committees (NHCs) and Community Development Societies (CDS). These community-based structures empower women in the urban areas to provide community leadership by way of participation in urban affairs on a day-to-day basis. The SJSRY aims not only at economic empowerment of the women but also social, political and psychological empowerment as well.

The SJSRY, *inter-alia,* requires active participation of the people particularly the beneficiaries themselves in the designing and implementation process. In order to make the implementation process look effective, the participation of beneficiaries in the designing and implementation process is absolutely desirable. For this purpose, Community-based structures are set up. These are:

### (1) *Neighbourhood Groups* (NHCs)

This is an informal association of women living in mohalla or basti or neighbourhood group of manageable size (preferably to 10 to 40 represent urban poor or slum families), geographic contiguity and homogeneity should be the basis to carve out the boundaries of the NHCs. At least one women resident among them who is willing to serve as a volunteer should be selected as a Resident Community Volunteer (RCV) through community consensus or election or any other democratic process. There should be a change or rotation (if need be) of such volunteers at periodical intervals. The responsibilities of other RCVs include to:

(a) Serve as a channel of information and communication among the families in the cluster;
(b) Represent the views of the groups in the neighbourhood committees and community development societies and other forums;
(c) Support planning, implementation and monitoring of activities at the neighbourhood level;
(d) Foster and encourage participation in community improvement, and
(e) Motivate the community for being members of thrift and credit society and to contribute to community development fund.[8]

### (2) *Neighbourhood Committees* (NHCs)

A Neighbourhood Committee (NHC) is a more formal association of women from the above neighbourhood groups located in close proximity and as far as feasible within the same electoral ward. The committee should consist of all the RCVs from the neighbourhood groups as executives (with voting right) of NHC as well as one female member (without voting rights) from each family, which falls under the jurisdiction of NHC concerned. There can also be provision for honorary membership without a voting right for Community Organisers (COs), representatives from other sectoral programmes in the community like ICDS supervisor, school teacher, ANM, etc. The Convener/President of the NHC is to be selected/elected by the executive members of the NHC. The convener will ensure that the meetings are convened on regular basis. The NHC would be responsible to:

(a) Identify local problems and priorities;
(b) Provide suggestions for groups involvement in meeting community needs and goals (mini-plans);
(c) Support local action with partnership of responsible agencies including community contracts;
(d) Provide feedback to agencies of programme effectiveness and outreach especially for children and women;
(e) Develop community capacity through training in association with COs, NGOs and other sectoral departments;
(f) Develop community-based thrift and credit system as well as neighbourhood development fund;
(g) Facilitate the recovery of loans from the beneficiaries in time; and
(h) Assist/carry out community surveys in accordance with the guidelines.[9]

The NHC may be registered under the Societies Registration Act, or other appropriate Acts if so desired. If registered, these NHC may also apply for grants-in-aid under various schemes.

### (3) *Community Development Society* (*CDS*)

The CDS is a formal association of all the neighbourhood development committes at the town level based on common goals and objectives. The CDS may consist of elected/selected representatives of NHCs as executive members (with voting right) as well as one female member from each family (without voting right) which falls under the jurisdiction of CDS; and other members with honorary membership (with no voting right) which may include community organisers, representatives of NGOs, sectoral department, leading citizens, elected representatives of the area and other resource persons. The Community Development Society (CDS) should be registered under the Societies Registration Act or other appropriate Acts to provide access to grant-in-aid under various schemes and for a wider Financial and credit base. The CDS would be responsible to:

(a) Represent needs of all the communities, especially women and children;
(b) Liaise and link-up with agencies and departments to promote action in the community towards fulfilment of their needs;
(c) Identify specific training and arrange for their organisation;
(d) Facilitate community surveys to be carried out to identify the genuine beneficiaries for economic and shelter benefits;
(e) Prepare community plans and proposals, mobilising resources from the community, town or other sectoral departments;
(f) Extend help to Bank in co-ordination with UPE Cell, for ensuring repayment of loans by the beneficiaries; and
(g) Create small community assets in low-income areas in consultation with town UPE Cell and Urban Local Body (ULB).[10]

The policy framework adopted by the Government of India also mentions "a frontal attack on poverty is an important element in development policy. This is the main rationale for anti-poverty programmes".

## Progress of SJSRY in Haryana

The State Urban Development Society, Haryana is presently implementing the scheme of SJSRY. This scheme relies on creation of suitable community structures based on the UBSP programme like NGSs, NHCs and CDS. One of the prominent feature of the SJSRY is formation of the DWCUA groups through the scheme for Development of Women and Children in the Urban Areas and shall be entitled to a subsidy of Rs.1.25 lakh or 50 per cent of the cost of the project whichever is less. This amount is to be spent on the purchase of raw materials and marketing; infrastructure support for income generation and other group activities; one time expense on child care activity, etc. The CDS are the focal point for purpose of identification of beneficiaries, preparation of applications, monitoring of recovery and other support whichever is necessary for the programme. The CDS will also identify viable projects suitable for that particular area. The Government of India (GOI) has issued guidelines for to all the Deputy Commissioners-cum-Chairman District Urban Development Agencies and the Additional Deputy Commissioners-cum-Chief Executive Officers, District Urban Development Agencies in Haryana.

In order to identify the urban poor families and to constitute the community structures, a Below Poverty Line (BPL) Survey for each town of the State has already been carried out. The Planning Commission has revised the income criteria for the identification of BPL families, which is Rs.337.42 per capita per month. The ADC-cum-CEO of the DUDA were asked to conduct a fresh BPL Survey and a proforma for the BPL Survey should be in conformity with the poverty ratios determined by the Planning Commission. The DUDAs were allocated funds for conducting the BPL Surveys in the month of April 1998 to the tune of Rs.4.60 lakh of the Centre and Rs.1.53 lakh as the State share on the basis of population. Further out of the unspent balance of the previous schemes the component-wise allocation was made to the DUDAs as indicated in the Table 1 and the corresponding achievements have been elucidated in Table 2.

**TABLE 1**

| Components | Amount (Rs. in lakhs) |
|---|---|
| Community Structures | 4.60 |
| UWEP | 11.54022 |
| USEP | |
| Subsidy | 42.53 |
| Training | 11.35 |
| Infrastructure | 1.15 |
| DWCUA | |
| Subsidy | 11.35 |
| T&CS | 4.05 |
| Grand Total | 86.87022 |

*Source:* O/o Project Director, SJSRY and SUDSH.

The unspent balance of the old schemes amounting to Rs.276.62 lakh was treated as opening balance of the new scheme. Initially, the implementation of the scheme was slow

The component-wise physical/achievement is as under:

**TABLE 2**

| Components | Target | | Achievements | |
|---|---|---|---|---|
| | 1998-99 | 1999-2000 | 1998-99 | 1999-00 |
| USEP (L&S) | | | | |
| Loan and Subsidy | 2164 | 3618 | 966 | 2816 |
| Training | 981 | 1000 | 960 | 1654 |
| DWCUA | 19 | 40 | 12 | 38 |
| T&CS | 20 | 60 | 16 | 87 |
| UWEP | 138983 | 37411 | 37056 | 36417 |

*Source:* O/o Project Director, SJSRY and SUDSH.

because due to change in economic criteria a fresh BPL survey was conducted. The Government of India has also laid down certain non-economic criteria and seeking of clarifications, training of staff, etc., took considerable time. The survey was completed in November 1998. Thereafter, the Community Structures like NHGs, NHCs, CDSs were constituted. As such the actual implementation of the scheme started with effect from January 1999. The funds have been utilised during 1999-2000 and up to 31 April 2000 an expenditure of Rs.446.45 lakh has already been incurred on the scheme. An allocation of Rs.181 crore has been provided in 1999-2000 (BE).[11]

Up to 31 March 2000, 943 NHCs, 76 CDSs have been constituted, 38 DWCUA groups are constituted and 87 Thrift and Credit Societies are formed. The District-wise progress in constitution of the CDS and T&CS has been elicited in the Table 3. Table 4 indicates the number of RCVs appointed, NHCs and the DWCUA groups constituted in the districts under the SJSRY.

It can be analysed from Tables 3 and 4 that though the effort of the state government in constituting the community structures is appreciable yet keeping in view the population of the districts it can be said that nothing much has been done. Particular care is to be taken while constituting the DWCUA groups as to keep these groups in working shape homogeneity of these groups on the basis of caste; creed, religion, etc., must

**TABLE 3: District-wise Progress of Composition of CDS and T&CS till 31 March 2000**

| District | CDS | | T&CS |
|---|---|---|---|
| | Formed | Regd. | |
| Ambala | – | – | 3 |
| Bhiwani | 6 | – | 4 |
| Faridabad | 7 | – | 10 |
| Fatehabad | 5 | – | 8 |
| Gurgaon | 9 | 6 | 3 |
| Hisar | 2 | 1 | 4 |
| Jhajjar | 1 | 1 | 12 |
| Jind | – | – | 3 |
| Kaithal | – | – | – |
| Karnal | 7 | 7 | 6 |
| Kurukshetra | 5 | – | 1 |
| Narnaul | 4 | 4 | 2 |
| Panchkula | 2 | – | 12 |
| Panipat | 4 | 4 | 4 |
| Rewari | 1 | 1 | 2 |
| Rohtak | 7 | 7 | 6 |
| Sirsa | 7 | 7 | 5 |
| Sonepat | 3 | 3 | 6 |
| Yamunanagar | 5 | 5 | 5 |
| Total | 75 | 53 | 96 |

*Source:* O/o Project Director, SJSRY and SUDSH.

be taken care of. Albeit, these things may not matter much to the policy framers and seem superfluous yet in Haryana it can be said that a lot of importance is attached to these social institutions.

## Conclusions

The concept of good governance embraces empowerment, decentralisation and people's participation in the development activities. It can be seen from the above analysis that though the scheme of SJSRY is targeting the women beneficiaries and aims at empowering the urban poor women by constituting various community structures and opening up of avenues of self-employment through creation of self-help groups solely for the women

**TABLE 4: District-wise Progress of RCVs, NHCs and DWCUA groups as 31 March 2000**

| District | No. of RCVs | No. of NHCs | DWCUA | Population |
|---|---|---|---|---|
| Ambala | – | – | 7 | 285809 |
| Bhiwani | – | 449 | 4 | 196568 |
| Faridabad | 437 | 44 | 2 | 717513 |
| Fatehabad | 307 | 37 | 2 | 102958 |
| Gurgaon | 595 | 56 | 2 | 211239 |
| Hisar | 349 | 26 | – | 278017 |
| Jhajjar | 198 | 11 | 3 | 99436 |
| Jind | 4250 | 100 | 3 | 165544 |
| Kaithal | 130 | 30 | – | 120637 |
| Karnal | 270 | 14 | 3 | 255172 |
| Kurukshetra | 360 | 36 | – | 154134 |
| Narnaul | 122 | 12 | 2 | 169288 |
| Panchkula | 40 | 6 | 1 | 111185 |
| Panipat | 270 | 36 | 4 | 209596 |
| Rewari | 85 | 13 | 1 | 84352 |
| Rohtak | 530 | 16 | 4 | 245703 |
| Sirsa | 70 | – | 1 | 214534 |
| Sonepat | 410 | 41 | 1 | 210521 |
| Yamunanagar | 301 | 10 | – | 256917 |
| Total | 8784 | 943 | 40 | |

*Source:* O/o Project Director, SJSRY and SUDSH.

yet the scheme as envisaged is yet in the take off stage. The commitment of the local level bureaucracies and the political elite at the district level feel the pinch of the power being taken away from their hands. A lot has to be done in this regard and some attitudinal changes in both the bureaucracy and political elite will usher in some hope for the success of this scheme and to the concept of good governance and empowerment of women in the urban areas.

Following recommendations need to focused:

(a) Effective targeting using either a self-identification system or a selection process by community structures responsible for financing/recovery UPAPs, as faulty targeting will enhance income inequalities otherwise.

(b) A "bottom up", approach be adopted for UPAPs, which should be routed through community-based organisations. There should be effective participation of community institutions for extending loans and for aiding loan recoveries had under UPAPs.

(c) Since the problem of urban poverty is a manifestation of the higher incidence of marginal and low-income employment in the informal sector, it is essential to upgrade informal sector occupations. Hence there is a need for emphasis on generation of self-employment in processing and services sector, improving the access to technology and credit and above all improving the general legal and physical environment, which governs the working of the informal sector.

## REFERENCES

1. Asian Development Bank, "Good governance and anti-corruption: the road forward for Indonesia", paper presented at the eighth meeting of the consultative group on Indonesia, Paris, 1999, July 27 and 28, p. 7.
2. Asmeroon H.K., Borgman K. and Hoppe R. "Good Governance, Decentralisation and Democratisation in Post-Colonial States", *The Indian Journal of Public Administration,* 1995, July-September, vol. 44 (3), pp. 735-81.
3. Arora, R.K. (ed.) ,"People's Participation in Development Process", *HCM,* SIPA, Jaipur, 1979.
4. Barnabas, A.P, "People's Participation in Planning", *Prashasnika,* 1997, Jan.-June.
5. Bandyopadhyay, "Administration, Decentralisation and Good Governance", *Economic and Political Weekly,* 30 Nov., 1996.
6. Bata, K. Dey, "Defining Good Governance", *The Indian Journal of Public Administration,* 1998, July-September; vol. 44 (3), pp. 412-27.
7. Bhattacharya, Mohit, "Conceptualising Good Governance", *The Journal of Public Administration,* 1998, July-September; vol. 44 (3), p. 291.
8. Deborah, Brautigam, *Governance and Economy: A review,* 1991.
9. H. Schneider, "Participatory Governance: The Missing Link for Poverty Reduction", *Policy brief,* no. 17 (Paris, OECD Development Centre, 1999).
10. Mamadou, Dia, "A Governance Approach to Civil Service Reform in Sub-Saharan Africa", *The World Bank,* Washington D.C., 1993.

11. Maddick, Henry R, *Democracy, Decentralisation and Development,* New Delhi, Asia Publishing House, 1963.
12. Maheshwari S.R, *Local Government in India,* Agra, Lakshmi Narian Agrawal (2nd edition), 1996-97, p. 148.
13. Minocha, O.P., "Good Governance: New Public Management Perspective", *The Journal of Public Administration,* 1998, July-September; vol. 44 (3), pp. 271-72.
14. Mishra Sweta *Democratic Decentralisation in India: Study in Retrospect and Prospect,* Mittal Publishers, New Delhi, 1994.
15. Mukhopadhyay, Asok, "Reinventing government for good governance", *The Indian Journal of Public Administration,* 1998, July-September; vol. 44 (3), p. 282.
16. Nirja Gopal Jayal, "The Governance Agenda: Making Democratic Development Dispensable", *Economic and Political Weekly,* 1997, February 22, p. 407.
17. Reeta Choudhary Trembley "Growth with Justice: Understanding Poverty" in C. Steven La Rue (ed.) 1996-97, p. 99.
18. S. Franzway, D. Court and R.W. Connell *Staking A Claim: Feminism, Bureaucracy and the State,* Cambridge, Polity Press, 1989, p. 31.
19. World Bank, *Governance: The World Bank's experience,* Washington D.C., World Bank Publication, 1994.
20. World Bank, *Governance and Development,* Washington D.C., 1993.
21. World Bank (Africa Region), "UNCHS and Governance", Habitat Debate, Vice-President Edward Jaycox's Tom Mboya Memorial Lecture in Nairobi last year, cited in the *Sunday Nation,* 1995, 29 January, vol. 1 (1) Internet Site www.undp.org/un/habitat/news 1trs/debate 1. html

## NOTES

1. O.P. Minocha, "Good Governance: New Public Management Perspective", *Indian Journal of Public Administration,* July-September; vol. 44(3), pp. 271-72.
2. Asok Mukhopadhyay, "Reinventing government for good governance", *The Indian Journal of Public Administration,* 1998, July-September; Vol. 44 (3), p. 282.
3. World Bank (Africa Region) "UNCHS and Governance", Habitat Debate, Vice-President Edward Jaycox's Tom Mboya Memorial Lecture in Nairobi last year, cited in the *Sunday Nation,* 1995, 29 January, 1 (1) Internet Site www.undp.org/un/habitat/news 1trs/debate 1.html
4. Mohit Bhattacharya, "Conceptualising Good Governance", *Indian*

*Journal of Public Administration,* 1998, July-September; vol. 44 (3), p. 291.
5. Bata K. Dey, "Defining Good Governance", *Indian Journal of Public Administration,* 1998, July-September; vol. 44 (3), pp. 412-27.
6. Report of the Economic and Social Commission for Asia and the Pacific on its fifty-fourth session (*Official Records of the Economic and Social Council, 1998, Supplement No. 20)* (E/1998/40-E/ESCAP/1117), paras. 97 and 201; "*Report of the Committee on Socio-Economic Measures to Alleviate Poverty in Rural and Urban Areas on its second session*" (E/ESCAP/1169), para 8.
7. S.R. Maheshwari, *Local Government in India,* Agra, Lakshmi Narian Agrawal (2nd edition), 1996-97, p. 148.
8. Guidelines of SJSRY issued by Ministry of Urban Affairs and Employment, Government of India, New Delhi.
9. *Ibid.*
10. *Ibid.*
11. Budget India 2000 Economic Survey Poverty Alleviation and Employment (Internet Site http://www.economictimes.com/budget 2000/chap 1004.htm).

# Part 3

# Women Empowerment

# 16

# Women's Participation in Gram Panchayats: A Study in Haryana

*Manjusha Sharma*

## Introduction

There was a poster with the following words which tries to aware the women all over the world to listen to the cry of the rural women of the Third World countries that is:

> We are more than half the number we do more than half the work. We are more than half the poor. We have more than half the love. We have more than half the dreams.

She in her sphere does work as useful as man does in his. She has as much right to her freedom to develop her personality to the full as a man. With the dawn of independence, our constitution guaranteed equality to the genders. Indian culture has been so built that it has resulted in her complete extermination from the field of political and economic independence. The woman today, is poised to talk off. The voice from the kitchen is beginning to be heard at national and international platforms. Woman can do everything these days even can act like father. She holds the world in her work. In spite of this, she stands at the cross-roads and suffers untold miseries silently.

There is an important saying that "Where females are honoured, there the deities are pleased". But the question arises at this juncture is why are they dishonoured? Why are they not given the right to take part in political decision-making? How they can be empowered? How they can be promoted to take active participation in the struggle for development in political, economic and social fields, so that they should not be merely reduced to a paper-tag on our statute books. Over the years, government has made concerted efforts to empower the women both politically and economically. But even after 50 years of Independence, women wear a pathetic look. Despite the constitutional guarantee women have been subjected to deprivation, brutality and extortion. The Constitution (73rd Amendment) Act, 1992 passed by the parliament and made effective from 24th April 1993, is a major landmark in the constitutional history of India. In consonance the directive principles of State Policy, it has attempted to fulfil the dream. No doubt, it is a positive step for the development of women. But it is a matter of serious concern to probe into the status of women in a state like Haryana totally culturally bound.

In this paper, an attempt has been made to examine the trend in participation of women in Gram Panchayats. In general, participation at local level can be viewed from two angles, viz., quality and quantity. Quantitative aspects refer to the strength of participation and trend of participation in general and that of different groups like men, women, backward class, etc. As far as qualitative aspects is concerned, there are three levels of quality of participation:

1. **Passive Participation**: Simply attending the meetings of Gram Panchayats without any active role.
2. **Active Participation**: Participating actively as members of Gram Panchayats.
3. **Decision Participation**: Participating in the capacity of leaders like Chairperson of Gram Panchayat.

The present paper is confined to the participation of women in Gram Panchayats, which is a pre-requisite of empowerment. The present investigation is confined to Babain and Ladwa blocks of Kurukshetra district in Haryana and to the quality of participation of women in Gram Panchayat for which selected respondents were asked questions to elicit the information.

## Participation in Gram Panchayat

We have made an attempt to know and to find out the perception of selected respondents about their participation in Gram Panchayats. In this connection, some important issues were raised. The responses of the respondents are presented herewith.

## Awareness about Haryana Panchayat Raj Act

No institution can get success in its working if the persons involved are not aware of its literature. If we look to the figures pertaining to awareness among the Gram Panchayat, we find that majority of the female selected respondents, i.e., 27 (92.3 per cent) out of 28 were unaware of the basic knowledge of the Act and the power given to them under this Act. The main reason for this sorry state of affairs is illiteracy as 95 per cent were illiterate among them. Women chairpersons as well as members lack self-confidence due to illiteracy. As a result they do not dare to actively participate in the decision-making process.

## Hesitation in Attending the Meetings

Meetings are considered very important. If the elected representatives do not take active part in the meeting, the main objective of devolution of powers will forfeit. It is in this context that a question was put to the elected representatives about attending the meetings and campaigning for themselves during election days. It has been found that at Gram Panchayat level 78.57 per cent women answered in negative and only 21.42 per cent reported that they did go to attend the meetings with their sons or husbands. In case of campaign, 92.30 per cent said that they hesitate in facing the village male people due to cultural taboos. This clearly indicates that in many cases the work of attending the meetings and campaign is completed by male members of their families. Thus, women representatives hesitate in coming forward to show their strength. This position is not in case of Haryana only there are other states too, where women representatives do not attend the meetings regularly.

### Attitude of Males Towards Women Representatives

It is expected that male members of Panchayati Raj Institutions (PRIs) should have positive attitude towards their female counterparts. A question was put to the male elected representatives regarding their attitude towards working of women representatives. Of them 23 out of 28, i.e., 82.14 per cent replied that when they don't turn up for meeting then how can we motivate them? We are ready to cooperate but for this they have to make their place in PRIs. But it is seen that they are just the proxy candidates of their husbands as a result seat is also wasted and no development work could be performed. And even one member went to the extent of saying that there should be no back-door entry. They are of the view that harmony of home as well as of village is disturbed. Contrary to this statement, it was found that 91 per cent women representatives were of the view that prevailing male dominated power structures in villages are not ready to accept women as the chairpersons of Gram Panchayats. They have not changed their attitude in true sense.

### Views Regarding One-third Reservation

No doubt by giving one-third reservation, women are being inducted into leadership position and thereby into politics. The selected respondents were asked as to whether one-third reservation was sufficient and did they think that they could be got elected to PRIs, if there was no reservation? The responses show that 100 per cent women were of the opinion, if actually this reservation is availed then it is sufficient, otherwise it makes no sense as it is the males again who are performing the whole of work. In response to second question, 99 per cent women said that because the seats were reserved for women, so they had to fight the election. This clearly shows that self-motivation is needed so that they themselves should come forward to contest the elections.

### Performance of Responsibility

The elected representatives are expected to perform their responsibilities assigned without any fear but in the case of female representatives it is presumed if they are to go in an other village falling in the jurisdiction of the concerned Gram Panchayat, they do not dare going out of the respective village. To know the real position, a question, i.e., "Can you travel outside the village as a part of responsibility?", was asked. In response to this question, as many as 24 (71.0 per cent) out of 28 admitted that they did not go in other villages to perform the duties assigned. This is because of dominance of male members not allowing them to do so. If we are really interested in providing better services to the areas, we will have to motivate them through inculcating self-confidence.

### Feeling after Elections

It was hoped that the women elected representatives after being elected would feel happy and satisfied. But to our surprise, the position is entirely different. As many as 26 (92.85 per cent) out of 28 felt no change at all after being elected to the Gram Panchayat. It seems, as if they were forced to contest election and that is why their attitude has not become favourable.

### Women Welfare

Our past experience shows that women in majority had already been by-passed from the sharing of development benefits. After 73rd Amendment to the Constitution having one-third reservation provision, it is expected that the elected women will take keen interest in welfare of women. To know their views, they were asked as to whether they were interested in women welfare or not? It is a matter of great pleasure that all those contacted and interviewed were interested in women welfare, i.e., 21 (75 per cent) out of 28 agreed that girl schools, maternity homes, planning centre, etc., should figure in the meetings. But they accepted that in the meetings, they are unable to raise these issues. This only cannot go a long way in finding solutions to the problems as overwhelming majority of them do not take part in the meetings of the Gram Panchayats.

### Suggestions

To streamline the functioning of Gram Panchayats with effective participation of women, following suggestions can be put into practice:

1. First of all, we are very much in the need of removal of illiteracy among elected women representatives. For this purpose, we will have to revive our adult education centres in close cooperation with the rural society. It should be mandatory for both female and male illiterate representatives to attend the prescribed centres so that they are in a position to read and write. This has to be ensured through political will.
2. Training centres should be opened in the villages level itself and we can have cluster of villages for imparting the training. The training centres should have real significance and Panchayati Raj orientation. Those imparting training should first go in for training and then they should be assigned the job. Training should be on regular basis followed by proper monitoring and evaluation.
3. There has to be close relationship between male and female representatives. Both the sexes should have due regard vice versa. Efforts should be made to motivate those having indifferent attitudes. Those who are on the right track should be appreciated.
4. As regards time factor, the meetings of the Gram Panchayats should be fixed in consultations with the women representatives. Their conveniences should never be ignored. Those belonging to poor sections can be financially compensated on such days when they attend the meetings.
5. To check the practice of not attending the meetings by the women representatives, constant motivation followed by stern action can compel them to attend the meeting themselves on regular basis. Those who are already attending should be inspired and we can make use of their services to motivate others.
6. So far as confidence is concerned, it will definitely be built sooner or later, if concerted efforts are made. When they will be associated in the decision-making process and have enough say, they will ultimately have confidence.
7. As it has been observed that the male members of the families of women representatives do not allow them to attend

the meetings, therefore, we are in the need to persuade them. This persuasion can be arranged through public meetings by village level workers, teachers and volunteers. To start with their relatives may be allowed to accompany women representatives. And ultimately they themselves will change their attitudes.

8. There is an urgent need to involve voluntary organisations in this noble cause/task. We can assign this job to them and financial assistance can also be arranged for them out of Panchayat Raj funds. These voluntary organisations will definitely prove useful in coping with the problem which is considered as serious. The NGOs can help in creating congenial atmosphere. Such women representatives who really work honestly and dedicatedly should be publicly honoured.
9. The ultimate aim of participation of women is the empowerment of women. Capacity building at the grassroot level is a pre-requisite of empowerment. Thus, capacity can be built through simple neighbourhood groups, gram sabhas, Self-Help Groups, task forces, specialised Committees, NSS, Women Studies Centres, etc.
10. If we are really interested in the enhancement of women participation in the Gram Panchayats, a special centre for rural women should immediately be started and all rural developmental activities should be shown on this channel. The successful experience should also be telecast from time to time to motivate others.

## Conclusion

Participation and capacity building are the integral part of empowerment. Without either of these, empowerment will remain as quite a distant dream. Once the women are given a chance to participate in the development activities, the inertia is broken and it will let loose the unimaginable force required for social transformation.

# 17

# Women Empowerment

## *Shriniwas Joshi*

I am going back seventy years in quoting Anne Besant, the founder of Theosophical Society who had then said, "The rights of man have become an accepted doctrine, but unfortunately they are only rights of man in the exclusive sense of the word. They are sexual and not human rights and until they become human rights, society will never rest on a just foundation, ... to deny these rights—liberty, property, safety and resistance to tyranny—to women is either to deny them to humanity or to deny that women form a part of humanity".

How could it be that 48.1 per cent of population in India (49.23 per cent of population in Himachal Pradesh) does not form part of humanity? Literature and Art sing praises for women. Even our land of birth is Bharat Mata. Tamil language is personified as beautiful and noble woman. Pahari miniature art has substance in the exquisite delicacy of feminine forms. A woman is glorified as a symbol of Shakti. Manu proclaims, "By cherishing women one cherishes the goddess of prosperity herself, and by afflicting her, one is said to pain the goddess of prosperity." She, as wife, is *ardhangini* (equal partner). But then Manu directs, "Be a girl or be a young woman or be advanced in years, nothing must be done even in her own dwelling place according to her pleasure". And also, "She should do nothing independently in her own house even. In childhood, she is subject to her father, in youth to her husband and during her widowhood to her sons; she should never enjoy independence". Tulsidas says, "A drum, a lower human, a rustic and a woman require to be beaten". Even the English considered her "weaker sex". Shakespeare had said, "Frailty, thy name is woman".

This so-called frail woman in the hills has the following percentage share in Agricultural and Animal Husbandry activities as collected from Mountain Women Development Centre Records, 1995:

| | |
|---|---|
| ***Agriculture*** | |
| Land preparation and stone breaking | 85 |
| Sowing and transplanting | 72 |
| Gap filling | 100 |
| Inter-culture | 68 |
| Weeding | 94 |
| Irrigation | 50 |
| Fertiliser application | 45 |
| Harvesting | 71 |
| Threshing and winnowing | 58 |
| ***Animal Husbandry*** | |
| Tending cattle in shed | 95 |
| Grazing | 48 |
| Removing dung from shed | 100 |
| Fodder collection | 93 |
| Milking | 96 |

From the above Table it is clear that except "plough in" activity which is done 100 per cent by men, woman's hand in great measure is there in all other activities. Negi, Rana and Sharma (1997) conducted a study in Mahim and Kwarag Panchayats of Kandaghat Block. They record that during the peak agriculture season a woman's work hours per day are seventeen. An assessment by Shiva (1991) on the workload on one hectare of land in one year in the Indian Himalayas discloses that it is 1,064 hours for a pair of bullocks, 1,212 hours for a man and 3,485 hours for a woman. Despite all this toil of her, it is the man who enjoys the power of taking decisions in all matters concerning the family and housekeeping. A study of M.S. Swaminathan Research Foundation in Chennai has shown that in Pichavaram and Muthupet, two coastal villages near the temple town of Chidambaram, women take care of 75 per cent of the responsibilities but are involved in less than 30 per cent of the household decisions. Studies conducted in sub-Saharan Africa and a 1984 study in Botswana all reveal that 'She' works and 'He' takes decision. Do you think that such conditions can ever be conducive to sustainable development? Says Bina, "In spite of the key role of women in crop-husbandry, animal-husbandry, fisheries, forestry and post-harvest technology, those in charge of formulating packages of technologies, services and public policies for rural areas have often tended to neglect the productive role of women". M.S. Swaminathan goes a step ahead and says that women are, in fact, "the largest group of landless labourers, with little security in case of break-up of the family through death or divorce; inheritance laws and customs discriminate against them". Subbiah Arunachalam, a gender expert, apprehends that the conditions are deteriorating so fast that the women's share of the world's poor has risen steadily in the past two decades and stands close to 70 per cent today, making feminisation of poverty a major issue.

But then, who does not know, that India is a land of opposites. Several bright spots dot this gloomy scenario. The Constitution of India granting equality to women in various spheres creates the legal framework within which the Department of Women and Child Development, which came into being in the year 1985, functions for women's empowerment. The following are the major policy initiatives undertaken by the Department in the recent past:

- establishment of National Commission for Women (NCW) in 1992. It covers issues relating to safeguarding women's rights and promotion of their empowerment. It works for review of laws, intervention in specific individual complaints of atrocities and sexual harassment of women at workplace, and remedial actions to safeguard the interest of women;
- setting up of Rashtriya Mahila Kosh (RMK) in 1993 which extends credit facilities to poor and needy women in the

informal sectors. Since inception, the Kosh has sanctioned credit of Rs.57.09 crore through 367 NGOs to benefit 2,77,662 women;
- adoption of National Nutrition Policy (NNP);
- implementing the world's largest and unique outreach programme of Integrated Child Development Services Scheme (ICDS) since 1975-76. It provides a package of services comprising supplementary nutrition, immunisation, health check up and referral services, pre-school non-formal education, health and nutritional education;
- National Creche Fund, Indira Mahila Yojana, Balika Samriddhi Yojana (to change the community's attitude towards the girl child), Rural Women's Development and Empowerment Project (RWDEP) are a few other schemes taken up by the Department. RWDEP is a Project, started in 1998, and will strengthen the process of, and create an environment of women in the six States of Bihar, Haryana, Karnataka, Gujarat, Madhya Pradesh and Uttar Pradesh;
- The National Policy for Empowerment of Women is being finalised by the Department. The policy would prescribe strategies and action points to bridge the gap between the equal *de-jure* status and unequal *de-facto* position of the women in the country. It would seek to guide action at every level and in every sector by mainstreaming gender perspectives into laws, policies, programmes, regulations, and budgetary allocation of the Government;
- setting up of National Resource Centre for Women. This would be a nodal agency to maintain gender issues in policies and programmes for women by training, policy support, information dissemination, research and documentation.

All this shows that the approach of the Government towards women has also changed. In the first two decades after Independence, women were considered as "beneficiaries" and programmes were started for their "welfare". Later started the programmes for women development and now in the nineties the slogan is woman's empowerment. Woman is now considered as emissary of social change, at least on papers, where efforts are being made to involve her in various schemes—particularly in economic empowerment programmes.

Regarding political empowerment, while the political parties here are battling over whether or not the Women's Reservation Bill should be passed in Parliament, the Commonwealth Plan on Gender and Development specifically mentions India among those countries where actions have been taken to increase the critical mass of women in decision-making. With reservation in Panchayats, India ranks third in the series with 33.5 per cent representation of women. Seychelles betters its record with a 54 per cent and Uganda with 40.8 per cent women representation. As against this, India does not figure among the ten top reporting countries on Women's participation in the National Executive or Cabinet and Parliament. While New Zealand tops the list with 30 per cent of women in its National Parliament or Assembly, India has only 7.8 per cent women representation in the Parliament. The representation in the Ministry was a mere 8.57 per cent as against the Gambia's 30.8 per cent, the highest. Antigua and Barbuda with 17.8 per cent follow the Gambia.

Having had the background of the *de-jure* and *de-facto* position of women, especially in India, and the shape of things to come, let us concentrate on what is required to be done for women empowerment in the coming future.

## The Prominent Target

International Conference on Population and Development, 1994 at Cairo, World Summit for Social Development, 1995 at Copenhagen and UN Fourth World Conference on Women, 1995 held at Beijing, all agreed on a target of closing the gender gap in primary and secondary education by 2005. This has been widely emphasised as the target for progress towards gender equality and the empowerment of women.

## The Missing Target

There are no targets for improving women's economic position or reducing the feminisation of poverty. Not only the governments but also the people in general should address women's economic inequality and poverty, and to change macro-economic policies that hindered women from enjoying secure and sustainable livelihood.

**The Position Target**

The Beijing Platform for Action affirmed that women should have at least 30 per cent share of decision-making positions.

To assess the achievements made there is need of gender sensitive indicators. These have also been agreed to by the United Nations:

- ratio of girls enrolment to that of boys in secondary schools;
- female share of paid employment in non-agricultural activities (secondary and tertiary); Paid employment is important because it puts money in woman's hand. Women's share of paid employment has certainly increased in most regions from the mid-1980s to the late 1990s barring in some parts of Eastern Europe. But the quality of employment has not. Women's job tends to enjoy less social protection and employment rights than do men's job.
- Women's share of seats in national parliament and decision-making positions in the economy. It is rising but there is still a long way to go before it reaches 30 per cent or more in all countries. Her share of position as an employer or a self-employed worker was 30 per cent or more in only 28 countries in the 1990s. During the same period her share of administrative and managerial employment was 30 per cent or more in only 16 countries. The Law Ministry's Department of Company Affairs has mooted a proposal that a fifth of all Boards of Directors must be women. The move is intended to influence policy decisions in terms of moderation and the overall welfare of labour as well as the elimination of gender biases in offices.

The age of Information and Communications Technology has already started but women are still very much in minority among Internet users. In the International Year of Women Empowerment let an effort be made to reduce the imbalance in the ownership, control and regulation of these facilities so that women use them in a creative way:

- e-inclusion, to overcome the constraints of seclusion;
- e-campaigns, to mobilise-on-line for women's human rights and other objectives;
- e-commerce, to reach new markets;
- E-consultations, to get women's views made known.

The challenge is huge. One is reminded of Robert Frost's famous words, "And miles to go before I sleep".

# 18

# Women Empowerment

*Subhash C. Arora*

Women are an integral part of a society. They play an important role in determining the destiny of a nation. Therefore, due recognition to them in the society and their greater involvement in socio-economic and political affairs becomes all the more important. However, history reveals that women have not been given their due status in the society.

Socially, women are a harassed and ignored lot. They have been and still are the victim of various social taboos particularly in developing countries like India. Though they enjoy equality but this equality is more in legal terms than in reality. It is amazing that in a country like India where the highest object of worship is in the feminine form, crime against women should have assumed such alarming proportions. As per the information released by the Crime Record Bureau of the Home Ministry, there is a crime against the fair sex committed every six minutes.[1] Most of these cases are reported from rural areas where the literacy level is low and the women are unaware of their rights. According to the 1991 Census, Women's Literacy was reported at 39.62 per cent as against men's at 63.86.

To get a glimpse of their economic position, we cannot do better than quoting the U.N. Report on Women:

> The scales of world's equality are out of balance. The side

> marked women is weighted down with responsibility, while the side marked 'men' rides high with power. Tilting first under rules that say women must do all domestic work, the scales are tipped further by men's greater opportunities to earn wages. Advantage builds on advantage until today they are tilted so steeply that almost all of the world's wealth is on men's side, while most of the work is on women's.

This observation of the U.N. aptly applies in the case of India as the reconstruction of economy in the past decades has marginalised them within the workforce. Almost 90 per cent of women in employment are marginal workers and thus outside the purview of progressive labour laws. In the organised sector, of the 26.8 million employed, the number of women is just 3.8 million. Of these 2.4 million or 62 per cent are in the public sector and only 1.4 million in the private sector.[2]

Regarding their participation in political process the situation is no better. Though they constitute almost half of the world's population yet the number of those holding elected offices is very negligible. It is clear from the fact that in 1980 women made up just over 10 per cent of world's parliamentarians and less than 4 per cent of national cabinets. In 1993, just 6 nations had women as heads of government.[3] In the case of India, the situation is still worse. Despite the fact that about 48 per cent of India's population comprises of women and about 70 per cent of them are voters,[4] their representation in legislative bodies over the years have been very poor. Data reveal (see Table 1) that percentage of woman MPs has never touched the double figure mark in the Lok Sabha. In case of state legislatures the situation is all the more dismal as is clear from the fact that the average women's representation in them is just 4 per cent[5] (for detailed pattern of statewise changes in percentage of women representation from 1952 to 1997, see Table 2).

Further, a glance at data (see Table 3) regarding woman contestants for Lok Sabha elections held since 1952 show a broad picture of the trends of women's participation in national politics. The Table reveals that the average number of women contestant per seat, share of women among total contestants and their success ratio stand at 0.30, 3.7 per cent and 25.1 per cent respectively. It is evident that few women got elected because

**TABLE 1: Women's Representation in Lok Sabha 1952-1999**

| Year | Lok Sabha | | |
|---|---|---|---|
| | Seats | Women MPs | % of women MPs |
| 1952 | 499 | 22 | 4.4 |
| 1957 | 500 | 27 | 5.4 |
| 1962 | 503 | 34 | 6.8 |
| 1967 | 523 | 31 | 5.9 |
| 1971 | 521 | 22 | 4.2 |
| 1977 | 544 | 19 | 3.4 |
| 1980 | 544 | 28 | 7.9 |
| 1984 | 544 | 44 | 8.1 |
| 1989 | 517 | 27 | 5.3 |
| 1991 | 544 | 39 | 7.2 |
| 1996 | 543 | 39 | 7.2 |
| 1998 | 543 | 43 | 7.9 |
| 1999 | 543 | 37 | 6.8 |
| Average | 528 | 31.5 | 6.19 |

few women contested. Though the number of women contesting elections is going up steadily over the years but the increase is not very appreciable keeping in view the fact that there has been overall increase in the number of candidates both men and women. It is worth mentioning that the success ratio has steadily fallen over the years and ultimately nose-dived from 43.1 per cent in 1952 to just 6.8 per cent in 1999 elections.

From the preceding discussion, it is evident that the socio-economic and political position of women in India has been very deplorable. Keeping in view this painful reality there has been widespread feeling among the scholars, political leaders and social reformers to empower women politically to improve their lot. This feeling ultimately led to the passage of 73rd and 74th Constitutional Amendments in 1992, which provided one-third reservation to women in panchayati raj bodies and municipalities. These amendments were taken as a good beginning towards women empowerment. This step, thus, prompted the then United Front Government headed by H.D. Devagowda in 1996 to propose the 81st Amendment to the Constitution wherein women were to be given one-third reservation in Parliament and state

**TABLE 2: Women's Representation in State Legislatures 1952-1997 (% of women MLAs)**

| State | 1952** | 1957 | 1960-65 | 1967-69 | 1970-75 | 1977-78 | 1979-83 | 1984-88 | 1989-92 | 1993-97 | State Avg. |
|---|---|---|---|---|---|---|---|---|---|---|---|
| Andhra Pradesh | 2.9 | 3.7 | 3.3 | 3.8 | 9.1 | 3.4 | 4.1 | 3.4 | 3.7 | 2.7 | 4.0 |
| Arunachal Pradesh | – | – | – | – | – | 0.0 | 3.3 | 6.7 | 3.3 | 3.3 | 3.3 |
| Assam | 0.5 | 4.6 | 3.8 | 4.0 | 7.0 | 0.8 | 0.8 | 4.0 | 4.0 | 4.8 | 3.2 |
| Bihar | 3.6 | 9.4 | 7.9 | 2.2* | 3.8 | 4.0 | 3.7 | 4.6 | 2.8 | 3.4 | 4.3 |
| Goa | – | – | – | 6.7 | 3.3 | 3.3 | 0.0# | 0.0 | 5.0 | 10.0 | 4.3 |
| Gujrat | – | – | 8.4 | 4.8 | 3.2 | NE | 2.7 | 8.8 | 2.2 | 1.1 | 4.2 |
| Haryana | – | – | – | 7.4* | 6.2 | 4.4 | 7.8 | 5.6 | 6.7 | 4.4 | 6.2 |
| Himachal Pradesh | 0.0 | – | – | 0.0 | 5.9 | 1.5 | 4.4 | 4.4 | 5.9 | 4.4 | 3.6 |
| Jammmu & Kashmir | – | NE | 0.0 | 0.0 | 5.3 | 1.3 | 0.0 | 1.3 | NE | 2.3 | 1.5 |
| Karnataka | 2.0 | 8.7 | 8.7 | 3.2 | 5.1 | 4.0 | 0.9 | 3.6 | 4.5 | 3.1 | 4.5 |
| Kerala | 0.0 | 4.8 | 3.9* | 0.8 | 1.5 | 0.7 | 3.2 | 5.7 | 5.7 | 9.3 | 3.6 |
| Madhya Pradesh | 2.1 | 10.8 | 4.9 | 3.4 | 5.4 | 3.1 | 5.0 | 0.7 | 3.4 | 3.8 | 5.1 |
| Maharashtra | 1.9 | 6.3 | 4.9 | 3.3 | 9.3 | 2.8 | 6.6 | 5.6 | 2.1 | 3.8 | 4.7 |
| Manipur | – | NE | NE | 0.0 | 0.0* | NE | 0.0 | 0.0 | 1.7 | 0.0 | 0.3 |
| Meghalaya | – | – | – | – | 1.7 | 1.7 | 0.0 | 3.3 | NE | 1.7 | 1.7 |
| Mizoram | – | – | – | – | 0.0 | 3.3 | 3.3 | 2.5 | 0.0 | 0.0 | 1.4 |
| Nagaland | – | – | 0.0 | 0.0 | NE | 0.0 | 0.0 | 1.7 | 0.0 | 0.0 | 0.5 |
| Orissa | 9.6 | 3.6 | 1.4 | 3.6 | 1.4* | 4.8 | 3.4 | 6.1 | 4.8 | 5.4 | 4.0 |
| Punjab | 2.2 | 5.8 | 5.2 | 1.0* | 5.8 | 2.6 | 5.1 | 3.4 | 5.1 | 6.0 | 4.0 |
| Rajasthan | 0.0 | 5.1 | 4.5 | 3.3 | 7.1 | 4.0 | 5.0 | 8.0 | 5.5 | 4.5 | 4.8 |
| Sikkim | – | – | – | – | – | – | 0.0 | 0.0 | 6.3 | 3.1 | 2.3 |
| Tamil Nadu | 0.3 | 5.9 | 3.9 | 1.7 | 2.1 | 0.9 | 2.1 | 3.4 | 9.0 | 3.8 | 3.6 |

| | | | | | | | | | | | |
|---|---|---|---|---|---|---|---|---|---|---|---|
| Tripura | – | NE | NE | 0.0 | 3.3 | 1.7 | 6.7 | 3.3 | NE | 1.7 | 3.0 |
| Uttar Pradesh | 1.2 | 5.8 | 4.4 | 2.8* | 5.9 | 2.6 | 5.6 | 7.3 | 3.3* | 4.0* | 4.1 |
| West Bengal | 0.8 | 3.6 | 4.8 | 2.9* | 1.6* | 1.4 | 2.4 | 4.4 | 7.1 | 6.8 | 3.4 |
| Delhi | 4.2 | – | NE | NE | 7.1 | 7.1 | 7.1 | NE | NE | 4.3 | 5.9 |
| Pondicherry | – | – | 6.7 | 3.3 | 0.0 | 0.0 | 3.3 | 3.3 | 1.7 | 3.3 | 2.6 |
| Period Average | 1.8 | 6.3 | 4.9 | 2.9 | 4.4 | 2.8 | 3.8 | 5.3 | 4.5 | 4.0 | 4.0 |

Notes: Table entry stands for % of women MLAs elected to state legislatures in the relevant elections.
NE: No elections held in that year/period.
#States did not exist.
*Two elections held during this period. The figures given here is an average of the two.
**In 1952 the Election Commission did not recognise women as a separate category. The figures given here are based on name recognition and hence liable to under reporting of women representatives.

**TABLE 3: Women Contestants in Lok Sabha Elections 1952-1999**

| Year | Contestants per seat | Share among contestants (%) | Success ratio (%) |
|---|---|---|---|
| 1952 | 0.10 | 2.7 | 43.1 |
| 1957 | 0.14 | 4.4 | 38.6 |
| 1962 | 0.14 | 3.4 | 50.0 |
| 1967 | 0.13 | 2.8 | 47.0 |
| 1971 | 0.17 | 3.1 | 25.6 |
| 1977 | 0.13 | 2.9 | 27.1 |
| 1980 | 0.26 | 3.1 | 19.7 |
| 1984 | 0.29 | 2.9 | 27.7 |
| 1989 | 0.37 | 3.1 | 14.3 |
| 1991 | 0.60 | 3.7 | 12.0 |
| 1996 | 0.90 | 3.4 | 7.4 |
| 1998 | 0.49 | 5.6 | 7.9 |
| 1999 | 0.64 | 6..6 | 6.8 |
| Average | 0.30 | 3.7 | 25.1 |

Note for Table 3, 4, 5:

$$\text{Contestants per seat} = \frac{\text{number of women contestants}}{\text{total number of seats.}}$$

$$\text{Share among candidates} = \frac{\text{number of women contestants}}{\text{number of all contestants}} \times 100$$

$$\text{Success ratio} = \frac{\text{number of women elected}}{\text{number of women contestants}} \times 100$$

legislative assemblies on the pattern of 73rd and 74th Amendments.[6] The Amendment Bill provided that,

> not less than one-third (including the number of seats reserved for women belonging to SC and ST) of the total number of seats to be filled by direct election to the House of People in a state or union territory shall be reserved for women and such seats may be allotted by rotation to different constituencies in that state or union territory.

Likewise, the Bill provided one-third reservation for women in state legislative assembly. It was laid down that

> not less than one-third (including the number of seats reserved for women belonging to the SC and ST) of the

total number of seats to be filled by direct election in the legislative assembly in every state shall be reserved for women and such seats may be allotted by rotation to different constituencies in that state.[7]

The proposed Amendment Bill was introduced in the Lok Sabha in September, 1996. During the course of debate, the Bill did not find favour even with some of the MPs from United Front coalition, leaving aside the opposition. The bone of contention was the special quota for OBC women from the 33 per cent and a call for some percentage of reservation in Upper House. Consequently, the Bill was referred to the Joint Select Committee.[8] The Committee recommended as follows:

1. the words "not less than one-third" occurring in Bill are vague and liable to be interpreted differently and confer power to make reservation which may far exceed the limit of one-third. The Committee is, therefore, of the opinion that these words should be substituted by "as nearly as may be one-third".
2. the Bill should be amended so as to provide that one of the members nominated from the Anglo-Indian Community shall be a woman by rotation;
3. there should also be reservation of seats for women in Rajya Sabha and the legislative councils. The Committee, therefore, recommended that the Government should work out the modalities for this purpose and bring out suitable legislation in this regard at the appropriate time; and
4. The Bill, as amended, be passed without any delay.

Though the Joint Select Committee cleared the Bill in 1996 itself, several OBC members of the Committee expressed reservation to the Bill saying it would jeopardise the entry of OBCs into the legislature of the country.

Practically all the political parties except the Left seemed to view the Bill with hostility, the majority view was to split up the 33 per cent quota among all castes possible besides minorities. Consequently, the Bill went into hibernation. Meanwhile, a Committee on the Empowerment of Women was set up by the then Government. But before the Committee could start functioning, the government lost the confidence of the House, parliament was dissolved and fresh elections were declared in February, 1998 for the 12th Lok Sabha. In these elections, almost all the political parties in their respective election manifestoes blared loudly on women upliftment by promising to give one-third reservation to them but factual position was horrifying which speaks of hypocracy that has struck firm roots in Indian politics over the past 50 years.

The 1998 elections saw a total of 4756 candidates in the fray with only 267 women. Of the total 267 woman contestants, there were 115 party nominees with Congress heading the list with 39 followed by 30 of B.J.P. The number of woman nominees of other parties were J.D. 11, M.C.P. and S.P. 8 each, C.P.I. 6, T.D.P., R.J.P., S.P. (Samta Party) 3 each and SAD, AIADMK, H.L.D. (R), T.C. one each.[9]

Further, it is worth mentioning that out of 267 female contestants, just 43 found their way to the Lok Sabha which is 7.9 per cent only.[10] Almost the same story was repeated in the Elections for the 13th Lok Sabha held in 1999. Of the total 5231 contestants the number of women nominees was 347,[11] i.e. 6.6 per cent. Out of total 1298 candidates fielded by various political parties, the number of woman contestant was just 105 which comes to 8.09 per cent only. As regards the party-wise number of woman nominees, the Congress topped the list with 51 followed by B.J.P. 26, B.S.P 10, J.D. (S) 6, C.P.M. 5, C.P.I. 4 and J.D. 3.

It may not be out of place to mention that out of the 347 woman contestants who tried their luck in these elections only 37 were successful.[12] Clearly, even this time the position with regard to women representation in Lok Sabha was in no way better if compared with the earlier elections. This makes us to conclude that adequate representations to women in legislative bodies is direly needed in order to give them opportunity in the decision-making process.

The present BJP led N.D.A. Government has given top priority to the issue of women reservation in its National Agenda. It has given the word that the Bill will be passed in the Parliament as the first step. However, when the Bill was slated to be introduced in the Lok Sabha on July 11, 1998 serious roadblocks were witnessed, so much so that the Bill was snatched from the hands of the concerned Minister and the copy of the same was removed from the table of the Speaker.

Later on, though the Bill was introduced in the Parliament in December 1998, it failed to make any headway till date. Even in its Winter Session (2000) the determined section of the opposition, stalled its consideration. Members belonging to S.P., R.J.P. and B.S.P. demanded the withdrawal of the Bill and pressed for the introduction of sub-quota within the proposed legislation for the backward classes, scheduled castes/tribes and minorities. As against this, another section of opposition consisting of the Congress and the Left parties insisted that the Bill be taken up in its present form.[13] The Government too has rejected the demand for sub-quota and made it clear that the legislation would be taken up in its present form in the current Budget Session of Parliament.[14]

Thus the bone of contention regarding women's representation in legislative bodies appears to be the provision of sub-quota within quota. But it is not as simple as it appears to be. The real cause is deep-rooted in the minds of the male members as almost everyone of them suffers from fear psychosis that his constituency may not be reserved for a woman. Clearly both apparent and deep-rooted causes have stalled the clearance of the Bill so far.

However, in view of the compulsions of political correctness to provide adequate representation to women and to get rid of this morass, the N.D.A. Government, of late, toed with the Election Commission's proposal which implies shifting the onus of providing a minimum of 33 per cent seats to women on political parties.[15] As per the proposal it would be mandatory for a political party to provide a minimum of 33 per cent tickets to women candidates in the Parliament and assembly elections.

There is almost a consensus among most of the ruling and opposition members that Election Commission's formula is an improvement upon the proposed Bill. However, in our considered opinion, this formula is not an unmixed blessing as its applicability would open up a pandora box of newer and different type of problems. As per the spirit of the formula, providing representation to women would be the responsibility of a political party, it would be far more difficult for the party managers to strike a balance between this compulsion of political correctness and practical consideration of winning a seat. In such situation, it would be highly difficult, if not impossible for them to earmark the constituencies for women candidates as no male member of the party would cherish that his constituency is reserved for a woman. Certainly, it would lead to infighting within a party and promote indiscipline, factionalism and defections too. Above all, one should not overlook the factor of male chauvinism which has so far played a dubious role in the way of women empowerment.

The whole discussion lead one to observe that such a Bill or Formula whould hardly help the cause of women empowerment. What is required is that let the women awake and educate themselves, shed the social taboos, come forward to gain economic independence and organise themselves in a far better way to become a reckoning force to get their due.

## REFERENCES

1. Quoted from P.K. Palli, "Women Reservation Bill: Male chauvinism at its worst", *The Tribune*, Chandigarh, 15 January, 2000.
2. *Ibid.*
3. *U.N. Human Development Report*, 1993, Oxford University Press, p. 29.
4. M. Satyawati Raj Gopal, "Nari Shakti in Polls, Waiting to Exhale", *The Tribune*, Chandigarh, 31 January, 1998.
5. Chandrika Parmar, CSDS Data unit fact-file 1952-1997: *Seminar*, 457 September, 1997, p. 51.
6. Empowering Women: *Seminar*, 457, Sept., 1997, p. 56.
7. *Ibid.*
8. Towards Equality, Report of the Committee on the Status of Women in India, *Seminar*, 457, 1997, p. 58.
9. *Nav Bharat Times*, New Delhi, 13 March, 1998.
10. *Ibid.*
11. *The Tribune*, Chandigarh, 2 September, 1999.
12. Office of the Election Commission.
13. *The Tribune*, Chandigarh, 24 December, 2000.
14. *Ibid.*, 9 March, 2001.
15. *Ibid.*, 21 December, 2000.

# 19

# Women's Position and the Constitution

*S.C. Sharma*

Legislators, priests, philosophers, writers and scientists have striven to show that the subordinate position of woman is willed in heaven and advantageous on earth.

—*Simone de Beauvoir*

## The Position of Women

The question with respect to the position of women is ancient one and relates to the evaluation of man and society. To most of thinkers, philosophers and writers, woman is a symbol of sex as the man decrees her in that sense, thus she is called "the sex", by which is meant that she appears essentially to the male as a sexual being. For him she is sex-absolute sex, nothing less than that. In a society, dominated by man—He is the subject, i.e., he is the absolute where as she is the other. The otherness in ancient Greek philosophy, is considerd the same thing as negation, therefore, Evil. Thus, the religion and codes of law treat woman with hostility. Furthermore, the Roman code puts her under guardianship and asserts her "imbelicity".

The Muslim law treats woman with utter scorn and this is reflected by what can be termed as a contractual relations between man and woman. The *Sariat* law postulates, "Man have authority over woman because *Allah* has made the one superior to the other and because they spend their wealth to maintain them. Good women are obedient so for those whom you fear disobedient admonish them and send them beds and beat them". Marriage in Muslim law is based on contract theory.

Manu, the originator of Hindu law sees women as a vile thing who should be held in slavery.

### Women in Primitive Society

What was the position of women in primitive society? No one has been able to project the forthright answer of this crucial question because the historians have not been able to tap the traces of the happenings and operations during that period. Due to the frail physical position, she carried the burdens in the shape of the bondage of reproduction which was a terrible handicap in their dealings with the society. Three factors, i.e., menstruation, pregnancy and child birth, have reduced their capacity to work and at times made them fully depended upon men for protection and food. Thus, women's subordination began with the development of society. It is the work of a man which is appreciated in compsrison to a woman's thus further drawing a line of demarcation betweeen the two.

Despite all this, there have been a host of woman in Ancient India both in early Vedic as well as later Vedic period, who, not only carved out a sacred and pivotal place for womanhood (or to be more respectfully the motherhood) but had shown greater wisdom and tolerance to guide the destiny of mankind as a whole thereby undoing the notion of submitting passively to the biologic fate.

### Historical Materialism and Woman

According to historical materialism, human being is not only an animal species, but a historical reality. In their opinion woman could not be treated simply as a sexual organism, their position has also been determined by techniques, attainment and economic organisation. This view has been supported by Engels who has retraced the history of woman according to this perspective. He explains that in the stone age, when land was common to everyone in the clan, the rudimentary character of the spade and hoe limited the possibilities of agriculture, so that woman's strength was adequate for gardening. Thus the two sexes constituted two classes in the primitive type of division of labour and there appears to be equality between these classes. But with the passage of time, the man appeared to have dominated the scene, called/designated as the proprietor of woman. This movement of males can be termed as "the greatest historical defeat of the feminine sex". It upsets the earlier division of labour. Thus the maternal authority gave into paternal authority thereby began the subjugation of woman.

The categorisation of woman as "other", in later stages, tended to assume the reciprocal relation between the two sexes. Woman was seen as Earth, Mother or Goddess, but not as fellow creative in man's eyes. It was "beyond" the human realm that her power was affirmed. Though there have been exception to this notion as during *Medieval period* some women have adorned the thrones of mighty empires. Even then the society, be it English or Indian remained unchanged as women became the subject or symbol of less dignity and prey to males. In fact, the crux is that the two sexes have never shared the world equally.

In India, the position of women by virtue of their position being in disadvantageous position took to a worse turn under the Muslim rule as being a second rate subject/citizen. This subcontinent has seen those days when women were treated like slaves. This must have been due to the fact that from the beginning of humanity, men's biological advantage has enabled them to confirm their status as sole and sovereign subjects. Again the denial of rights to woman in society including her place and status has always been assigned by men and at no time, has she ever imposed her own law. This notion might be on the analogy of land's ownership, which predominantly that of man so man claimed also ownership of woman—a sad but well accepted notion of all. To fortify this notion further, we have seen and read history which speaks in volumes of *orthodox* customs like, *sati pratha*, child marriages, female infanticide, etc. Rapes have also been committed by mighty on helpless females (minor as well as major woman) thereby negativating the correct and legal evaluation of society. Might be on the consideration that they are living sub-human existence. The gender inequality have hampered their development.

Many historians have defined the working class "de facto" as working men. Occupations, skills, wages and the labour process itself, have been and still are discussed as if social productions were exclusive made prerogative of men.

With the developing trends in society and emergence of industries all around the world, the ideal womanhood emerged out of this revolutionary ideology. The role of woman as wife and mother was centralised and as a consequence it was expected from them to guard all the religious and socio-cultural values and thus women's wage work was supposed to be in harmony with the home, the family and domesticity. Thus, "home" became their primary occupation even if they take a secondary salaried job outside the home.

On this drastic change, Lenin has to comment, To quote him:

> Housework is most unproductive, the most barbarous and the most arduous work, a woman can do. It is exceptionally petty and does not include anything that would in anyway promote the development of the women.

But it cannot be forgotten that the house-work is essentially to sustain our social and economic structure, where the family is the basic unit of production. It is highly labour intensive yet it is unpaid. From this, flow the idea that the economic interdependence on men should be lessoned so that the woman can think of becoming the part of decision-making process. This idea has come in from various stages and ongoing process of the development of society through evolution stages stretching from one decade to another and so on from one century to other. Thus the patterns of employment of woman stood changed from the traditional to capitalist era with the advancement/development of industries which gave rise to the labour unions hence coming into force the labour laws for various types of labourers involving men and women notwithstanding the discrimination among men and women. (Attempts have been made in recent years for removing such discrimination). In certain matters, the women were considered as reserve army of labour. This is because of the fact that woman has been considered as an easy source of cheap labour and being low paid by making out a difference between skilled and unskilled labour which appears to be one of the main features of women's employment. For part-time work today, the statistics show improvements in women's economic participation. Although female labour is increasing, but they are getting jobs as part-timers. It is worthwhile to mention here that the condition of woman workers of India is much worse than that of the Western woman. Industrialisation in India began to take roots by 1850. As a result, the jute, cotton and textile industries come into existence and expanded. Women constituted a major chunk of the labour force in these industries right from their inceptions. Even in new industries whether small or big, the working conditions of the women workers are depressingly inhuman. The worldwide economic recession have proved fatal for female workers. Firstly and fastely, the women workers were being victimised. Gender biases are more acute in Industries settings. The socio-cultural prescriptions create hurdles in women's educational achievements. With inadequate qualifications women face difficulty in competing with the men in the labour market. Thus, they settle for any work that fetches remuneration. In rural India, where agriculture is the central source of livelihood, the subsistence production of women become an essential requirement. As agriculture do not provide round the year employment, the burden of family survival falls on the shoulders of the women folks. Such poor woman burn their energy in handicrafts, stitching, embroidery of saries and dresses, etc., but the money in return is too less to buy even a square meal of one person.

The relationship between women and men has become subject to men's use of their position in the political, legal, academic and economic institutions. Like these important institutions, history is also male dominated since it recorded only what men did or achieved (with exception of some elite woman who have excelled themselves in the art of administration like queen Victoria, etc.). Thus gender biases are also reflected in historical experiences too up to the stage of the rise in labour and before the dawn of twentieth century.

### Women in Twentieth Century

The dawn of twentieth century has brought many eventful

changes across the world. In India, with everybody was involving in the freedom struggle to say good-bye to the British empire, the role played by womenfolk could not be minimised. The women freedom fighters were so much involved in the freedom struggle that they outclassed male freedom fighters, viz., the role of "BA" (Kasturba Gandhi) who not only played a valiant role but had inspired the "Father of Nation". Similarly Kamla Nehru, even from her deathbed inspired Pandit Jawaharlal Nehru whereas other illustrious daughter Smt. Indira Gandhi as a weak child played her role by organizing *Banar Sena*. The names of personalities like Sarojini Naidu, Aruna Asaf Ali, Mrinal Gore, Vijaylaxmi Pandit could not be forgotten as these women had not only fought the British but had also done their best to remove the unnecessary bondage of rigid customs with their becoming part and parcel of law building process. By seeing the pros and cons of India being multi-languages, multi-religion, castes, races and multi-customs society, the laws framed here are not sufficient to improve the lots of women. To bring about social change thereby enhancing the status of women, more concrete steps are required to be there to abridge the gap among the citizens of India which should be in complete harmony with the preamble to the Constitution in general and further in complete uniformity with the Fundamental Rights and Directive Principles of state policy. The Constitution of India as it stands today is the result of the experience and noble thoughts of the founding fathers of the Constitution a long way process itself.

While elaborating the status of women, the first Prime Minister of India Late Sh. Jawaharlal Nehru has highlighted the position of woman dating back to 1928. To quote him:

> One could judge the degree of civilisation of a country by the social and political position of women.

He has further added that the "building of India as a nation will also be judged by the position of Indian women". He was the firm believer of the high status of Indian women, i.e., at par with men. This plea of the "Builder of modern India" was supported by Mahatma Gandhi who professed for equality between daughters and sons. He wrote,

> I am uncompromising in the matter of women's rights. In my opinion, she should labour under no legal disability not suffered by man. I should treat the daughters and sons on a footing of equality.

Further this clearily reflects the deep concern for women's upliftment in the minds and hearts of the two nation-builders which echoed in Karachi resolution on Fundamental Rights and Duties which were later on incorporated in the Constitution of India. It was, at that time propounded that:

(a) All citizens are equal before the law, irrespective of religion, caste, creed or sex;
(b) No disability attaches to any citizen by reason of his or her religion, caste, creed or sex in regard to public employment, office or power or honour in the experience of any trade or calling.

It was, thus inevitable that free India would made these duties and fundamental rights an integral part of its Constitution. The social domination of women by men was pointed out by Pandit Jawaharlal Nehru prior to Independence when he stated,

> Our civilization, our customs, our laws, have all been made by man and he has taken good care to keep himself in a superior position and to treat woman as a chattel and a plaything to be exploited for his own advantage and amusement.

So in the Constitution, it has been provided that states should look after the rights of women and children and such special provisions should be made which may not be violative of the fundamental rights of equality.

To improve the lots of women workers, labour laws have special provisions. Further women specific laws, i.e., the Equal Remuneration Act, 1976, and Maternity Benefit Act, 1961 have been enacted and these are on the side of industrial workers whereas in respect of working women on government side, there are service rules and regulations for their benefit which are sufficient under the present circumstances. Whether these are purposeful or not? The answer to this is partly yes and partly no. Despite the various legal securities for women workers, the situation reflects lots of discrimination and exploitation. The National Commission of Self-Employment have echoed such opinion in its report in the year 1988. The planning process itself has its limitations as all the developmental plans, generally refer to men. Many developmental plans/schemes have been formulated and put in action to improve the conditions of woman whether working or not and for the purpose, massive programmes have been undertaken by the Rural Integrated Department of the Government of India and state governments for the upliftment of the conditions of women for their all-round development including that of literacy amongst women. This has been reflected in the Nairobi Forward Looking strategies for the advancement of women which had laid emphasis in the following words;

> What is now needed; the political will.
>
> The Strategy for the advancement of women seeks first and foremost to alter the current unequal conditions and structures that continue to define women as secondary person and give women's issue a low priority. Development should now move to another plane in which women's pivotal role in society is recognised and given its true value.

## Women and Constitution of India

The framing of the constitution for the people of India was a big exercise aimed at to accelerate the all-round development of the citizens of India. The word "Citizen" does include the woman as there is no distinction having been made in respect of sex. The framers/founding fathers of the Constitution have taken a note of the happenings around India while framing the constitution. It was in 1945 when the United Nations Organisation came into being which spell out its objectives by reaffirming faith:

(a) in the human rights;
(b) in the dignity and worth of the human beings; and
(c) in the equal rights of man and woman.

Thus, the United Nations have spoken of human rights and the dignity and worth of human beings. It has laid emphasis in the equal rights of men and women. These objectives have further been incorporated in the Universal Declaration of Human Rights in 1948 with no discrimination to either of the sex. In fact, no distinction have been made between men and women. The universal declaration of Human Rights 1948 envisages:

> All human beings are born free and equal in dignity and rights.

It *inter alia* postulates equality amongst the mankind. So while enacting/framing of the constitution the positions of women have been taken care in matters of employment without there being distinction in respect of religion, caste and creed.

The constitution of India can be judged from the preamble itself which is as under:

> We the people of India, having solemnly resolved to constitute India into a Sovereign Socialist Secular Democratic Republic and to secure to all its citizens:
>
> JUSTICE, social, economic and political;
> LIBERTY of thought, expression, belief, faith and worship;
> EQUALITY of status and of opportunity; and to promote among them all;
> FRATERNITY assuring the dignity of the individual and the unity and integrity of the Nation.

In real sense, Constitution of India presents a true picture of the Indian policy which speaks of India—a welfare state. Wherein equal legal rights have been given to all the Indian citizens.

To wipe out the discrimination, our Constitution provides:

***Right to Equality***

(i) Equality before law (Article 14).
(ii) Prohibition of discrimination on grounds of religion, race, caste, sex or place of birth (Article 15).

(iii) Equality of opportunity in matters of public employment. (Article 16).

***Right to Freedom***

(iv) Six freedoms (Article 19).
(v) Protection of life and personal liberty (Article 21).
(vi) Prohibition of traffic of human beings and forced labour (Article 23).

These rights are common to all citizens and no distinction have been made out.

Right to freedom of religion and in respect of other fundamental rights, specific guidelines following Apex Court's decisions have been provided highlighting the rights of the women *vis-a-vis* their status and positions in society.

Hon'ble Supreme Court and State's High Court's are competent to hear and try writs under Article 32 and Article 226/227 of the Constitution for the removal of hardships in matters of importance against bias thereby affording reasonable opportunities. In recent past, these courts used to hear matters under public interest litigation in order to safeguard the fundamental rights (basic rights) as the Supreme Court is the ultimate guardian of fundamental rights.

In order to protect the interests of the weaker sections of the society which include the conditions to ameliorate the lots of women, the Constitution of India has provided a set of certain principles to be followed by the State, both in the matter of administration as well as in making the laws. They embody the objects of the state under the Constitution as it proclaims India as a Sovereign Socialist Secular Democratic Republic which clearly makes India a welfare state. As such most of the directives aim at the establishment of the economic and social democracy which is pledged for, in the preamble.

Further the protection, envisaged under Directive Principles of State Policy for women are as under:

(i) State to secure a social order for the promotion of the welfare of the people (Article 38).
(ii) Equal justice and free legal aid (Article 29A).

(iii) Organisation of village Panchayats (Article 40).

(New laws have been enacted thereby reserving 33 per cent seats to women, i.e., sphere of the participation of women in day-to-day working of Panachayats, Zila Parishads and other local bodies increased so that they could also be a part and parcel of policy formulation at grass-root level but due to political drudgery, the reservation of seats, i.e., 33 per cent of the seats in Legislators is a question, the solution/answer is required at this stage by making suitable amendment in the Constitution to meet the aspirations of women).

(iv) Right to work, to education, and to the public assistance in certain cases (Article 41).
(v) Provision for just and human conditions of work and maternity relief (Article 42).
(vi) Living wages, etc., for worker (Article 43) still require special attention of the planners and government to eradicate the prevalent discrimination.
(vii) Uniform civil code for the citizens (Article 44).

It is essentially required so as to put an end to different civil codes which are in existence separately for Hindus, Muslims and citizens of other religions.Though the framers of the Constitution has vigorously spoke about uniform civil code but despite 51 years of coming into force of the Constitution, the question remained unanswered. In one of the recent judgements, the Hon'ble Supreme Court has ruled/mandated that the mother can sell the share of a minor for his/her benefit which must go a long way towards equality between men and women.

(viii) Provision for free and compulsory education for children (Article 45). The Government of India as well as nearly all the state governments have made provisions for free education up to the levels of the degree courses.
(ix) Duty of the state to raise the level of nutrition and the standard of living and to improve public health (Article 47).

Women were considered as a symbol of innocence, purity and incarnation of the Goddess of power. This belief has been originated from Vedic period but for the Adivasis, illiterates and in other tribal areas, the women have been considered as a prey to men. Such a notion, when we have placed our steps in twenty-first century, has to be discarded and for this purpose efforts should be undertaken on war footings to improve the lots of the women thereby dismantling this unequal barrier prevailing in our society through bold initiatives and firm decisions to achieve the objectives enshrined in the Constitution.

Laws and regulations have been framed to safeguard the women from the powerful in the society. Even the pronouncement made by the highest court, i.e., Supreme Court makes the position of women as embodiment of innocence and further in sexual crimes, the Hon'ble Apex Court, in numerous decisions have handed down guidelines to the judges of lower courts, public prosecutors and lawyers in respect of the conduct of trials where the victim is female to observe certain norms, i.e., holding of trial in camera, names of the prosecutrix should not be disclosed, defence should not be allowed to put questions which are irrelevant and minute details of the crime to be avoided so that the prosecutrix could feel hereself at home while being questioned in cross-examination during trial.

## Social Change is Required to Meet the Challenge

Having regard to the position of women and the anxiety of all who are working to formulate plans and policies, the administrators, writers, philosophers and social workers have been pondering over this crucial question keeping in view the recent World Bank Annual Report in which it has been stated very fairly in regard to the poverty and under-development of India. The World Bank in its annual report has stated:

> Only way to lift India from poverty and under development is by enhancing the status of women by educating them.

The convention on elimination of all forms of discrimination against women which has come into force in the year 1981 calls for radical reforms in this directions. This is because, India being a party to the convention obliges it to adopt temporary special measures aimed at accelerating equality between men and women. Needless to add here as the constitutional provisions have clearly envisaged the goals and objectives set out in the Preamble itself.

No doubt, there is discrimination against women. The discrimination tantamount to the violation of the principles of equality of rights and respect of human dignity and as such this has to be removed by taking cogent and legal steps by making suitable laws within the four walls of the constitutional provisions to achieve social justice as it include the gender justice also.

We, the Indian have to remember the words of Gurudev Rabindra Nath Tagore who, in his own right was one of the illustrious devoted son amongst the greatest sons of India had remarked about the reality, i.e., the status of women:

> Do not keep me as a pedestal to be worshipped,
> nor under your feet to be trampled,
> but keep me at your side to share,
> And to dare in facing this world.
>
> —Tagore in *Chitra*

Let the noble thought of the illustrious son of this great country be put in practice by all citizens to make India strong, literate and vibrant in the comity of nations in the new millennium.

# 20

# Empowerment of Women

*S.S. Dhaliwal*

The problem and challenges facing humanity are global but occur and have to be dealt with at the local level. Women have the equal right to freedom from poverty, discrimination, environmental degradation and insecurity. To fight these problems and to meet the challenges of sustainable human development, it is crucial that women be empowered and involved in local government as decision-makers, planners and managers.

*—International Union of Local Authorities (IULA)*

## Status of Women

"That society would be highly developed and prosperous where women have their rightful place" expounds Manu. The status of women varies enormously from one part of the world to another. However, nowhere to do women enjoy equal status with men. But in the developing countries like Africa, the Middle East, Asia and Latin America, the status of women is so low as cannot be imagined by women in the developed countries.

The woman is the pivot around which the family, the society and humanity itself revolves. It is well said that the hands that rock the cradle rules the world. Women play a significant role in the development of their offspring. Truly, if a man is educated one person is educated but if the woman is educated, the whole family is educated.

Status is a relative term. In sociological expression, it denotes neither rank nor hierarchy but only position *vis-a-vis* others in terms of rights and obligations.[1] In the ultimate analysis, status is "the conjunction of positions a woman occupies ... as a worker, student, wife, mother ... the power and prestige attached to these positions and the rights and duties she is expected to exercise."[2]

Women's status can then be analysed in terms of their participation in decision-making, access to opportunities in education, training, employment and income.[3] In recent years, there has been an increasing recognition of the interface between women's ability to control their fertility and their exercise and enjoyment of other options in life.

In the ancient India women held a high place of respect in the society as mentioned in *Rigveda* and other scriptures.[4] Volumes can be written about the status of our women and their heroic deeds from the Vedic period to the modern times. But later on, because of social, political and economic changes, women lost their status and were relegated to the background. Many evil customs and traditions stepped in which enslaved the women and tied them to boundaries of the house. The untold miseries and sufferings of women of the nineteenth century awakened the conscience of mankind. Many reformers like Raja Rammohun Roy, Swami Dayanand, Justice Ranade, Mahatma Gandhi, and other championed the cause of the emancipation of women. The Constitution of India also prohibits any discrimination on grounds of sex.[5] Many laws have also been enacted by the Government of India to protect the rights of women.[6]

Jagmohan, former Minister of Urban Development and Poverty Alleviation, GOI, suggests the need of involving women in urban affairs affecting their lives. To quote him:

> As we know the problems and challenges facing humanity are global but occur and have to be dealt with at the local level. Women have the equal right to freedom from poverty, discrimination, environmental degradation and insecurity. To fight these problems and to meet the challenges of

> sustainable human development, it is crucial that women be empowered and involved in local government as decision-makers, planners and managers.[7]

Anna Kajumulo Tibaijuka, Executive Director (UNCHS), says:

> Where women are not involved in public decision-making, the quality of services deteriorates. It is time for change from the practice of leaving women to do only the dirty work. We are aware that women have been instrumental in the urban social movements that aim at improving urban poor neighbourhoods. They do this because they want to protect their families' health and create livable communities. These numerous women's initiatives must be recognised. This must be done, first, by involving them in governance structures. And second, by addressing the things they care about in urban policy, planning and management. Women and men have specific and different needs, in areas such as transport, public space use, the implementation of by-laws, and security. These must all be addressed.[8]

The 74th Amendment of the Indian Constitution in 1992, ushered in a new era in the democratic process of the nation as it not only provided constitutional status to municipal bodies but also provided an enabling environment for women to take direct part in the process of local self-government and brought women to the forefront and centre of city development.

International Union of Local Authorities has also asserted this point. To quote:

> The systematic integration of women arguments the democratic basis, the efficiency and the equality of the activities of local government. If local government is to meet the needs of both men and women, it must build on the experiences of both men and women, through an equal representation at all levels and in all fields of decision-making, covering the wide range of responsibilities of local governments.

The members of IULA, representing local governments worldwide, firmly believe that:

1. Democratic local self-government has a critical role to play in securing social, economic and political justice for all citizens of every community in the world and that all members of society, women and men, must be included in the governance process;
2. Women and men as citizens have equal human rights, duties and opportunities, as well as the equal right to exercise them. The right to vote, to be eligible for election and to hold public office at all levels are human rights that apply equally to women and men;
3. The problems and challenges facing humanity are global but occur and have to be dealt with at the local level. Women have the equal right to freedom from poverty, discrimination, environmental degradation and insecurity. To fight these prolems and to meet the challenges of sustainable human development, it is crucial that woman be empowered and involved in local government as decision-makers, planners and managers;
4. Local government is in a unique position to contribute to the global struggle for gender equality and can have a great impact on the status of women and the status of gender equality around the world, in its capacities as the level of governance closest to the citizens, as a service provider and as an employer;
5. The systematic integration of women augments the democratic basis, the efficiency and the quality of the activities of local government. If local government is to meet the needs of both women and men, it must build on the experiences of both women and men, through an equal representation at all levels and in all fields of decision-making, covering the wide range of responsibilities of local governments;
6. In orders to create sustainable, equal and democratic local governments, where women and men have equal access to decision-making, equal access to services and equal treatment in these services, the gender perspective must be mainstreamed into all areas of policy-making and management in local government.

Local government as a service provider and enabler of sound living conditions

7. Women have the right to equal access to the services of local governments, as well as the right to be treated equally in these services and to be able to influence the initiation, development, management and monitoring of services. The provision of services such as education, welfare governments, should aim to see women and men as equally responsible for matters related both to the family and to public life, and avoid perpetuating stereotypes of women and men;
8. Women have the equal right to sound environment living conditions, housing, water distribution and sanitation facilities, as well as to affordable public transportation. Women's needs and living conditions must be made visible and taken into account at all times in planning;
9. Women have the right to equal access to the territory and geographical space of local governments, ranging from the right to own land, to the right to move freely and without fear in public spaces and on public transport;
10. Local governments has a role to play in ensuring the reproductive rights of women and the rights of women to freedom from domestic violence and other forms of physical, psychological and sexual violence and abuse;

Local governments as an employer and in a strategic position of influence local society

11. Women have the equal right to employment in local government and equality in recruitment procedures. As employees in local government women and men have the right to equal pay, equal access to benefits, promotion and training, as well as the right to equal working conditions and treatment in the evaluation of their work;
12. Women's often heavy workload of paid and unpaid work is a barrier to their ability to take part in decision-making. Local government has an important role to play in providing affordable, professional and safe care services for children, older people and people with disabilities, be that directly or in partnership with the private or the voluntary sectors, and in promoting the sharing of household tasks by women and men on an equal basis. Men have the equal

right and responsibility to care for their children and relatives and should be encouraged to do so;[9]

Dr. (Smt.) Kalawati Tripathi, President, AIWE also emphasised that:

> Women, as disadvantaged sector with a low economic and social status need to be empowered and gender equality promoted. The NGOs have highlighted this during various national and international conference. The NGOs have a very important role to play in empowering women and participating in the governance of the growing cities. NGOs partnership with the administrative, official, regional and municipal institutions will help to surmount the challenges and improve the quality of urban living. We have realised that programmes of human settlements must ensure greater participation of women in decision-making at the planning, implementation and the management level.[10]

**International Initiatives**

Understanding the need to participation and empowerment of women at the level of local self-government, let us first enumerate the important initiatives taken by international institutions.

The issue of empowerment of women came to the forefront with the Convention on the Political Rights of Women (1952) and the International Covenant on Civil and Political Rights (1966), aimed at providing women equal opportunity in the public life. The declaration of 1975 as the International Women's Year was an important point. The Nairobi Conference in 1985 advocated the "forward looking strategies for the advancement of women's".

The 1992 UN Conference on Environment and Development at Rio de Janeiro, the Habitat II Conference at Istanbul in 1996, and OECD Roundtable Conference held in 1996 highlighted the major actions for improving the contribution of women to urban policies:

- Enhance the theme of "citizenship" to recognise women's right to participate fully in all spheres of activity in cities.

- Improve the representation and participation of women, especially of elected officials, at all levels of public life, in decision-making bodies which affect urban policies, and in urban planning and related professions.
- Develop and introduce the use of time series gender-sensitive indicators and targets for use in the formulation of urban policies, and for monitoring and improving the representation of women in public life and in decision-making bodies.
- Establish and seek appropriate financing for networks at the local, regional, national and international level: to develop a policy research agenda; to improve the formulation of urban policy issues and responses from the viewpoint of women; to organise links between experts and grassroot movements, between different countries and regions, and between different levels of political representation.
- Make better known, via the media and new information technologies, innovations in urban policy desired by women relating to environmental and social issues to key urban policy sectors such as transport, housing and economic activity and The Fourth World Conference on Women in Beijing, China in 1995 and The Huairou Commission established as a follow-up had moved the grassroot women to the centre of international policy-making.

The "World-Wide Declaration of Women in Local Government" by the International Union of Local Authorities in 1998, identified the local bodies as the most accessible and best suitable launching pad for the involvement of women in governance.

## Indian Initiative

Based upon the Indian constitution, which provides equal role to Indian women in development and partnership, the following were initiated:

(i) ***Setting up of National Commission for Women:*** In 1992 "The National Commission for Women" was set up as a national apex statutory level body to review the constitutional and legal safeguards for women; recommended remedial legislative measures; facilitate redressal of grievances and advise government on all policy matters affecting women.

The composition of the commission as laid down in the Act, provides for the appointment of a chairperson committed to the cause of women, five members who are nominated from amongst social scientists, experts in legislation, trade union movement, industrial management, administration, socio-economic development, and so on, and a member secretary.

To begin with, the Commission set up and organised its secretariat and established institutional linkages with government agencies, Members of Parliament, Non-Government Organisation and others concerned with women's issues. The Commission took several initiatives to discharge its statutory function.[11]

(ii) ***Blue Print of Action Points and National Plan of Action for Women.***

(iii) ***New Legislation to Promote Women Welfare:*** The Constitution of India not only grants equality to women but also empowers the State to adopt measures of positive discrimination in favour of women for neutralising the cumulative socio-economic, educational and political disadvantages faced by them.

The Preamble to the Constitution resolves to secure to all its citizens, justice, social, economic and political, liberty of thought, expression, belief, faith and worship, equality of status and of opportunity and to promote among them all, fraternity, assuring the dignity of the individual and the unity and integrity of the nation.

Article 14 of the Constitution of India, confers equal rights and opportunities on men and women in the political, economic and social spheres. While Article 15 prohibits discrimination on the grounds of religion, race, caste, sex, etc., a provision under Article 15(3) enables the State to allow affirmative discrimination in favour of women. Article 16 guarantees equality of opportunity in public employment. The State also imposes a fundamental duty on every citizen to renounce practices derogatory to the dignity of women.

To uphold the constitutional mandate, the State has enacted various legislative measures intended to ensure equal rights, to counter social discrimination and various forms of violence and atrocities and to provide support services especially to working women.[12]

(iv) ***Implementing Programmes like ICDS, Swarna Jayanti Shahari Rozgar Yojana, etc.***, to uplift the status of women especially disadvantaged women living in slums.

During the First and Second Five Year Plans, there was a strong focus on comprehensive social welfare programmes to facilitate women to fulfil their legitimate role within the family and the community. The Fifth Plan supported economic development, employment and training for women as principal forces for their socio-economic development. Sixth Plan, for women's development and for the first time gave a co-ordinated picture to provide a nodal point on matters like protection to women against discrimination, exploitation, etc. The Eighth Plan extended the reach of services to women both quantitatively and qualitatively.

Ninth Plan gave the objectives Empowering Women as the Agents of Social Change and Development Strategies:

- To create an enabling environment for women to exercise their rights, both within and outside home, as equal partners along with men, through early adoption of "National Policy for Empowerment of Women".
- To legislate reservation of not less than 1/3 seats for women in the Lok Sabha and in the State Legislative Assemblies and thus ensure adequate representation of women in decision-making;
- To adopt an integrated approach towards empowering women through effective convergence of existing services, resources, infrastructure and manpower in both women-specific and women-related sectors;
- To adopt a special strategy of "Women's Component Plan" to ensure that not less than 30 per cent of funds/benefits flow to women from other development sectors;
- To organise women into Self-Help Groups and thus mark the beginning of a major process of empowering women;

- To accord high priority to reproductive child health services and thus ensure easy access to maternal and child health services;
- To universalise the on-going supplementary feeding programme—Special Nutrition Programme (SNP) and Mid-Day Meals (MDM);
- To ensure easy and equal access to education for women and girls through the commitments of the Special Action Plan of 1998;
- To initiate steps to eliminate gender bias in all educational programmes;
- To institute plans for free education for girls up to college level, including professional courses;
- To equip women with necessary skills in the modern upcoming trades which could keep them gainfully engaged besides making them economically independent and self-reliant; and
- To increase acccss to credit through setting up of a Development Bank for Women Entrepreneurs' in small and tiny sectors.[13]

Other programmes are:

1. National Perspective Plan for Women (1998)
2. Sharamshakti—the Report of the National Commission for Self-Employed Women and Women in the Informal Sector (1988)
3. Report of the National Expert Committee on Women Prisoners (1986)
4. The National Plan of Action for the Girl Child (1991-2000)
5. Reservation for Women in Grass-root Level Democratic Institutions (1993)
6. Poverty Eradication Programmes
7. Mahila Samriddhi Yojana (MSY) (1993)
8. National Credit Fund for Women (1993)
9. Support to Training and Employment Programmes (STEP)
10. Training-cum-Employment-cum-Production Centres
11. Socio-Economic Programme (SEP)
12. Condensed Courses of Education and Vocational Training for Adult Women (CCE&VT)

13. Monitoring of Beneficiary Oriented Schemes (BOS) for Women
14. Gender Sensitisation and Awareness Generation
15. Gender Sensitisation of 1991 Census
16. Support Services
17. Legal Literacy Manuals (LLMs)
18. National Resource Centre for Women.

The impact of various developmental policies, programmes and institutional mechanisms is to be gauged from the perceptible improvement in the socio-economic status of women in the country. The challenge before government, the women's movement and the voluntary sector is to translate this concern into a wider societal awareness, which can then shape praxis at all levels.[14]

*Experiments*

Let us first discuss the community-based structures under the SJSRY with special reference to Punjab.

**Community-based Structures under the SJSRY**

The community-based organisations include Neighbourhood Groups (NHGs): Neighbourhood Committees (NHCs) and Community Development Society (CDS).

*Neighbourhood Group (NHG)*

This is an informal association of women living in a mohalla or a basti or neighbourhood group of manageable size (preferably the 10 to 40 per cent representing urban poor or slum families). Geographic contiguity and homogeneity should be the basis to carve out the boundaries of the NHGs. At least one woman resident among them who is willing to serve as a volunteer should be selected as a Resident Community Volunteer (RCV) through community consensus or election or any other democratic process. There should be a change or rotation (if need be) of such volunteers at periodical intervals. The responsibilities of RCVs include:

## Organisational Set Up

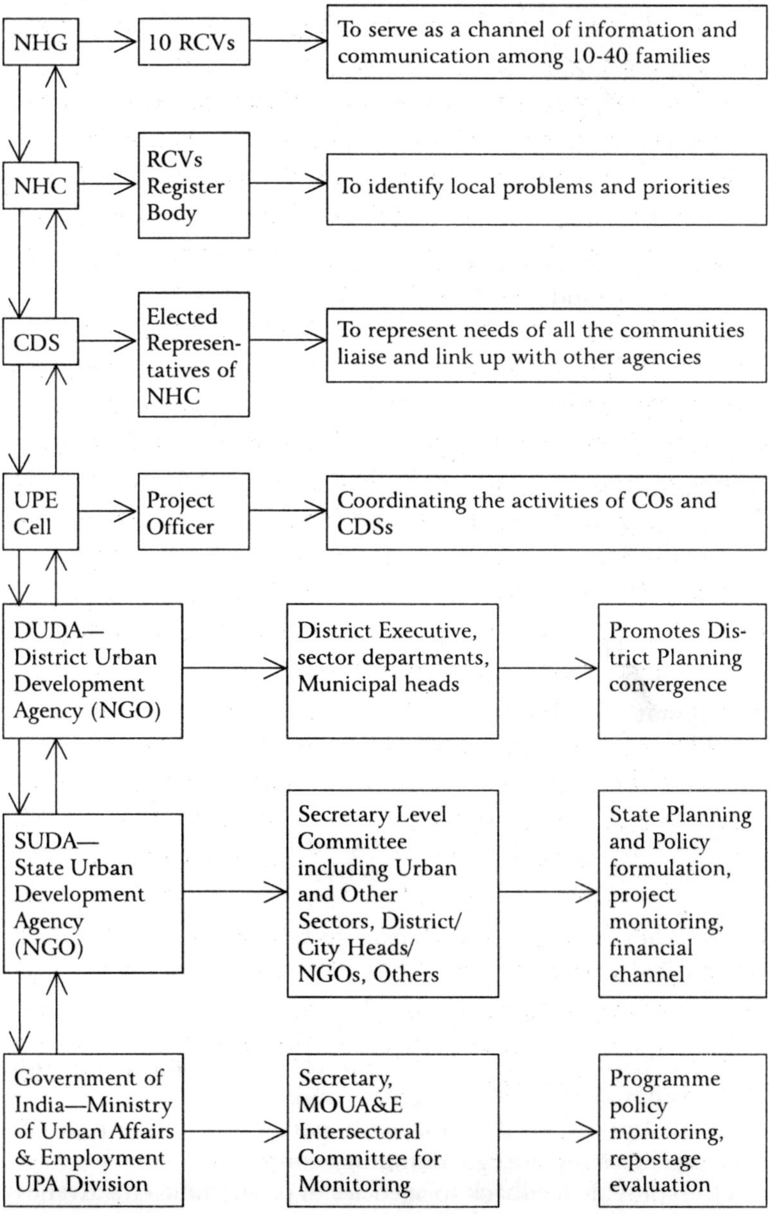

(i) to serve as a channel of information and communication among the families in the cluster;
(ii) to represent the views of the groups in the neighbourhood committees and community development societies and other forums;
(iii) to support planning, implementation and monitoring of activities at the neighbourhood level;
(iv) to foster and encourage participation in community improvement; and
(v) to motivate the community for being members of thrift and credit society; and to contribute to community development fund.

### *Neighbourhood Committees (NHCs)*

A Neighbourhood Committee (NHC) is a more formal association of women from the above neighbourhood groups located in close proximity and as far as feasible within the same electoral ward. The Committee should consist of all the RCVs from the neighbourhood groups as executives (with voting right) of NHC as well as one female member (without voting rights) from each family, which falls under the jurisdiction of NHC concerned. There can also be provision for honorary membership without a voting right for Community Organiser (CO), representatives from other sectoral programmes in the community like ICDS supervisor, school teacher, ANM, etc. The Convener/President of the NHC will be selected/elected by the executive members of the NHC. The Convener will ensure that the meetings are convened on regular basis. The NHC would be responsible for the following activities:

*Infrastructure and function of community-based structures at municipal level*

(i) to identify local problems and priorities;
(ii) to provide suggestions for groups involvement in meeting community needs and goals (mini-plans);
(iii) to support local action with partnership of responsible agencies including community contracts;
(iv) to provide feedback to agencies of programme effectiveness

and outreach especially for children and women;
(v) to develop community capacity through training in association with Cos, NGOs and other sectoral departments;
(vi) to develop community-based thrift and credit system as well as neighbourhood development fund;
(vii) to facilitate the recovery of loans from the beneficiaries in time; and
(viii) to assist/carry out community surveys in accordance with the guidelines.

The NHC may be registered under the Societies Registration Act, or other appropriate Acts if so desired. If registered, these NHC may also apply for grants-in-aid under various schemes.

### *Community Development Society* (*CDS*)

The CDS is a formal association of all the neighbourhood development committees at the town level based on common goals and objectives. The CDS may consist of elected/selected representatives of NHCs as executive members (with voting right) as well as one female member from each family (without voting right) which falls under the jurisdiction of CDS; and other members with honorary membership (with no voting right) which may include community organisers, representatives of NGOs, sectoral department, leading citizens elected-representatives of the area and other resource persons. The Community Development Society (CDS) should be registered under the Societies Registration Act or other appropriate Acts to provide access to grant-in-aid under various schemes and for a wider financial and credit base. The CDS would be responsible:

(i) to represent needs of all the communities, especially women and children;
(ii) liaise and link-up with agencies and departments to promote action in the community towards fulfilment of their needs;
(iii) to identify specific training and arrange for their organisation;
(iv) to facilitate community surveys to be carried out to identify

the genuine beneficiaries for economic and shelter benefits;

(v) to prepare community plans and proposals, mobilising resources from the community, town or other sectoral departments;

(vi) to extend help to Bank in co-ordination with UPE Cell, for ensuring repayment of loans by the beneficiaries in time; and

(vii) to create small community assets in low income areas in consultation with town UPE Cell and Urban Local Body (ULB).[15]

*Functions of the Community-based Structures*

(a) *Participation of beneficiaries:* Voluntary organisations are nearer to the people and get better response from them in the implementation of programmes than official agencies and thus they are in a better position to render effective service. By and large, they have a better knack of communicating with the beneficiaries than members of official agencies. This of course, is a natural manifestation of the ancient civilisation of India, which has attached the greatest importance to the participation of the people in decision-making. The mobilisation of the energies and resources of the beneficiaries themselves is the key factor in increasing their welfare and self-reliance. People's participation through voluntary agencies in the promotion and economic of social welfare means involvement of the people in the process of social welfare voluntarily and willingly. Such participation cannot be forced. People's involvement can be assured through the participation of the beneficiaries in the decision-making, implementation, monitoring and evaluation of development programmes carried out by the voluntary agencies. This will lay the solid foundation in the prevention and promotion of services and the people would become self-reliant rather than depend on the help from the Municipal Government. According to Dharma Vira:

> "Work of voluntary organisations and citizen participation are two sides of the same coin. Citizens work in the organisation but on there work depends the quality of the service the organisation render. Voluntary Organisations provide a

frame for citizen participation. Without effective participation, the organisation would only be empty forums".[16]

Municipal staff is supposed to provide facilities for community-based structures to function efficiently.

(b) *Creating a sense of responsibility through direct involvement:* Programme results are more successful and meaningful if the potential beneficiaries take part in their design and implementation through the forum of voluntary organisations. For example, if uncollected garbage draws flies, or drains become clogged and overflow or if dirt pathways become ankle-deep mud sloughs in the rainy season, voluntary agencies will like to do something to remedy the situation from complaining to the Municipal Health Department to dredging canals and filing in muddy pathways themselves.

The more important role of voluntary agencies is to stimulate active citizen participation in matters that concerns them and their community. How can this role be effectively played? Today, it is generally accepted that social and economic development cannot take place, unless these forms of traditional inertia are broken by municipal staff, so that the masses can be imbued with confidence in their capacity to solve their own daily problems.

(c) *Rectification of planner's misconception:* It is very difficult for people to let their views be known individually. And planners find it difficult to appreciate their needs. People's participation through voluntary agencies can rectify planning errors by making it possible for clients to point out to planners, policy-makers and administrators, what will work and what will not. Planning Agency created at the district level under 74th Amendment of the Constitution can really plan if the views of these community-based structures are taken into consideration. These views are based on reality and theory. If things are left only to the specialists, they would ignore the demands of the masses. The higher status experts thus set the framework of discussion and carry it through in categories meaningful to themselves but often incomprehensible to the ordinary, poor and lowly educated laymen.

(d) *Greater understanding and positive attitudes among the beneficiaries (formation of public opinion):* The involvement of the beneficiaries in the socio-economic development or city reconstruction is dependent to a great extent upon their enlightenment. This can take place when community based structures interpret and explain the issues and problems of municipal care administration to the public, e.g., family planning. The community based municipal structures are also trying to help by creating in the people an urge, an attitude to adopt new methods of development by arranging for the people services and opportunities to acquire new knowledge and techniques and by acting as a mediator between the people and the official machinery to interpret the problems and needs of the one to the other in order to develop better appreciation of each other.

(e) *Effective policy formation through interpretation of public opinion:* The community-based municipal structures can present the real needs of development of the peoplee to the various decision-making bodies to the Local Self-Government Department. Information is the policy-makers' raw material, forming the basis for his diagnosis, strengthening his projections and permitting him to evaluate the programmes, which have been planned. The degree to which a municipal planner will be able to plan in terms of needs will depend on the degree to which he is able to obtain information about them, which is valid and reliable. The information supplied by voluntary agencies can be reliable as it is based on the outcome of their intimate contacts with the population.

(f) *Flexibility and experimentation:* The voluntary agencies are autonomous in their functioning. They are not bound by well-defined laws and regulations, which are difficult to change. This gives the voluntary agencies an opportunity to experiment with a given programme and adjust it according to the environmental conditions. The programme must develop environmental linkages in order to be of lasting value and benefit to the people. The autonomous character of the voluntary agencies provide them flexibility to adopt their programme according to the needs and aspirations of the people. We know that the best structure can come up only in a congenial soil. The health problems of the people differ from city to city and hence, it is difficult to solve the problems for all the areas with the same solution. The voluntary organisations can experiment with different models in different areas and adopt and develop the best for the area for a given time dimension as the models of development are bound to change with the time dimension.

(g) *Initiative and leadership:* Voluntary agencies involve the people in the policy formulation and implementation of the programmes. This encourages the local potential leaders to develop as agents of socio-economic change. The people are not dependent on the initiative of the Municipal Government alone. They take the initiative and believe in self-help rather than help from outside.

(h) *Channelise human resources:* It is very difficult to provide all the social services to the people through the Municipal Government, as it is very costly. The voluntary agency can exploit the unused energies of the people for the development of the city. Energy of the people, if unused, cannot be preserved. This unused energy "like the unused vast water resources flowing down the Himalayas is not only wasted like those rivers, but also, like the river waters that take with them the top solid of the Himalayan region causing permanent losses in soil erosion, cause permanent damage to the human spirit and will in a community through dependence and frustration born out of ever-increasing level of abject poverty over the generations".[17]

We can explain this in the context of the provision of Primary Health Care Services. Voluntary health agencies can train the educated and willing workers in the art of elementary health care and health education. Such trained and motivated people in turn would be able to provide primary health care to the people. This would be cheaper and efficient as can be seen from the Chinese experience.

(i) *Advancing social legislation:* In a welfare state, social welfare laws are as essential as security laws. These come under the purview of social legislation. It is the tool with which the social administrator is able to help the community from hazards. The social legislation need radical changes to cover all the people.

Voluntary agencies can mobilise public opinion in support of such legislations. These agencies can prepare the people to act as a pressure group to motivate the government to enact legislations for the welfare of the masses. A political system remains in equilibrium only if it channelises the demands of the people into policies and decisions beneficial to the people.

(j) *Supplement the efforts of government:* The problems of development are so vast and stupendous that it is difficult to solve these problems with the efforts of the Municipal Government machinery alone. There is a need to share this responsibility and the voluntary sector, which possesses immense potential, can take up this burden. During the last three decades, the municipal governments have been trying to bring about socio-economic revolution but the progress has been halted because of the non-availability of needed resources. Thus, there is a need of a voluntary sector to supplement the efforts of the government. The working group appointed by the Planning Commission remarked that the country's social and economic problems are so vast and multifarious that the government's administrative machinery alone cannot tackle them. The establishment of a self-reliant society implies progressive curtailment of people's dependence on the government. From time immemorial voluntary agencies in our country have played a significant part in promoting people's welfare.[18] Government has to assume the major responsibility, not only for developmental programmes, but also in providing leadership and resources for voluntary agencies to continue their work. This partnership or complimentary relationship now needed eventually be lessened to a point where it can be possible to have a demarcation of roles.

(k) *Help in efficient programme implementation:* Community-based municipal structures agencies can help in the programme implementation, collaboration and co-ordination with other agencies. They can contribute to development in many ways through programme implementation. They can:[19]

1. Provide assistance to develop and/or strengthen local NGO capabilities and activities with particular attention to local community development groups.

2. Conduct reviews and assessment of existing development programmes and assist communities in the exercise of their own role in such reviews. A greater emphasis on evaluative techniques will render all new programmes more accountable to real community needs.
3. Develop innovative ideas in the context of comprehensive human development.
4. Ensure that their existing programmes and new initiatives promote full participation by individuals and communities in the planning, implementation and control of these programmes.
5. Expand their training efforts to respond to the needs of development, e.g., training of health workers, supervisors, administrators, planners and various agricultural and development workers.
6. Extend their efforts to develop locally sustainable and appropriate technologies and use of resources, with particular attention to energy, water, agriculture, sanitation and medical care.
7. Contribute to the creation of new and effective methods of health education, which enable both individuals and communities to assume greater responsibility for their own health.
8. Recognise the essential roles of women in health promotion and in the full range of community development concerns.

Further extend their capacity to work with poor, disadvantaged and remote populations enabling them to break the cycle of deprivation, and in this way contribute to the search for greater social justice.[20]

In the State of Punjab, there are 177 Community Development Societies and 1145 Neighbourhood Committees and 12865 RCVs are the part of the CDSs. UBSP, NRY and PMI-UPEP schemes, which were being implemented in the state, merged into SJSRY with effect from 1.12.1997.

Only 10-15 per cent CDSs are covered under this training programme. 36 new and refresher training programme were conducted for RCVs and CDs members. These training programmes are funded bv UNICEF under capacity building. 4 Orientation

Programmes were organised for UPA staff. Apart from this five programmes/workshops were organised for Field Functionaries, COs/APOs in the field and staff from Head Office.

Since inception SUDA through the Municipal Committees has been struggling to make the life of the people better especially those living in urban slums. It is a challenging task to remove urban poverty. Since the resources—financial, personnel and material were limited, therefore, SUDA, as per the scheme, has to resort to community help, but community was least interested. Therefore, the first step was to impart education and training to community volunteers and municipal staff.

*Refresher and New Trainings for RCVs*

The refresher and new training programmes, which were organised in the State benefited around 743 RCVs/CDS and the general public. The objectives of these programmes were:

- To make the RCVs aware about different welfare schemes implemented by various Sectoral Department.
- To show the RCVs how to take benefit out of these schemes.
- To uplift the standard of living of RCVs.
- To make the RCVs understand their roles and responsibilities.

To achieve the first objective the Resource Persons from different Sectoral Department like Health, Family & Child Welfare (ICDS) and Education were invited. The officials from lead bank were also invited in these programmes so that the formalities regarding sanctioning of loan could be made clear to the RCVs to make the achievement of 2nd and 3rd objective possible.

The official from SUDA office explained all the schemes and clarified all the queries regarding their roles and responsibilities and implementation of SJSRY and BSY.

A programme was organised on 28 March, 2000 at Municipal Corporation, Amritsar. Around 35 RCVs/CDS participated in the programme. The Resource Persons, i.e., CDPO from Family & Child Welfare, Medical Officer from Health Department and LDM from Bank institute participated in the programme. CDPO showed her interest in opening Anganwadi

Centre with the collaboration of CDS. The LDM also showed his interest in sanctioning loan to DWACUA group, because one DWACUA group was already running in Municipal Corporation area and the loan was being repaid regularly. The Medical Officer also made them aware about Maternal and Child Health and Hygiene and assured to give full support to CDS in organising Medical Camp. The queries regarding implementation of SJSRY were also answered by the SUDA official.

In this way the programme was organised with the convergence of different sectoral departments.

### *Training for UPA Staff*

The beneficiaries can avail benefit from UPA schemes through the Municipal Councils, therefore, the concept of Urban Poverty Alleviation Schemes should be made clear to the UPA staff, they are then able to guide the field staff, office staff and the beneficiaries properly. There workshops were organised for UPA staff during the year 2000. 2 two-days workshops were organised for Executive Officers and a one-day workshop for Sanitary Inspectors. Another two-days workshop was organised on 5th and 6th April 2000.

For this purpose Resource Persons from different Sectoral Departments were invited. The different Resource Persons informed the participants about the basic concepts of Town Planning, Financial, Personal and Health Management and Time Management. Therefore, around 55 beneficiaries were from these four programmes.

### *Training for APOs/COs*

Four training programmes were organised at headquarters and in field for APOs/COs on different topics. The objectives of the workshops were to update the Field Staff and improve the functioning of APOs/COs. All the COs/APOs benefited from these workshops. Two workshops of two-days were organised on PLA tools and two on SJSRY.

The objective of a two-days workshop that was organised on Participatory Learning and Action (PLA) tools on 4-5th October, 2000 at headquarter was to enhance the skills of

APOs/COs in working with the urban poor, so that participation of community in planning, initiating action and analyses may be sought and community may be able to express themselves. In this workshop 21 APOs/COs participated and the master trainers, who got training from NIUA training institute, were invited to impart training. The participants learnt the use of different PLA tools in this training. Therefore, for the better implementation of UPA schemes such workshops are very fruitful.

The experiment has been quite useful as is evident from the following:

Skill training
DWACUA
Thrift & Credit

In Andhra Pradesh, the Department of Municipal Administration has taken an initiative to enable the urban local bodies to entrust some of their basic functions involving community contracts to women groups formed under schemes such as the Swarn Jayanti Shahari Rozgar Yojna (SJSRY).[21]

Under this scheme, women groups are entrusted with the task of ensuring sanitation solid waste management, and hygiene of specified areas. They are paid an honorarium for their services, and provided with basic support mechanisms in the form of subsidised loans from financial institutions for executing their task. Women groups themselves select the works, prioritise their needs and execute the projects. Administrative approval for the works is granted by Municipal Councils, with technical approval from the Public Health Engineering Department. Women groups are imparted training in engineering skills and financial management, among other things. Fifteen per cent of the project cost is given as an advance and the savings generated by giving the work to community-based organisations form the capital of the women groups, to be used for micro credit interventions.

For the projects, which have so far been undertaken as part of this scheme, the women were selected from the poor areas and slums. More often than not, they were illiterate women from the scheduled and backward classes, living in distressed conditions, with an average family size of six members.

Today, there are 26 urban local bodies in Andhra Pradesh, which have organised 74 women groups and successfully maintained public sanitation in their allocated areas. Fifty more women groups from different civic bodies are very keen to undertake community sanitation. Works worth about Rs.84 crore have been earmarked to be undertaken as part of the community contract system, out of which work worth about Rs. 18 crore is already in progress.

There are, however, three major obstacles in implementing this scheme: psychological, political and economic. The first impediment is the lack of confidence among the women to undertake this project. The second factor pertains to the threat and pressure of the local contractor, who is often hand-in-glove with the local politician. And, finally, it is the fear of failure, which often deters the women from executing the project. The women groups also harbour doubts that if they were to fail in successfully implementing the project, they would be denied even the low wages that they were getting earlier. None of these obstacles is insurmountable and the Municipal Commissioners have worked hard to counter these pressures and instil self-confidence in the women groups.

The benefits of the scheme are manifold. First, its implementation has resulted in clean roads and improved sanitation. The garbage is cleared everyday, sometimes more than once a day, and there is a feeling of community ownership. In monetary terms, the schemes foster employment and asset creation, besides belping to increase family savings and income of the communities. Each member of the team gets a minimum daily wage of Rs.50, which is almost twice the wages that they were getting earlier. In some cases, the members have also doubled their family incomes. In one case, the municipality even started a thrift society for the members so that they could save from their increased monthly income and take loans. Community empowerment thus translated into better quality of assets, optimal utilisation of high quality and adequate construction material, higher mutual interaction and better understanding among the women groups, as also the enhancement of both their social status and monthly savings.

The growing self-confidence, increasing commitment, firm

determination to learn, the self-conscious pride as the movers of community and the consciousness that they are here as agents of socio-political changes, are writ large on the elected women's faces all over. The reconstruction of India's polity and local development is on the cards, if only the urban and educated people of India can back them up with the necessary information, political support and economic programmes. One does hope that the training and orientation programmes will provide this support, even while the democratic movements pursue doggedly to make the centre and state governments part with their economic resources and administrative control.[22]

Why even the bestowal of political empowerment on women has not proved to be effective? In order words, why being in the very decision-making bodies, women still remain on the periphery? The following explanations emerge:

- The pattern of patriarchy, beginning at home, stretches through educational, occupational economic worlds to the political—thus denying a centrality to women incumbents in the decision-making process;
- The persistent demarcation between private and public domains whereby the woman is supposed to limit her activities to the private sphere, with the public domain remaining a monopoly of the male. Political empowerment of women many a times symbolises pushing them into the public domain for the gains of their husbands, sons or father;
- An extremely antagonistic attitude of not only the males but even females among bureaucrats, superiors, subordinates, friends, family members and public at large against the women as competent candidates for decision-making positions. The evidence of such an antagonism gets reflected to through cases where women in powerful situations (in order to be taught a lesson) have been physically abused. In each such cases, some women have always accompanied male culprits. Such incidents bring the gender issue back to the biological attributes of women and leave a deep impact and push the women back into the private domain. Given these stark realities, how can constitutional provisions by themselves empower women?

- Misuse of the constitutional provision by the politicians mainly males, to retain the political power within the family by making female relatives contest elections and then act a as dummy incumbents, thus damaging the very spirit of the Constitution;
- An inhibition on the part of educated, articulate and competent women to enter the field;
- An extreme politicisation of the whole issue, with serious repercussions on reserved constituencies. For example, it may not be possible to successfully contest without political backing. Even if you were elected, it would be possible for you to function effectively without political support. Political affiliations normally overshadow or dilute the gender issues subsequently. This is the reason why women even after entering the political field, fail to play a constructive role. It is certain that political parties cannot be entrusted with empowering women with political power in the sense our Constitution aspires to do.
- It is going to be a much more difficult and challenging task for women to rise to high levels of political office, get into existing patriarchal structures, stay on and be effective. This is true mainly because women's empowerment is a political question, linked to change in power relations. Contemporary history indicates that in defining identities that have to be preserved, it is the perceptions of the male political leaders that rule the day.
- Special training programmes must be organised by the government for women councillors in order to impart communicative skills and professionalism among them.
- Some minimum levels of educational qualifications should be mandatory for both men and women aspiring to contest elections to Municipal Corporations, to ensure meaningful participation in municipal governance.[23]

The biggest gains of these schemes, therefore, accrue to the target community through the women groups, who are involved in the projects from conception to implementation. These groups gain self-confidence through the process and acquire relevant skills in construction, engineering, material and financial management. The fact that about 26 urban local bodies have already initiated the process to implement the programme within the first year indicates that the scheme is replicable.[24]

## Conclusion

As per the International Union of Local Authorities (IULA): "The systematic integration of women augments the democratic basis, the efficiency and the equality of the activities of local government. If local government is to meet the needs of both men and women, it must build on the experiences of both men and women through, an equal representation at all levels and in all fields of decision-making, covering the wide range of responsibilities of local governments".[25]

What, then has been the experience of women once in local government? They responded as follows:

1. No proper orientation about municipal acts and civic administration.
2. No experience about dealing with urban development/civic issues and its complexities.
3. Lack of knowledge about technical inputs related to urban service delivery system.
4. Lack of support from senior male/female colleagues in the party/municipal body.
5. Less co-operation from municipal officials.
6. Less understanding about various facets of the budgeting, allocation of budget at ward level and at central level, etc.
7. Lack of party support at local level.
8. Lack of confidence in public speaking.
9. Local political atmosphere.
10. Lack of resources to cultivate own base at local level.[26]

The National Commission on Self-Employed Women and women in the informal sector has rightly mentioned that although at the planning level, there is consciousness about women's low status and the need to focus on women's needs in development, but at the implementation level, this awareness percolates very slowly. The delivery system is based on a stereotyped concept of women's development where women are object of pity or welfare and are given some benefits in a sporadic and haphazard manner.... If the political leadership decides that women's problems have to be tackled on a priority basis, the entire planning processes, implementing mechanisms and monitoring system will be geared in no time.

It's time for women to lead equally in urban governance—they know our homes and communities best.[27]

One of India's greatest poets, Rabindranath Tagore, had expressed the pain and inequity of the situation more than half a century ago, thus:

> "O Lord Why have you not given woman the
> right to conquer her destiny?
> Why does she have to wait head bowed,
> By the roadside, Waiting with tired patience,
> Hoping for a miracle in the morrow?"[28]

## REFERENCES

1. "Towards Equality", Report of the Committee on the Status of Women, p. 6.
2. Status of Women and Family Planning (C/C No. 6/5/75/Ref. No. E75/V5, 1975).
3. Women, Population and Development, Population Profiles No. 7, p. 10.
4. *Rigveda,* 2/17/71; 9/67/10.12.
5. Article 15(1), Constitution of India.
6. Special Marriage Act, 1954; Hindu Marriage and Divorce Act, 1955; Hindu Succession Act, 1956; The Hindu Guardianship Act, 1956, etc.
7. *Shelter* vol. III, no. 4, October 2000, p. iv.
8. *Ibid.*, p. xiv.
9. *Ibid.*, pp. 73-74.
10. *Ibid.*, p. 83.
11. Fourth World Conference on Women, Beijing, 1995, (GOI), p. 38.
12. *Ibid.*, p. 24.
13. *Shelter,* vol. III, no. 4, October, 2000, pp. 15-16.
14. Fourth World Conference on Women, Beijing, 1995, (GOI), p. 30.
15. Swarna Jayanti Shahari Rozgar Yojana (SJSRY) Guidelines, pp. 16-17.
16. Dharam Vira, "Citizen Participation" in *Encyclopaedia of Social Work,* vol. 1, p. 102.
17. Malhotra, R.C., *op. cit.*, p. 11.

18. GOI, Planning Commission, Report of the Working Group on Block Level Planning, 1978, pp. 139-40.
19. World Federation of Public Health Associations, *op. cit.*, pp. 45-46.
20. *Social Welfare Administration,* vol. 2.
21. Launched in 1997, this GOI employment programme had two main components—self-employment and wage employment. For both the components, actual activities are identified through community groups and poor women. Besides access to credit, SJSRY also incorporates a component for training women and elected leaders.
22. Women in Panchayat Elections, Susheela Kaushik, *Decentalisation and Local Politics,* p. 247.
23. *Urban India,* vol. XIX, no. 1 (1999) Seventy-Fourth Constitution Amendment and Political Empowerment of Women in Punjab: A study in Urban Governance, pp. 56-58.
24. Department for International Development, (DFID) 31 August 2000.
25. *Shelter,* vol. III, no. 4, October, 2000, p. 63.
26. *Ibid.*, p. 46.
27. *Ibid.,* p. 111.
28. Fourth World Conference on Women, p. 6.

# 21

# Awareness Among Rural Women and Their Development: A Study

*S.S. Chauhan*

Women constitute nearly 50 per cent share in the total population of India. Rural women in India as well as in other countries have been a neglected lot. They have not been actively involved in the mainstream of development even though they represent a bulk of population and labour force. Primarily women are the means of survival of their families but are generally unrecognised and undervalued being placed at the bottom of the pile. Ideologically as well as in practice women were considered completely inferior to males. Many areas of employment were completely shut for women. Socially she was kept in a state of utter subjugation, suppressed and oppressed. They have lesser access to asset resources, technology and credit.

The rural workforce in India constitutes a sizeable section of rural women such as housewives, artisans, agricultural labourers, cultivators, etc. Analysis of various studies on rural women reveals that they occupy a low position on all fronts in the society while effecting the development of the nation.

The inequalities prevalent in our traditional social fabric, based on caste, community and class, have a significant impact on the low status of women in different spheres. Therefore, the main issue which is still being discussed is the kind of strategy to be devised for improving the status and extent of participation in the process of development. For the rural women, the primary concern requires their economic upliftment, improving educational standard, self-awareness and political participation.

Many efforts have been made by the government since independence, towards changing the village as the most important unit of our social and economic life. Attempts have been made to rationalise the status of women through the execution of various plans and programmes, and enactment of statutory laws.

In the present paper attempt has been made to study the degree of awareness, participation in democratic processes, and socio-economic conditions, etc., of women in a remote and backward panchayat—Thachadhar in Mandi district of Himachal Pradesh.

The data was collected through structured questionnaire. One hundred women respondents in the age-group of 20 to 60 years were selected from the Panchayat through simple random sampling technique. Variables like, social, economic, political and personal were included in the study. The data was also collected through personal interview and observation methods.

## The Panchayat

Thachadhar village panchayat is named after biggest village "Thachadhar". It also includes many other small villages within its jurisdiction as in hilly state of H.P. villages are very-very small. Headquarter of said gram panchayat is located at Gada Gusain which is small market place linked by road which is 160 km by road from block headquarter and 90 km from district headquarter.

The village panchayat has been fully electrified but none of the village has been touched by road. Road facility is available up to its headquarter. There is one senior secondary school, four primary schools, one primary health centre and one sub-centre within the jurisdiction of this panchayat area. The nearest college and hospital is 90 km away.

This panchayat is inhabited by families of many castes but of single religion. It has a total population of nearly, 3,050.

## Social Conditions of Women

In the present study attempt was made to study the social status of women of Thachadhar village panchayat. For this purpose social variable like age, education nature of women work were studied in details.

**TABLE 1: Age-wise breakup of sample women respondents (Nos. 100)**

| Age | Number | Percentage |
|---|---|---|
| 20-30 | 32 | 32 |
| 30-40 | 28 | 28 |
| 40-50 | 20 | 20 |
| 50-60 | 20 | 20 |
| Total | 100 | 100 |

Age-wise distribution of sample women reveals that women between age-group of 20 to 30 years comprised 32 per cent of the total which was followed by women of age-group of 30 to 40 years, women between the age-group of 40-50 and 50-60 years comprised equal percentage, viz., 20 per cent each.

**TABLE 2: Literacy rate of women in the Thachadhar Panchayat on the basis of Different Education levels**

| Category | L.P. | U.P. | M.E. | Matric | +2 | Total | Graduation and P.G. | Total |
|---|---|---|---|---|---|---|---|---|
| Male | 356 | 175 | 45 | 52 | 15 | 2 | 10 | 655 |
| Female | 152 | 60 | 35 | 24 | 5 | 3 | NIL | 279 |
| Total | 508 | 235 | 80 | 76 | 20 | 5 | 10 | 934 |

Table 2 depicts the literacy rate among males and females in Thachadhar panchayat. Out of total population of Gram Panchayat Thachadhar (3,050) only 934 were illiterates which is 30.6 per cent of the total. Sex-wise distribution of illiterates revealed that there were 655 male and 279 female literates in the said panchayat. Majority literates had education up to lower primary and upper primary level. High education was found confined among male population only. From above analysis it is clear that spread of education is still very very low among women in rural areas.

**TABLE 3: Opinion of sample rural women regarding adult education**

| Variable | Number | Percentage |
|---|---|---|
| Useful and Participate | 78 | 78 |
| Not useful and Do not participate | 12 | 12 |
| No opinion | 10 | 10 |
| Total | 100 | 100 |

Above table reveals about opinion of sample rural women regarding usefulness of adult education. Majority sample respondents, i.e., 78 per cent opined that adult education is very useful and they have participated in it. Whereas 12 per cent respondents replied that it is not useful for them and they do not participate in it. Ten per cent gave no opinion. From the analysis it is found that majority rural women population is now aware of usefulness of education.

In our country there is widespread illiteracy among rural people, particularly among rural women. It is due to conservative social system, poverty, low level of awareness and many beliefs. Present study was carried out among rural women in Thachadhar panchayat to know their opinion regarding women education and find out reasons, behind their opposition towards women education. Table 4 depicts opinion for and against of sample rural women regarding education among rural women. Table reveals that 70 sample women, i.e., 70 per cent of the total were in favour of female education. Out of 70 per cent sample women 40 per cent opined that education is helpful to know 3R's, viz., reading, writing and arithmatics, 23 per cent opined that education is helpful in improving their social status. They revealed that educated rural women is respected by all majority population in their panchayat. During panchayat elections educated women were elected to different bodies in panchayati raj system. Only

**TABLE 4: Opinion of sample women respondents in favour and against female education**

| | Frequency | Percentage |
|---|---|---|
| **In favour** | | |
| 1. For better marital alliance | 5 | 7 |
| 2. Knowledge of 3R's must | 28 | 40 |
| 3. Education helpful during crisis | 13 | 18.5 |
| 4. It improves their status | 16 | 23 |
| 5. To participate in decision making | 8 | 11.5 |
| Total | 70 | |
| **Against** | | |
| 1. No need since she has to confine within the four walls of the house after marriage | 16 | 53.4 |
| 2. It adds to their poverty | 4 | 13.3 |
| 3. Education creates problems in finding suitable match | 4 | 13.3 |
| 4. No benefit of education | 6 | 20 |
| Total | 30 | |
| Grant Total | 100 | |

reason behind their election to different bodies was their being educated. Eighteen percent sample respondents opined that education can be helpful during crisis, i.e., family crisis, social crisis and economic crisis, etc., and nearly 12 per cent respondents revealed that education was helpful in taking decision. Only 7 per cent women opined that education is helpful in finding out suitable match and for better marital relationships.

Out of total 100 sample women respondents 30 women (30 per cent) were found against female education. In support of their opinion they have given many reasons. Out of total 30 women 16 respondents (53.4 per cent) opined that there is no utility of education because after their marriage they have to confine themselves within the four walls of the house. Thirteen per cent women opined that education among females adds their poverty. And equal per cent of respondents, replied that it creates problems in finding out the suitable match because educated females do not want to get married with illiterates which adds their problems.

**TABLE 5: Breakup of nature of work of women in village panchayat Thachadhar**

| Nature of work | Frequency | Percentage |
|---|---|---|
| 1. Household work with agriculture | 850 | 61 |
| 2. Agriculture labour | 135 | 9.6 |
| 3. Mannual workers with P.W.D. | 75 | 5.4 |
| 4. Forest Labour | 62 | 4.4 |
| 5. Government Job | 8 | 0.6 |
| 6. Other | 265 | 19 |
| Total | 1395 | 100 |

In the present study attempt has been made to study the nature of work performed by women of sample panchayat. Out of total women population of 1395 large number of said population—850 women—were found engaged in household work with agriculture work which is 61 per cent of the total women population. Another area where large women population engaged was agriculture sector. One hundred thirty three, i.e., 9.6. per cent women were found working as agriculture labourer, 75 women out of total women population were found working as manual workers and 62 were working as forest labourers. Their share in government employment was only 8 which is 0.6 per cent of the total population. It was due to the fact that literacy rate among women was very low in sample area. Nearly 265 women were found engaged in other types of activities.

From above analysis it is evident that still the nature of women work had not changed and were performing old demarcated activities which rural women were performing since early socialisation.

Table 6 depicts the nature of work performed by sample respondents in village panchayat Thachadhar. Highest number of sample respondents were found engaged in household work with agricultural activities. They comprised 38 per cent of the total respondents studied. There were 35 per cent respondents who were engaged entirely in household work. There was single respondent who was in government job and also performed household work during holidays. Considerable number of sample respondents, viz., 24 (24 per cent) out of total 100 interviewed were found performing household work along with

**TABLE 6: Nature of work of sample women**

| Variables | Frequency | Percentage |
|---|---|---|
| 1. Household work with agriculture | 38 | 38 |
| 2. Only household work | 35 | 35 |
| 3. Household work with business | 2 | 2 |
| 4. Household work with government job | 1 | 1 |
| 5. Household work with manual labour | 24 | 24 |
| Total | 100 | 100 |

manual labour. Above analysis reveals that women in rural areas have been performing multifarious activities.

For rural women household work is their primary job and with it they have to perform other activities also. It also reveals that women have been contributing lot toward augmentation of family income by putting her labour in different spheres.

## Economic Conditions

The fundamental challenge that women's development now faces is to ensure economic empowerment and self-reliance for women. Rural women perform a host of activities which helps in augmentation of their family income. But in spite of that the economic condition of rural women is still not up to the mark. In the present paper we have made an attempt to study the economic condition of rural sample women. For this purpose certain important variable were identified and studied in detail.

Table 7 reveals that the monthly income of sample women respondents is quite low as 25 per cent of the total women respondents interviewed revealed that the monthly income from all sources was less than 200 rupees. There were large number of respondents, i.e., 38 (30 per cent) out of total 100 whose income ranged between 200-400 rupees. Twenty-two per cent sample women revealed that their monthly income ranged between 400-600 rupees. There were only 3 per cent sample respondents whose income was above 100 rupees. These respondents were either in government service or running business. As a whole the income of rural women in sample rural area is

**TABLE 7: Monthly Income of Sample Women respondents**

| Income (Rs.) | Frequency | Percentage |
|---|---|---|
| Less than 200 | 25 | 25 |
| 200-400 | 38 | 38 |
| 400-600 | 22 | 22 |
| 600-800 | 7 | 7 |
| 800-1000 | 5 | 5 |
| Above 1000 | 3 | 3 |
| Total | 100 | 100 |

quite meager. It is due to the fact that employment opportunities are not available.

Study was also conducted to find out the sources of income of sample rural women respondents. Study revealed that main source of their income was from agriculture labour, forest and manual labour. As it is evident from Table 8 that out of total 100 women replied that their main source of income was from agriculture, forest and manual labour from forests they collect various types of herbs, woods and other types of medicinal plants and sell them in the local market. Still for considerable section of women (i.e., 25 per cent) the cottage industries, was still their main source of income. For seventeen per cent women respondents the source of earning was from agriculture produce like potato, green peas and grass footwears. There were only two sample respondents who were running business and only

**TABLE 8: Sources of income of sample women respondents**

| Sources | Frequency | Percentage |
|---|---|---|
| 1. Agriculture, forest and manual labour | 55 | 55 |
| 2. Cottage industry | 25 | 25 |
| 3. Agriculture produce | 17 | 17 |
| 4. Business | 2 | 2 |
| 5. Government job | 1 | 1 |
| Total | 100 | 100 |

one respondent was in government employment. As a whole the source of earning of sample respondents was from manual labour, cottage industries and from agriculture produce.

Table 9 depicts the monthly expenditure of sample respondents. Majority number of sample respondents, i.e., 78 out of the total interviewed replied that their monthly expenditure ranged between 100 to 200 rupees. This expenditure was mostly on medicine, cosmetics, sweets and clothing, etc. This low level of expenditure was due to their low level of income and certain part was deposited by them in saving accounts. For 12 per cent women monthly expenditure ranged between 200 to 300 rupees and 6 per cent women were found spending between 300 to 400 rupees and 3 per cent women used to spend between 400 to 500 rupees per month. There was only respondent who was found spending above 500 rupees per month. Due to low level of earning the monthly expenditure of sample women respondents was also low. Now there is improvement in the level of awareness among the rural women. Whatever amount they could spare is saved by them for certain occasions in future course of time.

**TABLE 9: Monthly expenditure of sample rural women**

| Expenditure in Rs. | No | Percentage |
|---|---|---|
| Less than 200 | 78 | 78 |
| 200 to 300 | 12 | 12 |
| 300 to 400 | 6 | 6 |
| 400 to 500 | 3 | 3 |
| Above 500 | 1 | 1 |

As we have discussed earlier that the rural womenfolk is now awakened. She is aware of usefulness of saving. Whatever amout is spare with her is now deposited either in the bank account or in the post office or is kept with herself for future contingencies. Table 10 reveals that there were 82 per cent sample respondents who were saving in different sources, viz., post office, bank or keeping with them. There were 35 per cent respondents who were saving less than 200 rupees per month, 20 per cent respondents saving between 200 to 400 rupees, 18 per cent respondents were found saving between 400 to 600

**TABLE 10: Saving of Sample Rural Women**

| Amount | Frequency | Percentage |
|---|---|---|
| No saving | 18 | 18 |
| Less than 200 | 35 | 35 |
| 200 to 400 | 20 | 20 |
| 400 to 600 | 18 | 18 |
| 600 to 800 | 6 | 6 |
| 800 to 1000 | 2 | 2 |
| Above 1000 | 1 | 1 |
| Total | 100 | 100 |

rupees per month. There were 8 per cent respondents whose monthly saving ranged between 600 to less than 1000 rupees per month. Single respondent was found saving above 1000 rupees per month. There were certain section of the sample women respondents who were not saving at all, because their sources of income were very meagre and whatever amount they were earning was spent on basic necessities.

## Decision-Making and Women

Women are an important segment of the family's economy because of their active participation in home, farm and other activities. Rural women play a vital role in decision-making regarding household resources which are especially used by them. Their influence and decision-making in household affairs is affected due to certain factors like the degree of economic independence, socio-cultural pressures, demographic factors and physical settings, etc. Table 11 indicates women's participation in socio-economic life of the villagers.

**TABLE 11: Family Expenditure/Other Decision Making Processes**

| Opinion sought on | Frequency | Percentage |
|---|---|---|
| 1. Male members only manage the family affairs | 72 | 72 |
| 2. Females manage the family affairs | 18 | 18 |
| 3. Both manage | 9 | 9 |
| 4. No reply | 1 | 1 |
| Total | 100 | 100 |

In rural areas from ancient times male members have been dominating the social systems. As far as decision-making in regard to family affairs is concerned in majority cases male members have been dominating the decision-making process. As it is evident from Table 11, that in case of 72 sample respondents the male members, only takes the decisions. There were 18 respondents who replied that in their cases women manage the family affairs and in the case of nine respondents both manage the said affairs. As a whole in our social system male members have been dominating the family affairs, but slowly women have been showing their presence in the decision-making processes are far as family affairs are concerned.

## Level of Awareness

Our rural society as a whole has a poor level of awareness about various developmental programmes, provisions of various legislations, benefits of education small family norms and various other developmental opportunities. This is all due to illiteracy, poverty, various disbeliefs and conservative social system. In the present study attempt has been made to study the level of awareness among rural women in a sample village panchayat.

Table 12 depicts the level of awareness among sample women respondents regarding provisions in Panchayati Raj Act for women representation. There were 12 per cent respondents who were fully aware of said provisions and 28 per cent were partially aware of provisions in the Act for women representation. Whereas considerable number of respondents, viz. 60 per cent were not at all aware of such provisions in the PR Act. It may be due to the fact that large number of women in rural

**TABLE 12: Awareness regarding provisions in Panchayat Raj Act for women representation**

| Variable | Frequency | Percentage |
|---|---|---|
| Fully Aware/know | 12 | 12 |
| Partially know | 28 | 28 |
| Don't know at all | 60 | 60 |
| Total | 100 | 100 |

areas are illiterates and do not find time to gain knowledge about such provisions.

**TABLE 13: Awareness about various developmental programmes**

| Variable | Frequency | Percentage |
|---|---|---|
| Fully Aware | 6 | 6 |
| Partially Aware | 24 | 24 |
| Don't know at all | 70 | 70 |
| Total | 100 | 100 |

The Government of India and various state governments have started various developmental programmes for rural people. There are certain programmes which have been implemented for women population. These developmental programmes can be successful if beneficiaries are aware of them and actively participates in them. But generally it is found that beneficiaries are not aware of such programmes. In the present study it was found that only 6 per cent women respondents were fully aware, 24 per cent were partially aware and large number of respondents, viz., 70 per cent were not at all aware of any programme.

The knowledge of legal provisions too is very very poor among rural people in our country particularly among women. In the present paper sample women respondents were asked about certain legal provisions which are directly related to them, to ascertain their awareness level. There was no respondent

**TABLE 14: Awareness about Various Protective Legislations/Legal Provisions for Women**

| Awareness about | Frequency | Percentage |
|---|---|---|
| 1. Law against atrocities | NIL | NIL |
| 2. Law deal with rape | 5 | 5 |
| 3. Law dealing with divorce & maintenance | 32 | 32 |
| 4. Knowledge about industrial laws for women | 3 | 3 |
| 5. No. of respondents who are not aware of above provisions | 60 | 60 |
| Total | 100 | 100 |

aware of legal provisions providing protection against atrocities. Majority number of women respondents, i.e., 32 per cent were having little knowledge of law dealing with divorce and maintenance and only 5 per cent women were found having little knowledge about law dealing with rape. Three per cent women had knowledge of certain industrial laws. These women were working in industrial employment as casual labourers. From the above analysis it can be concluded that level of awareness among rural women pertaining to protective legislations is very very poor. It may be due to widespread illiteracy among women population in our rural India.

Population of our country is fast increasing which is resulting widespread poverty, diseases and umemployment. Despite tremendous governmental efforts the population explosion could not be controlled. It can be successful only if citizens of this country are aware of its side-effect. Now due to spread of education, propagation of small family norm, the level of awareness regarding family planning is fast catching up among people in our country. Table 15 depicts that out of total 100 sample respondents 45 respondents were in favour of family planning and wants to keep their family small but still large section of respondents, viz., 35 were against it. They have certain types of apprehensions about the side-effects of family planning. Need is to educate such people about the misgivings about various methods of family planning programmes.

In our rural society existence of male child is still very important and without male child family is thought to be incomplete. The present study also revealed this notion. Table 16 reveals that there were 15 sample women respondents who would try for male child till it is possible. No respondent even

**TABLE 15: Respondent's response to family planning programmes**

| Response | Frequency | Percentage |
|---|---|---|
| Favour | 45 | 45 |
| Against | 35 | 35 |
| No reply | 20 | 20 |
| Total | 100 | 100 |

**TABLE 16: Opinion regarding number of child/ children in the family**

| No. of children | Frequency | Percentage |
|---|---|---|
| One male child only | NIL | NIL |
| One boy and one girl | 12 | 12 |
| Two boys only | 35 | 35 |
| Two boys and one girl | 38 | 38 |
| No limit till male child | 15 | 15 |
| Total | 100 | 100 |

wants single male child and wants to have two male childs one female child. But as a whole there is change among rural women regarding size of family. Majority respondents wants to restrict their family size between 2 to 3 children.

## PRI and Women's Participation

In the political system the village panchayat is there at the grassroot level to obtain women's participation in democratic processes. The village has always remained as the most important unit of social and economic life.

The very important step toward political empowerment of women has been initiated with reservation of 33.3 per cent of total seats in Panchayati Raj Institutions (PRIs) under the 73rd Constitutional Amendment in 1992.

In the panchayat elections held in December 1996 in the wake of the new enactment five women members were elected to the Thachadhar village panchayat, one member was elected unanimously to the Seraj Block Samiti. Post of panchayat pradhan was reserved for women. In these elections rural women voters took keen interest. Women population of this village panchayat was very happy with the provisions of 73rd Constitutional Amendment. They opined that, earlier male population did not want to share political power with females. Women of this village panchayat revealed that now their husbands or parents did not object to contest the election rather than encouraged them to contest the same and provided full financial as well as moral support. Only elderly section of women population was against women participation in political activities.

From the election results of various women candidates it was revealed that rural population has chosen such candidates who were comparatively better qualified. All seven women elected to different positions in different bodies were found above matric. The above discussion reveals that women in village panchayat Thachadhar are not encouraged to participate in various development programmes by the male dominated society. Literacy rate among women was found to be quite low and majority of women were found performing traditional types of job. Their level of earning was also found to be quite low. Level of awakening was found at a very low level but there is gradual improvement in level of awareness among sample rural women in certain fields. Now women wants to have small family size, adult education has become popular among them and have actively participated in panchayati raj institutions. This participation could be possible due to reservation of seats under the provisions of 73rd Constitutional Amendment. But still in economic, educational health and political fields, their participation is very negligible.

Thus for the overall development of women it is essential to encourage their active participation in various development programmes. Their participation in various democratic institutions needs to be encouraged. For this purpose spread of education is must among said section of the society. Women needs to be educated about merits of small family norms and abuses of large family size. Further more employment opportunities must be created for rural women so that their level of earning could be improved and they could be made self-dependent only then they can show their presence felt in the decision-making processes at different levels on different issues. Through workshop the state governments should enlighten women regarding various protective legislation and varieties of developmental programmes which have been provided by the government especially for women. Only then atrocities against women can be minimised and active participation of women in development can be increased and social, economic and political status of such a large section of population can be improved.

# 22

# Women Development—Strategies, Challenges and Prospects

*Mamta Kaushal*

> "Suffer women once to arrive at equality with you and they will from that moment on become your superior".
>
> —*Cato the elder, 195 BC*

The role women plays in society and image we have of them have developed not simply from exigencies of biology and social situations. These are deep-rooted in the myths and legend and the religion of culture.

"Women is the builder and moulder of nation's destiny. Though delicate and soft as a lily she has a heart far stronger and bolder than man—she is the supreme inspiration for man's onward march, an embodiment of love, pity and compassion" (Tagore). But all through the ages, she has been walking on the flames of atrocities pleasing the society which is deaf, dumb and cruel. Her exultations and feelings are trampled underfoot just as a terrible storm scatters the petals of a beautiful flower. Women seems to be a burden on society which survives because of women only.

Post-colonial period in a backward capitalist country like India has generated contradictory currents. On the one hand growth of economic development and socio-political movements resulted in generating a liberal attitude towards access to education and employment for middle-class women. These currents further led to social awareness against inhuman anti-woman social practices like sati, femal infanticide, prohibition of widow remarriage, etc. While on the other hand new problems have been created such as dowry murders, increasing sexual atrocities against women, marginalisation of women workers, religious revivalism, caste and communal riots leading to devalution of women.

Various policies and programmes were implemented to improve the condition of women, to uplift them and to empower them. In this paper, an attempt has been made to examine the programmes and perspectives of government organisations in connection with women development.

## Constitutional Provisions for Women

The Constitution of India guarantees fundamental rights to all its citizens. The preamble of the Constitution resolves to ensure justice, social, economic and political, liberty of thought, expression, belief, faith and worship, equality of status and opportunity and to promote among them all fraternity assuring the dignity of the individual and the unity and integrity of the nation.

A look at the Constitution of India gives an insight into the constitutional provisions for women. The Articles relating to the Fundamental Rights of women are:

Article 14 ensures that the State shall not deny to any person equality before the law or equal protection of the laws within the territory of India.

Article 15 prohibits discrimination against any citizen on ground of religion, race, caste, sex, place of birth or any of them.

Article 15(3) empowers the State to make any special provision for women and children. This has resulted in legislations like Factories Act, Mines Act, etc.

Article 16(1) states that there shall be equality of opportunity for all citizens in matters relating to employment or appointment in any office under the State.

Article 16(2) guarantees that no citizen shall on grounds only of religion, race, caste, sex, descent place of birth, residence or any of them be ineligible for or discriminated against in respect of any employment or office under the State.

Directive Principles of State Policy embody the major policy goals of the Welfare State. The Directive Principles of State Policy concerning women and having a special bearing on their status are:

Article 39(a) which directs the State to frame its policy for ensuring that the citizens, men and women equally have the right to an adequate means of livelihood. Article 39(d) directs the State to ensure equal pay for equal work for both men and women.

Article 39(e) directs the State to ensure that the health and strength of workers—men and women—are safeguarded and children of tender age are not abused and that they are not forced by economic necessity to enter avocations unsuited to their age.

Article 42 directs the State to ensure just and humane conditions of work and maternity relief.

It can be seen from the above that the Fundamental Rights of Constitution and the Directive Principles of State Policy accord equality to women in all fields. Thus constitutional provisions safeguard women and protect their rights from being trampled in the male dominated society.

## Five Year Plans and Women Development

***First Five Year Plan (1951-56)***

(i) Establishment of the Central Social Welfare Board.
(ii) Organisation of Mahila Mandals.
(iii) Community Development Programme.

***Second Five Year Plan (1956-61)***

Welfare measures for women persisted during this plan period.

***Third Five Year Plan (1961-66)***

(i) Supported female education.
(ii) Rural welfare services and condensed courses of education had priority besides provisions of service for maternal and child welfare, health, education, nutrition and family planning.

***Fourth Five Year Plan (1969-74)***

The outlay for family planning was stepped up and highest priority was accorded to immunisation and supplementary feeding programmes.

***Fifth Five Year Plan (1974-79)***

(i) Emphasised the need to train women in need of income and protection.
(ii) Functional Literacy Programme got the top priority.
(iii) Women Welfare and Development Bureau were set up in 1976 under the Ministry of Social Welfare.

***Sixth Five Year Plan (1980-85)***

(i) It was a definite shift from welfare to development.
(ii) It recognised women's lack of access to resources as a critical factor impending their growth.
(iii) A programme for joint pattas to men and women was initiated.

***Seventh Five Year Plan (1985-90)***

(i) Operationalised the concern for equity and empowerment.
(ii) Emphasis was on qualitative aspects such as inculcation of confidence generation of awareness with regards to rights and training in skills for better employment.
(iii) Emphasised the need to open new avenues of work for women.
(iv) Recognition was also given to the need for organising women for safeguarding their rights.

***Eighth Five Year Plan (1990-95)***

It focused on empowering women especially at the grass-root level through Panchayati Raj Institutions.

## Legislation and Women

The series of liberal and progressive sounding legislations affecting women enacted in our country over the period of the last one decade are the outcome of continuous struggle launched by women's group, sensitive lawyers and democratic right groups. Some of these laws are given here:

Legislations for women.
Hindu Law of Inheritance Act, 1929.
The Hindu Marriage Disability Removal Act, 1946.
The Hindu Women Right of Property Act, 1937.
The Special Marriage Act, 1954.
The Hindu Marriage Act, 1955.
The Hindu Succession Act.
Hindu Adoption and Maintenance Act, 1956.
The Dowry Prohibition Act, 1961.
The Maternity Benefits Act, 1961.
The Equal Remuneration Act, 1976.
The Criminal Law Amendment, 1983.
Immoral Traffic (Prevention Act), 1986.
Indecent Representation of Women (Prohibition) Act, 1986.
Muslim Women (Protection of Rights on Divorce) Act, 1986.
The Sati Prevention Act, 1987.

Significant activity during the decade is not legislation only but rather the role of the judiciary in proclaiming path-breaking judgements; as well as the use of law and law courts by many women's groups—not merely to get justice but also to highlight women's issue.

In pursuance of a Supreme Court judgement dated 13 August, 1997 on sexual harassment of women at work place, the Ministries/Department of the Government of India have set up Complaints Committees for redressal of grievances of female employees. The conduct rules applicable to the Central Government employees have been amended to include "sexual harassment" as a specific offence liable for punishment.

Supreme Court in a landmark judgement on the guardianship of "a minor" under section 6(a) of the Hindu Minorities and Guardianship Act, 1890 has ruled that mother can act as natural guardian of the minor children.

### Approaches to Women's Development

There can be two major approaches to women's development:

(i) Governmental; and
(ii) Non-Governmental.

Government programmes for women's development began as early as 1954 in India. Although the beginning was made in 1954, the actual participation of women in mainstream economic activities began only in 1974 with the report of the Committee on the Status of Women in India. In the seventies, the government dealt with women's development issues as part of the wider category of poverty alleviation. Numerous initiatives in the later half of the eighties demonstrated the Indian Government increasing concern about women. These initiatives includes the setting up of:

(i) National Commission on Self-employed Women and Women in the Informal Sector (NCSW).
(ii) Formulation of National Perspective Plan for Women (NAPPW).
(iii) Support to Employment Programmes for Women (STEP).
(iv) Pilot Mahila Samakya Programme—Women's access to information and participation in development.
(v) Network of State Level Women's Development Corporation.
(vi) Women's Credit Fund.
(vii) Training-cum-Production Centre for Women.
(viii) Awareness generation camps for rural and poor women.
(ix) Women's Training Centres or Institutes for Rehabilitation of Women in distress.
(x) Voluntary Action Bureau and Family Counselling Centres.
(xi) Short Stay Homes for Women and Girls.
(xii) Free legal aid and para legal training.
(xiii) Working Women's Hostels.

## Department of Women and Child Development

The Department of Women and Child Development, Ministry of Human Resource Development has wide range of programmes aimed at the welfare and development of rural women. To tackle the problem of rural women the Department of Women and Child Development initiated a nation-wide debate on the National Perspective Plan for Women 1998-2000.

## National Commission for Women

It is a statutory body created during January, 1992 under the Act of Parliament to facilitate redressal of grievances and to accelerate the socio-economic development of country.

Special studies of National Commission for Women focused on:

(a) Women of weaker sections.
(b) Widows of Vrindavan.
(c) Project Mangalam.
(d) Issues concerning prostitution.
(e) Study of mentally disabled women.
(f) Agenda of political empowerment.

Focus areas of Commission in 1999 were:

(i) Launched Dahej Mukti Abhiyan.
(ii) Prison reforms for women undertrials.
(iii) Gender sensitisation workshops for police, judiciary, doctors through training modules.
(iv) To study problems relating to women and disabilities.

Policies made for Women Welfare:

(i) National Plan of Action for Women, 1976.
(ii) National Health Policy, 1983.
(iii) National Policy on Education, 1986.
(iv) National Perspective Plan for Women 1988-2000.
(v) National Plan of Action for Child and Girl Child (1991-2000).
(vi) National Nutrition Policy, 1993.

In all these policies, efforts were made by government to identify women as special beneficiaries and to do welfare measures for them.

## DWCRA Programmes for Women Development

The programme for Development of Women and Children in Rural Areas (DWCRA) launched in 1982-83, inaugurated an era for systematically organising women in groups for enhancing their earning on a self-sustaining basis and increasing their access to and utilisation of services like health, child care and adult education among others. The programme called for formation of groups of 10-15 women who would collectively engage in an activity. A revolving fund of Rs.15,000 (presently enhanced to Rs.25,000) was made available to each group for credit and administrative need. Supplementing of staff by inclusion of an additional Gram Sevika and appointment of a lady officer to the post of Assistant Project Officer to oversee implementation to the programme were called for. Subsequently with a view to fortify the programme further and increasing awareness a Community Based Convergent Services (CBDS) Component and Information, Education and Communication (IEC) Component were included. Up to early 1996, over 1.3 lakh groups covering 2.2 million women were formed. Almost all the districts in the country (except a handful of exclusively urban ones) are presently covered under this programme.

### *Canadian International Development Agency (CIDA)*

Canadian International Development Agency was among the first national donor agency to integrate women in development (WID) strategy into its operation since adopting the strategy. CIDA has played a prominent role in ensuring the adoption of WID policies by such multilateral institutions as the UN Development Programmes and the Asian Development Bank.

### *Support to Training and Employment Programme (STEP)*

This programme was started in 1987 to up to date women skill and knowledge in agriculture, animal husbandry, fishery, handloom, handicraft, small-scale industry, sericulture and social forestry.

### *Mahila Samriddhi Yojana*

It was started in 1993 to encourage saving among rural women. Under this Yojana, 1.32 lakh rural Post Office were opened.

### *Rashtriya Mahila Kosh*

A Rashtriya Mahila Kosh was set-up in 1993 for extending credit with low transaction costs to poor and needy women and women's groups through non-governmental organisations. At present the scheme is being implemented in the fifteen States—Andhra Pradesh, Bihar, Haryana, Himachal Pradesh, Gujarat, Karnataka, Kerala, Maharashtra, Madhya Pradesh, Manipur, Orissa, Rajasthan, Tamil Nadu, Uttar Pradesh and West Bengal—through a network of one hundred and four non-governmental organisations.

### *The Indira Mahila Yojana*

The Indira Mahila Yojana launched in 1995 aims at co-ordinating and integrating sectoral programmes relevant to women like health, education, water, sanitation, housing and others at local, block and district levels and increasing their awareness and income through group activities and participation with the aim of empowering women. Indira Mahila Kendras would be established at village level and Indira Mahila Block Kendras at Block for this purpose. The programme would be centrally sponsored scheme. Non-governmental organisations would also be involved in this process. The programme has been sanctioned for a period of seven years commencing from 1995-96. During the inception year, it was to .cover 200 blocks on a pilot basis and a thousand blocks each year in the subsequent years. The central government would provide a one time grant of Rs.5000 to each Indira Mahila Kendra.

Other policies started for women welfare are:

(1) Bhagyashree Child Welfare Policy.
(2) Raj Rajeshwari Mahila Kalyan Yojana.

Although the efforts made by government are commendable still the common Indian women are amidst hunger, oppression, physical and mental torture, dishonour, illiteracy, disease and general neglect. The critical areas of concern that continue to impede gender equality are access to economic structure, decision-making and planning process, disadvantages faced by girl child and poverty of women. Women suffers from violence, poor wages, victimisation, criminal offences, molestation, abduction, dowry deaths, wifebattering, eve teasing and rape.

The State of World Population Report, 1997 released on 28 May, 1997 has brought to the light that in India there is a rape every 54 minutes, one molestation every 26 minutes, one reported dowy death every hour and 42 minutes and one act of cruelty after 33 minutes.

The participation of women in administration is less in number at the level of decision-making. There is only one woman judge in Supreme Court out of 21 and 14 women High Court judges out of total 419. Among the 75 secretaries to government, there are only a few women.

In Human Development Report, 1998, India ranks 128 in the gender related development index. Women earned income share is merely 24.8 per cent. India ranks a dismal 95 when it comes to gender empowerment measures. A mere 2.3 per cent women are administrators and managers, 20.5 per cent professional and technical workers.

The demand for dowry made even on professional educated women, imply that a son is preferable to a daughter because a son is an oldage pension for parents. Daughters don't inherit parental property. Despite the passage of 1994 amendment to the Hindu Succession Act.

The growing gap in the male-female ratio testifies to the discrimination against women. The skillful network between obliging doctors and conspiring family members makes at next to impossible to book the culprits doing legally prohibited sex determination tests. Now more sophisticated chromosome separation techniques make even an abortion unnecessary. In 1991 the female sex ratio in India hovered around 929. Preliminary surveys indicate that in the 2001 census, we will find only 920 women for 1000 men. The precipitous decline in India's female sex ratio can be traced to the rampant social evils of female infanticide, female foeticide and the depreciation of the girlchild.

More than 40 per cent of the married women in India are tortured by their husbands for silly reasons, according to Amnesty International Report which was released on the eve of International Women Day, 8 March, 2001.

## What More is to be Done

Thus as far as government efforts are concerned there is no doubt that the list of major initiatives taken over the years to improve the lot of women is a long one. But mere setting up of a Commission for women is just not enough. Education must be imparted.

(i) Education must be imparted to inculcate such values in our children as would make them consider men and women as equal in every sense of the term.
(ii) It should be understood clearly that women's development is not only women's responsibility but men have equal share and responsibility.
(iii) Women development should be taken as a national movement irrespective of political ideology.
(iv) Women should not remain passive spectators, they should struggle, they should demand and they should fight for the just cause.

### *Empowerment of Women*

(i) The name of the mother along with father should be included in every document.
(ii) Loans should be given to women in her individual capacity without the support of male members.
(iii) In the allotment of house, land, etc., the name of wife should also be included.

### *Women in Public Life*

(i) Women's issues to be included in Party manifestos.
(ii) Minimum 30 per cent of party tickets should be given to women by political parties.

(iii) Reservation of seats in Parliament and Assemblies.
(iv) Women should be increasingly involved in the decision-making process.
(v) Age relaxation should be given to women up to 5 years.
(vi) Women's representation should be ensured in all national bodies like Planning Commission and Public Service Commission.

### *Atrocities Against Women*

(i) Efforts to be made to minimise crimes against women.
(ii) Involvement of more and more women in policing.
(iii) Deterrent punishment for heinous crimes like rape, bride burning, etc.
(iv) Change in Evidence Act and Criminal Procedure Act to avoid loopholes.
(v) Girls in NCC to be encouraged.
(vi) Karate and judo to be introduced in girls schools and colleges.
(vii) Victims of rape to be rehabilitated properly.
(viii) The sikh clergy deserves to be congratulated on pronouncing a "Hukamnama" from Shri Akal Takhat asking the Sikhs to refrain from this evil of female infanticide. The Hukamnama says that a sikh should not kill his daughter nor should he maintain any relationship with such killers. Other religions should follow the sikh clergy because this is in the interest of humanity.

### *Women's Development*

(i) Proper monitoring of women development programmes.
(ii) A women's cell consisting of members other than government officials to be established in each department.
(iii) Women's organisation to take women's development as a movement and take the message from door to door.

### *Women's Participation*

(i) Empower women in poverty groups with information and education pertaining to factors affecting their status and situation as also to government schemes and intervention.

(ii) Facilitate group formation and action to improve women status.
(iii) Develop leadership and capacity among women to effectively participate in local bodies organisation.
(iv) Establish a network of resources agencies to provide technical inputs for initiating and sustaining the process.
(v) Promote positive understanding of women's need among policy-makers, peoples representatives and the public at large.

It should be remembered that howsoever intelligent doctor may be howsoever effective his medicine may be, he cann't cure the patient unless the patient himself wants to be cured. This applies to the women as well. The women are the patient here and indiscrimination, inequality and atrocities are their desease. Only when the women both individually and collectively, sincerely and genuinely want to get rid of this disease can an abiding remedy be found.

> "Buck up women, the World is at your feet if only you dare and act".

## REFERENCES

Aleem Shamim, *Women Development—Problems and Prospects,* APH Publishing Corporation, New Delhi, 1996.

Desai Neera and Patel Vibhuti, *Indian Women—Changes and Challenges in the International Decade 1975-85,* Popular Prakashan, Bombay, 1985.

Jha Shankar Uma, Mehta Arati & Menon Latika, *Status of Indian Women—Crisis and Conflict in Gender Issues,* volume-I. Kanishka Publishers and Distributors, New Delhi, 1998.

Joseph Molly, *Women Participation and Development Strategies,* Kanishka Publishers, Distributors, New Delhi, 1997.

Roy Kalpana, *Women and Their Environment,* Rajat Publications, New Delhi, 1999.

Forward Looking Strategies for the Advancement of Women. The World Conference of Review and Appraise the Achievements of the United Nations Decade for Women: Equality, Development and Peace, Nairobi (Kenya) 1985. Ministry of Human Resource Development, Department of Women Welfare.

National Perspective Plan for Women, 1988-2000 AD, Department of Women and Child Development, Ministry of Human Resource Development, Government of India, 1988.

Towards Equality: Report of the Committee on the Status of Women in India-1974. Ministry of Education and Social Welfare; Department of Social Welfare.

# 23

# Women Empowerment at Grassroot Level

*S.L. Kaushik & Kiran Hooda*

The term empowerment indicates the process of "giving power to", developing conditions for "generating power within", facilitating "acquisition of power" and lastly "building capacities for utilisation of power".[1] Thus, empowerment has multi-dimensional focus and its success depends on environmental factors in a given society.

Women power means having control, organising further control, having a say and being listened to, being able to define and create from a women's perspective, being able to influence social choices and decision affecting the whole society (not just areas of society accepted as women's place), being organised and respected as equal citizens and human beings with a contribution to make.[2]

Addressing the inaugural session of a three-day International seminar on "Decentralisation; Devolution and Participation", at Calcutta on 28 December, 1998, Nobel Laureate Prof. Amartya Sen said that the four fundamentals of decentralisation were information, autonomy and incentives, competition and empowerment of women. While citing the example of Bangladesh where the rate of population growth has shown a marked decline, he said that enhancing the decision-making powers of women in rural areas and the preference given to women for loans at the micro-level had hastened the process of decentralisation as well as development.[3] The primary challenge facing women today, therefore, is to increase their participation so that they get hold of the situation and become actively involved in the process of decision-making. To elaborate further women's development can be viewed in terms of five levels of equality.[4]

1. Welfare address only the basic needs of women without recognising or attempting to solve the underlying structural causes, which necessitate provisions of welfare services.
2. Access—involves equality of access to resources, such as educational opportunities, land and credit.
3. Conscientisation—Woman must recognise the role they can play in reinforcing the system that restricts their growth.
4. Participation—is the point where women are taking decisions alongside men equally.
5. Control is the ultimate level of equality and empowerment. The contributions of women are fully recognised and researched.

As one moves towards higher levels of empowerment there is bound to be resistance and conflict, as exclusive male privileges are threatened.

The issue of women's empowerment cannot be viewed in isolation from the general position of women in society. The whole issue needs to be placed in a historical perspective with a view to examine the status assigned to them by tradition, religion and social structure.

## Women in Ancient and Medieval Period

In Vedic age woman was viewed not as a thing of pleasure but as a partner in the religious duties of a man. Women capable of carrying religious discussions were admitted into assemblies.[5] However, in the later Vedic period, their position deteriorated. There exists evidence of sati, dowry system and polygamy. Even Manu regarded women as more emotional and less rational than man and advocated for their protection throughout their life.[6] Buddha regarded women as easy victims to the senses, passions, anger, greed, etc.[7] and hence man and woman were not considered equal.

The position of Hindu women registered a gradual decline after the advent of Muslim rule in India. The medieval period strengthened the atrocious practice of female infanticide, child-marriage, sati, parda and polygamy. It is interesting to note that while the status of women had deteriorated in the society, women in high positions proved to be good administrators and writers of distinction. Some of the famous personalities of this era are Gulbadan Begum, Jahan-Ara, Razia-Sultana, Nur-Jahan, Zibunnisa, Begum Hazrat-Mahal, Chand Bibi, Sahabji, etc.[8]

## Women in India's Freedom Struggle

The period between 1857-1900 is marked by the political awakening. There was a political and administrative unification of the country, which was further promoted and strengthened by the modern means of communication and transport, Western education, religious organisations like the Brahmo-Samaj, Arya-Samaj, Theosophical Society worked for social reforms.

In 1919, under the Montague-Chelmsford reforms, women obtained the voting right. However, they exercised their franchise for the first time in 1932. Till 1926, no woman ever got into any legislature. Muthulakshmi Reddy of Madras, a dedicated social worker was the first woman to be nominated to the Madras Legislative Council and she was also elected as the Deputy Chairperson of the Council. The initiative of introducing the Devdasi Bill was taken by her. Kamla Devi Chattopadhyaya, a pioneer in the women's movement was the first to contest a seat from the South Kanar Constituency in Karnataka in 1926.[9]

The Swadeshi Movement, the Non-Cooperation Movement and the Civil Disobedience Movement drew them out from the seclusion of home and made them direct participant in the struggle.

Women also involved themselves in the making of the Constitution. The Constituent Assembly was set up in October, 1946, had amongst its members some of the noted personalities like Sarojini Naidu, Durgabhai Deshmukh, Renuka Roy and Hansa Mehta.[10]

### Women in Post-Independent India

With the process of modernisation and increasing education, we can see women taking active part in politics and holding high offices. There have been woman Prime Minister, women ambassadors and delegates to international bodies, women governors, women chief ministers, ministers and legislators who have shaped the history of our country. Some of the famous names are Vijay Lakshmi Pandit, Indira Gandhi, Sarojini Naidu, Sucheta Kriplani, Nandini Satpathy, Raj Kumari Amrit Kaur, V.S. Rama Devi etc.

The Constitution of India guarantees both rights and privileges to women through Fundamental Rights and Directive Principles. Article 14 confers on men and women equal rights and opportunities in political, economic and social spheres. Article 15 prohibits discrimination against any citizen on grounds of religion, race, caste, sex, etc. Article 15(3) makes a special provision enabling the State to make affirmative discrimination in favour of women. Article 16 provides for equality of opportunities. Article 39(a) ensures equal rights to means of livelihood and Article 39(c) ensures equal pay for equal work. Article 42 directs state to provide for just and humane conditions of work and maternity relief. Above all, the Constitution imposes a fundamental duty on every citizen through Article 51 (a) (c) to denounce practices derogatory to the dignity of women.

A number of laws have been enacted to ensure equality and improve the status of women. Some of these are Hindu Succession Act, 1956, Remuneration Act, 1976, Hindu Marriage Act amended in 1976, The Immoral Traffic (Prevention) Act, 1956 (amended in 1986), Dowry Prohibition Act, 1961 (amended in 1986), The Child Marriage Restraint Act of 1976, The Factories Act, 1948 (amended in 1976), The (Prevention) Act, 1987, etc.

Besides the social legislations, planned change played an important role in creating awareness amongst women. The government adopted a multi-disciplinary approach with a three-pronged thrust on health, education and employment of women. The four decades of planned development in India through the seven five-year plans had hardly achieved much where women especially rural women were concerned. The approach of the Eighth Plan marked a shift from development to empowerment of women. It recommended 30 per cent reservation for women at all levels of government. The Ninth Five-Year Plan (1997-2002) has focused on two aspects. The first is the listing of empowerment of women as a major plan objective and the other is to propose inclusion of a Women's Component Plan in the Plan of all Central Ministries/Departments.

Many policy instruments have been brought forth over the years. Some of the important policy guiding documents include—The National Plan of Action for Women, 1976, a National Perspective Plan for Women (1988-2000), Shram Shakti—The Report of the National Commission on Self-Employed Women and Women in Informal Sector (1988), The National Expert Committee on Women Prisoners (1986), The National Plan of Action for the Girl Child (1991-2000), etc. Government has adopted various strategies for empowering women. It set up the Central Social Welfare Board in 1956; Department of Women and Child Development was set up in 1985; the National Commission for Women (NCW) was set up in 1992 for safeguarding the rights of women. The Rashtriya Mahila Kosh (RMK) was set up in 1993 to extend credit to poor. Various programmes like Mahila Samriddhi Yojna (1993), Indira Mahila Yojna (1995), Hostels for Working Women, Reservations under Poverty Alleviation Programmes, etc., are started to empower women.[11]

The (73rd and 74th) Constitutional Amendment Bills passed in 1992 by the Parliament marks a major event in the lives of Indian Women as amendments ensure one-third of total seats (33.3 per cent) for women in all elected offices of local bodies. About 0.8 million women have emerged as leaders/decision-makers, of these about 76,200 are chairwomen at the village, block and district levels.[12]

## Women in Panchayati Raj Institutions

The committees which recommended the creation and improvement of Panchayati Raj Institutions had nothing much to say on the role of women in the Panchayati Raj Institutions. The only mention made by the Balwantray Mehta Committee, in regard to women was the recommendation that in the constitution of Panchayat, provision may be made for the co-option of two women members. The Ashok Mehta team had mentioned that two women securing highest number of votes among the women candidates in the election could take the seats reserved for them, i.e., a method of cooption by election.

The seats reserved for women in Panchayati Raj Institutions have been so low that women could hardly influence the political process. In view of the 73rd Constitutional Amendment, the Panchayati Raj System, has got a new look. Out of total number of seats reserved for scheduled castes and scheduled tribes, not less than 1/3rd seats shall be reserved for women belonging to the scheduled castes and scheduled tribes. Out of total number of seats to be filled by direct election in every panchayat not less than 1/3rd seats shall be reserved for women. Similarly, not less than 1/3rd of the total number of the offices of chairperson in the Panchayati Raj Institutions shall be reserved for women.

Now with 33 per cent reservation and 33 per cent of women already present in Panchayati Raj Institutions, they are expected to make their impact felt in local policy-making. Various studies have been conducted to assess the influence women are exerting in local policy making and to identify factors that facilitate or prevent women from playing a more effective role through Panchayati Raj Institutions.

There are various studies at grass-root level which confirm the low level of political participation of women members. Some of these are, study conducted in Bangalore rural district in the State of Karnataka,[13] Himachal Pradesh,[14] Jalandhar district of Punjab,[15] Haryana[16] and Jabalpur district of Madhya Pradesh.[17] Variety of constraints were reported in their effective functioning, like socio-cultural, norms of society, negative reactions of men, lack of interest and awareness, illiteracy, poverty and social institutional barriers. The Rajasthan Panchayati Raj Act, 1994, which ensured for the woman a place in the top positions in the local bodies, has failed to protect them from humiliation and harassment and forced resignations. The male deputy chairpersons working under women chairpersons in the Panchayati Raj Institutions have taken advantage of this provision in the Act to get them ousted from their positions.

61 no-confidence motions were brought for hearing between March, 1997 and February, 1998.[18]

A study conducted by the Human Rights Advocacy and Research Foundation in Tamilnadu shows how male members and clerks try to get a semi-literate women president dismissed under Section 205 of Chapter 10 of the Panchayat Act, which is used by a District Collector in dismissing "errant and non-performing panchayat members".[19]

In contract to the findings of the studies mentioned earlier, in Karnataka,[20] it was revealed that majority of women members of Panchayati Raj Institutions had put up fairly better development role performance (between 1987 and 1992). They secured development benefits to the people of their villages mainly in the field of agriculture, public works and civic amenities, welfare and education.

Fatima Bi, Sarpanch of Kalva village in Kurnool district of Andhra Pradesh was selected for the United Nations Development Programme's International Race against Poverty Award for her outstanding contribution to strengthen the poverty alleviation programmes in the State. The award was presented to her by the UN Secretary General on 17 October, 1998 at New York.[21]

There is much to be achieved in the area of women emancipation and empowerment. Drawing lessons from experiences and case studies at both national and international level is important.

The low literacy level of women is most often given as a reason for their invisibility. In Kerala the female literacy is 86.9 per cent and yet women's participation in the State Assembly is not more than 5.7 per cent whereas in Rajasthan where the female literacy level is 20 per cent, women's participation in Assembly has touched 8 per cent mark.[22] So, education is not the only factor which influences women's emancipation.

Self-reliance is important as it leads to self-confidence. But economic independence does not lead to their increased participation in PRIs. Reviews of cross cultural research lead to universal conclusion that all cultures distinguish between behaviours considered appropriate for males and females and reinforce it through differential socialisation of males and females. Men are considered more desirable to act as leader, to be aggressive, ambitious, competitive and dominant. It is considered more desirable for women to be sensitive to the need of others, tender, warm, affectionate, polite and submissive. Both tend to go into gender-stereotypic occupations.[23]

An appropriate question which need to be answered is, can one expect empowerment of women through legal and constitutional measures in system where both the state structures and the institutions of civil society are feudal and patriarchal. The study was conducted in a few villages in the Shivalik foothills to explore the impact of integrated watershed management projects on the role and position of women in comparison with men. It was found that as a result of project activities, achievement levels of both women and men increased, but the burden of ecological change had fallen disproportionately on females. Their contribution to farm activities increased by 157 per cent whereas that of men by only 85 per cent.[24] The suggestion is that any assessment of the role and problems of women in Indian economy has to take note that the nature and structure of Indian economy is largely based in agriculture with its characteristic feature of labour utilisation and the social position of women in rural areas.

There is hardly any activity in crop, animal husbandry and other household chores in which females of rural areas do not contribute right from cooking in household to post-harvest operations in agriculture. The struggle of farm women is not only for food but also for firewood and water. A study conducted by Thakur *et al.* (1992) in mountainous region revealed that women contribute more than 50 per cent in almost all the agricultural activities except ploughing; while in animal husbandry related works, rural women share as much as 90 per cent of the burden. According to National Commission for Women Report (1994) a pair of bullock works for 1064 hrs, a man for 1212 hrs, whereas a women works for 3495 hrs on one hectare farm annually.[25] The emanicipation requires women's freedom from the drudgery of existence in rural areas.

Empowerment is a socio-political concept and it goes beyond political participation. Political behaviour is outside one's specified job requirement. Politics is always concerned with power. As Pfiffner writes, "if power is a force, a store of potential influence through which events can be affected, politics involves those activities or behaviours through which power is developed and used in organisational settings.[26] To influence and lead effectively, leader must develop and use power. To empower is giving women the capacity to influence the decison-making process by integrating them into our political system. Reserving seats for women in political institutions provide them an opportunity for political participation and involves them in political, economic and social life of a nation. But effective participation is a function of both higher level support and the capacity and willingness of women to lend a helping hand to local community efforts. Hence empowerment of women can be made possible not only through reservations but it also requires the removing of causes of disempowerment which can be social, political or psychological. Even after 50 years of independence, there exist growing violence against women—rape, wife battering, family violence, dowry deaths, ghunghat phenomenon and prostitution. Empowerment would involve understanding of the conditions of subordination and powerlessness and the causes of such conditions in society. According to Paul Friere "empowerment" would involve enabling the oppressed to become active and reflective about their reality (conscientisation process) to create social capacity to transform existential reality.[27] It expresses on inner attitude of strength which make room for transformation by getting over phelplessness grown out of adverse process of socialisation.

We, therefore, emphasise that empowerment process requires social change by organising and mobilising the women groups for struggle. The Mahila Mandal's should be formed in all the villages and the existing ones need to be strengthened. Political education and training is necessary for them to overcome many of their obstacles to empowerment. Any development strategy which perceives women as a specific interest issue and designs programmes for them will not serve the purpose until and unless the multidimensional processes and structures that marginalise them are examined and tackled.

## REFERENCES

1. Jain, S.P. "Empowerment of Rual Women through Local Self-Government in Afro-Asian Countries", *Journal of Rural Reconstruction*, 31:2 (1998) 38.

2. Sahay, Sushma, *Women and Empowerment: Approach and Strategies*, New Delhi, Discovery Publishing House, 1998, p. 22.
3. *Panchayat Raj Update*, New Delhi, Institute of Social Sciences, 1998, p. 1.
4. Sahay, Sushma, *op. cit.*, pp. 39-40.
5. Shastri, Shakuntala Rao, *Women in the Vedic Age*, Bombay, Bhartiya Vidya Bhawan, 1960, pp. 186-90.
6. Das, Ram Mohan, *Women in Manu's Philosophy*, New Delhi, ABS Publications, 1993, p. 2.
7. Shastri, Shakuntala Rao, *op. cit.*, pp. 7-9.
8. Jharta, Bhawana, *Women and Politics in India*, New Delhi, Deep & Deep Publications, 1996, p. 53.
9. Jharta, Bhawana, *op. cit.*, p. 57.
10. Baig, Tara Ali, *India's Women Power*, New Delhi, S. Chand & Company, 1976, p. 218.
11. Das, Asha, Child Development and Empowering Women in India, *Indian Journal of Public Administration*, XLIII:3 (July-Sept. 1997), pp. 369-94.
12. *Ibid.*, 392.
13. Vidya, K.C., *Political Empowerment of Women at the Grassroots*, New Delhi, Kanishka Publishers, 1997, p. 248.
14. Jharta, Bhawana, *op. cit.*, p. 221.
15. Harsukhjit Kaur, "Women Leadership at the Grassroot Level in Punjab, A Case Study of Jalandhar District", Unpublished Ph.D. Thesis, Chandigarh, Punjab University, 1994. p. 248.
16. Duhan, Kiran, "Women Leadership in Panchayati Raj Institutions in the State of Haryana", Unpublished Ph.D. Thesis, Chandigarh, Punjab University, 2000.
17. Tremblay, Reeta Chowdhari, *et al.*, Governance and Representation: A Study of Women and Local Self-Government, *Indian Journal of Public Administration*, (Sept.) 1998.
18. *Panchayati Raj Update*, New Delhi, Institute of Social Science, (Aug. 1998), p. 6.
19. *Ibid.* (Nov. 2000), p. 5.
20. Gowda, S. Govinda, *et al.*, "Developmental Role of Women Members of PRIs: A Study of Karnataka", *Journal of Rural Development*, 15:1 (April-June 1996), pp. 249-59.
21. *Panchayati Raj Update*, New Delhi, Institute of Social Sciences, (Sept. 1980), p. 1.
22. Naryana, Shashi S, "The Reservations of Women in Decision Making Bodies", *Social Action*, 48:2 (April-June 1998) 154.
23. Ghadially, Rehana, *Women in Indian Society*, New Delhi, Sage Publications, 1998.

24. Mittal, S.P. *et al.*, *Fifty Years of Research On Sustainable Resource Management in Shivaliks,* Chandigarh, Central Social and Water Conservation Research and Training Institute, 2000, pp. 209-16.
25. *Ibid.*, p. 210.
26. Sudha, G.S., *Organisational Behaviours: A Psychological Framework,* Jaipur, National Publication House, 1996, p. 195.
27. Bhattacharya, Mohit, *Development Administration*, New Delhi, Jawahar Publishers, 1997, p. 93.

# 24

# Reservation and Political Empowerment of Women: A Vital Issue

*Mohan Jharta & Bhawana Jharta*

One of the components of good polity and society is the equality of access to political rights i.e. the right to vote, to hold public office, to speak up and challenge incumbent leadership and to associate freely with one's fellow citizens in political activity. The availability of political rights, however, is justified in terms of their consequences. In a democratic set up, there may be equal rights for every citizen but there may not be equal access to these rights. Although most of the modern democratic constitutions of the world have established the equality of men and women in matters of political rights, yet in actual practice their participation in active politics is not very encouraging. It must be acknowledged that political participation is the hallmark of any given democratic set up. In order to inject a new life in such a set up, it becomes imperative that women's participation in politics is given due recognition. Gender equality is a pre-requisite for effective participation of women in strengthening the institutional structure of democracy. It would be an ideal set up, if women in large numbers come forward to take part in politics. The general experience in most of the countries of the world is that not many of them come to the forefront. They largely remain inactive and indifferent towards politics.

Same is the case with Indian women. India, the world's largest democracy has only about 7 per cent representation of women in politics.

Women who constitute nearly half of the total population of the country have not been able to participate effectively in various walks of their lives including the political. There prevails a gender discrimination and women's lot in the society is not what it should be and is not getting what is due to them. It is thus half a democracy if women do not have a real share in decision-making at all levels. With the advent of independence, gender equality, gender justice and equal participation of women in the socio-economic and political processes have been the concern of our leaders and policy-makers. Gender discrimination has been banned by the constitution suggesting that all men and women enjoy equal opportunities for their multidimensional growth. Women have been guaranteed political equality with men. The constitution has recognised the need for a free and active participation of women in politics and anticipated their political empowerment so that they could contribute in the nation-building and its alround development. However, even after more than 50 years of independence, women are still marginal to the actual political process. They have been marginalised because of several socio-economic constraints. The number of women in leadership positions at different levels is still not commensurate with their numbers in society.[1]

In the context of the changing socio-economic and political scenario of the country, the gender discourse has shifted from a concern for women's welfare to women's development and now to women's empowerment. Now-a-days, women's empowerment is a new phrase in the vocabulary of gender literature. It has been given currency and recognition by UN agencies and received fillip in the recent years only. The phrase is used in two broad senses i.e. general and specific. In a general sense, it refers to empowering women to be self-dependent by providing them access to all those freedoms and opportunities which they were denied in the past only because of their being a woman. In a specific sense, women's empowerment refers to enhancing their position in the power structure of society. In other words, it means increase in their access to the structures of decision-making process which have otherwise been dominated by men.

We are concerned herewith women's empowerment in the specific sense of the term.

The scholars have suggested two main approaches to women's empowerment namely, 'from-above' and 'from-below'. The first is concerned with the efforts made by the government in order to enhance women's power in public affairs whereas the second focuses on the self-striving of women to get a respectable place for themselves in the given power structure of the society. It is indeed an empowerment through self-struggle. It is believed that true empowerment of women can take place through women's own efforts to mobilise and organise themselves by way of mass women's movements. It may be mentioned here that the track record of India in respect of women's empowerment is comparatively better than that of the so-called developed countries of the world.[2]

In India, women's participation in political activities has increased and improved especially after independence. With the process of modernisation and increasing education, the mental horizon of women have broadened and they have come to know the outside world. Consequently, they have started taking part in politics and holding high offices in the government. Though their number is not very high but their efficiency in administrative and political matters has been well recognised. There have been a Woman Prime Minister, women governors, ambassadors and delegates to international bodies, chief ministers, ministers and legislators who have shaped the history of our country. However, a few sparrows do not make a summer. The overall situation is not very satisfactory. There is a difference between the constitutional rights and the rights enjoyed in reality by women. More then fifty years of independence have made very little impact on women's active participation in politics. Their performance quantitatively has been rather insignificant. Barring a few exceptions, women have remained outside the domain of power and political authority. Women constitute about half of the citizenry and over the years their participation by way of voting has increased and is not too low in comparison to men. However, their participation and representation in law-making and law-implementing bodies is not very satisfactory. Although the 73rd and 74th constitutional Amendment Acts have provided access to women in the decision-making process at the grassroot level, yet their representation in the Parliament and State assemblies is woefully poor as is evident from the following brief analysis.[3]

It may be pointed out that from 1952 to 1999, the overall representation of women in the Lok Sabha remained too low barely between 4 to 8 per cent in comparison to their about 50 per cent share in voting population. In the first Lok Sabha in 1952, their number was 23 which increased to 44 in 1984 and it was 43 in the 12th Lok Sabha of 1998. However, their number is highest ever (47) in the present 13th Lok Sabha. Similarly in the Rajya Sabha also, women's strength remained marginal in comparison to men. Their strength was highest (38) in 1991 and after this a downward trend started and presently there are about 20 women in Rajya Sabha. Thus, in comparison to their voting strength, the number of women is much less in Lok Sabha and Rajya Sabha.

One of the reasons for the poor representation of women in Parliament is that there has always been a very small number of women contestants. There were only 51 women contestants out of the total 1874 in the first general election held in 1952 which increased to 599 in 1996. The number decreased to 252 out of the total 4693 contestants in 1998 which further decreased to 247 out of the total 4648 contestants in the 1999 Lok Sabha election.[4] It is observed that most of the women contestants are either wives or daughters or daughters-in-law of important political functionaries. This is evident from the list of women candidates released by the various political parties during the Assembly and Parliament elections. The political parties follow a trend of dynastic politics. The veteran politicians groom their wives, siblings and relatives to don the mantle of power.

The same is the position of women's representation in the state legislative assemblies (1993-2001) where the percentage of women MLAs vary from one to nine approximately. The political parties seem very reluctant to field women candidates. The imperative of 'winnability' seems to have been used to justify the denial of the tickets to the women except when they are sure winning bets. The political parties dominated by men perhaps do not want to share power with women. Women are at a great disadvantage in power politics. Their numerical strength is also marginal in decision-making bodies. Only a few women have succeeded in getting into the council of ministers so far. In the 13th Lok Sabha, there are 8 women in the council of ministers. Their number never exceeded nine and that was in 1991. Interestingly, there had never been more than one woman cabinet minister. Most of the women ministers had been of the rank of state ministers or deputy ministers.

The same is the case of women in Judiciary, the third organ of the government. The position of women in Judiciary is also not satisfactory. There are only 19 women judges out of a sanctioned strength of 647 judges in various high courts in the country. The Supreme Court has only one woman judge against a total of 26 Judges. The Bombay High Court tops the list with just four women judges followed by the Madras High Court and the Kerala High Court with three women Judges each.[5]

This shows that the actual power is a male monopoly with just a few crumbs thrown to women. There is no deliberate and consistent policy to ensure an adequate participation of women in the higher echelons of power. Some cosmetic steps have been taken in this regard. The government has drawn up National Perspective Plan (1988-2000 AD) which seeks 30 per cent reservation of seats for women in Parliament, State legislatures and at grassroot level in order to ensure effective participation and empowerment of women in democratic institutions. The NPP urged all political parties to ensure at least 30 per cent women among the candidates put up for election, but no party has met the target so far. Some of the notable aspects of women's political participation in post-independent India are as under:[6]

- 'Bibi-Beti-Bahu' syndrome is in operation. Most women MPs, MLAs and other women who are active in politics are either wives, widows, daughters, daughters-in-law, sisters or relatives of prominent politicians or big-wigs or come from politically active families. They remain name lenders for their husbands, fathers, fathers-in-law, brothers or relatives.
- Women are still non-political by nature. They largely remain inactive and indifferent towards politics. A large number of women are reluctant to join politics because of the lack of political interest, political education, unfavourable family as well as societal attitudes and

atmosphere, and their pre-occupation with domestic responsibilities. Women themselves have yet to realise the value of their political role.

- It is not only the incapacity of women to join politics but men also do not want to encourage them. They like to retain their monopoly of power. This keeps women out of political activities and is the cause of their general political backwardness.

As we know, Indian society is male dominated in every aspect of its life. As a result, Indian women suffer all types of socio-cultural, economic and political disadvantages and discriminations. The injustice done to the women over the ages urgently needs to be redressed. Socio-economic and political powers should not be denied to them any longer. In recent years, there has been an awakening among women about their rights. There are proposals for a greater role for women and their empowerment i.e. to give them powers that they deserve. The various feminist organisations, activist women, political parties and leaders are demanding an honourable share for women in the Parliament, state Legislatures and other decision-making bodies. The question arises, how greater participation of women in politics can be achieved in the new century? This is indeed a great challenge before all of us. Generally, the measure suggested is the political empowerment of women by making suitable reservation for them in all walks of public life. The political empowerment of women is perceived as a powerful and indispensable tool for the uplift of women and eliminating gender inequality and discrimination.

Keeping in view the appallingly low representation of women in the law-making and law-implementing bodies, the need for increasing their proportion through reservation can not be over-ruled. It is maintained that our development strategy has been neglecting the cause of womenfolk and has also been exploitative of them. This may be one of the justifications to a cause for reservation for women in the Parliament and state Legislatures. The 73rd and 74th Constitution Amendment Acts of 1992 provide for effective participation of women in Panchayati Raj Institutions and municipalities respectively by making special reservation for women. These are the steps in the right direction and represent a landmark in the history of efforts for empowering women through 33 per cent reservation of seats in municipal and panchayat bodies. This representation at the grassroot level has opened up new horizons for women's participation in the country's politics. It is hoped that these amendments in the constitution will usher in a new era of women's empowerment.

The reservation for women in the Parliament and state Legislatures has become a vital issue of debate. It is debated that a Constitution Amendment Bill (Women's Reservation Bill) providing for 33 per cent reservation of seats for women in the Parliament and state Legislatures be introduced in the Parliament in order to ensure women's empowerment and their full participation in decision-making process which would help them to get respectable position in the society. But, as we know, Women's Reservation Bill is hanging fire for about four years in the Parliament. It may be recalled that the attempts made by the previous Gowda and Gujral governments to introduce the Women's Reservation Bill (the 81st Constitutional Amendment Bill) had failed twice in the Lok Sabha (1996) in the past and later when it was introduced in the Rajya Sabha, it was referred to the Joint Select Committee of Parliament which prepared the Bill. However, the Bill lapsed with the dissolution of the 11th Lok Sabha.[7]

The 84th Constitution Amendment Bill (Women's Reservation Bill) providing for 33 per cent reservation of seats for women in the Parliament and state Legislatures was being proposed to be introduced by the Vajpayee Government in the Parliament as it is. However, the Bill could not be moved in the budget session of Parliament (1998) and met the same fate as in the 11th Lok Sabha as MPs belonging to the Samajwadi Party, the Rashtriya Janata Dal, the Bahujan Samaj Party and some other political parties like the National Conference, the IUML and the MIM protested against it in its present form and the Bill ran into a rough weather. The introduction of the Bill was deferred by the government for the time-being due to objections raised by various political parties and to enable them to arrive at a consensus on the issue. The main objections raised by them include to provide quota for women belonging to Other Backward Classes and minorities within the provision of 33 per cent; the reservation of seats to be slashed from 33 per cent to 15 per cent beside some other changes. So, a demand for reservation within reservation. The result was that the fate of the Bill remained undecided.

The government renewed its attempt to introduce the Jinxed Women's Reservation Bill in the winter session of Parliament (1998) and finally amid pandemonium and turmoil, the Bill was introduced in the Lok Sabha. This time also, it lapsed with the dissolution of the 12th Lok Sabha.[8] In the present 13th Lok Sabha, amid protests, slogan shouting and confusion, the 85th Constitution Amendment Bill providing for one-third reservation for women in Parliament and state Legislative Assemblies was re-introduced by the Vajpayee government on December 23, 1999, the last day of the winter session of Parliament. This time also, some political parties like SP, RJD, BSP, etc. opposed the introduction of the Bill in its present form and demanded that the proposed legislation should include sub-quotas for women belonging to the OBCs, minorities, SCs and STs. However, the major political parties like BJP, Congress, TDP, etc. are favouring the Bill in its present form. Before the House was adjourned sine die, the Prime Minister said the Bill introduced in the Lok Sabha was not the last word and a solution to the demand for a sub-quota for women belonging to the OBCs, minorities, SCs and STs by some political parties would be found. However, he regretted that the unseemly incidents in the Parliament over the Bill had lowered the image and dignity of the highest Legislative Forum.[9] It is pertinent to mention here that the issue should be discussed thoroughly with the leaders of various political parties to reach a broad consensus on the Bill. Let us hope for the very best that the controversy-ridden Women's Reservation Bill would be passed by the both houses of Parliament without any further delay with the dawn of the 21st century.

It may be mentioned here that none of the political parties is opposing the Women's Reservation Bill in principle and a few disagreeing with its content. In the context of the rapidly changing political scenario of the country, it would not be so easy to pass the Women's Reservation Bill in its present form in view of some political parties going back on their commitment. Some of the political parties which had earlier pledged their support to the Bill have come under the tremendous pressure of their male MPs in general who feel insecure of their political future on account of one-third seats (about 180 of the 544) being reserved for women. Hence, the probability of the Bill becoming an act seems bleak at the moment. Therefore, it is not certain whether the Bill would be passed in the Parliament in the near future or it would be put in cold store in view of the widespread demand for quota for the OBC and minority women. It was really unfortunate that the Women's Quota Bill was prevented from being admitted in the Parliament. It is an important step towards women's empowerment in the country as it proposes 33 per cent reservation for women in the Parliament and state Legislatures as against their strength of about fifty per cent in the total population of the country. Such is the sorrow state of affairs of the gender bias even in modern India which has entered in the new millennium.[10] The following remedial measures may be suggested in order to ensure effective participation and empowerment of women in democratic institutions.

- As a transitional measure, 'reservation of seats' for women in the Parliament and State Legislatures would be a welcome step in order to provide a corrective to the gender imbalance in power structure. The quantum of reservation for women should be decided by consensus by all political parties (whether 33 per cent or 15 per cent) and it should be made mandatory to them to compulsorily reserve the prescribed number of seats for women of the total number of seats being contested by them, failing which they would be derecognised. The election commission can be empowered to enforce this. However, instead of allowing the Election Commission to decide on which seats to be reserved for women, the same should be done by the political parties. The Election Commission should not impose upon the political parties which of the constituencies would be reserved for women. By allowing this freedom to the political parties, the effective participation of women in politics can be ensured. The political parties would be forced to field those politically conscious and educated women as candidates from their respective parties whom they think are the sure winning bets. Thus, the imperative of 'winnability' will be taken into account by the political parties. In addition to the prescribed quota for women, the political parties may go beyond this quota and may bring other potential women candidates into the election fray, who have the capacity to win from whatsoever constituency they belong.

- In a democracy, political parties have a very important role to play. They should take such measures which would facilitate more participation of women in politics. The political parties should encourage women to come into the mainstream of political arena. They should reach the women masses, inspire them to join public life and improve their tainted image. They should not discriminate against women in providing important offices in party hierarchies, in government and various other decision-making bodies and in allotting them party tickets to contest elections. Such a political motivation would provide an impetus to women's initiation into politics. However, mere reservation will not solve the problem unless and until women members are given commensurate powers to function effectively.
- The reservation especially on grounds of religion may be avoided as it may add a communal aspect to the issue. It may be mentioned here that even the constitution-makers had also rejected reservations on the grounds of religion. However, they did make special provisions for the scheduled castes and tribes. It may be pointed out that the reservation for women should not become a lasting feature as has been the experience with reservations for SCs and STs.
- The efforts of the government for empowering women can be neither effective nor adequate unless women themselves become more conscious and aware of their rights and duties. Women in themselves should develop a favourable attitude towards politics and should take interest in it. They should not confine to the four walls and should come out of the clutches of their traditional role assignments and spare time to take part in political activities. They must take upon themselves the task of

participation in political affairs with commitment and a sense of challenge.

- As we know, Indian society is still bounded by traditions which cast women in a secondary role. There is a need for a change of values and behaviour in the society, a need for positive socio-cultural and economic empowerment and above all the will-power and strong determination of women to join politics. Education can play a vital role in bringing about the desirable behaviourable changes among the women and make them well equipped in terms of knowledge, competence and capacity to deal with different political problems.
- Women will have to empower themselves 'from below' in order to compel the government to empower them 'from-above'. They should launch a joint forum and lobby together to ensure a collective voice to demand political empowerment for themselves. The equal participation of women in decision-making processes and institutions at all levels would be a step towards empowering women and reforming and restructuring the unequal structure of the society. It is hoped that in due course of time the changes in the socio-political structure of the society will take place and more and more women will come into the mainstream of political arena.

To sum up the foregoing discussion, it may be said that the reservation of seats for women in the Parliament and State Legislatures through an amendment in the constitution would be a significant step towards political empowerment of women and bringing about gender equality and distributive justice in the society provided the reservation for women is effectively adopted and implemented in letter and spirit.

## REFERENCES

1. Bhawana Jharta, *Women and Politics in India* (New Delhi: Deep & Deep, 1996).
2. S.L. Sharma, "Reservations for Women's Empowerment", *Competition Affairs*, September 1998, p. 3.
3. Rita Manchanda, "A Dwindling Presence", *Frontline*, March 20,

1998, pp. 101-4; *India Today*, February 16, 1998 (p. 42), March 16, 1998 (p. 48) and April 6, 1998 (p. 16).

4. *India Today*, October 18, 1999, p. 24.
5. *The Tribune*, May 6, 2001, p. 8.
6. Bhawana Jharta, "Women and Politics in India: A Historical Perspective, *Punjab Journal of Politics*, Vol. XX, Nos. 1 and 2, 1996, pp. 66-68.
7. *The Tribune*, July 14, 1998, p. 1.
8. *The Tribune*, December 15, 1998, p. 1.
9. *The Tribune*, December 23-24, 1999.
10. S.L. Sharma, *op. cit.*, p. 5.

# Part 4

# Disaster Management

# 25

# An Approach to Disaster Management

*Virender Singh Tonk*

## Introduction

Mankind has faced many a challenge since times immemorial. History is replete with instances of disasters, which have challenged survival. Disasters of the natural or man-made kind are a worldwide phenomenon. Natural disasters are a part of the environment, in which we live. The magnitude of disaster however, varies in accordance with the degree of human negligence. Human activity invariably aggravates the risks through insufficient attention to "where and how" settlements are built. Rapid urbanisation and unplanned expansion of townships, coupled with environmental degradation have increased disaster risks manifold. All countries and areas are exposed to some natural occurrences like drought, cyclones, floods, earthquakes, volcanic eruptions, tornadoes etc. at one time or the other. Frequencies and magnitude of such occurrences may vary in accordance with the environmental conditions peculiar to the concerned areas. These are quite often aided by human failings and acts of omission. Very often, they take a heavy toll of human life and property, and cause serious disruptions in the developmental processes.

Varied nature of terrain, industrial and climatic conditions in India, make us vulnerable to almost all kinds of disasters, be they natural or the man-made kinds. While some parts of the country face floods, there are others facing drought conditions. Cyclones, cloudbursts, flash flood, landslides, earthquakes, avalanches, internal disturbances, arson, accidents (including the industrial kinds), fires, deforestation and epidemics are common occurrences in our country. We are disaster prone. Our ever increasing population further aggravates the adverse effects of disasters. While some disasters like accidents may be localised, wherein the administrative machinery is able to concentrate all resources, specially those from unaffected sectors, in the event of disasters like the earthquakes of Uttar Kashi, Latur and Gujarat, such a luxury is not available to the administration of the District/State. Resources in terms of manpower/specialist personnel, equipment, food supplies and medical resources, etc., will not only get committed *in situ*, but will also be partially immobilised as they themselves will suffer casualties/damages. Management of such disasters needs foresight, planning and great coordination. While the administrative machinery would generally get time to gear up its act in calamities like drought, excessive rain/snow disasters, floods and epidemics, etc., an earthquake would literally catch the administration unawares.

Year after year, our people get subjected to miseries caused by numerous disasters, yet our efforts at disaster management remain inadequate. We have not been able to constitute or workable disaster management organisation at the national, state or district level to conduct coordinated prevention, mitigation, response and recovery activities. Our approach is generally not anticipatory and systematic. It is generally reactive and consequently unplanned. There is therefore, a need for management of disasters through a dynamic process.

### State Responsibility

Disasters would generally have wide-ranging effects on the state, its government and the people. It needs to be emphasised therefore, that coping with disasters is primarily a government responsibility. The government is responsible to the people for management of the needs created by disaster in the same way that it is responsible for other aspects of national life. However, a government may, and usually does need assistance from non-governmental organisations, private sector, the general public and outside agencies/governments. It is the government organisation and government resources which necessarily have to bear the brunt of counter disaster actions. An assessment of the scale of organisational planning and other measures which need to be undertaken to deal with a disaster, can be made by the range of responsibilities and tasks which need to be addressed. Some of the important ones are as under:

(a) Provision and dissemination of warning.
(b) Search and rescue.
(c) Survey, assessment and reporting of disaster effects.
(d) Treatment and care of victims.
(e) Clearance of debris and rehabilitation of roads, airfields, railway systems, and other key areas.
(f) Provision of emergency food and water supplies.
(g) Provision of shelter.
(h) Evacuation of individuals, groups and communities; and livestock.
(i) Provision of health and sanitation measures.
(j) Restoration of essential services such as communications, water supply and power supply.
(k) Direction and coordination of counter-disaster measures.
(l) Information and advice to the public.
(m) Immediate financial assistance to victims.
(n) Maintenance of public morale.
(o) Counselling of victims and relatives.
(p) Control and distribution of emergency supplies.
(q) Liaison with the media.
(r) Rehabilitation and subsistence.
(s) Emergency building programmes.
(t) Measures for long-term recovery.
(u) Application of emergency regulations.

It is also important to bear in mind that the disaster management organisation does not duplicate the normal government organisation, it does not act independently of the government, it does not control other government departments and it acts within the charter laid down by the government. This organisation is essentially, an adjunct of the government system, designed to enable the government to deal effectively with special demands which may arise from disasters. The system is not some form of specialised setup superimposed on the existing resources for disaster purposes. It would normally comprise of senior government officials (e.g., Heads of departments and representatives of NGOs) because they are the best people to understand and be responsible for the utilisation of available resources in their respective spheres. The system utilises the existing government structure from state level, down to local government and community level. As this structure, by its nature, is permanent, it is best suited for disaster related purposes.

Handling of disaster situations in emergencies calls for a high degree of initiative and coordinated efforts by various departments at different levels. Concerned authorities must not waste time in getting their act together on occurrence of disasters. A well organised predetermined structure becomes a prerequisite for prompt and well coordinated action to face disasters.

At the national level a nodal ministry is assigned the task of coordinating all activities of the state and district administration and the other support departments/ministries. The Ministry of Agriculture has been designated as the nodal ministry by the Central Government for dealing with natural disasters management. The Central Relief Commissioner functions as the nodal officer to coordinate relief operations for all natural disasters. The nodal ministry is supported by other ministries like Home, Defence, Finance, Health and Family Welfare, etc., also, based on requirements.

While we do have crisis management committees at various levels starting from the National Crisis Management Committee down to the district level, we lack quick response capabilities.

## Shortcomings Noticed in Disaster Management during Earthquake in Gujarat

Our people seem to have short memories, and we also do not take lessons from others mistakes. Or else, the devastation in Gujarat would not have been so severe. The earthquakes of Latur, Uttar Kashi and Jabalpur should have cautioned people in seismic prone regions, to undertake safeguards and preventive actions, formulate suitable preparatory and response plans, tie up coordination aspects and so on. This however, had not been done. Some of the major shortcomings are as follows:

(a) ***Preventive Actions:*** The most glaring human error/negligence in the Gujarat earthquake was the poor construction norms followed by builders while constructing high-rise residential blocks. Having known the vulnerability of Gujarat to earthquakes, seismic-proof construction norms should have been ensured.

(b) ***Response:*** It appears that no worthwhile disaster management plans existed in the state, to cater for such eventualities. Hence, the response to the calamity was slow and delayed. There was a lack of planning, coordination and direction.

 (i) Coordination between various relief agencies was lacking. The nation and the world at large flooded Gujarat with relief personnel and material, but these could not reach the affected areas/people with desired speed.

 (ii) There were no dedicated disaster management resources. All relief work commenced in an ad hoc manner. Order was restored only when resources poured in from outside the state.

 (iii) Management of relief supplies left much to be desired. In spite of relief material pouring in, the administration was not able to provide these to affected people due to lack of coordination.

 (iv) Plant and equipment for clearance of debris were not available in adequate numbers. This resulted in excessive casualties.

 (v) Medical aid too was inadequate. This further aggravated matters.

 (vi) There was a general shortage of drinking water, food supplies, warm clothing and other such basic needs.

(c) ***Communications:*** Total disruption in communications precluded quick response to the calamity. The import of the disaster was not known to the nation till mid-day 26 January 2001. The responses at all levels were therefore, woefully slow and delayed.

(d) ***A Paralysed State Administration:*** It seems the administration itself was in a state of trauma, after the earthquake struck. A quicker response from the national disaster management committee would have helped. The armed forces and NGOs played a stellar role in relief and rescue.

(e) ***Slow Mobilisation of Resources:*** There were no dedicated resources like medicines, equipment, technical help, shelters, plant and machinery, etc., for an earthquake disaster. These had to be mustered in an unplanned manner, further delaying relief work.

## An Approach for Management of Disasters

### *Anticipatory Actions*

***Prevention and Mitigation:*** Disaster prevention and preparedness consists of a wide range of measures both long-term and short-term, which are designed to save lives and restrict losses to the minimum. Prevention is concerned with the long-term policies and programmes to prevent or eliminate the occurrence of disasters. Disasters cannot be prevented/eliminated, but their disastrous effects can be mitigated. There is a need to rectify the existing situation in vulnerable areas to safeguard valuable life and property in the event of disaster. Land-use legislation and other regulations of the town planning departments exist but these have been disregarded and flouted by private enterprise. The government has to enforce existing regulations. Several broad strategies need to be incorporated into a general safety programme such as reducing structural vulnerability, land-use regulation and public information programmes. Although these cannot guarantee total safety against loss of life from disaster, they certainly can reduce damage to life and property.

(a) The government and administration should:
   (i) Establish vulnerable geographic zones and populations through hazard mapping and collection of other related information.
   (ii) Establish an extensive public awareness programme disseminating information about earthquakes, cyclones and related hazards, and disaster mitigation and preparedness measures.
   (iii) Establish a technical programme including architectural and engineering inputs to improve building design,

construction and siting, demonstrating the techniques, and training local residents.

(b) Following actions will help reduce disaster related damage:
   (i) Develop seismic or cyclone resistant construction techniques.
   (ii) Conduct a programme to introduce improved construction techniques to the building industries and educating the general public.
   (iii) Analysing soil types and geological structure to determine relative safety of construction sites.
   (iv) Instituting incentives to remove unsafe buildings or buildings on unsafe sites or more feasibly, to upgrade their level of safety.
   (v) Instituting incentives to encourage future development on safer sites and safer methods of construction, through:
      1. Land-use control and zoning.
      2. Building codes and standards and means of enforcing them.
      3. Favourable taxation, loans and subsidies for qualified building sites and use of building methods.
      4. Land development incentives.

(c) Reducing possible damage from secondary effects by:
   (i) Identifying possible landslide sites in hills and banning construction in these areas.
   (ii) Installing devices that will keep breakages in electrical lines from producing fire.
   (iii) Ban construction in cascading fashion on steep slopes, in hills.

***Preparedness:*** Disaster preparedness is the detailed planning for prompt and efficient response, once disaster strikes. It is concerned with operational planning, education and training of the population, especially of the disaster prone areas, and technical as well as management training of the personnel who will be required to help in a disaster situation with respect to relief operations, stocking of supplies and other arrangements. The more effectively these tasks are carried out well in advance, the more readily will it be possible to take the required action during emergency phase and later during post-disaster phase such as relief, rehabilitation and reconstruction. Disaster preparedness involves a wide variety of different services and skills, all of which must work harmoniously, aiming to get right things to right place in the right quantity and in time for managing a disaster. Hence, interdependence on each other is necessary.

(a) ***Preparation of Disaster Management Plans:*** There is need to prepare a disaster management plans for likely disasters. The plans must formalise the composition of the disaster management committee and their duties in detail. It is recommended that contingency plans be made to counter disaster situations, keeping in view, options for move of resources in terms of manpower, equipment and relief material as permissible in specific disaster scenarios. An important factor to be considered is that some of the key personnel of the disaster management committee and a fair portion of the relief personnel, would also be affected by the disaster and may not be in a position to help in countering the disaster effects. There would therefore be a need for training larger number of people for shouldering responsibilities for countering disasters. In the case of a District Headquarters it is pertinent to bear in mind that they are the nerve centre of the state government, as well as the district. Crisis situation in the nerve centre itself is likely to jeopardise or at least slow down the response for the counter disaster actions as coordination and directions will get affected. It is therefore vital, that a fair degree of decentralised actions be authorised in such a situation, viz., earthquake disaster. Optimum arrangements should be established for direction/coordination.

(b) ***Viability of Plans:*** Once plans are finalised and approved, continuous attention needs to be given to them, to maintain their viability. This can be achieved by:

   (i) ***Exercises and Tests:*** The plans must be put to test by simulating disaster conditions and exercising the departments/personnel in some or all aspects of disaster management as feasible. If not much, at least activation and mobilisation of resources can be exercised. This would help improve the plans.

   (ii) ***Functional and Readiness Checks:*** These need to be done periodically, to ensure that key facilities and systems are serviceable and ready for use (e.g., emergency shelters, health centres, etc.)

(iii) ***Training Activities:*** All training activities (in addition to exercises and tests) be based on the plan so as to develop and maintain awareness of the plan and its key role in disaster management.

(iv) ***Public Awareness Activities:*** Some public awareness activities offer a good opportunity for maintaining viability of the plan. Designating one day in the year as 'Earthquake Preparedness Day' to raise the level of awareness of both official agencies and the community, can pay rich dividends. On such a well-publicised day all government officials having responsibilities under the plan would check all aspects of planning, preparedness and response relevant to these responsibilities. Non-government organisations should be asked to do likewise. Test activation should be carried out. Public places like bazaars, hospitals, and schools, etc., can also be tested by simulated activities. Involvement of officials and community at large in such an activity will improve general awareness as also test the viability of the plans.

(v) ***Publicity on Preparedness:*** Suitable media coverage should be given to various aspects of disaster preparedness measures for public awareness.

(vi) ***Education in Schools:*** There is a need to introduce appropriate disaster preparedness education into school syllabi. This can be based on relevant plans to assist community awareness.

(vii) The plan itself should be attractively presented, clear and easy to read so that people refer to it. A badly presented document, with confusing language, with a mass of statistics will not be read by anyone.

(c) ***Provision for Emergency Actions:*** The administration should undertake following actions to support their emergency action plans:

(i) Review the structural soundness of vital facilities for counter-disaster response, such as hospitals, fire stations, communication installations, vital bridges on the roads and upgrade their strength if needed.

(ii) Identify safe sites in close vicinity of cities where vulnerable population can be relocated.

(iii) Plan the alternate water supply means like wells, hand pumps, water tankers, temporary pipelines, etc.

(iv) Relocation of medical aid centres, recovery vehicles, dozers, mechanical excavators, and other earth moving plants keeping in view the accessibility of vulnerable areas.

(v) Storage of emergency food supplies for public distribution in emergency. The sites for storage would need to be least vulnerable and should have an easy access.

(vi) Stocking of warm clothing, blankets, tents and tarpaulins for the homeless. These would be need to be close to areas selected for relocation of the homeless.

(vii) Means of transportation, air/helicopter-based supplies and evacuation.

(viii) Training of personnel in trauma care, street clearance and excavation, search and rescue operations.

(d) ***Education of the Public:*** An important aspect of disaster preparedness is the training and education of the population of the disaster prone area. This would greatly improve the response to disaster emergencies and prepare the public to face disaster challenges with confidence.

(i) ***Information to be Communicated to the Public:*** The information to be communicated to the public can be divided into the following categories:

1. ***Basic Community Needs:***
   - What the earthquake or cyclone disaster will do.
   - The best immediate action to take personally and by families and other kin groups.
   - How best to help other members of the community.
   - What the government has planned to do, to assists the community.
   - How to participate effectively in the disaster communication and warning process.
   - How to improvise shelter and sustenance until assistance is available.

2. ***Information of Government Assistance Programmes:*** May include:
   - Community relevant details of the disaster management system.
   - Any essential information required to amplify the

above-mentioned basic community needs. This could include special warning signals, designated shelters or safe areas, evacuation process and so on.

- Government limitations e.g., logistic problems in providing relief supplies, and priorities for relief measures.
- Any other information which is applicable to particular circumstances.

3. Periodic preparedness reminders to keep the public updated.

(ii) ***Information Format:*** The format for communicating information to the public can vary. Some of the possible methods are as under:

1. Notices.
2. Posters.
3. Cartoons.
4. Photographs.
5. Films, film clips and videos.
6. Inserts into ongoing programmes on other subjects.
7. Short radio and TV features.
8. Talks or presentations at different fora like community gathering/meeting and religious places like Temples, Church, Gurudwara, etc.
9. School programmes, which offer good long-term dividends.

(iii) ***Effectiveness of Information:*** It is important to check where possible, the effectiveness of public awareness programmes. The programmes must have the ability to gain and maintain the interest of the target population. The information should also be received by the public in the intended sense.

(iv) ***Maintenance of Awareness Levels:*** There is a need to continuously monitor the adequacy of awareness levels to ensure that public interest does not fade.

(e) ***Training:*** Training is a means to improve performance and problem solving capabilities of people. It is a continuous process to build capability in sufficient number of concerned individuals, to bring about planned changes in the system. Besides education of the general public, there is a need for technical training for utilising specialised skills to greater extent, and management training for disaster managers and planners.

(i) ***Training Needs:***

1. The range of functions and skills which need to be addressed by training may include:
   - Planning and organisation.
   - Day-to-day management activities.
   - Counter-disaster operations.
   - Crises management activities.
   - Logistic functions.
   - Recovery management.
   - Participation in major programmes such as development, prevention and mitigation.
   - Specialist skills applicable to rescue, first aid, assessment, emergency relief and welfare, communications, information management and so on.
2. All the above-mentioned skills do not call for specialist full scale training because a certain degree of competence already exists. The government departments entrusted with disaster management responsibilities would already be proficient in their basic roles. For instance the public works department do not need training for clearance of debris from roads, fire department and police department too are trained in their respective tasks in crises. Hence, they do not need further specialised training in their specialised roles. Nor do government officials need training in day-to-day management aspects.
3. The types of training which need to be conducted are as follows:
   - ***Disaster Related Management Tasks:*** Training for existing or potential managers (both government and NGOs) in order to equip them for specialist disaster related tasks and to orientate them to various aspects of crises management.
   - ***Skills Training:*** Training of those people from government agencies, NGOs and community volunteers who may be required to undergo duties in:
     - Emergency operation centre.

- Rescue.
- First aid.
- Emergency feeding and welfare.
- Communications.
- Damage assessments and survey of needs.
- Auxiliary support for police, fire department, rescue teams, etc.

- ***Coordination Training:*** Training for coordinated disaster management is required for all key personnel in:
  - Standard emergency services.
  - Government departments and agencies.
  - NGOs.
  - Community/Private sector groups.

  (Combined exercises periodically would give best results).
- ***Specialised Training:*** Training can be organised through workshops and seminars to cover specialised subjects such as mitigation, review of disaster preparedness, evolution of new concepts and plans.

(ii) ***Training Strategy:*** Disaster preparedness training should be based on the following lines:

1. *Institutionalisation of Training Efforts:* Training efforts should be institutionalised at the state level. For this, there should be an apex institution, through which training can be imparted regularly and in a sustained manner. Efforts should also be made to include significant aspects of disaster preparedness in the curriculum of school and college education.
2. *Training of Trainers:* Preparing a state cadre of experienced trainers in various fields of disaster management is the first step. This will be an ongoing process, given the variety of disciplines that disaster preparedness encompasses and its expanding scope. The first few batches may be trained at the disaster management institute, Bhopal, National Civil Defence College, Nagpur; Administrative Staff College of India, Hyderabad and so on. Once a core group is trained further training can be organised at the state level through courses, workshops etc.

3. *Training Courses, Workshops, Seminars and Exercises:* To create awareness and develop skills necessary for disaster preparedness, a variety of training courses, workshops, seminars, and exercises should be organised for general and specific target groups.
4. *Developing of New Areas of Technical Expertise:* Having established a mechanism for transmitting general skills, efforts should be concentrated on developing new areas of technical expertise. Training programmes and material should be dynamic and up to date.
5. *Development of Training and Educational Material:* Training and educational material should be developed in the form of books, pamphlets, films/video cassettes, etc., by reputed agencies, institutes and experts on specific disaster fields. This material should be used for various training programme, to make the "multiplier effects" of training, a success. A "Centre for Lessons Learnt" must be established at the state level Disaster Management Institute, which must collect data on disasters from within and outside state, so as to draw lessons from previous experiences and suggest changes in disaster management/ preparedness techniques. This process of evolution of techniques would need validation at seminars through discussions by experts.

(f) ***Resources' Utilisation:*** One hard fact which emerges from analysis of previous disasters is that resources are seldom adequate to cope with the requirements. In an earthquake disaster, high priority requirements would be for heavy earth moving equipment, search and rescue and special medical skills. Optimum utilisation of available resources entails:

(i) Maintenance of an accurate and up to date inventory of all available resource organisations e.g., Government Departments, NGOs, outside assured help.

(ii) Clear allocation of roles and responsibilities which resource organisations are required to undertake during response operations and recovery phase.

(iii) Suitable preparedness arrangements within resource organisations to ensure that they are able to fulfil their roles when required.

(iv) Periodic monitoring of capabilities of resource organisations to ensure operational preparedness.
(v) Drawing of plans for reception, storage and distribution of relief commodities; utilisation of assistance teams like rescue workers, medical personnel, technical teams, etc.

## Response

Immediately on occurrence of an earthquake disaster the Disaster Management Committee will convene and meet under the Chairman. If planning and preparedness has been properly carried out, the majority of the response tasks (as designated before hand to appropriate government departments and other resource organisations) would automatically get activated. For example, PWD would undertake clearance of debris on access roads; the medical and health department would undertake triage, police would maintain law and order and enforce security, etc. The disaster management committee would need to meet other emergency conditions, which are other than routine and allocate priorities for implementation of response tasks. Major response aspects which will need to be addressed are:

(a) ***Rescue:*** Persons who may be trapped in buildings under debris would need to be rescued and evacuated for medical attention. Others rendered homeless will need to be evacuated to safer places.
(b) ***Treatment and Care of Victims:*** Establish casualty collection points:
  (i) To render first aid.
  (ii) Arrange medical evacuation, hospitalisation, and treatment.
  (iii) Identification and tagging of casualties.
  (iv) Disposal of the dead.
(c) ***Evacuation:*** To determine the need for evacuation of affected people to safer places.
(d) ***Shelter:*** Provide shelter for victims whose housing has been destroyed and the floating population like tourists/other visitors in need of shelter.
  (i) Arrange for temporary shelters like tents, sheds, tarpaulins, community buildings, etc.

(ii) Arrange urgent repairs of houses where required/feasible.

(e) ***Food:*** Organise and distribute food to disaster victims and emergency workers.

(f) ***Communications:*** Re-establish essential radio and telephone links.

(g) ***Clearance of Roads and Access:*** Arrange clearance of key roads, railway line, and access to air fields and helipads including repair of bridges and construction of temporary bridges where required.

(h) ***Water and Power Supply:*** Potable water will need to be provided to the affected population at priority. Alternative measures like water purifying equipment will need to be ensured. Power failures are also very likely. Alternate power supply, specially for emergency services, will need to be made through use of captive generators.

(j) ***Fire Fighting Arrangements:*** Fires are likely to be a great source of concern as secondary affects of an earthquake. The fire department, will be hard pressed due to lack of road access post-disaster, non-availability of water due to disruption in water supply and its limited resources. Priority will need to be allocated to safeguard against excessive casualties.

(k) ***Health and Sanitation:*** The health department will need to maintain sanitation facilities, specially in congested and worst affected areas to safeguard health of the people.

(l) ***Temporary Subsistence Supplies:*** The administration will need to provide supplies such as clothing, disaster kits, cooking utensils and plastic sheets in addition to food, to enable victims to subsist temporarily in their own areas/safe areas.

(m) ***Security:*** The police will need to provide security against looting and law and order problems. Assistance from paramilitary forces/civil defence agencies will need to be requisitioned for these.

(n) ***Public Information:*** The administration will need to keep the community informed on what they should do, specially in terms of self help and what action is being taken to assist them. Efforts will also need to be made to prevent spread of rumours and panic.

(o) ***Construction Requirements:*** High priority building repairs will need to be estimated and work undertaken on a war footing.

(p) ***Maintenance of Public Morale:*** Welfare bodies, religious organisations and other appropriate organisations will need to provide moral and spiritual support to the stricken people to sustain them in the prevailing circumstances.

(q) ***Requisition of Army Assistance:*** The magnitude of earthquake disaster will dictate the need for requisition of army assistance. The armed forces are well-organised to provide support to a full range of public services such as public works, communications, transport, health and emergency medical services, rescue and support activities. They can react quickly and respond rapidly in a fully self-contained and self-sufficient manner. The armed forces may be called upon to provide following type of assistance:

(i) ***Infrastructure for Command and Control:*** The army could set up a command and control organisation at a suitable location. This would involve provision of communications, both telephone, radio and specialist manpower.

(ii) ***Medical Aid:*** Army can provide medical care with the help of medical teams in affected areas and treatment at the Military Hospitals.

(iii) ***Transportation of Relief Material:*** Provision of logistics backup aircraft/helicopters and vehicles for transportation of relief material to/from supply bases, etc.

(iv) ***Establishment of Relief Camps:*** Setting up and running of relief camps can be undertaken by the army.

(v) ***Construction and Repair of Roads and Bridges:*** Army engineers can undertake repair of roads and bridges including provision of technical and plant equipment such as cranes, bulldozers, bridging equipment, etc.

(vi) ***Maintenance of Essential Services:*** Repair and maintenance and running of essential services like electricity, water supply and communications can be undertaken in the initial stages of disaster relief.

(vii) ***Evacuation of People to Safer Areas:*** One of the important tasks which can be handled by the army is to assist in evacuation of people to safer places.

(viii) ***Stage Management of Relief Supplies:*** The army can also be entrusted with the task of stage management and handling of relief supplies from outside agencies to affected areas.

***Resource Mobilisation:*** A sudden disaster of the natural or man-made kind, is a distinct possibility in our vast country. Our response to an earthquake or a nuclear strike should be quick and spontaneous, to be able to save valuable human lives. For other calamities too, dedicated resources could pay better dividends. Disasters like floods, cyclones, droughts, epidemics are a common annual feature in our country. Should we therefore not have dedicated Task Forces to deal with such calamities? These could be established as dual purpose organisations i.e., they could undertake developmental tasks, under normal conditions but be able to mobilise to affected disaster struck areas with speed when called for. They would need to be staffed, equipped and trained accordingly. It is recommended that the Task Forces be raised and organised on the lines of the Territorial Army. Two to three Battalions each of the following units, be raised in each state.

(a) ***Ecological Battalion:*** To be financed by Forest and Environment Departments. Undertake tasks related to environmental protection and afforestation during normal times. Help in relief and rescue work in times of disasters.
(b) ***Engineering Services Battalions:*** To be financed by the PWD. Undertake construction tasks like roads, bridges, canals, etc., during normal times. To be equipped with plant and machinery accordingly. Assist in relief, rescue and reconstruction during disasters, to include provision of temporary shelters to the displaced population.
(c) ***Medical Battalions:*** These should be financed by the Department of Health. During normal times, these units should be employed for providing medical cover including well appointed hospitals in rural areas. They should have access to stocks of medicines, to cater for preventive and curative needs in times of calamities.
(d) ***Store Holding Organisations:*** These must be created to maintain stocks of stores, equipment and plant at the state level which could be issued to the various departments in

normal course. Reserves should be maintained to cater for disasters. Procurement of stores could be financed by the department concerned.

(e) ***Communication Infrastructure:*** It would be best suited to build-up the communication network alongside/within the State Police department. Resources in terms of radio equipment must be held in reserve, to cater for calamities. There is also a need to organise coordination of all communication facilities to include All India Radio, Doordarshan, Satellite communication, P&T and NGOs.

***Resource Management:*** The National Disaster Management Council should coordinate in mobilisation and deployment of the above-mentioned Support Battalions from various states. Means for mobilisation by air or surface transport would need to be catered for. Speed would be of essence. At the state level, it would need to be ensured that resources are deployed in correct places without delay, by proper planning, coordination and direction.

## Concluding Remarks

Disaster occurrences of the man-made or the natural kinds, are an increasing phenomenon, with expanding population, urbanisation, industrialisation and other modern human activities. It is therefore imperative, that disaster management be given its rightful place in administration, by the government. Preparatory actions would always pay better dividends in terms of safeguarding human life and property, than post-disaster reconstruction and rehabilitation. Anticipatory actions, evolution of suitable plans to deal with various contingencies and enforcement of safety norms, would greatly mitigate disaster impact. Involvement of both, the administration and the public in implementation of safety norms, and facing disaster situations with confidence is called for.

Public awareness about vulnerability to disasters, their consequences and how best to cope with such eventualities by the people themselves are important aspects of disaster management. Precautionary steps taken by the general public as part of their civic responsibilities can help reduce disaster impact.

## REFERENCES

Army Training Command, *Policy Approach and Various Organisations for Disaster Management in India,* ARTRAC, Shimla, 1998.

Carter, W. Nick, *Disaster Management: A Disaster Manager's Hand Book,* Asian Development Bank, Manila, Philippines, 1992.

Misra, Girish K. and Mathur, G.C. (ed.), *Natural Disaster Reduction,* Reliance Publishing House, Ranjit Nagar, New Delhi, 1993.

Narain, M.K. (ed.), *Fourth Training Workshop on Earthquake Disaster Mitigation,* Indian Institute of Public Administration, Indraprastha Estate, New Delhi, 1999.

Sahni, Ashok, *Disaster and Emergencies: Preparedness and Management of Health Services,* Indian Society of Health Administrators, Bangalore, 1997.

IGNOU, School of Social Sciences, CDM-01 publications.

# 26

# Disaster Management

*Rakesh Kanwar*

Asia-Pacific region is exposed to almost every type of natural disaster. More than 60 per cent of the major natural disasters, reported in the world, occur in this region. Besides, man-made disasters take millions of lives in the region every year. The vulnerability to disasters, both natural and man-made, is increasing every year with increasing population densities, unplanned growth, urbanisation, industrialisation and other global phenomena such as green house effect, social violence, terrorism, civil unrest and conflict.[1]

**Major Earthquakes**

| Location | Date | Fatalities | Magnitude |
|---|---|---|---|
| **India (Bhuj)** | **26.01.2001** | **50,000** | **6.9 (8.0)** |
| Taiwan | 21.09.1999 | 2,000 | 7.3 |
| Turkey | 17.08.1999 | 15,000 | 7.4 |
| Colombia | 25.01.1999 | 1,200 | 6.3 |
| Afghanistan | 30.05.1998 | 3,000 | 6.9 |
| Afghanistan | 4.02.1998 | 4,500 | 6.1 |
| Russia | 28.03.1995 | 2,000 | 7.5 |
| Japan | 17.01.1995 | 5,500 | 6.5 |
| **India (Latur)** | **30.09.1993** | **22,000** | **6.4** |
| Indonesia | 12.12.1992 | 2,200 | 6.8 |
| Philippines | 16.07.1990 | 2,000 | 7.7 |
| Iran | 21.06.1990 | 35,000 | 7.7 |

The academic distinction between natural and man-made disasters is of no consequence when it comes to the destruction and loss caused by the disasters. Moreover, the *naturalness* of many *disasters* is itself questionable. Even earthquake, the most natural of disasters, does not kill people, the buildings do.

Our world is prone to more disaster threats than our ancestor's. While the traditional disaster threats such as earthquakes, cyclones, volcanic eruptions, floods, droughts, fires and accidents still persist, new threats are looming large over humanity. In fact, the damage caused by the old enemies has increased manifold. Growing population alone has forced people to live in disaster prone areas which, previously would not have been regarded as habitable. What is often seen as progress can, in fact, represent a backward step.

New disaster threats that have developed, particularly since Second World War, are far more destructive in their potential than the traditional threats. Increased social violence including trans-border terrorism has drastically affected many nations and communities. Threats from production, transportation and dumping of hazardous materials and substances endanger unprotected and unaware people. Atomic and nuclear sources pose yet another threat. The possibility of use of nuclear weapons has added a new dimension to the problem of disaster management and mitigation.

## Conceptual Framework

There is no doubt that hazards are integral aspects of our environment. For centuries man considered disasters as the work of the evil spirits and tried to please them with magic and other rituals but later he started manipulating nature. Paradoxically this attempt to control nature has exposed the humanity to new threats. Disasters may be result of natural or human-induced processes or events with the potential to create loss but exposure to a hazard need not necessarily mean disaster. It is the level of vulnerability of those exposed to the hazard that increases risk and the likelihood of a disastrous occurrence.

Disaster management is normally viewed as a post-disaster intervention focusing on rescue, relief and rehabilitation in the events such as earthquakes, cyclones, floods, droughts and fires.

While this has indeed been the dominant approach to disaster management, its effectiveness in dealing with the problem is limited. This post-event approach is not only short-term but short-sighted also. Fire-fighting can never be a substitute for fire prevention.

It has been realised during the 1990s that effects of disasters on human populations can be reduced, if not averted altogether, through integrating disaster prevention and mitigation with development planning. Taking into account the hazard-vulnerability analysis of an area and implementing focused development plans can reduce disaster threats considerably.

The development perspective does not view disasters as isolated random acts. Rather, these are viewed as expected consequence of poor risk management over long-term. They are the outcome of inter-connected social and physical processes that increase risk and vulnerability to even modest threats.

Both risk reduction and disaster management are multi-disciplinary processes, engaging experts from various fields and the civil society at large. Any hazard reduction planning must integrate existing development strategies, plans and programmes to achieve sustainable, environment-friendly development.

In global terms, disasters need to be mitigated and managed to the optimum extent possible by mutual cooperation. World is already facing a range of environmental and subsistence crisis. Disasters don't care for man-made boundaries therefore nations must join hands to make a safer world. It is being realised that the political, economic and social stability of the world depends significantly on bridging the great north and south divide.

In national terms the impact of disaster results in direct loss of existing national assets in various forms and in diversion of national resources and effort away from ongoing subsistence and development in order to achieve satisfactory recovery.

This indicates that nations need to develop comprehensive approach to disaster management. To be effective this approach clearly needs to cover all aspects of the disaster management and to include an appropriate balance of prevention, mitigation, preparedness, response, recovery and disaster related development.

In practical terms, there is pressing need for focused, professional approach at all levels of government. But at the same time governments must realise that disaster management to be effective has to be a community based response system with disaster driven strategic planning. Disaster management must account for things such as:[2]

- Possible threats
- Resources available
- Organisational requirements
- Planning needs
- Action required in relation to sectors of the disaster management cycle
- Training

Nations must have systems in which both government and non-government organisations are blended together to provide a thoroughly professional disaster management capability.

Yokohama Strategy and Plan of Action for a safer world, which was adopted in the World Conference on Natural Disaster Reduction, held in Japan on May 23-27, 1994 has laid down the basic framework for the nations for disaster management. The conference highlighted the importance of disaster prevention and community involvement. The principles laid down by the conference are of utmost importance as these emphasise risk assessment, disaster prevention and preparedness while integrating development plans at national, regional, bilateral, multilateral and international levels in the entire planning process. The declaration lists out the actions required at various levels. At national level it calls mainly for political commitment increased resource mobilisation and involvement of NGOs for disaster management.[3]

## The Indian Scenario

The geophysical profile of the nation is alarming. India is prone to almost all the disaster threats. Fifty-six per cent of the area is liable to substantial earthquake damage. Eight thousand kilometre long coastline is prone to severe cyclonic formations. India is one of the most flood-prone countries in the world and accounts for one-fifth of the global death count due to floods. Over 30 million people are displaced annually. On an average 16 per cent of the total area of the country is prone to droughts, about

68 per cent of the total sown area gets affected due to various levels of droughts affecting about 50 million people annually. Landslides and avalanches; various types of fires; air, road, and rail accidents; epidemics and industrial accidents are other disasters that threaten the country.

Destruction to life and property annually due to these disasters is enormous. Every year India is struck by one or more major disasters besides innumerable minor ones. Every time a disaster strikes, the post-disaster management turns out to be disastrous management.

**Major Disasters of 1990-2001**

| | |
|---|---|
| 1990 | Cyclone in Andhra Pradesh |
| 1991 | Earthquake in Uttar Pradesh |
| 1992 | Floods |
| 1993 | Earthquake in Maharashtra |
| 1994 | Cyclone in Andhra Pradesh |
| 1995 | Floods in Western India |
| 1996 | Cyclone in Andhra Pradesh |
| 1997 | Earthquake in Madhya Pradesh |
| 1998 | Cyclone in Gujarat,<br>Landslide in Uttar Pradesh<br>Severe Flooding in Eastern Parts |
| 1999 | Earthquake in Uttar Pradesh<br>Flooding in Eastern Parts |
| 1999 | Orissa Cyclone |
| 2001 | Gujarat Earthquake |

*Source:* National Disaster Management Cell, IIPA, New Delhi.

Major flood-years in India were 1955, 1971, 1978, 1988 and 1996. In 1996, 7,420 million hectare land was submerged, 39.4 million people were affected and over 2000 people died. In 1988, 16 million hectare land was submerged and over 4,500 people were killed. Estimated economic loss was rupees 1.8 billion in 1996.[4]

In Orissa Cyclone (1999) over 17 lakh houses were damaged. Official death toll is 10,000 people and 45,000 cattle heads. Accidents are the other major killers. Death by accident is reported every 2.35 minutes. 37 per cent of road accident victims are pedestrians in Delhi.[5]

How poor planning and lack of social responsibility results

**Human Lives Lost due to Various Disasters in India**

| Year | Floods | Cyclones/ Floods | Hail- storm | Earth- quakes | Total |
|---|---|---|---|---|---|
| 1990-91 | 1,320 | 979 | – | – | 2,299 |
| 1991-92 | 1,185 | 304 | – | 768 | 2,257 |
| 1992-93 | 1,193 | 497 | – | – | 1,690 |
| 1993-94 | 1,690 | 318 | – | 7,938 | 9,946 |
| 1994-95 | 2,038 | 247 | 59 | – | 2,344 |
| 1995-96 | 2,072 | 361 | 31 | – | 2,464 |
| 1996-97 | 2,069 | 1,719 | 40 | – | 3,828 |
| 1997-98 | 1,560 | 216 | 247 | 39 | 2,062 |
| Total | 13,127 | 4,641 | 377 | 8,745 | 26,890 |

*Source:* National Disaster Management Cell, IIPA, New Delhi.

in disasters is illustrated by fires. It is estimated that 35-40 per cent urban fires are caused by electric faults and in urban areas faulty wiring accounts for residential fires in 33 per cent cases.[6] Fires at Mandi Dabwali and Upahar Cinema are prime examples of tragedies on account of carelessness and casual attitude.

Country's high vulnerability to a wide array of disasters requires a systematic, planned and professional approach at all levels. But no one can beat us when it comes to not doing right things at right moment. We, as a nation, are notorious for having the best databases but being the worst managers in almost all fields and disaster management is no exception. India has the National Hazard Vulnerability Atlas that has exhaustive data on every possible hazard that threatens each and every district of the country. We also have plans to tackle disaster situations. But when it comes calling we are found groping in the dark.

Every tragedy leaves us painfully aware that we need to tighten our belts but every time we don't learn the lessons and it takes another disaster to shake us from slumber. And it is not the government alone that has to be blamed for it as has become too fashionable these days. It is we the people who must share the blame collectively as individuals and as institutions. The civil society at large is responsible for the ills we have. It is aptly said that we get the systems we deserve.

Given the fact that almost all the districts of the country

are prone to at least one major disaster and 139 districts are multi-hazard prone, it is ironic that the country does not have Disaster Management Plans at national, state, district and sub-district levels.

## High Power Committee on Disaster Management

Ironically we do not have a nationwide network to handle disasters in a professional manner even today. Nothing more can highlight this than the fact that government of India set up a High Power Committee (HPC) only in August, 1999 to prepare Disaster Management Plan for the country for natural disasters, to comprise of national, state and district level plans. The terms of reference of the HPC have been modified in February 2000 to include all types of disasters. The committee has already submitted its interim report. It has identified more than thirty disaster threats and these have been grouped into five categories (Annexure 1).

The Committee has suggested that the district plan would be the main plan to deal with the disasters to which the district is prone. It would lay out prevention, mitigation, preparedness and response plans for the district including plans for corporations and municipalities. Mega corporations will have their separate plans.

The state level plans will have two parts. The first part will have essential details with historical perspective and current data for the each group of disasters. Second part will lay out state-wise or region-wise prevention plan and prevention strategy; mitigation plan and mitigation strategy; preparedness plan and response plan.

The National Plan is supposed to be primarily a Response Plan for the five sub-groups with (a) prevention plan of interstate and sub-continental features, (b) prevention strategy of interstate and international issues, (c) mitigation plan and mitigation strategy of inter-state and international issues, (d) preparedness plan at the national level and (e) SAARC and international initiative in this regard.

High Power Committee has recommended that every year 'last week of April' be observed as 'updating the plan' week and every year 'first week of May' be observed as 'rehearsing the plan' week throughout the country. It is also suggested that school, college and universities systems be integrated with disaster preparedness and response mechanism. Involvement of NGOs, CBOs, PRIs and other institutions is also envisaged.

Another concept advocated by the HPC is Trigger Mechanism (TM) to minimise response time when disaster strikes. Establishment of a Civil Defence Warden System involving panchayat members as wardens and providing communication network through wireless stations and HAM (Help All Mankind) radio systems is also key thrust area.

The HPC has also suggested a State Disaster Management Act like the Representation of Peoples Act that would give overriding powers to the government to deal with the crisis situations.[7]

It is indeed a welcome thing that the government has finally woken up to have a national perspective on disaster management. Hopefully it would lead to better management of disasters. But there are many questions that remain. Given the record of government in handling things of importance, are we really going to have professional system in place? Will the annual rehearsals proposed serve real purpose or turn out to be empty rituals like *van mahotsavas*? Will the systems work in real situations? More important than all this is the mind-set and attitude of the people in general and agencies (both government and non-government), systems and organisations responsible for delivering the goods. Shall we rise to the occasion?

A well-made disaster management plan will not be more than a piece of paper unless the people who have to execute it give their due.

First is the political executive. Will they act responsibly or keep on regularising the illegal skyscrapers that would turn out to be graves for thousands of innocent people? Are they willing to integrate the disaster prevention and mitigation plans into the development strategies or will continue to be guided by short-term political gains? Are they serious to break the nexus that exists between their fraternity and other thugs? What is the guarantee that our beloved politicians would not politicise the post-disaster rescue and relief work? Will the publicity hungry, so-called VVIP, politicians not descend like vultures on the disaster scene?

Then comes bureaucracy that fails every time it is needed. Are they willing to stand up to the politician when it comes to the choice between the good and the bad policies? Are they willing to discharge their duties honestly? Will they not be missing in action next time around?

Normally the buck stops at these two scapegoats. But what about the media that wishes to act as the watch-dog of democracy but ends up as a sensationalising agent? Is the responsibility of media limited to serving gory pictures and grotesque details of death, deprivation and human suffering? Will the media undertake the massive job of educating people about disaster threats, the dos and don'ts at the time of disaster? What about the non-transparent fund hungry non-government organisations that keep on asking the government to be transparent every time? They are best at picking up holes but know that their criticism comes without any responsibility. Shall the seekers of a code of conduct from the government conduct themselves first?

There are other questions as well. The thrust given by the HPC on plans at all levels is well meaning but is there any guarantee that it would not lead to more and more commissions, committees, subcommittees, action groups, sub-groups and host of other institutions that would generate tons and tons of paper work and forget the real job at hand.

Besides, disaster management is not a post-disaster activity, it is also important to have pre-disaster interventions, both structural and non-structural, so that impact of disaster is minimised.

The role of government becomes important in this regard. But the experience has shown the government agencies in a very poor light. Disaster management becomes a management disaster. Bhopal (1984), Andhra Cyclone (1990), Latur (1993), Jabalpur (1997), Orissa Cyclone (1999) and Gujarat Earthquake (2001) have all shown that government fails miserably in management of post-disaster situations. Annual recurrence of major disasters also highlights that governments do nothing worthwhile in the peacetime to prevent or mitigate the disasters. Many times the golden rule is: call the army. Civil administration must be trained to handle disaster situations on its own.

Earthquake and cyclones don't give much response time but the massive destruction caused by these points out towards callous attitude as regards prevention, mitigation and preparedness aspects of disaster management.

Floods and droughts are also badly managed. Drought, which is known as a creeping disaster, occurs every year. Floods devastate millions of hectare of land in same parts of the country in same regions during the monsoons every year but we are unable to do anything. Even though the vulnerable flood and drought-prone areas are familiar just like the back of our hand nothing seems to be moving.

Whatever little has been done has proved counter-productive. For example, it is believed that dams and embankments can help curtail floods. But reality is that embankments prolong waterlogging by obstructing the retreat of floodwaters.[8]

Gujarat earthquake has made us realise painfully once again that disaster management is something that should not be left to the bureaucrats alone. There is no doubt about it that the role of government is very important in disaster management, but unless NGOs, CBOs, and all other local organisations are actively involved in the process the results will not be to the satisfaction. In advanced countries there are family disaster management plans, that kind of preparedness is required. The families are supposed to have supply of high energy dry food items ready along with other essentials such as flash light, signal devices, etc. All the members are trained to act in particular manner in disaster situation to save not only their own life but also the life of other members of family and community. The members must have local and outstation phone numbers, common meeting place, contact addresses to reach out to other members of family in case of emergency. We too must strive in the same direction.

## Disaster and Development

Disasters and development affect one another. Disasters disrupt normal life, leave tales of loss, misery and suffering behind them and create challenges for those engaged in public management. Disasters affect the economy negatively. However the disasters also present development initiatives. Disasters do highlight high-risk areas where action must be taken before another disaster strikes. The realisation of vulnerability after the occurrence of a disaster can motivate policy-makers and the public to participate in risk-reduction activities.

Sometimes development increases the vulnerability of communities, e.g., by creating employment opportunities, you attract scores of people who flock to urban areas to look for jobs and settle on dangerous locations.

Disasters know no boundaries. Unless disaster management and risk-reduction are effectively driven at central, state and local government level and are made compulsory, disasters will be extremely difficult and costly to manage.

## Disaster Management: Key Issues

World over disaster management is seen as an evolving process. There cannot be a single model or approach towards management of disasters. Much depends on the type of disaster, however all efforts and processes must keep the disaster management cycle given below in mind. There is a saying in the forces that the more you sweat in peace the less you bleed in war. It applies to the management of disasters as well. Here too prevention is better than cure.

## Prevention

Government has a vital role to play in this area. Having a techno-legal regime that is enforced strictly is a precondition and falls exclusively in the domain of either the government or local bodies. But it is here that the failure of state as a regulatory body is the most glaring. Disaster after disaster we learn in the most bizarre manner that the government fails in areas where it must excel. The Gujarat earthquake has brought into forefront the politician-builder-bureaucrat nexus. Everyone proclaims with pride that the laws are meant to be broken. Public accountability is missing. Where to be spineless is the criterion of excellence it is foolish to expect standards of performance. The story of innumerable Indian towns and cities runs like this: first illegal constructions are allowed to mushroom then orders are issued for demolition and after a lot of politicking these are regularised. And when disaster strikes the political game of allegations and counter allegations starts.

Myopic plans do not lead towards a safer tomorrow. But along with the failure of government it is the failure of our civil society. The kind of social capital we have built over the years has made the things worse. Incidents of looting and arson are common place after the disasters, hooligans flood the area and relief supplies are diverted to other places.

After all people must realise that social responsibility does not end by organising relief supplies to the disaster-hit areas. If the civil society does not demand answers now and would elect the same set of people who keep the lives of people for ransom then we the people are at fault. And we cannot absolve ourselves by blaming the system for every ill.

That prevention planning becomes an integral part of everything we do is the aim for which the all the agencies, viz., government, industry, elected bodies, non-government organisations and community-based organisations must strive.

Community participation can work wonders. Hosts of examples in watershed development and rainwater harvesting are there to show the path. Attempts are being made by way of people's committees to manage natural resources in more and more eco-friendly manner. More thrust needs to be given to these.

## Mitigation

Disaster mitigation refers to measures that can be taken to minimise destructive and disruptive effects of hazards and thus lessen the scale of a possible disaster.

This again is a matter that has to be linked to the entire planning and implementation process. The 73rd and 74th Constitutional amendments are a milestone in Indian context, as these have started the process of decentralisation by giving powers to panchayats to formulate and execute local level plans. All the local bodies and Panchayati Raj Institutions (PRIs) must be oriented so that the prevention and mitigation aspects are interwoven in the local plans. Capacity building of all the institutions is also a prerequisite. Not only that they must be trained to handle post-disaster scenarios.

## Preparedness

Preparedness measures such as the maintenance of inventories of resources and the training of personnel to manage disasters are vital components of managing a disaster. Furthermore, this should be an ongoing, regular function of all the government departments at all levels in active collaboration of people. These measures can be described as logistical readiness to deal with disasters and can be enhanced by having response mechanisms and procedures, rehearsals, developing long-term and short-term strategies, public education and building early warning systems.

Preparedness is the core area after the plans have been taken care of. There has to be Standard Operating Procedures for every likely and unlikely scenario. There must be *what if* and *worst case* planning. The plan is as good as it is rehearsed. The communication networks, the alternate communication channels, the information flow mechanisms and an efficient management information system are some key points that need to be taken care of.

How prepared are we if a disaster of severe magnitude strikes any part of the country? We don't have to be experts to know the answer. Orissa and then Gujarat have exposed each one of us. More than that is the apathy and inaction on the part of everyone between these two disasters.

Delhi will be flattened within a few seconds even if the earthquake strikes the Himalaya.[9] If an earthquake of magnitude 8.0 (the same scale that struck Kangra in 1905) on Richter scale strikes today in Kangra region, the destruction will be beyond imagination. Dr. (Prof.) A.S. Arya, Professor Emeritus Department of Earthquake Engineering, Roorkee University presents following scenario in his paper on "Earthquake Risk and Disaster Mitigation in Himachal Pradesh":

| | |
|---|---|
| Completely collapsed houses | 1,36,000 |
| Those partly destroyed but will require reconstruction | 2,63,000 |
| Those with partial collapse but repairable | 9,16,000 |
| Small cracks and repairable without evacuation | 3,58,000 |
| Fine cracks or no damage | 1,43,000 |

The paper has estimated the loss to life on the basis of 1991 census to be 65,000. The month and time of earthquake may increase the number of deaths and the loss to property considerably. And the damage caused by the above disaster will not be confined to Himachal alone, it would affect J&K, Punjab, Haryana, Uttar Pradesh and Uttranchal.

Kind of preparedness required for this kind of disaster is enormous and it cannot be government based. Entire nation will have to be an active party to the frightening post-disaster scenario mentioned above.

How prepared are we exactly? It is shocking to learn that the Rashtrapati Bhawan and the PMO are not earthquake proof structures.[10] Are our hospitals, community buildings, government offices, communication installations, dams, bridges, power houses, food godowns, police stations, educational institutions and other important institutions earthquake resistant? Not only that how much attention we pay towards checking the fitness of our resources? Many times the fire personnel are unable to find the hydrants and even if these are located they do not function. Such *routine* matters reflect upon our preparedness. It is well known that the community responds to the disaster first then why not train a group of volunteers in each locality to carry out the rescue and relief operations in the area after the event. Presently the response is emotive, people come in large number to help their fellow citizens but it would be much better if they were professionally trained to manage such situations.

Apart from police, home guards, NCC, scouts and guides volunteers from each locality must be trained and educated about the rescue and relief operations.

## Response

Delayed response in the event of a disaster is criminal. Delays occur if the agencies responsible for handling the disaster situations have no clear plans. A well-managed professionally trained team that knows where to go, what to do ... should always be there that can assemble at the shortest possible notice.

Search and rescue plans need to be clear and all role players need to know their role and function. Basic needs such as shelter, water, food and medical care also have to be provided and a plan needs to be in place. Many times our response is ad hoc and casual. Response (including rescue and evacuation) in a non-normal situation is specialised matter and nothing should be left to chance.

## Relief and Rehabilitation

Interventions are also needed after a disaster occurs. In many ways this is the most difficult period for the victims. Immediate rescue and relief should in a systematic way lead to job-producing activities, construction works and public works programmes may be needed. The victims cannot be forgotten once the immediate disaster has passed. The economy must be brought back on the rails.

Every disaster tells us that there is no dearth of relief material but the distribution is mismanaged.

## Required: A Professional Approach

Disaster management requires effort and commitment by all stakeholders. The capacity must be built to handle such events, and training programmes are essential. Duplication of efforts should be minimised and financial resources appropriately controlled. Disasters being non-routine events require non-routine response. Governments cannot rely on normal procedures to implement appropriate responses—they will need to learn special skills, techniques and attitudes in dealing with disasters.

Disaster management as a professional team-based effort must be coordinated up to the village level in rural areas and ward level in the urban areas where a team of volunteers must be in readiness to tackle the immediate impact of disasters and at the same time there should be standing instructions to all the administrators in adjoining districts and states to rush to the disaster site with all resources without any formal orders. Normal bureaucratic channels should be bypassed in these crisis situations.

## Afterword

Carl Sagan in his magnificent, awe inspiring work *Cosmos* has described human predicament and dilemmas that surround us in the most thought provoking manner:

The earth is a lovely and more or less placid place. Things change, but slowly. We can lead a full life and never personally encounter a natural disaster more violent than a storm. And so we become complacent, relaxed, unconcerned. But in the history of Nature, the record is clear. Worlds have been devastated. Even we humans have achieved the dubious technical distinction of being able to make our own disasters, both intentional and inadvertent. On the landscapes of other planets where the records of the past have been preserved there is abundant evidence of major catastrophes. It is all matter of time scale. And even that would be unthinkable is a hundred years may be inevitable in a hundred million.

Our lovely blue planet, the Earth, is the only home we know. Venus is too hot. Mars is too cold. But the Earth is just right, a heaven for humans. After all, we evolved here. But our congenial climate may be unstable. We are perturbing our poor planet in serious and contradictory ways. Is there any danger of driving the environment of the Earth toward the planetary Hell of Venus or the global ice age of Mars? The simple answer is that nobody knows. The study of the global climate, the comparison of the Earth with other worlds, are subjects in their earliest stages of development. They are fields that are poorly and grudgingly funded. In our ignorance, we continue to push and pull, to pollute the atmosphere and brighten the land, oblivious of the fact that the long-term consequences are largely unknown.

A few million years ago, when human beings first evolved on Earth, it was already a middle-aged world, 4.6 billion years along from the catastrophes and impetuosities of its youth. But we humans now represent a new and perhaps decisive factor. Our intelligence and our technology have given us the power to affect the climate. How will we use this power? Are we willing to tolerate ignorance and complacency in matters that affect the entire human family? Do we value short-term advantages above the welfare of the Earth? Or will we think on longer time scales, with concern for our children and our grandchildren, to understand and protect the complex life-support system of our planet? The Earth is a tiny and fragile world. It needs to be cherished".

## ANNEXURE 1

### List of Disasters Identified by the High Powered Committee

I. Water and climate related disasters
   1. Floods and drainage management
   2. Cyclones
   3. Tornadoes and hurricanes
   4. Hailstorm
   5. Cloudburst
   6. Heat wave and cold wave
   7. Snow Avalanches
   8. Droughts
   9. Sea erosion
   10. Thunder and lightening

II. Geologically related disasters
   1. Landslides and mudflows
   2. Earthquakes
   3. Dam failures/dam bursts
   4. Mine fires

III. Biological related disasters
   1. Biological disasters and epidemics
   2. Pest attacks
   3. Cattle epidemics
   4. Food poisoning

IV. Chemical, industrial and nuclear related disasters
   1. Chemical and industrial disasters
   2. Nuclear disasters

V. Accident related disasters
   1. Forest fires
   2. Urban fires
   3. Mine flooding
   4. Oil spill
   5. Major building collapse
   6. Serial bomb blasts
   7. Festival related disasters
   8. Electrical disasters and fires
   9. Air, road and rail accidents
   10. Boat capsizing
   11. Village fire

## REFERENCES


1. Carter W. Nick, *Disaster Management: A Disaster Manager's Handbook*, Manila: ADB, 1991.
2. *Ibid.*
3. *Yokohama Strategy and Plan of Action for a Safer World*, United Nations, New York and Geneva, 1995.
4. *Source Book on District Disaster Management*, Ministry of Agriculture and Cooperation, Government of India.
5. *Ibid.*
6. *Ibid.*
7. Interim Report of High Powered Committee for Preparation of Disaster Management Plan, New Delhi, 2000.
8. *Source Book on District Disaster Management*, Ministry of Agriculture and Cooperation, Government of India.
9. *Down To Earth*, February 28, 2001.
10. *The Times of India*, February 25, 2001.

# 27

# Environment Protection and Sustainable Development

*Mohinder Singh & Suman Gupta*

Today, environment is at the forefront of development. Development has been the watchword of the fifties and sixties while environment is the watchword of eighties and nineties. Industrial revolution brought remarkable achievements but without paying attention to environment. It was considered that the sky was too vast and clear to change its colour, our water sources so big and their water so plentiful that no amount of human activity could ever change their quality and our natural forests were too plentiful to finish. In the shift from traditional to modern society, developmental process in India, has neglected the environment. On the other hand, there was a time when we Indian remained the worshipper of environment. Our ancestors worshipped the trees like *peepal,* rivers like the *Ganga,* mountains like the *Kailash,* animals like *cow*. They knew the fact that without a proper "natural" atmosphere, human life was very difficult. The *Rigveda*, which is the oldest scripture of India, describes the beauty and glory of the morning which must be worshipped. The continued degradation of human environment is the result of modern living, technological advancement, industrialisation, urbanisation and population explosion. The economic development now enjoyed by the developed states was sometimes achieved without giving due regard to the preservation of environment. The situation is that more economic and industrial development endangered the environment. All these actions of man have led to an unsustainable environment.

In this paper, we have focused on the basic concepts such as environment and sustainable development. An attempt has been made to highlight the problems pertaining to environment protection and sustainable development. Finally, some suggestions have been given to upgrade environment for attaining sustainable development.

The term environment has gained a significant importance throughout the world in the second half of twentieth century. It is an aggregate of all external conditions and influences affecting the life and development of human beings, animals and plants. It includes air, climate, culture, water, noise, temperature, soil, etc., which affect the health and development of life. Thus, it is more than the air we breathe and water we drink.

## Environment Defined

In the words of Douglas and Holland, "Environment is a word which describes, in the aggregate, all of the external forces, influences and conditions which affect the life, nature, behaviour and growth, development and maturation of living organism." Macmillan Dictionary meaning of environment, "The physical, chemical and biotic conditions surrounding a living organism." Internal environment contains the physical and chemical conditions inside the body of a plant or animal.

Environment in its entirety is the consolidation of physical, chemical, organic and non-organic components of the atmosphere, lithosphere, and oceans. It reflects the interests, biases and perspectives of the users. So the environment must be life supporting, useful and beautiful. Man's demands should be restricted in such a way that natural environment is able to sustain the need for development. The environment protection demands concern much more seriously than ever, to both developed and developing countries. It must be people-oriented as it revolves round the people.

## Deterioration of Environment

Our well-being is surely jeopardised not only when air, water or food becomes contaminated but also when war destroys our cities or free passage on the roads is interrupted whether by increasing traffic or a choaked water drain or poorly maintained roads. Acid rains, increasing hole in the ozone layer, etc., have compelled us to think seriously about the alarming danger created by ourselves.

The Central Groundwater Board says that water exploitation level is over 98 per cent in Punjab and 80 per cent in Haryana. Today, India's about 175 million hectare, out of 329 million hectare, land is threatened by degradation. The Stockholm Conference held in June 1972 on "Human Environment" brought consciousness among developing countries about the deterioration of the environment caused by increasing population, urbanisation, and industrialisation. The conference motivated both developed and developing countries to take preventive measures in order to achieve sustainable development.

## Concept of Sustainable Development

The World Bank's Report on "World Development" has highlighted the complementary aspects of economic development and sound environment management in 1997. The report portrays the difficulties created by environmental problems. The sustainable development means neither to yield things less nor more than the needs of the society. Under the sustainable development, we change our way of living in such a way that the natural resources would be able to fulfil the needs not only of the present but the posterity generation also.

Sustainable development has become the buzz word of 1970s. The term was first used in 1987. Time and again new legislations are being enacted so to impose restrictions and codifying economic activity with the objective of sustainability. Sustainable development refers to achieve the goal of economic development which is sustainable within the context of the planet's eco-system and human society. Thus, it is a multi-dimensional concept interacting with the different angles—ecology, economics and ethics. It can be achieved only when we would be ecologically secured, economically efficient and socially equal. Only getting sustainability of the environment and resource system is not sustainable development rather it also requires the sustainability of economic and social systems.

Economic sustainability can be defined in terms of variables such as levels of unemployment, personal incomes, affordability of services, viability of firms and financial performance of regional and national economies. From the social point of view, it includes freedom of individuals, united community, easily availability of jobs, maintenance of services (accommodation, education, law and order); and preservation of cultural diversity and heritage values.

In a narrow sense, the sustainable development can be achieved by "locking up" resources, but for economic growth and development, to provide goods and services, and to create employment for increasing population, there is a need of such management that will use resources in such a way that wastes must be absorbed by the environment without creating any imbalances.

The Report of the World Commission on Environment and Development (1987) has defined the term, "In essence, sustainable development is a process of change in which exploitation of resources, the direction of investments, the orientation of technological development, and institutional change, are all in harmony and enhance both current and future potential to most human needs and aspirations." Thus 1992 UNDP report states, "Sustainable development is a process in which economic, fiscal, trade, energy, agriculture and industrial policies are all designed to bring about a development that is economically, socially and ecologically sustainable."

Environment has neither political nor geographical boundaries. In this context, every nation is equal whether it may be developed, developing or underdeveloped. Man is responsible to push this planet to the brink of disaster. A person may be able to afford energy consumptive automobile and a couple may desire to have some children but can our planet afford carbon-emitting automobiles and how many automobiles can the planet afford? How many children can afford our planet per family? Is it not our right to preserve the animal's species and biological heritage for our future generations. For sustainable development, the leaders and the community should join hands. Some of the factors responsible for causing harm to the environment, the measures taken by our government to protect the environment and control the pollution are also highlighted.

## Deforestation

There was a time when 70 per cent area of the land was covered with forests but now it has reduced to mere 16 per cent. In India, deforestation has been accelerated to meet developmental projects of railways, industries, mining, river valley projects, defence, etc. Urbanisation and expansion of agricultural activities are also responsible for the exploitation of forest cover. Our country is lossing 1.3 million hectares forest annually. The states of Haryana, Punjab and Rajasthan have lost over one-half of the forest cover and the states like Himachal Pradesh and Jammu & Kashmir have lost over one-third of their forest cover. The effect of deforestation can be seen in the form of micro-climate change, increase in temperature and decrease in rainfall, soil erosion and increase in floods. Despite three national forest policies, our forest cover has reduced.

A scientific land-use policy can ensure sustained production, ecological balance and environmental benefits. It is a time when environmental policy should be reviewed and a new strategy should be adopted for conservation including preservation, maintenance, sustainable utilisation, restoration and enrichment of the environment.

In hilly areas, where the effects of deforestation have been felt acutely, scientists have developed a field-based technology. A thorny bush "Agva Cantula" has gained popularity because of its multipurpose use. A survey conducted in some villages revealed the fact that loss of crop due to wild animals has come down from 55 per cent to 15 per cent. It not only saves the crops of the hilly areas but also helps in making fancy articles from the fibers extracted from the leaves of this plant.

## Energy

Excess energy production is responsible for bringing the change in the climate of the earth. Through this process, a huge amount of carbon dioxide is emitted into the atmosphere. If it is going on without any change, its quantity may be doubled by AD 2010. World's 64 per cent energy is being produced from fossil fuels and in doing so 27 per cent carbon dioxide gas is emitted into the atmosphere. Every year 17 per cent energy is generated while 250 million tonnes carbon dioxide gas is emitted.

Hofemeister and Resenfeld are of the view that a little attention on the part of our policy-makers and electric engineers may cut 75 per cent consumption of electricity with present technology. By using compact fluorescent bulbs, the efficiency of lighting can be increased more than double.

### Disaster

Earthquakes bring disaster to a large extent. They are produced by the passage of vibratory waves through the rocks of the earth. Building of large dams across rivers are also responsible for bringing earthquakes. The most recent earthquake occurred on 26th January, 2001 in Gujarat in which heavy loss of property and life was reported.

### Soil Erosion

In India, where a large number of population is vegetarian, the use of pesticides in agriculture is increasing. The farmers are using the pesticides, fertilisers, harmones carelessly to increase their production. Agricultural wastes, including manure and crop residue, act as environmental pollutants and recycling of these wastes minimises the problem to a great extent. They don't know that in doing this they not only degrade the ferti-lity of the soil but the ground water also. In our country, about 53 per cent area is suffering from the problem of soil erosion.

Farmers should be educated regarding the dangers of indiscriminate use of chemicals. Use of organic manure—through mulching, green manuring and composting of rural and urban waste of biological origin, etc., providing all the nutrients in the soil for better plant growth and upgrade the soil by managing organic matter can prove useful. The focus of these methods is to nurture the soil rather than a particular crop. Water is necessary for irrigation of the crop but scarcity of water is a major problem. To remove this problem, the Centre of Science for Villages at Wardha, Maharashtra has introduced "Clay Emitter Method" for small and marginal farmers. Through this method within the same amount of water, the emitter could irrigate five times the area than in flow irrigation and twice more area than the most efficient drip irrigation. The main objective of agriculture should be to extreme benefits from existing agricultural assets by using environment friendly technology. Vermitechnology can be used as it converts waste management, resources recovery and environment conservation. Sustainable agriculture should therefore, provide farmers with a choice of cost-effective farming system including the systems that minimise environmental hazards. It can be achieved by combining traditional conservation-oriented farming techniques with modern technologies.

## Harmful Effluents

After industrialisation, the use of unlimited commodities is increasing both in developed as well as developing countries. For example, sugar manufacture is one of the largest industries in India and it ranks fourth in the world. A study indicated that raw distillery waste water is very toxic to the soil micro-organisms which are vitally important in the eco-system. In India, most distilleries are not treating their waste water due to non-availability of a proven process under Indian conditions. The damage they bring is incalculable to environment and ecology. In Haryana, all five distilleries are now closed for alleged failure to take anti-pollution measures. Industrial wastes and toxic substances are thrown in water course or openly. These wastes accumulate in the environment and upset the growth of micro-organism. Some of these wastes are not degradable and causing problems for the environment. Through gene engineering, new strains of bacteria and other micro-organisms are being bred to decompose harmful industrial effluents into non-toxic agents.

As development and environment are inseparable, therefore, development should be eco-friendly. Over the years, lack of proper sewage facilities, depletion of vegetation, unplanned construction are held responsible for unsustainable environment. Environmental friendly technology would fulfil the needs of increasing population on one side and it would protect the environment for the future generation on the other side. If the domestic waste is disposed of in landfills, the result would be the production of explosive methane gas and the soil as well as the ground-water would be contaminated. No doubt, it is a cheap way but if the wastes contain toxic substances then it must be disposed through composting. According to an estimate, 90 per cent solid wastes are being disposed through landfills. On this process, the expenditure is only Rs.10 per tonne. On the other hand, compositing cost of disposal of one tonne wastes is about Rs.250. This compositing technology is very costly for municipalities. Through incineration process not only air is polluted but this process produces ash with toxic heavy metals. A survey conducted by the Haryana State Pollution Control Board in 1990 reveals the fact that 65 per cent organic pollution is being caused by municipal committees. Although municipal sewage treatment plants can remove large floating matter, settleable solids and through physico-chemical and biological processes organic matter can be broken and in this way harmful microbes can be removed yet without proper sewage facilities and treatment plant untreated sewage water is allowed to enter in nearby water bodies. That is why all the holy rivers of the world, like the Elke, the Ganga and the Yamuna have become highly polluted.

After the Stockholm Conference, our government passed the Water (Prevention and Control of Pollution) Act, 1974. Under this Act, the Central Pollution Control Board and State Pollution Control Boards were established. In 1976 through 42nd Amendment, environmental protection was given Constitutional status.

Now several techniques have been adopted for sewage treatment and to extract water for irrigation, fodder, fuel and fertilizers from it. Efforts are also being made to use sewage to improve the farm lands. Sewage water can be used for fish farming. It is very common in Germany, Poland, Russian, Hungary, China, USA like countries. India too should take steps in this direction.

The fly ash is used in building material, manufacture of PPC cement, road making like constructive activities. Steel slag is also being utilised in making cement. Now maximum power stations and other plants are being equipped with effective utilisation of waste because it is necessary to utilise industrial waste.

One can live sometime without drinking water but he cannot live without breathing for a minute. The most important gaseous pollutants are carbon monoxide, oxides of sulphur, hydrogen sulphide, hydrocarbons, oxides of nitrogen, ozone and other oxidants. Carbon monoxide is emitted into the atmosphere mainly from automobiles. In cities, 70 per cent air pollution is caused by automobiles. Oil refineries, fertiliser industries, paper and pulp industries release significant amount of sulphur dioxide. It is causing not only health problems but also having a damaging effect on the famous Taj Mahal. Hydrogen sulphide and organic sulphide cause odour problem. Natural Gas refining, manufacture of paper and distillation of petroleum, etc., produce hydrogen sulphide.

To control air pollution, the Air (Prevention and Control of Pollution) Act, 1981 was passed. The Ministry of Petroleum and Natural Gas has been considering for reducing the sulphur content from diesel stock in the existing refineries in the country. They have incorporated sulphur reduction facilities. Many iron foundries have discontinued the use of coal and have switched over to gas.

## Technology and Environmental Degradation

Now-a-days developing economies are attracting foreign investment without caring safety and health aspects. Environmental laws of developed countries are much more strict in comparison to the developing countries. Due to this state of affairs, the multinational companies are coming in India and other developing countries to produce such goods which they could not produce in their own countries because of stringent rules and regulations. Developed countries have adopted the policy "polluters pay". But the developing countries do not know that the lack of strict environmental law can reverse the economic progress in the coming period. Many industrial units are being set up in the new areas causing destruction of forests, diversion of fertile lands and displacement of local population due to industrial pollution. We cannot forget the 1984 Bhopal Gas tragedy. Technology transfer from developed countries to Third World countries has also become another cause of environmental degradation because of improper management. The measures of sustainable development may be different in developed and developing countries to their level of technological and economic development. There is lack of proper monitoring and accountability.

Multinational companies should be allowed to set up industries only after careful evaluation by the expert group. These companies should disclose all the information which endanger public health. Only uncultivable wasteland areas should be allowed to establish these industries.

## Absence of Strict Laws

The World Development Report, 1992 has highlighted the causes of environmental degradation. This report has pointed out that the main causes are the low prices of resources, lack of accountability, lack of monitoring, no strict laws, etc. No doubt loopholes are being left in the environmental laws by some of our corrupt politicians. They do so with the hope that the affected parties would be in a condition to save themselves and provide funds to them for the elections.

## Suggestions

At the outset, it is suggested that the community as a whole should be enlightened and made aware of the serious consequences of environmental degradation. A joint campaign on the part of governmental and non-governmental institutions should be launched and the whole country should be covered in a phased manner. Micro approach may be adopted to take start from the grass-root and in doing so those who are concerned should not forget regular monitoring of judging the impact of awareness.

Unless we adopt an approach of sustainable development, the objective of environmental protection cannot be achieved. Now it has become the need of the hour to bring sustainable revolution. We can go in for such technology as will minimise the use of raw materials as well as air, water, land and produce minimum wastes. Sustainable technology should be used in using non-renewable, fossil fuels to take advantage of renewable energies like the sun, wind and biomass.

As the aim of sustainable development is to bring maximum welfare to human being without endangering the life support system, therefore, it is suggested that forest policies should be implemented strictly. Research projects should be sponsored on environmental issues. Economical methods should be adopted for salvaging hazardous industrial wastes. The Central Pollution Control Board and the State Pollution Control Boards should be made independent and empowered. They should not succumb to any political pressure and also should try to adopt unbiased approach in handling the delicate matters pertaining to environmental protection.

Some small-scale industries are causing a huge amount of pollution. Therefore, it is suggested that a comprehensive study should be conducted by some reputed non-governmental organisations to know the extent to which industries have not been inventorised by the State Pollution Control Boards. Such industries, as are polluting the water to a great extent, should not be allowed to do so and as there is a provision of "treatment plants", they must instal and ensure that no water pollution takes place. Moreover, financial aid, if need be can be provided to those industries as are not financially sound in the establishment of effluent treatment plants. The findings and the recommendations of the study should not be shelved but they must be used in the larger interest of the people.

It has been observed that most of the municipalities do not strictly adhere to rules and regulations relating to environmental protection. Such institutions should not be spared at all and heavy penalty must be imposed on them so that others should also learn lessons from them.

We have already established courts to deal with the problems of environmental degradation. But these courts are also not expediting their functioning in the timely disposal of cases referred to them. It is suggested that there should be a time schedule for early disposal of cases.

As it is mandatory for the industrial units to get consent of the State Pollution Control Board, in this connection, it has been found that generally they do not get the consent in time because of indifferent attitude of the functionaries. Gratification also plays its own role.

Those found indulging in corrupt practices should be

brought to book and there should not be any let up of leniency in doing so. This approach will require hard decisions on the part of those who are at the helm of affairs.

Every country is spending a huge amount of money on "defence" expenses. In the world more than a trillion dollars are being spent on "defence". The nations sitting over the citadels of development process an armory of 42,000 nuclear weapons. If mere one-half of the present expenditure is spent on environmental protection and to redesign the technology, then we shall be able to hope for the better future for the forthcoming generation.

Environmental education should be made a compulsory part in school and college curriculum. Solar energy should be promoted, environmental-friendly products should be encouraged. For sustainable development there must be proper environmental management including regular monitoring and accountability.

As the environmental degradation is exceeding its limits, therefore, the policy-makers, the planners and the executors should sit together to apply their minds jointly to find out permanent solution to the problem and ensure sustainable development for intergenerational equity of the natural resources.

## REFERENCES

1. Agarwal, Sunil K., "Appropriate Technology Transfer and Eco-Sustainable Development", *Kurukshetra,* vol. 45 (4 & 5), Jan-Feb. 1997.
2. Bhattacharya, Gautam, "People's Participation in Environmental Protection: A Case Study", *Yojana,* vol. 44 (6), June 1999.
3. Brigs, H.S. and Harison, S.R. "Indicators For Monitoring of Ecologically Sustainable Development" in Ron Moore et al. (eds.), *Sustainable Development Policy and Practice,* New Delhi: New Age International (P) Ltd., 1995.
4. Dhanagare, D.N., "Sustainable Development, Environment and Social Science Research in India", *The Indian Journal of Public Administration,* vol. 39(3), July-Sept., 1993.
5. Hamm, Bernd, et al. (eds.) *"Sustainable Development and the Future of Cities",* London: Intermediate Technology Publications, 1998.
6. Joshi, Navin Chandra, "Land Reforms Through Wasteland Development", *Kurukshetra,*vol. 48(12), September, 2000.
7. Kamalamma, N. and E.K.N.V. Raja (1991a): Technology for Rural

Development, Series-2, *Spil-Water Recycling,* Gandhigram Rural Institute, Gandhigram, TN, India.
8. Lahiry, Amitab, "Is Sustainable Development is a Mirage?", *Kurukshetra,* vol. 45 (4 & 5), Jan.-Feb. 1997.
9. Lahiry, S.C., "Sustainable Economic Development", *Kurukshetra,* vol. 45 (4 & 5), Jan.-Feb. 1997.
10. Manivasakam, N., "Environmental Pollution", New Delhi; National Book Trust, 1999.
11. Moore, Ron, "Economic Growth, Ecology and Sustainable Development: Theory and Policy with Reference to Australia" in Ron Moore et al. (eds.), *Sustainable Development Policy and Practice,* New Delhi: New Age International P. Ltd., 1995.
12. Nath, Kamal, "Environment and Development", *Kurukshetra,* vol. 43(3), December, 1994.
13. Pollution: Ominous Partend, *Yojana,* vol. 45(2), Feb., 2001.
14. Rai, Adhikesh, "The Problem of Co-ordination between Environment and Economic Development", *Kurukshetra,* vol. 46(4), Feb., 2001.
15. Santosh Vasudevan, P. and Arya, R.S. "Compositing of Solid Waste of Villages for Disposal and Fertiliser Production, Changing Villages", 9(2), 1990.
16. Saxena, H.M., "Sustainable Development" in *Environmental Geography,* Jaipur & New Delhi: Rawat Publications, 1999.
17. Vajpayee, Atal Bihari, "Food, Nutrition and Environmental Security", *Employment News,* vol. 25 (46), 10,16 Feb., 2K1.
18. Verma, S.S., "Environmental Pollution", *Employment News,* vol. 25(10), 3, 9 June 2000 (Weekly).
19. World Commission on Environment, Our Common Future (Second Impression), Oxford, Oxford University Press, 1987.

# 28

# Role of Education and Training in Disaster Management

*Sudesh Negi & Rajinder Singh Chauhan*

Disaster is defined as "a serious disruption of the functioning of a society, causing widespread human, human material or environmental losses which exceed the ability of the affected society to cope using its own resources".

The traditional view is that earthquakes, floods, famines, etc., are extreme natural phenomena that cause damage and loss of life, i.e., that the more severe the force of the phenomena the greater the losses. It is a sudden calamitous event disrupting normal life pattern. The frequency of disasters has gone up in the recent past due to uncontrolled and unplanned activities. Disasters are not caused only due to natural hazards, but a combination of natural forces and human activities, which affect the environment.

Due to increased pressure on land, numerous people are settling down in the earthquake-prone areas, flood plains and coastal area, making these communities highly vulnerable for damages.

Experience of recent disasters in the country like the one in Gujarat on 26 Jan. 2001 reveals the following characteristics of the damage scenarios in the aftermath of any disaster:

- It is the poorer sections of society who suffer severely.

- It is the weaker sections of society, i.e. woman, children, old people, who feel the severity most.
- It is rural or underdeveloped/undeveloped area which suffer the most.

The Indian subcontinent is highly prone to drought, floods, cyclones, earthquakes and land-slides, though avalanches and bush fire too occur in the Himalayan region. Among 34 states/ union territories in the country, 22 are disaster prone. With a wide range of climatic and topographic conditions, the country is subjected to one or other type of disaster very often. The year 2000-2001 saw the occurrence of Natural Calamities of unprecedented magnitude at both the national level as well as in our state. The unprecedented floods on the night of 31 July, 2000 in the Satluj valley and in other parts of state, caused a loss of Rs.1730.89 crore to the state. Several people were either homeless or washed away in the flood. The Hindustan Tibet Road in Kinnaur was completely disrupted. But the promptness and efficiency demonstrated by the government in relief and rehabilitation operations in the Satluj valley has never been witnessed in the past. The people of Kinnaur organized themselves to contribute their own physical labour in the process of restoration of communication will surely came to be quoted as an example for others.

The earthquake on Republic Day, i.e., January 26, 2001 in Gujarat was the fourth major earthquake in the past decade which disrupted completely all types of the communication system along with numerous casualties of human beings.

In a country like India, majority of disaster related problems are basically the unsolved development problems. Here, disaster prevention is not an aspect of development. Without solving the basic problems of population growth, housing, employment and environmental degradation, much talked about technical measures, like housing by laws, regulations and land-use planning are of no use. The various problems regarding disaster management cannot be solved in isolation. These have to be linked with poverty alleviation, proper environmental management and overall development activities.

There is no readymade solution for disaster management and even the models of one country cannot solve the problems of another country. A number of developed countries are suffering from severe disasters. But the losses are minimum. The countries like U.S.A. and Japan are at the top in the effective disaster management approach list. The countries adopted a long-term planning to combat the adverse impacts of disasters. These countries developed a well drawn programme to undertake research studies in the area related to Disaster Management. Based on the outcome of research and the lessons learnt from the past events, these countries were able to formulate the policy related to education in their respective countries. A number of developed countries are still following the long-term policy to combat the disaster solution.

Communication is an important component of management. Disaster management also has certain communication tasks inherent in it. Whether it is awareness building through forecasting and warning or education and training during the pre-disaster state, there is a communication task involved in it. It is in reference to this, the paper focuses on Role of Education and Training in Disaster Management. Communication can play a meaningful role during the disaster and pre-disaster stages.

In the developing country like India, there is a need for evolving a strategy to mitigate the impact of disasters by initiating the preparedness measures through education and training. The declaration of 1990s as the International Decade for Natural Disaster Reduction (IDNDR) by Limited Nations General Assembly was very timely. The objective of the decade was to reduce through concerted international co-operation and efforts the damage to property and social and economic disruption caused by natural disasters. The IDNDR has requested the government, NGOs, research education institutions to pay more attention to evolving effective ways for migrating disasters. At present, in the country, there is a high demand for the institutions of higher learning to develop and launch such programmes, which besides training of functionaries of government agencies and NGOs, could generate necessary awareness among the masses. Such education programmes may take the following forms.

## I. Public Education

Education represents formal, informal and non-formal approaches to learning for developing the knowledge base, among to help a person in:

- understanding the intended subject
- forming independent opinion
- establishing priorities and last
- knowing relevant methodologies.

It is, indeed, a long-term programme under which standard curricula for school/college and university students should be drawn. It should include the necessary information to counter the disaster threat.

## II. Training Programmes

Training involves a set of learning activities oriented to objectives of improving knowledge, skills and attitude of individuals to carry out specific tasks based on accepted methodology with appropriate techniques. Thus, this may include the short-term training programmes and exchange of knowledge through seminars, conferences, expert group meetings, etc. There is a need to design special training workshops for adult population either to be organised specially a integrated with ongoing programmes like, adult education.

## III. Extension Programmes

Community or village-based outreach worker can be trained to provide relevant information. For the purpose of public information, radio, T.V. and printed with well-designed and projected messages can be of great help.

The process of training and education for living and working in disater prone areas requires a continuous improvement and knowledge transfer between the various stake holders, like researchers, community leaders and volunteers. Training and education programmes in the area of Disaster Management are multidisciplinary and should the following:

- education and training programme in disaster management/ mitigation

- oriented towards the most vulnerable sections of the community
- institutionalised as ongoing process.
- based upon the outcome of training need analysis
- specific for subject-matter and target groups in local languages.
- participating in nature ensuring active community participation.

Education and training must be based on the training need analysis and must correlate with the specific problems of particular region or community. Disaster management training programmes should have the following basic requirements:

- Public information and awareness including the over-view of potential hazards in a particular region and locality.
- Vulnerability analysis and risk features involved for various hazards.
- Prediction and warning systems available and the proper utilisation for the appropriate safeguard against the potential hazard.
- post-disaster relief and recovery mechanism.
- emergency management including do's and don'ts during the disaster situations.

Long-term recovery plans and role identification for various actors.

An important aspect of disaster management education and training is the target group programme. The various target groups may include.

1. Policy Makers
   - Central Governments/ State Government officials
   - Other senior level administration.
2. Professionals
   - Engineers/ Architects
   - Physical planners
   - Trainers/ Researchers.
3. Voluntary Groups
   - N.G.O. representatives working in the field of disaster management

   - various religious organisations involved in disaster management NCC/NSS representatives.
   - individual volunteers involved in social work and interested disaster management activities.
   - representatives from various clubs and social organisation.
4. Community Groups
   - community leaders including religious heads.
   - school teachers and student community
   - general masses.

Considering the status of various target groups the education and training programmes must suit their level of understanding and requirements.

The various education and training programmes can be grouped into two major streams, i.e., the formal education system in colleges and universities and non-formal short-term training programmes. The major contributions from formal education system can be made in the following three areas.

### 1. *Research*

The institutes of higher learning are involved in conducting research in traditional sciences and social sciences which should include the area of disaster management. The research findings may form the basis for formulating policy and may also open certain commercial ventures.

### 2. *Technical Advises*

Concerted efforts may be based from vast human resource potential for conducting research and socio-economic analysis on disaster events. Though senior faculty members of reputed universities/colleges are being consulted by various government, non-government, public and private organisations for their expertise in the relevant fields.

### 3. *Knowledge Transfer*

Course work in the subjects related to disaster management can shape the careers and minds of young professionals and also can accelerate their enthusiasm for working in this field.

In our country number of academic institutions are conducting programmes in areas related to disaster management. The university of Roorkee is having post-graduate courses in earthquake engineering, since the sixties. IITs at Delhi, Kanpur and Mumbai, Anna University in Chennai and colleges like Delhi College of Engineering and Madan Mohan Malaviya Engineering College are working in the areas of earthquake related studies. A good work has done in the field of floods and drought in the universities of Kolkata, Patna, Mysore, Madras, Utkal, Andhra Pradesh, etc. Research on landslides and related areas is being conducted at the universities of Himachal Pradesh, Delhi and the Jawaharlal Nehru University.

Besides the traditional universities, a number of research institutes like CBRI, RRI, SERCs, the Wadia Institute of Himalayan Geology are engaged in educational programmes in the areas of disaster management. IGNOU has started a course on disaster management through correspondence.

Under the category of non-formal short-term training programmes, the Government of India has taken the initiative of setting up the National Centre of Disaster Management at the Indian Institute of Public Administration (IIPA) and Disaster Management Cells in all the states. At the moment about thirteen states have already started Disaster Management cells in their respective public administration institution. Other organisations involved in short-term disaster management training are the administrative staff college and the CWC Delhi.

To conclude, I would like to recommend few suggestions in relation to education and training for disaster management and these are as follows:

1. NDM should form an integral part of formal, non-formal and adult education programmes.
2. Modules generated in disaster management may be used in the pre-service and inservice training programmes of the DIET.
3. NDM should be introduced as an activity based programme and not as a scholastic one.
4. At the college level it can be incorporated in the course. Content of the Diploma course in environment education.

5. Existing agencies like DAE, SRC, leading voluntary agencies and university departments may develop material related to disaster management.
6. The NGOs should work hard in hand with government department in disaster preparedness mitigation programmes, relief and rehabilitation.
7. The NGOs having been closed to community can prove an asset in imparting training and education for well prepared community.
8. The NGOs can be trained in specific skills like search and rescue, first-aid and in providing temporary rehabilitation.

## REFERENCES

Budget Speech of Chief Minister, H.P. Government Presented on 9 March, 2001.

Contingency Action Plan for Natural Calamities, Ministry of Agriculture, Govt. of India, 1990.

B.S. Padmanabhan, "Disaster, Health and Development", Media Oriented Symposium on Natural Disaster Reduction, New Delhi, 15 January, 1993.

Health Services in Disaster Management, Keynote address by Dr. Olaivi Elo, WHO Representative to India, Media, Orientation, Symposium on "Natural Disaster Reduction", New Delhi, 15 January, 1993.

*Indian Journal of Adult Education,* July-September, 1998.

Natural Disaster Reduction South Asian Regional Report, Ministry of Agriculture, Government of India, 1994.

The UNESCO Courier, Special Issue on "Natural Disaster"—Prepared October, 1997, UNESCO Press.

S. Suri and M. Sivanand, "Voices That Span the Globe", *The Reader's Digest,* Sept. 1992.

# 29

# Noise Pollution and its Effect on Educational Institutions

## A Challenge to the New Millennium

*Pradeep Vaid & Himani Vaid*

The problem of environmental pollution has in recent times engaged the attention of various organisations, agencies and institutions. Man's activities have now acquired the potential of artificially due to development of technology, scientific advancement, growth in population and industrialisation disturb the delicate balance of biosphere. Introduction of large amounts of pollutants causes serious problems for the life on the earth. Today, the problem of noise pollution is emerging as a serious matter on the earth and institutions in particular. Researches have proved that a loud noise during the peak working hours creates tiredness, irritation and impairs brain activities so as to reduce thinking and working capacities. Loud noises destroy delicate receptor cells which convey sounds to the brain. With years of exposure to blaring music or thundering machinery, more and more of these cells die.

At present most educational institutions consisting of teachers, student and employees have a rather noisy inside environment. Noise as a pollutant, produces contaminated environment which becomes a nuisance and effects the working environment of educational institutions like universities, colleges and other related institutions and thus teachers, students and administrative staff are apparent victims of this pollution.

## What Noise Pollution Is?

*Encyclopedia Americanna* defines it as:

> Noise by definition is unwanted sound; what is pleasant to some ears may be extremely unpleasant to others, depending on a number of psychological factors. The sweetest music, if it disturbs a person who is trying to concentrate or to sleep, is a noise to him, just as the sound of a pneumatic riveting hammer is noise to nearly everyone.

Noise is sound without value and is of an unwanted obnoxious and disturbing nature. The pollution by noise which is the product of the modern age has increased in multifarious directions. How dangerous is noise pollution to human beings? The answer depends on the kind of pollutants and their conservation in the aquatic system of interest. Noise is an audible acoustic energy that adversely effects the physiological or psychological well-being of the people.

The level of noise is increasing in Indian cities and working institutions day by day. A collaborative study on the prevalence and actiology of hearing impairment conducted by the Indian Council of Medical Research (ICMR) and Department of Science and Technology (DOCT) shows an increase in hearing disabilities among workers employed in noisy environment for more than 10 years.

## Effect on the Educational Institutions

Today, generally most of the educational institutions like schools, colleges, universities and other related institutions are mostly located in or around the cities where the noise pollution is much higher and it disturb the healthy teaching and research environment in these institutions due to communication gaps, loss of hearing, behaviour changes and deconcentration produced by noise.

Noise levels are measured in decibels, one decibel is the threshold of hearing, 30 decibels denotes the whispering range and 60 decibels is the level normal talk, 90-95 decibels may cause irreversible changes in the automatic nervous system.[1]

At present most of the educational institutions are facing noise in the inside environment. This noisy environment rises due to high noise pollution around these educational institutions. These sounds create feelings of negative emotions, startle, fear, anger, frustration, etc., in the students and teachers because of unexpectedness or other meanings the sound convey or because of the annoyance caused to concentration in the study and research. It is generally believed that the continued exposure to noise concentration in the study or research can be a source of physiological stress that can be possible capable of causing situation is beyond imagination. Interruption during delivering lecture by the teachers to the students may impair performance, lead to errors and lower the output and the efficiency of the students. Apart from this, the students and teachers of these noise polluted institutions may develop a habit of shouting in the classrooms.

The following factors are generally responsible for noise pollution around the educational institutions:

(i) Use of high volume loud speakers on many occasions continuously for hours together with their loudest capacity.
(ii) High traffic density around the educational institutions contribute towards noise pollution because no regulation is observed in blowing of electric horns of high intensity by the modern vehicles.
(iii) Construction of new residential and commercial complexes results in vibration of sounds which always make the educational institution a victim of noise pollution.
(iv) Adjoining residential complexes and shops near educational institutions play their audio with high volume/watts throughout the day, causing noise pollution. Further, the TV disc connections are also creating a serious challenge to noise pollution.
(v) Increase in industrialisation leads to noise pollution where machines are working and this noise pollution also disturb the smooth working of the educational institutions.

(vi) Nowadays all the educational institutions are becoming the centre of political activities where the different political organisations arrange their speeches, manage dharnas and other established causes only to disturb these institutions.

(vii) Finally, educational institutions' campuses are generally becoming visiting centres by the local residents which means multiplication of sound and noise of all kinds and intensity in the institutional campuses.

## Avoidance of Noise Pollution: An Institutional Approach

Since the noise pollution adversely effects the educational institutes, it is, therefore, necessary that various steps should be taken to reduce level of noise to the optimum. An organised effort on the part of students and teachers, engaged in the educational institutions is required to keep a check on noise pollution within and around these institutions for educational efficiency and effectiveness.

While planning the structure of educational institutions, proper attention is to be paid to this problem of noise pollution. For this purpose, there should be co-operation between planners and environmentalists. Educational institutions should be planned in such a way that these should be away from residential areas and commercial places or other public services like railway stations, bus stands etc.

To increase awareness among the students, regarding environmental pollution, environment education is an important subject which makes students fully aware of the problems. Further, teacher training in terms of orientation programmes and refresher courses relating to environmental education is also an important factor in carrying out this task successfully.

## Teacher's Participation—An Accountability

Apart from the students and teachers participation to fight with environment pollution, there is growing need to regulate pollution through legislative measures, so that the environment can be saved from being polluted in the interest of educational institutions. The various legislative measures towards protection and control of the noise pollution have been taken by the courts. It is the responsibility of the teachers to make aware the students of the colleges and uiniversities to know about the legislative measures regarding the noise pollution and make the society more informed through them. The various enactments regarding the noise pollution are:

> No persons shall use and play a loudspeaker.[2]

Within such distance as may be prescribed from any educational institution maintained, managed, recognized or controlled by the State Government, or University established under any law for the time being in force, or a local authority, or admitted to such university, or any hostel maintained, managed or recognised by such institution when such institution or hostel is in the use of students.

Further, Indian Penal Code also has provisions to regulate pollution on the ground of nuisance. Motors Vehicle Act, 1939 (Amended, 1988) also provided certain restrictions on noise produced by horns and it also requires a silencer. A landmark verdict of Himachal Pradesh High Court through a Public Interest Litigation (PIL) suit on significant aspect to attitude of public functionaries and their duties.[3] It said:

> When loudspeakers are allowed to disturb the neighbourhood, it is the duty of the Police and Deputy Commissioner to take appropriate action against those creating a nuisance and not wait for the suffering public to protest to the Police.

The another important act regarding the noise pollution has been introduced in India Called Air Act[4] of 1986. This Act provides certain comprehensive measures for protection and improve the environment pollution in the country.

## Conclusions and Policy Implications

It is important to maintain the environment of educational institutions free from pollution especially from noise. Formation of "Noise Free Zones" around all schools, colleges, universities and other related institutions is required. Further, noise abatement zones should also be formed when noise pollution is very high to reduce it to the optimum minimum levels. Laws were made and laws are being framed, but more important is the proper implementation of these laws to achieve the desired results. Proper implementation does not only require a proper management and techniques, but also an active involvement and formation of various committees or bodies with members from students and teachers with the help of citizens, local administration, the pressure groups like NGOs and expertise definitely to help in avoidance of noise pollution. Such bodies should be given sufficient powers for doing the needful.

A healthy environment provides a healthy body and a healthy mind. Today, the emerging role of the educational institutions is becoming more challenging in the context of Nation Building and human society and its development. Last but not the least, participatory role of the Head of the Institution is also significant and meaningful in measures to making the pollution free environment. This would definitely, improve the educational environment of these institutions.

## REFERENCES


1. Ehrlich and Ehrlich, *Population, Resources and Environment,* 1970.
2. Rajasthan and Bihar, *Section 3 of Bihar Controls of Use and Play of Loudspeakers Act, 1955* provides use and play of Loudspeakers it reads.
3. *AIR, 1984,* NOC 137, HP.
4. Ministry of Environment and Forests, Government of India, "The Environment (Protection) Act, 1986", No. 29, 23rd May, 1985.

Part 5

# Administrative Reforms

# 30

# Administrative Ethics

*S.L. Goel & Aruna Goel*

Essentials of Ethics are depicted in the word WATCH

| | | |
|---|---|---|
| W | – | Watch your Words |
| A | – | Watch your Actions |
| T | – | Watch your Thoughts |
| C | – | Watch your Character |
| H | – | Watch your Heart |

**Prevailing Environment of Unethical Values**

We are passing through critical times when the environment all around is unethical. K.R. Narayanan, President of India, while delivering his address, on the eve of Independence Day, on 14th August, 2000, was critical of the nexus between politicians and criminals and in the process polluting the environment of the country. The malpractices in every sphere have become cancerous and are engulfing the entire system geared to provide good standard of living to people. T.N. Chaturvedi in his Editorial on the Special Number on Ethics in Public life of the *Indian Journal of Public Administration* (July-September, 1995) has rightly remarked.[1]

The potential damage and threat to the political fabric of a system is not dependent on the character of government, i.e., whether it is an activist or limited in scope. History shows that neither a capitalist nor a socialist nor a welfare state is immune to the corrosive evil of corruption. The standards of conduct and behaviour of people in political authority have their malignant influence in other walks of life in society. The ethical dimensions of how influential and powerful people conduct themselves in private life and the public domain set a precedent for the lesser human beings and groups in society to follow or to seek justification for their own self-seeking or even scandalous conduct. The perniciousness ripple-effect encompasses all segments of society. It is not only the public systems that are under attack. The people harbour grievances against trade, industry, business, academia, medical and other professional groups and organisations. The evil within and outside the government circle, is thus, not limited to any narrow confines. Similarly, the influence of ethical conduct in positive terms is also not contained or concerned with only some specific sections and select groups but is relevant to the entirety of society and its wider network of relationships. As is often said, the moral basis for the unity and stability of society demands that ethical restraints must operate not only in respect of individuals but also organised groups—be they industrial, business and trade associations, labour unions, political parties, military and civil services, judiciary, non-governmental organisations, academic or professional associations, agriculturists organisations, etc.—apart from government itself. The all-pervading and inter-locking nature of ethics in public life is to be comprehended in all its manifestations and dimensions. This is borne out by history in different times and ages and also by the prowess of civilisation today.

The scandals and cases of corruption, kickbacks, bribery, extortions, lying and deception by government all over the world, in both developed and developing countries at different times, are too many and too well-known to need any enumeration. In the wake of many cases of nepotism, influence peddling, corporate bribery, corruption, illicit operations, business malpractices, and unhealthy nexus between politics, administration and business coming of public notice at the time of the Second World War, the US Senate set up a subcommittee under Senator Paul Doughlas, which submitted its report, commonly known as the Report on Ethical Standards in Government. This attracted attention all over the world and the various nuances of ethics in governance were discussed, researched and commented upon in various forums.

Vohra Committee has been quite vocal in portraying the decaying environment engulfing the basic framework of the Indian constitution and social life of the people.

To quote from the Vohra Committee:

> The big smuggling Syndicates, having international linkages, have spread into and infected the various economic and financial activities, including havala transactions, circulation of black money and operations of a vicious parallel economy causing serious damage to the economic fibre of the country. The Syndicates have acquired substantial financial and muscle power and social respectability and have successfully corrupted the Government machinery at all levels and wield enough influence to make the task of Investigating and Prosecuting agencies extremely difficult; even the members of the Judicial system have not escaped the embrace of the Mafia.[2]

Justice V.R. Krishna Iyer has even blamed the elite clan for joining the criminals and make the nation stink by their frivolous activities. To quote him.

> Lawyer, Doctors, Company Secretaries, Chartered Accountants, Engineers and Scientists, not to speak of the talented bureaucrats, are all slowly selling their souls for a mess of pottage. Even the leaders in the professions have let us down. In Browning's verse:
>
> Just for a handful of silver he left us,
> Just for a riband to stick in his coat,
> We that had loved him so, followed him, honored him,
> Lived in his mild and magnificent eye,
> Learned his great language, caught his clear accents,
> Made him our pattern to live and to die![3]

## Meaning and Nature of Ethics

Let us now understand the meaning and contents of ethics

which need to be ingrained into the Politico-Administrative machinery of the Government.

The word "Ethics" is defined by the *Concise Oxford Dictionary* as "the science of morals in human conduct: moral philosophy: moral principles: rules of conduct". The utility of ethics rests on the fact that it requires one to reason, to analyse and to search for morally correct position while taking a decision. Ethics in the area of public services is called administrative ethics. Chester Bernard has described moral behaviour as "governed by beliefs or feelings of what is right or wrong regardless of self-interest or immediate consequences of a decision to do or not to do specific things under particular conditions". S.K. Chakraborty[4] has suggested work ethics where everybody is motivated by the ethical and moral values and works with the doctrine of *nishkama-karma*. The salient features of *nishkama-karma* have been identified as under: (a) Psychological energy conservation, (b) Reactionless steady action, (c) Perfection (as the aim), (d) Inner autonomy, (e) Freedom (*swaadheen*), (f) Socio-Economically appropriate, (g) Work Commitment, (h) Work as Worship for excellence, (i) Mind-Enrichment, and (j) Leads to yoga with the transcendent/higher Self. *Nishkam-karma* will bring holistic transformation in work and will culminate in the following results: (1) a stress-free mind at work, (2) a feeling for works as acts of consecration, (3) a pure, transparent mind, (4) an abiding instinct for ethical rectitude, (5) an inner sanctuary of fullness, and (6) an all-embracing, other-related mind.

Manoj Pandey[5] rightly defines that moral values, in simple terms, are the values that tell us what is the right, proper and acceptable way of behaving. Moral values are indispensable for good governance. An efficient and technologically sound administrative machinery, unless it stands on high moral pedestal, does not serve the public, but it services a self-perpetuating and exploitative system.

Unfortunately, the Indian Government sector cannot boast of high moral standards. Superior courts have made highly critical comments on the conduct of bureaucracts, and the media is full of reports of high-handedness, corruption and other forms of inappropriate conduct of the bureaucrats. Honest and upright civil servants themselves are concerned about the low morality of the bureaucracy and have been voicing concern at various fora.

## Techniques to Inculcate Administrative Ethics

### 1. *Need of Reforming the Environment Responsible for Unethical Practices*

Bata K. Dey, has sounded an alarming bell to save the nation from the onslaughts of unethical values dominating all walks of life and spoiling the entire fabric of the society. To quote him

> Public life is in a desperate state today, with vice-regal regalia dominating it with its fierce ferocity and crushing criminality, sounding the death-knell of ethicality, morality, and value-system. There is dire need to save it. Public men—at whatever station of life they function—must be "men" for the public; leaders must lead; and; most importantly, politicians must stop "politicking". Public opinion—which is often branded as meaning neither public nor opinion—must be built up against acceptance and tolerance of unethical behaviour and action by anybody, howsoever high and mighty he may be. Crisis of confidence—which admittedly is a function of culture—must be restored in public life; otherwise, the ancient civilisation that we boast of will be no more; there will remain no public, no life, worth living, without ethics.[6]

Prashant Bhushan feels that the prevailing environment is full of corrupt practices at all levels. "Corruption has steeped into every pore of this country's public life. From top to bottom, Prime Minister to a peon, cutting across almost every office or organisation of all Governments, Central, State or local, the vast majority of public officials in this country has become corrupt."[7]

S.R. Maheshwari suggests immediate measures to root out this growing menace of unethical practices to save the nation. To quote him:

> Low ethics, today, is no doubt a worldwide phenomenon but its effects are most pernicious in developing countries, like India, characterised as these are by vulnerable economies. The country's policy-makers must realise that its

> economic and social costs are virtually devastating: it demoralises the civil service and adversely affects its performance. It must be fought. Otherwise, the society will be forced to resort to extraordinary measures, like violence, to deal with the evil.[8]

An analysis of above statements by eminent scholars, experts and administrators reveal that there cannot be any development until and unless, we can inject morality in the Government machinery. The writing on the wall is clear that the nation is going to follow the dictates of criminals giving rise to violence, unrest and explosive situations. The recent Supreme Court judgement in Veerapan Case against Karnataka Government is a pointer in this very direction. Supreme Court held in a very clear verdict that if Govt. cannot tackle such criminal menace, they must leave.

O.P. Dwivedi, an eminent scholar, suggests the need of moral base for the Government to save the country from further degradation. To quote him:

> No country is immune from the moral disarray which we have seen recently. Even in the People's Republic of China, which was hailed as a paragon of public virtue and morality by some, cases of public service unethical activities and corruption have been reported. In many nations, a widespread sense of moral disarray exists, neither industrial nor Third World countries are exempt from this disarray. Everywhere, instances are on the rise detailing the collapse of standard and quality of service. This has contributed to the public cynicism; but at the same time, public is clamouring for a new set of bases for public morality and decent moral standards. Because, if we don't wish to be swallowed by the sea of amorality and self-centered hedonism, there will have to be some agreement (or consensus) about the behaviour of individuals, particularly those holding public offices.[9]

The vacuum created because of traditional and "old-fashioned" values drawn from religious sources and based on common sense being discarded in favour of materialism and selfish individualism, clearly points to the need for a code of ethics. As a matter of fact, no specific standards were left sacred against which the conduct of public officials (as well as business people) could be measured. And as clergy and religious leaders were told to keep out of the state affairs, the protective layer of public morality was left exposed to the onslaught of corruption, dishonesty, sleaziness, deception and selfish individualism. That protective layer in the body politic is needed back. For no nation or a society, irrespective of its political and religious orientation, can live in a moral vacuum. There have to be some articles of faith (drawn from the societal culture, traditions, and religions) governing our lives, which must be resurrected and strengthened. We already know that one cannot legislate honesty and good behaviour; these have to come from within. For that, one has to look to our religions where such attributes are considered sacred. But, one does not acquire such attributes by thinking alone; these have to be drilled in the thinking process of the officials. But that could be possible if their moral consciousness is raised so that they are able to fight against the forces of corruption, favouritism, and malpractice. Otherwise, they will continue to be adrift in the sea of amoralism, of which the prevailing administrative culture has come to symbolise. It is to prevent further decay that they ought to think in terms of drawing on their priceless spiritual and cultural heritage. Thus there is a need within the secular domain of the administrative culture to seek the spiritual guidance. Only by demonstrating high standards of personal integrity, fairness, justice, and by regarding their work as *dharma*, public officials may be able to arrest those insidious forces which have penetrated the foundation as well as the structure of India's administration. Such is the requisite of a moral government.[10]

Moral values, in simple terms, are the values that tell us what is the right, proper and acceptable way of behaving. Moral values are indispensable for good governance. An efficient and technologically sound administrative machinery, unless it stands on high moral pedestal, does not serve the public, but it services a self-perpetuating and exploitative system.

Unfortunately, the Indian Government sector cannot boast of high moral standards. Superior courts have made highly critical comments on the conduct of bureaucrats, and the media is full of reports of high-handedness, corruption and other forms of inappropriate conduct of the bureaucrats. Honest and upright civil servants themselves are concerned about the low morality of the bureaucracy and have been voicing concern at various fora.

### 2. *Understanding Religious Foundation for Administrative Culture (Ethics)*

The scriptures of many world religions contain pearls of wisdom about how one should behave in the public office, or what is expected of those who govern people. When scriptures were written, the world had rule of kings; hence advice is rendered for the king and his servants. Hindu religion is no exception to this pattern; except that unlike some other religions, edicts and codes are not handed down either by Govt. or by His prophets. The religious foundation of the duties and conduct of public officials as described in some scriptures of the Hindu religion is examined here. Let us begin by quoting:

Krishna in *Gita*:

> One ought to understand what is duty
> and what is forbidden in the regulations laid down by the scriptures *(Shastras)*.
> Knowing such rules and regulations, one
> should behave accordingly.
>
> (*Gita,* Chapter XVI, Verse 24)

Lord Krishna further says:

> O Partha! that understanding by
> which one knows what ought to be done
> and what ought not to be done,
> what is to be feared and what is not,
> what is obligatory and what is permitted,
> leads to the righteous path
>
> (*Gita,* Chapter XVIII, Verse 30)

That righteous path in Hindu religion is called *dharma*. How does one know the righteous path for specific functions or duties, Hindu scriptures *(Shastras)* provide guidelines. These guidelines or rules of *dharma* have been prescribed by great many seers, each according to his or her wisdom.

### 3. *Practice of Ethics in Management*

Col. D.S. Cheema stated that since a manager is expected to get desired and specified results from and through people, the focus of attention of management and that of the managers is on results. There is no doubt that the manager should be result-oriented, yet it appears that almost exclusive emphasis is laid on results and results alone. Many a management thinkers believe that the solution to the problems of managerial obsession with results and its undesirable effects lies in our heritage, traditions and ethos. It is relevant to mention here the concept of *"Karmayoga"* and *"Sthitha Pragnya"* as propounded in the *Bhagvad Gita*. It is well known that *Karmayoga* calls for action without expecting the results and *Sthitha Pragnya* denotes equanimity whether the results are achieved or not. A manager should aim at professional commitment when it is action and emotional detachment when it is the results.[11]

Pursuing material and spiritual happiness and the welfare of mankind can lead any organisation confidently into the future. The essence of all this is "management from the heart" and it is much closer to our way of life than anybody else.

Kamala Prasad[12] has beautifully defined the concept of Ethics and morality which needs to be understood and practised to usher in a moral Government.

This will call for defining morality for governance. Morality signifies pursuit of ethical conduct and performance of duties assigned in such a manner that the declared purpose is realised. In the Greek tradition, it implied the development of the latent capabilities of an individual for the full flowering of his/her personality to deliver public good. To this end, there was rigorous training and preparation for the holders of public office so that the aims of public office were served. *Dharma,* in the Indian tradition, commands morality in the sense of righteous conduct. As propagated by Emperor Ashok, it further implied inculcation and practice of virtue in the performance of assigned duties. To an extent, the normative morality would subjugate personal interests to community interests and particular aims to general aims of the society. Mahatma Gandhi has raised *dharma* to a higher pedestal, signifying a quality through which we know "our duty in human life and our relation with otherselves".

Thus, ethics in public life is important to understand our place in society and the duties we owe to the society by virtue of what society gives us. The common people may not articulate it in as many words but this is built into their thinking process when they make an assessment of the conduct pattern of their representatives and leaders and the system over which the representatives have command.

> While considering a charter of Ethics for public servants in India, there has to be a multi-dimensional approach, covering corruption, serving the Government, serving the public solving conflict of interests, etc. Each of these attributes has an ethical connotation, and unless these are examined in depth, a holistic approach will not be visible.

Responsive and clean administration depends, *inter alia,* on adherence of the employee in public service to ethical standards and the basic principles of the Constitution such as secularism, social justice, attention to the needs of weaker sections and vulnerable groups, equality and rule of law. Both Centre and State Governments, no doubt have notified regulations governing the conduct of employees in various services which address the issues. However, they are more in nature of formulations of 'do's and dont's and do not represent a positive statement of values and believes that they should govern the private conduct of civil servants. In this context, Ministry of Personnel, Public Grievances and Pensions has formulated a draft code of ethics which have already been endorsed in the Chief Ministers Conference and at present is being given a legal shape. The objective of the code is to prescribe standards of integrity and conduct in the public services. It would apply to all services, generalist and technical.

The key Public Service Regulations provide that an officer should perform with skill, care, diligence and impartiality, the duties of his office, to the best of his ability, comply with any lawful and reasonable direction given by a person having authority to give the direction, treat members of the public and other officers with courtesy and sensitivity to their rights, duties, and aspirations, avoid waste or extravagance in the use of public resources, not take improper advantage of any official information acquired as a consequence of employment, etc.

All modern governments suffer from the persistent preoccupation with procedures and functional rationality to the exclusion of ethical values and standards. It is not surprising, then, to see that public servants view their domain as a rational, objective, and value-free, where expediency and technical considerations dominate the policy decisions of vital socio-economic consequences. Ethical dilemmas faced by a public servant include many issues of contention, for example, if there is a conflict between an individual's privately held convictions and publicly held obligations; as determined by his organisation, what should he do? Should he interpret government policies and programmes according to his personal sense of right and wrong? Or, when a public servant feels that there is a clear-cut conflict between what he is required (by his senior officials or by the political leadership) to do and what he really thinks is right, where should his loyalty lie? Is a public servant committed to keeping information secret that might be embarrassing to the government of the day? What should an employee do when he finds certain indications of deliberate inefficiency, protection of incompetence, extravagant and unreasonable use of public funds, use of government equipment and machinery for personal use or subjective criteria used in recruitment or in the award of government grants or favours?[13]

To what extent, should a public servant support the political ideology practised by the current political leadership of the government? Or, when a person accepts public service employment, how much should be subordinate or abdicate his claims to private life, property and values?[14] Obviously, neither the traditional concept of "bureaucratic neutrality" nor a "code of bureaucratic conduct" can cover all such situations or resolve such dilemmas. In addition to certain code of public ethics (determined in accordance with the prevailing socio-cultural political norms in the society), a public servant needs to develop an inner sense of professional responsibility, refined by the considerations of "humanism", "responsiveness" and "public good". As Dwivedi has so emphatically put it, "public responsibility" is multi-dimensional in nature, it flows upward and downward as well as outward and inward. Such a complex notion is bound to create dilemmas; consequently a responsible administrator would be well advised to be on guard against forces which might attempt to influence him to act otherwise".[15]

It has been noted by many observers that Singapore has succeeded in developing a Public Service ethos which emphasises merit, equity, probity, integrity, and ethical conduct, apart from leadership, quality, and productivity.

In Malaysia, the Government has always insisted on the highest levels of discipline in its employees, discipline meaning adherence or conformance to set work ethics and value systems.

It is clear that the existing legal provisions as well as the elaborate rules, regulations, standing instructions, etc., have not been able to prevent large-scale administrative corruption in India. There are some objective and impartial observers who are of the view that in the last two decades, administrative corruption has increased in tandem with growing corruption among elected officials in India. They feel that without tackling political corruption, administrative corruption cannot be contained in India. While, in theory, one has to admit that political corruption on a large-scale will have repercussions on the administrative set-up, the two need not necessarily go hand in hand, as the Japanese example illustrates. But it is certain that if political corruption is negligible and there is strong political determination, administrative transparency is insisted upon and norms of political as well as administrative behaviour are well publicised, making them known to the general public including the Press, there is a good chance that corruption can be contained if not eliminated.

### 4. *Practice of Ethical and Moral Values*

According to Chinmaya, be a noble person in life. The tides of circumstances and the tussle of happenings may toss us hither and thither, may buffet us up and downs, but stay noble in your thoughts and actions—you will be ever safe.

Let us discuss the various aspects of it.

(a) ***Serving the Government as per the Constitution:*** Public service must be committed to the philosophy and programmes of the present government. They should tender their unbiased advice and implement the policies of the Government sincerely.

(b) ***Serving the people:*** Public servants should serve the people efficiently and effectively. Almost by definition, a democracy demands a responsive administration accountable to the people. It means that administration must be sensitive to the needs of the people, it must ensure its credibility and prestige.

(c) ***Integrity:*** Integrity is essential in dealing with administrative activities. The importance of character, dedication and sense of service are the important attributes of integrity.

(d) ***Transparency:*** Since the civil services in India is the major instrument of the Government for the implementation of policies for economic growth and the delivery of services, the restructuring of the civil service and the reorientation of its attitudes and value systems are essential components of a responsive administration. While there are striking examples of officials with demonstrated excellence, motivation and commitment to the cause of the underprivileged, these have been perceived by the public as outnumbered by inaccessibility, indifference to the public, undue emphasis on procedures and regulations, lack of quality and promptitude, proneness to corruption, and the lack of accountability for results. The associations of civil servants, on the other hand, complain about demoralisation, political interference and lack of motivation. The assumption of an executive role by the judiciary in recent years is seen as arising from the failure of the civil service in different levels of Government in the proper and responsive performance of assigned functions and in conforming to the code of conduct. The need is to function in the above framework of Ethics to usher in an Era of citizen-friendly administration.

(e) ***Taking active interest and not be indifferent and apathetic:*** Shekhar Singh in his Article "Ethics and Administration" rightly mentions that there is also a class of apathetic officers who, though they refuse to participate in or condone corruption, are not willing to fight it. Very often such officers are erstwhile fighters who have been beaten down or have become cynical. They withdraw into themselves and are often marginalised within the system. They sometimes take to other, non-administrative, pursuits, and try to revive their sagging spirits and sense of self worth by excelling in the arts, or as intellectuals or sports persons.

Their immorality lies in the fact that they continue to be public servants without serving the public. They don't directly seek any benefits from their office except their salaries, their legitimate perks, and the freedom to do their own thing. But even in doing so, they take their due from the public, without in return giving the public its due.[16]

(f) ***Need of creating climate to promote ethical values:*** B. Rattan Reddy opines that there is no doubt that Indian administration needs a strong core of dynamic values to transform its ethos at all levels. Laws can be enacted and rules framed to this end. Enforcement agencies can prosecute and the system can punish. This will have an impact. Nonetheless, enforcement of morality through law will largely remain an external process that can at best delineate a framework for public behaviour that should not be transgressed. But beyond that, laws or rules have inherent limitations in addressing the question of societal and individual change. As such, lasting public morality and ethics cannot be forced from outside. These must take roots and grow within the system itself. People have to understand and accept it so that change becomes organic.

(g) ***Code of ethics for the public services in india:*** The document prepared by Department of Administrative Reforms and public grievances has chalked out a code of Ethics which need implementation. The objective of Code is to prescribe standards of integrity and conduct that are to apply in the public services. The principles stated below underlie and supplement the rules and laws to regulate the public and private conduct of various public services.

***Selflessness:*** Holders of public office should take decisions solely in terms of the public interest. They should not do so in order to gain financial or other material

benfits for themselves, their family, or their friends.
***Integrity:*** Holders of public office should not place themselves under any financial or other obligation to outside individuals or organisations that might influence them in the performance of their official duties.
***Objective:*** In carrying out public business, including making public appointments, awarding contracts, or recommending individuals for rewards and benefits, holders of public office should make choice on merit.
***Accountability:*** Holders of public office are accountable for their decisions and actions to the public and must submit themselves to whatever scrutiny is appropriate to their office.
***Openness:*** Holders of public office should be as open as possible about all the decisions and actions that they take. They should give reasons for their decisions and restrict information only when the wider public interest clearly demands.
***Honesty:*** Holders of public office have a duty to declare any private interest relating to their public duties and to take steps to resolve any conflicts arising in a way that protects the public interest.
***Leadership:*** Holders of public office should promote and support these principles by leadership and example.

These principles apply to all aspects of public life. The Committee has set them out here for the benefits of all who serve the public in any way. Even the chambers of commerce has formulated a code of Ethics and the important features of the Code of Ethics promulgated by the PHD chamber read as follows:

- Business must maintain highest standards of behaviour so that their actions and decisions result in the benefits for industry, employees, customers, shareholders and society.
- Goods and service must conform to the commitment promised to customers. Business must be realistic and truthful in stating claims.
- Customers must be given best possible service and treated with respect and fairness.

- Best way of promoting high standards of business practices is through self-regulation. The Code has been designed as an instrument of self-regulation to serve as voluntary guideline towards better quality of life and higher standards of business practices.

(i) *Obligation to Government and the Constitution*

The Constitutional and administrative role of the Public Services is to assist the duly constituted government, of whatever political colour, in formulating and implementing policies of the government and in administering the public services under the Central Government in the most effective and efficient manner, within the framework of the Indian Constitution.

It is the obligation of every employee in the public services to uphold the Rule of Law and respect for human rights, and to act solely in the public interest while making recommendations or exercising administrative authority. He or she must maintain the highest standards of probity and integrity.

In relation to the general public, employees in the public services should conduct themselves in such a manner that the public feels that the decisions taken or the recommendations made by them are objective and transparent, and are not calculated to promote improper gains for the political party in power, for themselves or for any third party.

Employees in the public services should not seek to frustrate or undermine the policies, decisions and actions taken in the public interest by a duly constituted Government by, declining or abstaining from action which flows from ministerial decision or statutory obligations. Where, following the instruction of the superior authority implementation of such decisions or action would appear to conflict with the exercise of impartial professional judgement, or affect the efficient administration of the department or undertaking, the employee should set out the points of disagreement clearly and courteously in writing to the superior authority, and seek explicit written instruction thereon.

Where an employee in public services has reasonable grounds to believe that he or she is being required by the superior authority to act in a manner which is illegal or against prescribed rules and regulations, or if any legal infringement comes to his or her notice, he or she should decline to implement the instruction. He or she would also have a right to bring the facts to the notice of the Head of Department or the chief secretary (cabinet secretary in the central government) or the Minister. It shall be incumbent on the chief secretary (cabinet secretary in the case of Central Government) to examine the issue carefully and advise the chief minister (prime minister in the case of central government) appropriately.

(ii) *Right of Public Comment*

Generally, employees in public services have the same rights of free speech and independence in the conduct of their private affairs as other members of the public. However, they also have a duty not to compromise the government by public criticism of, or comment on policies. They should, therefore, ensure that their contribution to any public debate or discussion on such matters maintains the discretion appropriate to the position they hold, and is compatible with the need to maintain a politically neutral public service.

(iii) *Conflict of Interest and Peer Pressure*

Employees in public services should refrain from decision in respect of which they have reason to believe that they are calculated to benefit any particular person or party at the expense of the public interest.

Every employee in the public services shall disclose any clash of interest when there is conflict between public interest and private interest, or he or she is likely to benefit from any act of omission or commission while discharging his or her functions.

Employees in public services should be alert to analytical or potential conflict of interest, financial or otherwise, and should disclose this to their superiors, whether the conflict covers them or their family members.

Employees in public services should maintain their independence, dignity and impartiality by not approaching politicians and outsiders in respect of service matters or private benefit, and exercise peer pressure to dissuade those within their own cadre who do so, and to set in motion disciplinary proceedings against such persons. Any such approach on his or her behalf in such matters would be deemed to be at the instance of the employee.

(iv) *Accountability and Responsiveness to the Public*

Consistent with accountability to the superior officers and the Ministers in accordance with Constitutional provisions, employees in the public services should be accessible to the people and practice accountability to them in terms of quality of service, timeliness, courtesy, people orientation, and readiness to encourage participation of, and from partnerships with, citizen groups, for responsive government.

Employees in the public services should be consistent, equitable and honest in their treatment of the members of the public, with particular care for the weaker sections of society, and should not ever be, or appear to be, unfair or discriminatory. Decisions in pursuit of discretionary powers should be justifiable on the basis of non-arbitrary and objective criteria.

Employees in the public services should accept the obligation to recognise and enforce the citizen's right for speedy redressal of grievances and commit themselves to provide service of declared quality and standards to the citizens.

Employees in public services should respect the right of the public to information on all Government activities and transactions except where they are debarred from releasing information by provisions of law or valid instructions.

(v) *Concern for the Value of Public Assets and Funds*

Employees in public services should avoid wastage and extravagance, ensure effective and efficient use of public money within their control, and endeavour that the benefits of schemes for disadvantaged and poor sections of society are not wasted or diverted for the benefit of others. They should avoid ostentation and set examples of austerity for others.

(vi) *Non-Abuse of Official Position*

Since employees in public services have a responsibility to take decisions on merits, and they are in a position of trust, they must not use their official position to influence any person to enter into financial or other arrangements with them, or with anyone else. They must not abuse official position to obtain a benefit for themselves or for someone else, in financial or other forms.

(vii) *Safeguards in Release of Information*

Employees in the public services should not unauthorisedly release information which is not permitted by law, or compromise private or business interests, or the privacy of an individual when such information has been received in confidence. They should not take improper advantage of official information acquired in the course of their work, for unwarranted gain for themselves or others.

(viii) *Integrative Role*

Every employee in public services should recognise the integrative role of public services in national development, and resist internal and external attempts to fragment public services and society on caste, communal or religious lines. He or she should cultivate national outlook to rise above sectarian, service, cadre of departmental loyalties.

(ix) *Continuous Improvement through Professionalism and Teamwork*

Every employee in the public services should continuously upgrade his or her skills and knowledge, strive for creativity and innovation and nurture values of team working and harmony.

All employees in public services should promote and exhibit public and private conduct in keeping with the appropriate behaviour and standards of excellence and integrity. They should support the juniors in the latter's efforts to resist wrong or illegal directives and in abiding by the Code of Ethics. At the same time, they should reward good work and punish any dereliction of duty or obligations, based on objective and transparent criteria.

The government at the union and state levels should pursue

ethical and moral values to develop the country on a permanent footing. The government must stop the rot crept into public life and improve the moral and ethical fibre of the society.[17]

(x) *Practice of Ethical Values at Top Level*

O.P. Dwivedi, a doyen on moral and ethical work, suggests the need of selfless service by the people in government. To quote him:

> Holding of a public office requires that its incumbent is willing not only to acknowledge the moral responsibility for his/her actions but also to accept the accountability for such actions. Deflecting responsibility does not make action and its consequences disappear. Nothing is more damaging to public trust than justifying fraud and deception in the name of national security, government needs, or nation-building. Problems are more pervasive at the top simply because it is there where more is to be gained. That is why moral leadership had to come from people at the top. The absence of such leadership breeds cynicism and generates tolerance of hypocrisy, greed, and self-indulgence. The State (and finally society at large) becomes the victim of those individuals holding public offices who are unable to put the public business above their selfish leanings.[18]

Enlightened citizens believing in Ethical values. Without the co-operation of citizens, nothing can be achieved. They have to be vigilant and enlightened. T.N. Chaturvedi has cautioned that moral and ethical fibre of society can be upgraded only with the co-operation of the citizens. To quote him.

> The need for organisation, activation, articulation and assertion of public opinion and enlightened citizenship is the life-breath of any vibrant democratic system. Public apathy leads to moral decay. Public vigilance and public awareness of its role and responsibilities provides a safeguard to the sustenance of ethical conduct of public affairs.[19]

It is well to recall here what the then United States Secretary of the Interior Harold Lacks said during the hearings of the Ethics Committee: "Within my knowledge, no public officer has bribed himself", and he went on to emphasis the fact that official morality is more than a political problem. "By all means let us consider how to assist in the establishment of higher moral standards in the official conduct of the Government, but at the same time let us realise that we cannot hope to assist the Government in this regard unless we are willing to assist ourselves and each other in the establishment of higher moral standards as between man and man in private life. Politics is an important part, an integral part, but only a part of the whole pattern of life." (George A Graham, *Morality in American Politics*.)

### 5. *Creation of Enlightened Organisations based on Ethical Values*

The ultimate purpose of all these reforms would be to set up spiritual or enlightened organisation as narrated by Jaideep Singh. To quote him.

The Englightened Organisation would be intensely imbued with a sense of spiritual mission. Take the case of a company producing, say; shoes. It would experience itself not merely in the business of manufacturing and selling shoes, but, simultaneously, in the spiritual mission of protecting and taking care of human feet.[20] The degree to which members of the organisation feel themselves involved in a spiritual mission will bring to them the deep psychic experience of living a worthwhile, meaningful life and will be reflected directly in their level of motivation and co-operation. This is so because the deeper biological layers of man, as Professor Abraham Maslow has identified in his *Theory of the Hierarchy of Human Needs,* are Self-Actualisation. Being Needs, i.e., the needs for Truth, Goodness, Beauty, Justice, Perfection, Completeness, Unity, Uniqueness, Meaningfulness, etc., and it is precisely these propulsion that we have traditionally called the spiritual thirst of man.

### 6. *Need of Developing Ethical Traditions and Practices*

Justice R.S. Pathak has rightly sensed the need of ethical traditions. To quote him:

> A code of ethical principles is particularly related to each public office, but in general there are common principles applicable to all public offices. Those principles do not require enumeration, they are well known and undisputed. In large measure, continuing traditions indicate the identity and scope of ethical principles and determine the ethos controlling the exercise of all public power. And when I refer to traditions, I refer to traditions, which have been classically evolved as most appropriate for the exercise of public power. It is for that reason that it becomes necessary to educate novitiates in the ethical traditions of their office.

It is important to remember that when state power is channelised through a network of public institutions and public offices, it is intended to create a functioning system held in organic balance and unity, a system which in its holistic operation gives to the nation the intended opportunities for development and secures to the citizen his dignity and worth and the possibility of personal growth. It is vital that the constitutional system be kept in equilibrium. It may lose that organic balance and unity if its channels are clogged in consequence of the misuse or abuse or non-use of power in one or more of its constituent offices. The higher and more significant the office in the hierarchy within the system, the greater the potential for damage to the system.[21]

### 7. *Universities can Act as Centres of Generating Ethical Values*

Universities can play great role in imparting value education. L.P. Singh in a Document *Morality in Public Affairs* has rightly stressed the role of universities in this direction. To quote him:

> A university has the unique opportunity of imparting its values and disciplines to the youth, who are potentially the most creative a part of a society, and who are at the stage when the mind is most capable of imbuing the right ideas and principles. The number of boys and girls passing out of our universities every year runs into several lakhs, and it is from these that our ministers and most of our legislator (compared to legislature of many democratic countries the

> Lok Sabha has a higher percentage of members who are graduates or have higher degrees) are drawn. It is from the annually enlarging pool of educated youth that our civil services, learned professions, and business and industries at the higher levels, are manned. And what is of immense importance, it is graduates of universities who, in vast numbers, become teachers in schools, where they can start the process of moulding the minds and character of our adolescents. The universities have been and can again become radiating centres not only of knowledge, but also values. They can provide to our talented scholars an environment in which they can realise creative potentialities; they now do so in most cases only when they go out to work in foreign universities where they earn great distinction. A high standard of creative work can help our universities to regain their soul.

Our universities can, over a period, make a decisive contribution to the enlightenment of the public mind, and restoration of ethical standards. I believe that if we succeed in taking care of standards and values in our universities, the moral problems of the rest of society will take care of themselves. You members of two universities community have great challenge before you, and it is for you to respond to it.

## Conclusion

Ethics is the moving spirit of a welfare state. All the problems emanating today in a family or a society or government are the product of ignoring ethics for selfish motives. Ethical government may appear to be harsh for temporary period but is the only alternative for a permanent beneficial government. "One could argue that ethical behaviour should in itself be rewarding. However, there are tangible benefits as well. Business is built on relationships with the suppliers, customers, employees, and other groups. The strength of these relationships is largely a function of the amount of trust the parties have in each other.... Studies have shown that the firms which maintain ethical standards perform much better than others due to the good relationships they have with their suppliers, customers, employees and general public. Thus, ethics are cornerstone of business success.[22]

We get a moral government by creating those conditions within which a moral government can operate. This is done by making it possible for officials to acquire the necessary traits and by the practice of the same. An exemplary public servants, to be specific, is not simply one who obeys the laws and behaves within the confines of law but is also one who strives for a moral government. Such is the duty of those who wish to be involved in the difficult and complex world of government. This is the essence and basis of a moral state.[23]

Public life is in a desperate state today, with vice-regal regalia dominating it with its fierce ferocity and crushing criminality, sounding the deathknell of ethicality, morality, and value-system. There is dire need to save it. Public men—at whatever station of life they function—must be men for the public; leaders must lead; and, most importantly, politicians must stop "politicking". Public opinion—which is often branded as meaning neither public nor opinion—must be built up against acceptance and tolerance of unethical behaviour and action by anybody, howsoever high and mighty he may be. Crisis of confidence—which admittedly is a function of culture—must be restored in public life; otherwise, the ancient civilisation that we boast of will be no more; there will remain no public, no life, worth living, without ethics.[24]

We must remember that it is the top men in each department who set the tone of the administration. It is they who set the example for those under them to emulate. When the acts of those at the top become tainted, when their reputation becomes shady, they will not be able to enforce high standards of integrity in those below them. It is, therefore, imperative that men at the top should personify the highest standards of personal integrity, probity and rectitude. As Sir Ivor Jennings observed, the most elementary qualification demanded of a minister is honesty and incorruptibility. It is, in addition, necessary not only that he should possess this qualification but also that he should appear to possess it.[25]

An action is noble because of the ideal which one strives, in itself an action is neither good nor bad. It is the motive in the heart of man that makes an act either good or bad. Once we are careful to choose for ourselves the right type of motive to inspire our activities, the achievement is not only spectacular, but the entire effort becomes rewarding in terms of the feeling of peace and sense of fulfilment that floods the bosom. When we work joyously to gain a great ideal or goal. Our efficiency increases.—Chinmaya

Administrators if works with ethics in their heart and soul are sure to make India, a heaven on this earth where people from other parts of the world would seek spiritual, ethical and moral pleasure.

## REFERENCES

1. T.N. Chaturvedi, Editorial, *IJPA,* July-Sept. 1995, pp. ix-x.
2. India, Report of Vohra Committee (Chairman N.N. Vohra), para 6.2
3. Justice V.P. Krishna Iyer, "Ethical Entropy in Public life", in *IJPA,* July to Sept, 1995, p. 350.
4. S.K. Chakraborty, *Ethics in Management,* Delhi, Oxford, 1996. (A book review by Krishan Mohan Mathur, in *IJPA,* Jan.-March, 1997, p. 102.
5. Manoj Pandey, "Assessing Moral Values for Higher Civil Service. Selection in India" in *IJPA,* April-June, 2000, p. 219.
6. Bata K. Dey, "Ethics—Maladies and Remedies", in *IJPA,* July-Sept., 1995, p. 461.
7. Prashant Bhushan, "Stemming the Tide of Corruption" in *IJPA,* July-Sept., 1995, p. 472.
8. S.R. Maheshwari, "Ethics for Civil Service in India", in *IJPA,* July to Sept., 1995, p. 505.
9. O.P. Dwivedi, "Administrative Theology", *IJPA,* July-Sept. 1990, pp. 418-19.
10. N.R. Ranganathan, A Charter of Ethics, Reading material for Trainees (Some abstracts)
11. Col. D.S. Cheema, "The Ethics in Management: The Indian Scene", *The Daily Tribune,* 12th Sept. 2000.
12. Kamla Prasad, "India's Pursuit of Public Good and the Democratic Dilemma", in *IJPA,* July-Sept. 1995.
13. See O.P. Dwivedi and R.B. Jain, *India's Administrative State,* New Delhi, Gitanjali Publishing House, 1985, p. 257.
14. *Ibid.*
15. Quoted in R.B. Jain, "Political Control of Bureaucracy", in *IJPA,* Jan-March, 1986, p. 16.
16. Shekhar Singh, "Ethics and Administration", *IJPA,* July-Sept., 1997, p. 334.

17. L.P. Singh, "Morality in Public Affairs", *IJPA,* July-Sept., 1995, p. 633.
18. O.P. Dwivedi, "Reflection on Moral Government", *IJPA,* July-Sept., 1995, p. 30.
19. T.N. Chaturvedi, *op. cit.*, pp. xvii & xviii.
20. Jaideep Singh, "The Enlightened Organisation", *IJPA,* April-June, 1979, p. 44
21. Ministry of Personnel, Public Grievances and Pensions, New Delhi, Nov. 1997, p. 15.
22. Atul Dhingra and MRP Singh, "Ethics is making all the Difference" *Indian Management,* July, 2000.
23. O.P. Dwivedi, "Conclusion: A Comparative Analysis of Ethics, Public and Public service", James S. Bowman and F.A. Elliston (eds.) *Ethics, Government and Public Policy,* New York, Greenwood Press, 1988, p. 318.
24. Bata K. Dey, "Ethics—Maladies and Remedies", *IJPA,* July-Sept., 1995, p. 461.
25. H.R. Khanna, "Ethics in Public Life, Issues and Remedy", *IJPA,* July-Sept. 1995, p. 357.

# 31

# Administrative Reforms in India During 1990s

*Arvind K. Sharma*

## I. The Overarching Emphasis

Efforts to transform an aloof, impersonal and paternalistic bureaucracy into one which is citizen-focused and sensitive to user-needs have been at the centre of the reform of public systems which was unfolded in India during the decade of nineties. The three defining pillars of this reform, subsumed under the label of new public management, are localisation, externalisation and debureaucratisation.

Localisation, in stressing the processes of devolution and deconcentration, has lent a new identity to the local elected fora and spurred a variety of initiatives designed to empower the operational managements within the organisations. The immediately relevant implication of localisation is that the flow of power (in the larger societal terms as well as from the narrow intra-organisational standpoint) is directed downwards; so also the flow of information. Therefore, a significant expertise must get built at vertically lower levels of the pyramid. These levels will, through the process of power relocation, gain in strategic importance. These must, equally, experience a growing pressure for answerability and quality by virtue of the physical proximity they achieve with the users of public services.

Externalisation espouses contracting out of the service-production-and-delivery functions to non-public providers or, in the immediate present, to arms-length agencies within, which operate under business style regimes. Relieved from the details of execution, government under this scenario devotes itself exclusively to the task of policy management. The implication of externalisation for public management is that a monolithic supplier gets replaced by competing providers. The imperious and impervious monopolist, whom the citizens cannot discipline, is substituted by a range of providers who compete for customers. And, of course, competition among the providers brings about an increased choice and enhanced quality, and builds consumer sovereignty.

The term debureaucratisation has a variety of meanings and nuances attached to it. Downsizing, delayering (moves towards flatter hierarchies), splitting up internally into more autonomous units, decentralisation designed to enhance the importance of the lower levels of the organisational pyramid, and empowerment of the cutting edge functionaries constitute some of the forms that debureaucratisation has taken. The term has also been used to connote efforts to secure attitudinal change (from "take it or leave it orientation" to "how may I help you attitude"), remove bureaupathologies (red tape, delays), and install strategies to demystify governance (simplification of procedures). A more fundamental usage views debureaucratisation as a process that encourages search for alternatives to bureaucracy and brings about a reduction in the role of the state. This is best illustrated by the growing advocacy of small government, devoted to policy management with service delivery functions devolved on the non-public providers.

These emerging emphasis might well be regarded as breakthroughs of sorts in that they dramatically change the substance and style of governance. The traditional pyramid is, as it were, made to stand on its head. Centralisation and top-downism get edged out, with strong compulsions for innovation dictating empowerment of functionaries at the cutting-edge. With the flow of power directed downwards, the frontline employees grow in strategic importance. Pressures for performance unleashed by the logic of localisation further reinforce the role of the customer-contact employees. Supported by vibrant local institutions, the people at large achieve a new identity that moves the government-citizen relationship into a bilateral mould.

In this backdrop, two distinct emphasis in the administrative reforms domain have emerged in the country during the decade of the nineties: (a) revitalisation of the institutions of local self-governance, and (b) a thorough revamping of the country's civil services designed to induce in them a conscious citizen focus.

## II. Revitalisation of the Local Self-Governing Institutions

The first of the above-stated two emphasis, in which relocation of power in favour of the localities has received increasing attention, has arisen from explorations that catapulted the "politics of poverty" to the centre of the development discourse. To the Alternative Development theorists is attributed the invocation of the power dimension of poverty. Poverty, according to this line of thinking, did not stem simply from an unequal distribution of economic resources; its roots instead lay in perpetuating an oppressive system of governance that disallowed the society's poor access to the elected assemblies. That this powerlessness, or the lack of voice in political processes and fora was a critical dimension of poverty, resulting in the inability of the vast excluded and oppressed sections to control the forces that determined access to resources and opportunities. That, ultimately, it was the uneven distribution of political power in society which lay at the back of the phenomenon of mass poverty. The task of removing poverty, therefore, entailed a realignment of the power equations in favour of the society's underprivileged. This was, in essence, an argument for fostering participation of the poor in the society's power structure, and over a period of time built into a staunch advocacy of political devolution. This intellectual effort has profoundly influenced the contemporary perspective on local self-governing institutions (LSGIs) by compelling a reconceptualisation of local government as a lever of redistributive politics, i.e., a device to provide a level playing field for the diverse social groups, particularly the disadvantaged ones, in the governance process. Concomitantly, as an instrument to physically relocate power through a system of power-sharing which would permit scattered localities a role in the society's governance. The distinctness of this specific perspective lies in stressing a point of unique significance: the need to bridge the gulf between power and people; the people who live in the localities and the power which is concentrated at the centre. Localities, endowed with elected local assemblies, emerge as a power centre to contain the centre's hegemony. And the unilateral sway of the centre is substituted by a bilateral central-local dialogue.

The momentous 73rd and 74th Constitutional Amendments of December, 1992, in fact, arose from the perspective outlined above. In terms of these developments, constitutional recognition was accorded to rual and urban local bodies, state-level election commissions as also finance commissions were created, gram sabhas were accorded a mandatory status, 33 per cent reservation for scheduled castes and scheduled tribes was provided for, so on.

A legal framework for a far more radical devolution to rural self-governing institutions became available in the form of "Provision of Panchayats (Extension to Scheduled Areas) Act, 1996". While this legislation was meant to cover the country's Schedule-5 areas, in practice, over the previous two years, there has developed a strong advocacy in favour of adopting the provisions of the 1996 Act for non-scheduled areas as well. The Ministry of Rural Development, through a March 1999 communication, addressed to the chief ministers of states and union territories, has stressed the need to adopt the 1996 legislation as the basis for amending the states' existing (the post-73rd Amendment) panchayat legislations to bring them in conformity with its provisions. Following this, the Government of Madhya Pradesh has amended its panchayat law in 1999. Government of Rajasthan followed suit in the year 2000.

### III. Efforts to Achieve a Citizen-Centred Bureaucracy

If the 73rd and 74th Constitutional Amendments denote the political route to people's empowerment, India's "Effective and

Responsive Administration" package—arising from the May 1997 Conference of the Chief Ministers at New Delhi—might be thought to represent the managerial route to redefine power equations between the government and the citizen. This is, actually, a comprehensive reform package designed to streamline delivery systems, foster transparency and openness in public transactions, allow citizens an easy, unhasseled access to public services, improve the quality of citizen-administration interface, and, ultimately, realign the provider-recipient power equations to the citizen's advantage so as to augment the prospects of an accountable and responsive governance.

This, therefore, is a multifaceted plan of action, involving a diverse range of initiatives impinging upon the responsiveness question. Three sets of measures are discernible in this managerial reform package. While admittedly there is an element of overlap as regards the concern(s) a particular component addresses, for the sake of academic understanding these may nevertheless be classified in separate categories, as follows: (i) accountability-fostering measures, (ii) measures for promoting transparency and openness, and (iii) measures directed at civil service performance and integrity.

### *Bureaucratic Accountability*

This category comprises: (a) introduction of citizen's charters, (b) measures to strengthen and streamline procedures for redressal of public grievances, and (c) steps directed at reviewing the existing legislations, rules and procedures; the exercise is essentially aimed at establishing or rationalising "frameworks" for responsive governance. While these measures are recounted, mention in the passing may be made of the union government's efforts towards enacting the Lokpal legislation.

### *Transparency and Openness*

The "freedom of information" legislations form the crowning feature of reforms under this category. Freedom of information acts have been legislated in some of the states. At the centre, the freedom of information bill is currently under the consideration of a committee of the Parliament.

Other initiatives by central ministries in regard to transparency and openness, which have become operational, include the following two.

The first involves computerisation of the departmental operations. The aim is three-fold: (a) to facilitate tracking of receipts and files and effective monitoring of pendencies; (b) to ensure easy public access to requisite information; and (c) to promote inter-agency and intra-agency co-ordination.

The second concerns measures to secure a wide dissemination of information. These include recourse to user-guides, publications, notice-board displays, and so forth. Besides, information and facilitation countres (IFCs) in various ministries have also been set-up. The IFCs provide information to users regarding the scope of activities of the concerned organisation, the schemes it operates, stipulated procedures to be followed, the status of petitions/complaints, and so on. All IFCs are computerised; and these are located outside the security zone to obviate the need, on the part of the visitor, to obtain an entry-pass.

### *Civil Service Performance and Integrity*

Initiatives in this category include the following: (i) measures to curb corruption, (ii) efforts towards evolving a civil service code of ethics, (iii) contracting out of public services, and (iv) steps towards simplification of procedures.

Arising from the above efforts, by December 2000, 65 union ministries had formulated their citizen's charters. At the state level, at the corresponding point of time, 19 states and union territories had formulated a total of 310 charters covering select (state/UT-level) departments and agencies. Alongside, by this time, 65 information and facilitation counters had become functional at the union government level. The union government's Department of Administrative Reforms and Public Grievances (AR&PG) constitutes the nodal agency for the reforms outlined above.

In 1997, while the Department of AR&PG announced these initiatives under the "Effective and Responsive Administration" rubric, the Fifth Central Pay Commission, in volume-1of its three-volume report, emerged with some radical proposals. These *inter alia* include recommendations for downsizing of the bureaucracy; delayering; contractual appointments in civil service; incentive pays; multi-skilling of the Group-D staff; constitution of the civil service boards; and a renewed emphasis on performance appraisal, with a view to making it an ongoing, round-the-year exercise. These are recommendations of far-reaching consequences on which the union government has, however, yet to take a view.

# 32

# Reforms for Whom and for What: Need for a Paradigm Shift

*Balram Dogra*

As we know, reforms in India were started in 1991 in the background of acute "foreign exchange" crisis, not as a matter of choice but under compulsion because we immediately needed to correct the "balance of payment" position through raising loans from the IMF, World Bank and other sources in the international financial market. The short-term measures initiated at that time produced desired results and the situation was considerably retrieved. The attempts for modernisation and technological upgradation improved the competitiveness of Indian industry. The exports started increasing at a faster rate and the foreign exchange reserves' position became comfortable. The industrial growth also started picking up and for sometime, it seemed that Indian economy is finally going to make breakthrough in breaking the "vicious circle of poverty" and the country is going to have a responsive government. But did it happen? Did the quality of life of an average citizen improve? Does the file in government offices move fastly now? Is our education system today better organised to train and prepare the youngsters to face the life more confidently? Are we better equipped to handle the national calamities like floods, draughts, cloud bursts, earthquakes, storms, etc.? Has our government become more responsive to the aspiration of its citizens?

Many of us supported reforms in the belief that they will make life easier for the common man but today, after a decade of reforms and seeing their consequences, every thinking Indian is being bothered by above-mentioned questions. So, before, we vigorously start implementing the "second generation reforms", we need to introspect for finding answers to these questions. And, after an honest introspection, even a strong supporter of the reforms would not find affirmative answers. If it is so, where did we go wrong? Why, gradually a scenario has started developing in which common man has started feeling that reforms are not meant to provide any benefits to him or her? People have already started looking towards future with despair and hence, an objective appraisal of the reforms, their real beneficiaries and desirable direction is needed.

All these reforms were initiated with the declared objective of cutting down the fiscal deficit, which, in fact, required either increase in revenue of the governemnt or reduction in its expenditure or both. But, factually speaking, except for 1-2 years, the fiscal deficit went on increasing during all these years, primarily because of the increasing expenditure of the government and lack of political will in taking bold decisions for "downsizing" or more appropriately "rightsizing" the government. Instead of formulating and implementing an optimum strategy for identifying the surplus workforce and its redeployment with an objective of reducing the cost of governance, the government opted for an easy route of cutting down subsidies on education, health, and other social welfare measures as if this was the only "wasteful" expenditure which could be dispensed with without any adverse effects on development! Even people "below poverty line" were not spared and the prices of all items supplied through the 'Public Distribution System' have been increased on the same plea of cutting down "unproductive expenditure" of the government in order to bring down the fiscal deficit. The disinvestment or outright sale of PSUs is also being advocated on the same logic even without giving a serious thought to the plight of the employees and their families working in these units. But, despite all these measures, directly hitting the masses hard, the fiscal deficit is not being reduced.

Ironically, while taking all these decisions affecting adversely the life of common man, no sincere and serious efforts seems to have been made to recover the total tax outstandings amounting to about Rs.60,000 crore on account of income tax, corporate tax, customs and central excise duty. If we add to these outstandings, about Rs.50,000 crore of debt which nationalised banks have to recover from different industrialists and businessmen, this makes a staggering amount of Rs.1,10,000 crore of public money which if recovered, can go a long way in increasing the government revenue and thereby reducing the fiscal deficit considerably. In fact, over a period of time, a bias against poor seems to have creeped into the system—affecting the very terminology itself, i.e., the benefits for the agriculture sector, the farmers/poor persons are being named as "subsidy" whereas the benefits meant for the industry and service sectors/business are known as "incentives". So, implicitly, incentives should continue as they are required for growth and development and subsidies need to be cut down as they are unproductive and wasteful. This intellectual apathy and biasedness seems to have been guiding the process of reforms and the socio-economic development of this country and that is why, common man is getting alienated from this entire process.

As is widely known, these reforms basically aimed at opening up the economy and lessening controls/regulations so that the "industry" could come up in a big way but in reality, the reforms have already started leading to "de-industrialisation" of the traditional industries in India. On the name of "foreign investment", by and large, the foreign companies are just following "merger & acquisition" route to enter Indian market and sell their products here, exploiting to the maximum the known Indian weakness for any "foreign-made" label. Moreover, under the garb of reforms and privatisation, it seems that the government and its officials have abdicated their responsibility of regulating and getting various laws enforced. This widespread "abdication" is evident if we examine the wages which labour contractors are paying to their workers, private transport operators are paying to their drivers/conductors, construction contractors are paying to their engineers/supervisors/workers, factories are paying to their workers or private educational institutions are paying to their employees, teachers/trainers and no official of the government is getting the minimum wages Act enforced. Besides, the reforms have started adversely affecting the masses involved in the agriculture, horticulture and dairy farming because in the West, these products are highly subsidised and hence cost-effective and cheaper to our products. It is a fact that if the present trend is allowed to continue, all these products may be "dumped" in the Indian market with serious consequences for the Indian farmers, horticulturists, dairy owners and other common people involved in these sectors. So, what is the way out?

It is felt that along with controlling and changing the direction of on-giving reforms, we also need to make them more deeper, covering all aspects of social, economic and political life. It is all the more important if we want these reforms to benefit the people and thereby get their support in getting the reforms implemented at a faster pace. The "industry" and "service"-driven reforms cannot influence the socio-economic development in a significant manner and they have also been bringing lop-sided development in the country because other sectors like agriculture, horticulture, etc., still continue to be more critical to the economy. So, reforms are required to be brought in those areas as well in order to ensure that the benefits of development percolate to the common people. Even the methods of governance and administration are required to be examined and corrected to make administration more responsive to the needs of the people. A comprehensive "national policy", covering all aspects of reforms is required to be drafted and implemented after developing national consensus on all facets of reforms. Hard decisions, with national perspective in mind, are required to be taken in the national interests so that the cost of administration is reduced while improving the quality of governance and bringing down the level of fiscal deficit of the government.

Rather than blindly implementing privatisation, we need to learn lessons in "management" from the corporate world and private sector and apply the same techniques of "Total Quality Management" (TQM) in governmental affairs so that the services are provided to the satisfaction of the common people. A serious effort is required to be made to reduce the government expenditure by cutting down the apparatus of governance and the number of employees at different levels. To achieve this objective and send an appropriate message to the masses, the government has to start from the top. No more "States" or "Union Territories" or "Districts" be created. The numbers and sizes of ministries and departments should be reduced and no new ministry/department be created either at the "Union" level or at the level of "States". Professional consultants and management experts should be hired to determine and suggest appropriate re-organisation of the ministries/departments and identify the "surplus staff" in each of them. After identifying the surplus staff, they should be re-trained for new jobs and redeployed accordingly in different ministries or departments. To check the government expenditure, the government should also stop the practice of giving "counter guarantees" to the MNCs and they should be provided a "level playing field" with the local firms/companies. Another important area for reducing the government expenditure is the rationalisation of material procurement for the government offices. It is felt that different types of material should be procured keeping in mind the current needs and the alternative sources of the material. To make any significant contribution and ensure success, this entire policy should be supported and supervised by the top, i.e., the Prime Minister himself at the Union level and the Chief Minister at the state level so that the quality of life of an average citizen is improved.

While attempting rejuvenation of the nation and giving "human face" to the reforms, all the seven S's, i.e., the Structure, Strategy, Systems, Skills, Staff, Style and the Shared Values of the government functioning are required to be critically examined and re-oriented to the national goal of carrying reforms in all facets of national life so that the quality of life of an average citizen is improved and the objective of national integration is achieved in the true sense of the term. The entire focus has to be on building the "shared values" in the government staff—the attempts are required to be made in inculcating the values of equality, fraternity, liberty service, secularism and scientific outlook. The widespread "non-working" culture in the offices has to be replaced with the "work and quality" orientation in all spheres of socio-economic life. Those who think that it may not be possible in our country, have to be reminded that nowhere in the world, such a big effort for "social engineering" aiming at empowering SCs, STs and other weaker sections of society has been made as in India since Independence and considerable success has been achieved in it. There is now almost a national consensus on this policy. This experience proves that if proper policies are formulated and implemented, people get the benefits and such progressive policies get the support of masses as well. But this can be achieved only if there is a clear policy and the leadership is determined in backing it.

It is obvious that any system and its paraphrenelia can survive in the long-run if it serves the interests of the larger percentage of population and if it is perceived as just, equitable and relatively open in terms of opportunities for upward mobility. So, it is in the interest of all of us if spending on "social sector", like education, health, and social welfare is increased in order to continue to assure the common man that his/her interests are well secured in the system. This higher spending on "social sector" is not being recommended for ensuring social justice only but also because it makes economic sense as well as healthier and well-educated and skilled workforce is a prerequisite for development and it can be an added attraction for foreigners to create manufacturing facilities in our country. Therefore, the government should try to improve health care facilities, improve the quality of education, especially the technical/professional education and ensure that it remains within the reach of common people.

Hence, while reducing the cost of governance, we also have to re-orient the government functioning to the needs of the common man. These steps will go a long way in winning back the support of the common people for the reforms and this way, we can continue our march to higher and higher stages of advancement. Otherwise, the "widening gap" between the rich and the poor on account of the reforms coupled with the "communication gap" will not ensure the stability of the reforms or the system itself. The increasing "arrogance" and "apathy" of the rich and "indifference" and "hate" of the poor has to be checked and replaced with the "compassion", "empathy" and a shared vision to build a strong, modern, democratic and secular India with scientific outlook and equitable society. Thus, the pace, direction and areas of reforms have to be controlled and continuously monitored so that they go more deeper and improve the quality of life of an average citizen of the country, while carrying forward the march of nation on subsequent stages of growth and development.

# 33

# New Directions in Administrative Reforms in India

*R.B. Jain*

## Introduction

The problem of administration reforms has received continuing attention in India both at the centre and in the states during the last five decades of its Independence.[1] Indeed since the British period, there has been a time-honoured practice of examining particularly areas of administration and to make recommendations for improvement.[2] Since Independence, there have been a large number of changes in the structure, work methods, and procedures of the administrative organisations. Although these changes have been gradual, at times not too perceptible, they do indicate the efforts made by the government to affect procedural and policy innovation in the administrative system and to keep pace with the changed situation, growing needs and exigencies of the government. In order to understand the impact of such changes, it is appropriate to recount some of the important suggestions made by the various committees, commissions and experts on the subject of administrative reforms.

## The Aftermath of Independence

Beginning with the Tottenham Committee's Report immediately

after the Second World War in 1945,[3] which sharply advocated a proper division between secretarial departments on the one hand and executive directorate and services on the other, with liberal delegation of powers to the heads of departments, the question of secretariat organisation was further debated by the Secretariat Reorganisation Committee, headed by Girija Shanker Bajpai immediately after Independence in 1947. The Committee suggested a reorganisation of the methods of work in the secretariat. In 1948, the Economy Committee headed by a prominent industrialist Katurbhai Lalbhai, made many suggestions for effecting economy in central administration and to tune up general efficiency and mould of the civil service.[4] Shortly thereafter, the first comprehensive review of the central government was undertaken by the committee headed by N. Gopalsawmy Ayyangar in 1949. It dealt with organisational changes, improvement in the calibre of personnel, and in the methods of transaction of governmental business. One of the recommendations that was adopted by the Government was the strengthening of the organisation of the cabinet through the constitution of the standing committees of the cabinet such as the Defence Committee. Economic Committee, Parliamentary and Legal Committee, etc.

## The Appleby Efforts at Reforms

However, none of the above attempts at administrative improvement received as much public attention in 1950s as did the three subsequent reports. Gorwala Committee Report of 1951, and Paul Appleby's two reports on the Indian administration in 1953 and 1956. Gorwala Committee, headed by a former ICS officer, A.D. Gorwala was appointed by the Planning Commission in 1951 to assess the adequacy to meet the requirements of planned development.[5] Gorwala's report on the Planning Commission served as the basis for the formulation of certain crucial administrative proposals which were later included in the First Five Year Plan. In the same year, Gorwala submitted another report relating to the efficient conduct of State Enterprises. Appleby's two reports in 1953 and 1956 made significant impact on the thinking and interest in administrative reforms amongst the government officials, educated elites and the academics, primarily because it was perhaps the first appraisal of the Indian Administrative system by a foreign expert. Although Reports were critical of the administrative machinery, they were complementary of the administrative system as a whole, Appleby's first report dealt more with changes in the basic principles and concepts including the structural changes in the Indian administration rather than with details of administrate machinery[6]—the two main recommendations of Appleby, relating to the setting up of an Institute of Public Administration at the national level and the other, the creation of O and M organisations at different levels of administration, which were implemented immediately, helped the nation towards developing necessary infrastructure for research, teaching and improvement in public administration. In his second report, Appleby made several proposals for streamlining the administration, work procedures, recruitment and training, and relationship of administration with Parliament, the Planning Commission, and the Comptroller and Auditor General of India: Appleby also underlined the need for delegation of powers.[7]

## The Post-Appleby Period: The Administrative Reforms Commission and Administrative Development

In the Post-Appleby period (1953-66) a number of other Committees and Commissions made piecemeal recommendations relating to the qualification for public services, salary structure of public services, district administration, work procedures, corruption and reorganisation of foreign service, but no comprehensive study of the administrative system was attempted before the appointment of the Administrative Reform Commission in 1966.[8] The attempts at reforms until now had been far too narrow in their scope to make any appreciable impact on the administrative system as a whole. Because of the widespread deterioration in administrative efficiency and standards, the idea of setting up an independent commission on the pattern of Hoover Commission in USA gained ground.[9] Accordingly, the Administrative Reforms Commission (ARC) was appointed on 2 January 1966 under the Chairmanship of Morarji Desai (who was later replaced by K Hanumanthaiya).

The objectives laid down to guide the Commission's investigations were (a) "to give consideration to the need for ensuring the highest standards of efficiency and integrity in the public service", (b) to take into account the need "for making public administration a fit instrument for carrying out the social and economic policies of the government and achieving social and economic goals of development" and (c) to make the administration "responsive to the people".[10] The two additional objectives, were implicit in the Commission's terms of reference, viz. the promotion of national integration and the maintenance of efficient standards of administration throughout the country.

The ARC had stressed that in the above recommendations it was guided by certain basic considerations, such as:

> the intensity or magnitude of the administrative deficiency or inadequacy, the requirements of adapting the administrative system or procedure to the demands of developmental functions or tasks, the availability of the proposed reforms in terms of administrative social and political challenges the need for improving efficiency, effecting economy and raising administrative standards, the need for maintaining a balance between administrative innovation and change and administrative stability, the need for improving the responsiveness of the administration to the people, the urgency for reform, and finally the demands of the present and the needs of the future.[11]

Some of the most significant recommendations made by the ARC pertained to the (a) the appointment of Lok Pal (at the centre) and Lokayuktas (in the states) to deal with complaints of corruption and public grievances; (b) constitution of inter-state councils under Article 263 of the Constitution of dealing with centre-state relations; (c) establishment of a central personnel agency at the centre (Department of Personnel and Administrative Reforms) under the cabinet secretariat and independent personnel departments in each ministry, (d) introduction of the concept and technique of performance budgeting; (c) procedural reforms relating to the elimination of delays in sanctioning of pensions to retired officials and payment thereof; (f) constitution of a policy advisory committee, policy cells and policy officers in each department or ministry; (g) establishment of internal standing committee on planning and planning cells in each ministry, constitution of state planning boards, and preparation of project manuals and training programme for project management; (h) the constitution of several corporations for management of the public sector; and (i) constitution of consumer consultative committees. Perhaps the two most important areas touched upon by the ARC in its reports were: (a) minister-civil servants relationships, wherein the ARC emphasised the need for the depoliticisation of the services, and (b) the creation of a climate and culture of administration, that would help arrest the growth of unhealthy personal relationship between civil servants and the minister.

Another important but at the same time the most controversial recommendations, which if implemented would have meant a radical departure from the past traditions and structure of the civil services, was to change the character of the Indian Administrate Service (IAS). The ARC had suggested the regrouping of all the present services in the Government of India into eight functional categories, so that the IAS shall no more be a generalist service, but shall have a purely functional role of revenue administration.[12] This recommendation which could have changed the entire civil service structure from being based on generalist character to a specialist system of service and would have ended the primacy of the erstwhile "steel-frame" had evoked sharp and bitter reaction from amongst the top hierarchy of the civil services,[13] no wonder, the proposal was not only shelved, but perhaps was responsible to some extent in the development of an indifferent and apathetic attitude amongst the top civil services for the implementation of the recommendations of the ARC.

In retrospect, it seems that despite the extensive work done by the ARC extending over a period of four years, it failed to make any real impact on the administrative structure. There was no attempt made to overhaul the original administrative structure. The ARC seemed to have no philosophy of administration and made no attempt to articulate one. Indeed it had no overall core report on public administration as a whole. It did not ask such basic questions as what constitutes good administration and in reference to those norms of good administration, what could be considered to be the major reforms in Indian administration. In not raising these basic issues of administrative reforms, the ARC lost a major opportunity to suggest some fundamental changes in Indian administrative system.[14]

Most of the ARC's recommendations had failed to arouse the authorities to take positive action to implement them. But the fact, as observed by a political commentator was that the Commission never came to tight grips with the day-to-day administrative lacuna, lapses and shortcomings, much less produced a single, coherent report spelling out in precise and concrete terms the steps needed for effecting a complete overhaul—a real breakthrough in civil administration. The eminent individuals who headed the various study teams and their learned colleagues took only an overall view of the issues entrusted to them and dealt with the larger questions of administrative policies and procedures, but lost sight of specific issues affecting the core of administration. As a result, whatever reforms they have recommended and acted upon by the government—have hardly touched the core of administration, which remains as cumbersome out-of-date and red-tape ridden as it was before the Commission was brought into being.[15]

### The Post-ARC Reform Efforts

After the Administration Reforms Commission, there have been no major committees or commission on administrate reforms *per se* except for three isolated attempts: (a) to improve the examination pattern of combined services by introducing a preliminary tests to eliminate a large number of candidates having less potential for success, as a sequel to the Kothari Committee Report;[16] (b) to revitalise the Panchayati Raj System at the grassroot level by converting the three-tier structure into two-tier structure;[17] (c) to change the system of economic and fiscal administration.[18] In 1983, the Government appointed a high powered commission led by Justice Sarkaria to enquire into the entire gamut of Centre-State relations. The Sarkaria Commission regarded federalism as basically a functional arrangement for co-operative action rather than a static institutional concept. It emphasised the need for decentralisation of the planning process. Nevertheless, action on the above recommendations has been very slow because the centre-state relations are still being conducted in the same old hierarchical top-down approach. However, another development in the history of administrative reforms in India has been the appointment of Satish Chandra Committee to review the civil services Examination system. The Committee reported in 1989, and some of its major recommendations have been put in operation effective 1993 competitive examinations for All India and Central Services.[19]

One of the reasons for such a lack of interest had been the domination of administration by politics in the 1970s, and the political leaders being too much preoccupied with buttressing their positions rather than be interested in administrative reforms. There was some toning up of administration in the period during the Emergency (1975-77), but this was more due to draconian measures taken to impose the discipline rather than through any systematic reform of administration. All these improvements were washed away in the backlash after the emergency, and administration actually lapsed into a still greater measure of inefficiency. This only reiterates the danger and futility of undertaking ad hoc measures to tone up administration.

### The Era of Liberalisation

During the 1990s, after adopting policies of economic liberalisation and structural adjustment, a number of expert committees (such as the Raja Chelliah Committee on Tax Reforms, the Rangarajan Committee on Foreign Investment, and the Goswami Committee on Industrial Sickness and Corporate Restructuring) were appointed to study and make recommendations on various policy measures related to economic reforms. Despite these committees' recommendations and the emergence of a somewhat deregulated industrial system, clearance and approval of investment proposals still take time because of powerful inherent roadblocks.

In 1997, the Government of India's Department of Administrative Reforms had organised a national debate on the issues of making administration responsive, accountable and effective and assuring its adherence to constitutional principles. On the basis of responses received from officials, experts, voluntary agencies, citizen's groups, media, etc., and Action Plan was evolved which was discussed in the Conference of Chief Ministers convened by the then Prime Minister on 24 May 1997. Simultaneously, in order to make public agencies more responsive to citizen's needs, a number of citizen's charters have been instituted by a number of central departments/agencies and state governments.

## The Emerging Administrative Style

Mapping the political and administrative history of India over a period of fifty years is indeed a difficult exercise. Obviously, there have been changes in administrative institutions, structures, style and cultures in post-Independent India, and some distinct changes do carry the mark of the political leadership then in power. Thus, administrative development has been an uneven process; and it can best be understood only in the context of the totality of politico-administrative environment.

The first ten years of the Republic represent a period of remarkably smooth change and adaptation from the British Raj to a democratic parliamentary system during which a bold attempt was made by the political leadership to change the character and values of the administrative system, while preserving its essential characteristics of an effective framework to cope with new problems and situations. There were no visible cracks in the system, rather it developed the necessary resilience, and the capacity to both mend, mould, and build itself. The processes of change from this situation were manifest in the next ten years of the growth of the Republic, which is up to the end the period of Lal Bahadur Shastri's term as Prime Minister and the beginning of Indira Gandhi's era (1966). During her time, a new generation of politicians emerged, who were not so much oriented to liberal traditions or values as the first post-independence political leadership. Despite this generational change, and the many stresses and strains that marked the itinerary of the political system, the trend and temper of the administrative procedures and style of the preceding decade were substantially unchanged.

It was, however, after 1967, that one witnessed the beginning of erosion of most of the fundamental values of the administrative system that were consolidated during the earlier years of the Republic. This period marks the beginning of uncertainty and instability in the political system. Whether this happened because of the personal struggle amongst leaders for consolidating and preserving their power-base, or changing economic, local or institutional condition, is a matter for speculation, but the net consequences of this uncertainty was that the policy-making administrative apparatus got disoriented and replaced by some kind of a "shot-gun" approach to administration. The administration and the administrators reached the lowest ebb both in their performance and efficiency at the time of the heightened crisis posed by the imposition of the nation-wide emergency in 1975. The post-Emergency period also did not help to restore the erstwhile standards and morale in the public services.

## Changes in the Administrative System

Basically, there have been a number of visible changes in the administrative system and style since the British times. The "district" as the fundamental unit of administration has undergone a metamorphosis both in terms of the importance and the position and status of its chief executive. The importance of both the district and district officer have been reduced owing to the fragmented expansions of governmental activities on the one hand, and to the growth of "mafia" politics on the other. Much of a district officer's time is now simply wasted in listening, persuading and arguing in the anti-social elements (with whom local political leadership seems to be in companionship), while the regular official work remains unattended. These developments, coupled with enormous responsibilities that are now put on a youngish district officer have eroded whatever autonomy and authority he used to employ with respect to his assigned duties in the past. An ambitious officer now wants to complete his compulsory tenure at district as early and smoothly as he can and looks forward to the day he is posted to a position at the state capital, away from the rough and tumble of the district politics, with the result that district and local administration has suffered heavily at the delivery point and at the cutting edge.

Along with the decline of the district level of administration, there has been a simultaneous decline in the strength and morale of the main public service—the so-called "steel frame" of the British administration. Although the Indian Administrate Service still maintains its dominant position despite the various attempts by the Administrative Reform Commission and the Pay Commissions to water it down, its position and prestige in general has suffered, due to various socio-political factors referred to above. Public and political reactions, values, judgements and even sentiments and prejudices have affected the performance and morale of public bureaucracy in India. There seems to be at present a strong reaction and suspicion against the power of the bureaucracy, and the constant hammering that it has received at the hands of politicians, has earned it the name of a "villain" in the public eyes, who regard it as a big impediment in the attainment of the socio-economic millennium promised to them by politicians. The ethical values of politicians, businessmen and the bureaucrats have gone down so low that there is no aspect of public life today which is free from the incidence of corruption or black money. People in authority seems to have acquired dual personalities; their private actions ill-match their public pronouncements.[21]

Finally, political interference, influence peddling, growing nexus between politicians, criminals and bureaucracy, pervading corruption in all walks of public life, muscle-flexing through the unions have made even the most legitimate means of control and accountability meaningless in the administrative perlance. The emerging administrative style and culture of India does not seem to provide any positive orientation to help the ordinary citizenary.[22]

## The Positive Achievements of Administrative Reforms

The above analyses of changes in the style and culture of administration in India may seem to the pessimistic. However, it is not meant to undermine the achievements and the performance of the administrative system. It has been a fine machine, capable of rendering some excellent performances in the sphere of policy-making and implementation. It has over the years sustained the working of the most politically conscious people. It has been able to maintain its strength, and achieved a strong industrial base for the nation through a system of planned development. There have been an absolute growth in terms of literacy, education, scientific and technical knowledge and even relative prosperity. The bureaucracy in India has responded well in times of crisis and particularly when it was given clearly defined objectives and unambiguous priorities. All these give a ray of hope for further improvement in the style and operations of administrative system in India. But this is only a hope because until now, even taking into consideration the ten years of economic reforms (between 1990 and 2000), one thing which has resisted all suggested administrative reforms is the government's own style of functioning. Prone to overstaffing, slow action, the bureaucracy in India tends to be seen as an agency meant to ameliorate the unemployment situation and therefore, not necessarily designed to produced results or be accountable for its decisions. Oversize administration tends to promote lethargy, inefficiency and corruption. The government administration of post-liberalisation era in India will have to be result-oriented, service-driven and accountable. This is possible, but only if the political leadership changes its style of operation, and cleanse-up its greedy and corrupt way of governing the nation.

## New Directions for Administrative Reforms

Given the political will, therefore, the need of the hour in India at present seems to be to adopt a normative model of *Good Management Approach* towards administrative reforms. This should include (a) A more strategic or result-oriented (efficiency, effectiveness and service quality) orientation to decision-making (b) Replacement of highly centralised organisational structures with decentralised management environment integrating with the new Panchayati Raj and Municipal Institutions, where decisions on resource allocation and service delivery are taken close to the point of delivery, (c) Flexibility to explore alternatives to direct public provision which might provide more cost-effective policy outcomes, (d) Focussing attention on the matching of authority and responsibility as a key to improving performance, including mechanism of explicit performance contracting, (e) Creating of competitive environments within and between public service organisations, (f) Strengthening of strategic capacities at the Centre to steer government to respond to external changes and diverse interests quickly, flexibly and at least costs, (g) Greater accountability and transparency through requirements to report on results and their full costs, (h) Service-wide budgeting and management systems to support and encourage these changes, and (i) The most important task to break the growing nexus of bureaucrats, politicians and criminals leading not only to a breakdown of the total system but also to a sense of cynicism amongst the citizenry, (j) Adapting of innovations and evolving suitable mechanism to eliminate corruption at both political and administrative levels and strengthen citizen's grievance redressal system, (k) Improving the system of delivery at the cutting edge of administration by replacing the existing archaic bureaucratic procedures by absorbing some appropriate precepts inherent in the philosophy of New Public Management, and (l) Making improvements in the working atmosphere of the government institutions and offices to reflect a new work culture and a changed administrative behaviour incorporating the principles of transparency, responsiveness, accountability, participative and citizen-friendly management.

## Concluding Observations

In conclusion, however, it should be remembered that no amount of planning and thinking in all these areas would be useful unless the government is capable enough to take hard and unpleasant decisions and has the will and capacity to implement and continuously monitor and evaluate their impact. At the same time, the political leadership has to demonstrate its strong determination to undertake reforms by first cleaning its own stable from corrupt and criminal influences, and setting ethical standards of good governance both at political and administrative levels. Given the present political milieu, can the present government rise to the occasion—is a big question?

## REFERENCES

1. This section of the Paper is based on O.P. Dwivedi and R.P. Jain, "The Administrative State of India" in Yogendra Malik (ed.), *India After 50 Years of Independence,* 1998.
2. See for Details, B.B. Mishra, *Government and Bureaucracy in India,* Delhi, Oxford University Press, 1986.
3. See, R. Tottenham, *Reports on the Reorganisation of the Central Government, 1945-46,* New Delhi, Government of India, 1946.
4. This Report was discussed during the Constituent Assembly Debates, See Indian Constituent Assembly Debates, New Delhi, Government of India, 1949.
5. Paul H. Appleby, Public Administration in India, Report of a Survey, New Delhi, Government of India, 1953.
6. Paul H. Appleby, Reorganisation of India's Administrative System with Special Reference to Administration of Government's Industrial and Commercial Enterprises, New Delhi, Government of India, 1956.
7. For Further Reference, see the following reports: India, Report on the Public Service (Qualification for Recruitment) Committee, New Delhi, Ministry of Education [Mudaliar Committee], 1956; India, Commission of Inquiry on Enrolments and Conditions of Service of Central Government Employees, 1957-59; India, Report on Indian New Delhi State Administrative Services and Problems of District Administration, New Delhi: Government of India, [Krishnamachari Report], 1962, India, Report of the Committee on Prevention of Corruption, New Delhi: Ministry of Home Affairs, [Sanathanam Committee] 1964; and India Report of the Committee on The India Foreign Service, New Delhi; Ministry of External Affairs [Pillai Committee Report], 1966.
8. R.B. Jain, *Contemporary Issues in Indian Administration,* New Delhi; Vital Publications, 1976, pp. 398-434.
9. India, Ministry of Home Affairs, Department of Administrative Reforms, Resolution No. 40, 165-AR (P), 5 January 1966.
10. India, the Administrative Reforms Commission and Its Work: A Brief Survey, New Delhi; Administrative Reform Commission, p. 8.
11. India, Report on Personnel Administration, New Delhi: Administrative Reforms Commission, 1969, p. 24.
12. B. Sivaraman, "Generalist and Specialist in Administration" *Indian Journal of Public Administration,* vol. 17, July-September 1971, 9, 384.
13. P.R. Dubhashi, "Administrative Reforms in Perspective", Dr John

Mathai Endowment Lecture, published by the University of Kerala, Trivendrum, 1985.

14. P.S. Narayanan, "ARC Goes: Core in Administration Remains Untouched", *Northern India Patrika,* Allahabad, 1970.
15. D.S. Kothari, Report of the Committee on Recruitment Policy and Selection Methods, New Delhi, Union Public Service Commission, 1976.
16. Ashoka Mehta Committee Report on Panchayati Raj, New Delhi, Government of India, 1979.
17. L.K. Jha Committee Report on Economic Administration, New Delhi, Government of India.
18. S.R. Maheshwari, *Administrative Reforms in India,* New Delhi: Jawahar Publishers, 1993, p. 148.
19. See, Government of India, Ministry of Personnel, Public Grievances and Pensions, Annual Report, 1997-98, New Delhi, 1998, pp. i-vii.
20. O.P. Dwivedi and R.B. Jain, *India's Administrative State,* New Delhi, Gitanjali Publishing House, 1985, pp. 122-23.
21. O.P. Dwivedi and R.B. Jain, "Bureaucratic Morality in India", *International Political Science Review,* vol. 9, no. 3, 1988, pp. 205-14.
22. 25 February 2000/Reviewed and sent for HPU Shimla Seminar 1.4.01.

# 34

# Administrative Reforms in India: Problems and Solutions

*S.S. Tiwana*

The problem of administrative reforms has received continuing attention in India both at the national and state levels during the last five decades of its Independence. Indeed since the British period, there has been a time-honoured practice of examining particularly areas of administration and to make recommendations for its improvement. There have been a large number of changes in the structure, work methods, and procedures of the administrative organisations after Independence. Although these changes have been gradual, at times not too perceptible, they do indicate the efforts made by the Government to affect procedural and policy innovations in the administrative system and to keep pace with the changed situation, growing needs and exigencies of the government.

The first ten years of the Republic represented a period of remarkably smooth change and adaptation from the British Raj to a democratic parliamentary system, during which a bold attempt was made by the political leadership to change the character and values of the administrative system, while preserving its essential characteristics of an effective framework to cope with new problems and situations. There were no visible cracks in the system, rather it developed the necessary resilience, and the capacity to both mend, mould, and build itself. The processes of change from this situation were manifest in the next ten years of the growth of the Republic, that is up to the end of the period of Lal Bahadur Shastri's term as Prime Minister and the beginning of Indira Gandhi's era (1966). During her time, a new generation of politicians emerged, who were not so much oriented to liberal traditions or values as the first post-Independence political leadership.

It was, however, after 1967, that one witnessed the beginning of erosion of most of the fundamental values of the administrative system that were consolidated during the earlier years of the Republic. This period marks the beginning of uncertainty and instability in the political system. The net consequences of this uncertainty was that the policy-making administrative apparatus got disoriented and replaced by some kind of a "shot-gun" approach to administration. The administration reached the lowest ebb both in its performance and efficiency at the time of the heightened crisis posed by the imposition of the nation-wide emergency in 1975. The post-emergency period also did not help to restore the erstwhile standards and morale in the public services.

## Changing Scenario of Administrative System in India

Basically, there have been a number of visible changes in the administrative system and style since the British times. The "district" as the fundamental unit of administration has undergone a metamorphosis both in terms of the importance and the position of its chief executive. The importance of both the district and district officer has been reduced owing to the fragmented expansions of governmental activities on the one hand, and the growth of "mafia" politics on the other. These developments, coupled with enormous responsibilities that are now put on a youngish district officer, have eroded whatever autonomy and authority he used to employ with respect to his assigned duties in the past.

Along with decline of the district level administration, there has been a simultaneous decline in the strength and morale of the main public service—the so-called "steel frame" of the British administration. The Indian Administration Service still continues to maintain its dominant position, but its position and prestige in general has suffered due to the degradation of moral values.

The performance and morale of public bureaucracy has been effected due to unhindered interference of the politicians in the day-to-day activities of the administration. The ethical values of the politicians, businessmen and the bureaucrats have gone down so low that there is no aspect of public life today which is free from the incidence of corruption and black money. People in authority seems to have acquired dual personality; their private actions ill-matched their public pronouncements.

Finally, political interference, influence peddling, growing nexus between politicians, criminals and bureaucracy, pervading corruption in all walks of public life, muscle-flexing through the unions have made even the most legitimate means of control and accountability in administration meaningless. The emerging administrative style and culture in the country does not seem to provide any positive orientation to help the ordinary citizenary.

## Achievements and Performance of Administrative System

One may have a pessimistic view of changes in the style and culture of administration in India, but still one has to acknowledge the achievements and the performance of the administrative system. The administration has worked quite satisfactorily in the sphere of policy-making and implementation. It has enabled the nation to achieve a strong industrial base for the nation through a system of planned development. There have been significant growth in terms of literacy, education, scientific and technical knowledge and even relative prosperity. The bureaucracy in India has responded well in times of crisis particularly when it was given clearly defined objectives and unambiguous priorities. All these give a ray of hope for further improvement in the style and operations of administrative system in India. But this is only a hope because until now, even taking into consideration the ten years of economic reforms (between 1990 and 2000), one thing which has resisted all suggested administrative reforms is the government's own style of functioning. Prone to overstaffing, slow action, the bureaucracy in India tends to be seen as an agency meant to ameliorate the unemployment situation and therefore, not necessary designed to produced results or be accountable for its decisions. Oversize administration tends to promote lethargy, inefficiency and corruption. The government administration of post-liberalisation era in India will have to be result-oriented, service-driven and accountable. This is possible, but only if the political leadership changes its style of functioning, and gives up its greedy and corrupt way of governing the nation.

## New Directions for Administrative Reforms

The Department of Administration Reforms and Public Grievances organised a Conference of Chief Secretaries of States and Union Territories on 20 November, 1996 to discuss the issue of making administration responsive, accountable and effective, cleansing the civil services and ensuring its adherence to constitutional principles. The Conference of the Chief Ministers convened by the Prime Minister in May 1997 endorsed the Action Plan focused on:

(i) accountability and citizen-friendly administration;
(ii) transparency and Right to Information; and
(iii) improving performance and integrity of civil services.

"Effective and Responsive Administration" package arising from the May 1997 Conference of Chief Ministers held at New Delhi—might be thought to represent the managerial route to redefine power equations between the Government and the citizens. This is actually, a comprehensive reform package designed to streamline delivery systems, foster transparency and openness in public transactions, allow citizens an easy unhasseled access to public services, improve the quality of citizen—administration interface, and ultimately realign the provider—receipt power equations to the citizen's advantage so as to augment the prospects of an accountable and responsive governance.

## Follow Up Action

**(a) *Transparency and Openness***

The "Right to Information" legislations form the important feature of reform under this category. Some of the states like

Tamilnadu and Goa have already enacted a legislation for Right to Information. At the national level, the Right to Information Bill is under the consideration of the Committee of the Parliament. Apart from improved efforts for strengthening the grievance redressal machinery at all levels, computerised monitoring of replies and designation of nodal officers, there is a growing effort for taking administration to the people. It is quite common for the District Collectors and all district officials in a number of states to visit the villages and blocks on pre-announced dates and deal with all the grievances on the spot or ensure redressal before the next visit. It is realised that the availability of independent machinery such as Lokayukta for grievance redressal will need to be supplemented by an efficient and prompt internal system for prompt attention to problems faced by the people and the promotion of information required by them.

**(b) *Greater Responsiveness to the People***

This category comprises:

(i) introduction of citizen's charters;
(ii) measures to strengthen and streamline procedures for redressal of public grievances; and
(iii) steps directed at reviewing the existing legislations, rules and procedures; the exercise is essentially aimed at establishing or rationalising frameworks for responsive governance.

**(c) *Changes in the Regulatory Framework***

Most of the central ministeries and departments have taken up a major exercise for the review of laws and regulations operated by them and improvements have already been effected in the existing system in consistent with the requirements of liberalisation, Information and Facilitation Counters (IFCs) in various ministries have also been set-up. The IFCs provide information to the users regarding the scope of activities of concerned organisation, the schemes it operates, stipulated procedure to be followed, the status of petitions/complaints and so on. All IFCs are computerised; and these are located outside the security zone to obviate the need, on the part of visitors to obtain an entrypass.

**(d) *Civil Service Reforms***

Reforms in this category include·

(i) measures to curb corruption;
(ii) evolving a civil service code of ethics;
(iii) contracting out public service; and
(iv) steps towards simplification of procedures.

Arising from the above efforts, by December 2000, 65 Union Ministries had formulated their Citizen's Charters and 19 States and Union Territories had formulated a total of 310 Charters covering select (State/UT-level) departments and agencies. Apart from it, by this time, 65 Information and Facilitation Counters (IFCs) had become functional at the union level. The Union Government's Department of Administrative Reforms and Public Grievances constitutes the nodal agency for the reforms outlined above.

In 1997, while the Department of Administrative Reforms and Public Grievances announced these initiatives under the "Effective and Responsive Administration", the Fifth Central Pay Commission, in volume I of its three volume report, emerged with some radical proposals. There *inter alia* include recommendations for downsizing of bureaucracy, delayering, contractual appointments in civil service, incentive pays, multi-skilling of Group-D staff, constitution of civil service boards and a renewed emphasis on performance appraisal. There are recommendations of far-reaching consequences on which the Union Government has, however, yet to take a view.

**(e) *Normative Model of Good Management Approach***

Given the political will, therefore, the need of the hour at present seems to be to adopt a normative model of good management approach towards administrative reforms in India. This should include

(i) a more strategic or result-oriented (efficiency, effectiveness and service quality) orientation to decision-making,
(ii) replacement of highly centralised organisational structures

with decentralised management environment integrating with the new panchayati raj and municipal institutions, where decisions on resource allocation and service delivery are taken close to the point of delivery;

(iii) creating of competitive environment within and between public service organisations;

(iv) strengthening of strategic capacities at the centre to steer government to respond to external changes and diverse interests quickly, flexibly and at minimum costs;

(v) breaking the growing nexus among bureaucrats, politicians and criminals leading not only to a breakdown of the total system but also to a sense of cynicism amongst the citizenry;

(vi) evolving innovative and effective mechanism to eliminate corruption both at the political and administrative levels and strengthen citizens' grievance redressal system;

(vii) improving the system of delivery at the cutting edge of administration by replacing the existing archaic bureaucratic procedures by absorbing some appropriate precepts inherent in the philosophy of New Public Management; and

(viii) making improvements in the working atmosphere of the government institutions and offices to reflect a new work culture and a changed administrative behaviour incorporating the principles of transparency, responsiveness, accountability, participative and citizen-friendly management.

To conclude, the debate on administrative reforms in India has been a continuous process starting from the comprehensive Report of Administrative Reform Commission. The suggestions made in the Report of the Fifth Central Pay Commission on a variety of issues relating the public service management also indicate the directions in which the reforms should proceed. But in a vast country like India, consisting of states with varied administrative practices and local conditions, it is difficult to be prescriptive about the extent of reform. However, there is a considerable agreement on the thrust areas in reform and the immediate priorities especially the need to make administration more people-centred, open, decentralised, flexible and free from corruption. However, it should be remembered that no amount of planning and thinking in all these areas would be useful unless the government is capable enough to take hard and unpleasant decisions and has the will and capacity to implement and continuously monitor and evaluate their impact. At the same time, the political leadership has to demonstrate its strong determination to undertake reforms by first cleaning themselves from corrupt and criminal influences and setting ethical standards of good governance both at the political and administrative levels.

# 35

# New Economic Policy and Administrative Reforms in India

*Pradeep Saxena*

## Introduction

The new global economic system has become a big problem to the developing economies. Such economies are passing through a period of dilemmas, contradictions and social challenges. The reasons may be attributed to the pressures exercised by the developed economies through WTO, structural adjustments, competitive markets, regionalisation of economies and domestic realities. The new global economic system has emerged as a problem rather than solution to the developing economies. It has generated more poverty than affluence, social disorders, heavy unemployment, and administrative corruption. Developing economies more specifically big and overpopulated countries like India have become the victims and loosing their properties, culture, heritage, export, social identity, etc. On the other hand, the new global economic system has become a method of exploitation, earning, market, political interference, etc. In sum, developing economies are loosing everything while developed countries are getting everything. In the Asia-Pacific region, most of the developing countries are under heavy debt of the IMF and the World Bank. In such state of affairs, India is struggling to save its own socio-economic system, in order to find a suitable strategy in the reign of dilemmas, contradictions and challenges.

Since India is a poverty-ridden, overpopulated and a big country in the South-Asian region, the administrative system is solely responsible to find out a solution of the problems generated by the new economic system. Several economists,[1] many international conferences, have outlined the role of the state in development more specifically in the global economic system. Most of the economists have advocated the role of the state as "information-cum-service delivery state", "level playing" and "regulatory mechanic". These advocacies were designed in the specific context of the technologically advanced and industrialised countries. For the developing countries privatisation and liberalisation of the welfare services sector was advocated. Several top economists of the developing countries have attracted the attention of the developed countries and the international donor agencies over the problems of the developing countries in the adoption of market economy as well as clearing the ground for privatisation and liberalisation. They argued that history cannot be settled down into any single mold. Therefore, the developed countries' emphasis upon market economy and privatisation of state liabilities will not be as much effective as in their own countries. Developing countries have to evolve their own strategies of development. For example, finance and structural adjustment programmes are difficult to balance in a developing society like India. Administrative reforms, a part of structural adjustments, are required to be seen in the light of the burden being carried out by the developing countries as the welfare state. After the debackle of some of the East-Asian economies in the late 1997 is to justify the plea of the developing countries.[3] Further, the cost of administrative reforms will also be a major factor in the politico-economic crises. Beside this, the later-effects of administrative reforms are also to be managed in a very careful way as these effects may cause the national integrity and the culture. Administrative reforms are also required to be supported by the domestic economic environment and the culture besides the public support and institutions. Some of studies[4] on the collapse of East-Asian economies in 1997 have pointed out that the administrative reforms in these countries (Indonesia, Malaysia, Thailand) were not carried out efficiently and therefore have not yielded efficiency to satisfy the peoples' expectations after the adoption of new economic system. It is also argued that the administrative reforms were focused in the economic sector and other sectors were not touchd in order to support the economic administrative reforms. Consequently, such reforms could not get success and were made ineffective in the whole administrative system. Last but not least, administrative reforms must be supported by political stability and democratic ways of operation. In developing countries, political consensus on administrative reforms, political stability and matured outlook on the democratic ways of operation have yet not emerged due to political compulsions, party agendas, and coalition governments. The question of political stability is a very complex problem of India, it can be pointed out that the introduction of new economic policy in 1991 has brought political instability in itself as the previous governments have not been able to convince the masses about the market economy. Strong political and mass movements against the market economy have brought in its wake political instability after 1996 and India has undergone twice for general elections between 1996 to 1998 but political instability is continuing in the political sphere. In a country where 45 per cent population is below poverty line, the introduction of market economy needs a careful implementation at the administrative level. Administrative support to the new economic policy is still a far dream of the market directed administrative reforms. Widespread strikes in central and state governments, public sector enterprises mainly in banking and financial sector have again cautioned the governments to be very careful in implementing the GATT/WTO agreements in the administrative system like disinvestments in public sector, opening of insurance and media sector to foreign investors, merger of banks, etc. The administrative reforms being carried out in India were aimed to redesign the administrative system consistently in order to achieve the aims of the market economy. The "rational choice" approach to the political economy of public institutions is governed by the "rent seeking" forces. And there was a major thrust in the administrative reforms that what would/should be the role of the administrative institutions in the "rent-allocation" process in a market economy. However the political instability in India has not provided much choices to the political leaders to make a balance between the rentier and their interests and also the competing interests of the masses, consumers, producers and the capitalists. Most of the administrative reforms in India, therefore, have been directed by the political implications than the administrative efficiency, service or market choices. For example, trade in services policy was outrightly rejected by the Indian voters in 1998 general elections.[5] The role of government as "rent-allocator" was also discarded by the domestic industrial sector as the economic depression in the Indian markets could not be ended even after the introduction of independent regulatory mechanisms and reforming the administrative institutions. For example, Indian primary and secondary capital market was depressed after 1994 till today and the establishment of Securities Exchange Board of India (SEBI) and the changes brought in banking and non-banking financial institutions failed to generate the market.[6] Administrative reforms were also introduced to generate more professionalism in the government services but the non-material determinants of reforms like caste, religion, regionalism, language, etc., have been more influential than professional commitments and administrative efficiency and effectiveness have remained the far-reaching dreams. For example, reservation policy for scheduled castes and tribes, backward classes have created obstacles in the way of professionalism, as it is not based purely on merit but on the reservation of positions for such castes/classes. Merit is the backbone of Professionalism in any services. Reservation for such castes and classes in government services is around 47 per cent. Since the issue of reservation is related to votes in general elections and hence political power is committed and sustained by the votes of such castes and classes, no political party is seemed to go for its abolition. Another reservation problem is to emerge from the reservation for women (minimum 20 and maximum 33 per cent) in government jobs. Such kind of policies are to question the implications of administrative reforms for the global competition. In developing countries like India, the question of administrative reforms is concerned with the accountability of the government and its administration to a poverty ridden society. In such societies, the general tendency is to use the public office for private means which negates the spirit of administrative reforms. Corruption is a worldwide phenomenon and does exist in all societies, however, the level of efficiency in providing world class services in a competitive world is to become a parameter as well as an attraction when the developing countries aspire to collaborate with the MNCs or the administration of the developed countries more particularly in the foreign direct investments in the infrastructure sector.[7] Delays in decision-making, lengthy procedures, over-controlled mechanism and poor management of development plans are to raise the questions pertaining to accountability of public servants. The experiences of the East-Asian economies and their crisis tell us—that more collaboration with MNCs and dependency on FDI is not good in long-run to the developing countries like India. To avoid such situations, administrative reforms must be aimed to gear up for accountability so that such situations will not come to India. Beside the financial crisis situations, administrative accountability is also related with the social cost as the consequences of liberalisation on social modernisation and social destruction as well as cultural decay pose the problem of accountability. Public services are required to be accountable to the social cost emerging from the social change. Therefore, administrative reforms must be carried out in the context of the social cost also.

New economic system in developing countries is to be understood in terms of administrative modernisation. Technology is a key variable of it. In these countries, the conflict between the use of technology and the availability of huge manpower is a major issue of administrative reforms. For example, Computerisation of office-work, procedures and records is severely opposed by employees organisations/unions in view of the emerging unemployment market. Since India is passing through a period of economic depression, unemployment will become a major problem of the country as the technology is replacing the man. Another related problem is of deliberate avoidence of technology by the government employees in their respective organisations as it prevents them to adopt corrupt practices. Involvement of employees in the maximum use of technology is a problem of administrative modernisation.

In a centrally planned economy, administrative decentralisation and deconcentration is a vital issue of administrative reforms. In the adoption of liberalisation and privatisation of service sector, decentralisation is considered a highly risky method of reforms. Decentralisation in developing economies is generally considered a synonym of corruption, inefficiency and discretion. Therefore, decentralisation is avoided and done with great care and cautions. For example, state governments have not been authorised to clear foreign direct investments proposals. After a long time, state governments were authorised to clear such proposals in power (electricity) sector only at their own level but such clearances will be subjected to the final clearance of the central government and the State Electricity Board Regulatory Authority. In such situations, administrative decentralisation is to become a crucial issue. Deconcentration of administrative structures in metro and big cities of the country is a point of administrative reforms in order to provide services to the masses as well as to make realistic planning and strategy of development. A very thoughtful exercise is needed to deconcentrate administrative structures as these are practical and human problems involving several complex situations in the deconcentration processes.

The issue of cutting down the size of staff in the government services is a very sensitive problem and it has its own several dimensions. However, the arguments of developed countries and donor agencies are difficult to accept both at the government and the staff level. At the government level, down sizing the administration is against the idea of welfare state in a highly poverty ridden country and government will not be able to carry out its social development programmes. The new ways of carrying out such programmes like involvement of non-governmental organisations (NGOs), voluntary organisations and the private sector have not been very effective in the Indian conditions and the cultural setting of the country.[8] The question of human rights and trust of Indian poor masses are the crucial issues which need to be understood in the context of downsizing the staff strength in government. On the staff side, it is not acceptable as it will affect the morale and motivation of government employees.

Another very significant issue of administrative reforms is

concerned with the legal structure of the country. In an era of privatisation, macro regulation by an independent institution more particularly in the situation of conflict between government and the private sector is considered as maintaining balance of economic aggregates, promoting optimum economic structures and ushering in a new and modern economic systems. Such macro-regulation is also trusted both by the private and foreign investors. However the exclusive powers of the general courts to intervene and direct such independent regulatory authorities as well as jurisdiction of general courts over these authorities has now become a problem in administrative reforms. Such independent authorities, face difficulties in the delivery of services to the customers in a competitive market. The concepts of "Welfare state" and "Model employer" imposed by general courts on the entrepreneurial government in market economy has generated a debate over the legal structural reforms in India. It is being argued that the jurisdiction of general courts in a competitive economic era be restricted and more autonomy and independence be provided to such independent regulatory authorities.

In developing countries like India, introduction of market economy and restructuring the administration to suit the needs of the economic system has started debate over the conventional or the monocratic role of administration as characterised by instrumentality, unity and rationality to a "transfigured administration" through "market type mechanism". In a vast, overpopulated, poverty-ridden and culturally diversified country, the new role of public administration has become a issue of debate, analysis and criticism. Political instability, economic depression and dominance of MNCs or foreign investors has put more burden on the shoulders of public administration in India. In such situation, a very careful and cautious strategy of administrative reforms is needed in India. The experiences of South and East Asian economies have also made government to become extra careful in devising a proper and more suitable strategy of administrative reforms in the country.

Since the beginning of new economic system in 1991 till 30 April 1998, the basic strategy of administrative reforms has been to continue the old British administrative services and structures in the regulatory system of administration, evolution of policy framework in government activities, decentralisation of developmental decision-centres and activities, creation of trade organisations in service and business sector, privatisation of non-essential and consumer services, participation of private sector in commercial and business administration, establishment of independent authorities to regulate commercial and business contracts and agreements in government services, abolition of inspectors system, minimising discretionary powers of authorities, abolition of bureaucratic obstacles and bottlenecks, more transparency in government decisions, activities and contracts, grant of right to information, simplification of laws, rules and regulations, procedures, deconcentration of administrative structures, downsizing the staff, involvement of technology in office management more specifically computerisation of procedures, records and correspondence, and minimising the chances of corruption in administration, avoiding legal battles, abolition of unnecessary administrative organisations, tax and tariff reforms and redesigning the economic organisations and institutions, etc. In this reform strategy, major emphasis was laid down on policy designs and framework. However, policy reforms are not on priority. Policy choices and alternatives were not evolved. Policy-making centres are confined to administrative officials. Peoples participation and specialised and professional organisations are being still ignored or not prioritised. Imbalance between the regulatory and developmental role of administration is also an area of policy evaluation in the study of new economic policy and administrative reforms. In these reforms, internationally competitive government organisations to protect the interest and property rights of the country were not seriously considered in designing the administrative reforms for the implications of GATT/WTO and human rights declarations and conventions. Consequently, India is facing losses of billions of dollars at the international level. Publicity of reforms at the international level was also ignored. Training was not properly catered to bring attitudinal and orientational changes in the administrative system. However, the administrative reforms process is still going on and a significant change in the Indian administrative system can be seen.

## Major Administrative Reforms

### *Administrative Reforms* (1991-98)

In 1991, India's adoption of new economic policy was not implemented speedily as the Narasimha Rao's government was not equipped with full majority in the Parliament. Due to minority government till 1996, administrative reforms were carried out with the consent of the opposition parties and the administrative officials and staff. After the general elections in 1996 & 1998, coalition governments headed by three successive Prime Ministers, i.e., Mr. Devegowda, Mr. I.K. Gujral (1996-98) and Mr. A.B. Bajpai (from 19 March to till today) were also not prompt and active in bringing drastic changes in administration. The major focus of minority and coalition governments was to evolve a general policy framework and simplification of administrative process and to provide some policy as well as administrative facilities to the private and foreign investors. However a brief review of administrative reforms is given below in order to have a basic understanding of correlation between the new economic policy and the administrative apparatus.

1. *The Policy Framework in Major Areas of Administration*

In the last 7 years (1991-98), the major thrust of governments was to evolve policy framework in the major areas affecting the total economy of the country. Several policies were announced during this period like Industrial Policy, Export-Import Policy, Agriculture Policy, Banking Policy. Tourism Policy, Health Policy, Foreign Direct Investment Policy, Power Sector Policy, Water Policy, Environment Policy, Motor Vehicle Policy, Railway Gauge Conversion Policy, Media Policy, Insurance Policy, Rural Development Policy, Air Transport Policy, Surface Transport Policy, Sales Tax Policy, Income Tax Policy, etc. In evolving the policy framework, the major emphasis was put on the development of infrastructure sector with the collaboration of private and foreign investors in order to generate more employment and to reduce the number of below poverty line people. Joint vantures were promoted in core and consumer items and the investors were motivated to initiate in the market economy. These policy frameworks have provided a set of directives to the administrative officials to act on the thrust of such policies. Necessary amendments/modifications are made in several laws, rules and regulations to abolish bureaucratic discretion, obstacles, delays, redtapism, problems, etc. Further, policy reforms were also introduced to provide a suitable environment for development.

2. *Establishment of New Administrative Organisations*

To implement several policies, a major reshuffle was carried out in the Union Government ministries/departments as well as some new organisations were also created. However, the Ministry of Finance, Home Affairs, Commerce, Education, Personnel, Pension, and Administrative Reforms, Civil Aviation, Transport, Environment, etc., were redesigned to suit the needs of the new economic system. Some of the administrative positions were either abolished, redesigned or renamed to cutdown the size of ministries and bring efficiency and effectiveness in the administrative operations and activities. Agency system was also introduced in the ministries of Agriculture, Tourism, Civil Aviation, Media (Television & Radio), Telecommunication, etc., to reach at the downtrodden areas and people of the country. Agency system was a partially successful experiment to deliver services/goods in rural areas and to the poor people. It (Agency) has also generated employment in non-governmental sector to deliver government services, and reduced the burden on government both in terms of money and staff. Some of the ministries have also been reoriented for privatisation and foreign collaboration or joint ventures like Civil Aviation, Telecommunication, Broadcasting, Power (electricity), etc. In some of the ministries, new administrative organisations and institutions were created:

1. Ministry of Finance
   (a) Securities Exchange Board of India (SEBI)
   (b) Banking LokPal (Ombudsman) of India
   (c) Export Processing Zones Council
   (d) Foreign Direct Investment Board

2. Ministry of Home Affairs
   (a) Special separate Department for Jammu & Kashmir State for Development purposes and Tourism,
   (b) Special cell for scheduled castes/tribes and women and children,
   (c) Special force for communal riots, conflicts and problem areas,
   (d) Special cell for identifying infiltrators in Assam State and to control insurgency in north-east states.
3. Ministry of Commerce & Industry
   (a) Over the Counter Agreements
   (b) Single Window Lincence System for Export
   (c) Export-Incentives System
   (d) Patents Review Board
   (e) Intellectual Property Rights Protection Board
   (f) Monopolies Restricted Trade Practices Commission (MRTPC)
   (g) Trade & Tariff Review Council
4. Ministry of Power
   (a) Central Electricity Authority (for Technical Aspects)
   (b) Central Electricity Regulatgory Commission (27 April 1998 for tariff purposes)
   (c) State Electricity Regulatory Commissions
   (d) High-Power Committee to clear Power Sector Projects in Private Sector.
5. Dept./Ministry of Telecommunication
   (a) Telecommunication Regulation Authority of India
   (b) Telecommunication Commission of India
6. Ministry of Information and Broadcasting
   (a) Prasar Bharti Act for more autonomy and independence in radio and television programmes.
   (b) Cable Operators Promotion System.
7. Ministry of Personnel, Pension and Public Grievances
   (a) Fifth Pay Commission for central government employees (report submitted in 1997 and implemented in March 1998)
   (b) Training of All India Services—divided among five, training institutes in the country:
   (c) New schemes for pension to central government employees were introduced.

(d) LokPal (Ombudsman) Bill to be introduced in the Parliament in June 1998 to redress public grievances against public servants;
(c) Right to Seek Information of Government Decisions which do not fall in the Official Secret Act:

Beside the some of above-mentioned administrative reforms in the major ministries of the central government (which were directly concerned with the new Economic Policy), some initiatives were also taken to improve the economic conditions in the different sectors and some independent institutions were created:

(a) Human Rights Commission
(b) Women's Development Commission
(c) Children Labour Exploitation Protection Board
(d) Minimum Wages for Agricultural Labour Commission
(e) Pay Committee for University and College Teachers in India
(f) Narsimhan Committee to reorganise the banking industry

In setting up these institutions, the major thrust of the government was to deregulate and decentralise the administrative system, we would discuss the major issues of it.

***Deregulation***

In the new economic system of the country, government has tried to deregulate some of the core and consumer areas where government regulation was creating obstacles in the development of industry like reregulation of cement, non-petroleum products, sugar, steel, milk-products, liquor, gold-silver, electronics, computer softwares, telecommunication equipments, paper, edible oils, soaps, cosmetic prices. Government is also considering to deregulate those areas where problems are more acute like urban land, co-operative, housing, drinking water resources, leather and shoe industry, medical and health care services, textile industry, refrigeration industry, etc. Government is also inclined to deregulate those areas where healthy competition can bring efficiency and foster development like bank interest rates, non-banking companies, environment-friendly companies, higher educational institutions more particularly foreign universities, foreign exchange, full convertibility of Indian rupee in current account, media-foreign newspapers publication in India, insurance (20 per cent deregulation proposed) sector, etc.

Although government is prepared to deregulate more sectors of economy in order to abolish licencing system, pricing, storage limits, transportation. There are three major problems to deregulate rapidly: (a) poor masses and unawared consumer; (b) lack of technology in marketing; and (c) large size of staff. Keeping these problems in mind, the government is deregulating the sectors on priority basis.

### *Decentralisation*

In a centrally planned economy, decentralisation is a big problem both politically and administratively. A major step was initiated in 1993-94 to create a third tier of Indian federation by constitutional amendments (73 & 74) in the urban and rural local governments.[10] These amendments have brought drastic changes in the Indian urban and rural local governments as these governments were empowered with constitutional rights, duties, resources, finances and representation. Political level of these governments was made more accountable, responsible, autonomous, and powerful than administrative level. Personnel of all-India services were brought under the control of the local government. District councils (Zila Parishads) and block councils (Panchayat Samities) were entrusted the task of planning and development. As such, decentralised planning was enlarged at the local level. Participatory democracy and governance system was evolved. In the new economic system, local authorities were encouraged to develop the region/area by industrialising or by marketing system. For the division of powers and resources, between the state and the local governments, state finance commissions were set up and separate financing institutions like banks were evolved to strengthen the local governments. Village Panchayats were also allowed to take up new measures to protect the small and medium farmers from the repercussions of the new market economy by providing incentives, subsidies and different assistance. On the whole, decentralisation of the governance structure has equipped the local governments to meet the challenges of the new market economy. New, the elected and administrative officials should try to extract the benefits of the new economic system of the country.

### *Ensuring the Use of Modern Technology*

One hundred fifty years old British patterned administrative system is being restructured, equipped and reoriented towards the new challenges of the economy.[11] The government has provided special funds for its modernisation through the use of modern technology like computers and various means of information technology. Office procedures, data-storing, records and preservation of several documents are being computerised. Communication technologies are being provided even at the village-level official machinery in order to link up the whole administration in a national network. More emphasis is laid on remote and hilly town to link up them with the district and state administration. Police and other security network is also being equipped with the latest technology of information, transportation and communication to meet the challenges of new economic system, ministries/departments were allowed to use the modern technology from the private sector or to privatise such services in their respective organisations. Although, the task of using modern technology needs huge funds, resources and satellite capabilities of the country but it may be hoped that the task will be completed in the Ninth Five-Year Plan (1998-2002).

### *Reform of Public Undertakings*

The constitutional guarantee of bringing "Socialism" and "welfare state" was ensured by a big set-up of public undertakings during the last 40 years. But in the announcements of new economic policy in 1991, 1996 public undertakings were considered as a burden on tax-payers as most of the public undertakings were incurring heavy losses and not helpful in competing the global economy. To redesign and restructure them in the new set up. Some of the public undertakings were partly sold through shares/debentures. A disinvestment commission was set up to review the government policy of investments in these undertakings. The commission's suggestions are being studied by the central government. However, investment in loss-making undertakings will be discouraged and investment will be on priority and service basis. Profit-making undertakings were also opened for joint ventures, or for private and foreign investors. Nine public sector/areas undertakings were declared "*Navratna*" (nine precious stones) as these were the base of economy, security and interest of the country. Beside this, to reform the public sector in India, the government's reform policy of public undertakings is mainly centred around the divestment or disinvestment, downsizing, privatising through various means and types of public sector, global competitiveness, profit, and priorities of the economy. Further, area or sectorwise regulatory system is also being evolved to sort out the differences between the ministries and the public undertakings, to protect the users and consumers, to decide the tariff and trade, to maintain a minimum standard of services, efficiency and effectiveness and to generate a system of trust in the public services.[12] In spite of all these efforts, public undertaking in India constitute a large part of economy, it is not a easy task to discard them. Public sector reforms will take a long time to produce good result in the Indian economy. The experiences of the East Asian economies are preventing the central government to take drastic steps in the public sector.

### *Ensuring Trust in the Civil Services*

The British legacies in the Indian administration have been very strong and influential and it is becoming very difficult to change the image of civil services in the Indian people. Civil services are considered the symbol of authority, corruption and favouritism rather than servants and meritocracy. In the present new economic scenerio, civil services have occupied more profitable positions in the society as the chances of security, corruption, favouritism, and discretion in civil services increased. To maintain a standard of services and to avoid these problems in the new economy, government has activated its anti-corruption machinery like C.B.I., anti-corruption Bureau and state level ombudsman (Lokayukta) in state administration and also considering to establish a national level Ombudsman (LokPal) to investigate such corruption charges. The scope of national Ombudsman will be extended to Prime Minister, elected representatives and government public officials. The definition of "Public Servant" is being enlarged to widen its scope of activities. Beside this, rules, regulations and official acts are being modified and amended to delimit the discretionery powers of the all India Services in public administration. Further, government has also provided legal right to its citizens to get information on administrative decisions which are not to come under official secrets Act. Parliamentary committees/commissions were also strengthered to control administrative machinery. Peoples councils/committees at district and block level will also be established to review the administrative discretion. Transparency in administrative activities will be ensured through publication and public notices, Janata Adalat (Peoples' Court) and open Janata camps, special measures suitable to the culture and the Indian rural and illiterate masses are being devised to settle disputes between administration and the citizens. Personal liability of administrative officials in the matters pertaining to public complaints and grievances is being fixed. Consumer protection courts have been set up in service sector like telecommunication, electricity, Railways, Roadways, Civil Aviation, etc. Police System is being revamped. A Police Reforms High Power Committee is being set up to restructure, reorient and redesign the police services. Citizen's rights in the case of arrest are being ensured to minimise Police atrocities and cruelty. Judiciary is also playing a key role in ensuring reliable, transparent and efficient public administrative system. Judicial activism has brought a significant change in administrative decisions and policy implementation.[13] Beside this, new ways of financing development plans and programmes are being devised.[14] In order to bring closer the administration and the citizens for mutual trust and understanding of practical problems in the Indian setting. These some of the measures may generate trust and confidence in civil services and will restablish a image of efficient and effective civil service. However, there is great need of bringing professionalism, specialism and secular outlook in the Indian administration which is still a lacunae in the Indian

Civil Services. Efforts in this direction are not very effective.

**Poverty Eradication Programme Machinery**

Since India has a huge Section of population (45 per cent) below poverty line due to overriding reasons, the government has established administrative machinery to abolish the below poverty line population by 2005. For this, Rural Reconstruction Ministry, Integrated Rural Development Programmes Department, 20-Point Programme Department, Urban Development Ministry, etc., are responsible to eradicate poverty in the Country. Beside this, similar departments, agencies and organisations are operating at the state level. However, the percentage of below poverty line population is not reducing in spite of heavy investments in poverty eradication programmes, as a large section of money is spent on the big administrative machinery and a very little amount of money reaches to these people. To cut such spending, the government has devised some new schemes and programmes in which the role of non-governmental organisations and voluntary organisations will be enhanced to implement poverty eradication programmes. Now, the government is reducing the number of employees in these organisations (ministries and departments) so that more money could be available to the programmes. Implementation of some programmes is solely privatised or is handed over to NGOs and VOs like family welfare programmes, vaccination of children and their mothers, hut-making, etc. Some of the programmes are started to be run with specialised agencies and NGOs like literacy programmes in rural areas, distribution of life saving medicines, eye care programmes, handicrafts making in rural areas, sale and purchase of rural products, unskilled workers' training programmes, the government departments cannot discard their responsibility. However, the efforts of government to reduce its burden is being shared by the NGOs but the sole responsibility lies with the government and its administrative machinery. The effects of the administrative reform to develop an alternative for socio-economic development was also appreciated by the World Bank and some other donor agencies.[15] In spite of these efforts, there is a very serious question to the market economy advocates whether global new economic system will reduce or increase poverty in overpopulated countries like India? India's Planning Commission's reports of 1992-96 clearly indicated that market economy approach is increasing the gap between the rich and the poor and the percentage of poor has increased during this period. The administrative reforms has not much contributed in the poverty eradication programmes. NGOs and voluntary organisations have not been successful to share the burden of government in poverty eradication due to socio-economic reasons.

## An Assessment

India's administrative reforms were carried out under the pressures of the World Bank and the other international donor institutions as a part of structural adjustment programme in the developing countries. Beside this, administrative reforms were also made to implement the WTO/GATT agreements in the economy of the country. However, it must be noted that: first, no basic change or reform was made in the basic structure of the civil services. The 150 years old British patterned structure was continued in the new economic policy; second, these reforms were made at the operational and procedural level but policy-making (Secretariat/Departments/Ministries) level was unaffected; third, such reforms were aimed for the economic system and the general public or masses were not facilitated by these reforms. For the public, the same old civil services are being continued; fourth, these reforms were not supported by the state administrative system both at state and local level. Hence, no significant change at these two levels was seen. And, lastly, the critical issues of reforms like downsizing, entrepreneurial and managerial civil services were not resolved due to political instability, minority governments and political differences.

Looking at the ministry level reforms, most of the reforms were regulative, contractual and procedural in nature, the creation of new institutions in various sectors of the Indian economy was to make sectoral planning, regulation and to providing services mainly to the private and foreign investors. Poverty ridden people were untouched and consequently poverty eradication programmes were not supported by the market economy. Administrative reforms were not able to bridge the gap between the market economy approach and the poverty eradication programmes. Institutional arrangements were made at the surface level of the Indian administrative system and a clear-cut and visible conflicts on the scope of rights between the central government ministeries/departments and the independent institutions can be seen (for examples, conflict between the central department of Telecommunications and the Telecommunication Regulatory Authority of India). The crisis in the last Asian economics has put a negative effect on administrative reforms and the structural adjustment programmes in India as several suspicions were expressed over the GATT/WTO agreements and the central government hesitated to make further reforms. However, committed to liberalisation in its announcements. Last but not least, it must be kept in mind that administrative reforms are ongoing processes and are conditioned by the socio-cultural setting of the country. Although the pace of reforms is slow but is concrete and solid in its effects on Indian administration.

## REFERENCES

1. Sen, Amartya, "Development Strategies: The Role of the state and the Private Sector" in proceedings of the World Bank Annual Conference on Development Economics, 1990.
2. Singh, Manmohan, "Development Policy Research: The Task Ahead", in the proceedings of the World Bank Annual Conference on Development Economics, 1989, See also I.G. Patel, "Limits of the Current Consensus on Development" in the proceedings of the World Bank Annual Conference on Development Economics, 1993.
3. Saxena, Pradeep "Managing the Transition: Foreign Direct Investment in India" A paper presented in the round table conference of the International Institute of Administrative Sciences in Quebee (Canada), 14-17 July, 1997. In this paper's presentation, it was feared that the economies based on FDI will later or sooner face the economic crisis.
4. *Ibid.*
5. Major ruling parties like Congress in Madhya Pradesh and Bharatiya Janata Party in Rajasthan, Haryana, Maharashtra States experienced unexpected defeats of their candidates as

these state governments have tried to introduce trade in services policy in their respective states. As such, India has shown that trade in service sector is not politically sustainable and may generate more political instability in the country.

6. Saxena, Pradeep, "Primary Capital Market and Regulatory institutions in India", A paper presented in the American Political Science Association Conference in Chicago (U.S.A.), 1-4 Sept 1995.
7. Israel, Arturo, "The Changing Role of the State: Institutional Dimensions", RPE working paper 495, World Bank, Washington, December 1990.
8. Saxena, Pradeep, "The Poor, Human Rights and Institutions", *Politics, Administration and Change (PAC),* No. 28, July-December, 1997, pp. 23-36.
9. Cheung B.H, "Understanding Public Sector Reforms: Global Trends and Diverse Agendas", *International Review of Administration Sciences*, vol. 63, no. 11, Dec. 1997, p. 130.
10. Saxena, Pradeep, "73rd and 74th Constitutional Amendments in India: Prospects of local Governments", A paper presented in the IASIA Conferences in Durban South Africa (1996) and Quebec-Canada (1997).
11. Saxena, Pradeep, "Information Technology: Market, Capability, and future Prospects in India", A paper presented in the IASIA Conference in Quebec (Canada) in July, 1997.
12. Saxena, Pradeep, "Government Owned Companies as an Instrument of Government Action; A paper presented in the IASIA Conference in Quebec (Canada) in July 1997 and published (in press) in *Sturt Nagel*, "Public Administration in Cross-Countries:. Policy Studies Organisation", University of Illinois/U.S.A.), 1998.
13. Saxena, Pradeep, "Law and Poverty Eradication Programmes in India", A paper for the CROP Workshop on Law, Poverty and State II in Madrid (Spain) 1996.
14. Saxena, Pradeep, "New Ways of Financing Social Development Programmes in India", A paper prepared for the World Bank Conference in 1997.
15. Asian Development Bank Report, 1997. See also the World Bank Report 1996-97.

Part 6

# Role of Information Technology in Administration

# 36

# Role of Information Technology in Public Administration

## Issues for E-Governance

*Charanjeev Singh & Devinderjit Kaur*

India adopted parliamentary form of government inherited on the colonial pattern, which is operated vertically rather than across. Various administrative structures like the Ministries and Administrative Departments have been set-up, as a response to a particular need of the citizenry. These supra-structures are largely characterised by large amount of paper work and file handing, time-consuming processes and several levels of explicit controls and approvals. In an attempted effort for greater interventions in the interest of development and improving citizen welfare measures government structures soemtimes moved from just governance to be pro-actively involved in social reforms and providers of basic services and utilities, thereby increasing the hierarchies and their associated costs.

The last decade of twentieth century witnessed Information Technology (IT) emerge as the most prominent technology to have a revolutionary affect on the lives of people across the world. IT has potential of converting our society into a truly knowledge-based society. Now, there is no area of human life, which is not affected by IT in one way or the other. In order to ensure that the citizenry at large reap the benefits of this development, it is imperative that the government evolves a coordianted strategy, which could affect all the facets of life of its citizens. With the incorporation of the latest technologies the Indian society got more and more information savvy. In its conventional sense, IT has been used as synonymous to computers. However, rapid advancement and convergence of various information delivery systems such as Radio, TV, Telephone, Newspapers, Fax and computers *per se* and networks, it is feasible to offer IT services, using conventional forms of information delivery systems. For the last many years the country has seen phenomenal growth with regard to spread of cable-TV and mobile telephony. It is through their integration with Internet has been a major facilitator of empowering people with information. It has ensured that the information delivered to people through Internet is available even in the remotest places in the country and that too without necessarily requiring computers, which have all along been the only devices to access Internet.

> The explosive growth of the information-intensive services sector is radically altering the world economic landscape. In the emerging knowledge-based global economy, the sustainable competitive advantage of nations will reside not in their possession of abundant natural resources or cheap labour force, but in their ability to harness their countries' intellectual assets.[1]

Indian people have realised the significance of information and communication, which has ushered in an era of qualitative and valuable transformation in social, economic and political sectors mainly as a result of free flow of information and sharing of knowledge. The networking of resources through innovative information and communication technologies is creating limitless opportunities for accessing all available forms of social learning and intelligence. The potential capacity of information and communication technologies to generate wealth, foreign exchange and employment has already caught the attention and imagination of the people, business community, industrialists, economists, bureaucracy and politicians. Earlier, our data and information were preserved on papers or some other modes creating enormous problems of space and reproducibility. Now these problems have been overcome as a result of introduction of cyber media having no space and time limitations. This paradigm shift is also heavily marked in the business sector through electronic commerce (E-commerce), government operations online (E-governance), online education (E-education), mailing through computers (E-mail), development of human interpersonal relationships (E-communities), data management and retrieval, etc. India's participation in IT developments is going to create a fundamental change in our value systems, quality of life, thoughts and visions and moreover to put the country in the path of acquiring a status of developed economy. Today, our skilled manpower driven software IT industries are at the top of the national agenda as government has increasingly realised that IT sector is the only cost-effective high quality and reliable medium to ensure speedy delivery of results, and moreover, the fact that the use of the state-of-art technologies in software development could enhance the ongoing economic reformation and modernisation process that country initiated during the last decade. The cumulative effect of the IT driven progress will be to surge in India's strength and self-confidence not only in economic but also in military and external relation sectors.

## Attitudinal Changes and Computer Literacy

With the Introduction of IT there is likely to be "paradigm shift from authoritarian approach to a more democratic people friendly approach. The new agenda for governance will be to achieve dramatic improvement in critical, contemporary measures of performance, such as cost, quality of service and speed of individual public organisations".[2] This would require changes not only in the attitude towards new technology but in work culture as well. The following steps need to be taken to improve productivity:

- Training on computer devices and the related hardware in a phased manner so as to eliminate the fear of new technology.
- Drastic change in work system and procedures, delegation of powers so as to empower the employees and to make them

accountable. Middle level management must be delegated with decision-making powers and free from budget and performance measurements so that the top-level administrators are free for strategic policy framing.

- Job related training programmes be initiated for each level. For operating levels exposure to working of specific transaction system, middle level for handling Management Information Systems (MIS) and senior level to emerging trends in IT.
- Incentives to be provided for the employees who excel in IT.
- New recruitment to be based on computer literacy.

## Areas of IT Applications

### *Poverty Alleviation Programmes and Empowerment*

Several centrally sponsored poverty alleviation programmes[3] are being implemented for both rural and urban poor at the state level. These schemes target the beneficiaries living below the poverty line (BPL) and provided credit for them. These schemes envisages eradicating poverty is via self-help groups of women. These women groups are encouraged to save money. The government steps in with revolving fund as well as bank credit. This method is found to be the most effective in delivering rural credit as well as eradicating poverty. One of the critical components of this scheme however involves tracking these beneficiaries who save money as well as receive subsidy from the government and credit from the banks. Every self-help group can be documented which will include the name of the beneficiary, the family particulars, contribution to the corpus, revolving fund received from the state agencies, credit received from the concerned bank, the interest due and paid, etc. These particulars can be computerised and stored in the respective bank branches where groups would be investing their savings. This would help the concerned officials and non-officials involved in the implementation of the programme for intensive review and monitoring.

### *Municipal Service*

The urban residents can benefit from the introduction of the

IT in the municipal services. All services provided by the urban local bodies (ULBs) can be computerised and residents have access to various departments of the ULBs online from the information kiosks, set up throughout the urban district. Public grievances will be given priority and resolved speedily by the use of computers and interconnectivity. Mapping of the urban area can be done and co-ordination between the various departments can be ensured to prevent repeated inconvenience to the public as and when digging or construction activities are carried out. Similarly, online payment of house tax bills, water and sewage charges and other municipal taxes and charges can be for the convenience of the public at large.

### *Licences and Registration*

All driving licences and registration certificates for all types of vehicles can be computerised and procedures for issuance of new licences and registration certificates and their renewal can be made convenient for the public through online connectivity. Delays can be totally eliminated as these documents can be provided the same day as the application is made. SMART Cards can be introduced for registration certificates and driving licences. SMART Card based citizens ID with multi-functions that enable citizens to interact with services, make payments, act as a Voter ID, obtain ration card, passport, driving licence, Arms licences, Births and Death Certificates, etc., can be introduced in association with the private sector.

### *Treasury*

The government treasury can be computerised and connected online with the Secretariat and other important offices. All bills and other documents can be computerised and manual processes minimised. This involves intensive computerisation of all the treasuries in the area. This system serves pensioners of government service, women, old age pensioners, freedom fighters, physically handicapped and destitute widows, etc. As the treasuries act as bankers to the ULBs and the Panchayati Raj Institutions (PRIs) comprehensive computerisation can be planned using the V-sat terminals. There will be a main database at the state capital and local headquarters at the district and block levels.

### *MIS for Different Levels of the Government*

An efficient and effective department specific IT based Decision Support System (DSS)/Management Information System (MIS) can be evolved concurrently with the process of reengineering in the government. Abstract on all developmental parameters, revenue collections, crime rate, key agricultural inputs, condition of irrigation facilities, status of power generation and distribution, social infrastructure, etc., can be integrated in this system. Wherever citizen interface is involved, Web enabled applications can be developed. On-line Analytical Processing (OLAP) can be developed for planning and decision-making.

### *Government Tendering/Procurement Process*

One of areas, which attracted a lot of attention, recently, again via IT is government tendering and procurement process. Electronic procurement and settlement system with supporting databases and transparent decision-making can replace the existing manual system, which can bring in greater transparency in government purchases and contracting.

### *Police*

Officers and officials of the police can be made IT savvy. Connectivity between all the police stations and the police headquarters can be established through V-SAT to ensure and these offices can further be connected with those of the Deputy Commissioner and Sub-Divisional Magistrate. The system as and when connected online can provide speedy communication and exchange of information for ensuring greater efficiency in policing.

### *Hospital Administration*

Even hospital services can be benefited from the use of IT. Hospitals without any paper or film are now not far. This is being experimented for the first time in India in a hospital at Fortis Heart Institute (FHI), Mohali[4,5]. FHI is working towards future hospital where only digitised records (case-histories), X-rays, laboratory reports, payment records will flow through IT. The deal is that a patient will not have to waste time waiting and collecting slips of paper from different hospital departments. Instead, everything will happen seamlessly via electronic devices instead of the conventional papers. In the initial stage three hospital departments will be integrated, viz., hospital information system (HIS), clinical (laboratory) information system and the radiology (imaging) department. HIS includes all the information that is generated daily in the hospital—from inventory status of the hospital supplies to detailed patient records. The front and the back-end operations of this system have been detailed in Plate 1.

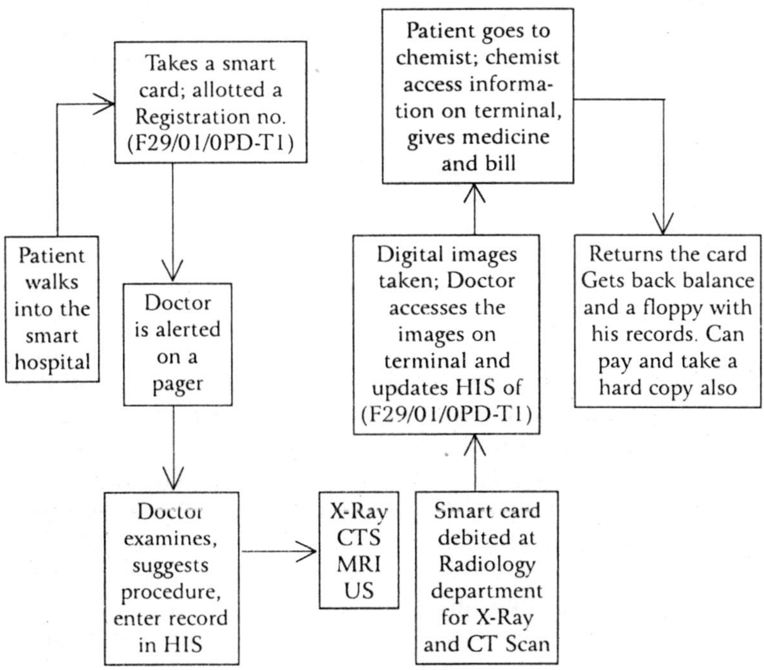


**PLATE 1: Front End Operations in HIS** (*Business World*, March 2001)

### *Telemedicine—A New Concept in the World of Medicine*

Telemedicine literally means medicine at a distance. It is more narrowly defined as the integration of telecommunications, information, human-machine interface, and medical-care technologies for the purpose of enhancing the delivery of health-care. It can include the transfer of basic patient information over computer networks (medical informatics), the exchange of images such as radiographs or pathologies among geographically separated specialists, remote patient interviews and examination through videoconferencing and remote monitoring, and educational activities. With the rapid growth in telecommunications and computer technology over the last few years, telemedicine has become an important part of medical development, with the potential to greatly improve the quality of future health care.[6] It is defined as the use of modern telecommunications and information technologies for the provision of clinical care to individuals at a distance and the transmission of information to provide that care. Telemedicine is not one specific technology but a means for providing health services at a distance using telecommunications and medical computer science. It spans every echelon of health care, from first responder/emergency medical systems to tertiary medical speciality consultations and home care.[7]

Telemedicine aims at bringing in more and better health care facilities even to the remore areas throughout the world. Furthermore, it can be used for educating medical professionals and keep them abreast with specialised information which otherwise would take a lot of time and resources in obtaining it. In India, the concept of telemedicine is gaining importance. In northern India for the first time three premier medical researches and education institutes namely All India Institute of Medical Sciences (AIIMS), New Delhi, Post Graduate Institute of Medical Education and Research (PGIMER), Chandigarh and Sanjay Gandhi Post Graduate Institute (SGPGI), Lucknow have been linked through a network for exchanging information regarding latest developments in medical education and research. This feat is likely to gain ground and spread over other medical institutes.

## IT and Administration—Concept of E-Governance

### *E-Governance Defined*

E-governance is provision of citizen services, re-engineered by technology, viz., Internet. It is now emerging, as governments and citizens around the world experiment with and learn to exploit new media and technologies. It involves new styles of leadership, new ways of debating and deciding policy and investment, new ways of accessing education, handling citizen grievances, organising and delivering information and services. A "joined up" government-community-citizen infrastructure has its own significance. A strong and effective information chain, comprising a choice of practical, accessible and manageable channels of communication has a dual benefit. Citizens enjoy a fast and convenient "service", whilst government not only becomes more integrated into the community itself, but also can focus its resources where they are needed most. Moreover, a culture of self-service enables citizens to "help themselves" wherever possible, saving time and money for all concerned.[8] E-governance applications need to enable online transactions between large number of users, across geographies and hierarchies, within each department and across departments and organisations—both within the government and external to the government. Ultimately, these applications should enable a large number of end-users, the citizens, to be able to transact with the government—anytime, anywhere.[9]

### *IT and E-Governance*

IT can help the administration to create a knowledge-based society. It envisages a scenario wherein every citizen shall be able to access the benefits of IT. The ultimate goal should be to use IT as a medium for effective interaction between the government and the public so that exchange of information and access to government departments is speedy and easy, leading to a better quality of life. It will help to improve processes in the government by using computing devices; communication systems associated electronics and software to provide better delivery systems to the citizens. It must be clearly understood that IT is not an end in itself but means to provide better quality of life to the citizens. It is not merely automating existing process but the target is to use IT to improve overall organisational efficiency and pass the benefits to the citizens. With the help of the IT the government can:

(i) Provide public service for the citizens through E-governance which is efficient, speedy and cost-effective;
(ii) Create enormous new employment opportunities by developing and training skilled manpower in the field of IT;
(iii) Promote industrial development through IT. Infrastructure relating to IT can be utilised for modernisation thus increasing productivity;
(iv) Train and develop skilled manpower in IT;
(v) Increase exports in IT thereby creating a platform for excellence in software development;
(vi) Provide information about the facilities like health, education, transport, etc., and about various developmental schemes/programmes; and
(vii) Make government-citizen interface more effective, efficient and transparent on the principle of SMART government (which stands for simple, moral, accountable, responsive and transparent government).[10]

As a matter of fact the use of IT will subserve dual purpose. Citizens can enjoy fast and convenient "service", while government not only becomes more integrated into the community itself, but also can focus its resources where they are needed most. Moreover, a culture of self-service enables citizens to "help themselves" wherever possible, saving time and money for all concerned.[11] Information would also be gathered much easier without duplication of efforts and many routine and repeated tasks could be simplified or totally eliminated. Taken together all these steps require a fundamental change to systems, procedures and processes so as to provide basic services to a broader segment of citizens with optimal quality and at a desired time place and cost.[12] This process would necessitate that:

1. All departments would prepare their IT Action Plan, with

one-year focus and a five-year perspective.

2. All departments would create databases of rules and other related information. This would include information such as budget, recruitment/service rules; plan achievements for various schemes, etc.
3. Each department will create web page in the web site to display grievance-handling procedure.
4. Certain inter-departmental projects, which have considerable significance as being underlying feature for all other IT related activities as well as of considerable importance for the well-being of the citizens, would be given a special status. This would include projects such as disaster management system, citizen's database, budget, etc. Inter-departmental committee to be appointed hereafter would monitor them.
5. To oversee implementation of IT strategies in the departments, each department will have Chief Information Officer (CIO) who would report directly to Secretary of the department.
6. Creation of E-mail system.
7. Creation of document imaging system to reduce paper work.
8. Development of software in local language.

For co-ordinating this enormous task independently an agency with fair amount of autonomy be set up for helping various players in IT field and in implementing IT Policy. Among other things, this organisation would also select consultants/specialists for providing services to various government departments/agencies under broad framework contracts. Some of these would include:

- Development of Information strategy.
- Networking and IT architectural design and communication.
- Programme and project management.
- Customer support system.
- Internet/intranet services.
- System security and system audit.
- Implementation of the architectural design and provision of services.
- Development, Training and Testing.

This proposed organisation would also help augmenting its finances from various resources including resource mobilisation from the domestic and foreign market. It would charge fees for the services rendered to the government departments/agencies; and take up activities such as acquisition of hardware, software development, training, and placement, etc. It would keep itself updated with the recent technological developments in the field of IT and keep the government and its agencies aware of the same. It would also work as an agency for identification of projects for private sector participation as participation of the private sector in IT sector is extremely important from two angles. It would involve first, attracting additional resources and second, imbibing sufficient competition. Private sector would also participate in creation of "information superhighways"; setting up of information kiosks for the use of the clientele and provision of services for creating of database-oriented services. Private participation may not be restricted at local level, whereas global partnership must be sought keeping in view the extent capital and human investment required. This would not only help in creating enormous job opportunities, economic development, absorbing the technical workforce but also help in setting up of high-tech cities and info-tech parks so as to generate software export-oriented markets. The essentials of E-governance can be visualised in Plate II.

## The Tasks Ahead

In order to introduce the portals of E-governance and creation of self-service solutions for the citizenry the government must fulfil the following:

### *Awareness*

For successful implementation of the concept of E-governance it is imperative for the government to create awareness among its citizenry about the information gateways available for them. While the government is taking number of pro-active steps to promote the growth of IT industry, it must be equally conscious that these developments do not create a new division in society—the digital divide. The gap between those who have access

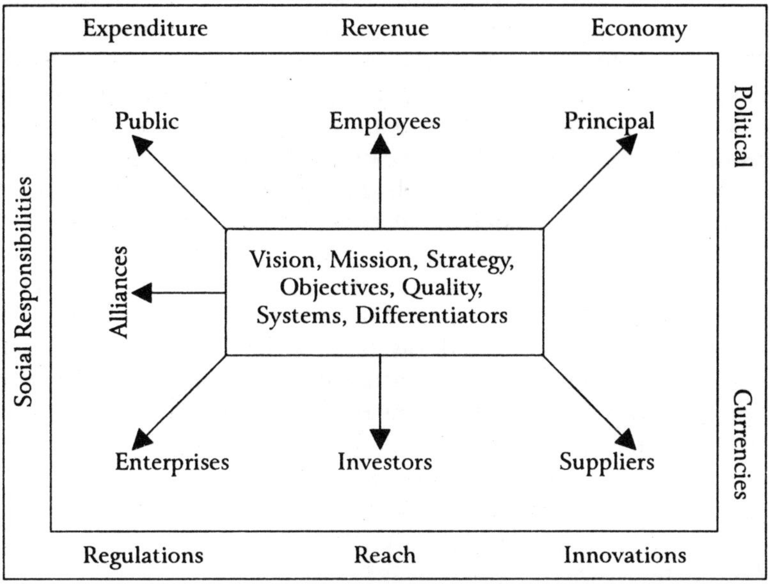


**PLATE II: E-Governance and factors acting on it**
(*Dataquest*, May 31 2000)

to IT-based services and those who do not. The endeavour of the government must be, therefore, to see that the benefits of IT do not concentrate and benefit only the elite—both educated and financial. As a matter of fact IT must be used as a potent tool to provide new opportunities to those sections of the citizenry who would otherwise develop a negative attitude towards it. The E-solutions available for the general public must be attractive and enticing so that the common man knows well about this channel to reach to the government. The services and facilities available on this portal must relieve the end user from hardships, which were encountered in the old system. This will not only enthuse the end-user but will invigorate the enterprise within government as well.

### *Accessibility*

The government at the doorstep must be the agenda for E-governance. This channel must be within easy reach of the end-user.

The availability of Internet services can be improved by encouraging healthy competition among the Internet Service Providers (ISPs) thus facilitating the end-user in getting more services at cheaper rates. As a matter of fact, the model of telephone revolution, which was brought in the late eighties, must be emulated. The "cyber kiosks" must be well equipped with all the facilities, which have direct association with IT, viz., videoconferencing, "chatting" which would enable the common man to come "face to face" yet sitting miles apart from any government office and using the value-added services provided by the government. For this purpose, hardware and software can be obtained on lease from the manufacturers for whom other benefits like tax holidays may be extended coupled with income/corporate tax relief for a limited period. Further, keeping in view the fragile and obsolence of the equipment the producers be made eligible for 100 per cent deprecation from the very first year.

***Usability***

One of the ingredients, which make any technology successful, is being user-friendly. The software and the information available with the citizenry must be such that should not require any specialised knowledge or skill. This can be ensured that the data retrieval through cyber kiosks be planned in such a manner that these are available at shopping centres, railway/bus stations, public libraries, Public Call Offices (PCOs), post offices and other places which are frequented by the common man.

***Content***

In order to provide a comprehensive, one-stop service the IT channel must provide all the information required and not simply one aspect of it. Care must be taken to integrate the new systems with the old systems and batabases so as to prepare comprehensive information systems. As a matter of fact, no information system can be visualised where proper support of various databases and data analysis is missing. These databases have to be complied before being pressed into service for the use of the citizenry and for this purpose databases must be shareable across all the platforms, languages, operating systems only then they can be converted to user interfaces.

***Reliability***

The E-solutions must be able to cope up with heavy traffic on the information super-highway and be available to the customer 24 hours a day for 365 days. This can be made possible with optimum bandwidth, both for local access and Internet connectivity as Internet is the backbone of all IT projects involved in E-governance portals. Serious constraints on the bandwidth cannot only severely limit activities like large file browsing/downloading, videoconferencing but as well making the end-user feel the uselessness of this potent tool. Frequent power failures can also sap out life from this portal, for this uninterrupted power supply is to be ensured.

***Functionality and Relevance***

The E-solutions available for the citizenry must be capable of carrying out transactions such as payment of bills of essential services, bookings and provision of relevant information, which is kept updated. For this purpose information be segregated on the basis of its being obsolete. Information relevant in its content and accurate will have any value for the citizenry.

***Security***

Security of the information from the "Internet hackers" is yet another area which is assuming importance. This should be the basic and integral part of the website design of any government department/agency. Hackers/intruders and all other illegal attempts to have access to the information must be punitive offence. "Security Shells" must be provided to guard against hacking and intrusion. Automated Practical Extraction and Reporting Language (PERL) scripts can be useful for this purpose. All-important information can be made secure by disabling the directory listings or have "index HTML" file in them, which can be blank or left with some irrelevant content that may mislead the potential intruder.

## Conclusions and Suggestions

Today many organisations be it government or private are embarking on the path to the prvision of E-solutions to the citizenry and the government is following the suit in the form of getting the administration to the door step of the common man yet the distance from the corridors of the secretariat to the threshold of the citizens seems to be wide. The IT revolution is facing a damp squip both internally as well externally. These threats come from within from the mindset of the bureaucracy, which is bewildered at the loss of power from their hands and from outside—the fall of dot.com companies world over. If centre or any of the state government wants to provide E-solutions then it must change the mindset of their bureaucracies rather than crying hoarse over the illiteracy and Internet backwardness of the people at large. The infrastructure on which the government is trying to portray to the world that India is a country where cyber kiosks are present even in the remotest of the areas fail to understand their presence though basic necessities for the survival are missing. No wonder that the newly created Ministry of Information Technology is going to yet any Ministry in the country which has the bureaucrats pushing the file and memos instead of updating their websites regularly. As a matter of fact, it is time for them to realise that IT is not merely a force to reckon with but such a growth engine, which would usher in an era and support other development activities and thus putting the economy back on the rails as India has huge potentials in both the end-users and the software and hardware technologies (see Plate III). It would thus be essential to create awareness among the people and the government itself of the role that IT can play in economic and social development information sharing and disseminating. To enable the PPP approach, i.e., public-private participation by seeking their help in creating awareness, innovation, capacity to invest and take pro-active steps in seamlessly delivering digital services—maximising the effects its IT portals, viz., decentralisation and empowerment. Towards the end

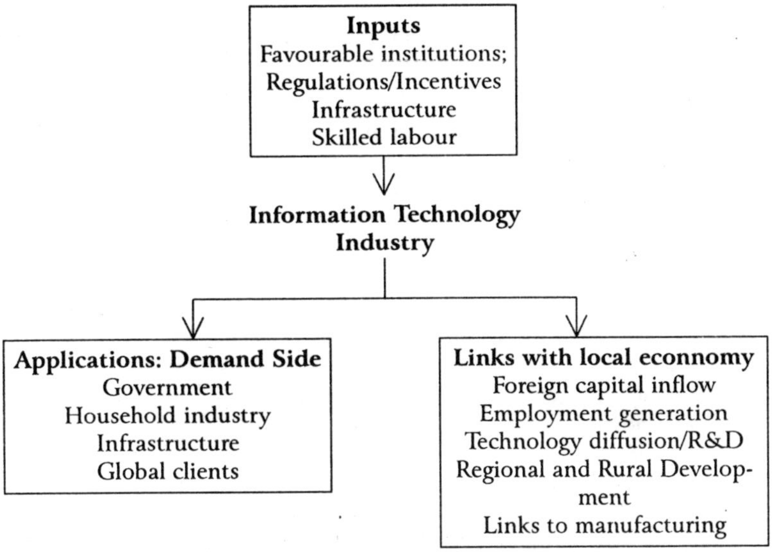


**PLATE III: IT and the Regional Economy**
(Nirupam Bajpai and Anupama Dokeniya, "Information Technology-Led Growth Policies: A Case Study of Tamilnadu", Discussion Paper No. 729, Harvard Institute for International Development, October 1999)

it is suggested that we substitute the word E-governance with "E-democracy" or "tele-democracy" as it would rather fit in more appropriately as we are the largest democracy in the world and it would also give support to the ideals enshrined in the Constitution of India.

## REFERENCES

1. Nirupam Bajpai and Navi Radjou, "Raising the global competitiveness of Tamil Nadu's information technology industry", Development Discussion Paper No. 728, Harvard Institute for International Development, Harvard University, October 1999. (Internet site http://www1.worldbank.org/).
2. Jagdish C. Kapoor, "IT and good governance", *Indian Journal of Public Administration*, 46(3), July September 2000, p. 389.
3. Schemes, viz., Swarna Jayanti Shahri Rozgar Yojana (SJSRY), Prime Minister Rozgar Yojana (PMRY) for urban poor and Swarna Jayanti Gram Swarozgar Yojana (SGSY) for rural poor.

4. Shelly Singh, "A Medical Thriller" *Business World,* 20(45), 19 March 2001.
5. *Ibid.*
6. Rex E. Gantenbein, "Clinical practices in the information age: An introduction to telemedicine technologies", Department of Computer Science/School of Human Medicine, University of Wyoming. (Internet site http://www/cs/uwyo.edu/-rex/).
7. *Ibid.*
8. Renu Budhiraja, *Electronic Governance—A Key Issue in the 21st Century,* (Internet site http://www.mit.gov.in).
9. *Dataquest*, 31 May, 2000.
10. Robert Schware, "IT and public sector management in developing countries: present status and future prospects", *Indian Journal of Public Administration,* 46(3), July-September 2000, p. 415. (Also see Subir Hari Singh and Renu Budhiraja).
11. Renu Budhiraja, *op. cit.*
12. Subir Hari Singh, *Ways and means of bridging the gap between developed and developing countries,* (A paper presented at High-level panel on Information Technology and Public Administration at United Nations, New York on 26 September 2000) (http:www.mit.gov.in).

# 37

# Challenges of Information Technology in Administration

## (With Special Reference to the State of Rajasthan)

*Ravindra Sharma*

The world has ushered in an era of "Information Technology". IT has affected all walks of human life. No part of human beings remained unaffected by it. Social, political, cultural, educational and economic parts of our life are getting changed day in and day out. Private and public administration too have been affected by IT. One can notice that on the one hand IT has facilitated economic administration, development administration, police administration, military administration, justice administration and general administration, on the other hand IT has placed challenges before these administrations. Before discussing IT, it would not be out of place first to define "communication" and have a bird's-eye view on the historical development of communication in the world.

### Definition and Historical Development of Communication

The word communication has been derived from the Latin word "communis", which means common. Communication refers to the sharing of ideas, facts, opinions, information and understanding. According to Leonard J. Kazmier communication is the transfer or transmission of some information and understanding from one person to another.[1]

McFarland defines communication as: "a process of meaningful interaction among human beings. More specifically, it is the process by which meanings are perceived and understandings are reached among human beings".[2] According to Brown communication is "a process of transmitting ideas or thoughts from one person to another ... for the purpose of creating understanding in the thinking of the person receiving the communication".[3]

Vardaman and Halterman gave a very comprehensive definition of communication. They said: "By communication we mean the flow of material, information, perception, and understanding between various parts and members of an organization ... all the methods, means and media of communication (communication technology), all the channels, network, and systems of communication (organisation structure), all the person-to-person interchange (interpersonal communication).... It includes all aspects of communication: up, down, lateral, speaking, writing, listening, reading, methods, media, modes, channels, networks, flow; inter-personal, inter-organisational".[4]

In a very simple manner communication may be said to be a process of transmitting information, thoughts, opinions, messages, facts, ideas or emotions and understanding from one person, place or thing to another person, place or thing.

In the early stages of civilisation men did not have language. They had sound merely. Man used to convey his feelings to other persons with the help of making sound. Examples of such communication can be seen amongst animals today. The development of language opened doors for the advancement of men. The tradition of transfer of knowledge from one generation to the other started with the help of language. Later on the development of script became a powerful means of communication. Innovation of paper in China made written communication easier. Earlier the cost of publication was too high. John Gutenburg, a goldsmith of Germany, developed a system of cheap publishing in his printing press in the year 1455.[5] The inventions one after the other in the field of communication took place thereafter. Radio, Wireless, Telegram, Telephone, Telex, Fax, Pager, Tele Vision, Mobile Phone, etc., made communication quick, cheap and effective. Satellite removed the distance and converted the whole world into a "Village" by introducing revolution in the field of IT. The latest technology named as "direct to home" (DTH) would make possible to receive programme directly on TV set from satellite. Internet is another mile-stone in the field of IT. This technology made possible to mutually exchange data and information by connecting computers. Internet may be said to be a great sea of knowledge. With the help of E-mail one can get information, data, documents, etc., without wasting time by establishing connection with any corner of the world. E-commerce and E-governance have been facili tated by the new means of communication.

## The Developments in Rajasthan State

The Government of Rajasthan established a Directorate of computers in 1987 with the key objectives ranging from formulating the policies, creating awareness, providing technical consultancy to the various departments of the state for recruitment and cadre management. In order to implement computerisation projects efficiently a separate cadre comprising computer professionals was created in the government. The Directorate of Information Technology (DoIT) is the nodal agency for computerisation in the state government today. The government of Rajasthan also established a consultancy and project implementation agency known as Rajasthan State Agency for Computer Services (Raj Comp) in the year 1989. The Chief Secretary is the head of the governing body of Raj Comp. The Director of DoIT is the Managing Director of Raj Comp.

The Chief Minister's Secretariat, Board of Revenue, Finance Department, State Insurance and PF Department, Agriculture Department, Commercial Taxes Department, Planning Department, Department of Personnel, Special Schemes Organisation and Integrated Rural Development Department were computerised in the first phase. Basic office automation applications were provided in these offices during the first phase.

During the second phase of computerisation, Rajasthan launched its own web-site. Emphasis is laid on developing web-enabled citizen-oriented applications to increase government-public interface. Government provided right of information to the citizens through E-governance. It is expected that E-governance would facilitate transparency in government operation and government-public interface and also improve the efficiency and effectiveness of government's delivery system and administration.

Information kiosk project was conceived and launched by the state government recently. It is named as Raj Nidhi.[6] It aims at delivering government information to citizens. It is developed in Hindi. Citizens can download forms required for availing government services like ration card, driving license, caste certificate, application for obtaining electricity connection, etc. Website Mandi Online developed for Rajasthan Agriculture Marketing Board which provides prices of agriculture products to farmers on an online basis. The offices like the Department of Registration and stamps, Rajasthan Housing Board, Transport Department and some Hospitals have recently been computerised.

## Challenge Before Police Administration

The IT has a negative side also. IT paved the way for anti-social and criminal activities in an unprecedented manner. It provides opportunities for law breaking and hide in no time. IT facilitated committing crimes at the global level. "The communication system and network are often used in the furtherance of criminal activity including organised crime, racketeering, extortion, kidnapping, espionage, terrorism and trafficking in illegal drugs".[7] Hence IT has emerged as a great challenge before police administration. "Recent and continuing advances in telephone technology and the introduction of new technology and transmission modes by telecommunication industry have made it increasingly difficult for government agencies to implement lawful orders and threaten the ability of such agencies effectively to enforce the laws and protect the national security".[8]

The cyber crime, which the world faces these days, may be said to be the byproduct of IT. Intentionally disturbing electronic transfer of information or money, illegally withdrawal of money from someone's account by decoding certain level of password and theft of information confidential to a corporate, institution or a security agency may be said to be cyber crime. Indians are masters in software as well as in misusing IT. It is interesting to note that among all the cyber crimes committed around the world in 1999 as high as 24 per cent were committed in India only. Only two cyber cells have so far been established in the whole country one by Bangalore and the other by the Maharashtra government. Only two cells are not enough for a huge country like India.

Another challenge for the police administration is lack of centralised database of all criminals in the country. In the developed countries every police van is equipped with a laptop loaded with database of all the criminals in the country, their addresses, their fingerprints, their faces, etc. It can be readily checked that any suspect has criminal records or not and has performed any crime similar in nature in other parts of the country.

Here in India this has become a very basic necessity to investigate a crime since the criminals today have a very great mobility. So lack of access to IT where it is required is another challenge for the police.

The ratio of solved cases out of total registered is very low in India. Out of total cases filed during 2000 guilty was proved only in 2 per cent. Hence persons in 98 per cent cases were acquitted. Our police could not collect adequate evidences against the criminals therefore they fail to prove the guilty in the courts.

Recently Bombay police identified a website which was being used to execute murder with the help of third party. "Supari" is being fixed and paid with the help of IT.

The person who wants to get someone killed has just to login to that website, paste the photograph and details of the person to be killed. Then he is informed on a given E-mail address that how much money is to be deposited in which bank account. As soon as the money is deposited the other party starts action. This website was maintained by an unidentified underworld. The beauty of the whole process is that nobody used to know each other. Names of the murderer and the person interested in getting murdered were neither mentioned nor required on the website and E-mail.

Another example of violating law is misuse of cell phones in criminal activities. Criminals perform crime at new location where they use cash card with cell phone and they throw away cash card and come back to their old place. At their old place they use another sim card. The police fails to trace the criminal even if they come to know the number since cash card has already been thrown away by the user.

### Internet for Jaipur, Bhilwara and Kota Cities

An internet—a computer network built using Internet technology, tools and standards—has been developed by DoIT. Initially this facility was developed for Jaipur city. Presently six police stations of Jaipur South, all the police stations of Jaipur North, two police stations of Bhilwara and one police station of Kota are availing the service of Internet. This is to be noted that there are 701 police stations in the whole state of Rajasthan. This innovative system has been named as "*Aarakshi*". It enables the field level officers to carry out online communication regarding crime data, criminals' photographs, etc. This to be noted that this internet facility in Rajasthan is available to only five police districts out of 37 in the state. It has been reported that no other state has this facility. The other states are planning to imitate it. The internet system developed in Rajasthan has been appreciated by NCRB, Delhi, and National Police Academy, Hyderabad. Providing internet to only four-five police districts in such a huge country may be said to be a drop in the ocean.

## REFERENCES

1. Kazmier, Leonard J., *Principles of Management: A Programmed Instructional Approach*, Tata-McGraw Hill Publishing Co. Ltd., 1977, p. 266.
2. McFarland, D.E., *Management: Principles and Practice*, p. 552.
3. Brown, C.A. "Communication Means Understanding", *Personnel Administration*, Jan.-Feb. 1958, pp. 12-16.
4. Vardaman, Georg T., and Carrol C. Halterman, *Managerial Control Through Communication*, John Wiley & Sons, New York, 1968, pp. 3-4.

5. Naveen Panth, Patra Suchna Karyalya, Bharat Sarkar, Special Article on Republic Day, 2001, on Sanchar Kranti, p. 2.
6. Document of Rajasthan Information Technology Policy, 2000, Government of Rajasthan, Jaipur.
7. Bill on Digital Telephony, 102nd session, American Congress, USA.
8. *Ibid*.

# 38

# Reforms in India: Towards E-Governance

*Rajbans Singh Gill*

## Introduction

An administrative system originally designed for the performance of the narrowly limited functions of an imperial government, but subsequently called upon to promote and work for the welfare of society, is bound to reveal inadequacies and deficiencies in its organisation, procedures and personnel, no less than its style and ethos. These shortcomings are apt to become increasingly frustrating with progressive escalation in the scale, variety and pace of development programmes. (S.R. Maheshwari) India being a federal country, reform in Public Administration is simultaneously—not sequentially—necessary at all the three levels of government—central, state as well as local.

## Reinventing Government

The proposal to reinvent Public Administration may seem presumptuous to those who see Public Administration as static and unchangeable. But, in fact, Publlic Administration constantly changes with changes in the philosophy of state, objectives of government and values of people. It is a dynamic apparatus of state, not a static instrument. Values of society have undergone drastic change and a New Society and a New Man with lofty ambitions and vaulting desires have emerged (Sofi Ali and Anita Rao).

The state has not been static and has metamorphosed from a political state to the Administrative state and to the Bureaucratic state and is today on the threshold of becoming a cybernetic state (Allen Shick). The governments all over the world are trying for a change-change for the future. The cybernetic state is the developing technology which is making in roads in the administrative system.

## Cybernatic State

In Cybernatic State, "government functions as a servo-mechanism, conjoining the polity and economy to achieve public objectives", and distinction between public and private disappears. The Cybernatic State envisages two changes in government: new forms of community government and new structures for cybernetic guidance, the former to ensure greater participation and the latter to keep the cybernetic processes on track.

IT revolution is sweeping the globe. Governments planning giants are being drawn into it. Transition to electronic delivery of services in government not only involves changes to the systems, procedures and processes of relevant services but also affects the way in which the public and business community deals with the government.

## E-Governance

E-Governance gives the extraordinary pace of changes in the IT industry, the term E-Governance itself is somewhat new and essentially implies upgradation of the efficiency and effectiveness of the administrative machinery through the combination of information technology and sophisticated multimedia to deliver better, cost-effective and speedy services to the citizens. We are, in fact, in the midst of one of the most rapidly changing periods in history. There has been a shift in importance from the traditional inputs of a production process to the processes involved in the creation, storage, dissemination and use of information. The new technology has already had a profound impact in the manner in which large organisations function.

Many of the organisations have had to restructure themselves to create a flatter-less hierarchical-structure. At the same time one of the principal efforts of all organisations have been devoted to creation and sustenance of environment of learning in view of the quantum increases in knowledge and changes in technology.

In Government the transition to electronic delivery of services will not only involve changes to the systems, procedures and processes of the relevant services but will also affect the way in which the public and the business community deals with the government. Customers will no longer need to interface directly with government officials in order to secure a particular service. They also do not need to know which agency is the service provider, as the service can be obtained through a kiosk or personal computer. What is important to them is to be able to secure the required service speedily and easily. These new trends will influence the nature of government administration and management, thereby reinventing the government to make its experience seamless to the citizens.

**Ministry of Personnel, Public Grievances and Pensions**

The Government of India has already issued guidelines that 2 to 3 per cent of every Ministry's/Department's Plan Budget should be utilised for the purpose of promoting Information Technology (Vasundhara Raje Scindia). The process of computerization is an expensive one. It is imperative that in a situation of scarce resources of the state, a systematic approach to introduction of computers and their effective use is adopted so that the scarce resources are not wasted in the acquisition of sophisticated high-end systems which lie around and end up with low utilisation. The process of introduction of IT is not one simply of automating the manual processes. It has to go in tandem with an overhaul of the existing manual processes so as to maximise the benefits of the use of new technology. Given the fact of such extraordinary technological change, greater innovations are possible. A very simple example, from Ministry of Personnel, Public Grievances And Pensions relates to the present system of updating the career and training records of IAS officers in the personnel information system database. It is presently done on the basis of orders/letters received from different cadre controlling authorities. This system can be fully decentralized so that a unified database located in Delhi can be accessed by each of the cadre controlling authorities located in the States who can update the records of their officers locally. This would considerably reduce errors and omissions in updating records and make the most recent information available online to the cadre controlling authorities for their use (Ministry of Personnel, Public Grievances and Pensions). It will be make things easier for the administrators.

## Recent Advances: Internet

The World Wide Web is only a few years old and has witnessed explosive growth in terms of the number of people connected and the amount of information available on it. It is now possible to make available an enormous amount of information to anyone with access to the Net and, increasingly, to carry out a variety of transactions from filling in and sending forms to ordering and paying for goods and services online. We need to harness the potential of the technologies available. But it is not simply a matter of creating web-based content: the content has to be useful, it must be easy to access and updated regularly. We also need to take special care to ensure that use of IT does not create a new class of haves and have nots. While, on the one hand, we increase the use of computers, we must also ensure that they are accessible and functional in the rural or remoter areas. This is extremely important because the technology makes it possible for a person in the remotest of areas to have access to the same information base on the internet as someone located in the heart of the most developed cities. However, if the rural communications and networking infrastructure as well as "information booths" are not put in place, the technology is of no use to the people living in those areas.

The recent advances in information technology have opened up opportunities to provide basic government services to a much broader segment of the population of optimal quality at desired time, place and cost. Some of the state governments have taken initiative to develop "one-stop shops" to deliver a host of services to the citizens, such as, domicile certificates, driving licence, payment of property tax, electricity and water bill, facility for lodging the FIR, etc. Similarly information kiosks with Internet connectivity are being integrated with the ISD/STD booths. All these are commendable initiatives to provide seamless governance at the door-steps of the citizens. However, for these mass customisation efforts to succeed on a large-scale, there is need to build capacities in government at all levels. The Government of India has, therefore, decided to set-up a National Institute of Smart Government to be the focal point of this capacity building exercise.

All reforms require a clear vision, leadership and a considerable amount of effort to bring about systematic changes in organisations so that their performance is improved and they create better ways of delivering services to the public. You need to harness the innate creative and innovative abilities of your colleagues and subordinates so that there is a collective and collaborative initiative to bring about the changes that technology has now made possible.

The Conference will explore four broad topics. These relate to technology alternatives, citizen-government transactions, the socio-economic perspective and resources planning. I am quite sure that given the quality of the speakers and the participants, this Conference will come up with practical suggestions to improve the quality of life of the citizens of this country through innovative usage of Information Technology.

## Case of Andhra Pradesh

The idea that Information Technology (IT) can be an enabling force, not only for business and trade but also for government, has now been widely accepted. However, a cursory glance at the existing initiatives in India seems to suggest a mixed picture. With the exception of the Railways Reservation System, IT applications seem to have had no remarkable effect on the manner in which citizen's benefit from the services of the government. Against this backdrop, the efforts of the State Government of Andhra Pradesh to harness Information Technology seem like a major initiative to deliver an improved administration.

The State Government of Andhra Pradesh has introduced

a series of Information Technology based interventions to improve the performance of select departments. The foundation of this effort was in the attempt to connect all district Headquarters and the State Government's offices in Hyderabad through APSWAN (AP State Wide Area Network). While there has been an extensive discussion on the scope of introducing IT and the projected benefits, the two major departments with large citizen interface where IT has been actually introduced are:

(a) Registrars offices
(b) Commercial Taxes

The third department where this process is in progress are the Mandal Revenue Offices.

Given the potential of what was being attempted, Public Affairs Centre (PAC) felt that a careful study of the situation in Andhra Pradesh would yield rich insights on whether and how computerisation had affected the life of the common person.

Computers existed only in Doordarshan. Until the village sarpanch, postman and headmaster in 20,000 hamlets of rural Maharashtra decided it was high time the local farm hands actually touched what townsfolk call a CPU and keyboard. (Ministry of Personnel, Public Grievances And Pensions)

When 3,78,000 Hindi, Marathi and Gujarati schools from the heart of rugged India in Maharashtra, Madhya Pradesh, Gujarat, Uttar Pradesh and Rajasthan wrote back gripped by information technology fever in response to only 31,000 mailers on computers and IT from Rural Relations, a Pune-based social organisation, they triggered a silent revolution this year.

### Village Cyber Cafe: Haryana

The internet is quietly bringing about a cyber revolution in the interiors of Haryana. Surfing on the net, Prof Avinash Kak, who teaches at Purdue University in United States, was amazed to find the website of a remote villages in south Haryana. Stirred, Prof. Kak shot off an E-mail to nangalchaudhary.8k.com. offering assistance for putting up one more computer and an air-conditioner at northern India's first village cyber cafe at Nangal

Chaudhary village, about 20 km from the district headquarters of Narnaul. This sleepy and backward village had indeed been noticed in the U.S. (*Hindustan Times*).

Today is the age of computers. Rapid advancements are taking place in the field of Information Technology all over the world. To keep pace with the world, we have introduced our Information Technology Policy which provides a number of incentives to industry and aims at effective E-governance besides accelerating the pace of development. An Information Technology Initiative Fund has also been created with an initial corpus of Rs.10 crore for E-governance and to promote the Information Technology in the state of Haryana. A corpus fund of Rs.5 crore for the setting up of an Indian Institute of Information Technology (IIIT) at Gurgaon (*The Tribune*). The state is spearheading in the field of E-governance.

## Citizens and IT

India, which is the largest democracy in the world, is presently undergoing a rapid economic transformation with the thrust on social justice. Good governance involves fulfilment of the expectations of the people from the Government. The expectations of the people include aspirations for good standard of living and superior access to essential services through rapid economic growth and social justice. This requires a model of governance based on cooperative federalism, decentralisation, accountability, social justice, economic reforms, respect for citizens' rights and transparency—all of which will benefit both the Nation and the individual citizen.

Good governance will involve focussing attention on the thrust areas, some of which will include formulation and implementation of Citizens' Charter; Right-sizing the Government; Use of Information Technology in the Government; Right to information; Redress of Public Grievances; Simplification of Rules and Procedures; and Capacity Building for Quality in Government.

## Capacity Building for IT Management

As information technology gradually permeates the working of the Central Government, need is being felt for capacity building for decentralised decision-making with regard to IT issues in various Ministries and Departments. Moreover, a large workforce also needs to be trained in the use of computers, etc. For this purpose, in addition to appointing IT Managers/Officers in individual departments/organisations, on the lines of the Grievances Officers, Vigilance Officers, etc., there is need for taking certain steps for capacity building in these and other personnel. Thus, short-term and long-term training programmes in IT Management may be developed for IT managers as well as Secretaries of IT in State Governments. Departmental IT Manuals would also, be developed. Learning Centres may be set up in various Ministries and Departments to provide opportunities for self-education.

## Conclusions

The initiative regarding strengthening of Public Grievance Redress Mechanism would be focused by merging the multiple agencies handling them into the institution of a Central Grievance Commission (Ombudsman) and empowering it to deal effectively with citizens' grievances. Information Technology can be an ideal vehicle for bringing about the required change in the work culture of government. For that a minimum agenda should be developed in a time bound manner. India needs "smart" governments and techno savvy politicians who have a feel about how the benefits of IT can be filtered down to the country's masses (Dewang Mehta). To start with the implementation of E-governance it is the mindset of the people which have to be adjusted. Many bureaucrats and civil servants are more concerned about individual departments than the larger picture. This has to be overcome by imparting correct knowledge, education and mindset of the concerned. However, the most important aspect is strong leadership, which invariably will overcome the inertia and mindset of the people.

Part 7

# Miscellaneous

# 39

# Research in Public Administration

*Satya Deva*

Public Administration, as part and instrument of the government, has to constantly adapt itself to the changing role of the State, particularly in a changing, developing, society. It has yet to shed many of its colonial features and to prepare adequately for its new responsibilities, like helping to promote growth of indigenous new technology and competitive industry in the face of globalisation, regulation of business in the interest of business itself (for example, through curbing monopolies) and in the interest of consumers, and protection of the environment, in addition to provision of social services and development of the infrastructure. Monitoring change requires better knowledge about the administration.

One of the obstacles in the way of knowledge is the separation between knowing and doing. In the history of medicine, competent physicians emerged only after hospitals were attached to medical colleges, thus bringing knowing and doing together. Administration, like medicine and engineering, is an applied subject. In the West, where the study of administration is advanced, there is frequent interchange of personnel among corporations, governments and universities. University teachers often teach for one semester and do consultancy in the next. Their publications derive from the interplay between theory and practice and are more down to earth. In India we still lack this culture in most fields: agriculture, engineering, architecture, business management, public administration. The need for greater interaction between governments, industries and universities has been felt for quite sometime. We need not wait, however, for changes at the institutional level. Action at the individual level, by teachers and practitioners, can begin to give results, and pave the way for changes at the institutional level. If we do pieces of research which are found to be useful by governments and industries, requests for consultancy should soon begin to pour in.

## The Problem-Solving Approach

The main difference between pure and applied disciplines is that while a pure discipline deals only with one aspect of the reality, an applied one deals with the whole. While a pure discipline aims only at building and testing theory thus advancing knowledge in general, an applied one aims at investigation and solution of particular problems. Since every problem in real life has various aspects, knowledge about all of them contained in the various relevant pure disciplines has to be brought together, in the process building a holistic science—the whole being greater than the sum of the parts. Thus while a psychologist studies the influence of job satisfaction in isolation on productivity, a student of administration finds that in practice there are other factors also, which tend to interfere with or enhance the relationship. It was thus that Herzberg discovered the "hygiene" factors some of which are economic or sociological in character. Similarly, a student of health administration must realise that a policy for dealing with widespread ill health of longstanding must provide not only for preventing the spread of infection through inoculation with vaccine or serum, but also for proper nutrition to build up vitality and sanitation for protection from secondry infection. Hence some attention to the economy and environment is also needed, requiring application of several social and natural sciences. Also, a student or practitioner of health administration must have some knowledge of the science of medicine. If such varied preparation seems to be a tall order, one should note how an engineer or doctor has to prepare himself by studying various sciences and their branches and sub-branches. It is such preparation that enables the practitioner or the researcher to deal with the various facets of a tricky practical problem with the necessary speed and effectiveness.

It is also of importance to note that in every applied discipline there is space for both general prectitioners and specialists. A specialist in an applied discipline also often requires in-depth knowledge of a pure discipline. Thus understanding of economic policy, which is so important in public administration nowadays, must be based upon a good knowledge of economics. As noted earlier, the boundary between research and practice is blurred. An adviser to a government in a certain field may be both. He is in demand like no one else, for he thinks in an ivory tower but works on the ground.

## Dig Where You Stand

We often postpone indefinitely taking up a research project for fear that it will require too much time and running about. Unfortunately, research has come to be identified with a big survey. This is part of the lure of bigness in modern civilization, deriving from association of status with size of a corporation in monopoly capitalism. However, many of the classical research studies in administration were small case studies. Thus Taylor mentions in lucid detail how he developed this theory by watching carefully just one labourer—the one who was like a "bull" and was the most productive.[1] The Hawthorne studies constituted a case study of the Western Electric Co., in much of which the work of only a small number of girls in a small room was studied.[2] Max Weber depends to a large extent upon the biography of one men, Benjamin Franklin, for the origin of his famous hypothesis that Puritanism (involving austerity leading to savings) helped the rise of modern capitalism, in *The Protestant Ethic and the Spirit of Capitalism*. Robert Michels studied just one political party to develop, in *Political Parties,* the classic theory that large-scale organisations tend to be oligarchic. Philip Selznick developed the valuable hypothesis that the rich and powerful get authority in the administrative system by being co-opted, through a case study in *The TVA and the Grass Roots*. S.M. Lipset built the hypothesis that the poor tend to revolt only after their condition improves somewhat by studying only one province of Canada, in *Agrarian Socialism*. This indicates that by studying just one organisation in-depth we may be able to build valuable hypotheses leading to a new theoretical framework, in addition to helping that organisation if requested.

### Be Your Own Investigator

The vogue of the large survey has given rise to the academic entrepreneur, who obtains a large grant from the UGC or the ICSSR and sets up a research organisation consisting of a horde of interviewers, a statistician who processes the data, and a deputy director who manages the show and writes the report, which is often later published as the work of the "director" who obtained the grant. What is often missing is the spark of creativity which would put life in the work—the set of new hypotheses which might give birth to a whole new vision. Unfortunately, our surveys often borrow their theories from abroad, and thus fail to break new ground. We all realise that our problems, complicated both by the partial continuation of feudal and colonial structures of the past, and the increasing impact of the new forces of globalisation, are different and much more acute than those faced in the developed countries. Perhaps this complexity, in addition to our educational upbringing in a system which teaches us mainly to reproduce materials rather than think for oursleves, frightens us into merely copying others, when the need precisely because of the unique complexity of the problems is to seek new vistas.

The right course for a committed researcher would be to start, not by setting up a research organisation, but by familiarising himself/herself with, say, a public undertaking through informal observation of its working, informal interviews with employees, clients and rulers, and the study of its reports, balance sheets and other documents. The researcher proceeds by seeking answers to questions, such as: Why is it that the main object for which the undertaking was set up is hardly being fulfilled (as is often the case)? Mainly whose interests is the undertaking serving? What is the role and contribution of those at the top? How much overstaffing is there? Who exploits whom? What need for reorganisation is there? What is the shape of things to come? What are the areas of conflict? and so on.

New hypotheses are likely to mainly arise from tentative answers to questions such as those posed above. The answers may come from the respondents in the course of informal interviews, and may also be suggested to the researcher himself as a result of his interaction. They may also be suggested to him by earlier studies of similar organisations. Another important source is grand theory. The contributions of great thinkers like Marx, Weber, Gandhi and Jayaprakash Narayan often contain seeds for the growth of new ideas. Thus Marx hypothesised (*Paris Manuscripts)* that instrumentally involves alientation indicated by immorality: an employee functions immorally on behalf of his employer. Weber, also known as bourgeois Marx, gave the related example ("Bureaucracy") of officials co-operating with the enemy in occupied territory. Gandhi theorised (*Hind Swaraj)* that "development", being capitalist ("Western") in character, involves human degradation, indicated by hypocrisy and selfishness, for example of members of Parliament. His alternative lies in deconcentration of power.

## The Survey

Basically, while the function of a case study is to help in developing hypotheses (which are also derived from grand theory and suggested by earlier research studies), that of a survey is to test the hypotheses. While analytically the distinction is clear, in practice it gets blurred. Thus a survey may be a part of a case study: the survey may help in refining the emerging hypotheses. This is true the other way round also: some case studies may be added on to a survey to throw light on unexplained phenomena. Thus after the survey, the cases of respondents exhibiting a high degree of divergence may be studied to find areas where the hypotheses do not seem to apply.

The nature and role of the survey has tended to change in the recent past. One of the reasons is the decline of positivism, so much that Anthony Giddens says that it has become a term of abuse.[3] The acceptance of positivism implies the use of the methods of natural sciences in human or social sciences.

Positivism consists mainly in belief in phenomenalism (the reality consists only of sense impressions), the verification principle (a statement is meaningful only if there is potentially some means of testing it), the duality of fact and value (the separation of facts and values, since empirical knowledge is logically discrepant from the pursuit of moral aims), and the unity of science (natural and social sciences share a common logical and methodological foundation).[4]

The attck on positivism has come from several directions. The Frankfurt School maintained that positivism involves instrumental rationality, so that scientific theories, instead of being true descriptions, are merely useful instruments. They pleaded for moral rationality. Thus while Max Weber had pleaded for the separation of facts and values, the Frankfurt School maintained that facts and values cannot be fully separated. For example, according to them,

> science already embodies value-judgements, such as the desirability of the technological domination of nature, which, though in fact questionable, seem so self-evident that they appear not to be value-judgements at all, but simply disinterested devotion to science. The postulate of value-freedom in effect insulates such well-entrenched value-judgements from criticism by disqualifying potential competitors.[5]

Jurgen Habermas, a second-generation member of the Frankfurt School, pointd out that by separating fact and value positivism condemns practical questions to irrationality or myth. Thus Herbert A. Simon tries to legitimate exploitation in the existing society by maintaining that workers accept a job at a certain wage only after rationally deciding that there is "equilibrium" between their contribution and the compensation they receive.[6] It is another matter that due to unemployment workers have often to accept a meagre wage just to keep body and soul together. According to Simon's argument, "exploitation" is a value-loaded term, while the worker's choice is a fact. By separating the fact and the value, exploitation is shown to be a myth according to positivist social science which does not make value-judgements.

Karl Popper attacked positivism by questioning induction

or generalisation from particular instances, to which scientists constantly resort, particularly while interpreting statistical data. Thus all significant correlations need not be indicative of cause-effect relationships. Thomas Kuhn argued that scientists work within and against the background of an unquestioned set of beliefs, namely a "paradigm", and tend to overlook findings that go against it.

The critique of positivism has on the whole focused on the inappropriateness of the methods of natural sciences in the human or social sciences. It is held that there are certain distinctive human attributes, such as consciousness, cultural norms, symbolic meaning and intentionality, which require a methodological gulf between natural science and human social life. As a result there now tends to be more emphasis on qualitative, as compared with quantitative data, particularly that related to human attributes such as intelligence, aptitude, attitudes and performance. Quantitative data continue to be important for the study of economic indicators; however, there is less emphasis on the use of measurement and statistical analysis in the study of psychological and socio-psychological aspects.

It is of great importance to realise that research methodology is deeply related to theory. Changes in theory lead to changes in research methodology also. In the history of administrative theory, the Scientific Management movement (1900-23), led by Frederick Taylor, encouraged the measurement of performance; the Human Relations movement (1925-55) emphasised the study of attitudes; Systems Rationalism (1955-80) (whose seeds were sown during Second World War, when the British and American military employed "operations research teams" of mathematicians, physicists, and statisticians to devise methods for solving logistical problems) involved the application of quantitative techniques for dealing with problems of planning and control, and the Organisational Culture and Product Quality movement (1980 onwards) emphasised the study of values, beliefs and emotions.[7]

Theory, in turn, grows and changes in the context of socio-economic situations. The Scientific Management movement arose when cheap migrant labour was available in the United States: workers could be forced to work faster and produce more and more or face removal. Hence the measurement of individual performance was the order of the day. After the rise of trade unionism workers could no longer be forced, and so the measurement of performance was not needed. The Human Relations movement resulted from the resurgence of welfare capitalism after First World War. It was argued that "workers were primarily social beings driven by a need for belonging and acceptance. Social interaction and group affiliation were deemed necessary for human fulfilment and, by implication, harmony in the workplace".[8] It was hoped that happy workers would produce and earn more too. Attitude surveys of workers were made to find out how far managers had been able to instil high motivation and group cohesion among them through developed communication skills and sensitivity in interpersonal relations. Attitude surveys were followed by training programmes and group psychotherapy for changing attitudes. However, it was found that attitudes could not be changed in this way. Frederick Herzberg, one of the foremost exponents of the ideology of human relations noted after about half a century of its rise as follows:

> Unfortunatley, this approach does not work. We have never changed attitudes to get motivated behavior. Incredible sums of money have been spent by organisations on morale surveys and attitudes change programmes, ranging from elaborate communications systems to group psychotherapy. This has been a scandalous waste. The whole premise is wrong. Attitudes do not lead to behavior. It is the other way round Behaviour leads to attitudes. Attitudes are a psychological confirmation and justification and rationalisation for the behavior that an individual manifests.[9]

In other words, attitudes are not the cause but the effect of the way a person function in a given situation. After this realisation grew, the study of attitudes lost importance and attitude surveys became rare. Quantitative techniques involved in operations research ceased to be used for another reason: it was found that queuing theory, network analysis, simulation techniques, and theories of linear and dynamic programming were usable only in large corporations, rare even in countries like the

United Kingdom. The measurement of human attributes associated with organisational culture similarly went out of vogue when it was found that Japanese corporate culture could not be replicated in other countries; also, Japanese firms could not maintain their success in the competition against firms in other countries for long.

We thus see that the use of quantitative techniques has been found to be no panacea, despite its repeated resurgence in the history of research and theory building. Added to it was the calling into question of the measurement of human attributes arising from the decline of positivism. It is also notable that there is now a tendency to work with smaller samples in survey research. Reduction in the emphasis on quantification also reduces emphasis on the quantum of the random sampling error, which would be less in large samples. A small sample is also amenable to study in greater depth qualitatively. These trends imply the recognition that a small survey, which does not require employing a team of investigators, can be quite valuable.

## Conclusion

What we aim at is in-depth study of our society and solution of its various problems in their different aspects and locations. With this object in view we have to build hypotheses to describe and explain social phenomena; the hypotheses later constitute new theories. One of the basic features of science is its continuing falsification in part and replacement by new theories. Hence being a scientist requires creativity for building new hypotheses and theories, and courage to test them in the field to see if they can be falsified, wholly or partially. At the same time, we must stand on the shoulders of scientists who have gone before, lest we begin the scientific endeavour from the beginning again and again. Hence if on the one hand we have always to be cognisant of the ground reality, we also have to be ambitious, imaginative and creative for breaking new ground.

## REFERENCES

1. F.W. Taylor, *The Principles of Scientific Management in Scientific Management*, New York, 1964, pp. 61-62.

2. F.J. Roethlisberger and W.J. Dickson, *Management and the Worker*, Cambridge, Mass., 1939.
3. Anthony Giddens, "Positivism and Its Critics" in Tom Bottomore and Robert Nisbet (eds.), *A History of Sociological Analysis,* London, 1979.
4. *Ibid.*
5. M.J. Inwood, "Frankfurt School" in Ted Honderich (ed.), *The Oxford Companion to Philosophy,* Oxford, 1995, 290. Technological domination of nature leads to sophisticated armaments, concentration of power, dictatorship, war and heightened exploitation through new machinery.
6. H.A. Simon, D.W. Smithburg and V.A. Thompson, *Public Administration,* New York, 1950, pp. 381-82.
7. Stephen R. Barley and Gideon Kunda, "Design and Devotion: Surges of Rational and Normative Ideologies of Control in Managerial Discourse", *Administrative Science Quarterly,* 37 (1992), pp. 363-99.
8. *Ibid.*, p. 374.
9. Frederick Herzberg, *The Managerial Choice: To Be Efficient and To Be Human,* Homewood, Ill, Dow Jones-Irwin, 1976.

# 40

# Depoliticise Civil Services: An Agenda for New Millennium

*Harbans Pathak & Parul Pathak*

India is a vast country. We are rich in resources. We have the second largest manpower in the world. We have seven times the population of Japan. We have 10 times its inhabitable area. We are heirs to a rich heritage. We have given the Vedas and Upanishads to the world. We have taught morality to mankind. We preach non-violence. We give sermons on peace. Yet, in spite of our resources, we continue to be one of the poorest nations in the world. We occupy a high position amongst the 10 most corrupt nations of the world. This nation of more than nine hundred million people cannot boast of even a single gold medalist at the Olympics. In fact, the supermacy that we had gained in the game of hockey prior to Independence has been slowly lost in the recent years. Even the two Nobel Prizes were won by the two Indians—Rabindranath Tagore and Sir C.V. Raman—in the years 1913 and 1930.[1]

With all this glorious past and rich heritage, the present scenario seems to be distressing. India is at crossroads. This is a well-known fact since most problems have stayed with us even as Governments have come and gone. The basic question is why is it so? A lack of vision and commitment to the people? Or is it because of the absence of a will to Govern? Good governance as a concept has suddenly entered the vocabulary of public administration since the 1990s.... The conference of Chief Secretaries held on November 20, 1996, all of a sudden woke up to the realisation that there was a crisis in Indian Administration.[2] The reality is our administrative system where the politico-bureaucratic order which rules most thrives on status—quoism of the negative type. This is a pity. The old order of 53 years has to change the challenges ahead in the new millennium call for a modern outlook and a totally fresh approach to the problems which have made this ancient land a prisoner of antiquated practices. The country priority areas need to be redefined. In this paper an attempt is made to make a plea to depoliticise our civil services by ensuring their independence and impartiality in the system of the country. This seems to be a mantra for the twenty-first century. The politicisation of the bureaucracy had climaxed in 1980s.[3]

In the post-Independence era, the Constitution of India provides the framework for the administration of the country through a uniform set of inter-related institutions. The Directive Principles of State Policy provide a non-justiciable foundation for a balanced and equitable socio-economic development. These principles are fundamental to the governance of the country, and the states are duty bound to follow them, enforcing the objectives through the enactment of necessary laws. The governance of the country is carried out through three vital instruments of the Constitution—the executive, legislature and judiciary.[4]

Before attempting any prognosis of the kind of changes in the administrative apparatus which may be required to meet the challenges of the twenty-first century, it would be useful to at least rapidly review the experience of the past five decades of national governance.

The federal administrative system bequeathed by the British was largely continued after the attainment of Independence.[5] Necessary changes, to meet arising requirements, were introduced in the subsequent years. The Indian Civil Service (ICS) and Indian Police (IP) were retained and legislation was enacted to create their successors, the Indian Administrative Service (IAS) and the Indian Police Service (IPS), and other required All-India Services (AIS). Sardar Patel, the then Home Minister, had to fight a hard battle not to disband the ICS and IP and to secure the creation of the new AIS.[6]

It was his conviction that officers selected on an All-India basis, from among the best available talent, will be most suited to man the vital posts in the states; as the AIS cadre would be managed by the Centre, these officers will not be easily subject to political pulls and pressures and would enjoy the requisite sense of security to discharge their duties without fear or favour. Their experience of dealing with the ground realities in the states would equip them to make valuable contribution to policy formulation when they came on deputation to serve the Centre; and their tenures at the Centre would engender a wider, national outlook which they would be able to inject in their work in the states. It was Sardar Patel's vision to strengthen cohesion and national unity through a strong and vibrant federal administrative system in which the AIS would play an important role.

The first two decades after Independence witnessed significant progress on many fronts. The work done by the Planning Commission and the National Development Council laid the basis for the Centre and the states undertaking a collaborative endeavour for securing equitable socio-economic development and uplift of the poverty-stricken masses. Among the many significant achievements were the implementation of the grow more food and the National Extension and Community Development Programmes, land reforms, consolidation of holdings, security of tenure for the farmers, construction of dams and enlargement of power and irrigation facilities, development of a nationwide network of rural co-operative credit and service societies, construction of fertiliser production units, development of high-yielding seeds, establishment of agricultural research stations and universities, and the subsequent outstanding success of the Green Revolution. Side by side, attention was devoted to industrial and infrastructural development—steel, cement, coal, power, roads, railways, ports, telecommunications, drugs and pharmaceuticals. Medical and health care services were enlarged; institutions of higher learning and research and universities were set up and facilities were created for the advancement of engineering, science, technology, space, atomic energy and oceanography.

Consequent to the humiliation faced in the 1962 Sino-Indian conflict various measures were taken to strengthen the armed forces. The military regained its honour in the 1965 Indo-Pak engagement and earned fresh laurels in the 1971 Bangladesh war. Meanwhile, planned action had been taken to strengthen and enlarge the indigenous capability for meeting defence requirements and to connect the borders with a network of roads and bridges. For improved border guarding and providing assistance to the states for internal security managements, several new central police organisations were created—the ITBP, the BSF and the CISF.

All in all, till about the late 60s (around the time the Congress started facing serious internal conflicts) the country seemed well set on the path of steady advancement. From then onwards governance in the states and the Centre started witnessing serious difficulties and consequent decline.

While one can advance innumerable reasons, a major factor for the deterioration has been the progressive loss of ideology and erosion of values among the political leadership. Indira Gandhi's resolve to stay in power at any cost, followed by the enforcement of the Emergency (1975-77), marked the dilution of the Cabinet system, and the beginning of the virtual abrogation of the rule of law. Mrs. Indira Gandhi became the undisputed leader of the country.[7] The ascendancy of extra legal elements in decision-making and the emergence of groups of unprincipled politicians and "committed" civil servants led to wanton exercise of authority which, protected by the highest echelons, led to encouragement of unaccountability and resort to corrupt practices. Whereas it would have been desirable that Public Service should exhibit a more adequate commitment to the public good than is generally expected of the Private Sector.[8]

Another factor which has had a deleterious affect on the much needed evolution of a mature and stable polity has related to our election system. Over the years, there has been continuing increase in the number of political parties in all parts of the country.[9]

In the last General Elections, with well over 600 political parties participating in the polls, every seat was contested by far too many candidates. This has involved large-scale deployment of security forces and a huge increase in the governmental expenditure on the conduct of the polls. Another, and a far more serious consequence of such confusing electoral contests has been that in many states no single party has been able to secure a clear majority. Since 1996, formation of a government at the Centre has faced a similar serious situation.

The lack of necessary checks and balances in our electoral system has generated continuing political instability in the states and, recently, at the Centre. To be able to lay claim to forming government the party which gains the highest tally in the elections is compelled to garner the requisite majority by seeking the support of disparate small groups and even individuals, notwithstanding the sharp variations in the political ideologies and agendas, if any, of such elements. Such "supporting" elements demand their proud of flesh on a daily basis, generating uncertainty about the longevity of the governments which they prop up.

A related and extremely worrying facet of our democratic process has been the large expenditure which a candidate has to bear for contesting a poll, specially if it relates to gaining a seat in the Legislature or in Parliament. While all political parties contesting elections collects funds through means fair or foul, to support their candidates, the parties in power in the states and at the centre and more advantageously placed. They have, over the years, adopted the simple approach of exploiting their official positions to collect funds not only from trade, business and industry but from the public at large on almost every occasion that it requires to deal with the governmental machinery—allotments, auctions, registrations, grant of licences, recruitment to any service, including the police, admissions to educational institutions, etc. The amounts collected generally relate to the degree of irregularity or illegality involved in the favour being done.

For example, if the existing customs regulations or excise or sales tax laws are compromised to specifically help the business interests of an Indian multinational, the rake-in may run into several hundred crore of rupees, some of which may be collected in foreign exchange in an undeclared foreign bank account (and this was the genesis of black money transactions and the 'hawala' business).

All such deviations from the norm are transacted through the officialdom; employees who quote rules or do not comply are promptly transferred and marginalised. Thus, over time, a strong nexus has grown between unprincipled politicians, pliant civil servants and the unseemly elements among those who perennially seek to support whichever political party is in power provided their unlawful demands are met.

Suffice it to say that the single-minded objective of political parties in power of retaining their position, brazenly indifferent to the misuse of authority, has led to their progressively identifying weak, compromising and aspiring elements in the civil, police and technical bureaucracies to subserve their unprincipled objectives. This has, over the years, led to the politicisation of the cadres of the states services and even those which comprise the All-India Services, specially the IAS and IPS. The politicisation of the services has resulted in vitiating the erstwhile command and control structures through which the state Chief Secretaries, Director-General of Police and other important heads of departments effectively managed the services under this charge. Peter Self compared the relationship and said it is which exists between means and ends. He explores three ways of distinguishing between politics and administration.[10]

The extraordinary precedence given by the political masters to the "committed" or "loyal" elements in the various services has resulted in thoroughly undoing the laid down principles, rules and regulations which govern recruitment, postings and appointments, tenures of field and secretarial posts, promotions, deputation for training at home or abroad et al. Officers who are not adequately malleable and ductile are transferred from post to post and station to station, in utter disregard of how this affects their training for handling higher responsibilities in due course, or how the repeated transfers of key functionaries disrupt the implementation of vital development programmes for which they are responsible, to say nothing about the effect on their morale and public esteem.

The rather frequent change of governments in some of the states has resulted in officers of various services, specially the Collectors and Superintendents of Police, being shifted time and again. This vicious malady has got to a stage where appointments to key posts—specially those involving handling of large budgets, having dealings with industry and commerce, and the vital posts of district chiefs on the civil and police side—are virtually put to auction. It would be puerile to expect that those who gain appointments on such terms of trade can even think of enforcing honestly, transparency and accountability in the areas of their respective functioning.

The disciplined and productive functioning of the cadres of various services in the states has been further vitiated by considerations of caste, community and ethnicity.

The emergence of caste groups among the services has created serious problems in their functioning and further diminished and espirit-de-corps of the cadres. The progressive politicisation, communalisation and exploitation of the services has left them exposed, unprotected and leaderless, resulting in loss of morale and cynicism among their constituents.

The growth of regionalism, increasing demand for larger autonomies for the states, alongside a growingly weaker centre, have considerably reduced the strength of the concerned central authorities in enforcing compliance by the state governments of the statutory rules and regulations relating the management of the AIS cadres. The unfettered manner in which the states have managed the Indian Administrative, Police and Forest Services has resulted in eroding the image and credibility of those who man them. Except issuing hapless advisories to the state governments, the centre has been able to do no better than watch the continuing mismanagement of the AIS which, despite the serious constraints under which they operate, still provides vital support to the states and the centre and help in holding the country together.

Notwithstanding the outstanding successes achieved on many fronts, our country has still a long way to go in achieving its avowed goals. A dent has still to be made in containing our population growth, half of our population is illiterate; several hundred million of our people exist below the poverty line; millions continue to remain unemployed; health care and housing programmes continue to lag far behind the ever increasing demands: agricultural production is not increasing at the expected rate; we have a large public debt, a growing fiscal deficit and dwindling foreign exchange reserves, and serious problems on many other fronts.

Failures of governance have generated continuing debate and criticism. One view, often expressed, is that the existing failures in the functioning of the executive can be set right if the country shifts from the Cabinet system to a Presidential form of government. Whatever be the merits of such argumentation, it must be remembered that almost three quarters of our vast population still lives in the villages. Thus, whatever may be done to make the functioning of the centre more effective, we have to remain most seriously concerned about the quality of administration at the ground level, from which all our problems originate and some of which, due to sustained mismanagement, develop into national issues.

Any change in the form of government at the Centre shall not automatically result in curing the serious ailments in the administrative apparatus across the length and breadth of our vast country.

The government and Parliament understand the need to enforce wide-ranging reforms in the continuing system of elections. After the wide publicity given to the N.N. Vohra criminal/nexus report, there was focused debate regarding the various measures required to at least keep persons with known criminal backgrounds out of the state legislatrues and Parliament. Even this limited objective has still to see fruition, to say nothing of the other important reforms, required in the electoral process.

Several parts of the country face serious internal security problems which have continued to receive, sustained abetment and systematic support from Pakistan's ISI.

Professionally planned action, fully co-ordinated between the Centre and the states, and executed by loyal and competent civil and police services, would be required to liquidate the espionage and subversive networks established by the adversary intelligence agency. Such serious problems cannot be politicised and tossed around between the states and the Centre as, unfortunately, has happened in the recent past. No more time can be lost. The Centre must act firmly, and fast.

In the backdrop of the continuation failures of the executives and the disability of a splintered Parliament to provide the much needed direction, the judiciary has attempted to fill the yawning gaps in the governance of the country. While the recent phenomenon of "judicial activism" generated considerable satisfaction among the public at large, it would be unwise to expect one of the instruments of the Constitution, which has a well-defined role, to take over the responsibilities of the executive and Parliament and seek to remedy the failures of both. In any case, those who comprise the judiciary, executive and parliament are drawn from the same society.

In the aforesaid background no time and energy may be wasted in embarking upon any approach which assumes that mere structural changes in the administrative apparatus will result in improving the governance of our vast country. We have spent the past several decades in negating the Constitution, abrogating the rule of law and systematically subverting the application of well-laid down rules of government business and systems of functioning.

Let us do no more than spending the next few years in honestly and assiduously restoring the essentials of governance.[11] Towards this end, it would be necessary to launch all necessary initiatives to start tackling the ailments of our polity which have already infected our society and denigrated governance and to introduce civil service reforms in order to check the decline of civil service.[12]

There is no need for expending time and energy in thinking of inducting exotic concepts to restore good governance in the country. During the past five decades excellent experience has been gained in the entire field of development administration. We have highly competent, resourceful and honest functionaries in all services, all over the country.

All that we need to do is to ensure that such elements are provided recognition, the requisite security of tenures, and the opportunity of putting the system back on the rails. All those who cannot perform or are dishonest must be ruthlessly weeded out under whatever new legal framework which may be required to do this.

## REFERENCES

1. For more information, refer *General Studies Manual,* New Delhi, Tata McGraw-Hill Publishing Company, 2000.
2. Mohit Bhattacharya, "Conceptualising Good Governance", *Indian*

*Journal of Public Administration,* vol XLIV, no. 3, July-September 1998, p. 289.

3. Harbans Pathak, "Politicised Bureaucracy", in Hoshiar Singh (ed.), *Higher Civil Services in India,* Kurukshetra, Nirmal Book Agency, 1995, p. 138.
4. For details, refer J.C. Johari, *The Constitution of India: A Politico-legal Study,* New Delhi, Sterling Publishers, 1996.
5. See B.B. Mishra, *The Administrative History of India,* New Delhi, Oxford University Press, 1970.
6. A. Avasthi, *Central Administration,* New Delhi, Macmillan, 1980.
7. Kuldip Nayar, *India after Nehru,* Delhi, Vikas, 1975, p. 208.
8. O.P. Dwivedi and R.B. Jain, *India's Administrative State,* New Delhi, Gitanjali Publishing House, 1985, p. 93.
9. For various aspects concerning elections, refer *Indian Journal of Public Administration,* vol. XXXVII, no. 3, July-September 1991 (Special issue on Administering Elections in India).
10. Peter Self, *Administrative Theories and Politics,* London, George Allen and Unwin, 1979, pp. 149-51.
11. O.P. Minocha, Good governance: Concept and operational issues, management in Government, October-December, 1997.
12. Harbans Pathak, "The Decline of Civil Service" in R.B. Jain (ed.), *Public Services in a Democratic Context,* Indian Institute of Public Administration, 1983, pp. 286-91.

# 41

# Bureaucracy in the New Millennium

*C.S. Panwar*

As we move into a new millennium almost every country and society is facing a challenge and change of looking back and also ahead. India on the threshold of the twenty-first century is currently experiencing an information explosion, thanks to the dramatic advance of information technology which is sure of affect various aspects of life including Bureaucracy.

The very concepts of structure and processes of bureaucracy is already undergoing significant changes under the impact of information technology. More significant however will be its impact on the administrative culture. Administrative culture basically refers to the nature and style of public administration. It includes bureaucratic culture and is, in its turn influenced by the broader political culture refers to the mode of functioning of the bureaucrats who as public servants in the higher echelon of administration are called upon to provide policy counsel, assist in formulation of programmes, and engage in the management and direction of human resources in the interest of translating policy hopes into realities.

With the use of information technology, the role and functioning of bureaucrats and other public servants is coming under effective public scrutiny. People are becoming more exposed to the merit and attitude of public servants. This attitude would help free the administrative culture of colonial administration and despotic government. Further it would lessen red tapism and corruption in public service management.

### Change in Administrative Process

All the development in information technology have had a dramatic input on overall organisation culture and job design of an individual employees. IT has led to flattening and denon sizing of today's organisations, eliminating the need for levels a bureaucracy and a long chain of command. In short organisations become flatter and less hierarchial. The need for "information keepers", "number crunchers" and "paper pushers" is eliminated people are replaced by technology and the organisation is able to down-size or rather right size which is the process of reducing the number of people in the organization. In the traditional administrative process in India, the middle management level constitutes the mainstay of bureaucracy and the impact of IT is felt mainly at the middle management level.

Another factor affecting bureaucracy is the co-ordinating activity computers have made co-ordinating better and cheaper. By using data communication networks, it will be possible to track work done in big office headquarters and in its field offices and also to take note of the grievances of the citizens and consumers. This has led to administrative decentralisation. Now the decision-making would be done quickly and cheaply. Administrative efficiency will improve the standard of services rendered.

However the paradoxical situation that is emerging in the country is that even though IT has a great impact on the bureaucratic structure but still the general public been harassed in their relationship with the government. The age-old process of endless forms, regulations, paperwork, delays, negativism still persists and so they would like to out of all these nightmarish experiences. They need a good governance and this can be possible through E-governance.

Now the country has moved to a new journey of hope, promise and opportunity and people cannot go without good governance. Thus while moving into the new millennium, Indian state needs to be welfare oriented, people directed and service driven. And Government can justify this only through providing good governance and effective governance.

Although efforts have been made to restructure the role of bureaucracy, to reform the deformity and to remove the dysfunctionality but it is a slow process.

Another factor which needs more attention in the bureaucratic structure is to provide degree of protection to its weaker and disadvantaged section of the society. As a democratic nation, we are committed to the cause of improving socio-economic status of downtrodden sections of our society specially the scheduled castes, scheduled tribes and uphold the principle of justice.

Although the Indian constitution provides an elaborate and effective framework to administer the protective, preferential and developmental constitutional provisions for the downtrodden sections of the society. It lays down in particular the policy goals and objective, guidelines for physical infrastructure and financial support. But equality of status and of opportunity is still not persistent. Therefore the task before our bureaucracy is to provide them social justice. Bureaucrats as an instrument of state should play a pivotal role in planning of social and economic life of its citizens with a view to establish egalitarian social and economic order for distributive justice. The bureaucracy has to understand its position and responsibilities in a democratic system. A system has to be developed where accountability informs the upper echelons of administration and understanding shows that authority resides with the lower levels.

However one negative impact on the bureaucracy is that of the process of liberalisation and globalisation. Caught in the glare of globalisation and liberalisation, bureaucrats are either demanding very high emoluments or joining the multinational corporations. In competition with the transnational corporations, the Indian bureaucracy has accepted its subordinate and subservient position and many important members of the higher bureaucracy are standing in a queue to join global corporations. This has a great impact on the structure on Indian bureaucracy as it is internally weakening the bureaucratic structure.

# 42

# Dilemma of Politicisation of Police Force in India

*P.P.S. Gill & Rajesh Kumar*

Maintenance of "Law in Order" is the basic function of the state. Police is one of the most important law enforcing agencies. Developmental and welfare activities can be undertaken successfully only if the foundation of law and order are well laid and well looked after. Police work is valuable like any other developmental work and thus, progress is possible, if peace and tranquillity exist and persist. The law and order situation immensely affect the functioning and structure of administration besides having larger social and political overtones.

Police and political environment, is a sum-total of institutional interactions and complex political processes and leadership behaviours and rules, which produce a symbolic web of relationship between various groups of people in society. The Indian situation confronts a phenomenon, where in the transplant of sophisticated Western institutions in the traditional milieu of an oriental country presents a striking paradox of glaring contradictions that defy instant solutions. It has puzzled the prophets of doom, who have expressed their despondency in predicting a Hungry Future.[1]

The nature of this political environment conditions the police system in several ways. First, the mass frustration explodes in violent political outbreaks and adds to the already difficult challenges of police jobs. The police has to cope up with these trying situations within their scarce resources and often have to suffer in men and materials against heavy odds. This kind of law-breaking as a daily bread severely strains the priorities of police work and the basic duties in a police station often go unattended because of the expected and threatened incidence of political violence. Second, the political atmosphere, surfeit with corruption and nihilism, gets reflected in the day-to-day behaviours of the demoralised constabulary. The political ethos weakens their discipline and they tend to take resort to political bargaining for the redressal to their organisational grievances. It is common knowledge that politicisation process has made deep inroad into the ranks and the strivings of the constabulary to organise themselves into police associations is a reflection of the political milieu, which has made the demand respectable as well legitimate. Third, the fact of over politicisation of the environment overtly needs and demands political intervention in police administration and goes to the extent of even condoning corruption as a necessary evil.

It has gravely weakened the leadership of senior officials, especially the I.G.P. and the S.P., who have been rendered passive spectators of the game. The corrupt ones in the lower ranks are difficult to be punished and worse still, the models of integrity and dedicated public service are recending from the scene. The corrupt and the suffocating atmosphere around offers new and increased opportunities to fall and the temptations for doing as well as not doing the routine public jobs in normal course of time are simply alluring.

The frustrated people and not demoralised policemen make a sick team and the innocent persons and weaker sections of the society are made to suffer due to lack of popular vigilence and social spiritedness in public life.[2]

The common man's understanding of national security and his fear about the deteriorating law and order situation is more realistic. Criminals are much better organised and equipped nowadays. The growing nexus between them, the police and politics posing a serious threat to our polity. One does not have to be a security expert to realise how the recent "Hawala case" and the many other scams are undermining national security.

Huge funds are being brought in or siphoned out through dubious channels, some of which are known to have links with foreign intelligence agencies.[3]

The political environment of lawlessness and cynicism provokes the people to be violent. They antagonise the police by taking law in their own hands. The instances of mob hysteria, lynching policemen on duty have shocked the police and it has thrown its wrath on people in return by being extra cruel and high handed. Asking for unilateral restraints from an armed force in the midst of provocative situations is not a rational proposition. Naturally, the ding-dong battle between the police and political miscreants continue to be increasingly aggressive, causing physical violence and untold misery to the weak, the poor, the ignorant and the innocent.[4]

The deterioration that we have witnessed in the past three decades is the direct result of the rapid politicisation of the police force across the land. Democracy at work in our country has subordinated efficiency and professionalism to politics. Officers even, at the senior level are being tempted to toe the political line with the promise of plum posting and important assignments and undeserved honours. The results is that discipline has suffered, moral is low everyone looks after his own selfish interests and the law is enforced selectively according to the wishes of the political masters.[5]

The situation is, however, not as hopeless as it appears. To start with the role and functions of the police need to be redefined in the present context. It is indeed strange that the police working is still governed by an antiquated legislation enacted in 1861 whose main objective was to uphold and subserve that interest of the British Raj. Unfortunately, the situation continues to this day, the only difference being that the alien power has been replaced by indigenous ruling parties. It is high time that the role of the police is redefined in the present context, emphasising that the police has a paramount obligation and duty to function according to the Constitution, the laws of the land and democratic aspirations of the people and a new Police Act incorporating these ideals is drafted.

Having done that it would be necessary to depoliticise the police. Three things would need to be done. First, State Security Commission should be set up in every state and a National

Security Commission at the central level. These apex bodies should comprise persons of integrity drawn from different walks of life and should be entrusted with laying down the broad policy guidelines for the state and central police organisation.[6]

Systematic effort have been made by the political leadership to undermine the professional efficiency of the force. Recruitment to all ranks police constables, sub-inspector and deputy superintendent of police, promotions and transfers were used as a means of political patronage and source of corruption. The pliant police leadership not only helped politicians in this game but also helped itself. Thus, undesirable elements with questionable record of integrity and professional competence came to occupy plum postings. Upright officers mostly of the IPS, were sidelined and shunted off to the Government of India on deputation. To reward loyalty to political masters, parallel police. Decorations were instituted in the state with hefty cash awards and were awarded to favourites by the political elite.

Once the police leadership and rank and file knew that supplication and servility were the passports for personal advancement, psychophancy and selected law enforcement for the benefits of the ruling party, became the order of the day. We witnessed the sorry spectacle of the chief of police issuing a circular on the eve of the general election to everyone in the department to highlight the achievements of the ruling party to the policemen during their daily briefing roll call. This, in short, was canvassing votes for the ruling party.

The National Police Commission appointed by the Janata Government in 1977 had come out with excellent recommendations to insulate the police from political interference. Congress government in the centre never wanted to implement them and the report is gathering dust in the archive of the union Home Ministry. For the shake of the future of Indian democracy energetic steps are called for to depoliticise the police in India.[7]

Even Ved Marwah has written that the new breed of politicians was not encumbered by any sense of idealism. They were also not so sure of their political base. Political power for them only a means to make money and gain power for themselves. The police with its presence at the grassroot level for strengthening their political base by rewarding their friends and punishing their foes. Over the year, the police has been seen increasingly used as an instrument of oppression in the hands of unscrupulous politicians.[8]

## Summing Up

Today, majority of the police personnel do not like to be controlled by the public representatives because they feel that their fair and independent functioning will be affected by it and public instead of thinking police as the protectors of the society may treat police as a "Political Force". Political interference at times, creates hurdles in the smooth functioning of the police force. Sometimes the politicians use the police to settle their scores and negative interferences leads to the incredibility of the police force.

DSP and above ranking police officials do not face that sort of political pressure which tend to make them an instrument in the hands of the politicians, but the core category of police, i.e., ASIs, SIs and SHOs are regular victims of political pressure and at times they play into the hands of political masters due to their own weaknesses and consequently, become an instrument in the hands of politicians. It is a common knowledge that with the change of government heavy dose of transfers and posting is administered due to lack of any rational personnel policy which most of the time leads to the lowering of morale and consequently the performance of police personnel. The level of police performance today stands vanquished owing to debased political culture and disappearance of leaders with values and ethos. It will not be an outlandish remark to debunk the Indian polity as a weak debased social institutions with the total disregard for value, norms and ethics. Moreover, the entry of inexperienced and immature people is labyrinth of Indian polity which has impaired the quality of political leadership. The poor quality of political leadership has led to the perverse conditions of police system. Criminalisation of politics has severely affected the functioning of the police force. The involvement of the people with criminal background in political activity brings in its wake anti-social elements who exploit their proximity with the politicians to gain protection from possible police action under law. The political party in power has got habituated to take direct hand in directing and influencing police action in such situations. Many times politicians create onerous circumstances for the police officials where they are forced to make compromise with political supremacy which has its genesis in the threat of transfers or some backyard posting. The collusion with the degraded politicians is done in order to secure political patronage which facilitates plum postings and no transfers. The police force itself to be blamed for getting brow beaten by the political masters and that too, where a close nexus between the criminals and politicians have emerged which has reduced the political force to an extension ruling political party.

## REFERENCES

1. Harrison Brown, *et al, The Next Hundred Years,* Viking Press, 1957. For differences with these projections, see George Rosen's calculations in for Eastern Survey July, 1958, p. 10. from P.D. Sharma, *Police Polity and People in India*, Uppal Publishing House, New Delhi, 1981, pp. 135-36.
2. Rangaswamy, K., "Police Revolt in Uttar Pradesh", *Rising Sun*, 15 June, 1973, pp. 4-7 from P.D. Sharma, *Police, Polity and People in India*, Uppal Publishing House, New Delhi, 1981, p. 138.
3. Ved Marwah, "Motivating the Police", *The Indian Express*, 3 July, 1996.
4. Rangaswamy. K., "Police Revolt in Uttar Pradesh", *Rising Sun*, 15 June, 1973, pp. 45-53 from P.D. Sharma, *Police, Polity and People in India*, Uppal Publishing House, New Delhi, 1981, p. 138.
5. Julio Rebeiro, "Indian Police, Reflecting Social Ills", *The Indian Express*, 4 August, 1995.
6. Prakash Singh, "Police Reforms Cannot take place in a Vacuum", *The Indian Express*, 8 August, 1996.
7. S. Subramanian, "Depoliticising the Police", 11 June, 1996.
8. Ved Marwah, "Using, Misusing Police for Partisan Ends Law Enforcer, Yes; Law Unto Itself, No", *The Tribune*, Friday, 13 March, 1998.

# 43

# Morale, Motivation and Job Satisfaction Affecting Human Resource Management

*Simmi Agnihotri*

## Introduction

This period is a period of change in management practices. Organisation have to be more competitive to meet the challenges from international competitors, tough economic conditions, macroeconomic reforms and restructure of management practices. In particular organisations in the public sector, banking and information technology (IT) industries have experienced these pressures and have restructured their management practices in order to complete more successfully. To manage change successfully, these organisations have placed an emphasis on linking their human resource (HR) strategies with organisational strategies. The importance placed on people issues in organisational strategies is consistent with the resource based view of the firm

The globalisation phenomenon has led to the emergence of the "survival of the fittest" syndrome all over. Probably, never in the history of global business such a keen sense of competition was noticeable among the corporates. It is now increasingly being realised that machines, technologies and systems have only limited competitive potential. And, uncertainty in the business environment is simply chaotic. Technological innovations are no more of strategy importance, even as they are a fundamental necessity. It is believed that human resource is the only factor in the value creation process, which has immeasurable growth potential and is being viewed as the most critical to competitive success. Thus has emerged the subject of human resource management (HRM) virtually replacing the tradition of personnel management (PM) and industrial relations (IR). HRM envisages that human capital is capable of being further enhanced by developing competencies and managing them proactively. The HRM area has assumed critical and strategic importance in corporate success. Moreover HR practices are emerging to cope with the new workplace realities.

### Organisation Effectiveness through HRD

> Other thing being the same, an organisation that has competent, satisfied, committed and dynamic people is likely to do better than an organisation that scores low on HRD outcome variables. In the same way, an organisation that has better HRD climate and processes is likely to be more effective than an organisation that does not have them. It is stressed that HRD outcome variables are a step closer to organisations effectiveness. This relationship is depicted in a model linking HRD instruments processes and outcomes and organisational effectiveness.
>
> —*Indian Journal of Industrial Relations*, vol. 36, p. 102, July 2000

It is believed that psychological contract between the new entrants and the organisations needs to be built right from the day one of their entry into the organisations. The probability and potential for growth depends on the aptitude, resourcefulness, integrity, coverage and dedication of men at all levels.

### Strategic HRM

The use of strategic HRM is a function of factors such as:

1. Size of the organisations.

2. Overall sophistication in the use of business planning.
3. Involvement of HR managers in the business planning process.
4. Intensity of research and development activity.
5. Stability of the organisation employment.

A number of factors that influence the extent of strategic integration within the organisations were identified:

1. The ability of HRM to get policies in place.
2. The role of the senior HRM executive.
3. The support of top management for strategic HRM.
4. The existence of a strategic mindset within the HRM function.

**1. *The ability to get HRM policies in place***

To be effective, the HRM department must improve its profile within the organisations. This can be done by customising its services to other line department and effective delivery of the products and services.

**2. *The role of the senior HRM executive within the organisations***

The presence of the senior HRM managers in the top management team is not the only reason for success in the organisations but the participation of the HRM executive as an active business partner within their organisation must also be achieved.

Human resources as basically defined, cover both quantitative and qualitative aspects. While quantitative aspect refers to the members involved, the qualitative aspect encompasses attributes such as initiatives enterprise capacity for sustained work, interests and attitudes towards work which have a direct correlation with output and productivity and as such these contributes towards economic growth. Viewed in this manner, human resource is an adjunct of capital investment and these together have the potential to help the process of growth of the country. An imaginative human resource development strategy would contribute substantively to the objectives of the Seventh Plan, viz., food, work and productivity. While productivity would be helped by the fuller utilisation of capacities created in the facts of production, the other two objectives, viz., food and work would be faciliated by the creation of additional employment and better compensation to employment through productivity investments.

## What is HRM?

HRM is the term increasingly used to refer to the philosophy, policies, procedures and practices related to the management of people within an organisation. The term p.m. as perhaps modern P.M.—means the same thing.

A broad based view of human resources management has great practical value. With such a perspective, it is possible to understand the interrelations of all human resource management activities and to appreciate how they contribute to the overall success of an organisation. Within the organisations, such an awareness increases the effectiveness with which human resources are used to achieve desired outcomes that benefit employees and the organisations in which they work. According to the process systems view, human resource management is the systematic planning, development and control of a network of interrelated process affecting and involving all members of an organisation. These processes include:

1. HR Planning.
2. Job and work design.
3. Staffing.
4. Training and development.
5. Performance appraisal and review.
6. Compensation and reward.
7. Employee protection and representation.
8. Organisation improvement.

To effectively manage these processes, human resource systems are planned, developed and implemented through the combined efforts of all managers and human resource specialists—and frequently all employee—in an organisations. Overall the systems are intended to achieve organisation-wide goals and contribute to organisational effectiveness and productivity.

How do we motivate our employees? How can we get people to do a better job? Why did she quit? Why is he so upset? Questions like these and the answers arrived at by management underline many all the personal policies and practices in a given organisation. But the reality is that asking these questions is far easier than answering them.

The success or failure of an organisation depends, to a great extent upon the administrative capability, morale and motivation of its top leadership. Work is highly complex phenomena in our present stage of technological development. To understand work, we need to recognise this rather than assume an oversimplified push-button concept. Work may be a task, a duty, or an accomplishment. It may be a mental, physical or both. It may be a repetitive or creative. Its end product is often evaluated differently by different people. In other words, work takes a different shade of meaning and most important is the intrinsic meaning that it has for the individual performance and the group with which he identifies regardless of its meaning, work cannot be considered a part from the individual who performs it. His motives, experiences and social inter-relations with his family, company and community must always be considered.

Most workers find work as a social thing. It occurs in the presence of others and occupies much of working life. The spirit and willingness with which that work is done constitute job morale. Without high morale, work is drudgery and supervision is mere slave driving.

## The Complexity of Motivation

To understand the employee and employer effectively, we must start with a knowledge of the complexity of motivation and the ways in which motive differs for different people. Age, education, marital status and the host of personal character also contribute to the different meanings that certain incentives have.

An understanding of motivation will contribute knowledge to the way a person perceives his role in society. By further understanding his attitudes, job satisfaction and the way he relates to his work group we can then begin to approximate a meaningful prospective on the variety of problems confronting men in his work a day world.

The one thing that psychologists know is that an individual rarely if ever behaves or responds in a situation as a result of a single motive. They clearly recognise the complexity of human behaviour and understand that a person often does not know the true reason for his behaviour. Because of this complex behaviour, an individual is, in many instances, unpredictable.

Motivation is truly complex. Different forms of behaviour are sometime similarly motivated. A desire to be outstanding or to acquire prestige may cause one person to write an book, another may decide to achieve this by dressing effectively another by marrying well and still another by remaining single. The next person may decide to fulfil this desire by acquiring wealth.

The vocabulary of motivation is large. Such terms as motive, purpose, desire, goal, preference, perception, attitude and incentive all have their place. Regardless of the individual word applied at any given moment, a person is likely to have a number of motives, drives, incentives, desires, wishes and purposes operating at the same time. Drives and motives vary in strength not only from one individual to the next but within the same individual at different times.

One way of defining motivation is to talk in terms of a particular state of the individual—a state of imbalance—as defining a motivated person. The person is motivated to correct any such imbalance; that is, he seeks same way of obtaining relief.

## Frustration among Employees

If the structure of the work situation is such that it is not possible for an employee to select goals or to obtain goals which are necessary to satisfy his needs, then frustration-instigated behaviour is likely to occur. It is therefore, important that a system of goals or rewards be available to the employee that will be satisfactory in satisfying whatever needs he brings into the work situation. Eaten (1952) has listed seven different hypotheses about the origin of frustration in a work situation:

1. The worker is frustrated by the insignificance of his group.

2. The worker is frustrated by the absentee ownership of the production of his work.
3. The worker is frustrated by unfulfilled expectations of upward mobility which attend his labour.
4. The worker is frustrated by his lack of a defined role and by the many alternatives available in his work.
5. The worker is frustrated by the changing technology and conditions of his work.
6. The worker is frustrated by the isolation of his work within the community.
7. The worker is frustrated by the economic insecurity of his work.

### Incentives as a Motivating Force

Ever since, Taylor's time "experts" have concerted one wage incentive system after another, until there are literally hundreds of such systems. One of the most comprehensive reviews of wage incentives plans was offered by Lytle (1938), who believed that such plans were important in any cost production problem. According to him, incentive payments have two advantages:

1. an increase in production per unit.
2. an incentive in employee earning.

He believed that advantages of a properly selected well installed and ably managed wage payment plan acquire annually to employees and employers.

### Kinds of Incentives

The term incentive is used for a spurring face that is introduced as a means of achieving goal. An incentive blasters activity in the direction of the goal. An individual may introduce his own incentives, in which case they are extremely meaningful. When the incentive results in satisfaction for the employee and the achievement of the goal results in satisfaction for the employer.

Possibly the best means of understanding worker motivation is to consider the social meaning of work. In this respect short-term and long-term goals of employees and employers may affect production variously. Accordingly, giving attention to the manner in which incentives are perceived is preferable to assuming that an incentive means the same thing to all.

## Morale

Morale is a powerful driving force that plays a pivotal role in an organisation. The state of morale in any organisation can be judged by the degree of willingness its employees show towards their work. Basically, as with so many other aspects of efficiency much depends on the quality of the initial selection of staff, particularly for senior posts. But satisfaction of work is the principle factor in high morale which means that pay must represent on fair reward, the duties of the job must held the employee's interest.

The satisfaction or dissatisfaction from the job gives to the psychological problem of morale. Morale is a mental condition or attitude of individuals and groups which determines their willingness to co-operate. Good morale is defined by management, is evidenced by employee enthusiasm, voluntary conformance with regulations and others and willingness to co-operate with others in the accomplishment of organisation objectives. Poor morale is evidenced by surliness, cases of insubordination, discouragement and dislikes the job, company and associates. It is easy to recognise by observation the extremes of high or low morale.

## Concept

Morale is a state of mind, especially of persons associated with some enterprise with reference to confidence, courage, hope, zeal, etc. Good organisational morale is a condition in which individuals and groups voluntarily make a reasonable subordination of their personal objectives to the service and objectives of their organisation. Morale is the sum total of several psychic qualities which include courage, fortitude resolutions and above all confidence. It is obvious that men can perform their task only when they put their heart into their work. It is possible only when they feel inspired by the organisation, the objectives and the people they are working far. They may work what might appear as virtual miracles. If, on the other hand, the members are cold or indifferent, if not having an altogether hostile attitude towards work and the organisation, it will not prosper notwithstanding all its resources. It is, therefore, absolutely essential that the group as a whole is charged with enthusiasm about the work entrusted to it. Such zeal or enthusiasm is usually referred to as morale. It is the subjective feeling of employees. It is a continuous process that should be possessed throughout the life of the organisation.

Morale is a feeling of togetherness. There is a sense of identification with an interest in the elements of one's job, working conditions, fellow workers, supervisions, employer and company. Good employee morale is the mental attitude of the individual or of the group, which enables the employees to realise that the maximum satisfaction of his drives coincide with the fulfilment of the objectives of the organisation. Feeling, emotions and motives combine to provide certain attitude and behaviour on the part of the individual, which in term represents the employee's morale.

Morale is a feeling, zeal or enthusiasm. If employees appear to feel enthusiastic and optimistic about group activities, if they have a sense of mission about their job, if they are friendly with each other, they have high morale. If they seem to be a dissatisfied, irritated cranky, critical restless and pessimistic, they are having low morale.

Morale is the subjective feeling of the employees. The morale of the group is said to be high when the group shows an attitude of satisfaction. Morale is said to be good in group when each employee in that group believes that satisfaction of their needs are mutually dependent. High morale is confident spirit of wholehearted co-operation in a common effort while low morale generates an attitude of apathy non-involvement and non-cooperation.

Since morale is fundamentally the result of good human relations, its promotion is the primary responsibility of the management. High morale assists the management to overcome several problems. It also helps seek co-operation of the workers in the running of the organisation and thus getting higher production at minimum possible cost by reducing the wastage of time, man, machines and materials. It is in other sense as index of good industrial relations. The management has also recognised the importance of high morale and realised that low morale has long range effects, which are even more damaging to the organisation.

### Improving Morale

The effective functioning of any organisation depends more than anything else upon the co-operative action of its employees. Co-operative action of employees further depends upon the amount of satisfaction and morale they are driving from the job, they are performing. If employees in an organisation are not satisfied with their job and possessing a low morale, that organisation can never function properly. Whereas, high morale of an employee can make an organisation function properly even under adverse circumstances. Whenever something is found to be wrong with the workers, it is obvious that there must be same cause of this situation. In such cases, a three-fold action must be initiated. In the first step, it is essential to change the policy or to correct it immediately. Employees do not loose their respect for the boss, who admits his mistakes, but they cannot respect one who makes too many and they may have contempt for one who refuses to admit his mistakes. Second step, misconception should be removed and the correct position should be explained to the employees. Third, a reasonable attempt should be made to educate and convince the employees.

It is the sole responsibility of the management to take various steps to raise the morale of its employees to achieve the objectives of the organisation. Such measures like sound wage structure, security of job, sound promotion policy, grievance procedures, recognition, employee counselling, joint consultation, delegation of authority, etc.

Any organisation, however, cannot achieve common goal without effective utilisation of human resources. There must be a rational and effective blending of material and human resources to accomplish the basic objectives of an organisation.

### Job Satisfaction

Modern society is an organisational society. In this sense,

industry is also a social institution. Human resource is one of the most important and precious of all the resources on the earth and work is related with the fulfilment of the human needs. Job satisfaction is mainly based on the needs of the individual, the stronger the needs the more closely does job satisfaction depends upon its fulfilment. Work forms an essential part of human life and occupies too much of a man's life and the satisfaction and dissatisfaction with the job assigned can affect the individual in every walk of life.

Human being needs to occupy his life with same array of mental and physical activity and certainly, work is not the only means of satisfying this need, yet many men spend nearly half of their working hours. As in materialistic world nowadays; man has to meet the multifarious problems in his life. So, whatever he earns by the job is not necessary will be fulfilling his desires and needs. If an individual is not satisfied with the working conditions, office atmosphere, having no cordial relation with fellow employees as well as with the management, lack of promotional assurances, etc., there can never be job satisfaction in an organisation.

Job satisfaction is combination of psychological, physiological and environmental circumstances that, causes a person truthfully to say, "I am satisfied with my job". In a similar way job satisfaction has been defined as an attitude which results from a balancing summation of many specific likes and dislikes experienced in connection with the job. These evaluations may rest largely upon one's own success and failure in the achievement of personal objectives and upon the perceived contribution of the job and company towards these ends.

It can be stated that work forms an essential part of human activity. Work occupy so much of a man's life span that the satisfaction or dissatisfaction with it could affect the individual considerabley in all walks of life.

## Concept

Job satisfaction is, of course, basically an individual matter. Individuals look for these aspects of jobs which are related to their own value systems, some placing greater value on, say security, others as income, and some on the type of work, etc. But, while individuals vary in their sets of value, there some-times is at least moderate consistency in the values of individuals within specific groups. It should be added incidentally, that the values are subjected to at least moderate change depending upon economic, social and other influences.

Job satisfaction is the employees judgement of how well his job on the whole is satisfying his various needs. Job satisfaction depends upon the performance of work and emotional aspects of individuals experience towards the job. Job satisfaction is the perception an internal responses, i.e., feeling, etc. It is pleasurable or positive emotional state resulting from the appraisal of one's job as job experience.

As human beings, members of work-oriented organisation have thoughts and feelings which strongly influence their behaviour on the job. These thoughts and feelings are part of their conscious state and provide the inputs used by them to make decisions about their actions and reactions to their job. Job satisfaction is a specific subject of attitudes held by organisation members. It is the attitude one has towards his or her job. It is one's effective response to the job. General criteria seem important in the determination of levels of worker's job satisfaction:

1. The organisation itself.
2. The nature of work.
3. Level of the morale of the personal.
4. The supervision received.
5. The perception of self.
6. Workers perception of the past awards and future opportunities for rewards.
7. The employee's age.
8. The employee's educational level and occupational level.

Job satisfaction is a must and every organisation should make an effort to provide the facilities to personnel working there. If the employees are satisfied with their job and conditions are favourable the workers morale will naturally be high and they will feel a sense of satisfaction. The impact of work on man cannot be denied. It operates as a great stabilising, integrating, ego satisfying, central influence in the pattern of each persons life. If job fails to satisfy these needs of the individual, it is problematic whether man can find adequate substitutes to provide a sense of significance and achievement purpose and justification for his life. So every organisation should enquire about the factors that are associated with job satisfaction or dissatisfaction among their employees. If the employees will not feel secure and independent, working conditions are not better, it can never be presumed that employees will be satisfied in their respective duties. So, it is very important and essential for the smooth growth of the organisation.

To conclude with, it is very clear with the concepts of motivation, morale and job satisfaction that HRM techniques cannot be effective. Because, it is the employee only who will accept the policies and processes of HRM. If the same class is not satisfied with their job, automatically it will lead to low morale. If they will not be motivated towards their job, they cannot gain satisfaction. Thus all these processes are interrelated and interdependent.

## REFERENCES

1. Wendell French, *Human Resources Management*, 3rd edn. 1997, All India Publishers and Distributors.
2. John W. Newstrom and Keith Davis, *Organizational Behaviour, Human Behaviour at Work*, 10th edn., 1998, Tata McGraw Hill.
3. Yoder Dale, *Personnel Management and Industrial Relations*, 6th edn. 1972, Prentice Hall of India.
4. Norman R.F. Maier, *Psychology in Industry*, 3rd edn. 1965, Oxford and IBH Publishing Co. Milton L. Blum and James C. Nayi, *Industrial Psychology*, Harper International Ed. Harper and Row Publishers.
5. Fisher, Schoenfeldt, Show, *Human Resource Management*, 3rd edn. All India Publishers and Distributors.
6. Ph.D. Research Work.

# 44

# Sustainable Development: Gandhian Perspective

*Saroj Malik*

It has been universally recognised that development is the key to meet peoples' need and to improve the quality of life. Though the idea of development has dominated human thought for centuries, but it became a general human concern only after the industrial revolution. Most of the theories of development are based upon the assumption that industrialisation and continuous growth and technological advancement are the prerequisites for development. On the one hand, industrialisation has created an earthy utopia for the human being, by wiping out poverty, ignorance disease and illiteracy but on the other hand has contributed to smoke, pollution and suffocating the atmosphere. Man has been intervening in nature for a long time. However, the growth of industrialisation during the present century has accelerated the process of intervention to worrying levels. Human species is part of an immensly complex varigated and interrelated structure. What we sow in terms of industrial pollution, we will reap from the instability of the ecosphere. If our activities interfere too radically with the working of nature, then nature might no longer be capable of providing the benefit, we now take for granted and upon which our survival depends. All ecological schools are concerned to raise questions about the limits of economic growth in industrial societies. Hence the growth oriented theories must be replaced by sustainable theories, which will not damage but will exist harmoniously with the eco-system. Thus in the backdrop of this scenario, the present paper is divided into two parts:

(i) In the first part, an effort has been made to conceptualise the sustainable development and to establish its relationship with eco-system and other systems.
(ii) In the second part an attempt has been made to explore the compatibility of sustainable development and Gandhian development. Can they meet the present crises generated by industrialisation?

## I

### *Sustainable Development: Conceptual Framework*

Sustainable Development has become a buzzword of 1990s. It refers to creating a style of economic development, which is sustainable within the context of the planet's eco-system and human society. The concept is a synthesis of economic and ecological ideas.[1] This concept is being exploited by marketing and media type. It is a collection of concepts, ecological, economic, social and political that have been put together to address what is perceived by many to be a world environmental crises. It originated as a global concern in its embryonic form for cleaning up the effluent of affluent. (Stockholm, June 1972) matured in (UNEP) and defined in (Brundtland Commission in 1987) and comprehensively reviewed and chalked out its educational programmes on training and public awareness in (Earth Summit 1992).[2]

Sustainable Development was defined "as development that meet the needs of the present without compromising the ability of future generation to meet their own needs".[3]

At the ecological level, it is designed as a science dealing with systematic relation between plants and animals and their habitat or environment. From its beginning as a science, it has had powerful and fruitful cross-disciplinary connotations. It is inter-disciplinary and has a distinct scientific character which has been of interests not only to biologist but also to zoologist, geographer, physical scientists and social scientists.

The concept of sustainable development is not only an ideology but a movement and a vision too. At the levels of ideology not in the dogmatic but pragmatic sense, it has drawn our attention to the global responsibilities and indicated that human beings are inter-related with eco-sphere. Certainly it has a clear role to play in public policy-making. Like ecology, it has a concern for nature of reality, human nature and role of human in world evaluations and assessments of the constituents of the best political, economic and social life and a set of recommendations as what ought to be done in these spheres.

At the level of movement, it suggests a way of life and active participation of all the members of society. Science and technology are not inherently wrong but if the humans do not encapsulate them in right vision, we will use them to exploit the earth and other fellow beings, we can veer away from this malaise through the recovery of the nurturing bonds that connect us to the natural world.

It is based upon a total value shift in production consumption, habits, political structure, etc. It places more emphasis on moral responsibility of the individual at personal, social, national and universal level. The vision places a heavy emphasis on the virtue of personal moral responsibility of the individual.[4]

Before explaining the futuristic vision of sustainable society, it is essential to know the place of this society in the larger ecosystem. Though there is great diversity within the ecological movement but at philosophical and political levels, two broad tendencies can be identified. The first school is known as "Light Anthropocentrists", who believe that natural world has value because human beings give it value. Their major appeal is most usually based on the importance of retaining some aspects of the environment for the benefit or survival of human beings. They work within existing institutional framework and political process. The other school is known as "Bio-centrist" or "Deep Ecologist". They do not give primary value to human individual but to the eco-sphere as a whole of which man is a part. They are also called "Eco-centric". They want to set up alternative communities based upon alternative technology and bio-regionalism. The radical wing of ecologists are called "Eco-Fascist". But one common thread which binds them together is the central theme of sustainable development which will not damage but will exist harmoniously with the Eco System.

Closely linked with sustainable society is another question, as to how to achieve it and what kind of society will emerge out of it? Two visions of futuristic society can be identified:

(i) Maximum Sustainable Society,
(ii) Frugal sustainable society.[5]

Vision of Maximum Sustainable Society is supported by anthropocentrist. They are of the opinion that though market capitalism may have been part of the problem, it can also become a part of solution. For them, development is one, which via market adjust to recycle cleaner technologies, infrastructural investment and alternative energy which is also labelled as "The New Age Capitalism."

Frugal Sustainable Society—is the economic vision of a decentralised commune of Post-industrial age. James Robertson describes this as SHE (Sane, Human, Ecological) Economy as opposed to HE (Hyper Expansionist) Economy. They believe in personal self-sufficiency and voluntary frugality. It will link human beings intimately with nature. It put faith in decentralised commune life where needs and wants are reduced to bare minimum, concept of work will significantly change. It is a vision of self-reliance, self-help, decentralisation, labour intensive localised and small-scale in terms of technology, qualitative goals of a satisfying and meaningful life are seen as more important than quantitative values.[6] Extension of workers co-operatives, wealth will be measured not just by monetary value or capital interest but also by the health and well-being of people. The informal own work to replace the concept of formal employment. Conversely the New Economics is based upon different perception of reality itself, it embodies a change in outlook as fundamental. One of the central arguments of the New Economics is that they assume that growth can go on infinitely. But in a world where resources like non-renewable fuels are finite, how can growth be infinite. Sustainability from a social viewpoint is quarterly recognised as requiring equity, freedom of individuals, community cohesion availability of jobs, maintenance of services and preservation of cultural diversity and heritage value.

The vision of sustainable order varies. One vision poses a decentralised commune, agrarian and non-state order as the ideal. The other envision a technologically sophisticated, affluent ecological state order. Paritt and winner truly depicted the picture of Eco-capitalism. They say, "All that has happened is some companies are making a lot of money causing pollution and then making even more by cleaning up some of the mess."[7] Thus eco-capitalism is seen as a classic case of double standards, offering no answer to the massive destruction of the environment by industry. Like Paritt a half-hearted deep ecologist still does not want to do away with the State. A society needs to respect ecological carrying capacity. People need to dwell in place and it needs to be human scale. It is probable that only in the small community can a man or a woman be an individual. Thus introduction of the concept of environment in the context of development is still in the process of formation. It has drawn our attention to the global responsibilities and indicated that human beings are inter-related with eco-sphere. However, it is worth pointing out a number of damaging internal disjunctions within the concept of Sustainable Development since 1970s. While the fact of global environment deterioration is widely recognised, it is in many instances incremental. Its levels have yet to have disastrous consequences for most of the globe's present human inhabitants.

Due to its political origin the application of Sustainable Development tends to be the process oriented and bypass economics. It often starts with a political view and ends with codification of production processes without resort to economics in either the decision-making as its application. Tokar mentions of bio-region. They not only link social economic and political life with natural entity but also link the human beings instrumentally with nature. These small scale communities would be characterised by grass-roots participatory as opposed to representative democracy. The idea of decentralised public participatory assembly meeting within bio region to decide on policy appears as the central feature. This will be a totally egalitarian Post Patriarchal society envisages an eco-empire. But whether this overarching state will be democratic or authoritarian is not clear. Coming over to the second part of the paper, an attempt will be made to explore the compatibility of Sustainable Development with Gandhian Development.

## II

Though the concept of Sustainable Development is the outcome of 1970s. But Gandhi warned about the havoc created by industrialisation in his book *Hind Swaraj* in 1909. External pressures generated by over-exploitation of natural resources, consumerism, rapid growth of population and change in the production pattern caused by new technology have primarily been responsible for pollution and environmental degradation. Industrial development is no answer to environmental problems, they can provide temporary success but they cannot provide lasting solutions. He mentions, we need a development which is free from external dichotomies arisen out of environment degradation, economic disparities and social tensions. Environment protection and economic development "both reinforce each other. Environment quality is itself part of the improvement in welfare that development attempts to bring. Environment damage can undermines future productivity, soils that are degraded, ozone layer which is depleted and the ecosystems that are destroyed in the name of rising income today can jeopardise the prospects for earning tomorrow.[8]

Though he was not a system builder, but he had a scheme of concepts on the basis of which a most appropriate model of sustainable development could be built. There is no finality in the Gandhian approach. He himself kept on modifying, elaborating and enriching his own concepts on the basis of his experience.[9] He attempted to evolve a comprehensive system which denounce both capitalism and bureaucratic statism. His sustainable development was a holistic paradigm which lays stress on all round development of individual and society in harmony with nature. On the pillars of truth and non-violence, he erected a moral, social, economic and political structure. His entire thinking was based on the ethical vision in which individual had the central position. Material progress beyond the requirement of the satisfaction of basic needs and comforts leads to the deterioration in the inner self of man. He stated that, "If inward change is achieved, outward change takes care of itself."[10]

The individual as perceived in the Western society is self-centred entity, separated from each other by the motive of selfishness. False needs are superimposed on the individual by social interests of the capitalists. Excessive pursuit of wealth makes a monster of man. The greater the possession of riches, the greater was the moral turpitude.[11] Real development is moral.

He believes the nature of environment is dynamic holistic, which continually underwent change. Whole universe is interconnected, inter-related and interdependent. The physical bodies of all creatures, human beings, birds, animals and plants are composed of five great elements (*panch mahabhutas*), that is earth, water, fire, sky and wind. No one is an island, we are interwoven in the intricate tapestry of life. Cause of our civilizational crisis lies in our disconnectedness with nature. Bateson has referred to this alarming individualism as the epistemological error of Western civilization. Berry and Brain Swimme have attempted to build a new cosmo-vision through integrating evolutionary theory and a spirituality of connectedness with the earth and the universe. David Abram mentions, we are human only in contact and conviviality with what is not human. Our humanity can be completed only through a sensuous and fulfilling relationship with nature.[12] Suchumacher the proponent of sustainable development emphasised on meeting human need and caring for the environment. This would be a society where energy would come from renewable sources like the sun and wind and all non-renewable energy would be conserved and recycled technologies would be appropriate not harmful.

The rise of modern technology has assumed the shape of large-scale machinery with the result that its production requires large functions. Naturally those who can undertake to finance the production of such a large technology control it. Thus power and control tend to be concentrated in the hands of financier. Such a concentration of economic power in the hands of few is bad, because it leads to the process of exploitation and alienation. Gandhi stated that "Concentration of wealth should not be in the hands of few but in the hands of all. Today machinery merely helps a few to ride on the back of millions."[13] Any mechanism may be misused, but if it is, the moral evil is in the man, who misuse it not in the mechanism.[14]

He comes very close to the ideal of *Vasudhaiva Kutumbkam*—

the whole universe is the family. His principle of non-possession was designed both to create a quick rate of growth and full employment, less on the basis of individual profit incentives and more on the basis of joint efforts and community advantage. His ideas of bread labour trusteeship and *charkha* are answer to modern civilization. *Charkha* stood for a new lifestyle, a non-exploitative economy and technology which could be controlled by human being. A judicious shift from a "consumer society" to a "conserver society" seems to be the demand of modern age.[15] One may argue that the origin of the present global crises does not stem from inherent human weakness or human evil. The roots lie in a serious defect of vision that allows us to be callous to the earth and fellow human beings. He was of the opinion that there is enough in this world for everyone's need but there is nothing in this world for anyone's greed.

At political level, he dismissed liberal democracy as a fish market. He believed that consensus was the basis of Good Government and dissent is the oxygen of democracy. He believed in the qualitative and not quantitative aspect of democracy. He pleaded for decentralisation of power in society. He believed that power resides in the people. He visualised Swaraj at the individual level, Gram Ganraj at the local level and Sarvodya at global level. He pleaded for decentralisation of power in society and gave the concept of "oceanic circle". In his political set-up village was to be made nucleus of all life. Village should be economically self-supporting and politically self-governing. He stressed on moral values in politics.. For him, there is no politics bereft of religion, but religion for him is the identification with the universe and with the service to all. He had given for post-Independence India the process of knitting the nation and people as communities living in harmony, where each one would have been able to complement the life of the other and serve the nation with a spirit of true voluntarism. He had a very valid logic behind this thinking.

For Gandhi all activities of man constituted an indivisible whole. But today we dichotomise life into exclusive compartments of politics, economics, society and religion, which are devoid of morality. There is a lack of harmony between man and man, class and class, nation and nation and between man and nature. Consequently our present miseries are mainly due to lack of a holistic approach. When all life is one and whole universe including everybody is the manifestation of God, then why these petty conflicts should arise? Absolute truth justifies man's being, consequently devotion to truth is the sole justification for our existence.[16] The entire cosmos is co-operative. The sun, the moon and the stars live together as a co-operative. The same is true for humans, animals and trees, and the earth. When we realise that the world is a mutual, interdependent, co-operative enterprise, then we can build a noble environment. If our lives are not based on this truth, then we shall perish, only the common spiritual field of our inter being with the natural world can give us the fulfilment necessary to distance outselves from the over-determination of material and technological props.

The future of global understanding and co-operation may be in these endeavours. The idea of inter-connection and interdependence of all creatures, holistic view of development, mutual co-operation as a way to sustainable development of which the world community is talking today—have already been focused and incorporated in Gandhian philosophy.

It can therefore, be concluded that the growth models based on conserver philosophy will be suitable for environmentally sustainable development and developing such models is a big task as well as a challenge before all humanity. Despite their widespread promotion by many different and politically diverse groups throughout the twentieth century, it is accidental conjunction of circumstances, individuals and events in the 1970s has provided a dynamic reforms for the ecological vocabulary. Think globally and act locally in a world that has shrunk metamorphically into a village because of communication technologies and global economies. Future of Sustainable Development lies somewhere between the two extremes acting as a pure and good conscience for environmentalism which has become a part of the developmental policies of the present-day nation states. It will continue to play an active role in the environment movements throughout the globe. Because of the economic growth, environmental nexus, the future of all countries industrial and agrarian are inextricably linked together.

Gandhiji's ideas and Sustainable Development are closely linked with each other. Interpretations may be different but they are alike in essence and form. Like an old reformer, he did not systematise his ideas. No one should be misled into believing that his actions were sporadic or merely contextual unsupported by vision or thought. He himself said, "The root of all actions is in thought. Right action has its roots in right thoughts. Thought is never complete unless it finds expression in action and action limits your thought."[17] His philosophy is contained in politics and politics is praxis. Praxis in turn is unity—a unity of theory and practice, thought and action, subjective and objective arrived at dialectically. It is only when there is a perfect accord between the two that there is full natural life. In his life precept and practice went hand in hand that is why he said. My life is my message.

## REFERENCES

1. Ron Moore & Jan Ryan, *Sustainable Development Policy and Practice*, New Age International Publishers, New Delhi, 1995, p. 2.
2. Global concern regarding the steadily deteriorating state of the environment was first seriously manifested in the form of the United Nations Conference on Human Environment held in Stockholm in June 1972. It led to the establishment of the United Nations Environment Programme (UNEP). The World Commission on Environment and Development (Brundtland Commission was established in Dec. 1983 and it presented in 1987 a remarkable report "Our Common Future". The report was extensively debated in the UN in 1989 led to the UN Conference on Environment and Development better known as Earth Summit 92 at Rio De Janeiro, Brazil in June 1992. At this conference, a comprehensive educational programme including training and public awareness was chalked out. The role of universities was discussed at Conference on University Action for Sustainable Development held at Dalhousie Univ., Halifax, Canada in Dec. 1991.
3. *Ibid.*, p. 3.
4. Andrew Vincent, *Modern Political Ideology*, Blackwell, USA, 1992, p. 227.
5. D. Pirages (ed.), *Sustainable Society: Implications for Limited Growth* Prager, N.Y., 1977, pp. 162-63.
6. Andrew Vincent, op.cit., pp. 233-34.
7. *Ibid.*
8. Narayan Prasad, "Development Philosophy of Gita", *Gandhi Marg*, vol. 18, no. 4, Jan-March, 1977, p. 471.

9. J.D. Sethi, *Gandhi Today,* Vikas Publishing House, New Delhi, 1978, p. x.
10. *Collected Works of Mahatma Gandhi*, vol. 34, Publication Division, Govt. of India, New Delhi, p. 506.
11. D.G. Tendulkar, *Mahatma Gandhi: Life of M.K. Gandhi,* vol. 1, Jhaveri K., Vithalbhai, Bombay, p. 236.
12. *The Hindu,* 8 April, 2001.
13. M.K. Gandhi, *Hind Swaraj or Indian Home Rule,* Navjivan Publishing House, Ahmedabad, 1938, p. 8.
14. *Ibid.*, p. 7.
15. P.L. Dhar and R.R. Gaur, "Technology and the Crises in the West", *Gandhi Marg,* vol. 7, no. 10, Jan. 1986, p. 681.
16. *Harijan,* December 24, 1938.
17. *Collected Works of Mahatma Gandhi,* vol. 3, p. 426.

# 45

# Peoples Participation in Family Planning Programme: A Study of Role of Voluntary Organisations

*Hiteshwar Singh Thakur & S.S. Chauhan*

## Introduction

Population explosion is one of the critical issues in India as in many other developing countries. The pressure of population growth is adversely affecting the national development efforts and acting as a deterrent to structural changes in the economy. The problem of rapid population growth is one of the most serious problems confronting mankind and it has gradually assumed frightening proportions. The history of the growth of world population from the early beginnings of homo sapiens up to the recent times can only be based on speculation because evidence in support of it is quite scanty. Even for the present times, it is difficult task to arrive at a reliable estimate of the world population and the population of its various regions. The population growth prior to 1650, the human race had increased at a very slow pace. The population started increasing fairly rapidly from 1650 onwards, the rate of population growth increasing from 0.1 per cent to 0.6 per cent per year.

The world population had started increasing rapidly in the

twentieth century and the annual rate of growth had also increased consistently except from the period 1940-50. During the period 1900-50, the average annual rate of world population growth was 0.8 per cent. The rate rose to 1.9 per cent during 1950-70, that is more than twice the rate in the earlier period. The population in the developing countries increased rapidly with the annual growth rate of 2.22 per cent. The rate of growth in developed countries was also increasing at the average rate of 45 per cent, lower than that in developing countries. An important change in the growth rate of world population has been observed during 1965-75. The average annual rate of growth has begun to show down reversing the longstanding trend of accelerating growth rate. While the average annual rate of population growth during 1960-65 was 1.9 per cent, the highest ever recorded in the world the recent data indicate that this rate was 1.84 for the period 1970-75, a decline of 0.15 points. This may be taken as a hopeful sign and should be considered an important landmark in the history of world population growth.

An increase in the population of a country is ascertained by only three factors, fertility, mortality and migration. For the growth of population in India migration has never been an important factor. The contribution of other two factors, fertility and mortality, has therefore to be considered.

India is the most populous country in the world. According to the 1981 census, the population of India was 685 million and in 1991 census it is 84,39,30,861 million and further expected to cross 100 billion by 2001. The population of India is next only to that of People's Republic of China. The density of population in India according to census of 1981 was 21 persons per square kilometre and has increased from 267 persons per square kilometre in 1991 to 324 in 2001. The other contributory factor to the growth of India's effective widespread family planning programme particularly among the rural population.

In December 1970, parliament passed the bill to make Himachal Pradesh a full-fledged state. The population of Himachal Pradesh which was 19,20,294 according to 1901 census and has increased according to 1981 census to 42.81 lakh and further increased 51.71 lakh according to 1991 census and in the current census the population has crossed 60 lakh mark

(17.53 per cent increase). The density of population in 1901 was 35 square kilometre has increased in 1981 to 77 square kilometre and according to 1991 census it reached to 93 square kilometre and at present it has increased to 109 persons per square kilometre. The decline in birth rate in 1991 reached to 28.4 per thousand and death rate up to 8.9 per thousand and infant mortality rate is 75 per thousand. There is a 20.79 per cent decennial growth rate in population in Himachal Pradesh according to 1991 population census. During 1981-95 the decennial rate of growth of population in Himachal Pradesh was 20.79 per cent, whereas, it was 23.71 per cent during 1971-81.

## Concept of Family Planning

The Government of India has started Family Planning Programme in 1952 as an integral part of the socio-economic development of the country. It is a national programme and India has received aid from several parts of the world for the adoption of this programme. All kinds of devices have been used and the efforts is to approach all eligible couples to accept any of them.

Since April 1966 a separate department of Family Planning Programme has been constituted at the centre to give proper directions and to effect coordination of the various facets of the Family Planning Programme at the centre as well as the state. Voluntary organisations are encouraged to undertake Family Planning Programme work and are given full support. In the programme of family planning, the stage has come where there is need to take stock of the achievements and limitations, review the strategy, and evolve new ways to give the programme a greater push and drive in order to achieve the objectives.

Himachal Pradesh is passing through demographic phase which is marked by a fairly high fertility and moderate mortality. According to the Sample Registration System (SRS) the provisional birth rate of H.P. for the year 1999 is 23.8 per thousand, death rate is 7.3 per thousand and infant mortality rate is 62 per thousand.

## Need for People's Participation

India has a great tradition in voluntary work. The tragedy is that after four decades of planning, the role of voluntary action is yet to be understood. Community participation in health care system is regarded as a fundamental and essential prerequisite. The purpose of community participation is clear and genuine. After four decades of building the physical infrastructure for health care, training and developing manpower of various categories, and generating the medical knowledge and technology for health services, the government health services have failed to provide basic health care to a large section of the country's population. The measures taken for population control so far have met with partial success. On the positive side, the programme has been able to remove, by and large, the inhibitions in the minds of the people and now they come forward to discuss family planning methods. On the other hand, the family planning programme has not yet become a people's programme so that it could be sustained on its own, counting on people's initiative. The family planning programme has suffered from the same defects as other programmes, like top-down approach, target orientation and lack of people's participation. In order to convert family planning programme into a people's programme, it is necessary to take local communities into confidence so that they are sufficiently motivated to prepare their own plans, fix their own targets and operationalise the plan with the help of government functionaries. In this scheme of things, the role of government functionaries gets restricted to motivation of community and providing support in terms of supply of knowledge and information. They have to act as facilitators or enablers in participatory management of family planning programmes. They have to concentrate or make efforts to maintain the participatory character of the programme ensuring participation of all sections of society without exception.

However, it is clear that people's participation requires a forum or an institution which makes participation as well as the programme sustainable. Development of local institutions to mobilise the community and to build its own capability for management of the programme is therefore a necessary condition to make it acceptable to majority of members. It is the community's own organising capability which can be utilised in not only solving the current problems but also in developing sufficient confidence to meet the future challenges.

### Need for Greater Involvement of NGOs

The increased collaboration between the government and the NGOs will be able to give correct image to the programme that it is for the overall welfare of the people. The NGOs can help make this programme community's programme. Though this has been the realisation all through because of rich tradition of voluntary action in India it was the Fifth Five Year Plan (1974-79) which included a specific programme for the promotion of voluntary schemes and social action programmes through the provision of financial assistance directly to the NGOs and to the State Governments for this purpose. The effects had been made to involve voluntary agencies in various developmental programmes. The potential of NGOs in health and family welfare sector has been well recognised. The government has shown increasing commitment in their involvement the decision on their extensive involvement has been taken at the highest level. The efforts is to make family welfare activity as people's programme with support of government, from its present status where it is a government programme with some support of people. There is a need to introduce basic changes in the policy regarding involvement of NGOs in the programmes.

1. Decentralisation so that local officials are given flexibility to operate the programme as per needs of the local people and the area.
2. Greater collaboration between government and the local NGOs so that harnessed for increasing acceptance of this programme.
3. Strengthening the monitoring system so that all components of the programme are continuously monitored an corrective measures are taken to rectify the problems.

The government of India has made some efforts to involve NGOs in the programme. Several grants-in-aid schemes have been initiated whereby NGOs could get funds from the government to promote health and family welfare activities in the area of their operation. Such schemes exist both for the organisations working with health units and those working with the community.

### Reasons for Inadequate Involvement of NGOs

There are following reasons which reflects collaboration between government and NGOs:

1. Large proportion of the NGOs are not familiar with government grants-in-aid schemes.
2. There is too much rigidity in the schemes and therefore experience of NGOs could not be utilised effectively. Too much interference of government in the funded schemes which affect flexibility and innovativeness of NGOs.
3. The application procedures for grants is reported to be very lengthy and cumbersome. Processing is slow, release of grants are often delayed and there is no response to their correspondence and enquiries.
4. There is a need to develop a mechanism so that monitoring and release of grant may not too far from them.
5. There is a need to change attitude of government officers at local level towards NGOs. They are no supportive role of NGOs to promote family planning programme.

### Role of NGOs to Promote Family Planning Programme

1. To bridge the gap between the officials and the public.
2. To educate the public to make family planning as much the need of the individual as it is a national need.
3. To break through the wall of superstitions and traditions.
4. To remove doubts and soft-pedal the resistance of non-responsive groups.
5. To make available supervisory staff when needed.
6. To utilise propaganda material properly.
7. To act as stockist for contraceptives.
8. To organise clinical service where there is none.
9. To take the services and the message of family planning to the doorsteps of the people especially in backward areas and tribal areas.
10. To make family planning a priority programme among their activities.
11. To conduct seminars and camps.

12. To create public opinion on the need of social reforms connected with family planning like raising of the age of marriage etc.
13. To coordinate the expert service of the officials with that of honorary workers and make it integrated with welfare programmes.
14. To reach the most vulnerable section of the society—the women.

## Role of Panchayats and NGOs in Family Planning Programme: Empirical Evidence

In order to make the family planning programme more effective, the importance of people's participation and role of gram panchayats and non-government organisations (NGOs) in the family planning programme cannot be over emphasised.

The present study highlights the people's participation in promoting family planning programme of sampled respondents from two districts i.e. Kangra and Mandi in Himachal Pradesh (on the basis of highest population). The present data on some of salient characteristics of Gram Panchayats, Mahila Mandals and Yuvak Mandals which formed the sample of the present study.

## Educational Status

Data relating to literacy and education in respect of sampled members of Panchayats. Mahila Mandals, and Yuvak Mandals were collected through the questionnaire is given in Table 1.

The study revealed that 71 i.e. 44.38 per cent sample respondents out of total 160 sample members studied in the said institution and organisation were illiterate. Highest number of illiterates were found among Mahila Mandal sample respondents followed by Yuvak Mandal members. As far as literacy among sample members in said selected organisations was concerned it was found that 89 i.e. 55.63 per cent out of total 160 respondents were found literate. It comprised 46 below matric, 31 above matric and 12 graduates. No member was found possessing postgraduate or above qualification. From the study it is clear that literates in more and more numbers are participating

**Table 1: Educational Status of Members of Panchayats, Mahila Mandals and Yuvak Mandals (N = 160)**

| Educational status | Members Panchayats | | Members Mahila Mandals | | Members Yuvak Mandals | | Total | |
|---|---|---|---|---|---|---|---|---|
| | N | %age | N | %age | N | %age | N | %age |
| Illiterate | 25 | 31.25 | 28 | 70.00 | 18 | 45.00 | 71 | 44.38 |
| Below matric | 28 | 35.00 | 8 | 20.00 | 10 | 25.00 | 46 | 28.75 |
| Above matric | 19 | 23.75 | 4 | 10.00 | 8 | 20.00 | 31 | 19.37 |
| Graduate | 8 | 10.00 | | – | 4 | 10.00 | 12 | 7.50 |
| Postgraduate | | – | | – | – | – | | – |
| Total respondents | 80 | 100.00 | 40 | 100.00 | 40 | 100.00 | 160 | 100.00 |

**Table 2: Occupation-wise Distribution of Members of Panchayats, Mahila Mandals and Yuvak Mandals (N = 160)**

| Occupational status | Members Panchayats | | Members Mahila Mandals | | Members Yuvak Mandals | | Total | |
|---|---|---|---|---|---|---|---|---|
| | N | %age | N | %age | N | %age | N | %age |
| Agriculturist | 40 | 50.00 | 25 | 62.50 | 25 | 62.50 | 90 | 56.25 |
| Business | 12 | 15.00 | 2 | 5.00 | 5 | 12.50 | 19 | 11.87 |
| Labourer | 15 | 18.75 | 3 | 7.50 | 5 | 12.50 | 23 | 14.38 |
| Others | 13 | 16.25 | 10 | 25.00 | 5 | 12.50 | 28 | 17.50 |
| Total respondents | 80 | 100.00 | 40 | 100.00 | 40 | 100.00 | 160 | 100.00 |

through different community development organisations. It may be due to the expansion of education in the rural areas of Himachal Pradesh.

## Occupational Status

Table 2 depicts the occupation-wise distribution of sampled members in selected Panchayats, Mahila Mandals, and Yuvak Mandals.

It was found that agriculture was their main occupation. There were 90 i.e. 56.25 per cent out of total 160 sample respondents in said selected organisations/institutions followed by manual labourers i.e. 23 (14.38 per cent). Business was found as their occupation among 19 sample respondent members. Lastly there were 28 i.e. 17.5 per cent respondent members out of total 160 studied were tailors, carpenters and self-employed etc.

From the above analysis it is evident that agriculture is still the main occupation of these respondents living in rural areas. It may be further stated that due to the fact that these institutions are for the rural people, of the rural people and are run by the rural people which are engaged in community development in our country.

## Purpose of Joining

Table 3 reveals the purpose of joining the concerned organisations/institutions of sample members in selected Panchayats, Mahila Mandals and Yuvak Mandals.

The purpose of 23 respondents i.e. 14.38 per cent of the total 160 sample respondents studied in said organisations/institutions was to serve the nation. The highest number of 137 respondents i.e. 85.62 per cent out of total 160 sampled respondents in said selected organisations/institutions were found that their motive to join these organisations/institutions was to serve the people living in the rural areas. There was no member in these organisations with the purpose to gain political motive.

From the above analysis it is clear that more and more number of rural people are joining these organisations/institutions to serve the population living in rural areas.

**Table 3: Purpose of Joining Concerned Organisation/Institution (N = 160)**

| Occupational status | Members Panchayats | | Members Mahila Mandals | | Members Yuvak Mandals | | Total | |
|---|---|---|---|---|---|---|---|---|
| | N | %age | N | %age | N | %age | N | %age |
| To serve the Nation | 10 | 12.50 | 5 | 12.50 | 8 | 20.00 | 23 | 14.38 |
| To serve the society | 70 | 87.50 | 35 | 87.50 | 32 | 80.00 | 137 | 85.62 |
| To gain political motive | | – | | – | | – | | – |
| Total respondents | 80 | 100.00 | 40 | 100.00 | 40 | 100.00 | 160 | 100.00 |

**Table 4: Factor which Motivated them to join NGO (N = 160)**

| Issues | Members Panchayats | | Members Mahila Mandals | | Members Yuvak Mandals | | Total | |
|---|---|---|---|---|---|---|---|---|
| | N | %age | N | %age | N | %age | N | %age |
| Reading newspapers | 18 | 22.50 | | – | 5 | 12.50 | 23 | 14.38 |
| People motivated to join | 50 | 62.50 | 30 | 75.00 | 25 | 62.50 | 105 | 65.62 |
| After seeing it functioning in other parts of the country | 12 | 15.00 | 10 | 25.00 | 10 | 25.00 | 32 | 20.00 |
| Total respondents | 80 | 100.00 | 40 | 100.00 | 40 | 100.00 | 160 | 100.00 |

## Motivation behind Joining the Organisation/Institution

Table 4 shows the factors which motivated sample respondents to join NGO institution like; Panchayats, Mahila Mandals and Yuvak Mandals.

It was found that 23 respondents i.e. 14.38 per cent out of total 160 sample members studied in said organisations/institutions shows factors which motivate them to join these organisations/institutions after reading in the newspapers except members of Mahila Mandals. There were 105 respondents i.e. 65.62 per cent out of total 160 sample members studied in said organisations/institutions were motivated by the peoples of that areas to join these organisations/institutions followed by 32 respondents i.e. 20 per cent out of total 160 respondents were found that the factor behind joining concerned organisations/institutions in the other parts of the country.

From the above analysis it is clear now that the factor behind joining the concerned organisations/institutions is the motivation of the people of that areas, on the other hand the factor to join these organisations/institutions through newspapers and after seeing the functioning in the other parts of the country seems to be ineffective.

## Problems in Implementing Family Planning Programme

Table 5 depicts the problems faced by the sample members of Panchayats, Mahila Mandals and Yuvak Mandals in promoting small family norms.

It was found that 9 respondents that is 5.63 per cent out of total 160 sample respondents in said selected organisations/institutions were facing religion as a problem to promote the small family norms. There was 36 respondents i.e. 16.25 per cent out of total 160 respondents were facing problem of poverty among the acceptors of small family norms. It was found that 20 respondents i.e. 12.5 per cent out of total 160 sample respondents were facing problem of old age insecurity among the acceptors of small family norms. There was 31 respondents i.e. 19.37 per cent out of 160 sample respondents were facing problem of illiteracy among the acceptors of family planning programme. There was 9 respondents i.e. 5.63 per cent out of

**Table 5: Problems Faced by Members in Promoting Small Family Norms (N = 160)**

| Problems | Members Panchayats | | Members Mahila Mandals | | Members Yuvak Mandals | | Total | |
|---|---|---|---|---|---|---|---|---|
| | N | %age | N | %age | N | %age | N | %age |
| Religions | 5 | 6.25 | 2 | 5.00 | 2 | 5.00 | 9 | 5.63 |
| Poverty | 15 | 18.75 | 5 | 12.50 | 6 | 15.00 | 26 | 16.25 |
| Old age insecurity | 10 | 12.50 | 5 | 12.50 | 5 | 12.50 | 20 | 12.50 |
| Less education | 15 | 18.75 | 8 | 20.00 | 8 | 20.00 | 31 | 19.37 |
| Lack of administrative support | 5 | 6.25 | 2 | 5.00 | 2 | 5.00 | 9 | 5.63 |
| Health hazards | 5 | 6.25 | 5 | 12.50 | 3 | 7.50 | 13 | 8.13 |
| Less incentives by the government | 10 | 12.50 | 9 | 22.50 | 10 | 25.00 | 29 | 18.12 |
| Other problems | 15 | 18.75 | 4 | 10.00 | 4 | 10.00 | 23 | 14.37 |
| Total respondents | 80 | 100.00 | 40 | 100.00 | 40 | 100.00 | 160 | 100.00 |

total 160 sample respondents were facing problem due to lack of administrative support from the government in promoting the family planning programme. It was found that 13 respondent i.e. 8.13 per cent out of total 160 sample respondents were facing problem in promoting small family norms due to health hazards/standards. There was 29 respondents i.e. 18.12 per cent out of total 160 sampled respondents were facing problem due to the less incentives announced by the government to adopt family planning programme. It was found that 23 respondents i.e. 14.37 per cent out of total 160 sample respondents were facing other problems like desirability of male child, fear psychosis, complications etc.

From the above analysis it is evident that the social factors like religion, poverty, old age insecurity, illiteracy and health hazardness are the main problems faced by member of Panchayats, Mahila Mandal and Yuvak Mandal in promoting the small family norms. In addition desirability of male child, fear psychosis, complications and awareness among the adapters of family planning programme are also the problems in the way of promoting family planning. The lack of administrative support and less incentives given by the government are the other problems which the members of Panchayats, Mahila Mandals and Yuvak Mandals are facing to promote the small family norms.

## Morale of Fellow Members

Table 6 reveals the morale of fellow members of sample members in selected Panchayats, Mahila Mandals and Yuvak Mandals.

It was found that the morale of fellow members i.e. 35 respondents (21.88 per cent) out of total 160 sample respondents in said selected organisations/institutions were highly enthusiastic in promoting the family planning programme. There was 73 respondents i.e. 45.62 per cent out of total 160 sample respondents the morale fellow members was enthusiastic to promote family planning programme. It was found that the morale of fellow members i.e. 27 respondents (16.87 per cent) out of total 160 sample respondents was low in promoting the family planning programme. There was 25 respondents i.e. 15.63 per cent out of total 160 respondents gave no opinion in respect to

**Table 6: Morale of fellow members (N = 160)**

| Morale | Members Panchayats | | Members Mahila Mandals | | Members Yuvak Mandals | | Total | |
|---|---|---|---|---|---|---|---|---|
| | N | %age | N | %age | N | %age | N | %age |
| Highly enthusiastic | 15 | 18.75 | 10 | 25.00 | 10 | 25.00 | 35 | 21.88 |
| Enthusiastic | 35 | 43.75 | 20 | 50.00 | 18 | 45.00 | 73 | 45.62 |
| Low | 15 | 18.75 | 5 | 12.50 | 7 | 17.50 | 27 | 16.87 |
| No opinion | 15 | 18.75 | 5 | 12.50 | 5 | 12.50 | 25 | 15.63 |
| Total respondents | 80 | 100.00 | 40 | 100.00 | 40 | 100.00 | 160 | 100.00 |

the morale of their fellow members in promoting the family planning programme.

From the above analysis it is evident that the majority of the fellow members have very enthusiastic morale to promote this programme. There is also a percentage however of small fellow members having low morale to promote the family planning programme. Others have given no opinion about the morale of their fellow numbers.

### Methods Suggested for Adoption

Table 7 depicts the methods applied to encourage people to adopt family planning measures by sample members in selected Panchayats, Mahila Mandals and Yuvak Mandals.

It was found that 30 respondent i.e. 18.75 per cent out of total 160 sample respondents in said selected organisations/institutions were encouraged to adopt temporary methods of family planning. It comprised 13 respondents (8.13 per cent) for condoms, 13 respondents (8.12 per cent) for copper-T and 4 respondents (2.5 per cent) for contraceptive pills. There were 80 respondents i.e. 50 per cent out of total 160 sample respondents were encouraged to adopt permanent methods of family planning. It comprised 30 respondents (18.75 per cent) for sterilisation and 50 respondents (31.25 per cent) for vasectomy. It was found that 50 per cent i.e. 31.25 per cent out of total sample respondents were encouraged to adopt both methods of family planning.

From the above analysis it is evident that the sample respondents in said selected organisations/institutions are encouraging the people to adopt permanent methods to stop the population growth and also suggest them to opt temporary methods in spacing of children. The main objective is to encourage the people to adopt these methods to further control the population growth.

### Methods Applied for Motivating People to Adopt Family Planning Programme

Table 8 shows that methods applied by sample members in selected Panchayats, Mahila Mandals, and Yuvak Mandals to

**Table 7: Methods of Family Planning Programme Suggested for Adoption (N= 160)**

| Methods | Members Panchayats | | Members Mahila Mandals | | Members Yuvak Mandals | | Total | |
|---|---|---|---|---|---|---|---|---|
| | N | %age | N | %age | N | %age | N | %age |
| Temporary methods | 20 | 25.00 | 5 | 12.50 | 5 | 12.50 | 30 | 18.75 |
| (a) Condom | 18 | 10.00 | 2 | 5.00 | 3 | 7.50 | 13 | 8.13 |
| (b) Copper-T | 10 | 12.50 | 2 | 5.00 | 1 | 2.50 | 13 | 8.13 |
| (c) Pills | 2 | 2.50 | 1 | 2.50 | 1 | 2.50 | 4 | 2.50 |
| Permanent methods | 40 | 50.00 | 25 | 62.50 | 15 | 37.50 | 80 | 50.00 |
| (a) Sterilisation | 10 | 12.50 | 10 | 25.00 | 10 | 25.00 | 30 | 18.75 |
| (b) Vasectomy | 30 | 37.50 | 15 | 37.50 | 5 | 12.50 | 50 | 31.25 |
| Both methods | 20 | 25.00 | 10 | 25.00 | 20 | 50.00 | 50 | 31.25 |
| Total respondents | 80 | 100.00 | 40 | 100.00 | 40 | 100.00 | 160 | 100.00 |

motivate the people to adopt family planning programme.

There was 28 respondents i.e. 17.5 per cent out of total 160 sample respondents in said selected organisations/institutions were applying method through house visits to motivate the people to adopt family planning programme. It was found that 22 respondents i.e. 13.75 per cent out of total 160 sample respondents were applying method through private counselling to motivate the people to adopt family planning programme. There was 22 respondents i.e. 13.75 per cent out of total 160 sample respondents were applying method through general meetings to motivate the people to adopt family planning programme. It was found that 16 respondents i.e. 10 per cent out of total 160 sample respondents were motivating the people through camps to adopt family planning programme. There were 45 respondents i.e. 28.12 per cent out of total 160 sample respondents were applying methods through monetary benefits to motivate the people to adopt family planning programme. It was found that 27 respondents i.e. 16.88 per cent out of total 160 sample respondents were applying methods by assuring money and other benefits to motivate the people to adopt family planning programme. No member was found applying methods by exercising authority and through cultural activities to motivate the people to adopt family planning programme.

From the above analysis it is clear that the 88 respondents (55 per cent) out of total sample respondents are applying the methods through home visits, general meetings, and personal counselling while others are motivating through monetary and other benefits i.e. 45 per cent sampled respondents to adopt family planning programmes. Both the methods are to motivate the common masses to adopt family planning programme to avoid further increase in the population.

## Views Regarding People's Response

Table 9 reveals the response of general public regarding the efforts of sample members in selected Panchayats, Mahila Mandals and Yuvak Mandals in promoting family planning programme.

There were 54 respondents i.e. 33.75 per cent out of total 160 sample respondents were agreed with their efforts in promoting family planning programme. It was found that 40

**Table 8: Method Applied by Sample Respondents to Motivate the People to Adopt Family Planning Programme (N = 160)**

| Methods adopted for motivation | Members Panchayats | | Members Mahila Mandals | | Members Yuvak Mandals | | Total | |
|---|---|---|---|---|---|---|---|---|
| | N | %age | N | %age | N | %age | N | %age |
| Through home visits | 10 | 12.50 | 8 | 20.00 | 10 | 25.00 | 28 | 17.50 |
| Through private counseling | 15 | 18.50 | 2 | 5.00 | 5 | 12.50 | 22 | 13.75 |
| Through general meetings | 10 | 12.50 | 7 | 17.50 | 5 | 12.50 | 22 | 13.75 |
| Through family planning campaigns | 10 | 12.50 | 3 | 7.50 | 3 | 7.50 | 16 | 10.00 |
| Through cultural activities | | – | | – | | – | | – |
| Through monetary benefits | 25 | 31.25 | 10 | 25.00 | 10 | 25.00 | 45 | 28.12 |
| By exercising authority (pressure/forced) | | – | | – | | – | | – |
| Assuring money and other benefits | 10 | 12.50 | 10 | 25.00 | 7 | 17.50 | 27 | 16.88 |
| Total respondents | 80 | 100.00 | 40 | 100.00 | 40 | 100.00 | 160 | 100.00 |

respondents i.e. 25 per cent out of total 160 sample respondents were sometimes did not agree with their efforts in promoting family planning programme. There was 17 respondents i.e. 16.63 per cent out of total 160 sample respondents were agreed to adopt temporary method of family planning with their efforts. There were 27 respondent i.e. 16.87 per cent out of total 160 sample respondents agreed with their efforts to adopt permanent methods of family planning. It was found that 22 respondents i.e. 13.75 per cent out of total 160 sample respondents remained indifferent in their efforts in promoting family planning programme.

From the above analysis it is evident that large number of the respondents i.e. 61.25 per cent agreed with their efforts and ready to adopt any method either temporary or permanent and others remained indifferent and did not agree to their efforts in promoting family planning programme.

## Opinion Regarding Restriction on Non-Adopters in Democratic Institution

Table 10 reveals the opinion of sample respondent members of Panchayats, Mahila Mandals and Yuvak Mandals regarding no representation in Parliament, State Legislature and Panchayati Raj Institution to those who have more then three children.

There were 65 respondents i.e. 40.62 per cent out of total 160 sample respondents in said selected organisations/institutions strongly agree with this opinion. It was found 20 respondents i.e. 12.5 per cent out of total 160 sample respondents strongly disagree with the opinion of no representation in Parliament, State Legislatures and Panchayati Raj Institutions. There were 40 respondents i.e. 25 per cent out of total 160 sample respondents of the opinion that this should be implemented prospectively. It was found that 15 respondents i.e. 9.38 per cent of total 160 sample respondents found it undemocratic. There were 20 respondents i.e. 12.5 per cent out of total 160 sample respondents had no opinion in this regard.

From the above analysis it is evident that majority of the respondents are in favour of the opinion that those who have more than three children should not be given representation in Parliament, State Legislatures and Panchayati Raj Institutions,

**Table 9: Response of General Public Regarding Efforts in Promoting Family Planning Programme (N = 160)**

| Response | Members Panchayats | | Members Mahila Mandals | | Members Yuvak Mandals | | Total | |
|---|---|---|---|---|---|---|---|---|
| | N | %age | N | %age | N | %age | N | %age |
| Sometimes agree | 30 | 37.50 | 12 | 30.00 | 12 | 30.00 | 54 | 33.75 |
| Sometimes do not agree | 18 | 22.50 | 10 | 25.00 | 12 | 30.00 | 40 | 25.00 |
| Agree to adopt temporary methods | 4 | 5.00 | 7 | 17.50 | 6 | 15.00 | 17 | 10.63 |
| Agree to adopt permanent methods | 16 | 20.00 | 4 | 10.00 | 7 | 17.50 | 27 | 16.87 |
| Remains indifferent | 12 | 15.00 | 7 | 17.50 | 3 | 7.50 | 22 | 13.75 |
| Total respondents | 80 | 100.00 | 40 | 100.00 | 40 | 100.00 | 160 | 100.00 |

**Table 10: Opinion of Sample Respondents Regarding no Representation in Parliament, State Legislative and Panchayati Raj Institution to those who have more than three Children (N = 160)**

| Opinion | Members Panchayats | | Members Mahila Mandals | | Members Yuvak Mandals | | Total | |
|---|---|---|---|---|---|---|---|---|
| | N | %age | N | %age | N | %age | N | %age |
| Strongly agree | 40 | 50.00 | 15 | 37.50 | 10 | 25.00 | 65 | 40.62 |
| Strongly disagree | 10 | 12.50 | 5 | 12.50 | 5 | 12.50 | 20 | 12.50 |
| Should be implemented prospectively | 20 | 25.00 | 10 | 25.00 | 10 | 25.00 | 40 | 25.00 |
| Undemocratic | 5 | 6.25 | 5 | 12.50 | 5 | 12.50 | 15 | 9.38 |
| No opinion | 5 | 6.25 | 5 | 12.50 | 10 | 25.00 | 20 | 12.50 |
| Total respondents | 80 | 100.00 | 40 | 100.00 | 40 | 100.00 | 160 | 100.00 |

but it should be implemented prospectively. Other were of the opinion that it is an undemocratic norm in a democratic country.

### Opinion Regarding Governmental Aid to Institutions for Promoting Family Planning Programme

Table 11 shows that opinion of the sample members in selected Panchayats, Mahila Mandals and Yuvak Mandals regarding governmental financial aid to their organisations/institutions for propagating family planning programme.

It was found that 95 respondents i.e. 59.37 per cent out of total 160 sample respondents were of the opinion that there was no financial aid from the government to their organisations/ institutions to propagate the family planning programme. There was 35 respondents i.e. 21.88 per cent out of total 160 sample respondents were not knowing about financial aid to their organisations/institutions to propagate the family planning programme. It was found that 30 respondents i.e. 18.75 per cent out of total 160 sample respondents were of no opinion regarding financial aid to their organisations/institutions to propagate this programme.

From the above analysis it is evident that the government is not giving financial aid to these organisations/institutions to propagate the family planning programme.

### Opinion Regarding Type of Benefits/ Assistance to Institutions

Table 12 reveals the opinion of respondents of sample members in selected Panchayats, Mahila Mandal and Yuvak Mandals regarding type of benefit/assistance to their organisations/ institutions by the government to promote family planning programme.

There were 65 respondents .i.e. 40.62 per cent out of total 160 sample respondents were of the opinion that monetary benefit/assistance like cash to their organisations/institutions must be given by the government to promote family planning programme. It was found that 55 respondents i.e. 34.37 per cent out of total 160 sample respondents were of the view that

**Table 11: Opinion Regarding Governmental Financial Aid to their Respective Organisation/Institution for Propagating Family Planning Programme (N=160)**

| Opinion | Members Panchayats | | Members Mahila Mandals | | Members Yuvak Mandals | | Total | |
|---|---|---|---|---|---|---|---|---|
| | N | %age | N | %age | N | %age | N | %age |
| Yes | | – | | – | | – | | – |
| No | 50 | 62.50 | 25 | 62.50 | 20 | 50.00 | 95 | 59.37 |
| Do not know | 20 | 25.00 | 5 | 12.50 | 10 | 25.00 | 35 | 21.88 |
| No opinion | 10 | 12.50 | 10 | 25.00 | 10 | 25.00 | 30 | 18.75 |
| Total respondents | 80 | 100.00 | 40 | 100.00 | 40 | 100.00 | 160 | 100.00 |

**Table 12: Opinion of Respondent Members Regarding Type of Benefits/Assistance to their Organisation/Institution they Feel should be given by the Government to Promote Family Planning Programme (N = 160)**

| Mode of aid | Members Panchayats | | Members Mahila Mandals | | Members Yuvak Mandals | | Total | |
|---|---|---|---|---|---|---|---|---|
| | N | %age | N | %age | N | %age | N | %age |
| Monetary | 40 | 50.00 | 15 | 37.50 | 10 | 25.00 | 65 | 40.62 |
| Non-monetary | 30 | 37.50 | 10 | 25.00 | 15 | 37.50 | 55 | 34.37 |
| Award | 5 | 6.25 | 5 | 12.50 | 7 | 17.50 | 17 | 10.63 |
| Prize | 5 | 6.25 | 10 | 25.00 | 8 | 20.00 | 23 | 14.38 |
| Total respondents | 80 | 100.00 | 40 | 100.00 | 40 | 100.00 | 160 | 100.00 |

non-monetary benefits/assistance like schemes etc. must be given by the government to their organisations/institutions to promote family planning programme. There were 17 respondents i.e. 10.63 per cent out of total 160 sample respondent were of the opinion that awards such as benefits/assistance must be given to their organisations/institutions to promote family planning programme. I't was found that 23 respondents i.e. 14.38 per cent out of total 160 sample respondents were of the view that prizes such as benefits/assistance must be given to their organisations/ institutions to promote family planning programme.

From the above analysis it is clear that majority of the respondents i.e. 75 per cent are of the view that either monetary or non-monetary benefits should be given to their organisations/institutions, so that the morale of members remain high in promoting the family planning programme. On the other hand 25 per cent feels that awards and prizes can also boost up the morale of the members in promoting family planning programme.

## Opinion Regarding Running the Family Planning Programme without Governmental Assistance

Table 13 depicts the opinion regarding carrying out this programme vigorously by the sample members in selected Panchayats, Mahila Mandals, and Yuvak Mandals without the assistance of the government.

There were 113 respondents i.e. 70.62 per cent out of total 160 sample respondents were carrying out this family planning programme vigorously without the government assistance. It was found that 47 respondents i.e. 29.38 per cent were of no opinion in carrying out the family planning programme without government assistance.

From the above analysis it is evident that majority of the respondents are willing to carry out the family planning programme without government assistance.

## Attitude of Common Masses

Table 14 shows that opinion regarding any considerable change in the attitude of common masses after the efforts by sample

**Table 13: Opinion Regarding Carrying out this Programme Vigorously without Government Assistance (N=160)**

| Willingness | Members Panchayats | | Members Mahila Mandals | | Members Yuvak Mandals | | Total | |
|---|---|---|---|---|---|---|---|---|
| | N | %age | N | %age | N | %age | N | %age |
| Yes | 60 | 75.00 | 25 | 62.50 | 28 | 70.00 | 113 | 70.62 |
| No | | – | | – | | – | | – |
| No opinion | 20 | 25.00 | 15 | 37.50 | 12 | 30.00 | 47 | 29.38 |
| Total respondents | 80 | 100.00 | 40 | 100.00 | 40 | 100.00 | 160 | 100.00 |

**Table 14: Opinion Regarding any Considerable Change in the Attitude of Common Masses after their efforts in this Direction (N=160)**

| Attitude | Members Panchayats | | Members Mahila Mandals | | Members Yuvak Mandals | | Total | |
|---|---|---|---|---|---|---|---|---|
| | N | %age | N | %age | N | %age | N | %age |
| Yes | 40 | 50.00 | 20 | 50.00 | 25 | 62.50 | 85 | 53.12 |
| No | 10 | 12.50 | 5 | 12.50 | 5 | 12.50 | 20 | 12.50 |
| No opinion | 30 | 37.50 | 15 | 37.50 | 10 | 25.00 | 55 | 34.38 |
| Total respondents | 80 | 100.00 | 40 | 100.00 | 40 | 100.00 | 160 | 100.00 |

members in selected Panchayats, Mahila Mandals and Yuvak Mandals.

There were 85 respondents i.e. 53.12 per cent out of total 160 sample respondents were of the opinion that there was considerable change in the attitude of common masses after efforts of their organisations/institutions in the direction of adopting family planning programme. It was found that 20 respondents i.e. 12.5 per cent out of total 160 sample respondents were of the view that there was no change in the attitude of common masses regarding family planning programme. There was 55 respondents i.e. 34.38 per cent were of no opinion regarding any considerable change in the attitude of common masses after the efforts of their organisations/institutions in the direction of adopting family planning programme.

From the above analysis it is evident that maximum member i.e. 53.12 per cent of respondents are of the opinion that there is considerable change in the attitude of common masses after their efforts in promoting family planning programme and on the other hand 34.38 per cent respondents are of no opinion and remaining respondents have negative opinion on this issue.

## Level of Satisfaction

Table 15 shows the level of satisfaction of sample members on selected Panchayats, Mahila Mandals and Yuvak Mandals in promoting family planning programme.

There were 115 respondents i.e. 71.87 per cent out of total 160 sample respondents were highly satisfied with their performance in the field of family planning programme. It was found that 40 respondents i.e. 25 per cent out of total 160 sample respondents were satisfied with the performance in this direction. There were 5 respondents i.e. 3.13 per cent were dissatisfied with what they were doing in the field of family planning programme.

From the above analysis it is clear that maximum respondents are fully satisfied with what they have done and what they are doing in promoting the family planning programme. A few respondents are not satisfied with their performance in promoting the family planning programme.

**Table 15: Opinion Regarding their Satisfaction with what they have Done and what they are Doing in this Direction (N=160)**

| Satisfaction level | Members Panchayats | | Members Mahila Mandals | | Members Yuvak Mandals | | Total | |
|---|---|---|---|---|---|---|---|---|
| | N | %age | N | %age | N | %age | N | %age |
| Highly satisfied | 60 | 75.00 | 25 | 62.50 | 30 | 75.00 | 115 | 71.87 |
| Satisfied | 15 | 18.75 | 15 | 37.50 | 10 | 25.00 | 40 | 25.00 |
| Dissatisfied | 5 | 6.25 | | – | | – | 5 | 3.13 |
| Total respondents | 80 | 100.00 | 40 | 100.00 | 40 | 100.00 | 160 | 100.00 |

**Table 16: Views Regarding Attitude of Official Agencies towards the Efforts of Respondent Members in Promoting Family Planning Programme (N=160)**

| Views | Members Panchayats | | Members Mahila Mandals | | Members Yuvak Mandals | | Total | |
|---|---|---|---|---|---|---|---|---|
| | N | %age | N | %age | N | %age | N | %age |
| Appreciate our role | 25 | 31.25 | 18 | 45.00 | 20 | 50.00 | 63 | 39.37 |
| Do not appreciate our role | 20 | 25.00 | 5 | 12.50 | 5 | 12.50 | 30 | 18.75 |
| Indifferent about our role | 15 | 18.75 | 7 | 17.50 | 5 | 12.50 | 27 | 16.88 |
| Very keen to involve us whenever needed | 20 | 25.00 | 10 | 25.00 | 10 | 25.00 | 40 | 25.00 |
| Total respondents | 80 | 100.00 | 40 | 100.00 | 40 | 100.00 | 160 | 100.00 |

## Views Regarding Attitude of Official Agencies

Table 16 reveals the views of official agencies towards the efforts of sample members in selected Panchayats, Mahila Mandals and Yuvak Mandals in promoting family planning programme.

There were 63 respondents i.e. 39.37 per cent out of total 160 sample respondents were of the opinion that official agencies appreciated our role in promoting the family planning programme. It was found that 30 respondents i.e. 18.75 per cent of total 160 sample respondents were of the view that the official agencies do not appreciate our role in this field. There were 27 respondents i.e. 16.88 per cent out of total 160 sample respondents were of the opinion that the attitude of official agencies was indifferent about our role in promoting the family planning programme. It was found 40 respondents i.e. 25 per cent out of total 160 sample respondents were of the view that the official agencies were very keen to involve us whenever they required us in promoting family planning programme.

From the above analysis it is evident that a large number of respondent i.e. 64.38 per cent were of the view that the official agencies appreciate our role and they are keen to involve us whenever needed in promoting the family planning programme. On the other hand 35.62 per cent were of the view that the official agencies remains indifferent and do not appreciate our role in promoting the family planning programme.

## Views Regarding Role of Mass-Media

Table 17 shows the views of sample members in selected Panchayats, Mahila Mandals and Yuvak Mandals regarding role of mass media in promoting family planning programme.

There were 78 respondents i.e. 48.75 per cent out of total 160 sample respondents were of the view that the role of mass-media was excellent in promoting the family planning programme. It was found that 38 respondents i.e. 23.75 per cent of total 160 sample respondents were of the opinion that role of mass-media was very good. There were 22 respondents i.e. 13.75 per cent out of total 160 sample respondents were of the view that role of mass-media in promoting the family planning programme was good. It was found that 33 respondents i.e. 13.75 per cent out of total 160 sample respondents were of the opinion that the role of mass-media in promoting family planning programme was not up to the mark.

From the above analysis it is evident that 86.25 per cent out of sample respondents are of the view that mass-media has played a vital role in promoting the family planning programme, whereas 13.75 per cent out of sample respondents are not satisfied with the performance of mass-media in promoting the family planning programme.

## An Appraisal

Thus, after analysing the tables, it can be summarised that the educational background of the respondents is very poor, but now more and more educated people are coming forward to join such organisations/institutions. The majority of respondents are agriculturist. The ideas of respondents are to serve the society at a large, but they also wanted to serve the nation by way of joining such organisations. The large number of respondents are motivated by the people to join these organisations, but on the other have they are also inspired by the newspapers and after seeing the functioning of such organisation in the other part of the country. The majority of the respondents feel that poverty, poor education, old age insecurity, health hazards, lack of administrative support and less incentives by the government reflects the problems in promoting family planning programme even without the financial help from the government. They also encourage the common masses to adopt family planning methods through home visits, general meeting, personal counselling and monetary benefits announced by the government and it is found that majority of the people agreed to their advise, but a little percentage remains indifferent. It is a strong opinion that those who have more than three children should not be given representation in Parliament, State legislatures and Panchayati Raj Institutions and it should be implemented prospectively, but on the other hand people say it is undemocratic. Even without the financial aid to such organisations to promote the family planning programme, the

**Table 17: Views Regarding Role of Mass-Media in Promoting Family Planning Programme (N = 160)**

| Views | Members Panchayats | | Members Mahila Mandals | | Members Yuvak Mandals | | Total | |
|---|---|---|---|---|---|---|---|---|
| | N | %age | N | %age | N | %age | N | %age |
| Excellent | 40 | 50.00 | 18 | 45.00 | 20 | 50.00 | 78 | 48.75 |
| Very good | 20 | 25.00 | 8 | 20.00 | 10 | 25.00 | 38 | 23.75 |
| Good | 10 | 12.50 | 7 | 17.50 | 5 | 12.50 | 22 | 13.75 |
| Not up to the mark | 10 | 12.50 | 7 | 17.50 | 5 | 12.50 | 22 | 13.75 |
| Total respondents | 80 | 100.00 | 40 | 100.00 | 40 | 100.00 | 160 | 100.00 |

respondents are interested to carry out this programme vigorously, but they are of the opinion that some monetary or non-monetary benefits must be given to such organisations to boost their morale, so that they can promote this programme with full strength. But on the other hand the respondents feels that awards or prizes should also be given on the basis of merits of their work in the field of family planning. They also feel that there is a considerable change in the attitude of the common masses of the their efforts in this field of family planning. But the respondents are highly satisfied with what they have done or what they are doing in the field of family planning. The official agencies also appreciate their role and even they involve them whenever they need their help in implementing family planning programme. They are of the opinion that the role of mass-media is excellent, but not up to that mark as it should be.

To sum up we can say that people's participation can be initiated by the combined efforts of Panchayats, Mahila Mandals, Yuvak Mandals and Government agencies. The government should reorganise the present setup with better programmes, so that non-government organisations and Panchayats can motivate and educate the common masses to adopt the small family norms. The social, economic and political constraints also comes in the way of mass participation. Participation depends mainly on three factors, for which people need to be conscientised. Basic changes are needed in the socio-economic structure to enable the poor rural people to gain the capacity to participate. Some of the other constraints that comes in the way (i) ignorance of people about the benefits (ii) lack of information among people (iii) lack of initiative and ability to execute (iv) erroneous impression among people about this programme.

It should also be remembered that the Family Planning Programme is part of a family welfare scheme. The local bodies, Panchayats, Mahila Mandals, Yuvak Mandals, Trade Unions, Cooperatives, Professional Associations, Industrial Labour and Voluntary agencies engaged in Family Planning Programme should get together for mutual consultations from time to time and avoid overlapping of activities. The initiative should be taken by official agencies. The collaboration of Government and Non-Government agencies can only make Family Planning Programme a success.

On the back drop of above discussion it can be concluded that people's participation and cooperation can only motivate people to adopt Family Planning Programme.

## REFERENCES

Kingsley Davis, *Population of India and Pakistan,* New York: Russell and Russell, 1968.

R.A. Gopalswami, *Census of India,* 1951. Vol. 1, India Part I—A Report, p. 124.

*Economic Review,* Directorate of Economics and Statistics, Himachal Pradesh, Shimla.

Achievements under National Family Welfare Programmes, Demographic and Evaluation Cell, State Family Welfare Bureau, Shimla, 1991-92.

Achievements under National Family Welfare Programmes, Demographic and Evaluation Cell, State Family Welfare Bureau, Shimla, 1992-93, p. 9.

Ajai Paul Chandel, Unpublished Ph.D. Thesis, *Health Administration in Himachal Pradesh, A Case Study of Shimla and Chamba District,* Department of Public Administration, H.P. University, Shimla-5, p. 241.

P.N. Sharma, "Participatory Management in Family Welfare Programmes", *Yojana,* November, 1995, pp. 23-25.

Leela Damodara Menon, "Role of Voluntary Agencies in Family Planning", in V. Jagannadham (ed.) *Family Planning in India, Policy and Administration.* The Indian Institute of Public Administration, Indraprastha Estate, Ring Road, New Delhi, pp. 214-17.

Prem P. Talwar, "Policy of Greater Involvement of NGOs: Need for Concrete Measures". *The Indian Journal of Public Administration,* Vol. XXXVIII, No. 3, July-September, 1992, pp. 297-310.

Bandyopadhyay, P.K. "Population and Development", *Yojana,* Vol. 38, No. 16, September, 1994, pp. 4, 6-10.

Chandrasekhar, S., *Infant Mortality, Population, Growth and Family Planning in India.* London: George Allen and Unwin Ltd., Ruskin House Museum, Street, 1972.

Chassen, R.H., *India: Population, Economy, Society*, London and Basingstoke: The MacMillan Press Ltd., 1978.

*Economic Review.* Directorate of Economics and Statistics Department. Himachal Pradesh, Shimla, 1995.

*Family Planning Programme: Year Book (1997-98).* Demographic and

Evaluation Cell, State Family Welfare Bureau, Shimla, 1998.

*Family Planning Programme: Year Book (1993-94).* Demographic and Evaluation Cell, State Family Welfare Bureau, Shimla, 1994.

Ghosh, B., *The Indian Population Problem: A Household Economics Approach,* New Delhi, Sage Publications India Pvt. Ltd., 1990.

Goel, S.L., *Public Health Administration.* New Delhi, Sterling Publishers Pvt. Ltd., 1984

# 46

# Role of Women in Joint Forest Management in Himachal Pradesh

*Ompal Sharma*

Formerly, women were prepared for their activities in the home. Today, one of the objectives of development programmes is to train and empower women to carry out all development activities, other than subsistence activities, on the same level as man. It is vital to gear these efforts to action. This will not only help the sustainable development of forests but may also improve the standard of living of the people. This article examines the Role of the Women in Joint Forest Management in Himachal Pradesh. It identifies the issues of women's representation at institutional and the community level. The article suggests that the role of the Women in Joint Forest Management requires wider examination in Himachal Pradesh.

## Introduction

The forest resources in Himachal Pradesh are degrading fast while demand for forest products are increasing. The major factor responsible for the degradation of forests is the increasing biotic pressure. Enforcement of strict control cannot protect the forests resources to provide environmental security and cannot regenerate and improve these resources to meet the people's demand for these resources. Active involvement of people, especially the women, is imperative for the protection and development of forest resources. The last few years have witnessed several approaches tried for securing people's participation in forest resource management. Many innovative approaches have been tried with varying degrees of success in Himachal Pradesh. It has been endorsed that the major premise of community management is that local communities, especially the women have a central role in forest management. Giving responsibility of forest management to primary user group who rely on the resource base for survival over the long-term will encourage sustainable resource use practices. An argument is supported by an assertion that community management will empower local communities, secure livelihood strategies and be more equitable than other property regimes. Community management, where women play a vital role, is therefore attractive to policy-makers since it purports to integrate development and environment objectives.

## Policy Perspective

The forests of Himachal Pradesh have been governed by National Forest Policy as enunciated from time to time. The Forest Policy of 1952 and 1980 is closely followed in the management of forests in the State. It is laid down in the policy that two-third of the land area should be under forests in the Hill in our country. In H.P. about 68 per cent of the total land mass is declared as a legally classified forests. Legal control over forests of the State is affected under IFA, 1927.

## Institutional Framework

Like other parts of India, Himachal Pradesh forests from early times were conceived as a source of revenue for the rulers but open for bona-fide domestic requirements of the local communities. The foundation of organised forestry were laid down by Sir Dietrich Brandis in 1864. The three cornerstone of administration lie on Forest Policy, forest law and forest services and the basic structure of forest bureaucracy remains the same even to dates from the days of Dr. Brandis.

After independence the "Forests" was put on concurrent list through a constitutional amendment in 1980. The Ministry of Environment and Forests is now the ultimate authority in forest administration. It directly carries out recruitment, training and State-wise allocation of IFS officers and also has ultimate disciplinary control over them. It has a strict control over deforestation through Forest Conservation Act of 1980 and indirectly it influences the forest management through fund allotment and monitoring under various plan schemes. Like other States in India, Himachal Pradesh have a Pr. Chief Conservator of Forests (PCCF), who is assisted by Add. PCCF, CCFs, CFs, middle and lower level field functionaries.

### Perspective Changes

On closer inspection, there is little evidence to suggest that planners and foresters are aware of how to proceed with plans to involve women in decision-making process, either at grassroot or institutional level. There is an enormous gap between the field of gender related studies and forests, resulting in ignorance of gender issues approaches in forestry institutions. Even NGO's involved in these programmes are usually unaware of gender dimensions of their work. There is every fear that due to this lack of knowledge and skills in gender analysis and planning, the community-based projects are simply reinforcing existing gender relations without giving much thought to such impacts.

Planning to involve women in forest management at both grassroot level and institutional level cannot proceed without considering the process of internal reorientation at the institutional level. To make organisations gender-responsive, it is necessary to bridge the gap between gender issues and scientific management of forests and natural resources. This requires not recruiting more women staff and allowing their voices to be heard in senior-level decision-making forums, but also integrating the needs and perspectives of community women forum at the very inception of programme planning. So the professional women employed in male dominated institutions like forests require a more supportive working environment. So in the period of widespread global awareness of gender and development concerns, it is not sufficient for people-oriented forestry programmes to simply add a few women to their staff and users groups. They must become aware of the cost of gender-blind programming to safeguarding the State's forest resources and to the status of rural women themselves.

## Joint Forest Management

In 1990, the Ministry of Environment of Forests, Government of India complemented the 1983 policy with another government order to all States. The message was to adopt participatory forest management on degraded forest lands with communities and NGO's. This was a major shift from the early history at authoritarian forest management. This official sanction is known Joint Forest Management. This is a particular variant of community forestry in which responsibility and benefits are shared by local user groups with the government departments.

In Himachal Pradesh, the experimentation began about 25 years back when *three D forestry* was introduced. Thereafter, programmes like *Social Forestry, Van Lagao Rozi Kamao,* came into existence. *Sanjhi Van Yojna* and *Parishram Hamara Van Hamara* are the latest community forestry schemes going on in the State. Although, in all these schemes, there is a provision of women's participation yet no capacity building programme were notably fostered.

It has been argued by some foresters that women present a major problem for male field staff. Their problematic nature comprises the fact that they are often "offenders" and that they are "nearly impossible" to approach for duel reasons of their shyness and risk of accusations of sexual harassment (Raju, 1994). The policy statements regarding women's role or entitlements are narrowly conceived within Joint Forest management at the State Level (Catherine locke, 1997). Aside from token references to involving women, attention to women in joint forest management has revolved around issues of formal representation in local institutions and are often assumed that women are an undifferentiated group. Formal representation assumes that such woman may unproblematically seek to advance their interests. The issue needs thorough examination.

The community women of Himachal Pradesh are the prime

collectors, processors and users of forest products. This dependence of women on forestry products result in more intimate knowledge of forests than men. In my experience with village forest development society "NANOO" in Balag forest beat of Theog Forest Division in Shimla district, revealed that the compulsory minimum membership of women in society truly reflects the potential role which can be played by women. Because of an active involvement of the women, the society succeeded in raising 7 ha beautiful plantation near Nanoo village. The usufruct sharing is mainly done by the women. Two important points emerged during informal discussions with the society members. One, local women folk's mild threat of taking over male public space motivated local men to take society's work more seriously and second, village women prefer for working with women extension worker. This reflected the department's need to recruit more women staff.

The success of many projects has been jeopardised simply because they failed to recognise women's priorities (Archna, 1992). So far in Himachal Pradesh, women have been involved to a limited extent in managing the existing forest resources. Handful of lady foresters, few women actively involved in NGO activities, a very few dynamic Mahila Mandals leaders are delivering their roles as managers, motivators and trainees. Still seldom are women's opinion sought in matters involving decision-making. Thus women have important roles to play both in and outside the government. State government realising the departments constraints that due to lack of women staff in its positions of contact with villagers, amended rules to facilitate entry of women as forest Rangers. With this women can enter forest service at all level. This process needs to be further strengthened.

## Conclusion

In the present Joint Forest Management schemes in Himachal Pradesh, there is a need to find ways in which women can institutionalise the few bargaining strengths they have. Also to overcome the challenge in the changed scenario of the forestry sector, due recognition is required to be given to the catalytic role of the women in forest development of the State. More women foresters are required to be recruited. Existing foresters requires training relating to gender issues so that they could make best use of their new skills and new job descriptions. There is a need to widely examine the role of a women at community and institutional levels.

## REFERENCES


Bochet, Jean Jacques (1986), "Management of Upland Watersheds: Participation of the mountain communities", FAO Conservation Guide No. 8.

Catherine Locke (1997), "Constructing a Gender Policy for Joint Forest Management in India" Paper presented at the workshop on social construction of Community Participation in JFM, New Delhi (9-11 April).

FAO (1987), "Forestry for local community development", Forestry Paper No. 7, Rome.

FAO (1985), "Tree growing by rural people", Forestry paper, No. 64, Rome.

FAO (1986), "Forestry extension organisation", Forestry paper No. 66, Rome.

Hobley, M. (1996), "Participatory Forestry; The Process of Change in India and Nepal". *ODA*. Rural Development Forestry Study Guide 3, London, ODI.

H.P. Forest Department (1961), "Himachal Pradesh Forest Centenary (1861-1961)", Shimla, H.P.

H.P. Forest Department (1992), "Convention of Forest Officers" Talland, Shimla, H.P.

H.P. Forest Department (1995), "Back to People" Joint Forest Management Status Document, No. 1, Indo-UK Forestry Project, Kullu Forest Circle.

H.P. Forest Department (2000), "Himachal Pradesh Forest Sector Review", Talland, Shimla, H.P.

*Indian Forester* (1999), vol. 125, no. 1, Dehra Dun (UP), India.

Mahat, T.B.S. (1987), "Forestry-Farming Linkages in Mountain", ICIMOD occasional Paper No. 7. Kathmandu, Nepal.

MOEF (Ministry of Environment and Forests) (1989), "Selected Readings" Academy of Administration, Bhopal, India.

Sood, Minkesh Paul. (1999), "Change in Indian Forest Policy at the National Level", University of Wales, Swansea, U.K.

Raju, M.S. (1994), "Women's Involvement in People's Institution", in G. Raju (ed.) *People's Institutions in Forest Management,* Ahmedabad.